Cases in Marketing Management

THE IRWIN SERIES IN MARKETING

Cases in Marketing Management

SEVENTH EDITION

Kenneth L. Bernhardt
College of Business Administration
Georgia State University

Thomas C. Kinnear
School of Business Administration
University of Michigan

IRWIN

Chicago · Bogotá · Boston · Buenos Aires · Caracas
London · Madrid · Mexico City · Sydney · Toronto

McGraw-Hill

A Division of The McGraw·Hill Companies

CASES IN MARKETING MANAGEMENT

Copyright © 1997 by The McGraw Hill Companies, Inc. All rights reserved. Previous editions © 1978, 1981, 1985, 1988, 1991, and 1994, by Richard D. Irwin, a Times Mirror Higher Education Group, Inc. company. Printed in the United States of America. Except as permitted under the United States Copyright Act of 1976, no part of this publication may be reproduced or distributed in any form or by any means, or stored in a data base or retrieval system, without the prior written permission of the publisher.

1 2 3 4 5 6 7 8 9 0 DOC DOC 0 9 8 7 6

ISBN 0–256–120464–0

Irwin Book Team

Sponsoring editor: *Nina McGuffin*
Editorial coordinator: *Andrea Hlavacek*
Marketing manager: *Colleen J. Suljic*
Senior project supervisor: *Jean Lou Hess*
Senior production supervisor: *Bob Lange*
Designer: *Matthew Baldwin*
Prepress Buyer: *Jon Christopher*
Compositor: *Carlisle Communications, Ltd.*
Typeface: *10½/12 Times Roman*
Printer: R. R. Donnelley and Sons Co.

Library of Congress Cataloging–in–Publication Data

Bernhardt, Kenneth L.
    Cases in marketing management / Kenneth L. Bernhardt, Thomas   C. Kinnear. — 7th ed.
      p.   cm. — (The Irwin series in marketing)
    Includes bibliographical references (p.   ).
    ISBN 0–256–20464–0
    1. Marketing—Management—Case studies.   2. Marketing—Decision making–Case studies.   I. Kinnear, Thomas C., (date)   .   II. Title.
III. Series.
HF5415. 13.B448   1997
658.9—dc21   96–37108

http://www.mhcollege.com

To Kathy and Karen
To Connie, Maggie, and Jamie

Preface

With the publication of this, the seventh edition of *Cases in Marketing Management,* the world of marketing continues to change in new and exciting ways. Unfortunately, much of the excitement is hidden among the definitions and descriptions of concepts that are a necessary part of basic marketing textbooks. We believe that one way to make the study of marketing exciting and dynamic is to use cases. Cases allow the student to work on real marketing problems, to develop an appreciation for the types of problems that exist in the real world of marketing, and to develop the skills of analysis and decision making so necessary for success in marketing and other areas of business. Cases represent as close an approximation of the realities of actually working in marketing as is possible without taking a job in the field.

Your task as a user of this casebook is to work hard to develop well-reasoned solutions to the problems confronting the decision maker in each of the cases. A framework to assist you in developing solutions is presented in Part One of this book. Essentially, you will be using this, or some other framework suggested by your instructor, to analyze the cases in this book. By applying this framework to each case that you are assigned, you will develop your analytic skills. Like all skills, you will find this difficult at first. However, as you practice, you will get better, until it will become second nature to you. This is exactly the same way one develops athletic or musical skills.

The cases in this book represent a broad range of marketing problems. The book contains consumer and industrial cases, profit and nonprofit cases, social marketing cases, specific marketing area cases such as services marketing, and general cases, plus cases on marketing and public policy. Each case is designed to fit into a specific section of a course in marketing management. The cases are long and complex enough to require good analysis, but not so long and complex as to be overly burdensome. Within sections, cases vary in terms of difficulty and complexity.

Users of the first six editions will note that the fundamental thrust and positioning remains the same in this edition. However, we do note the following changes. First, 40% of the cases are new or updated to give students more timely case examples and learning tools. Second, the authors have replaced some of the product cases with services cases. Third, we have added new cases in a number of key areas: technology, service, and global marketing to reflect the issues that are most prevalent in today's business world. Lastly, we have a new case in Part 6 that focuses on integrated marketing communications.

This book contains 34 cases and 2 case-related exercises. Fifteen of the cases and both of the exercises were written by the authors of this book. In some instances we had a coauthor, and we have noted the names of the coauthors on the title pages of the cases concerned. We wish to thank these coauthors for their assistance and for allowing us to use the cases: Danny N. Bellenger, Craig F. Ehrnst, Tom Ingram, Constance Kinnear, Brian Murray, Joanne E. Novak, James Novo, James Scott, Jos Viehoff, and John S. Wright.

We would like to thank the executives of the organizations who allowed us to develop cases about their situations and who have released these cases for use in this book.

The remaining 21 cases were written by many distinguished marketing case writers. We appreciate their allowing us to reproduce their cases here. The names of each of these persons are noted on the title page of the cases concerned. They are: Eric Andrew, M. Edgar Barrett, Christopher D. Buehler, Elizabeth Carducci, William Carner, Eva Cid, Pantea Denoyelle, Mort Ettinger, Peter Faricy, Christopher Gale, Alfred H. Heineken, Akiko Horikawa, Tony Hughes, Shreekant G. Joag, Carla Johnson, Pranati Kapadia, Fred W. Kniffen, Aylin Kunt, Janet Lahey, Zarrel V. Lambert, Lawrence M. Lamont, Chris Lane, Jean-Claude Larreche, Daniel Lindley, Neil Miller, David B. Montgomery, Rowland T. Moriarty, Jr., James E. Nelson, Adrian Ryans, Martin Schreiber, Anne Senausky, Ronald Stiff, Elizabeth W. Storey, George Taucher, Mark Vendenbosch.

We were helped in selecting cases over the last two editions by the following people who responded to our surveys:

Dr. Newell Chiesl, Indiana State University; Professor William Hess, Golden Gate University; Dr. Karen Kaigler-Walker, Woodbury University; Professor Martie R. Kazura, Berea College; Dr. Rick Lewis, LeTourneau University; Professor Peter M. Lynagh, University of Baltimore; Dr. O. Karl Mann, Tennessee Technological University; Professor David J. Moore, The University of Michigan; Professor Robert S. Russell, Stonehill College; Professor John O. Young, Wayne State University; and Dr. Abdall M. Yousry, Bowie State University; Wendy L. Acker, Avila College; Julian Andorka, DePaul University; Thomas J. Babb, West Liberty State College; Joseph A. Bellizzi, Arizona State University–West; Deirdre Bird, Northeastern University; Charles Born, Golden Gate University; Mary Lynn Buck, Ferris State University; Robert E. Burnkrant, The Ohio State University; Charles R. Canedy III, University of Hartford; W. Fred Chatman, Jr., Presbyterian College; Henry C.K. Chen, University of West Florida; Yusaf A. Choudhoy, University of Baltimore; Susan Cisco, Oakton Community College; Paul Cohen, Castleton State College; Richard Cooley, California State University–Chico; Jerry A. Cooper, Southern Oregon State College; Philip Cooper, Loyola College; Michael W. Couture, University of Missouri-Columbia; Melvin R. Crask, University of Georgia; Roger Davis, Baylor University; M. Wayne DeLozier, Nicholls State University; Peter R. Dickson, The

Ohio State University; Robert A. Fischer, Northeastern University; Heidi Foreman, Columbia College; Irene R. Foster, Vanderbilt University; George Galiouridis, Webber College; Robert L. Goldman, Golden Gate University; John R. Grabner, The Ohio State University; Jim Hazeltine, Northeastern Illinois University; Tony L. Henthorne, University of Southern Mississippi; Susan Hibbins, John Carroll University; William G. Hines, Northeastern University; Thomas F. Hitzelberger, Southern Oregon State College; John W. Hummel, St. Michael's College; Don Jackson, Ferris State University; Keren Ami Johnson, Old Dominion University; Kissan Joseph, Purdue University; Norman Kangun, Clemson University; Debora A. Kielcover, Calvin College; John A. Kuehn, University of Missouri-Columbia; Virginia Langrehr, Valparaiso University; Robert Brock Lawes, Chaminade University; Paul A. Lawhorne, Bowie State University; Robert Lawrence, South Carolina State University; David Lohmann, Hawaii Pacific University; Peter M. Lynagh, University of Baltimore; Terry A. Madoch, Elmhurst College; Ernest Maier, Lawrence Technological University; Jennifer Meoli, Elizabethtown College; Stephen J. Miller, Oklahoma State University; Anusree Mitra, American University; Janet B. Monroe, Wayne State University; Janet Y. Murray, University of Missouri-Columbia; Harold E. Oakley, Belleville Area College; Christie H. Paksoy, University of North Carolina-Charlotte; Yigang Pan, DePaul University; A. William Pollman, University of Wisconsin-LaCrosse; Jay E. Poutinen, University of Wisconsin-Stevens Point; Marco Protano, Northeastern University; Pradeep A. Rau, George Washington University; Nina M. Ray, Boise State University; Mary Anne Raymond, American University; Irving E. Richards, Cuyahoga Community College; Lee Richardson, University of Baltimore; Donald P. Robin, Southern Mississippi University; Robert S. Russell, Northeastern University; William J. Schmid, Northeastern University: Harold S. Sekiguchi, University of Nevada; William L. Shanklin, Kent State University; Alan Terrence Shao, University of North Carolina-Charlotte; Richard Siedlecki, Emory University and Georgia State University; Stanley F. Slater, University of Colorado-Colorado Springs; James V. Spiers, Arizona State University; Vlasis Stathakopoulos, University of Hartford; John E. Swan, University of Alabama-Birmingham; Fred Trawick, University of Albama-Birmingham; Frances G. Tucker, Syracuse University; John S. Wagle, Northern Illinois University; Jay C. Wayne, Golden Gate University; James E. Welch, Kentucky Wesleyan College; Richard Wilcox, Rockford College; Edward D. Wirth, Jr., Florida Institute of Technology; and George M. Zinkhan, University of Houston.

We would also like to thank our colleagues at Georgia State University and the University of Michigan, and the Case Research Association for their helpful comments and their classroom testing cases. Finally, we would like to acknowledge the help in many tasks associated with the development, editing and production of the book we received from Nina McGuffin, Andrea Hlavacek, Colleen Suljic, Jean Lou Hess, and Norma Duncan.

Kenneth L. Bernhardt
Thomas C. Kinnear

Contents

PART 3

Marketing Information and Forecasting

PART 4

Product and Brand Management Decisions

PART 5

Distribution Decisions

PART 6

Promotion Decisions

PART 7

Pricing Decisions

Cases in Marketing Management

Part 1

An Orientation to the Case Method

Chapter 1

Note to the Student on the Case Method

The case method is different from other methods of teaching, and it requires that students take an active role rather than a passive one. The case method places the student in a simulated business environment and substitutes the student in the place of the business manager as the person required to make a set of decisions. To define it, a case is:

> typically a record of a business issue which actually has been faced by business executives, together with surrounding facts, opinions, and prejudices upon which the executives had to depend. These real and particularized cases are presented to students for considered analysis, open discussion, and final decision as to the type of action which should be taken.[1]

With the case method, the process of arriving at an answer is what is important. The instructor's expectation is that the student will develop an ability to make decisions, to support those decisions with appropriate analysis, and to learn to communicate ideas both orally and in writing. The student is required to determine the problem as well as the solution. This method of teaching thus shifts much of the responsibility to the student, and a great deal of time is required on the part of the student.

The case method often causes a great deal of insecurity on the part of students who are required to make decisions, often with very little information and limited time. There is no single right answer to any of the cases in this book, an additional source of insecurity. The goal is not to develop a set of right answers, but to learn to reason well with the data available. This process is truly learning by doing.

Studying under the case method will result in the development of skills in critical thinking. The student will learn how to effectively reason when dealing with specific problems. The development of communication skills is

---

[1]Charles I. Gragg, "Because Wisdom Can't Be Told," *Harvard Alumni Bulletin,* October 19, 1940.

also important, and students will learn to present their analysis in a cogent and convincing manner. They must defend their analysis and plan of action against the criticism of others in the class. In the class discussion, individual students may find that the opinions of other members of the class differ from their own. In some cases this will be because the individual has overlooked certain important points or that some factors have been weighted more heavily compared to the weighting used by other students. The process of presenting and defending conflicting points of view causes individual members of the class to reconsider the views they had of the case before the discussion began. This leads to a clearer perception of problems, a recognition of the many and often conflicting interpretations of the facts and events in the case, and a greater awareness of the complexities with which management decisions are reached.

In preparing for class using the case method, the student should first read the case quickly. The goal is to gain a feel for the type of problem presented in the case, the type of organization involved, and so on. Next, the student should read the case thoroughly to learn all the key facts in the case. The student should not blindly accept all the data presented, as not all information is equally reliable or relevant. As part of the process of mastering the facts, it frequently will be desirable to utilize the numerical data presented in the case to make any possible calculations and comparisons that will help analyze the problems involved in the case. The case will have to be read a number of times before the analysis is completed.

The student must add to the facts by making reasonable assumptions regarding many aspects of the situation. Business decision making is rarely based on perfect information. All of the cases in this book are actual business cases, and the student is provided with all the information that the executives involved had at their disposal. Often students cannot believe the low level of information available for decision making, but this is often the case. What is required in those situations is the making of reasonable assumptions and learning to make decisions under uncertainty. There is often a strong reluctance on the part of the student to do this, but the ability to make decisions based on well-reasoned assumptions is a skill that must be developed for a manager to be truly effective.

Once the student has mastered the facts in the case, the next step is to identify and specify the issues and problems toward which the executive involved should be directing his or her attention. The issues may be very obscure. Learning to separate problems from symptoms is an important skill to learn. Often there will be a number of subissues involved, and it will be necessary to break the problem down into component parts.

The next step in the student's case preparation is to identify alternative courses of action. Usually there are a number of possible solutions to the problems in the case, and the student should be careful not to lock in on only one alternative before several possible alternatives have been thoroughly evaluated.

The next step is to evaluate each of the alternative plans of action. It is at this stage of the analysis that the student is required to marshall and analyze all the facts for each alternative program. The assumptions the student is required to make are very important here, and the student must apply all the analytical skills possible, including both qualitative and quantitative.

After all the alternatives have been thoroughly analyzed, the student must make a decision concerning the specific course of action to take. It should be recognized that several of the alternatives may "work," and that there are a number of different ways of resolving the issues in the case. The important consideration is that the plan of action actually decided upon has been thoroughly analyzed from all angles, is internally consistent, and has a high probability of meeting the manager's objectives.

Once an overall strategy has been determined, it is important that consideration be given to the implementation of that strategy. At this stage, the student must determine who is to do what, when, and how. A professor may start out a class by asking the question, "What should Mr. Jones do tomorrow?" Unless the students have given some thought to the implementation of the strategy decided upon, they will be unprepared for such a question. Improper implementation of an excellent strategy may doom it to failure, so it is important to follow through with appropriate analysis at this stage.

During the class discussion, the instructor will act more as a moderator than a lecturer, guiding the discussion and calling on students for their opinions. A significant amount of learning will take place by participating in the discussion. The goal is for the students to integrate all their ideas, relating them to the goals of the company, the strengths and weaknesses of the company and its competition, the way consumers buy, and the resources available. A suggested framework for the integration of these ideas is presented in the next chapter of this book, in the appendix titled "Outline for Case Analysis."

The student's classroom discussion should avoid the rehashing, without analysis, of case facts. Students should recognize that the professor and all the other students in the class have thoroughly read the case and are familiar with the facts. The objective, therefore, is to interpret the facts and use them to support the proposed plan of action. The case method obviously requires a great deal of preparation time by the student. The payoff is that, after spending this time adequately preparing each of the steps described, the student will have developed the ability to make sound marketing management decisions.

Chapter 2

Introduction to Marketing Decision Making

In Chapter 1, you were introduced to your role in the execution of an effective case course in marketing. In summary, the primary task is to complete a competent analysis of the cases assigned to you. If you have never undertaken the analysis of a marketing case before, you are probably wondering just how you should go about doing this. Is there some framework that is appropriate for this task? Indeed, there are a number of such frameworks. The purpose of this chapter is to present one such framework to you. We think you will find it useful in analyzing the cases in this book.

An Outline for Case Analysis

The appendix to this chapter is the summary document for the approach we believe that you should use for case analysis. We suggest that you apply the types of questions listed there in your analysis. Figure 2-1 provides an overview of this outline. Basically, we are suggesting that you begin by doing a complete analysis of the *situation* facing the organization in the case. This *situation analysis* includes an assessment of (1) the nature of demand for the product, (2) the extent of demand, (3) the nature of competition, (4) the environmental climate, (5) the stage of the life cycle for the product, (6) the skills of the firm, (7) the financial resources of the firm, and (8) the distribution structure. In some cases, legal aspects may also form part of a good situation analysis. The premise here is that one cannot begin to make decisions until a thorough understanding of the situation at hand is obtained.

Once a detailed situation analysis is prepared, one is in a position to summarize the *problems* and *opportunities* that arise out of the situation analysis. These problems and opportunities provide an organized summary of the situation analysis. This in turn should lead to the generation of a set of *alternatives* that are worthy of being considered as solutions to the problems and actualizers of the opportunities.

These alternatives are then *evaluated* using arguments generated from (1) the detailed situation analysis, (2) the summary statement of problems and

FIGURE 2-1   Overview of a framework for case analysis

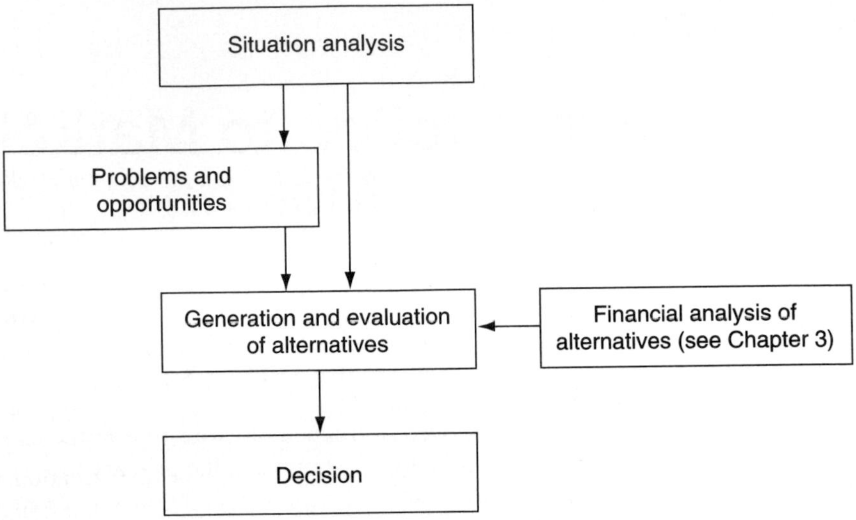

```
                    ┌─────────────────────────┐
                    │    Situation analysis    │
                    └─────────────────────────┘
                          │          │
                          ▼          │
          ┌─────────────────────┐    │
          │     Problems and    │    │
          │    opportunities    │    │
          └─────────────────────┘    │
                          │          │
                          ▼          ▼
          ┌─────────────────────────┐     ┌─────────────────────────┐
          │ Generation and evaluation│◄────│    Financial analysis of │
          │     of alternatives      │     │ alternatives (see Chapter 3)│
          └─────────────────────────┘     └─────────────────────────┘
                          │
                          ▼
                ┌─────────────────────┐
                │       Decision       │
                └─────────────────────┘
```

opportunities, and (3) relevant financial analysis (break-even points, market shares, and so on). The use of financial analysis is discussed in Chapter 3. The point here is that we use the situation analysis to generate and evaluate alternative programs. The pros and cons of each alternative are weighed as part of this evaluation, and a *decision* is then reached.

A Good Case Analysis

The question naturally arises: In applying the outline in the appendix to a case, how do I know when I have done a good analysis? The purpose of this section is to raise some points that are often used by instructors to evaluate either an oral or written analysis.

1. Be complete. It is imperative that the case analysis be complete. There are two dimensions to this issue. First is that each area of the situation analysis must be discussed, problems and opportunities must be identified, alternatives must be presented and evaluated using the situation analysis and relevant financial analysis, and a decision must be made. An analysis that omits parts of the situation analysis, or only recognizes one alternative, is not a good analysis. Second, each area above must be covered in good depth and with insight.

2. Avoid rehashing case facts. Every case has a lot of factual information. A good analysis uses facts that are relevant to the situation at hand to make summary points of analysis. A poor analysis just restates or rehashes these facts without making relevant summary comments. Consider the use of a set of financial facts that might appear in a case:

> Rehash: The current ratio is 1.5:1, cash on hand is $15,000, retained earnings are $50,000.
>
> Analysis: Because of a very weak financial position, as demonstrated by a poor cash position and current ratio, the firm will be constrained in the activities it can undertake to ones requiring little immediate cash outlay.

3. Make reasonable assumptions. Every case is incomplete in terms of some piece of information that you would like to have. We would, of course, like to have all the necessary information presented to us in each case. This is not possible for two reasons. First, it would make the cases far too long to be capable of being analyzed in a reasonable period of time. Second, and more important, incomplete information is an accurate reflection of the real world. All marketing decisions are made on the basis of incomplete information. Often, it just costs too much or takes too long to collect the desired information.

A good case analysis must make realistic assumptions to fill in the gaps of information in the case. For example, the case may not describe the purchase decision process for the product of interest. A poor analysis would either omit mentioning this or just state that no information is available. A good analysis would attempt to present this purchase decision process by classifying the product (a shopping good?) and drawing on the student's real-life experience. Could you not describe the purchase decision process for carpeting, even though you have never read a research report about it?

The reasonableness of your assumptions will be challenged by your fellow students and instructor. This is one of the things that makes case discussions exciting. The point is that it is better to make your assumptions explicit and incorporate them in your analysis than to use them implicitly or not make them at all. If we make explicit assumptions, we can later come back and see if our assumptions were correct or not.

4. Don't confuse symptoms with problems. In summarizing a firm's problems, a poor analysis confuses the symptoms with real problems. For example, one might list two problems as (1) sales are down and (2) sales force turnover is high. This would not be correct. These are symptoms, The real problem is identified by answering the question: Why are sales down or why is sales force turnover high? For example, sales force turnover may be high due to inadequate sales training. But this may not yet be the root problem. You still need to ask: Why is sales training inadequate? It may be that the sales manager has ignored this area through his or her lack of knowledge of how to train people. What you do is keep asking "why" until you are satisfied that you have identified the root problem.

5. *Don't confuse opportunities with taking action.* One can recognize an opportunity but not take any action related to it. For example, a large market for a product may exist. This is an opportunity. However, a firm may decide not to compete in this market due to lack of resources or skills or the existence of strong competition. Decisions involve the complex trading-off of many problems and opportunities. Thus, don't make statements that direct action—"target to. . . , promote as. . . ," and the like—as opportunity statements.

6. *Deal with objectives realistically.* Most cases present a statement from management about their objectives. For example, it might say they want a sales growth rate of 25 percent per year. Good analysis critically evaluates statements of objectives and revises them if necessary. Then it uses these revised objectives as part of the argument about which alternative to select. Poor analysis either ignores the stated objectives or accepts them at face value.

7. *Recognize alternatives.* A good analysis explicitly recognizes and discusses alternative action plans. In some cases, these alternatives are stated in the case. In other cases, the student must develop alternatives beyond those stated in the case. A poor analysis explicitly recognizes only one or two alternatives, or only takes the ones explicitly stated in the case.

8. *Don't be assertive.* In some case analyses, the decision that was made is clear to the reader or listener in about the first sentence of the situation analysis. The whole rest of the analysis is then a justification of the desired solution. This type of analysis is very poor. It has asserted an answer before completing a situation analysis. Usually, other alternatives are ignored or treated as all bad, and the desired solution is treated as all good. You must do your situation analysis and recognize alternatives before evaluating them and reaching a decision.

9. *Discuss the pros and cons of each alternative.* Every alternative always has pros and cons. A good analysis explicitly discusses these. In a poor analysis, there is no explicit discussion of the pros and cons of each alternative. Problem and opportunity statements serve as the basis of your pro (opportunities) and con (problems) discussion. Different ones relate to specific alternatives.

10. *Make effective use of financial and other quantitative information.* Financial data (break-even points and so on) and information derived from other quantitative analyses can add a great deal to a good case analysis. Totally ignoring these aspects or handling them improperly results in a poor case analysis. This analysis should be presented in detail in a written appendix or in class if asked for. However, in the body of a paper or in an oral discussion, present only the summary conclusions out of the analysis. Say "The break-even point is 220,000 units," and be prepared to present the detail if asked.

11. Reach a clear decision. You must reach a clear decision. You might like to hedge your bets and say "maybe this, maybe that." However, part of the skill of decision making is to be forced to reach a decision under ambiguous circumstances and then be prepared to defend this decision. This does not mean that you do not recognize limitations of your position or positive aspects of other positions. It just means that despite all that, you have reached a particular decision.

12. Make good use of evidence developed in your situation analysis. In reaching a decision, a good analysis reaches a decision that is logically consistent with the situation analysis that was done. This is the ultimate test of an analysis. Other students may disagree with your situation analysis and thus your resultant conclusion, but they should not be able to fault the logical connection between your situation analysis and decision. If they can, you have a poor case analysis.

The "Outline for Case Analysis" contained in the Appendix is designed to assist you in doing case analysis. You should keep the points stressed in this section in mind when you apply this outline.

Appendix
Outline for Case Analysis[1]

Overview of Analysis Structure

   I. Situation analysis
- A. Nature of demand.
- B. Extent of demand.
- C. Nature of competition.
- D. Environmental climate.
- E. Stage of product life cycle.
- F. Cost structure of the industry.
- G. Skills of the firm.
- H. Financial resources of the firm.
- I. Distribution structure.

  II. Problems and opportunities
- A. Key problem areas.
- B. Key opportunities.
- C. On balance, the situation is.

 III. Generation and evaluation of alternative marketing programs
- A. Objectives defined.
- B. Marketing mix/program decisions.

 IV. Decision

Details of Analysis Structure

I. SITUATION ANALYSIS
A. Nature of demand

The purpose of this section is to make *explicit* your beliefs and assumptions regarding the nature of the purchase decision process (consumer or industrial) for the goods or services under investigation. In case analysis, we are concerned primarily with developing your *skills* of analysis in identifying areas of problems and opportunities and in developing well-supported marketing program recommendations. Conflicting student beliefs and assumptions should lead to interesting and enlightening class discussion regarding the nature of the purchase decision process and its implication for marketing programs. We hope that through this type of class discussion, you will increase your sensitivity to, and understanding of, buyers and

---

[1]This outline is adapted from an unpublished note by Professor James R. Taylor of the University of Michigan. Used with permission.

their behavior. Again, the value of this type of analysis concerns its application to better *reasoned* and *supported* marketing program decisions. Hopefully, the development of your skills in this area has value in improving your *judgment capabilities* and in increasing your understanding of marketing decision making.

Analysis areas and questions:

1. How do buyers (consumer and industrial) *currently* go about buying existing products or services? Describe the main types of behavior patterns and attitudes.

    a. Number of stores shopped or industrial sources considered.
    b. Degree of overt information seeking.
    c. Degree of brand awareness and loyalty.
    d. Location of product category decision—home or point of sale.
    e. Location of brand decision—home or point of sale.
    f. Sources of product information and current awareness and knowledge levels.
    g. Who makes the purchase decision—male, female, adult, child, purchasing agent, buying committee, so on?
    h. Who influences the decision maker?
    i. Individual or group decision (computers versus candy bar).
    j. Duration of the decision process (repeat, infrequent, or new purchase situation).
    k. Buyer's interest, personal involvement, or excitement regarding the purchase (hairpins versus trip to Caribbean).
    l. Risk or uncertainty of negative purchase outcome—high, medium, or low (specialized machinery versus hacksaw blades) (pencil versus hair coloring).
    m. Functional versus psychosocial considerations (electric drill versus new dress).
    n. Time of consumption (gum versus dining room furniture).

Basically, we are attempting to determine the *who, what, where, when, why,* and *how* of the purchase decision.

Note: The key to using the above analysis is to ask what are the implications for marketing programs. For example, if the purchase (brand) decision is made in the store and branding is not important to the buyers, what implication does this have for national TV advertising versus in-store display? Do you see how you might *use* this information to support a recommendation for intensive distribution and point-of-purchase promotion and display?

2. Can the market be meaningfully segmented or broken into several homogeneous groups with respect to "what they want" and "how they buy"? Criteria:

    a. Age.
    b. Family life cycle.

    c. Geographic location.
    d. Heavy versus light users.
    e. Nature of the buying process.
    f. Product usage.

Note: For each case situation, you should determine whether a more effective marketing program could be developed for each segment versus having an overall program for all segments. The real issue is whether tailoring your program to a segment will give you a competitive advantage. Of course, there may be negatives to this strategy in terms of volume and cost considerations.

B. Extent of demand
    The purpose of this section is to evaluate demand in an aggregate and quantitative sense. We are basically concerned with the actual or potential size of the overall market and developing sound estimates of company sales potential.

Analysis areas and questions:
1. What is the size of the market (units and dollars) now and what will the future hold?
2. What are the current market shares, and what are the selective demand trends (units and dollars)?
3. Is it best to analyze the market on an aggregate or on a segmented basis?

Note: We are basically concerned with making *explicit* assumptions regarding primary and selective demand trends. These estimates are critical to determining the profit (loss) potential of alternative marketing programs.

C. Nature of competition
    The purpose of this section is to evaluate the present and future structure of competition. The key is to understand how the buyer evaluates alternative products or services relative to his or her needs.

Analysis areas and questions:
1. What is the present and future structure of competition?
    a. Number of competitors (5 versus 2,000).
    b. Market shares.
    c. Financial resources.
    d. Marketing resources and skills.
    e. Production resources and skills.
2. What are the current marketing programs of established competitors? Why are they successful or unsuccessful?
3. Is there an opportunity for another competitor? Why?
4. What are the anticipated retaliatory moves of competitors? Can they neutralize different marketing programs we might develop?

Note: Failure to correctly evaluate demand and competition is one common reason for unprofitable marketing programs. Also, Sections A, B, and C are analysis areas particularly important in making decisions concerning "positioning" your product and developing the marketing program to support your positioning strategy.

D. Environmental climate

It's not hard to identify current marketing programs that have been highly disrupted by a changing environmental climate. The energy crisis, together with pollution, safety, and consumerism concerns, can bring many such examples to mind. We are sure you can identify firms that have benefited from the energy crisis. The point is that the environment is constantly changing, and those organizations that can adapt to change are the ones which enjoy long-run success.

Analysis areas and questions:

1. What are the relevant social, political, economic, and technological trends?
2. How do you evaluate these trends? Do they represent opportunities or problems?

E. Stage of product life cycle

The purpose of this section is to make explicit assumptions about where a product is in its life cycle. This is important because the effectiveness of particular marketing variables may vary by stages of the life cycle.

Analysis areas and questions:

1. In what stage of the life cycle is the product category?
    a. What is the chronological age of the product category? (Younger more favorable than older?)
    b. What is the state of the consumers' knowledge of the product category? (More complete the knowledge—more unfavorable?)
2. What market characteristics support your stage of life-cycle evaluation?

F. Cost structure of the industry

Here we are concerned with the amount and composition of the marginal or additional cost of supplying increased output. It can be argued that the lower these costs, the easier it may be to cover the costs of developing an effective marketing program (see accompanying table). Basically, one is relating the level of fixed cost to variable cost.

	Marginal costs	
	High*	Low†
Selling price per unit	$1.00	$1.00
Variable costs per unit	0.80	0.10
Contribution per unit	$0.20	$0.90

*Such as the garment and auto industries.
†Such as the hotel and telephone industries.

G. Skills of the firm

The purpose of this section is to critically evaluate the organization making the decision. Here, we effectively place limits on what they are capable of accomplishing.

Analysis areas and questions:
1. Do we have the skills and experience to perform the functions necessary to be in this business?
   a. Marketing skills.
   b. Production skills.
   c. Management skills.
   d. Financial skills.
   e. R&D skills.
2. How do our skills compare to competitors?
   a. Production fit.
   b. Marketing fit.
   c. Etc.

H. Financial resources of the firm

Analysis areas and questions:
1. Do we have the funds to support an effective marketing program?
2. Where are the funds coming from, and when will they be available?

I. Distribution structure

The purpose of this area is to identify and evaluate the availability of channels of distribution.

Analysis areas and questions:
1. What channels exist, and can we gain access to the channels?
2. Cost versus revenue from different channels?
3. Feasibility of using multiple channels?
4. Nature and degree of within- and between-channel competition?
5. Trends in channel structure?
6. Requirements of different channels for promotion and margin?
7. Will it be profitable for particular channels to handle my product?

II. PROBLEMS AND OPPORTUNITIES

Here we prepare a definite listing of *key* problems and opportunities identified from the situation analysis which relate to the specific issues or decision questions faced by management.

A. Key problem areas
B. Key opportunities
C. On balance, the situation is:
1. Very favorable.
2. Somewhat favorable.
3. Neutral.
4. Somewhat unfavorable.
5. Very unfavorable.

Note: At this point, the critical issue is whether a profitable marketing program can be formulated, or whether a current marketing program needs to be changed in order to overcome the problem areas and/or take advantage of opportunities.

III. GENERATION AND EVALUATION OF ALTERNATIVE MARKETING PROGRAMS

A marketing program consists of a series of marketing-mix decisions which represent an integrated and consistent "action plan" for achieving predetermined goals. Different marketing programs may be required for various target segments. For a given target segment, alternative programs should be formulated and evaluated as to the effectiveness of each in achieving predetermined goals.

A. Objectives defined
1. Target market segments identified.
2. Volume to be sold (dollars or units).
3. Profit analysis (contribution analysis, break-even analysis, ROI, etc.).

B. Marketing mix/program decisions
1. Product decisions:
   a. Develop new product(s).
   b. Change current product(s).
   c. Add or drop product from line.
   d. Product positioning.
   e. Branding (national, private, secondary).
2. Distribution decisions:
   a. Intensity of distribution (intensive to exclusive).
   b. Multiple channels.
   c. Types of wholesalers and retailers (discounters, etc.).
   d. Degree of channel directness.
3. Promotion decisions:
   a. Mix of personal selling, advertising, dealer incentives, and sales promotion.
   b. Branding—family versus individual.
   c. Budget.
   d. Message.
   e. Media.
4. Price decisions:
   a. Price level (above, same, or below).
   b. Price variation (discount structure, geographic).
   c. Margins.
   d. Administration of price level.
   e. Price leadership.

Note: The above four decision areas involve specific strategy issues which, together, form a marketing program.

The key to effective marketing decision making is to evaluate alternative marketing programs using information from the situation analysis. The pros and cons for each alternative should be presented and discussed.

IV. DECISION

The outcome of the evaluation of alternatives is a decision. You must make a decision. Case analysis is designed to develop your skills in making well-supported and reasoned marketing decisions. The quality of your reasoning is much more important than reaching any particular decision. Generally, if your situation analysis is different (you perceive the facts differently and have made different assumptions) from someone else's, you should reach different decisions.

Chapter 3

Financial Analysis for Marketing Decision Making

In Chapter 2, we laid out an approach to marketing decision making. The "Outline for Case Analysis" summarized this approach. There is, however, one more important aspect of a competent case analysis that was not presented in that outline. This is the financial analysis of the alternatives presented in a case.

The ultimate goals of all marketing activities are usually expressed in financial terms. The company has a particular return on investment in mind, or growth in earnings per share. Proposed marketing activities must thus be evaluated for their financial implications. Can you imagine asking your boss for $1 million for a new distribution center or an advertising program without having to present the financial implications of such a request? It does not happen in the real marketing world, nor should it happen in a good case analysis.

Financial analysis can be complex. Our purpose here is to present some simple financial calculations that can be useful in case analysis. More sophisticated financial techniques are left to courses in financial management. Basically, the advanced techniques add little to the understanding of the cases in this book and take too much time and effort for the reader to implement.

It should clearly be understood that financial considerations are only one aspect in the evaluation of marketing alternatives. Marketing alternatives cannot be reduced to a set of numbers. Qualitative aspects derived from the situation analysis are also relevant. Sometimes the qualitative aspects are consistent in terms of pointing to an alternative to select. In other cases, they may point to different alternatives. The task of the student is to formulate both types of arguments for each alternative, and to select an alternative based upon which arguments the student thinks should carry the most weight.

This chapter assumes that the student is familiar with elementary financial accounting concepts. What we will present here are some useful concepts not usually presented in basic accounting courses.

Contribution

Contribution per unit is defined as the difference between the selling price of an item and the variable costs of producing and selling that item. It is in essence the amount of money per unit available to the marketer to cover fixed production costs and corporate overhead, and, having done that, to yield a profit. So, if a manufacturer sells an item for $12.00, and the variable costs are $8.40, then

$$\text{Contribution per unit} = \text{Selling price} - \text{Variable costs}$$
$$= \$12.00 - \$8.40$$
$$= \$3.60$$

Each unit this company sells gives it $3.60 to cover fixed costs.

Total contribution is the contribution per unit times the number of units sold. So, if this firm sold 20,000 units:

$$\text{Total contribution} = \text{Contribution per unit} \times \text{Units sold}$$
$$= \$3.60 \times 20,000$$
$$= \$72,000$$

If the total relevant fixed costs of this product were $42,000, the *profit* earned by this product would be:

$$\text{Profit} = \text{Total contribution} - \text{Fixed costs}$$
$$= \$72,000 - \$42,000$$
$$= \$30,000$$

Costs

In determining contributions and profit, we used the terms *variable cost* and *fixed cost*. At this point, we want to define them more formally. Variable costs are those costs that are fixed *per unit* and, therefore, vary in their total amount depending upon the number of units produced and sold. That is, it takes a certain amount of raw materials and labor to produce a unit of product. The more we produce, the more total variable costs are.

Fixed costs are costs that remain constant in *total amount* despite changes in the volume of production or sales. These costs would thus vary per unit depending upon the number of units produced or sold.

Sorting out which costs are variable and fixed is important in good case analysis. The rule to apply is: if it varies in *total* as volume changes, it is a variable cost. Thus, labor, raw materials, packaging, and salespersons' commissions would be variable costs. Note that all marketing costs except commissions would be considered fixed costs. Don't be fooled if a marketing cost or other fixed cost is presented in a per-unit form. It may look like a variable cost, but it is not. It is only that much per unit at one given volume. For example, if we are told that advertising cost per unit will be $1, this means that at the end of the year, when we divide total sales into advertising expenditures, the result is expected to be $1 per unit. What we must be told is at what volume advertising is expected to be $1 per unit. If the expected volume level is 300,000 units, we then know that the firm intends to spend $300,000 ($1 × 300,000 units) on advertising. This $300,000 is a fixed cost. Note that if they sold less than 300,000 units, the cost per unit would exceed $1, and vice versa. So beware of fixed costs that are allocated to units and presented in a per-unit form.

Break Even

A solid perspective on many marketing alternatives can often be obtained by determining the unit or dollar sales necessary to cover all relevant fixed costs. This sales level is called the break-even point. We define

1. $\text{Break-even point in units} = \dfrac{\text{Total fixed costs}}{\text{Contribution per unit}}$

2. $\text{Break-even point in dollars} = \dfrac{\text{Total fixed costs}}{1 - \dfrac{\text{Variable cost per unit}}{\text{Selling price per unit}}}$

or

$$= \begin{matrix}\text{Break-even point} \\ \text{in units}\end{matrix} \times \begin{matrix}\text{Selling price} \\ \text{per unit}\end{matrix}$$

Let's illustrate these definitions. Suppose that (1) direct labor is $7.50 per unit, (2) raw materials are $2 per unit, (3) selling price is $22 per unit, (4) advertising and sales force costs are $400,000, and (5) other relevant fixed costs are $100,000.

$$\begin{aligned}
\text{Contribution per unit} &= \text{Selling price} - \text{Variable costs} \\
&= \$22.00 - (\$7.50 + \$2.00) \\
&= \$22.00 - \$9.50 \\
&= \$12.50
\end{aligned}$$

$$\begin{aligned}
\text{Break-even point in units} &= \frac{\text{Total fixed costs}}{\text{Contribution per unit}} \\
&= \frac{\$400,000 + \$100,000}{\$12.50} \\
&= 40,000 \text{ units}
\end{aligned}$$

$$\begin{aligned}
\text{Break-even point in dollars} &= \frac{\$500,000}{1 - \dfrac{\$9.50}{\$22.00}} \\
&= \frac{\$500,000}{1 - 0.4318181} = \$880,000
\end{aligned}$$

Alternatively

$$\begin{aligned}
\text{Break-even point in dollars} &= 40,000 \times \$22.00 \text{ per unit} \\
&= \$880,000
\end{aligned}$$

Profit Targets

Breaking even is not as much fun as making a profit. Thus, we often want to incorporate a profit target level into our calculations. Basically, we are answering the question: At what volume do we earn X profits? Covering a profit target is just like covering a fixed cost. So in the previous example, if we set $60,000 as our profit target, we would have to sell an additional number of units equal to:

$$\text{Units to cover profit target} = \frac{\text{Profit target}}{\text{Contribution per unit}}$$

$$= \frac{\$60,000}{\$12.50} = 4,800 \text{ units}$$

Total units to reach this target is

$$40,000 + 4,800 = 44,800 \text{ or } \frac{\$500,000 + \$60,000}{\$12.50} = 44,800$$

Break-even analysis is a useful tool for comparing alternative marketing programs. It tells us how many units must be sold, but does not help us with the critical question of how many units will be sold.

Market Share

$$\text{Market share} = \frac{\text{Company sales level}}{\text{Total market sales}}$$

This calculation adds perspective to proposed action plans. Suppose that the total market sales are 290,000 units and our sales level needed to break even is 40,000 units. Thus, the required market share to break even is:

$$\frac{40,000}{290,000} = 13.8\%$$

The question then to ask is whether this market share can be obtained with the proposed marketing program.

Capital Expenditures

Often, a particular marketing program proposes expenditures for capital equipment. These would be fixed costs associated with the proposed program. Typically, they should not all be charged to the relevant fixed cost for that proposal. For example, suppose that $5 million are to be expended for equipment that will last 10 years. If we charge all this to the break-even calculation in year one, it will be very high. Further, for years 2 through 10, the break-even point will fall substantially. It is better to allocate this $5 million equally over the 10 years. Thus, $500,000 would be a relevant fixed cost in each year associated with the equipment. What one needs to do is to make some reasonable assumption about the useful life of capital assets, and divide the total cost over this time period.

Relevant Costs

The issue often arises as to what fixed costs are relevant to a particular proposal. The rule to use is: A fixed cost is relevant if the expenditure varies due to the acceptance of that proposal. Thus, new equipment, new research and development, and so on, are relevant. Last year's advertising, or previous research and development dollars, for example, do not vary with the current decision, and thus are not a relevant cost of the proposed program. Past expenditures are referred to as *sunk costs*. They should not enter into current decisions. Decisions are future-oriented.

Corporate overhead presents a special problem. Generally, it does not vary with a particular decision. We don't fire the president in selecting between marketing programs. However, in some instances, some overhead may be directly attributable to a particular decision. In this instance, it would be a relevant cost. We should recognize that, to stay in business, a firm must cover all its costs in the long run. Also, from a financial accounting point of view, all costs are relevant. This type of accounting is concerned with preparing income statements and balance sheets for reporting to investors. In marketing decision making, we are interested in managerial, not financial, accounting. Managerial accounting is concerned with providing relevant information for decision making. It, therefore, only presents costs that are relevant to the decision being considered. Such things as allocated overhead or amortized research and development costs only serve to confuse future-oriented decisions.

Margins

Often a case will present us with a retail selling price, when what we really want to know is the manufacturer's selling price. To be able to work back to get the manufacturer's selling price, we must understand how channel margins work.

When firms buy a product at a particular price and attempt to sell it at a higher price, the difference between the cost price and the selling price is called margin or markup or mark-on. Thus,

$$\text{Selling price} = \text{Cost price} + \text{Margin}$$

An example could be:

$$\$1.00 = \$0.80 + \$0.20$$

So a company has bought a product for \$0.80, added on a \$0.20 margin, and is charging \$1.00 for the product.

Margins are usually expressed as percentages. This raises the question as to the base on which the margin percentage should be expressed: the cost price or the selling price. Here, if the \$0.20 margin is expressed as a percentage of selling price, the margin is \$0.20/\$1.00 = 20 percent. If it were expressed as a percentage of cost price, the margin is \$0.20/\$0.80 = 25 percent. The most common practice in marketing is to express margins as a percentage of selling price. Margins expressed in this fashion are easier to work with, especially in a multilevel channel situation. Unless explicitly stated otherwise, you may assume that all margins in the cases in this book use selling price as the relevant base.

A number of different types of margin-related problems arise. They include:

1. Determining the selling price, given you know the cost price and the percentage margin on selling price. Suppose that a retailer buys an appliance for $15 and wants to obtain a margin on selling price of 40 percent. What selling price must be charged? The answer $21 is not correct because this margin ($6 = $15 × 0.4) would be on cost price. To answer this question, we must remember one fundamental relationship:

$$\text{Selling price} = \text{Cost price} + \text{Margin}$$

Here we are taking selling price as the base equal to 100 percent, so we can write

$$100\% = \$15 + 40\%$$

That is, the cost price plus the margin must add to 100 percent. Clearly, the $15 must then be 60 percent of the desired selling price. Thus,

$$\text{Derived selling price} = \$15/60\%$$
$$= \$25$$

The dollar margin is then $10, which is $10/$25 = 40 percent of selling price.

The general rule then is to divide 1 minus the percentage margin expressed as a decimal on selling price, into the cost price. For example, if cost price is $105 and the margin on selling price is 22.5 percent, then the desired selling price is $105/(1 − 0.225) = $105/0.775 = $135.48.

2. Conversion of margin bases. Sometimes a margin is given on a cost-price basis, and we wish to convert it to a selling-price base, or vice versa. How do we make the conversion? Suppose that a product costs $4.50 and sells for $6.00. The margin is $1.50. On a selling-price basis, the margin is $1.50/$6.00 = 25 percent. On a cost-price basis, the margin is $1.50/$4.50 = 33.33 percent. The conversion from one percentage margin to the other is easy if we remember that selling price is composed of two parts: margin and cost.

For selling-price base:

$$\text{Selling price} = \text{Margin} + \text{Cost}$$
$$\$6.00 = \$1.50 + \$4.50$$

or more important

$$100\% = 25\% + 75\%$$

For cost-price base:

$$\text{Selling price} = \text{Margin} + \text{Cost}$$
$$\$6.00 = \$1.50 + \$4.50$$

but here the cost is the 100-percent base, so

$$\$6.00 = \$1.50 + 100\%$$

or

$$133.33\% = 33.33\% + 100\%$$

That is, the selling price should be thought of as 133.33 percent of the cost price.
Conversion from selling-price to cost-price base:

$$\text{Selling price} = \text{Margin} + \text{Cost}$$
$$100\% = 25\% + 75\%$$

So, if we want to convert the 25 percent margin to a cost-price basis, the 75 percent that is the cost becomes the relevant base and

$$\text{Margin as a percentage of cost price} = \frac{25\%}{75\%} = 33.33\%$$

Note that this is exactly the same as dividing $1.50 by $4.50.
    A simple formula for making this conversion is

$$\text{Percentage margin on cost price} = \frac{\text{Percentage margin on selling price}}{100\% - \text{Percentage margin on selling price}}$$

In our example, this is

$$\frac{25\%}{100\% - 25\%} = \frac{25\%}{75\%} = 33.33\%$$

Note that the only piece of information that we need to make this conversion is the margin percentage on selling price.
Conversion from cost-price to selling-price base:

$$\text{Selling price} = \text{Margin} + \text{Cost}$$
$$133.33\% = 33.33\% + 100\%$$

The margin is 33.33 percent and the relevant selling price base is 133.33 percent, so

$$\text{Margin as a percentage of selling price} = \frac{33.33\%}{133.33\%} = 25\%$$

Note that this is exactly the same as dividing $1.50 by $6.00.
    A simple formula for making this conversion is

$$\text{Percentage margin on selling price} = \frac{\text{Percentage margin on cost price}}{100\% + \text{Percentage margin on cost price}}$$

In our example, this is

$$\frac{33.33\%}{100\% + 33.33\%} = \frac{33.33\%}{133.33\%} = 25\%$$

Note that the only piece of information that we need to make this conversion is the margin percentage on cost price.

Multiple Margins

Often a manufacturer gives a suggested retail selling price and suggested retail and wholesale margins. For example, the suggested retail price may be $7.50, with a retail margin of 20 percent and a wholesale margin of 15 percent. To determine the manufacturer's selling price in this situation, we simply take the appropriate margins off one at a time. Thus,

Retail selling price	$7.50
Less retail margin (20% of $7.50)	−1.50
Equals retail cost price or wholesale selling price	$6.00
Less wholesale margin (15% of $6.00)	−0.90
Equals wholesale cost price or manufacturer's selling price	$5.10

No matter how many levels there are in the channel, the approach is the same. We simply take the margins off one at a time. Note that we cannot just add up the margins and subtract this amount. Here 20% + 15% = 35%, and 35% of $7.50 is $2.63, making the manufacturer's selling price $7.50 − $2.63 = $4.87. This is not correct.

This chapter has outlined some financial concepts that add greatly to our abilities to make sound marketing decisions. These concepts should be applied where needed in the cases in this book.

Chapter 4

A Case with a Student Analysis

The fundamental premise of this book is that one learns by doing. However, one can also learn from example. The purpose of this chapter is to give an example of a case analysis. The framework of analysis presented in the previous two chapters will be used here in order to clarify how one can use the framework.

The case presented in this chapter, "Crow, Pope, and Land Enterprises," is a broad-issue marketing case that has no textbook or single "correct" answer. A student analysis of the case follows the case presentation, and in the last section of the chapter we present our commentary on the case analysis.

We suggest the following steps in using this chapter:

1. Read and prepare your analysis of "Crow, Pope, and Land Enterprises." This will give you a better perspective on the case analysis presented in this chapter.
2. Read and evaluate the analysis presented here. You may wish to use the points that constitute a good case analysis, as presented in Chapter 2.
3. Read our commentary on the case analysis. Compare our view with yours.

Case

Crow, Pope, and Land Enterprises*

In early August 1973, Mr. Dan Thatcher, vice president of CPL Condominium Enterprises, a subsidiary of Crow, Pope, and Land Enterprises, was planning his strategy for a new condominium project in Jacksonville, Florida. The project was an important one, since it was the company's first attempt to diversify out of the Atlanta area with nonresort condominiums. Earlier in the year, Mr. Thatcher had arranged the purchase of an option on a 40-acre tract just outside the city limits of Jacksonville, and the company had to renew the option in the next week or they would lose their earnest money. Before the senior officers of the firm would approve the final purchase of the land for approximately $700,000, Mr. Thatcher had to prepare a report discussing the proposed marketing strategy for the condominiums to be built there. His report was to include discussions of the target market, the specifications of the units to be built, the price range of the condominiums, and the promotional strategy to be used in marketing the units.

Company Background

Crow, Pope, and Land Enterprises, Inc., is a developer of residential, commercial, and motel/hotel real estate property, with projects located throughout the world. Headquartered in Atlanta, Georgia, the company was incorporated on January 14, 1967, under the name Lincoln Construction Company. Trammell Crow of Dallas, Ewell Pope of Atlanta, and Frank Carter of Atlanta were the shareholders of the company. Mr. Pope and Mr. Carter had been partners in the real estate brokerage firm, Pope and Carter Company, which had acted as the leasing agent for several of Trammell Crow's developments, namely, Chattahoochee Industrial Park and Greenbriar Shopping Center. These two ventures had proved so successful that the three men decided to strengthen their association and form Lincoln Construction Company.

---

*This case was written by Kenneth L. Bernhardt and John S. Wright, Professor of Marketing, Georgia State University. Copyright © 1975 by Kenneth L. Bernhardt.

In June 1972, Mr. Pope and Mr. Carter decided to establish separate organizations, both of which were formed in association with Mr. Crow. Crow and Carter started Crow, Carter, and Associates, Inc., and Crow and Pope, in association with A. J. Land, Jr., became owners of the continuing company, Crow, Pope, and Land Enterprises, Inc.

The company is organized on a project-management basis, with a managing partner who oversees and is responsible for every phase of the development assigned to each project. The manager of each project acts very much like the president of a small company, with the exception that he has the resources of a much larger corporation to draw upon when it is felt that added expertise would be of assistance. Most of the project managers, including Mr. Thatcher, are young, aggressive MBA graduates from leading schools of business administration.

The projects in which the company is involved range from the development of apartment complexes, condominium complexes, office parks, and shopping centers, to "total community" complexes complete with apartments, condominiums, single-family houses, retail outlets, parks, schools, office buildings, and recreational facilities. The firm has recently become active in the development of urban community centers containing a mixture of such features as commercial high-rise office buildings, luxury hotels, retail shopping facilities, and other pedestrian conveniences designed for high architectural impact in downtown environments. Examples of some of the company's projects include the $100 million Atlanta Center project (a large Hilton Hotel together with office buildings and shopping areas in downtown Atlanta), the $40 million Sheraton Hong Kong Hotel and shopping mall complex, and the Cumberland, Fairington, and Northlake total community complexes in Atlanta. Cumberland, a $65 million joint venture development with the Metropolitan Life Insurance Company, will, upon its completion in 1978, include a 1-million-square-foot enclosed shopping center, 750,000 square feet of office space, 1,800 apartments and condominiums situated around a 17-acre lake, an indoor tennis center, and hotel/motel facilities.

Crow, Pope, and Land has built a number of condominium and apartment complexes in Atlanta, and has built more condominiums than any other developer in the area. Among the projects currently being sold in the Atlanta area are projects oriented toward retired couples, young swingers, sports-minded couples and families, and couples who want to own their own residences but cannot afford single-family detached housing. The company also has several resort projects in Florida.

Background on the Jacksonville Project

The original idea for the Jacksonville project came out of a meeting Mr. Thatcher had in early 1973 with Lindsay Freeman, another vice president of CPL Condominium Enterprises. In discussing the future goals and directions for the subsidiary, they decided that a high priority should be placed on reducing their dependence on the Atlanta condominium market, where all nine of their projects were located. Since different geographic areas often were at different stages of the business cycle, they felt expansion into new geographical areas would provide a hedge against economic downturns as well as opening up profitable new markets for their products.

The first decision made was that they should concentrate on the Southeast, within a 400-mile radius of Atlanta, allowing greater control from the Atlanta headquarters. Also, projections of housing market demand indicated that this region of the country would experience rapid growth in the coming few years.

A number of cities, including Memphis, Louisville, Chattanooga, Mobile, and Birmingham, were investigated as possible sites for a condominium project. Several criteria were established. The area had to have several condominium projects already in existence since they did not want to be the first project in the area. Their experience had shown that the pioneers had to undertake a large educational effort, which usually took two years and a lot of money. The city should have a population of at least 250,000 so it could absorb a large number of condominiums if the company decided to add other projects at a later date. Lastly, the area should have a large number of residents in the target market for condominiums—young married couples and "empty nesters," couples whose children are grown and have moved out of the home.

Using census data, information obtained from Chambers of Commerce, and other real estate research sources, Thatcher narrowed the choice to Charlotte, North Carolina, and Jacksonville, Florida. In both places, condominiums had been marketed for two to three years, and a number of developments were being built. In Charlotte, however, the only land that was available for immediate development was not particularly well suited for multifamily building. It had been decided that land that had been zoned for condominium development, with utilities easily accessible, would be favored to avoid the normal two-year period to get undeveloped raw land ready for development. Therefore, it was without reservation that Thatcher made the decision to expand into the Jacksonville market.

Background on the Jacksonville Area

Jacksonville is the most populated city in Florida and ranks second in the Southeast and 23rd in the United States. In October of 1968, the city adopted a new charter which consolidated the city and county governments. All of Duval County is now operated as one government, and the consolidation made the new city of Jacksonville the largest city in the continental United States with 840 square miles (537,664 acres). To put the figures into comparative terms, the city is two-thirds the size of the state of Rhode Island.

Recent growth has brought many young people to the Jacksonville area. In 1970, the median age of the population was 26 years, compared to 32.3 years for the state of Florida and 28.3 years for the total United States. Duval County has a large, rapidly growing economy, with a balanced employment profile and a rather diversified economic base. This diversification has produced a stable economy by minimizing its sensitivity to both industrial and national business cycles.

For a distance of approximately 100 miles in all directions, the area surrounding the city is predominantly rural in character. With over 500,000 residents, Jacksonville is the commercial and cultural center of northeast Florida and southeast Georgia. It is one of the principal distribution, insurance, and convention centers in the Southeast.

One of the major impacts on the city's economy is the presence of three large military installations in the area, particularly the Jacksonville Naval Air Station located in the southern part of the county on the St. Johns River just north of the city of Orange Park. This facility is one of the largest naval air bases in the United States. It is supported by a smaller air station, Cecil Field, located in the western part of the county, where several air squadrons operate in preparation for air carrier qualifications. The third facility, the Mayport Carrier Basin east of Jacksonville, has berthing capacity for three of the country's largest aircraft carriers. The military installations employ approximately 34,000 people, including some 5,000 civilians, 9,000 shore-based military personnel, and 20,000 mobile/afloat military. Another 5,000 military employees are expected to be transferred to these facilities in the next year or two.

Extensive bedroom areas are forming just outside Duval County, reflecting lower tax rates, lower land prices, an absence of restrictive zoning ordinances, and a preference for suburban living. Also, the city of Jacksonville was busing children to achieve racial integration in the schools, and many residents were moving to Orange Park and other areas of Clay County (just south of Duval County) where there was no busing of students. The impact of all these factors made Clay County, and the Orange Park area in particular, a rapidly growing area.

The city of Orange Park lies adjacent to and south of the Duval County line, and is approximately 15 miles from the central business district of Jacksonville. Exhibit 1 presents a map of the area, showing the location of Orange Park in relation to the naval air station, Cecil Field, and the business district of Jacksonville.

After talking with many real estate people in the area, and after reviewing the statistics presented in Exhibit 2, Mr. Thatcher decided to obtain an option on a 40-acre tract of land just west of the city limits of Orange Park. As shown in the exhibit, the residents of Orange Park had an above-average median family income for the area and were better educated than Duval County residents. Also, over half the population in the area worked outside the county (principally in Duval County). Thatcher thought the higher-income, better-educated people would be receptive to condominiums. Also, he felt that the close proximity to Duval County would be attractive to many potential purchasers.

Access to the site is off Blanding Boulevard (State Road 21 on the map), a heavily traveled two-lane thoroughfare with development, for the most part, consisting of commercial and single-family residential development. Within the past

EXHIBIT 1   Map of Jacksonville and Orange Park area

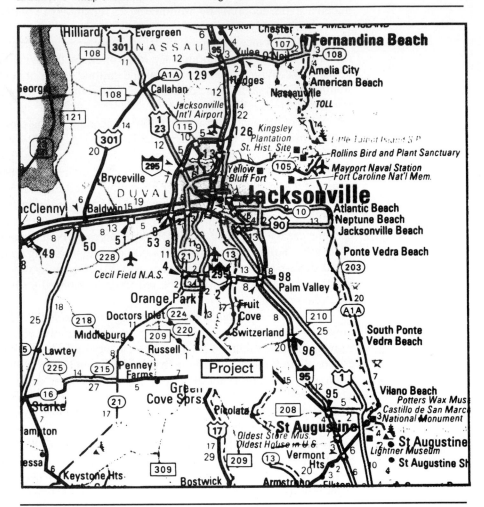

EXHIBIT 2   Selected statistics for Orange Park, Clay County, and Duval County/Jacksonville

	City of Orange Park	Clay County	Duval County/ Jacksonville
Total population, 1970	7,677	32,059	528,865
Median family income, 1970	$10,021	$8,430	$8,671
Median school years completed— 1970, adults	12.5	12.1	12.0
Percent of residents who work outside the county	—	53.5%	2.6%
Percent of residents who have lived in the same area for five years or more, 1970	30.0%	45.6%	67.1%

year, a considerable amount of multifamily development had occurred, but it was mainly concentrated further northeast in the vicinity of U.S. Highway 17.

Within one mile of the site to the north is a minor shopping center with a Winn-Dixie supermarket as the cornerstone tenant. Two and one-half miles north, a 1-million-square-foot regional shopping center is being developed and is scheduled to open in 1975. The school system in the area is rated excellent, and several elementary schools as well as junior and senior high schools are in close proximity to the site. Churches of all denominations and hospital and recreation facilities are all well represented in the area.

The current housing market in the Orange Park area is composed substantially of single-family houses, with prices of these units beginning at $32,000. Apartments in the vicinity of the site have achieved 100 percent occupancy, with many of the apartments renting for between $150 and $200 per month. There are a number of condominium projects in the area, as shown in Exhibit 3, although almost all of them are situated much farther north. The price range on these condominium projects typically begins in the low- $30,000 range and goes up to almost $60,000.

Marketing Strategy

The first question Thatcher had to resolve concerned the target market for the condominiums. There were three basic strategies he had been considering: (1) a specialty-type product with a large amenity package oriented toward active, young "swinging" couples; (2) a project oriented toward the retiree market; or (3) a project oriented toward families who wanted to purchase their residence but could not afford a single-family house. Crow, Pope, and Land had considerable experience in building all three types of condominiums in the Atlanta area, and Thatcher was reluctant to consider other types of condominiums that the company had not had experience with. He reasoned that undertaking a product that had worked elsewhere would reduce some of the risk of entering a new, relatively unknown market. Also, use of a product that the company had built in Atlanta would save the cost of architect's fees, and he would be in a better position to negotiate with a contractor to build the units because he would know in advance what the costs should be (building costs in the Jacksonville area were virtually the same as costs in Atlanta).

EXHIBIT 3   Condominium projects in the Orange Park area

Project	Rooms	Square feet	Price range
Bay Meadows	2BR,2B –3BR,3B	1,350–2,243	$34,850–$48,300
Solano Grove	1BR,1B –3BR,3B	874–2,006	26,100– 58,200
Regency Woods	2BR,2B –4BR,2½B	1,456–2,102	35,500– 45,900
Sutton Place	2BR,2½B–4BR,2½B	1,366–1,842	31,500– 38,000
Baytree	2BR,1½B–4BR,3½B	1,404–2,214	32,000– 46,750
The Lakes	2BR,2B –3BR,2½B	1,330–2,050	37,500– 59,400
Oxford Forest	2BR,1½B–3BR,2½B	1,282–1,622	28,500– 35,500

Thatcher had located a site along the St. Johns River that would be suitable for the specialty, high-amenity product. There might be some environmental problems with the Army Corps of Engineers, who had jurisdiction over the site, but he thought these could be worked out. The Orange Park site under option would not be suitable for this type of project, which Thatcher thought should be built around a body of water. With the high land cost for an appropriate site, and with the high cost for all the recreational amenities, the company would have to price the condominiums under this strategy at about $40,000 (the same price charged for the comparable Riverbend Condominiums in Atlanta).

The optioned site was also not acceptable for the second alternative, a project oriented toward the retirees' market. Experience in Atlanta had shown that retired couples preferred to purchase condominiums with a golf course on site, and the present site was not suited for development of a golf course. Thatcher had located several possible sites suitable for this alternative several miles south of the property under option. Because of the very large investment involved in building a golf course, he felt that a project oriented toward this market would have to be a large one to support the high fixed cost of the golf course.

If the company decided to purchase the property under option, about 12 units per acre could be constructed, or about 480 in total. As they did with almost all their projects, the units would be built in several phases, with phase I consisting of 50 units. Thatcher had determined that units built in the Fairgrounds project in Atlanta could be built and sold profitably in Orange Park for $24,900 for a 1,040-square-foot, two-bedroom unit and $29,900 for a 1,265-square-foot, three-bedroom unit. The price per square foot was comparable to the other condominium projects in the area, and the total price was well below most of them because of the smaller size. In addition to the difference in square footage and price, the Fairgrounds models also had different exteriors than the typical ones sold in the Jacksonville area; the Fairgrounds units used brick and aluminum siding, whereas most of the others had a stucco exterior. Although he basically believed that the Jacksonville condominium prospect was very similar to the Atlanta prospect, he wondered whether he should incorporate some stucco treatment into the exterior of the units if he should decide to follow through with this strategy.

Another issue he had not resolved concerned the extent to which the strategy should be oriented toward the large (and growing) military market. If he did define his target market as the military market, what impact would this have on the physical product and on his promotional strategy, which was still to be determined? Close to half of the residents of Orange Park worked at one of the three military installations in the area, and both the naval air station and Cecil Field were within seven miles of the proposed site. He was aware of the large word-of-mouth influence in the Navy—an apartment project not far from the site which was just beginning to lease new units had gone from 5 percent Navy to 30 percent Navy in less than two months.

Another question which concerned Thatcher was the low sales rate of the other condominiums in the area. He thought the reason was the relatively high prices, which caused them to compete directly against single-family housing. Also, he had shopped all the projects and found the on-site salesmen to be very uninformed and uninterested in selling the condominiums. He felt certain that this was hurting sales, but he was still not sure that the consumers in the Jacksonville/Orange Park area would buy condominiums, even in the price range he was proposing.

The senior officers of Crow, Pope, and Land would also expect a detailed promotional strategy as part of his report. In working with budget figures, he had determined that he could afford to spend $22,000 for promotion (1.5 percent of sales) for the first 50 units, which would be about 12 months' projected sales. Brochures, signs, business cards for salesmen, and other miscellaneous items would cost about $2,000, leaving $20,000 for media and production costs.

Crow, Pope, and Land used a small local advertising agency for all their apartment and condominium advertising in Atlanta. Thatcher was uncertain about the role he wanted the agency to play in this project and was worried that the agency was not attuned to the Jacksonville market. He wondered whether he should try to hire a Jacksonville agency, but he was afraid that the account was too small for anyone to pay much attention to it. Also, he felt that the retainer that any decent agency would want to handle the account, about $3,000, could be better spent on media. He had studied advertising and promotion in courses in college, and thought he should consider creating the advertising himself.

There were really only two alternatives for media strategy in the Jacksonville area—radio and newspaper. There were nine AM radio stations and four FM stations. The rates for the four largest stations were all about the same, between $25 and $30 for a one-minute spot during drive time (6–10 A.M. and 3–7 P.M.) and about 20 percent cheaper at other times, assuming 12 spots per week for 13 weeks. There were two daily newspapers in Jacksonville, a morning paper with 210,000 circulation and an evening paper with 148,000 circulation. As a result of common ownership, there was a combination rate available which was only 10 percent higher than the $13.16-per-column-inch rate for the morning paper alone. The morning paper had a Sunday edition, with a circulation of 182,000 and a cost per column inch of $13.72.

Mr. Thatcher was also concerned about what message to use in his promotional campaign. He was uncertain to what extent they should mention the fact that there was no busing to schools, an important advantage for many potential buyers. He was worried that other people might be upset with the implied racism in such a campaign. He was also concerned with the implications for the advertising creative strategy as a result of the target-market decision concerning whether or not to concentrate on the military market. Another advertising issue was the extent to which the copy should promote the fact that Crow, Pope, and Land was a large Atlanta developer, and that this was their first North Florida project.

The one decision Thatcher had made was that there was much opportunity for the company in the Jacksonville market, and, therefore, much opportunity for him personally to expand his responsibilities in the company. As a result, he wanted to make a recommendation that the company definitely enter the market; the only uncertainty was the strategy to be followed. The company had paid $1,000 for the initial option on the Orange Park property. Next week they had to either pay $20,000 to renew the option for 90 days or lose their $1,000 investment. If they decided to renew the option, this would give them time to arrange for the financing of the project and to arrange a production schedule with the contractors. They had to begin this planning immediately since it usually took at least six months to build condominiums, and that meant that they would have to act fast if they wanted to be selling condominiums by the height of the selling season in June. As he sat down to write the report containing his recommendations, Thatcher realized that a decision to renew the option would be a commitment to actually build the units he recommended.

Example Situation Analysis of Crow, Pope, and Land Enterprises (CPL)

CPL Condominium Enterprises, a subsidiary of CPL Enterprises, Inc., a residential housing and commercial builder, had built a number of *condominium* complexes in Atlanta, designed for specific segments such as retired couples, young swingers, families, and low-middle-income couples. In addition, they had several resort projects in Florida.

In order to reduce their dependence on the Atlanta condominium market, a *goal* of expanding into new geographic areas where profitable markets were opening up was developed by two CPL Condominium Enterprises VPs. The *tactics* were to choose a city of at least 250,000 population within a 400-mile radius of Atlanta, since forecasts of the housing market projected rapid growth in this general region in the coming few years. Dan Thatcher was to put together a marketing *strategy* discussing product, price, place, and promotion to pursue in reaching this goal. Since this discussion is centered around Dan Thatcher's review of the Orange Park condominium market, it will be assumed here that the product is *condominiums*. In the larger context of the company, which will be touched on at the end of this paper, the product considered is *housing*.

A. NATURE OF DEMAND

1. How do buyers currently go about buying condos?

In the search for housing, buyers will generally define the neighborhood they are interested in, then select among the alternatives within their price range. The decision to buy a condominium, rather than a single-family detached dwelling, may be influenced by several factors—price, ease of maintenance, amenities, and the like—which are discussed more thoroughly in Part 2. The buyer will seek information to a high degree through media, family, friends, co-workers, real estate brokers, and, if available, reports on developers of other condominium projects to ascertain their reputation and workmanship quality. After looking at a number of developments, the decision of which condo to buy will probably be made at home or after a second or third look at the property under consideration. Sources of information about condos in the Jacksonville/Orange Park area are probably newspapers, some broadcast coverage, and word of mouth. Although condos have existed for more than two years in this area, awareness level seems low due to the slow sales of condos in the area. In 1973, condos were not in vogue, and hence buyer knowledge and acceptability were not particularly well developed. The decision to purchase is made by the adults; if a couple, by a joint decision. This is the most important major purchase decision in most people's lives, thus much time, thought, and effort goes into the decision process. The buyer is highly influenced by the salesperson, the physical plant itself, friends, the real estate broker, and possibly the bank loan officer. This is usually a new purchase situation, evoking high interest, personal involvement, and excitement by the buyer. All of these factors contribute to a high risk associated with a poor purchase decision—it's hard to get rid of a condo that no one else wants either! A number of functional considerations enter into the decision, such as location, utilities, and convenience (more on this in Part 2). A number of psychosocial considerations also enter into the decision, such as aesthetics, social contact, safety, prestige, and self-esteem. This being a durable good, the consumption time is long term.

2.   Can the market be meaningfully segmented?

Due to CPL Condominium Enterprises' expertise in building condo complexes geared toward specific segments, and since Dan Thatcher desires to use an existing set of plans for the new condo development, it seems best to segment the market into those areas CPL can build for—namely, singles, retired couples, and young (low-middle-income) families. In addition, due to the demographic composition of the area (50 percent employed by the Navy), a Navy/military segment is also relevant. Attributes important to each segment are ranked in Table 1. Table 2 then ranks these attributes together with the housing options in the area, limited here to condos, single-family homes, and rental apartments, since these are the housing types mentioned in the case. Since the median age of Jacksonville is 26, below both the Florida and national medians, we can probably safely assume that there are many young couples and singles associated with the large military labor base, perhaps a growing number of babies and children (helping to lower the median), and that the family life-cycle stage is generally early. Additional data on average household size, the age distribution, and income versus age would be helpful in this analysis. The high turnover rate of Orange Park residents suggests either a very mobile population or a very fast-growing area.

Comparing Tables 1 and 2, there is not a one-to-one correlation between all the boxed attributes of Option: Condo and Segments. Note, however, that there is a correlation between Options: Apartment and Segment: Singles.

TABLE 1 Attributes important to the Navy/military segment

	Segments			
Attributes	Singles	Retirees	Young families	Navy (families)
Price	++++	++++	++++	+++++
Size	+	+	++++	+++
Neighborhood	++	+++	++++	++
Convenience to shopping	++	+++	+++	+
Schools	+	+	++++	+++
Social acceptability	++++	++	++	++
Social interaction	++++	+++	++	++
Recreation/amenities	++++	++++	+++	+++
Safety	++	++++	++++	++
Low tax base	+	++	++	++
Accessibility to work	++	+	++	++++
Mass transportation	++	+++	++	++
Access to entertainment	+++	++	++	++
Maintenance	++++	++++	+++	+++
Financing convenience*	++++	++	+++	+++
Public works	+	+++	+	+
Land availability	++	++	++++	++

*Defined as renting versus down payment/monthly mortgage commitments.

TABLE 2 Ranking of various housing options

	Options		
Attributes	Our condo	Rental apartment	Single-family home
Price	++++	++++	++
Size	+	++	++++
Neighborhood	+++	?	?
Convenience to shopping	+++	?	?
Schools	+	?	?
Social acceptability	++	+	++++
Social interaction	+++	+++	+
Recreation/amenities	++	+++?	+
Safety	++	+	++
Low tax base	+++?	+?	+++?
Accessibility to work	+++?	++?	++?
Mass transportation	+	+	+
Maintenance	++++	++++	+
Financing convenience*	+	++++	+
Land availability	++	++	++++
Equity	++++	+	++++

*Defined as renting versus down payment/monthly mortgage commitments.

B.   EXTENT OF DEMAND

1.   Sufficient demand for more condo housing?

Although there is limited information, one can still make some estimate of the total demand in the Jacksonville market. It is well known that, nationally, about 20 percent of the population moves each year. We also know from Exhibit 2 in the case that 32.9 percent of the population of Duval County (and a much higher percentage of Clay County) have lived there five years or less. On the basis of this information, we might expect about 5 percent of the households to be looking for a house; and, with an average of about 2.5 children and 4.7 people per family, the number of houses shifting hands may equal about 1 to 1.5 percent of the population, or in the neighborhood of 6,000 to 7,000 homes. Even if we recognize that a large proportion of the 20 percent of the population that move in a typical year consists of young people moving from one apartment to another, it would seem that this estimate of 6,000 to 7,000 homes is extremely conservative. Since Jacksonville is a very rapidly growing area full of economic activity, and since the "baby boomers" are just entering the age where they will be buying houses, we might raise this estimate to around 10,000 homes. With projected sales of 50 units the first year, Crow, Pope, and Land is trying to achieve around .5 percent of the market.

What part of this will be condos is the next issue to judge.

2.   Current market shares

We have no information to judge this. It appears that single-family home purchases dominate the purchasing mode, and that rental apartments are 100 percent occupied. There may exist excess demand for apartments. This can raise apartment rents (if no new apartments will soon be built), making the price advantage of renting less of a factor over time. Selective demand trends suggest that consumer awareness of condo developments is increasing, and, along with that, so is public acceptance. Since single-family homes start selling at $32,000, it could be that condos are not selling because people can just as easily afford single-family homes. Banks usually like housing to account for only 25 to 30 percent of one's gross income; hence these could be too high priced, even though they are less than the other alternatives. Purchasing the smaller condo at $24,000 would lead to the following results:

a.   12 percent, 20-year mortgage:

$$\frac{\$24,000}{7.469} = \frac{\$3,213.28, \text{ or } \$267.77/\text{month}}{32.1 \text{ percent of income.}}$$

b.   8 percent, 20-year mortgage:

$$\frac{\$24,000}{9.818} = \frac{\$2,444.49, \text{ or } \$203.71/\text{month}}{24.4 \text{ percent of income.}}$$

It would be difficult for the average person to finance anything but the lower-priced condo at the lower interest rate. Of course, when Thatcher needs to make his decision, he cannot foresee possible future increases in interest rates.

C. NATURE OF COMPETITION

1. Present and future structure of competition

Seven other condo projects in the general area, as well as numerous single-family home developments, exist. Market shares are unknown, although we know that rental apartments have 100 percent occupancy. Financial resources of competitors are unknown. Marketing resources and skills of condo competitors, judged by their salespeople, are poor. They lack interest, enthusiasm, and knowledge of the projects they are trying to sell. Production resources and skills of competitors are unknown.

2. Current marketing programs of established competitors

We do not know much but, judging from the slow sales, it might be reasonable to suppose that consumer awareness is low, knowledge of market needs is poor, and the salesperson's role is a very critical part of the competition's marketing program, although it seems to be unsuccessful.

3. Opportunity for another competitor?

The fact that the property Thatcher has an option to buy is *zoned* for condos indicates that the planning body of the county feels that condos will serve as one of the housing mixes for the area. Since the opportunity for CPL to drastically price-cut the market exists, there does seem to be opportunity for another competitor. Whether buyer demand exists is another question, however.

4. Retaliatory moves of competitors?

Competitors can probably drop their prices somewhat. The other developments appear to be a few miles away from this one, though, so perhaps another condo development may not greatly affect the competitors.

D. ENVIRONMENTAL CLIMATE

1. Relevant social, political, economic, and technological trends

Since this project is located in the South, busing is a hot issue. People opposed to busing (which is taking place in Jacksonville/Duval County) will want to live in an area with no forced busing. Condominiums are just hitting the market—they are in a young product life-cycle stage; thus social acceptability is currently in the developing stage.

The last lottery for the Vietnam War draft took place in 1973. The war is starting to wind down. In 1975, some military ships were mothballed. Hence the lifeblood of Orange Park, which is over half military, will soon be in a transition stage. Basing a project on military personnel housing demand is probably very risky at this time.

Some of these factors may increase the attractiveness of condos. People will want to live closer to work, but in an area with low land rates and a low tax base due to the ever-increasing squeeze on their pocketbooks. A condo may be easier to keep cool; the accessibility to a pool, which a condo development in Florida is likely to have, may further increase its attractiveness.

E. STAGE OF PRODUCT LIFE CYCLE

The product category, condominiums, is at an early life-cycle point. Some people are aware of their existence, but the concept is not yet so well tested that people are rushing out to buy condos. As the product ages and more people begin purchasing condos, social acceptability will increase. The slow sales of the present condo developments in the area are indicative of this lack of social acceptability due to the product's early life-cycle stage. Of course, other factors that are perhaps more important (price, location, etc.) enter into this, too. The fact that one of CPL's development criteria was that other condo projects should have existed in the area for at least two years supports the argument that an educational and acceptability process must first take place before the product sells well. The more knowledge the consumer has, the more he/she will want to buy this product.

F. COST STRUCTURE OF THE INDUSTRY

Comparing our project to the other projects' $/square feet range, the CPL project is about average in $/square foot price, although lower in total price due to the low square footage of the units. A comparison with competitors is presented in Table 3. The highs and lows are boxed. We know that $22,000 of selling costs equals 1.5 percent of sales. Hence, the first 50 units will bring in an expected revenue of

$$\frac{\$22,000}{.015} = \$1,466,667.$$

For sale of 480 units, total revenues would equal

$$\frac{480}{50} \times \$1,466,667 = \$14,080,003.$$

Other costs we know of:

Land = $721,000 (include $1,000 + $20,000 in option).
Selling costs = 1.5% = $210,000 ($14 million × .015).

TABLE 3 Comparison of cost by competitor

Project	Rooms	Sq. ft.	Price range	$/Sq. ft. range
Bay Meadows	2B2B –3B3B	1,350–2,243	$34,850–$48,300	$25.81–$21.53
Solano Grove	1B1B –3B3B	879–2,006	26,100– 58,200	29.86– 29.01
Regency Woods	2B2B –4B2½B	1,456–2,102	35,500– 45,900	24.38– 21.84
Sutton Place	2B2½B–4B2½B	1,366–1,842	31,500– 38,000	23.06– 20.63
Baytree	2B1½B–4B3½B	1,404–2,214	32,000– 46,150	22.79– 21.12
The Lakes	2B2B –3B2½B	1,330–2,050	37,500– 59,400	28.20– 28.98
Oxford Forest	2B1½B–3B2½B	1,282–1,622	28,500– 35,500	22.23– 21.89
CPL	2 Bdr	1,040	24,900	23.94
	3 Bdr	1,265	29,900	23.64
Single-family home		Assume 1,400	32,000	22.86

Assume construction is approximately $20/square foot:

1,000 square feet × 480 condos × $20/square foot
                    = $9,600,000 per condo, approximately.

Sales	$14,080,000	100%
CGS	− 9,600,000	68
Gross margin	$ 4,480,000	32
Sales	− 210,000	
Land	− 721,000	8
Other (guess)	− 100,000	
Net profit (pretax)	$ 3,449,000	24

The project looks profitable at this point, if these assumptions are valid. If the company highly leverages the development, this would be a very attractive investment indeed.

G.   SKILLS OF THE FIRM

1.   Marketing

Apparently, the firm as a whole has been quite successful, and much of this success for a real estate company must be attributed to marketing. A small Atlanta advertising agency is used for the Atlanta apartment and condominium advertising, but Thatcher is not sure the agency will be able to adequately and successfully come up with a Jacksonville marketing plan. To hire a local Jacksonville agency, about $3,000 would need to be spent on a retainer, which Thatcher thought could be better spent on media.

Since he had studied advertising and promotion in college courses, Thatcher thought he had the skills to create the advertising himself. If CPL commonly has its project managers create the advertising for projects, then I would question whether the marketing skills of the firm were really very good. I do not think Thatcher is who we want promoting a $14 million condo complex!

We do not know how successful CPL has been with its condo developments, but we can only assume that continued existence and expansion in the business means that it has been successful thus far, and hence its marketing is good.

2.   Production

Again, we don't have too much data to access this, but judging from the size of some of the projects, such as the Atlanta Center Project, the Sheraton Hong Kong Hotel, and the Cumberland, Fairington, and Northlake total community complexes, CPL must be able to "produce" buildings or else it wouldn't be undertaking such large efforts. Thatcher says that CPL has experience building the three condominium types in Atlanta (swinging singles, retirees, and young families) and could thus negotiate well with the contractor in Jacksonville, since he would have a good idea of what the actual costs would be. He also mentioned that this "product had worked"; therefore, he thought it could work again. Also, perhaps the use of brick and aluminum siding exteriors is popular and well liked, thus helping the firm to sell a slightly different product better than the stucco exterior norm in Jacksonville.

3. Management

Apparently, the company has a lot of MBA types and, due to the project-management emphasis, fairly aggressive self-starters. Crow and Pope had a good record of success in the real estate brokerage business prior to their forming CPL. It looks like we can assume the company has good management skills and talented, although perhaps overly confident, people on staff.

4. Financial

Their financial skills are probably very good, since the owners have over five years of experience in the business and the project managers, similar to Thatcher, have business training backgrounds/education. Due to the size of the projects the parent company is undertaking, we can assume it has a good financial relationship with its bank and must be doing well to continue getting large sums of financing. The subsidiary, CPL Condominiums, is thus backed by a strong parent company. The parent company is probably making nice profits from its hotel operations, as high margins are typically the rule in this area.

5. R&D

R&D in terms of a popular product design appears to be good, since it sounds like a brick and aluminum siding exterior condo is an attractive and long-lasting exterior. Modifying their developments to meet the needs of particular market segments in terms of amenities shows good insight in producing a product to meet the needs of the consumer.

However, the background research Thatcher has performed for judging the Jacksonville condo market is quite limited. He is basing his decision on very limited data. A much better decision could be reached with more research into demographic trends in the area, determining the mobility of the Navy personnel, and finding out how future road work will favorably or adversely affect this proposed condo development. The fact that apartments are 100 percent occupied but condo sales are slow should cause Thatcher to question whether condos are what is needed here. Perhaps apartments would be a better fit to community needs.

As far as comparing CPL's skills to the competitors, we do not know enough about the competitors, except that their marketing seems weak, to make a particularly valid comparison.

H. FINANCIAL RESOURCES OF THE FIRM

As the calculations in Part F show, the financial return on this investment looks very attractive. Since CPL Condominium Enterprises has the backing of the parent company, I think it is safe to assume that financing this project will pose no problem.

I. DISTRIBUTION/PROMOTIONAL STRUCTURE AVAILABLE

Classic distribution institutions are not a directly relevant dimension here. However, the existence of an institutional structure for promotion is important.

This is where media advertising comes in: A number of types could be utilized, under the constraint of $20,000 for the first year's promotional activities after spending $2,000 for brochures, wages, and business cards. Advertising on commute-time radio could take up most of this budget, if four radio stations are used, with 12 spots a week for 13 weeks (4 stations × $30/minute × 12 spots/week × 13 weeks = $18,700). Advertising in the newspaper only, using the Sunday rate of $13.72/column inch, would allow $20,000/$13.72/col. in. = 1,455 inches over 26 weeks. This is 56 column inches per week, which seems like a lot of newspaper coverage. A combination of these two mixes would probably be good. The Atlanta advertising agency would be able to determine what would be best. In addition, the agency might try to find a Navy newsletter to advertise in because this market, if encouraged to investigate the condo alternative, might through word of mouth be a very helpful advertising method. Also, the use of coupons in the paper to be exchanged for a gift upon coming to look at the development may further increase buying traffic. These media institutions are available for CPL use.

Problems and Opportunities

A. Problems
  1. Dan Thatcher:
    a. His inexperience in the Florida condominium market.
    b. His ambitiousness, possibly causing him to miss opportunities as he sees the "success" of this project promoting his career.
    c. His shortsightedness in only considering condominiums rather than apartments also, which may be more suited to the community needs.
  2. Economic dependence of the areas on the three military installations.
  3. Availability of close substitutes to condos, namely, similarly priced single-family housing.
  4. The instability of the Orange Park housing market, symptomized by the high turnover/mobility.
  5. Advertising agency located in Atlanta, with no promotion experience in this Florida, highly military market.
  6. High prices of the projects.
  7. Low social acceptability, as shown by the low demand.
  8. Transportation:
    a. The project under consideration is located on a heavy use corridor. More development will cause traffic problems.
    b. New freeway allowing easy access to the navy base is under construction, thus easy accessibility to work is not yet present.
  9. If the young swingers or retirees are the chosen market segment, need more land to put in amenities. Army Corps of Engineers may not approve other option plot if that one is pursued.
  10. Need better demographic data to properly evaluate the market, demand, and supply.
  11. Public still needs educating about the project itself.

B. Opportunities
  1. Very attractive area to build, as there are low taxes, low land rates, and no busing.

2. Military market is large.
3. The aluminum siding and brick exterior condo can provide a new look and style to the Jacksonville condo market.
4. Market for rental housing is excellent, due to low vacancy rates, a large influence of relatively mobile military personnel, and low median age of the area.
5. Good reputation and experience of CPL. They know housing construction and costs. Financial strength of CPL.
6. Market open to new competitor; fast-growing regions are the Southeast and Florida.
7. The plot under option is zoned for condos.

C. On balance, the situation is:
1. Very favorable for *housing*.
2. Neutral for *condo*.

Commentary on the Case Analysis

Table 4 presents our point-by-point summary evaluation of the case analysis. In our view, it is very well done, and our guess is you will agree. We should point out, however, that it is far easier to evaluate an analysis than to do one.

TABLE 4 Summary of the evaluation of the case analysis

Criteria	Analysis
1. Completeness	Very complete on all aspects of situation analysis structure
	Reasonable depth of analysis
2. Avoids rehash	Good
	Most points are made with an analysis purpose
3. Makes reasonable assumptions	Excellent
4. Proper problem statements	Excellent; has not confused them with symptoms
	Somewhat incomplete; e.g., competitors
5. Proper opportunity statements	Good; has not given action statements
6. Deals with objectives realistically	Very good; has questioned this issue
	Alternatives given and discussed
7. Recognizes alternatives	*
8. Is not assertive	Generally OK
	Some actions are implied in situation analysis, but not a big problem here
9. Discusses pros and cons of alternatives	*
10. Makes effective use of financial and other quantitative information	Excellent
	All options are given a good quantitative appraisal
11. Reaches a clear and logical decision	*
12. Makes good use of evidence developed in situation analysis	*
13. Overall appraisal	A very good situation analysis of a tough situation

*Not applicable as only situation analysis is presented.

Part 2

Introduction to Marketing Decision Making

In Part 1 of this book, you have studied how marketing decisions should be made. The cases in this section are designed to let you begin to apply this approach in decision making. These cases should be viewed as an opportunity to practice your skills on some broad-issue marketing cases before we go to other sections of this book, where we study cases that are more specifically tied to product or distribution, and so on.

Case 1

General Motors: Cadillac*

When Executive Vice President Lloyd Reuss took his job as the head of all North American car operations for General Motors (GM) in February 1986, he had a four-item list of goals. One of the four—clearly of the highest priority for GM—concerned a single division, Cadillac. The words were strong and simple: "Restore Cadillac products and image to where they are the standard of the world."[1] The task before Reuss was an ominous one. The U.S. auto market, General Motors, and Cadillac had all changed significantly since he joined GM in 1959. At that time, the U.S. market largely belonged to the "big three" domestic producers (GM 42 percent, Ford 28 percent, Chrysler 11 percent), and Cadillac *was* the "standard of the world." Now, 30 years later, things had changed. The three major domestic producers' market share has fallen to 67.8 percent, and Cadillac's share and reputation in the luxury market is being challenged not only by domestic competition but also by European and Asian competitors as well.

In order to analyze Cadillac's position in the market, Reuss must seek the answers to several questions. For example: Is it selling the right products? Are its products targeted at the right market? Does its image appeal to the buyers Cadillac seeks? Does Cadillac's advertising effectively reach the right market and convey Cadillac's desired image?

Current Environmental Factors

Throughout the 1950s and 1960s, while energy was plentiful and inexpensive, American car manufacturers enjoyed great success building cars that were large and powerful. During the 1970s, energy prices increased—the product of temporary shortages in the supply of oil. As a result, import manufacturers, many of

---

*This was prepared from public sources by Eric P. Andrew, under the supervision of Thomas C. Kinnear. Copyright © 1989 by Thomas C. Kinnear.

[1]Jerry Flint, "Hold the Velveeta—Please Pass the Brie," *Forbes* 8 (September 1986), p. 30.

which were building small, fuel-efficient automobiles, were in prime position to take advantage of the situation. With the influx of these fuel-thrifty imports, the domestic portion of the U.S. automobile market began to shrink from approximately 96.5 percent in 1957 to 85 percent in 1973, to 77 percent in 1979, and finally to approximately 68 percent in 1987.[2] Most of these imports were coming from Japan (Toyota, Nissan, Honda, etc.), now the world's largest producer of motor vehicles.

Western European countries also have been major suppliers of automobiles to the U.S. market. Makers such as Volkswagen, Mercedes-Benz, and BMW from West Germany; Volvo and Saab from Sweden; to a lesser degree, Peugeot and Renault from France; and, sporadically, Fiat, Lancia, and Alfa Romeo from Italy. Also, during the 1980s the Yugoslavians (Yugo) and the Koreans (Hyundai and partnerships through Ford and GM) began exporting cars to the United States. (See Exhibit 1 for 1987 import sales.)

Throughout the energy shortage and until the mid-1980s, the Japanese enjoyed favorable yen/dollar exchange rates and were, therefore, in large part able to offer vehicles that cost less than comparable U.S. or West European products. The Japanese manufacturers also had significant success in producing these small, fuel-

EXHIBIT 1   Selected 1987 U.S. import sales

Manufacturer	Country	Sales
Acura	Japan	109,470
Alfa Romeo	Italy	6,320
Audi	West Germany	41,322
BMW	West Germany	87,839
Eagle/Renault	France	13,991
Ford/Kia	South Korea	26,750
Honda	Japan	312,218
Hyundai	South Korea	263,610
Isuzu	Japan	39,587
Jaguar	Great Britain	22,919
Mazda	Japan	206,354
Mercedes-Benz	West Germany	89,918
Merkur	West Germany	14,301
Mitsubishi	Japan	67,954
Nissan	Japan	405,996
Peugeot	France	9,422
Saab	Sweden	45,106
Subaru	Japan	175,864
Toyota	Japan	583,809
Volkswagen	West Germany	130,641
Volvo	Sweden	106,539
Yugo	Yugoslavia	48,812

Source: *Automotive News,* 1988 Market Data Book.

---

[2]Sales/Registrations, "Market Shares for 36 Years," *Automotive Industries—1988 Market Data Book Issue,* May 25, 1988, p. 32.

efficient automobiles with high quality. However, the U.S. government, pressured by GM, Ford, and Chrysler, imposed a "voluntary restraint," or quota, on the number of Japanese cars which could be exported to the United States. With this quota and with the appreciation of the yen, which occurred in the mid- to late-1980s, Japanese manufacturers began to lose their ability to sell large volumes of small cars and still make desirable profit margins. These factors began to force the Japanese to adjust their product mix to include a greater percentage of the more profitable larger, upscale, and specialty automobiles.

While the Japanese first concentrated on small, fuel-efficient cars, the European car manufacturers, with Volkswagen as the possible exception, have targeted distinct market niches. Mercedes-Benz, BMW, Audi, Saab, and Volvo have all, to varying degrees, concentrated on the upper segments of the market. The Koreans and Yugoslavians have targeted the low-end market and, due to the strength of the Japanese yen against the U.S. dollar and other currencies, have replaced Japan as the low-cost automotive exporters to the U.S. market.

In response to the high cost of fuel in the mid-1970s, the U.S. big three began to downsize their products and increase the number of small and fuel-efficient models. As a result, cars in the 1980s are generally smaller and more fuel efficient than earlier models. However, when fuel prices in the mid- to late-1980s stabilized, manufacturers began to build and consumers began to purchase the larger and more powerful models as they had in previous years. These cars were, however, still more efficient than the vehicles of the 1960s.

Car sales are a function of the economy. When work forces are employed and the economic outlook is favorable, sales will more than likely be healthy. If gasoline prices are perceived as high or not stable, sales of small, fuel-efficient vehicles will rise. In the mid-80s, during a period of high interest rates and a slow economy, domestic automobile manufacturers offered large cash rebates and attractive low-interest financing (as low as 0 percent on a 24-month term by American Motors) to spur sales. During this period, when customers shopped, they not only shopped for the best model but for the best sale incentive.

Developments in the Luxury Car Market

Traditional versus Functional Luxury

The U.S. luxury car market can be classified into two segments: traditional and functional. U.S. manufacturers have typically produced entries to the traditional segment, and the Europeans, the functional segment. Traditional luxury cars have been represented primarily by Cadillacs and Lincolns in the first tier and Oldsmobile, Buick, Mercury, and Chrysler in the second. The functional luxury cars of Europe were primarily made up of Germany's Mercedes-Benz, BMW, and Audi; Britain's Rolls-Royce and Jaguar; and certain models of Sweden's Saab and Volvo.

Traditional luxury cars strive to make the driving experiences as effortless as possible. This has been accomplished by providing passengers with plush, living-room-style interiors and rides so smooth that Mercury commercials of the mid-1970s boasted that a Cartier jeweler could flawlessly cut a diamond while riding in the back seat of a Mercury luxury car. The functional luxury car, on the other hand, attempts to put the driver in touch with the road via steering and suspension systems that inform the driver of the immediate environment.

Throughout Cadillac's history, the division has had a variety of competitive products to contend with. In the 1930s, brands such as Packard, Pierce-Arrow, Auburn, Cord, Imperial, and Lincoln were vying for a piece of the luxury car market. By the early 1960s, most of these great marques had become memories, with only Ford's Lincoln division and Chrysler's Imperial (until 1985) left to offer a measurable amount of domestic competition.

Domestic Competition

As Cadillac plotted its strategy for the luxury car market, Ford's Lincoln wasn't far behind. In 1979, the Town Car/Coupe, Lincoln's equivalent to the de Ville, was downsized to dimensions similar to the Cadillac. (See Exhibit 2 for a description of models.) In that same year, the Mark V, competitor to the Eldorado, was also downsized. The new Mark VI (each new design of the Mark series advances one Roman numeral) in fact shared the same platform as the Town Car;

EXHIBIT 2   Descriptions of models, domestic comparison

	1978 target	*1988 target*
Cadillac		
de Ville/Fleetwood	Traditional large, 4-door, 6-passenger, rear wheel drive, V–8	New size traditional, 4-door, 6-passenger, front wheel drive, V–8
Brougham	N/A	Traditional large, 4-door, 6-passenger, rear wheel drive, V–8
Eldorado	Traditional large, 2-door, front wheel drive, V–8	International size, 2-door, front wheel drive, V–8
Seville	International size, 4-door, front wheel drive, V–8	International size, 4-door, front wheel drive, V–8
Allante	N/A	2-seat, coupe/convertible, functional
Lincoln		
Town Car	Traditional large, 4-door, 6-passenger, rear wheel drive, V–8	Traditional large, 4-door, 6-passenger, rear wheel drive, V–8
Mark V/VII	Traditional large, 2-door, rear wheel drive, V–8	Smaller, functional 2-door, rear wheel drive, V–8
Versailles/Continental	International size, 4-door, rear wheel drive, V–8, traditional market	International size, functional, 4-door, front wheel drive, V–6

therefore, it shared similar overall dimensions and was now for the first time available with four doors. In 1982, Lincoln introduced the Continental, the replacement for the poor-selling Versailles. Both cars were direct competition to Cadillac's Seville and attempted to emulate virtues of the Seville. The new Continental went so far as to borrow certain styling cues from the Seville, particularly the "bustle" style trunk.

In 1984, Lincoln's strategy began to change. This year Lincoln introduced the Mark VII. No longer built off the Town Car/Coupe chassis, the Mark VII was back to purely a two-door body style and offered two distinct versions: the traditional luxury model based on the Designer Series, and the functional luxury model—the LSC. The Mark VIIs used a newly developed air suspension system not found in any other car in the United States. The LSC version came with upgraded sport-oriented appointments such as European-style seats and a firmer version of the air suspension. Over the following years, a tachometer and a higher-output engine were also added to the LSC to increase its functional appeal.

In 1988, Lincoln introduced an all new design for the Continental. (See Exhibit 3.) Borrowing heavily on the functional theme of the Mark VII LSC, the Continental now seemed as eager to differentiate itself from the Seville as it was earlier to emulate it. According to Maryann N. Keller, automotive industry analyst and vice president of the New York brokerage firm Furman, Selz, Mager, Deltz and Birney, ". . . Lincoln's new Continental, priced just under $30,000, is demonstrating that an American car maker can produce an automobile that combines appealing features from two continents [Europe and North America]. The body style and interior appointments have a definite European flavor. The size and generous complement of creature comforts are distinctly American. Though it could use a more powerful engine, the Continental signals Ford's arrival as a real challenger in the functional luxury car market."[3]

Foreign Competition—European

As Cadillac moved through the 1960s and 70s, the European luxury cars were emerging as serious alternative types of luxury automobiles. Rolls-Royce of England, long recognized as providing expensive, hand-built luxury cars, was never a Cadillac alternative. Mercedes-Benz, however, was a different kind of luxury car. If Cadillacs were as plush as fine living rooms, the Mercedes-Benz was as functional as a well-appointed study. The Mercedes-Benz mission was not to surround the driver or passengers in cushions of soft velour or provide them with a silky smooth ride, but to provide firm, supportive seating and a controlled ride in an automobile engineered for traveling at high speeds on the German autobahn.

---

[3]Maryann N. Keller, "Streetwise Showdown in the High-Priced Sector," *Motor Trend*, October 1988, p. 138.

EXHIBIT 3   1988 Continental

"The new Continental will change the way the world thinks of American cars."
—*Car and Driver*

"Under the Continental's sleek sheetmetal lurks a suspension engineer's dream come true: computer-controlled air springs and dual-damping shocks at each wheel."—*Automobile*

"...it's a magic-carpet limo that shifts to tied-down sports sedan exactly when you want or need it to. Amazing!"
—*Motor Trend*

"This car translates much of the European standard of luxury into the American idiom. In so doing it redefines automotive luxury in the U.S. We think it will be a hit". —*AutoWeek*

The new Lincoln Continental. It's the world's most advanced luxury car. And that's not an opinion. It's a fact. For more information, call 1 800 822-9292.

LINCOLN
What a luxury car should be.

The Europeans would prefer we keep these opinions to ourselves.

LINCOLN-MERCURY DIVISION *Ford*
Buckle up—together we can save lives.

C O N T I N E N T A L

The heritage of today's Mercedes-Benz can be traced back to 1885 and the streets of Mannheim, Germany. It was then that Carl Friedrich Benz produced the world's first motor car. While others had pioneered and patented the gas engine, Benz applied it to a passenger-carrying vehicle.

Since the very beginning, Mercedes-Benz has stood for solid engineering. All of the company's automobiles are targeted to various price points in the functional luxury segment. While a $30,980 entry-level 190–D 2.5 model may share components with the top-of-the-line $79,840 560–SEC, there are no other "lesser" divisions that might require Mercedes-Benz components. This also affords Mercedes-Benz the luxury of maintaining a single automobile focus. However, the company is also one of the world's largest medium- and heavy-duty truck manufacturers.

As the 1970s progressed and the 1980s approached, additional European manufacturers began to market their products in the functional luxury segment. Bavarian Motor Works (BMW) of West Germany moved from exporting primarily two-door sports coupes to vehicles similar to Mercedes-Benz. BMW's strategy differed from Mercedes in that BMW catered even more so to the sport-oriented functional luxury buyer. The BMW product offerings begin with the small two- and four-door 3 series, the four-door midsize 5 series, large four-door 7 series, and the two-door 6 series. Over the past few years, BMW has broadened its product offering by introducing the previously mentioned 3 series four-door. The all new 1987 BMW 7 series includes a replacement for the 1986 735i model as well as an all-new model for 1988, the 750iL. The 750iL is the largest, and at $70,000 the most expensive, sedan BMW has ever sold in the United States. The 750iL is unique from the lesser 735i in its 4.5-inch-longer wheelbase, distinctive hood and grille treatment, and most notably its 12-cylinder engine. The 750iL is $13,000 more expensive than the 735i and is the only five-passenger sedan in the world to offer a 12-cylinder engine. (See Exhibit 4.)

As the functional luxury market has developed, Mercedes-Benz has also become considered by many to be the ultimate car in the luxury market. (However, it is recently being challenged by BMW.) According to the automotive research company J. D. Powers and Associates, Mercedes-Benz owners rated their cars and dealer service higher than Cadillac owners did when asked to rate the level of satisfaction of vehicle ownership and dealer service.[4] The Mercedes-Benz line is similar to that of the BMW. The 190 Class is similar in size to the BMW 3 series, the 300 Class the 5 series, and the S Class the 7 series. Mercedes-Benz also offers various two-door coupe and convertible models. In 1987, the combined U.S. sales of Mercedes-Benz and BMW reached approximately 178,000 vehicles, over half of Cadillac's current volume. (See Exhibit 5 for complete market segment sales analysis.)

---

[4]J. D. Powers reports from various years.

EXHIBIT 4   1988 BMW 735i and 1987 Mercedes-Benz S-Class

THE LUXURY CAR AS ONLY BMW COULD ENVISION IT.

When most automakers speak of vision, it's usually to discuss the rake of a windshield.

When BMW employs the term, it's to expound a philosophy.

One of unremitting zeal for performance, for which there is no greater thesis than the new BMW 735i.

A car which emerged after seven years, three million test miles and over 400 prototypes as not just a new luxury car. But a new conception of the luxury car.

That the BMW 735i heralds a new vision of the luxury car is proclaimed in every feature, from its largest component to its minutest detail.

LUXURY RETHOUGHT FROM MACROCOSM TO MICROCOSM.

From a torque-rich new 208-horsepower engine whose catalytic converter paradoxically enhances both fuel economy and performance," to electronic variable assist power steering that provides something rare in ultra-luxury cars: a feel of the road.

From a veritable brain trust of technology that optimizes driver, engine and brake performance (the check control alone monitors 26 functions on a single readout), to 9-mph bumpers at a time when the industry standard has dropped to 2.5 mph.

From computer-perfected front and rear crush zones, to a seat belt that adjusts itself automatically to the size of the driver.

From an elegantly sensuous interior swathed in supple, hand-crafted leather, to a buffer between suspension and chassis that banishes road noise from an already serene interior.

From air-conditioning considered the world's "strongest and most automated" (Auto Motor und Sport), to an electronic automatic transmission that lets you choose sport, economy or manual shifting modes.

And, finally, from a wider, longer, lower, more feline and aerodynamic body, to seats that "remember" positions for three different drivers, including outside mirror settings.

A 3,800-POUND WATCH.

To manufacture such a total rethink of the luxury car mandates a rethink of the whole assembly process. Engine tolerances one-fifth the thickness of a human hair.

A rigorous 37-step rust-proofing and painting regimen.

Inquisition-like inspections, demanding not a hundred or even a thousand steps, but a torturous 7,000-step process.

With a daily average of one quality control inspector for every car off the assembly line.

The result is the new BMW 735i. A luxury sedan more akin to a 3,800-lb. Swiss watch than an automobile.

A creation which could only be the handiwork of visionaries.

A group of whom invite you to relish in their vision. Which can be accomplished by a test drive of the new BMW 735i at your authorized BMW dealer.

THE ULTIMATE DRIVING MACHINE.

(continued)

EXHIBIT 4   1988 BMW 735i and 1987 Mercedes-Benz S-Class *(concluded)*

THE MERCEDES-BENZ S-CLASS:
THE ONE THING MORE IMPORTANT THAN THE TECHNOLOGY INSIDE IT IS THE TRADITION BEHIND IT.

A "big Mercedes" has crowned the line for almost as long as there has been a Mercedes-Benz.

This is Mercedes-Benz engineering at its most ambitious. And at its most assertive. From the 540 K of 1936 pictured at left, to the S-Class sedan of 1987 shown above, every big Mercedes and its performance has seemed to scale slightly larger than life.

The 540 K, for example, thundered into legend on the power of a supercharged eight-cylinder engine and the flamboyance of low-slung roadster coachwork. Half a century of technological progress later, the S-Class seems to glide rather than thunder over the road; in the case of the flagship 560 SEL Sedan on the roads of its native Europe, two tons of S-Class authority, capable of gliding along at 142 mph all day.

The Mercedes-Benz impulse to engineering masterstrokes marks the S-Class in other ways as well. In a body design that brilliantly combines large dimensions and low aerodynamic drag. In handling agility that large sedans have seldom aspired to, much less achieved. In vital technological innovations — an Anti-lock Braking System (ABS); and a Supplemental Restraint System (SRS) with driver's-side air bag and knee bolster, and emergency tensioning retractors at both front seat belts — that are gradually being emulated by other large sedans.

And laid over this bedrock of technical excellence, a thick layer of civilization and creature comfort. Experienced within a spacious cabin redolent of fine leathers, plush with velour carpeting, garnished with precious handworked woods.

Part limousine, part performance car — the uncommon versatility of the S-Class is reflected in its selection not only by connoisseurs of automotive luxury, but also by most of today's top-ranked Grand Prix motor racing fraternity.

The S-Class is available in three distinctive sedan models and as a two-plus-two closed coupe. You will find nothing to compare with them, in form or in function, wherever you look in the automotive world. They are unique, as is the tradition that spawned them.

Engineered like no other car in the world

EXHIBIT 5   Calendar year U.S. car sales

	1987	1986	1985	1984	1983
		Domestic luxury markets (units)			
Cadillac	261,284	304,057	298,762	320,017	300,337
Lincoln	166,037	177,584	165,138	151,475	101,574
Total domestic sales	7,081,262	8,214,897	8,204,542	7,951,523	6,795,295
		Luxury market (units)			
Domestic					
Cadillac (C)	261,284	304,057	298,762	320,017	300,337
Lincoln (L)	166,037	177,584	164,868	151,475	101,574
Import					
Acura (A)	109,470	52,869	*	*	*
Audi (AU)	41,322	59,797	74,061	71,237	47,936
BMW (B)	87,839	96,759	87,832	70,897	59,242
Jaguar (J)	22,919	24,464	20,528	18,044	15,815
Mercedes-Benz (M)	89,918	99,314	89,098	79,222	73,692
Total (C,L)	427,321	481,641	463,630	471,492	401,911
Total (A,AU,B,J,M)	351,468	333,203	271,519	239,400	196,685
Total luxury market	778,789	814,844	735,149	710,892	598,596
Total U.S. car sales	10,225,304	11,453,705	11,045,784	10,393,230	9,181,036

*Not in production.
Source: *Automotive News, 1988 Market Data Book. MYMA Motor Vehicle Facts & Figures '88.*

The third German player in the luxury car market is Audi. Audi reached an all-time-high U.S. sales volume of over 74,000 units in 1985 due in large part to the sleekly styled 5000 series (48,057 units). The size of a mid-Mercedes and BMW offering, the 5000 was priced lower and could be purchased with one of the first applications of four-wheel drive in a passenger car. However, in 1986, under reports that 5000s equipped with automatic transmissions could unintentionally accelerate, sales began to slide. In 1987, sales were off 44.2 percent from just two years earlier.

For the 1988 model year, in an effort to restore Audi's presence in the luxury car market, the company introduced an all new replacement for the 4000 series, now dubbed the 80 (as it is in Europe). For the 1989 model year, the Audi 5000 has been relaunched as the Audi 100 and 200 (depending on engine size). The 100 and 200 models do not differ from the 5000 series before them in exterior appearance. However, the interior has been redesigned, and the Audi engineers are quick to point out the new engineering developments that differentiate the 100/200 Audis from the old 5000 series.

Foreign Competition—Japanese

The mid- to late-1980s have been accompanied by generally stable fuel costs. As a result, manufacturers are again offering larger models and more powerful engines. In addition, the late 1980s has also included a weaker dollar against other Western currencies such as the West German mark and the Japanese yen. A weak dollar makes buying West German or Japanese imports more expensive. In an effort to maintain acceptable margins on their automobiles, many of the foreign manufacturers have raised prices. This upscale movement in prices by these manufacturers is accompanied, in many cases, by efforts to market models that are also further upscale in class and content.

In the late 1980s, a strong Japanese yen helped create a situation in which the Japanese were no longer the low-cost producers. No longer were the Japanese able to build entry-level cars and price them as competitively against domestic, Korean, and Yugoslavian entries as they had in previous years. The Japanese, unable to make their desired profit margins on these vehicles, began to expand their product line upward to include a greater proportion of compact and midsize cars. These cars include larger models of Honda Accord, Toyota Camry and Cressida, and Nissan Maxima.

Watching the Germans move further upscale in image and in price, Honda saw an opportunity to provide European-style functional luxury cars, but at the price of traditional domestic luxury models. Acura also places emphasis on dealer service. In combination with product quality, dealer service accounted for the number one rating in the 1988 J. D. Powers Consumer Satisfaction Index.

Acura, and other soon-to-be-released Japanese luxury cars from Toyota (Lexus) and Nissan (Infiniti), hope to appeal to those import buyers that have bought nonluxury imports in the past and now want to move upscale but maintain certain import virtues. Acura models include the midsize Legend. The Legend comes well equipped with four-wheel power disc brakes, air conditioning, power door locks and windows, and stereo radio with cassette tape deck—all standard. Like the European functional luxury cars, Acura also pays special attention to the vehicle's handling and performance. To that end, the Legend carries a high-tech racing-bred multivalve V–6 engine and a suspension not found in any other Honda vehicle. Of the Acura Legend, automotive analyst Maryann N. Keller said, "In less than three years, Honda's Acura division will surpass the magic 100,000-unit mark, which means it will outsell every high-priced European brand in the market."[5] Hans Jordan, head of U.S. marketing for Mercedes-Benz, says, "Acura is a legitimate contender in the $20,000 to $30,000 price range."[6] (See Exhibit 6.)

As Acura continues to establish itself in the U.S. luxury car market, Toyota and Nissan are in the process of launching their own luxury car divisions: Lexus and Infiniti, respectively. These new offerings will follow Acura's lead by initially introducing two products for each of the new divisions and selling them only in dealerships dedicated to that division. Acura, Lexus, and Infiniti will not

---

[5]Maryann N. Keller, "Streetwise Showdown in the High-Priced Sector," p. 138.
[6]Alex Taylor III, "Detroit versus New Upscale Imports," *Fortune,* April 27, 1987, p. 78.

EXHIBIT 6   Acura Legend

MOST AUTOMAKERS WOULD CALL THIS A VERY GOOD YEAR. WE'D CALL IT A VERY GOOD START.

1988 J.D. POWER & ASSOCIATES

C·S·I

CUSTOMER SATISFACTION
I N D E X

1. Acura
2. Mercedes
3. Honda

DEALER SATISFACTION INDEX

AUTO AGE, 1988

① Acura
② Mercedes
③ Honda
④ Saab

1 9 8 8

LUXURY IMPORT

S A L E S

Automotive News

1. Acura
2. Volvo
3. Mercedes
4. BMW

Number one in the J.D. Power Customer Satisfaction Index. Number one in Auto Age's first annual Dealer Satisfaction Index. Number one in sales for all luxury imports.*

There's no two ways about it: Acura automobiles and their dealers were an overwhelming success in 1988. But to our way of thinking, last year's performance is only the beginning.

From the day the very first Acura rolled off the assembly line, we've had a reputation for being innovative. And we have every intention of keeping it that way. Not only by continuing to improve the technology and craftsmanship that give Acura automobiles their edge, but also by striving to provide the highest level of satisfaction to our customers as well as our dealers.

Maintaining that reputation won't be easy. But we feel we already have the keys.

Namely, strong dealers whose sales, service and parts departments have consistently made customer satisfaction their top priority. Not to mention products of uncompromising quality.

1988 was unquestionably a year to remember. But the fact is, even if we wanted to rest on our laurels, we couldn't.

We're too busy working on next year.

ACURA
Precision crafted performance.

share facilities with the lesser Hondas, Toyotas, or Nissans as Lincoln does with Mercury or as Cadillac is allowed with other GM divisions. The Lexus and Infiniti models will also follow Acura by offering a high degree of Lexus/Infiniti "only" content and distinct styling not to be shared by Toyotas or Nissans.

Lexus' initial offering in 1990 will be an all new sedan with a modern multivalve V–8. (See Exhibit 7.) According to *Automobile Magazine,* the Lexus LS 400 "is a large, roomy, rather conservatively styled four-door sedan that appears to be an amalgam of BMW and Mercedes-Benz design cues, given an American spin with a Cadillacesque egg-crate grille, Detroit-style wood trim, and wrinkled leather upholstery. Its drag coefficient makes it the slipperiest of production sedans, and its four-liter, four-cam, 250-horsepower V–8 engine will push that slippery shape through the air at speeds guaranteed to keep Mercedes-Benz, BMW, and Jaguar engineers working late for the next decade or so."[7] The LS 400

EXHIBIT 7   1990 Lexus LS 400

is expected to be priced at approximately $35,000, roughly half of a comparable-size Mercedes-Benz or BMW.

Lexus will also introduce a midsize sedan derived from an existing Toyota, the midsize Camry. The ES250 will be powered by a high-tech multivalve V–6 similar to the Acura Legend. A year later, Lexus will debut a new coupe model.

Nissan's Infiniti brand will be introduced at roughly the same time as the Lexus. The introduction of the Infiniti brand will begin with a large sedan similar to the Lexus LS 400. The Infiniti Q45 will be powered by a 4.5 liter V–8 and sell for approximately $35,000. (See Exhibit 8.) Commenting on the image intentions of the sedan, Takashi Oka, senior project manager of the Q45, said, "We want to create a new definition of luxury and establish an international image beyond that of BMW and Mercedes." The Q45 will be joined at introduction with a smaller, less expensive two-door model based on the Japanese market Nissan Leopard. The new coupe will be powered by a multivalve V–6 and sell for around $25,000. A third model will join the Infiniti brand in 1991. A multivalve V–6 powered midsize sedan, based on the Nissan Maxima, will go head-to-head with the Lexus ES250 as well as the Acura

EXHIBIT 8   1990 Infiniti Q45

---

[7]David E. Davis, Jr., "First Look at Toyota's New Lexus." *Automobile Magazine,* January 1989, p. 74.

EXHIBIT 9   Comparison of key specifications

	Lexus LS 400	Infiniti Q-Series	BMW 735i	Mercedes 300-E	Cadillac de Ville	Cadillac Seville	1989 Lincoln Continental
Wheelbase	110.8	113.4	111.5	110.2	113.8	108	109
Length	197.6	199.8	193.3	187.2	205.3	190.8	205.1
Width	71.7	71.9	72.6	68.5	72.5	70.9	72.7
Height	55.1	56.3	55.6	56.9	55	53.5	55.6
Weight	3,800	3,860	3,835	3,195	3,470	3,449	3,626
Engine	V–8	V–8	I–6	I–6	V–8	V–8	V–6
Size (liters)	4	4.5	3.4	3	4.5	4.5	3.8
Horsepower	250	270	208	177	155	155	140

Source: *Automotive News,* December 5, 1988.

Legend. (See Exhibit 9 for a key specification comparison between the new Lexus/Infiniti models and selected competition.)

Both Lexus and Infiniti have targeted to sell approximately 100,000 units each when the full range of models is available. This contrasts to Acura's estimated sales of 300,000–400,000 by the mid-1990s.[8]

Cadillac

Cadillac Motor Car Division of General Motors got its start in 1899 as the Detroit Automobile Company and was renamed Cadillac in 1902. The car was named after the French adventurer who founded Detroit 200 years earlier. The force behind Cadillac's early years was Henry M. Leland, operator of Leland & Faulconer Mfg. Co., a precision manufacturer of automotive components. Unlike Henry Ford, who once worked for Leland, Leland was not interested in building an "everyman's" car. Leland and his company were devoted to building the best, and "despite record production of 4,307 vehicles in 1906, Cadillac management disregarded the lure of volume sales and dedicated the company to making quality automobiles. This lost Cadillac its position as a high-volume producer, but led to engineering accomplishments that made Cadillac one of the leading fine-car manufacturers."[9]

In 1909, Cadillac was purchased by the young General Motors Corporation. The Lelands, Henry and son Wilfred, stayed on to run Cadillac exactly as if it were their own. They did so until 1917 when they left to begin the Lincoln Motor Co. which was later sold to the Ford Motor Company.

The Lelands had left their impression on Cadillac. Their commitment to quality and innovation propelled Cadillac's status as the "standard of the world."

---

[8]Jesse Snyder, "INFINITI: Nissan Screening Luxury-Line Dealers," *Automotive News,* July 27, 1987, p. 65.
[9]Frank Gawronski, "Detroit's Oldest Auto Manufacturer," *Automotive News,* September 16, 1983, p. 98.

Innovations that helped to build this reputation included the self-starter in 1912, America's first V–8 engine in 1914, synchromesh gear boxes, and safety glass as standard equipment in 1929–30. In those same years a V–12 and the world's first production V–16 automobile engine were offered. In the late 1930s, as traditional coach building died out, GM used the Fisher and Fleetwood names to maintain the quality image of its prestige models. In 1941 Cadillac was the second manufacturer to offer a fully automatic transmission. In the 1950s Cadillac styling reigned supreme in the art of tail fins. (See Exhibit 10.) The 1960s brought longer, even more powerful luxury cars, and in 1966 Cadillac introduced its first front wheel drive (FWD) vehicle, the Eldorado, years before FWD was offered by any of Cadillac's non-GM competitors.

EXHIBIT 10   1959 Cadillac

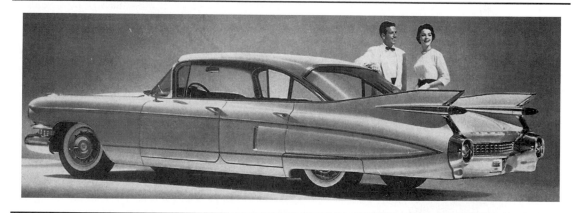

Through the "longer, lower, wider" years of the 1960s to late 1970s, Cadillac remained a distinguished luxury automobile. The Cadillac de Ville of the day weighed over 5,000 pounds, measured over 230 inches long, and was powered by an 8.2 liter engine. In comparison, the 1988 de Ville weighs only 3,437 pounds, is 196.5 inches long, and is powered by a V–8 engine that is 45 percent smaller than the 1976 model it replaces.

The trend toward smaller Cadillacs began in 1977, in reaction to the first oil embargo of 1973. The new de Villes and Fleetwoods were 8 to 12 inches shorter and averaged 950 pounds lighter than their 1976 counterparts. These models represented the first of the downsized Cadillacs. In 1979, the Eldorado received similar treatment. For 1979, the Eldorados were 20 inches shorter and 1,150 pounds lighter than the 1978 models. In 1985 and 1986, respectively, the de Villes and Eldorados underwent yet another round of downsizing to approximately the size they are today.

Cadillac customers are those who have demanded the best in traditional luxury cars. These traditional Cadillac consumers were most often professionals, above average in income and education, and in recent years an average of 58 years of age. (See Exhibit 11 for a demographic profile of the luxury car market.) These Cadillac buyers had also been accustomed to buying the biggest and most powerful. This, however, had begun to change over the course of the 1970s and 80s.

EXHIBIT 11   Demographics

	Median age	Age percent < 35	Median income ($000)	Percent college grad +
		Industry		
Domestic				
Cadillac	62	2.5%	$61.1	38.4%
Lincoln	59	4.4	66.3	39.9
Import				
Acura	35	50.4	55.5	74.6
Audi	41	27.7	78.4	70.8
BMW	42	24.0	98.4	68.3
Jaguar	50	7.9	>150.0	64.6
Mercedes-Benz	45	14.9	117.7	61.7
Saab	38	39.4	69.2	78.1
Volvo	38	36.0	61.7	67.5
		Domestic		
Cadillac				
Sedan de Ville	62	6.9	61.0	40.3
Brougham	65	0.3	53.2	27.4
Eldorado	60	4.1	70.2	39.7
Seville	63	1.6	90.0	47.2
Allante	54	6.1	150.0	47.1
Cimarron	60	9.5	45.2	47.0
Lincoln				
Town Car	60	3.2	58.6	35.6
Mark VII	50	10.2	71.3	45.0
Continental	61	3.6	95.2	49.6

Source: *Meritz 1988 Second Quarter Buyers' Study.*

In an effort to appeal to the younger upscale consumers who were not a part of the traditional Cadillac market, GM offered a new Cadillac in the 1970s. In May 1975, the Seville was a smaller, international-size Cadillac. Featuring a fuel-injected 5.7 liter V–8 as standard equipment along with a long list of other features, the Seville was one of the most well-equipped cars in the world. In 1981, GM introduced the smallest Cadillac ever, the Cimarron. Built on the "J" chassis shared by the Chevy Cavalier and Pontiac 2000, the Cimarron was introduced to take on the small "near luxury" imports such as the BMW 320 and later 325i. In 1985, the standard Cadillac, the Sedan de Ville/Coupe de

Ville, was thoroughly redesigned. The de Ville series was shortened and placed on a front-wheel-drive chassis shared with the Buick Electra and the Oldsmobile 98. (Sharing the chassis, or platform, among car divisions is a common automotive industry practice, particularly among U.S. manufacturers. Henry M. Leland recognized that this sharing of parts, or what he referred to as the "true interchangeability of parts," was the key to a great future for the automotive industry.)[10] In 1986, in a further attempt to appeal to the younger and the more functional-demanding customers, Cadillac began offering a functional luxury version to its de Ville series, the Touring Sedan. The Touring Sedan came complete with front air dam, fog lamps, rear deck lid spoiler, blackwell performance tires on 15-inch aluminum alloy wheels, higher spring rates, and faster ratio steering.

In 1986, Cadillac downsized its Eldorado and Seville (the Seville had grown larger from the 1979 model to the 1980 model year) models back to the international size. These two Cadillacs continue to share common platforms with Oldsmobile and Buick models.

Speaking of the 1986 Eldorado/Seville (E/S) models, Braz Pryor, Cadillac's general sales manager, says, "We [are] after a contemporary statement with international appeal for buyers young and old who want the luxury of a Cadillac in a more personal package."[11] GM's director of design, Chuck Jordan, calls the fourth-generation Eldorado "Cadillac's youthful sporty car," adding that "sporty elegance was the design theme."[12] Peter Levin, director of special marketing projects at Cadillac, offered some pertinent insights about the basic market philosophy behind the E/S models when he said, "Today, we're going through a revolution in customer expectations. We're after buyers of a certain mindset. . . . The challenge we gave our engineers was to create vehicles that were more responsive and refined but still retained outstanding comfort, because our buyers demand it."[13]

The 1987 model year Cadillac debuted one of its most unique automobiles, the Allante. The Allante, a two-seat, coupe/convertible, is built on a shortened Eldorado/Seville chassis that is assembled and mated in the United States to bodies and interiors that arrive twice weekly, via 747 cargo jets, from their designer/manufacturer, Pininfarina, in Italy. The Allante assumes the position as the flagship model in the Cadillac line. With a 1988 base price of $57,183 and limited to a supply of 6,000 units, it is the most expensive as well as one of the most exclusive Cadillacs ever produced.

Implementing this new strategy and striving to regain the aura of quality, technology, and exclusivity now associated with European luxury cars is not an easy task. John Grettenberger, Cadillac's general manager states, "We have to be very

---

[10]Ibid.

[11]Mary Ann Angeli, "86 Eldorado/Seville: Caddy's New Yuppie Lures?," *Automotive Industries,* November 1985, p. 40.

[12]Ibid.

[13]Bob Nagy, "Cadillacs across America," *Motor Trend,* June 1986, p. 91.

careful that we offer the right balance. If you go too far in either direction, a manufacturer like Cadillac could lose on either end of the spectrum. If we go too far in the high-tech direction, we could turn off some of our traditional buyers, but if we stick where we are then we won't appeal to the younger ones."[14]

To help achieve Cadillac's strategy of maintaining the traditional, as well as capturing new customers, Cadillac's 1987 advertising emphasized the "Spirit of Cadillac." (See Exhibit 12 for Cadillac's 1987 model line.) All Cadillac models shared a number of common themes including: making an "eloquent design statement," providing customers "worldwide Cadillac exclusives" (e.g., transverse-mounted V–8 engine), balanced performance, a commitment to security, and "the ultimate comfort: peace of mind" via "quality craftsmanship" and extensive warranties.[15]

From this common basis each Cadillac model has its own individual spirit. For example, the Allante is the "new spirit of Cadillac." The Allante was positioned to create a new class of performance that merges European road manners with Cadillac comfort and convenience.[16] The Sedan de Ville and Coupe de Ville are Cadillac's "contemporary spirits representing Cadillac's belief that today's luxury cars should reflect today's values."[17] The Fleetwood d'Elegance and Fleetwood Sixty Special are the "sophisticated spirits" of Cadillac. The d'Elegance's formal Cabriolet roof and opera lamps and the Sixty Special's five-inch extended wheelbase make these the most luxurious of the Cadillac "C-bodies" (chassis shared with the de Ville, Buick Electra, and Olds 98). Eldorado is the "driving spirit" while the Seville is the "elegant spirit." Sharing the same chassis, the Eldorado is a two-door coupe with a suspension system that delivers control with a minimum of body roll and sway, while the Seville is a four-door sedan that emphasizes supreme comfort and an exceptional array of standard luxury features. The Brougham d'Elegance is the "classic spirit" for this large, rear-wheel-drive Cadillac. It is a carryover from the model that the "C-body" cars were to have replaced. Because it and its competitor, the Lincoln Town Car, are in high demand, the Brougham has lived three years past its originally scheduled termination and will likely live on until the early 1990s. Last and certainly least in terms of size is the "sporty spirit" of Cadillac, the Cimarron. In 1988, the Cimarron was discontinued due to poor sales. In 1988, the spirit theme of Cadillac was also discontinued.

In all of 1987, Cadillac spent $35,334,300 on TV advertising to promote the "spirit of Cadillac," a 32.5 percent increase from the previous year. However, BMW's TV total was $45,498,700, and start-up Acura was almost even with Cadillac at $34,478,500.[18] Cadillac's TV budget in 1988 increased to $54,126,200.[19]

---

[14]John McElroy, "Cadillac's Grettenberger: Resetting the Standard," *Automotive Industries,* November 1985, p. 36.

[15]Cadillac 1987 (Detroit, Mich: Cadillac Motor Division, General Motors Corporation, 1986), pp. 2–3.

[16]Ibid.

[17]Ibid.

[18]"Et Cetera," *Automotive News, 1988 Market Data Book,* p. 208.

[19]Ibid.

EXHIBIT 12   1987 Cadillac Line

Allanté shown at the Music Center of Los Angeles County, Los Angeles, California.

Sedan de Ville shown at the Detroit Institute of Arts, Detroit, Michigan.

(continued)

EXHIBIT 12   1987 Cadillac Line *(continued)*

Fleetwood d'Elegance shown at the High Museum of Art, Atlanta, Georgia.

Eldorado shown at the Kitt Peak National Observatory, Kitt Peak, Arizona.

(continued)

EXHIBIT 12   1987 Cadillac Line *(concluded)*

Seville shown at the Adler Planetarium, Chicago, Illinois.

Cimarron shown at the Laumeier Sculpture Park, St. Louis, Missouri.

Cadillac is GM's luxury market division. Where it actually fits among the other GM divisions can be seen in the market plots of Exhibit 13. In 1986, Cadillac was positioned as the highest-priced division, offering the consumer automobiles that are conservative but not far from an even split between conservative and aggressive, and family and personal orientations. GM's goals for the

EXHIBIT 13   GM plots its markets

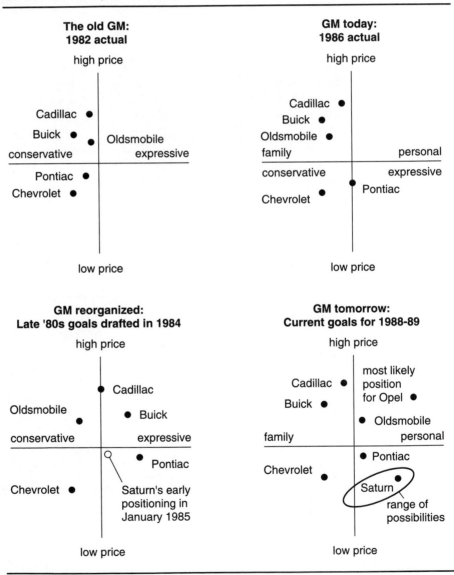

1988–89 model year show Cadillac maintaining its basic position except in terms of price, where it continues to move further upscale. According to General Manager Grettenberger, "Our vision is to move every Cadillac upscale in terms of its expressiveness, image, distinctiveness, and overall content. I don't see us having a sale-weighted average of $43,000–44,000 like Mercedes-Benz. But I would like to see Cadillacs move upscale."[20] Cadillac's 1989 model line ranges in price from approximately $25,000 for a Coupe de Ville, $26,000 for the Brougham, and $30,000–34,000 for the Fleetwood. The Eldorado begins at about $27,000 while the Seville begins at $30,000. The Allante is, of course, the high-price leader at $57,183.

The Problem

Throughout most of its existence, Cadillac has been synonymous with the finest in luxury automobiles. In the early years under the Leland family's leadership, the company won the Dewar Trophy from the Royal Automobile Club. Cadillac not only won this coveted prize for engineering excellence and innovation once, but also was the only car company to do it twice. After the Lelands left, and for quite some time, Cadillac managed to keep its eye trained on building the best luxury cars possible.

By the 1978 model year, Cadillac sales had hit an all-time record of 350,813 units. At that time and as recently as 1983, Cadillac accounted for over one-third of all luxury car sales. In 1987 Cadillac made up less than one-quarter of all such sales. Models that had been previously very popular were selling poorly. In 1985

EXHIBIT 14   Cadillac 15-year sales trend by model

Year	Cadillac	Eldorado	Seville	Cimarron	Allante
1987	203,487	21,470	24,266	12,295	2,517
1986	235,206	24,266	21,150	23,435	*
1985	187,664	58,310	29,034	23,754	*
1984	195,177	70,577	35,349	18,014	*
1983	176,003	71,624	33,522	19,188	*
1982	148,211	55,761	23,030	13,195	*
1981	134,765	53,233	23,054	13,406	*
1980	126,145	51,065	35,347	*	*
1979	202,681	61,000	44,216	*	*
1978	238,976	43,681	52,396	*	*
1977	238,066	45,206	42,452	*	*
1976	214,649	39,333	39,734	*	*
1975	189,034	44,363	22,738	*	*
1974	183,633	36,360	*	*	*
1973	235,504	50,205	*	*	*

Note: Sales for years 1973–1983 are represented by registrations.
*Not in production
Source: *Automotive News Annual Almanac Issues/Market Data Books.*

---

[20]Dave Zoia, "Cadillac Eyes an Allante Sedan," *Automotive News* 16 (February 1987), p. 37.

the Eldorado and Seville had sales of 66,863 and 32,986, respectively. During the following year, the smaller, redesigned models sold only 45 percent of the 1985 models they replaced; 1987 sales fared somewhat worse. Sales of the exclusive Allante have also been disappointing. The two-door coupe/convertible was expected to be a sellout its first year at 6,000 units, but by year's end the Allante tallied just over 2,500 units. (See Exhibit 14 for Cadillac's 1973–87 sales figures and Exhibit 15 for announced 1988 competitive car prices.)

EXHIBIT 15   1988 Luxury car manufacturers' suggested retail prices

U.S. domestic	4-door	2-door	European import	4-door	2-door
Cadillac			Audi		
Cimarron V–6	$16,071		80 Series 4	$18,600	
de Ville V–8	23,404	$23,049	80 Quattro 5	22,700	
Fleetwood d'Elegance V–8	28,024		90 Series 4	24,330	
Fleetwood Sixty Special V–8	34,750		90 Series 5	24,330	
Brougham V–8	23,846		90 Series Quattro 5	27,720	
Eldorado V–8		24,891	5000S 5	22,850	
Seville V–8	27,627		5000S Quattro 5	27,280	
Allante V–8		56,533	5000CS Turbo 5	30,910	
			5000CS Turbo Quattro 5	34,810	
Lincoln					
Town Car V–8	24,373		BMW		
Town Car Signature V–8	27,374		325 6	25,150	$24,350
Town Car Cartier V–8	28,520		325is6		28,950
Mark VII LSC V–8		26,380	325i6	28,950	
Mark VII Bill Blass V–8		26,380	325ix6		33,290
Continental V–6	26,078		M–3 4		34,800
Continental Signature V–6	27,944		528e6	31,950	
			535i6	36,700	
			535is6	37,800	
			M–5 6	47,500	
			635CSi6		46,000
			M–6 6		55,950
			735i6	54,000	
			750iL 12	69,000	
			Jaguar		
			XJ–6 6	43,500	
			Vanden Plas 6	47,500	
			XJ–S V–12		47,000
			XJ–SC V–12		50,450
			Mercedes Benz		
			190–E 2.3 4	29,190	
			190–D 2.5 5	29,960	
			190–E 2.6 6	33,500	
			260–E 6	37,845	
			300–E 6	43,365	
			300–CE 6		53,340
			300–SE 6	49,900	
			300–SEL 6	53,490	
			420–SEL V–8	59,080	
			560–SEL V–8	69,760	
			560–SL V–8		62,110
			560–SEC V–8		77,065

Source: *Automotive News, 1988 Market Data Book.*

What's more important to Cadillac and to Reuss, executive vice president of North American car operations, was the division's steadily declining reputation for luxury car excellence. On the surface the cause for the decline was multifaceted. First, Cadillac suffered from what the press called "look-alike cars." The Cadillac de Villes and Fleetwoods looked like Buick Electras and Oldsmobile Ninety Eights. This perception was even played up in a Lincoln Town Car television commercial where Cadillac, Buick, and Olds owners can't tell their cars apart at a restaurant when the valets bring the three cars forward. Concedes one GM man, "Cadillac, one could say, is selling 300,000 Buicks."[21]

Cadillac innovation in the late 1970s and early 1980s was also a cause for concern. The availability of a V–8 diesel engine, manufactured from a modified gasoline engine, was discontinued when its reliability proved disastrous. This same scenario played a second time, and in the same time period, with Cadillac's exclusive multidisplacement engine. The engine was programmed to run on 8, 6, or 4 cylinders depending on engine load demand. However, as with the diesel, lack of reliability killed the innovative engine.

On September 27, 1988, consumer activist Ralph Nader issued a report called "Cadillac—The Heartbreak of America."[22] According to Nader, "This report was written because of the large volume of mail we have received from indignant Cadillac purchasers who expect better quality from a $25,000 investment."[23] GM called the Nader document outdated, unfair, and inaccurate.

As Reuss looks over these problems and others, his task appears not to be an easy one. Could the quality and design of Cadillac's cars be the sole cause of the division's problems? Maybe advertising and imaging are being directed at the wrong customer, or perhaps the division has lost sight of just who the Cadillac customer is. Seeing the result of the problems may be easy, but finding solutions to their causes will be the real test to restoring Cadillac as the standard of the world.

---

[21]Flint, "Hold the Velveeta—Please Pass the Brie," p. 31.
[22]John E. Peterson, "The Heartbreak of America," *The Detroit News* 28 (September 1988), p. C1–2.
[23]Ibid.

Case 2

KitchenAid Small Appliances: Central Europe*

Introduction

In early 1995, David Robinson, the Director of KitchenAid small appliance sales in Europe, hung up the phone after talking with his supervisor, Keith English. English was the Worldwide Director of KitchenAid sales and marketing, based at the Small Appliance Business Unit (SABU) headquarters in St. Joseph, Michigan. KitchenAid was part of Whirlpool Corporation, the world's largest appliance manufacturer. Since coming from the Boston Consulting Group a year prior, Robinson had been given the challenging assignment of leading the expansion of KitchenAid-brand small appliances in Western Europe and the introduction of these same appliances into Central Europe.

In the phone call, Robinson and English had discussed the SABU strategic plan for Central Europe. As part of this ongoing discussion, Robinson wondered if it was the right time to enter the Central European countries of Poland, Hungary, and the Czech Republic. However, many questions remained to which English wanted answers. Was there a need for expensive kitchen appliances in these countries? Which product should lead the introduction? Should KitchenAid establish its own distribution network or sell its products through the newly established Whirlpool major appliance sales group? Should KitchenAid target the professional segment, the consumer segment, or both? What price should be charged in these countries? How much advertising and promotion was necessary to the trade and/or household consumers?

———
*Peter Faricy prepared this case under the direction of Professor Thomas C. Kinnear to provide material for class discussion. This case is not intended to illustrate either effective or ineffective treatment of a managerial decision. The authors have disguised certain names and data to protect confidentiality. Copyright © 1996 by the authors.

As he contemplated these questions, Robinson thought back over his experience at BCG and his first year at Whirlpool. As a consultant, he had helped numerous clients enter new markets. Yet, since coming to Whirlpool, he had worked solely on returning the KitchenAid Europa small appliance business unit to profitability. Entering these new Central European markets with a premium-priced product such as KitchenAid represented a considerable risk. Failure to understand consumers, competitors, and distribution dynamics in these markets could result in large financial losses for the KitchenAid Europa group. At the same time, Robinson wanted to enter these markets before his competitors, even if it could mean a few years of lower-than-expected profits. Since English agreed to review Robinson's Central Europe recommendations in May, the time to make the above decisions was imminent.

The U.S. and the Global Appliance Industry

In the 1980s, four manufacturers accounted for 92 percent of all major appliance sales in the United States. With little product differentiation, the appliance market had become a battle of lowering costs. Margins were being squeezed and manufacturers were scrambling to cut costs and provide more value to the consumer.

The appliance industry was structurally difficult due to the following factors:

- **Slow growth/high saturation.** As Exhibit 1 shows, the appliance industry was expected to grow slowly throughout the remainder of the decade. In addition, there was evidence that this slow growth was due to the U.S. market being saturated by appliances.
- **Highly concentrated and fiercely competitive.** The data in Exhibit 2(a) demonstrate that the U.S. appliance industry was dominated by five major appliance makers. With little product differentiation, competition was fierce for both distribution space and consumer sales.
- **Increasing power of retailers like Best Buy, Circuit City, and Fretter.** National retailers were growing in appliance market share and expected to control 65 percent of the market by 1997. Share of independent and medium retailers was expected to decline from 40 percent to 25 percent by 1997. The implication of this change was less power for manufacturers like Whirlpool, which contributed to lowering margins.
- **Increasing government regulation.** Government regulations such as those requiring removal of CFCs (freon gas in air conditioners, refrigerators, and freezers) were becoming increasingly important.
- **Low involvement, low technical products.** Consumer research indicates that appliances were not seen by consumers as being interesting or technically advanced products.

EXHIBIT 1   Appliance industry forecast

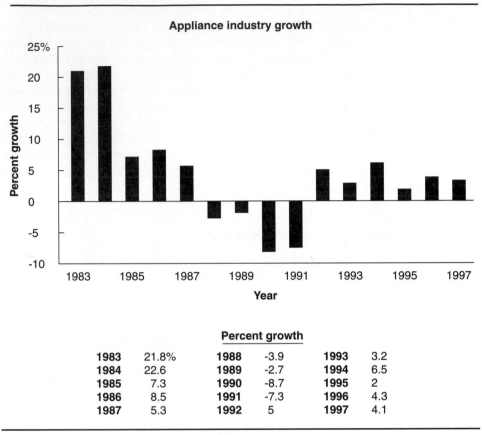

Appliance industry growth

Percent growth

1983	21.8%	1988	-3.9	1993	3.2
1984	22.6	1989	-2.7	1994	6.5
1985	7.3	1990	-8.7	1995	2
1986	8.5	1991	-7.3	1996	4.3
1987	5.3	1992	5	1997	4.1

Note: 1983–1993 is actual growth. 1994–1997 are forecasts.

As Exhibit 2(b) shows, this resulted in much lower prices relative to the consumer price index during the late 1980s and early 1990s. Margins which had been 10–20 percent fell to 2–9 percent during the late 1980s and early 1990s.

Whirlpool Corporation

Whirlpool is the world's leading manufacturer and marketer of major home appliances. It grew from humble beginnings to become a global leader. Headquartered in Benton Harbor, Michigan, Whirlpool began as a family-owned machine shop in 1911. The company now employs 39,590 people worldwide. In addition, Whirlpool currently manufactures in 11 countries and markets products under 10 brand names in more than 120 countries. Annual sales were over $7.5 billion in 1993 and were expected to continue to grow as the company expands its current lines of business and seeks opportunities in new markets around the world. Exhibit 3 details the Whirlpool milestones since 1911.

EXHIBIT 2   Appliance industry information

(a) U.S. industry concentration

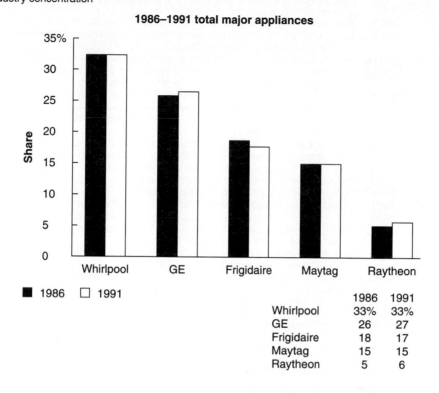

1986–1991 total major appliances

	1986	1991
Whirlpool	33%	33%
GE	26	27
Frigidaire	18	17
Maytag	15	15
Raytheon	5	6

(b) Prices

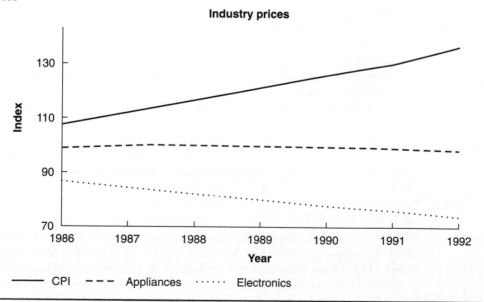

Industry prices

EXHIBIT 3   Whirlpool Corporation milestones*

1911	Upton Machine Co. is founded in St. Joseph, Michigan, to produce electric motor-driven wringer washers.
1916	First order of washers is sold to Sears, Roebuck and Co.
1929	Upton Machine merges with Nineteen Hundred Washer Co. of Binghamton, N.Y., forming the Nineteen Hundred Corp.
1947	The company's first automatic washer is introduced to the market by Sears.
1948	A Whirlpool-brand automatic washer is introduced, establishing dual distribution—one line of products for Sears, another for Nineteen Hundred.
1950	Nineteen Hundred Corp. is renamed Whirlpool Corp. Automatic dryers are added to the product line.
1951	Whirlpool merges with Clyde Porcelain Steeland and converts the Clyde, Ohio, plant to washer production.
1955	Whirlpool merges with Seeger Refrigeration Co. and the Estate range and air conditioning divisions of RCA. RCA Whirlpool is established as the brand name and Whirlpool Seeger Corp. is used as the company name.
1957	Company name is changed back to Whirlpool.
1967	RCA is dropped from the Whirlpool brand name.
1969	The Canadian appliance market is entered through the purchase of Inglis Ltd.
1986	The KitchenAid division of Hobart Corp. is purchased from Dart & Kraft.
1988	A joint venture is formed with Nitro S.A. of Monterrey, Mexico, to manufacture and market major home appliances for Mexico.
1989	The North American Appliance Group (NAAG) is formed to manage operations in the U.S., Canada, and Mexico.
1990	Estate brand of appliances is introduced to specific national accounts, including the Warehouse Club.
1992	The Small Appliance Business Unit (SABU) is formed.

*"Remake at Whirlpool Home Appliance," *Appliance Manufacture,* May 1994

Small Appliance Business Unit

In 1986, Whirlpool purchased the KitchenAid division of the Hobart Corporation. Initially, Whirlpool operated the division as a separate subsidiary. In 1992, Whirlpool established a separate Small Appliance Business Unit (SABU) to manufacture and market these small appliances. This group was independent of the large appliance groups which marketed major appliances like refrigerators and ranges under the Whirlpool, KitchenAid, and Roper brand names.

The SABU is responsible for products including stand mixers, hand mixers, blenders, and food processors marketed under the KitchenAid brand name. Almost 95 percent of the $139 million in 1994 sales of these products was domestic U.S. based. The remainder of sales came primarily from Western Europe, with France and Germany representing 70–80 percent of the business.

Changes at Whirlpool

In 1991, Whirlpool changed its strategy to be a more customer-focused company. Specifically, Whirlpool decided to create "a dominant consumer franchise." This meant understanding, designing, and delivering products that give customers a reason other than price to purchase its products. At that time, the

KitchenAid stand mixer was one of the few existing examples of an appliance not sold solely on price.

In addition, in 1991, Whirlpool purchased the floundering European appliance unit of N.V. Philips. This established the Whirlpool European Business Unit (WEBU) operations. Prior to the acquisition by Whirlpool, KitchenAid small appliances had been sold in Western Europe for many years by the Hobart Corporation. These small appliances were currently being sold as a small part of the Whirlpool European operations.

The KitchenAid brand was targeted toward two consumer segments, achievers and traditionalists. KitchenAid's objective with this strategy was to uniquely meet the needs of these two target groups by offering the best combination of style and performance.

KitchenAid Europe

The KitchenAid Europa group was a much younger and smaller operation than KitchenAid in the U.S.[1] As Exhibit 4 shows, KitchenAid Europa was a small part of KitchenAid, and even smaller compared to Whirlpool Europa.

EXHIBIT 4   KitchenAid sales and profits, 1994

	KitchenAid U.S.	KitchenAid Europa	Whirlpool Europa
1994 sales	$110 MM	$6.3 MM	$2.23 Billion
1994 operating profit	10%	1%	18%

Managing a younger and smaller organization was both an advantage and a disadvantage for Robinson. The advantage was the freedom to develop an entrepreneurial organization that could change very quickly and react to market or consumer demands.

The disadvantage was that KitchenAid was a small fish in the large Whirlpool pond. As Whirlpool executed its global expansion strategy, resources were precious. A small organization like KitchenAid Europa had to fight for both attention and resources.

Product

In 1995, KitchenAid Europa sold only the stand mixer. The stand mixer is a multi-functional mixer that mixes, whips, and kneads everything from egg whites to heavy bread dough. The sales brochure used to describe this appliance is shown in Exhibit 5.

---

[1]Note that figures represent KitchenAid small appliances only.

EXHIBIT 5   KitchenAid brochure

KitchenAid®
COMMERCIAL MIXER
MODEL KSMC50SWH

Put these commercial-duty features to work…for durability, convenience and professional mixing performance.

THERMAL OVERLOAD PROTECTION RESET BUTTON

CONVENIENT BOWL LIFT HANDLE

ATTRACTIVE ENAMEL FINISH

SAFETY GUARD PIN

SOLID-STATE, 5-SPEED PLUS STIR SPEED MIXING ACTION CONTROL

PROFESSIONAL PLANETARY MIXING ACTION MIXES THOROUGHLY AND FAST

5-QT. STAINLESS STEEL BOWL WITH SURE GRIP HANDLE

STAINLESS STEEL WIRE WHIP

6-FT., HEAVY-DUTY, 3-WIRE POWER CORD & PLUG

350 WATTS/110-115 VOLTS

DOUGH HOOK

FLAT BEATER

NSF TESTING LABORATORY NSF ANN ARBOR, MICH.

1 YEAR COMMERCIAL WARRANTY

EXHIBIT 5   KitchenAid brochure *(continued)*

   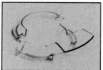

EXHIBIT 5   KitchenAid brochure *(continued)*

EXHIBIT 5 KitchenAid brochure *(concluded)*

KitchenAid®
Stand Mixers...
The Standard Of Quality For Generations!

KitchenAid multi-function mixers do it all...mix, whip and knead... everything from egg whites to heavy bread dough. Ten-speed, solid-state controls cover every need from gentle stirring to high-speed whipping. The unique KitchenAid planetary mixing action thoroughly blends ingredients...all the way to the edges...without ever rotating the bowl. The rugged, all-metal exterior construction and heavy-duty motor and transmission mean many years of trouble-free, dependable service.

(K45SS)

(KSM90)

(K5SS/KSM5)

Classic Series Stand Mixer

This is the mixer that the KitchenAid name was built on. Solidly constructed, powerful...a true timeless classic designed to deliver a lifetime of performance.

* 250 watts of power.
* Tilt-up mixer head makes bowl and attachment removal easy.
* 4 ½-qt. stainless steel bowl.
* Includes flat beater, dough hook, and wire whip.
* Available in white or almond cream.

Ultra Power Series Stand Mixer

With 20% more power than the Classic series and available in a wide variety of rich designer colors, this is the mixer of choice for the well-equipped kitchen.

* 300 watts of power.
* Tilt-up mixer head makes bowl and attachment removal easy.
* 4 ½-qt. polished stainless steel bowl features easy-grip handle.
* Includes flat beater, dough hook, wire whip, and a nonsealing bowl cover.
* Some models also available with pouring shield.
* White or designer colors.

Heavy Duty Series Stand Mixer

With its unique bowl lift handle and powerful 325 watt motor, the Heavy Duty series is built for serious cooks who use their mixers on a daily basis.

* 325 watts of power.
* Easy-to-use bowl lift handle.
* 5-qt. stainless steel bowl features easy-grip handle.
* Includes flat beater, dough hook, and wire whip.
* Some models also available with pouring shield or bowl cover.
* White or designer colors.

Every KitchenAid® stand mixer comes with these standard attachments

Flat Beater
Ideal for mixing cakes, cookies and batters.

Dough Hook
Specially designed for mixing and kneading yeast doughs.

Wire Whip
Produces maximum volume when whipping cream or egg whites.

The rationale behind only selling the stand mixer was based on two factors:

1. The stand mixer was the most successful KitchenAid small appliance worldwide.
2. Concentrating on one product simplified the marketing effort needed to introduce KitchenAid branded products into Europe.

In the United States, KitchenAid also sold hand mixers, blenders, and food processors. Published reports indicated that more appliances were likely to be added to the KitchenAid product line over the next few years. For example, coffeemakers were being tested for possible sale.

Advertising and Promotion

In the United States, the KitchenAid brand was well known and well established as an expensive, durable product. In Europe, however, the name was not well known. In Western Europe the name had some awareness, particularly with the kitchen staffs of premium restaurants. In Central Europe, the name was almost completely unknown.

The issue of brand awareness was complicated by lack of resources. Most of Whirlpool's resources were being used to establish the major appliance group in Europe and Asia. This left little money in Robinson's budget to fund an advertising effort. Robinson's advertising budget was $100,000 for all of Europe in 1995.

The little awareness that KitchenAid had in Europe was due to word-of-mouth, according to KitchenAid sales managers. Among those who were aware of the KitchenAid stand mixer, it was regarded as having excellent quality by both consumers and professionals alike. Robinson wondered if it would be possible to leverage this quality perception with the product into some greater awareness of the KitchenAid brand name. For example, if key professional influencers could be identified, KitchenAid could use these people as spokespersons to influence consumers.

Distribution

One very critical factor in introducing a product into central Europe was thought to be distribution. Unlike the United States appliance industry, distribution channels in Poland, the Czech Republic, and Hungary were not well developed. Exhibit 6 looks at some of the differences in distribution across Europe.

Robinson believed KitchenAid had three distribution options.

1. Utilize local distributors.
2. Develop KitchenAid distributors.
3. Some hybrid of the first two options.

Utilize local distributors. Distributors in Central European countries worked with diverse product lines. For example, an office equipment distributor sold everything from toilet paper to fine china to office furniture. In addition, lo-

EXHIBIT 6   Distribution spectrum

	*Distribution**	
Concentrated		*Fragmented*
U.K., France	Markets	Central Europe
Direct sales	Sales force	Use distributors
Specialty stores	Retailers	Regional independents
Department stores		

Distribution notes:*
- Care must be taken in choosing a distributor. Since privatization began, there are a growing number of distributors, but few are financially stable.
- Distributors expressed concern that KitchenAid had only one product to offer. In general, distributors preferred to partner with manufacturers who produced a full line of products.

*Notes taken from in-country interviews conducted by University of Michigan students in March 1995.

cal distributors often lacked basic computer and business tools and skills. Many distributed products from their apartments or homes. Even with these drawbacks, local distributors understood the local market extremely well. This understanding would take KitchenAid years to acquire on its own.

Establish KitchenAid distributors. KitchenAid also had the option to establish its own distributors. This was typically done by partnering with an existing distributor from another country like Bavarian Distributors from Germany. Another option was to finance a local group of distributors to distribute only KitchenAid brand appliances.

This option was appealing because it would have given KitchenAid more control of distribution while assuring that sophisticated business practices were followed. The drawback to this plan was the lack of market knowledge that outside distributors might have and the risk of financing an inexperienced group of distributors.

As part of the distribution decision, Robinson needed to decide how the appliances would be serviced and who would be authorized to provide the service. Also, Robinson considered if he should establish separate KitchenAid salespeople for the professional and consumer markets. Finally, would the salespeople be located within the Whirlpool national sales offices or separately to maintain their own identity? These questions needed to be answered before any effective country distribution effort could be implemented.

Price

In the United States, the stand mixer was priced at $200–$2,000, depending on the number of attachments and accessories. The stand mixer commanded the highest gross margin of any product in the Whirlpool Corporation at approximately 30 percent.

Pricing the stand mixer in Europe was more challenging. To begin with, KitchenAid's costs were higher due to the product being manufactured in Ohio and exported to Europe. In addition to transportation costs, tariffs were charged on appliances by every country in Europe. The basic stand mixer cost approximately $130 to manufacture. KitchenAid Europa then shipped the stand mixers to a warehouse in The Netherlands for $5.75 per unit. The products were then shipped directly to distributors or retailers in each country. Tariffs were 20 percent in Hungary, 25 percent in the Czech Republic, and 35 percent in Poland.

These higher costs were of even greater concern in the Central European market given that consumers there earned a fraction of that earned by consumers in the United States or Western Europe. Robinson had a difficult decision to make. Should KitchenAid charge a premium, or would this high price eliminate any potential sales in Central European countries?

Competition

As Exhibit 7 shows, KitchenAid had many general competitors, but few competing in the premium and small-volume segment of the consumer and professional markets. For example, the only competitor producing a premium stand mixer was Kenwood. The Kenwood mixer was made of some of the same durable materials that the KitchenAid mixer was and had a larger mixing capacity.

The other competitors, such as Bosch and Krefft, manufactured less-expensive plastic stand mixers made for light home use. None of the stand mixers were thought to compete with KitchenAid on quality. Not one of KitchenAid's competitors had made a strong effort to enter the professional market. Restaurants and hotels typically bought products from appliance makers like Hobart, who targeted large-scale professional accounts.

In the consumer market, KitchenAid's most direct competitors were slow to enter Central Europe. Kenwood, Bosch, and Braun were thought to be waiting

EXHIBIT 7   Competition by target market and product type by country

	Stand mixer	Food processor	Hand mixer/blender	Stand blender
Premium household	Kenwood (U.K., France, Benelux)	Magimix, Braun (U.K., France, Benelux)	Braun, Krups (U.K., France, Benelux, Germany)	Hamilton Beach (Germany)
	Bosch (Germany)	Braun, Bosch (Germany)	Bamix (France)	Waring (U.K., France)
			ESGE (Germany)	
Small professional	Kenwood (weak in Germany)	Robot Coupe (pan-European)	Bamix (not considered durable or strong enough for professional use)	Hamilton Beach (pan-European market leader)
	Hobart (not competitively priced)	Dito Sama (pan-European)		Waring (pan-European)
	Krefft (Germany only)			

for per capita incomes to rise. In general, these competitors did not believe consumers in Poland, Hungary, and the Czech Republic could afford their products. Mainstream competitors like Moulinex and Philips were having some success at selling relatively inexpensive appliances such as hand mixers and blenders in Central Europe.

Customers

In Western Europe, the market for small appliances could be generally divided into two categories, professionals and household consumers.

Professionals

The professional category consisted of three subgroups:

1. Bakery chefs.
2. Restaurant chefs.
3. Bartenders.

The needs of these segments are described in Exhibit 8.

The professional market was dominated by manufacturers like Hobart Corporation[2], which sold industrial-sized products. For example, the Hobart

---

EXHIBIT 8   Professional users

Bakery/Patisserie Chefs:
• Perform a limited number of tasks, i.e., stirring, kneading, mixing.
• Buy same product with different capacity levels.
• Satisfied with our stand mixer and had high awareness of KitchenAid brand name.

Restaurant Chefs:
• Perform a variety of tasks, i.e., mixing, grinding, slicing.
• Buy single-use, large-capacity products, but supplement with multi-function, small-capacity products.
• Satisfied with our stand mixer, but felt that attachments were not durable enough.
• Had high awareness of KitchenAid and were eager for line extensions.

Bartenders:
• Need products that are reliable and stylish because products are used and displayed in front of customers.
• Limited awareness of KitchenAid.

All professional customers take tremendous pride in their work and want a product that looks professional and not like a household product.

The greatest purchase influences for the professional are:
• The products that they used in school.
• Word of mouth from colleagues.

Advertising carries little weight.

---

[2]Note that Whirlpool had only purchased the KitchenAid part of Hobart in 1991. The Hobart brand continued as a competitor.

stand mixer had a 50-quart capacity. The KitchenAid stand mixer was much smaller and was used as a very flexible kitchen tool. For example, chefs might use the stand mixer to produce a low-volume specialty sauce or dressing.

The total consumer and professional market for small appliances such as mixers and blenders was thought to be about 12–15 million units throughout Europe in 1994. France, the U.K., and Germany accounted for about 6 million of this total. Good estimates for the size of the Central European market were not available. However, one manager's best estimate was that it was about 500,000 to 1 million units. The professional part of the market was thought to be about 15 to 20 percent of the total units sold. Estimates of the number of restaurants, hotels/motels, and boarding houses for Poland, Hungary, and the Czech Republic are presented in Exhibits 9, 10, and 11 respectively. The professional market was primarily made up of stand mixers and a very few hand mixers. The key influences in the professional market included which products the chefs used in cooking school and word of mouth from the most-respected chefs worldwide. Discussions with KitchenAid sales managers indicated that advertising carried little weight.

Household consumer

The consumer market was much larger. Research indicated that the premium small appliance segment that KitchenAid competed in was over 2.5 million products per year. The vast amount of these products were sold in France, Germany, and the U.K.

EXHIBIT 9   Poland profile

	Actual		Forecast			
	1993	*1994*	*1995*	*1996*	*1997*	*1998*
GDP change*	+$4	+$4	+$4.5	+$3.6	+$5	+$5.1
GDP per capita	$1,891	$2,013	$2,136	$2,248	$2,398	$2,560
Consumer prices	+35.3%	+30%	+25%	+18%	+16%	+16%
Unemployment	15.8%	16.5%	16.8%	17.5%	17.8%	18%
Exchange U.S. $	18,100	23,000	28,300	33,000	37,500	42,700

Population:	38.5 million
Population growth rate:	.26%
Percent living according to Western income standards:	5%
Percent of population = Polish:	99%
Average size of Polish household:	3.1
Literacy rate:	98%
Percent of labor force in state sector:	54%
Number of restaurants	4,500
Number of hotels/motels	200
Number of hotel/motel beds	74,600
Number of boarding houses	13,200

*GDP change in billions.

EXHIBIT 10   Hungary profile

	Actual		Forecast			
	1993	1994	1995	1996	1997	1998
GDP change*	−$1	+$1	+$3	+$4.2	+$5	+$5.6
GDP per capita	$3,500	$3,565	$3,956	$4,174	$4,696	$5,257
Consumer prices	+22.5%	+21%	+20%	+15%	+12%	+10%
Unemployment	12.1%	unavail.	unavail.	unavail.	unavail.	17%
Exchange U.S. $	92	109	120	136	142	148

Population:	10.3 million
Religions:	Catholic 69%, Calvinist 20%, Lutheran 5%
Government:	Multiparty parliamentary democracy
Language:	Hungarian; German and some English typically used in business
Workweek:	40 hours, Monday–Friday
Number of restaurants	9,500
Number of hotels/motels	550
Number of hotel/motel beds	85,600
Number of boarding houses	28,600

*GDP change in billions.

EXHIBIT 11   Czech Republic profile

	Actual		Forecast			
	1993	1994	1995	1996	1997	1998
GDP change*	−$0.5	+$3	+$4	+$4	+$4.3	+$4.5
GDP per capita	$3,073	$3,373	$3,937	$4,450	$4,992	$5,490
Consumer prices	+20.8%	+11%	+9%	+7%	+5%	+3.5%
Unemployment	3.5%	6%	7%	9%	9%	8%
Exchange U.S. $	29.2	30.4	29.5	29	28.3	27.8

Population:	10.3 million
Percent population urban:	7.3%
Population growth rate:	1.7%
Birth rate per 1,000:	11.8
Death rate per 1,000:	11.7
Net migration rate per 1,000:	0
Marriages per 1,000:	7.2
Divorce rate per 1,000:	2.8
Number of restaurants	5,400
Number of hotels/motels	410
Number of hotel/motel beds	19,100
Number of boarding houses	20,300

*GDP change in billions.

In the U.S., Whirlpool's marketing research had identified six discrete appliance segments.[3] As the list below demonstrates, KitchenAid was targeted at achievers and traditionalists. How or if this segmentation could be applied in

---

[3]"Remake at Whirlpool Home Appliances," *Appliance Manufacturer,* May 1994.

Europe was unclear, but Robinson believed that groups with similar needs to achievers and traditionalists existed in Europe.

1. *Achievers:* A small percentage of the population, but with a large percentage of buying power. The family is educated, has a high income level, entertains a lot, and sees appliances as an opportunity to display their good taste.
2. *Traditionalists:* Less than 20 percent of the population, they have a very strong home focus. Family is very important and cleaning and cooking are ways of showing that devotion to the family.
3. *Housework rebels:* The newest and fastest-growing segment. Their way of showing love is to hold down a full-time job and still get other homemaking responsibilities accomplished in an expedient fashion.
4. *Self-assureds:* Younger, well-educated families who have a low level of involvement with appliances and home. Value is extremely important.
5. *Proven conservatives:* Similar to the traditionalists, but younger.
6. *Homebound survivors:* Older adults, often living alone. Very conservative values and few outside interests.

Central Europe

There was a great deal of risk in marketing KitchenAid small appliances in Central Europe. These were still economies in transition from a communist control-type system to free markets. Within this broad context, each of the three countries had a distinct dynamic as follows.

Poland

Poland has the largest population of any of the three countries under consideration. As Exhibit 12 shows, Poland lagged behind Hungary and the Czech Republic in terms of spending growth, monthly salaries, and GDP per person. In addition, Poland had the highest tariffs of the emerging Central European countries. This was a large concern for KitchenAid since its products were only produced in the United States. Additional information about Poland is presented in Exhibit 9.

Despite these disadvantages, Poland was a very large and undeveloped country. Poland's population of 38.5 million was almost double that of Hungary and the Czech Republic combined. Also, reports estimated that 5 percent of the Polish population lived according to Western income standards.

Hungary

In general, the Hungarian market was much more appealing than Poland. Hungary was regarded as being the most politically stable of the Central European countries and was closest in thinking to the Western world. Overall,

EXHIBIT 12   Central Europe information

Changes in aggregate consumer spending

	Poland	*Hungary*	*Czech Republic*
1992	−2.50%	5.00%	11.10%
1993	0.00	5.50	1.50
1994	0.50	6.00	2.00
1995	3.00	6.00	3.00
1996	3.20	4.00	3.80

Average gross monthly salaries in February 1994

Poland	$79
Hungary	264
Czech Republic	219

GDP per capita

Poland	$1,895
Hungary	3,440
Czech Republic	2,470

Total GDP (1992)	*($ billion)*
Western Europe	$7,982
North America	6,526
Japan	3,735
Central Europe	166
Turkey	128

Source: *EIU Marketing in Europe,* August 1994, p. 65.

Hungary was economically more developed for premium-priced appliances. More detail is available in Exhibit 10.

However, Hungary had its disadvantages. To begin with, unemployment was relatively high and GDP growth was negative during the early 1990s. Also, housing was difficult to obtain and inflation was high.

Overall, Hungary did appear to be able to support premium-priced goods. For example, local estimates indicated that over 1,000 luxury automobiles such as BMW and Mercedes were sold in 1994. Whirlpool major appliance group estimated that Budapest had approximately 6,000 luxury households.

Czech Republic

The Czech Republic was clearly the most developed of the Central European countries. KitchenAid was actually selling approximately 1,000 units per year through a local distributor as a test market. Though the Czech Republic started privatization later than Hungary, it was much more economically developed.

The Czech Republic also had the most developed retailers and distributors. Kmart, for example, had three stores in Czech and, unlike Hungary or Poland, specialty retailers were opening. Economic statistics are provided in Exhibit 11.

Robinson's Decision

David Robinson needed to act quickly. Successful entry into Central Europe would give Robinson a large selling base and higher profits. At the same time, a poor entry would drain the few precious resources that Robinson had at his disposal.

As he contemplated his decision, he found himself wishing for more detailed market and competitive information on each of the three Central European countries. Unfortunately, he knew that good information was scarce and expensive to obtain in these markets. Time pressure would force him to prepare his marketing plan with the information he now had available. Keith English wanted his recommendations quickly.

Case 3

Compaq Computer Corporation*

On August 12, 1981, IBM Corporation entered the personal computer market with a blaze of advertising and public relations. Although the personal computer had emerged in the mid-1970s, many observers believed that the entry of IBM legitimized the fledgling industry and would propel the industry into the mainstream of American business. Mr. Markkula, the president of Apple Corporation, commented that the IBM entry would expand the personal computer market for all manufacturers. At the time of IBM's entry, Apple was the market leader with a 25 percent market share. Apple was followed closely by Tandy Corporation with its Radio Shack brand. Other players in 1981 included Xerox, Hewlett-Packard, and Commodore. Total sales of personal computers in 1981 were about $1.25 billion.

The IBM PC was based on the 16-bit Intel 8088 microprocessor, which was a faster and more powerful microprocessor than those used by IBM's competitors (they were all 8-bit). IBM had selected the MS-DOS operating system marketed by a small Seattle-based company called Microsoft. The earlier entrants into the personal computer industry had used a variety of operating systems. Apple Computer used its own proprietary operating system. The other popular operating system at the time was CP/M.

The initial reaction to the IBM PC was very positive and demand immediately began to outstrip the supply of computers. In early 1982, industry sources estimated that IBM PC sales in 1982 would be $400 to $600 million.

*Professors Adrian Ryans and Mark Vandenbosch, with the assistance of Neil Miller, prepared this case solely to provide material for class discussion. The case is not intended to illustrate either effective or ineffective handling of a managerial situation. Certain names and other identifying information may have been disguised to protect confidentiality. This material is not covered under authorization from CanCopy or any reproduction rights organization. Any form of reproduction, storage, or transmittal of this material is prohibited without written permission from Western Business School. Copyright © 1995 The University of Western Ontario.

Compaq's Entry and Early Growth

Compaq Computer Corporation was founded in February 1982 by three Texas Instruments alumni, Rod Canion, Bill Nurto, and Jim Harris. Canion had been considering several entrepreneurial ventures in 1981, when he realized that IBM was in the process of establishing an industry standard for personal computers. He believed that he could develop an IBM-compatible computer to take advantage of the emerging standard. The initial funding for Compaq was provided by Sevin-Rosen Management Company, a venture capital firm. Ben Rosen, the president of Sevin-Rosen, became the chairman of the board of directors of Compaq Computer Corporation.

With the successful entry of IBM into the personal computer industry, it became apparent to many other corporations and entrepreneurs that the open architecture of the IBM PC, based as it was on the Intel 8088 microprocessor and the MS-DOS operating system, provided them with a business opportunity. Literally dozens of companies began manufacturing personal computers using standard components and subsystems that were now becoming available from a variety of vendors. Some new entrants attempted to differentiate their offerings from IBM by offering proprietary operating systems or their own variants of the standard operating system. Other companies, among them Compaq, decided to try to be totally IBM-compatible. Not all were successful in achieving full compatibility, and end users were unable to use some of the programs developed for the IBM PC.

In order to assure total compatibility, Compaq immediately assigned a small team of programmers to develop a basic input/output system (BIOS) that would function identically to IBM's, while not copying the IBM code. While this development work was underway, Compaq moved ahead to establish the management infrastructure and manufacturing facility necessary to produce its first product, the Compaq Portable. This product, based on the Intel 8088 microprocessor, was announced in November 1982.

Launch Strategy

The initial target segments for the Compaq Portable were corporations and professionals who required portable (really "luggable") computers. Early adopters included auditors and salespersons.

Compaq distributed its portable computer only through retailers. It decided to focus on retailers who also sold IBM PCs. It was successful, in late 1982, in persuading both the Business Centers of Sears, Roebuck & Co. and the largest chain of computer specialty stores, Computerland, to carry its product. Unlike most of the other computer manufacturers, Compaq decided not to establish a direct sales force that would sell to large corporate accounts.

In addition to making the retail dealers its exclusive channel of distribution, Compaq also established its suggested retail and manufacturer selling prices so that retailers would be able to earn 36 percent to 38 percent margins on Compaq computers versus the 32 percent that IBM offered on its computers. Its prices were roughly equivalent to those charged by IBM for a comparable PC.

Compaq's field sales force was also very active in providing the retailers with sales training and other forms of retail support. In its second full year of operation, Compaq established a dealer advisory council, with representatives from many of its retailers, to provide feedback and advice to Compaq. Within its first year of selling personal computers, Compaq had established a dealer network of almost 1,000 dealers in North America. By targeting the high end of the corporate and professional market with a high-quality, fully compatible personal computer, Compaq was able to avoid some of the severe price pressures that were already starting to impact some of the other segments of the computer market.

Early Results

In its first year on the market, 1983, Compaq benefitted tremendously from the large market that IBM had created for its personal computers. With IBM unable to meet the demand it had created, there was rapid acceptance of the Compaq portable by both retailers and end users.

By late 1983, Compaq was enjoying considerable success. Sales had grown from $5 million in the first quarter of 1983 to $18 million in the second quarter and $36 million in the third quarter. In the third quarter, Compaq earned its first profit with a net income of $3.8 million dollars. In December 1983, Compaq made its first public offering of six million shares and raised $67 million.

Despite these early successes, many industry observers were not convinced that Compaq would continue to survive and prosper. They thought that Compaq's initial success was largely based on the inability of IBM to supply its computers. One analyst commented, "Compaq is a fine, well managed company, but can it sustain this extraordinary growth if IBM should double or triple production? All these IBM look-alike companies are racing towards a cliff. The only question is just how far down they will fall."[1]

Subsequent Moves

Late in 1983, Compaq introduced its second product, the Portable Plus. Exhibit 1 contains the approximate introduction date of major new Compaq products. This was the first personal computer on the market to have a 10-megabyte hard drive. Belatedly, IBM responded to Compaq's portable products with its own IBM Portable PC. However, the IBM product was not a success and didn't seem to significantly affect the sales of Compaq computers.

---

[1]"Compaq Computer Defies Cool Market, Plans Stock Sale," *The Wall Street Journal,* Wednesday, October 26, 1983, p. 44.

EXHIBIT 1   Major new product introductions by Compaq Computer Corporation

Date	Product
January 1983	Portable
Late 1983	Portable Plus
June 1984	Deskpro
April 1985	Deskpro 286 and Portable 286
September 1986	Deskpro 386
October 1988	SLT/286 (first battery-powered laptop)
October 1989	LTE (first notebook)
November 1989	Systempro file server (incorporates new EISA bus)
November 1989	First 80486 desktops
September 1991	Deskpro/M (modular easily upgradeable products)
June 1992	Prolinea desktop line
June 1992	Contura notebook line
October 1992	ProSignia low-cost servers
May 1993	First Pentium servers
August 1993	Presario line (first all-in-one Compaq for consumer market)
February 1994	Contura Aero (first subnotebook)

Source: Compiled from various company and non-company sources.

In June 1984, Compaq introduced its Deskpro series, its first desktop computers. The four initial models competed directly with the IBM PC family. The Deskpro product line was based on the new, more powerful, Intel 8086 microprocessor. As a result, the new Compaq products ran software two to three times faster than IBM's existing computers.

The most expensive computer in the Deskpro line incorporated a tape backup system, which made it much easier for users to back up their files. Compaq was the first company in the industry to incorporate this feature, and it was developed at the suggestion of one of Compaq's dealers. The Deskpro product line also benefitted from other dealer input. A few months prior to the Deskpro launch, dealers complained that the proposed four new models would take up too much storage space. In response, Compaq used one Deskpro chassis and the dealers could configure a particular model by putting in the right combination of disk drives and hard disks. The Compaq product return policy was one of the most liberal in the industry.

With the launch of the Deskpro line, Compaq began to promote the company and its product much more aggressively. In 1984, Compaq spent almost $20 million dollars on an advertising campaign and additional money in cooperative advertising with its dealers.

In 1984, Compaq also began its global expansion with its entry into Europe. It achieved sales of $20 million in Europe in 1984, and sales there continued to grow very rapidly.

Meanwhile, many of the other inexperienced startups, which had entered the market in the early 1980s, had fallen by the wayside. Even long-established companies, such as Hewlett-Packard and Digital Equipment Corporation, had underestimated the need to be totally IBM-compatible and achieved very disappointing results in their personal computer businesses.

Launch of the IBM PC AT Computers

In late 1984, IBM announced a new personal computer, the IBM PC AT, which was based on the Intel 80286 microprocessor. A few months later, several other personal computer manufacturers, including Texas Instruments and Zenith Electronics Corp., announced their own versions of the AT product. Other companies, including NCR, Hewlett-Packard, and Wang Laboratories, were expected to introduce AT products later in 1985. On April 30, 1985, Compaq unveiled two computers that utilized the 80286 microprocessor and were fully compatible with IBM's PC AT. Compaq's machines were priced from $4,500 to $6,300, equivalent to the prices charged for the comparable IBM models. Compaq claimed that both its new computers ran as much as 30 percent faster than the comparable IBM models.

Compaq ended 1985 with sales of more than $500 million, making it the first company in U.S. business history to reach the Fortune 500 in less than four years. Income statement data for 1983–1994 are included in Exhibits 2 and 3.

Drive for Product Leadership

On September 9, 1986, with great fanfare, Compaq announced its Deskpro 386 line of personal computers based on Intel's 80386 microprocessor. The launch of the Deskpro 386 represented a significant change in strategy for Compaq. Instead of waiting for IBM to take the lead in the mainstream 386 market, Compaq itself was setting the pace of innovation. Rod Canion commented in an interview with *The Wall Street Journal,* "We want the world to accept us as a technological innovator."[2] The Deskpro 386 claimed to run complex programs for IBM-compatible personal computers two to three times faster than the fastest available IBM personal computer in 1986.

In bringing the Deskpro 386 products to market, Compaq had worked closely with both Intel and Microsoft. Compaq had worked with Intel to ensure that all the programs that had been designed to run on the Intel 8086 and 80286 microprocessors would run on the new 80386 microprocessor. Compaq had also worked with Microsoft to help it adapt its operating system software to take advantage of the additional memory that would be available in a 386 computer. Gordon Moore, the chairman of Intel Corporation, and Bill Gates of Microsoft, as well as the presidents of several other major software manufacturers, were on the stage in New York City when Compaq made its announcement. Analysts estimated that Compaq had invested about $8 million in research and development and another $5 million to launch the Deskpro 386.[3]

---

[2]"Compaq Introduces Two Computers Using Intel's State-of-the-Art 386 Chip," *The Wall Street Journal,* September 9, 1986, p. 2.

[3]Bro Uttal, "Compaq Bids for PC Leadership," *Fortune,* September 29, 1986, pp. 30–32.

EXHIBIT 2   Consolidated income statement data ($ millions)

Year ended December 31	1983	1984	1985	1986	1987	1988	1989	1990	1991	1992	1993	1994
Sales	$111	$329	$504	$625	$1,224	$2,066	$2,876	$3,599	$3,271	$4,100	$7,191	$10,866
Cost of sales	80	232	326	360	717	1,234	1,715	2,058	2,053	2,905	5,493	8,139
	31	97	178	265	507	832	1,161	1,541	1,218	1,195	1,698	2,727
Research & development costs	4	11	16	27	47	75	132	186	197	173	169	226
Selling, general, & administrative expense	22	66	110	152	226	397	539	706	722	699	837	1,235
Unrealized gain on investment in affiliated company					(4)	(10)	(13)	(34)				
Other income & expense, net		3	8	9	10	3	19	42	145	28	76	94
	26	80	134	188	279	465	677	900	1,064	900	1,082	1,555
Income from consolidated companies before provision for income taxes	5	17	44	77	228	367	484	641	154	295	616	1,172
Provision for income taxes	2	4	17	32	93	119	165	216	43	97	154	305
Income from consolidated companies	3	13	27	45	135	248	319	425	111	198	462	867
Equity in net income (loss) of affiliated company				(2)	1	7	14	30	20	15		
Extraordinary item: Utilization of net operating loss carryforward	2											
Net income	$ 5	$ 13	$ 27	$ 43	$ 136	$ 255	$ 333	$ 455	$ 131	$ 213	$ 462	$ 867

Source: *Financial Fact Book*, Compaq Computer Corporation, 1994.

EXHIBIT 3 Consolidated income statement data (as a percentage of sales)

Year ended December 31	1983	1984	1985	1986	1987	1988	1989	1990	1991	1992	1993	1994
Sales	100.0%	100.0%	100.0%	100.0%	100.0%	100.0%	100.0%	100.0%	100.0%	100.0%	100.0%	100.0%
Cost of sales	72.1	70.5	64.7	57.6	58.6	59.7	59.6	57.2	62.8	70.9	76.4	74.9
	27.9	29.5	35.3	42.4	41.4	40.3	40.4	42.8	37.2	29.1	23.6	25.1
Research & development costs	3.6	3.3	3.2	4.3	3.8	3.6	4.6	5.2	6.0	4.2	2.3	2.1
Selling, general, & administrative expense	19.8	20.1	21.8	24.3	18.5	19.2	18.8	19.6	22.1	17.0	11.6	11.4
Unrealized gain on investment in affiliated company					(0.3)	(0.5)	(0.5)	(0.9)				
Other income & expense, net		0.9	1.6	1.5	0.8	0.2	0.7	1.1	4.4	0.7	1.1	0.8
Income from consolidated companies before provision for income taxes	4.5	5.2	8.7	12.3	18.6	17.8	16.8	17.8	4.7	7.2	8.6	10.8
Provision for income taxes	1.8	1.2	3.3	5.1	7.6	5.8	5.7	6.0	1.3	2.4	2.2	2.8
Income from consolidated companies	2.7	4.0	5.4	7.2	11.0	12.0	11.1	11.8	3.4	4.8	6.4	8.0
Equity in net income (loss) of affiliated company				(0.3)	0.1	0.3	0.5	0.8	0.6	0.4		
Extraordinary item: Utilization of net operating loss carry-forward	1.8											
Net income	4.5%	4.0%	5.4%	6.9%	11.1%	12.3%	11.6%	12.6%	4.0%	5.2%	6.4%	8.0%

Source: *Financial Fact Book,* Compaq Computer Corporation, 1994.

Compaq's Initial Strategy for the 386 Product Line

Compaq's Deskpro 386 personal computers were initially targeted at power users, many of whom were employed by large corporations. Prior to the launch of the Deskpro 386, almost half of Compaq's sales had been to large corporations. Typical applications for the Deskpro 386 machine were the manipulation of large spreadsheets or databases and computer-aided design (CAD) or computer-aided engineering (CAE). The first two Deskpro 386 models were sold at premium prices and could generate margins of over 40 percent for retailers. With heavy initial advertising and promotion, the Deskpro 386 achieved rapid adoption. Almost 50,000 units were sold in its first two quarters on the market, generating over $200 million in revenues.

IBM's Reaction

For several months there was no direct response from IBM. IBM was still, by far, the largest player in the IBM-compatible segment of the personal computer market. It continued to invest heavily in hardware and software upgrades for the IBM PC AT product line. Some analysts speculated that IBM was reluctant to move aggressively into the market for 386 personal computers, since these had the potential to cannibalize its engineering workstations and small minicomputer systems. Some analysts estimated that over $5 billion of IBM's non-PC revenues might be threatened by more powerful personal computers.

In April 1987, IBM responded and announced its PS/2 line of personal computers, with the 386 models in the line to be available in late 1987. At the same time that it announced the PS/2 line, IBM also announced a new operating system, the OS/2 operating system, for its more advanced personal computers. The OS/2 operating system, which had been developed by Microsoft for IBM, was expected to ship in early 1988. OS/2 promised to be a considerably more powerful and versatile operating system than MS-DOS, which was currently used on all IBM and IBM-compatible computers. The simultaneous announcement of the PS/2 product line and the OS/2 operating system caused considerable confusion in the market place. Many organizations and end users believed that the OS/2 operating system would only run on IBM's PS/2 line. In July 1987, Compaq moved to dispel this notion and announced that the OS/2 operating system would be available on its products. In fact, Rod Canion claimed that OS/2 would run better on Compaq computers than on IBM's new line, because of the higher performance of Compaq's personal computers.

In announcing the PS/2 line of personal computers, IBM included a number of features that it felt would enhance the performance of its personal computers. A major, and controversial, difference was IBM's Micro Channel bus, which was only incorporated in the high-end models in the PS/2 line. The Micro Channel was IBM's term for the pathway that connects the microprocessor and the other key subsystems or peripherals of the personal computer, such as its memory, disk storage, modem, and printer. The original bus on the IBM PC had become inadequate as the performance of the microprocessor and the other components in the personal computer increased. While the proprietary Micro Channel architecture solved many of these problems, it also meant that many of the components and add-in boards that were designed for the original 1981 architecture would no longer work with the PS/2 line. Other enhancements that IBM introduced included improved graphics and the use of 3 1/2″ floppy disks, rather than the standard 5 1/4″ disks.

Compaq's Subsequent Moves

In September 1987, Compaq announced a new Deskpro 386/20. This computer incorporated an improved bus. Compaq claimed that this new bus removed many of the bottlenecks caused by the original 1981 IBM bus design. Yet, unlike IBM's Micro Channel architecture, customers could continue to use cards and peripherals that were compatible with the old bus.

In January 1988, Compaq announced price cuts of 10 percent on some of its models. Compaq's "street" prices were at that time often considerably higher than those of IBM's comparable models. Although IBM's retail prices hadn't changed, it was reported in the industry that IBM's direct sales force was discounting its personal computers quite heavily for large customers.

In October 1988, Compaq introduced the SLT/286, its first battery-powered laptop. This product had been codeveloped with Citizen Co. of Japan. The laptop was the first one to incorporate VGA graphics (which created sharper images) and a fast-recharge battery. Although Compaq had continued to dominate the portable IBM-compatible personal computer market, it had seen its market share in the portable (including laptop) market slip rapidly in the preceding year to 50 percent. By late 1988, the laptop market was estimated to be worth at least $1 billion in sales. Toshiba and Zenith had beaten Compaq into the market by many months and had established strong competitive positions in this growth segment.

In July 1989, Compaq and eight other major manufacturers of IBM-compatible personal computers (but not IBM) introduced the Extended Industry Standard Architecture (EISA) bus. Compaq had played a leadership role in establishing the alliance to develop the bus. This new bus architecture solved many of the performance problems of the original IBM bus, while at the same time allowing customers to use components and add-in cards that had been designed for the original bus architecture. The EISA bus had been announced in mid-1988 and had been under development for more than a year. By announcing this new industry "standard," Compaq and the other manufacturers ("the Gang of Nine") hoped to demonstrate that IBM no longer had the power to dictate standards in the PC industry.[4]

---

[4]About this time, the business press started to use PC to refer to any personal computer. This convention is used here.

Other Developments at Compaq

From 1982 to 1989, the management team at Compaq was remarkably stable. Most of the top 20 managers at Compaq were, like Canion and his two co-founders, veterans of Texas Instruments. A consensus-type of management decision-making process had taken firm root at Compaq.

During the late 1980s, Compaq's research and development expenditures continued to be very low, averaging less than 5 percent of sales. IBM, on the other hand, spent almost 10 percent of its revenues on research and development. Because of its heavy reliance on its retail dealers, Compaq also invested less on sales and marketing than many of its competitors. IBM spent almost a third of its revenues on sales and marketing, whereas Compaq spent just over 11 percent.

There were signs of unrest emerging among some Compaq dealers. In February 1989, Compaq ended its six-year relationship with Businessland. Businessland was one of the leading suppliers of PCs to businesses. Dealers, like Businessland, had become increasingly important in the PC industry during the mid-1980s. It was estimated that about 70 percent of all business customers purchased most of their PCs through dealers. The termination of the relationship with Businessland was attributed to the demand by Businessland for better terms and margins from Compaq than Compaq was willing to give to its dealers. Businessland was also reported to be aggressively pushing IBM products and had adjusted its salesperson compensation schemes to encourage them to sell IBM solutions. Many other dealers continued to work effectively with Compaq, and Compaq continued to listen to and respect the views of its retail dealers. Every year it brought several hundred retail dealers to Houston to meet with its managers and product development teams.

Major New Products Introduced in 1989–91

The Intel 80486 microprocessor was unveiled in April 1989 by Intel. In September 1989, IBM began selling a plug-in card that allowed a user to convert a high-end PS/2 machine from a 386 microprocessor to a 486 microprocessor. Compaq announced its first 486 computers in November 1989, but the launch of the computers was delayed due to design flaws that had been detected in the Intel 80486 microprocessor.

In 1989, Compaq introduced its first SystemPro file server. Unlike the Deskpro, the SystemPro was a large machine designed to manage the mass storage system in a network of PCs. The original SystemPro server was based on an Intel 80386 microprocessor and was priced at $15,000. In July 1990, Compaq introduced three more SystemPro file servers based on both 80386 and 80486 microprocessors. The most expensive of these file servers cost $30,000. With these pioneering moves, Compaq created a new high-end market within the PC business.

In September 1991, Compaq announced its Deskpro/M family of easily up-gradeable personal computers. The various models in the line were based on both Intel 80386 and 80486 microprocessors.

Changing Retail Environment for PCs

By 1990, the growth of the customer base for PCs in North America had slowed and an increasing number of retailers were chasing these customers. This led to an intense price war among retailers. Even large retailers like Businessland were reporting poor financial results. Some retailers, encouraged by Apple and IBM, had begun to focus more on niche markets, such as desktop publishing or auto repair shops. Low-cost distribution channels, such as computer superstores and catalogue retailers, seemed to be gaining market share.

Compaq's Performance

In February 1988, Compaq reported 1987 sales of $1.2 billion, setting the record as the fastest company to reach that revenue level. European sales grew very dramatically, and by 1990, Compaq had higher revenues in Europe than it did in North America. See Exhibit 4 for Compaq sales by geographical area. The growth in Europe had led Compaq to open a manufacturing plant in Scotland in 1987, and to expand its manufacturing and service operations in Scotland in 1989. It had also established a manufacturing plant in Singapore in 1987. In 1990, Compaq achieved sales of almost $3.6 billion and after-tax net income of $455 million. By the end of the year, it had over 11,000 employees and almost 4,000 resellers. It was ranked 136th in the Fortune 500 ranking and 377th in the Global 500 ranking.

In 1990, the product mix was still overwhelmingly desktop computers. These generated about 65 percent of Compaq's revenue versus about 28 percent for its notebook and laptop computers, 4 percent for its SystemPro file servers, and 3 percent for its portables.

EXHIBIT 4   Compaq sales by geographical area ($ in millions)

Year	1984	1985	1986	1987	1988	1989	1990	1991	1992	1993	1994
North America	$309	$452	$506	$905	$1,256	$1,562	$1,641	$1,354	$1,831	$3,671	$5,473
Europe	20	52	119	319	810	1,314	1,958	1,725	1,889	2,718	3,828
Asia Pacific								159	244	469	737
Latin America								33	105	236	483
Japan									31	97	345
Total sales	$329	$504	$625	$1,224	$2,066	$2,876	$3,599	$3,271	$4,100	$7,191	$10,866

Source: *Financial Fact Book,* Compaq Computer Corporation, 1994.

Crash and Recovery

At a meeting of the Compaq board of directors on October 25, 1991, Rod Canion, Compaq's first and only president and CEO, was removed from his position and replaced by Eckhard Pfeiffer. Earlier in 1991, Pfeiffer had been named chief operating officer after a very successful career building up Compaq's European operations. Among the reasons given for Canion's dismissal was the failure of Compaq to adapt rapidly enough to the fast-changing PC industry environment. People, both inside and outside Compaq, felt that Compaq's premium price strategy was increasingly vulnerable to discounters such as Dell. Dell had been running very aggressive comparison advertising in 1991, demonstrating the large price differences between its computers and Compaq's. Price differences of up to $2,000 on notebooks had developed between Compaq and some of the more price-competitive players in the PC industry. Rod Canion's dismissal had been precipitated by a $70 million loss in the third quarter of 1991. Immediately after the announcement of the loss, the company had announced a massive restructuring and the layoff of 1,400 employees.

Compaq and the Changing Market Environment for PCs

By the early 1990s, the PC industry was being affected by a number of major environmental forces. The recession was having a significant impact on PC purchases. Many large corporations and small- and medium-sized businesses were reducing or delaying further investments in information technology. Many corporations and individual purchasers had also become more price-sensitive and were more likely to buy less expensive clones. These factors were having a significant impact on Compaq, which was a high-priced vendor focused heavily on the corporate community.

The PC market also seemed to be polarizing. There was rapid growth occurring in the low-end mass market, which was being serviced by computer superstores and some of the direct marketing organizations. Price was a very important purchase criterion in this segment of the market. Another segment that was growing quite rapidly was the high-end file server market. More and more, computers in the corporate environment were linked into local area networks with file servers. Considerable technical expertise was required to design, install, and service these networks. Unfortunately for Compaq, most of its computer dealers were not very effective at serving either of these growth segments in the PC market. They could neither compete effectively on price with the computer superstores and direct marketing organizations, nor service the needs of the high-end file server market. Many customers complained that the dealers simply didn't have the expertise to answer the technical questions that arose in designing and installing these networks. To help deal with this problem, in early 1991, Compaq announced that it was developing 10–20 percent of its dealers into specialists in the new file servers and was providing extensive training for them. In the fall of 1991, Compaq signed up Electronic Data

Systems Corp., a unit of General Motors, to market its machines, including its SystemPro file servers, to large corporations. This represented a major, albeit tentative, change in Compaq's strategy of relying totally on computer dealers.

Changes Initiated By Eckhard Pfeiffer

The board of directors of Compaq Corporation, including Ben Rosen, the chairperson, and Eckhard Pfeiffer, the new CEO, had concluded that a radical change in strategy was needed to correct Compaq's problems. These changes included a revamping of the product strategy and more dramatic cost cutting.

Shortly after Pfeiffer's appointment, he indicated to analysts the nature of the changes that he planned. Compaq would pursue new segments of the PC market, including home, education, and small business. He made it clear that Compaq would no longer simply follow Rod Canion's strategy of selling premium-priced PCs to large corporations. He said the company would continue to offer top-of-the-line hardware to corporate users, but would also develop low-priced PCs that would compete directly with the products of Dell Computer and AST Research Inc. The first group of these products was introduced in June 1992. In order to be able to price competitively with Dell, AST, and others, it was necessary to cut costs dramatically in order to try to maintain gross profit margins in the 30 percent range. Compaq also radically changed its distribution strategy. Merisel Inc. and Tech Data Corporation were appointed distributors of Compaq computers with the mandate to sell Compaq computers to specialized value-added resellers (VARs). These resellers were expected to bundle the computers with software and service to meet the needs of particular market segments. Compaq also contracted with General Electric and TRW to provide third-party on-site service for Compaq customers.

Within weeks of Eckhard Pfeiffer's appointment, five of Compaq's top officers resigned. All had been with Compaq since at least 1985.

Compaq's Strategy (1992–94)

A line of ProLinea desktop PCs and Contura notebook computers was introduced in June 1992. These products were targeted at home users and small businesses. At the same time, Compaq announced a number of new models and lower prices for its Deskpro product line. Compaq attempted to differentiate the Deskpro products from the ProLinea products on a number of different dimensions. See Exhibit 5 for a comparison of Deskpro and ProLinea computers. Because sales from the SystemPro line had been disappointing, Compaq added a much more competitive ProSignia line of file servers at dramatically lower prices. In August 1993, Compaq launched a new line of PCs called Presario. These were targeted at the first-time home PC buyer and represented Compaq's first all-in-one products. The Presario line launch was very successful, and the product rapidly gained market acceptance.

EXHIBIT 5   Comparison of Deskpro and Prolinea PCs

WHERE COMPAQ CUT OUT THE COSTS

DESKPRO 386/25M MODEL 60

▶ Modular design makes for easy upgrades, including microprocessor

▶ Five 32-bit expansion slots to handle high-performance add-ons

▶ More durable, heavy-duty, mechanical keyboard

▶ 240 watts of power for add-ons

▶ Audio board for sound

▶ Intel 386DX-25 chip, 60-megabyte Quantum disk drive

SUGGESTED LIST PRICE: $2,744

PROLINEA 3/25ZS

▶ Simpler, low-cost motherboard is reliable, but limits upgrades

▶ Only two 16-bit expansion slots, limiting hardware options

▶ Light membrane keyboard with fewer mechanical parts

▶ Standard 70-watt power supply

▶ No audio board

▶ Slightly slower Intel 386SX-25 chip, 40-megabyte Quantum disk drive

SUGGESTED LIST PRICE: $1,152

Both systems have color monitor, MS-DOS 5.0, and one-year on-site warranty

DATA: *BYTE* MAGAZINE, COMPAQ COMPUTER CORP.

Source: "Compaq: How It Made Its Impressive Move Out of the Doldrums," *Business Week,* November 2, 1992, pp. 146–151.

The significantly lower prices on the products introduced in June 1992 resulted in the gap between Compaq prices and those of the least-expensive PCs narrowing from over 30 percent to about 15 percent. The price cutting was not over. Compaq again cut prices by up to 30 percent in October 1992. In order to maintain profitability, Compaq continued the cost cutting that Canion had tentatively begun in October 1991. Pfeiffer and others in the company had concluded that many of the products in the Compaq product line were overengineered for the needs of their target customers. Compaq was building some subsystems and components in-house which could be bought at lower cost on the open market. For example, Compaq was one of the few PC manufacturers that built its own power supplies. Compaq engineers also redesigned its products for low-cost manufacturing. The number of chips in each computer was reduced, which not only lowered assembly costs, but increased the reliability of the product. A lot of attention was also devoted to reengineering the manufacturing process. By mid-1993, all three of Compaq's factories in Houston, Singapore, and Scotland had switched from one-shift operations to twenty-four-hour-per-day, three-shift operations.

Within one year of Pfeiffer assuming the leadership of Compaq, the company tripled the number of outlets for its computers around the world, and within two years had quintupled the number of outlets in North America. Besides adding value-added resellers, it also added mass merchandisers and superstores, such as Office Depot, CompUSA, and Circuit City. Additionally, it started selling Compaq computers in catalogues and via telemarketing. By late 1994, Compaq had almost 40,000 dealers worldwide.

Compaq replaced its advertising agency in North America in late 1991 and dramatically raised its advertising budgets around the world. In 1992, it spent almost $100 million on advertising.

Results of the New Strategy

Revenues at Compaq exploded between 1991 and 1994, exceeding $10 billion dollars in 1994. Net income grew from $131 million in 1991 to $867 million in 1994, although as a percentage of sales in 1994, net income was still below the levels achieved in the late 1980s. Sales per employee grew dramatically during this period, reaching $872,000 in 1994.

By January 1995, it was widely acknowledged that Compaq had reached the number one worldwide market share position in PCs, having sold 4.8 million computers in 1994.

As a result of the moves of Compaq and its competitors, the PC market had changed dramatically in the early 1990s. Average industry profit margins dropped by 75 percent, from 8 percent of sales in 1990 to 2 percent of sales in 1993. Some players, such as Everex and ComuAdd, were driven into bankruptcy, and several others were in serious financial difficulties.

The PC Marketplace in the Mid-1990s

Many analysts viewed the PC marketplace as a growth market for the rest of the decade. Intel's Pentium microprocessor (also known as the 80586 microprocessor) was introduced in the spring of 1993. Only a few hundred thousand units were shipped in the first year. However, with the introduction in 1994 of many new Pentium-based servers and desktop computer models by a number of manufacturers, the adoption of the new microprocessor began to grow rapidly in late 1994. In the final quarter of 1994, 17.6 percent of new home computers and 15.6 percent of new business computers in North America were based on the Pentium chip.[5] About 50 percent of the computers shipped in 1995 were expected to incorporate the Pentium. This was expected to stimulate new applications and the replacement of older computers in both the business and consumer segments. The home computer segment was booming and was spreading from North America to Europe and elsewhere as prices continued to drop and more applications became available. Even in North America, the penetration of the home market was only 30 percent in early 1995. The increased use of the Internet and E-mail was also expected to stimulate growth. Industry observers expected worldwide sales to grow from about 50 million units in 1994 to 60 million units in 1995.

The three different product segments that comprised the PC marketplace varied significantly in profitability. In 1994, analysts estimated that the gross margins on servers, notebooks, and desktop computers were 20–34 percent, 18–22 percent, and 15–18 percent, respectively.[6]

Key Suppliers to the PC Industry

Although there were a host of companies which provided components, subsystems, and software for the PC industry, the two most dominant and profitable suppliers were Microsoft and Intel.

Microsoft had, by 1995, become the dominant supplier of both operating system software and applications software for the PC industry. Windows 95 was finally launched globally in August 1995 with a massive and sustained advertising and public relations campaign. Microsoft estimated that it and the other companies who hoped to benefit from the introduction were spending $1 billion on advertising and promotion. The increasing complexity of the software that Microsoft and its competitors were selling required computers with fast microprocessors and large memories and encouraged the purchase of more sophisticated printers, CD-ROMs, and other peripheral equipment.

Intel was experiencing explosive growth based to a large degree on its microprocessor business and its other activities in the PC industry. With the mi-

---

[5]"The Laboratory in Your Lounge," *Economist,* May 5, 1995, p. 65.
[6]"Servers: A PC Money Machine," *Business Week,* March 28, 1994, pp. 166–67.

gration of customers to the Pentium microprocessor well underway, Intel was focussing a lot of its efforts on the next two microprocessor generations—the P6, which was expected to be available in some desktop computers in late 1995, and the P7. Intel's overall gross margins were about 55 percent and the margin on its microprocessors was estimated to be in the 80–90 percent range. The cost of the microprocessor typically represented about 20–25 percent of the selling price of a PC.

Increasingly, Intel was not content to manufacture just the microprocessor. As the microprocessors became more powerful, it was a major engineering challenge for a PC manufacturer to design and build the motherboard, which contained the microprocessor and other internal operating components of the computer. In fact, Compaq was one of the few companies that continued to design and build its own motherboards. Most PC manufacturers were buying at least some of their motherboards from Intel. Analysts estimated that Intel would sell 10–15 million motherboards in 1995. In addition, Intel was selling complete or "semi-complete" PCs to customers, such as AT&T, Digital Equipment Corporation, Carrefour (a French hypermarket chain), Reuters, and many others. From Intel's perspective, this allowed companies with limited engineering skills to bring the latest technology to market very quickly.

The above activities were not popular with Compaq. Compaq was Intel's largest customer and Intel was Compaq's largest supplier. Compaq had publicly expressed its unhappiness with Intel and had, in addition, complained that Intel's volume discounts on microprocessors were inadequate. Further souring the relationship with Compaq was Intel's massive advertising campaign for its microprocessors. In 1994, Intel spent $150 million advertising its microprocessors. Computer manufacturers who used Intel microprocessors and who promoted their computers with the "Intel Inside" logo could have up to half of their advertising costs paid by Intel. In certain circumstances, in late 1994, Intel was willing to pay 100 percent of the cost of manufacturer advertising if the PC manufacturer's advertisement focussed exclusively on Pentium PCs. In addition, Intel mounted a massive advertising campaign promoting the Pentium microprocessor, and, in some cases, even suggesting to end users that PCs based on the Intel 486 microprocessor would soon be made obsolete by the Pentium computers. See Exhibit 6 for a typical Intel Pentium advertisement.

Compaq's Major Competitors in 1995

Compaq faced dozens of direct and indirect competitors in the PC business in 1995. IBM continued to be a major factor in the industry, but was continuing to lose market share and often seemed unable to capitalize on some very attractive new products it had developed. Exhibit 7 contains estimated PC revenues for the major vendors.

EXHIBIT 6   Intel advertisement for Pentium processor

Create multimedia presentations.
Crunch financial planning scenarios.
Manage complex documents.
Share ideas face to face.
Etc., etc., etc.

Today's business software, from suites to groupware, places great demands on your PC. And with
even more sophisticated programs already being developed, that demand is only going to increase

Do you have
the power?

Fortunately, an Intel Pentium processor-based PC gives you the power to run today's
most demanding PC software while still having plenty in reserve for tomorrow's.   **intel.**

EXHIBIT 7   Estimated personal computer revenues for major vendors (revenues in millions)

	1982	1983	1984	1985	1986	1987	1988	1989	1990	1991	1992	1993	1994
IBM	$500	$2,600	$5,500	$5,500	$5,650	$6,500	$7,150	$8,343	$9,644	$8,505	$7,887	$9,728	$8,775
Compaq	—[1]	111.2	329	503.9	625.2	1,224	2,066	2,876	3,598	3,271	4,100	7,200	9,019
Apple	664	1,084	1,747	1,603	1,761	2,069	2,950	3,574	3,846	4,900	5,412	5,925	7,162
Packard Bell	—	—	—	—	—	—	—	—	518	641	878.8	1,250	2,600
AST	—	—	—	—	—	—	—	—	516.2	827.3	1,141	1,967	2,311
Gateway	—	—	—	—	—	—	—	—	275	626.8	1,107	1,732	2,700
H-P	258	399.4	500	400	450	499	670	—	625	715	725	889.2	1,152
Dell	—	—	—	—	—	—	—	—	546	667.4	1,813	2,583	2,870
NEC	—	1.6	305.1	338.6	697.3	933.2	2,492	3,117	3,620	5,280	3,987	—	—

[1]Company not in business, or data not presented in annual Datamation survey.
Source: Datamation (various dates).

Apple, in a major change in corporate strategy, had finally decided to license the Macintosh operating system to other companies. Several companics had signed licensing agreements with Apple, but total shipments of Mac clones in 1995 were expected to be only about 250,000 units. The PowerPC microprocessor that had been jointly developed by Apple, IBM, and Motorola was now the key microprocessor in the Macintosh product line, and it had speed and cost advantages over Pentium microprocessors.

Perhaps three of the most aggressive competitors Compaq faced in 1995 were Packard Bell, Hewlett-Packard, and Dell Computer.

Packard Bell Packard Bell was a privately held company that was founded in 1986 when three Israeli immigrants purchased the Packard Bell name from Teledyne Inc. Packard Bell had been a well-known manufacturer of radios and televisions in the 1950s. Initially, Packard Bell focussed on being a low-cost producer of PCs, and sold its computers to consumers and small- and medium-sized businesses largely through mass merchandise chains. Its annual sales did not reach $1 billion until 1993. By the mid-1990s, it had a very strong presence in most of the major mass merchandise chains, such as Wal-Mart and Sears, and in consumer electronics, such as Circuit City. In July 1993, Groupe Bull, a large French computer manufacturer, purchased a 20 percent stake in Packard Bell.

Packard Bell worked very closely with its retailers to ensure that they were successful with its computers. It provided sales training and developed in-store displays and demonstrations for its retailers to help them to be successful with the Packard Bell line. Its pricing was very aggressive, and, in 1995, its computers were 10–15 percent less expensive than comparable Compaq models. All of its advertising resources were spent on a very generous co-op advertising program for its retailers. It did no national advertising. It had a very liberal return policy. It also was one of the only PC manufacturers that offered its retailers several sub-brands, such as Forcc and Legend. This allowed the retailers more pricing flexibility because consumers found it more difficult to comparison shop on these products.

Packard Bell had been a leader in bringing new features and benefits to the consumer. It was the first manufacturer to deliver its computers with operating system software and some applications preinstalled. By working closely with Intel, it was the first PC manufacturer to bring Pentium-based computers to the consumer marketplace. It had also been very aggressive in bringing other new technology to the consumer, including "surround sound" and advanced CD-ROM drives. However, its reputation for customer service and product quality was not strong. It was trying to address this area. Its products were assembled in a highly automated plant in Sacramento, California.

Partly as a result of the strong shelf position it achieved in its retailers' stores and its aggressive promotion of its Pentium-based computers, Packard Bell gained a 50 percent share of the market for home computers sold through retail stores in late 1994 and early 1995, and was the overall leader in unit sales in the United States during this period. However, only 10 percent of its sales in 1994 came from outside of North America. In 1995, it was aggressively trying to build market share in Europe and Latin America. It was also developing a new line of computers targeted at the corporate market. This line was to be sold through computer store chains.

In September 1995, NEC, Japan's largest manufacturer of personal computers, bought a 20 percent stake in the company. Analysts believed the cash infusion would help finance its rapid expansion and its entry into the corporate market.

Hewlett-Packard Hewlett-Packard (HP) was a diversified electronics manufacturer producing a broad line of computer products and peripheral equipment, electronic test and measurement instruments, medical electronics, analytical instruments, and electronic components. HP had revenues of $25 billion ($20 billion in computer products) and after-tax profits of $1.6 billion in 1994. It was strong financially, with $1.7 billion of cash on its balance sheet. Analysts viewed it as a lean and efficient company with extremely strong R&D. HP invested about $2 billion per year in research and development. While it had been an active participant in the PC industry for fifteen years, its products, although sometimes quite innovative, had often been overpriced and poorly marketed. However, during this period it had achieved great success with large multiuser computers, with engineering workstations, and in computer peripherals, particularly laser and ink-jet printers. By 1995, HP was estimated to have a 50 percent share of the printer business in North America and 35 percent globally. Printer sales in 1994 were almost $8 billion. Most computer retailers around the world sold Hewlett-Packard printers.

In 1992, Hewlett-Packard restructured its PC business, closing most of its manufacturing plants and cutting its costs. Given its strong position in large multiuser computers and engineering workstations, it had strong relationships with many medium- and large-sized corporations. With good, well-engineered Vectra PCs it had moved to the #3 position in PCs in the corporate market by 1995, although it was still believed to be only #6 overall in the PC market. In the second quarter of

1995, it showed the fastest year-on-year growth of any major PC manufacturer in the world, and PCs were selling at an annual rate of more than $2 billion.

In October 1994, HP made the decision to enter the home computer market. A month later, it created its Home Products Division. Its first products were in-store trials early in 1995. In August 1995, it introduced the HP Pavilion line of home PCs and began selling them through nine major retail chains, including Circuit City. The new products were priced slightly above comparable Packard Bell computers, but below Compaq's products. The company hoped to sell 250,000 home PCs by the end of 1995. Another growth area that HP had targeted was full-function notebooks, where it already had some quite successful products.

In order to move quickly and to leverage on the skills of partners, HP made extensive use of outsourcing. All Pentium motherboards were purchased from Intel. The basic PC systems were built by a contract manufacturer in the United States, and HP added the disk drives and other components to the basic system. Low-end PCs in its product line were being manufactured for HP by a Taiwanese manufacturer.

Dell Computer Corporation Dell Computer was founded by Michael Dell, who began selling PCs over the telephone while he was a student at The University of Texas at Austin in 1983. His initial strategy was to acquire the excess inventory of computer dealers and to sell these computers to individuals and businesses by telephone and mail.

Dell Computers focused very heavily on sales and marketing activities, and outsourced much of the rest of its business. For example, while it did provide on-site service to its customers around the United States, this service was actually performed by Xerox Corporation. By the mid- to late-1980s, Dell was making significant inroads at the high end of the market. Here Dell was dealing with relatively sophisticated PC buyers who had a good understanding of their own needs and had the confidence to buy a PC over the telephone. In 1986, the company had achieved sales of almost $70 million. In calendar 1990, sales were about $500 million, rising to almost $2 billion in calendar 1992. The rapid growth in the early 1990s, together with an inexperienced management team and a disastrous situation with its notebook line, resulted in a loss of almost $36 million in fiscal 1994 (year ending January 31, 1994). The company was successful in recruiting a new, experienced management team, and both sales and net income resumed their rapid growth.

By 1995, Dell had refined its direct selling model with computers assembled only after the order was received. While it had experimented with selling through selected retail channels for PCs, it had abandoned this approach in 1994. The assemble-after-order approach resulted in Dell having inventory turns of 15 compared to the more typical 5.2 achieved by Compaq in 1994. The virtual absence of inventory meant that Dell could change its product mix very quickly or even move to the next generation of products. It could also take maximum advantage of the steadily declining prices of many PC components and subsystems (often 15 percent per annum).

By 1995, Dell was focusing very heavily on high-margin customers. About 75 percent of its sales were made to corporations and governments, which tended to buy higher-end PCs. Both its desktop and notebook designs were believed to be among the best in the industry. Partly as a result of its product mix, its average end-user price was almost 50 percent higher than Packard Bell's and about 15 percent higher than Compaq's. Much of its sales in 1995 were based on Pentium-based systems. By mid-1995, sales were growing very rapidly and were expected to exceed $5 billion for the fiscal year ending January 31, 1996. International sales, primarily in the United Kingdom, Eire, and Japan, were growing more rapidly than North American sales, but still only accounted for about 40 percent of revenues.

Distribution Channels for PCs

The distribution channels for PCs continued to evolve. Exhibit 8 contains the historical and projected unit shipments for PCs in the United States. Different segments of the market preferred to buy from different channels. The consumer segment purchased primarily from mass merchandisers, computer dealers, and computer superstores. Small businesses purchased from computer dealers, direct sales forces, value-added resellers, and direct from the manufacturer, office product dealers, and computer superstores. Medium and large corporations were most likely to purchase from direct sales forces, value-added resellers, and direct from the manufacturer and computer specialty stores or dealers.

EXHIBIT 8   Actual and projected unit shipments by distribution channel

Year	Direct outbound & response	Mail order	Mass merchant	Consumer electronics retailer	Office products retailer	Superstore
1989	1,772	309	363	425	NA	0
1992	2,234	470	941	706	235	588
1993	2,546	584	1,255	1,369	442	805
1994	2,565	855	1,539	1,539	342	1,026
1995E	2,633	1,129	1,693	1,693	376	1,129
1996E	2,839	1,014	2,028	1,825	406	1,217
1997E	2,586	1,078	2,371	2,155	431	1,293

Year	Computer specialty retailer	Corporate account reseller	Value added reseller	Systems integrator	Other	Total
1989	0	4,510	1,205	133	62	8,779
1992	588	3,764	1,647	353	235	11,761
1993	823	4,368	1,901	568	290	14,950
1994	1,539	4,788	2,223	342	342	17,100
1995E	1,693	5,079	2,633	376	376	18,810
1996E	2,028	5,273	2,839	406	406	20,280
1997E	2,371	5,388	3,017	431	431	21,550
1998E	2,491	5,661	3,170	453	453	22,645

Source: International Data Corporation 1994 (as reported in Smith Barney, "CompUSA Inc.—Company Report," May 8, 1995).

By 1995, some of the retailers selling PCs were large and quite powerful organizations. CompUSA, a superstore chain with more than 75 stores, had sales of over $2 billion. Circuit City, the largest consumer electronics chain, had total sales of more than $5 billion. A number of these retailers had computer and computer accessory sales of over $1 billion per annum. Wal-Mart, the largest retailer in the world, was estimated to sell over $1.5 billion of computers and computer accessories per year. Many of these large retailers were growing at close to 20 percent per annum. They clearly would become a more important factor in the industry over time.

Compaq in 1995

During the early 1990s, Intel and Compaq came more and more into conflict. Compaq chose not to participate in the "Intel Inside" campaign, saying it would rather promote its own brand name than somebody else's. In May 1994, Compaq announced two new Presario models that would use an Advanced Micro Devices microprocessor based on the Intel 486 design. In a major strategic decision, Compaq decided to continue to focus on PCs based on 486 microprocessors for the critical 1994 Christmas season, even though it had announced its first Pentium-based products in 1993. Its research suggested that the corporate market would not switch heavily to Pentium-based PCs until 1995, and it believed that the home market would respond more positively to 486-based computers selling for less than $2,000 rather than the more expensive Pentium-based computers. During the summer and fall of 1994, it built up massive inventories of 486-based Presario computers for the Christmas selling season. It claimed that the strategy had been successful, but it did leave a major opening for some of its competitors, such as Packard Bell, to build a strong position in the Pentium-based systems. In its advertising during this period, it tried to get the potential purchaser to focus on the experience of owning a Compaq computer and away from the microprocessor that was its heart. In March 1995, Compaq introduced 118 new computer models, most of them based on the Pentium microprocessor.

In order to reduce its dependence on Intel, Compaq was aggressively trying to develop new suppliers of microprocessors in addition to Advanced Micro Devices. In 1990, it had made a strategic equity investment in NextGen, a company that hoped to develop clones of Intel microprocessors. It had agreed to buy some microprocessors based on the Pentium design from NextGen in early 1995. It was also working closely with Cyrix, another company that promised to be able to clone Intel's microprocessors. As of the summer of 1995, none of these companies was expected to be able to produce Pentium clones in large volumes until late 1995 or early 1996. By then, Intel hoped to be starting the transition to the next generation of its microprocessors, the P6.

Compaq's aggressive push into international markets was proving to be very successful. Sales outside North America had grown very rapidly between 1992 and 1994. In 1994, it was the leading vendor of PCs in most major countries with the notable exceptions of Germany (where it was #2) and Japan. However, its growth in Japan had been spectacular over the previous two years as a result of very aggressive pricing and heavy promotion of its global market share position.

By 1995, Compaq was performing very well in two product segments, business desktops and servers, where it had achieved revenues in 1994 of $4.2 billion and $2.3 billion, respectively. It was reported to have a 35 percent share of the market for PC servers in early 1995. It was doing less well in the laptop/notebook and consumer segments, where its 1994 sales were $2.5 billion and $1.6 billion. It was reported to have about a 12 percent share of the laptop/notebook market, which was growing about twice as fast as the desktop market. In April 1995, Compaq announced plans to buy some laptops and consumer PCs from Taiwanese suppliers in order to plug the gaps in its product line quickly.

On July 20, 1995, Compaq reported first-half sales of $6.5 billion and net income of $462 million.

On September 15, 1995, Intel announced it was building a new plant in Dupont, Washington, to build personal computers. The personal computers would be sold under other companies' names. Andrew Grove, the CEO of Intel, had again reiterated that Intel had no plans to ever sell PCs under its own label.

Case 4

Exercise on Financial Analysis for Marketing Decision Making*

An important part of the analysis of alternatives facing marketing decision makers is the financial analysis of these alternatives. This exercise is designed to give students experience in handling the types of financial calculations that arise in marketing cases. If you can do the calculations in this exercise, you should be able to handle the financial calculations necessary to properly do the cases in this book.

1. You have just been appointed the product manager for the "Flexo" brand of electric razors in a large consumer products company. As part of your new job, you want to develop an understanding of the financial situation for your product. Your brand assistant has provided you with the following facts:

a.	Retail selling price	$60 per unit
b.	Retailer's margin	20%
c.	Jobber's margin	20%
d.	Wholesaler's* margin	15%
e.	Direct factory labor	$4 per unit
f.	Raw materials	$2 per unit
g.	All factory and administrative overheads	$2 per unit (at a 100,000 unit volume level)
h.	Salespersons' commissions	10% of manufacturer's selling price
i.	Sales force travel costs	$400,000
j.	Advertising	$1 million
k.	Total market for razors	1 million units
l.	Current yearly sales of Flexo	210,000 units

*An agent who sells to the jobbers, who in turn sell to the retailers.

Questions

1. What is the contribution per unit for the Flexo brand?
2. What is the break-even volume in units and in dollars?
3. What market share does the Flexo brand need to break even?

---

*Copyright © 1996 by Thomas C. Kinnear

4. What is the current total contribution?
5. What is the current before-tax profit of the Flexo brand?
6. What market share must Flexo obtain to contribute a before-tax profit of $4 million?

2. One of the first decisions you have to make as the brand manager for Flexo is whether or not to add a new line of razors, the "Super Flexo" line. This line would be marketed in addition to the original Flexo line. Your brand assistant has provided you with the following facts:

a.	Retail selling price	$80 per unit
b.	All margins the same as before	
c.	Direct factory labor	$6 per unit
d.	Raw materials	$4 per unit
e.	Additional factory and administrative overheads	$4 per unit (at a 50,000 unit volume level)
f.	Salespersons' commissions the same percent as before	
g.	Incremental sales force travel cost	$100,000
h.	Advertising for Super Flexo	$1 million
i.	New equipment needed	$1 million (to be depreciated over 10 years)
j.	Research and development spent up to now	$200,000
k.	Research and development to be spent this year to commercialize the product	$750,000 (to be amortized over five years)

Questions

1. What is the contribution per unit for the Super Flexo brand?
2. What is the break-even volume in units and in dollars?
3. What is the sales volume in units necessary for Super Flexo to yield, in the first year, a 20 percent return on the equipment to be invested in the project?

3. The $80 per unit selling price for Super Flexo seems high to you. You thought you might lower the price to $75 per unit and raise retail margin to 25 percent.

Question

What is the break-even volume in units?

Part 3

Marketing Information and Forecasting

Good information is essential for all marketing decision making. Most cases in this book present some information provided by marketing research. However, they also leave many points of uncertainty. The skill of marketing decision making is the use of the information that is available, along with explicit assumptions about uncertain points to make good decisions. The suggestion that we do marketing research has usually not been allowed in other parts of this text. In this section we turn to the undertaking of marketing research activity.

First, let us define marketing research. It is the systematic gathering, recording, and analyzing of data about problems relating to the marketing of goods and services. There are three kinds of marketing research: (1) exploratory, (2) conclusive, and (3) performance monitoring. Exploratory research is useful for identifying situations calling for a decision and for identifying alternative courses of action. Conclusive research is useful for evaluating alternative courses of action and selecting a course of action. Performance monitoring research is designed to provide the control function over marketing programs.

The marketing research process may be thought of as being composed of the following steps:

1. Establish the need for information.
2. Specify the research objectives and information needs.
3. Determine the sources of data.
4. Develop data collection forms.
5. Design a sample.
6. Collect the data.
7. Process the data.
8. Analyze the data.
9. Present research findings.

The responsibility for the execution of these stages is shared by the marketing manager and the marketing researcher. They both must be sure that the problem has been defined properly, that the objectives make sense, and so on. The researcher holds primary responsibility for the technical details of the study. However, he or she must always be prepared to explain these aspects to the manager in nontechnical terms.

Marketing research costs money. Before it is undertaken, it must be ascertained that the value of the information provided justifies the cost. Also, before research is undertaken, the use to which that research will be made should be clearly understood. A specific decision should be the target of the research, and the way the new information will be used in helping make the decision should be clearly understood.

This note and the cases in this section focus on the managerial aspects of marketing research. The technical details are mostly left for more advanced texts.

Case 5

*The Atlanta Journal and Constitution (A)**

Mr. Ferguson Rood, research and marketing director for *The Atlanta Journal* and the *Atlanta Constitution,* was still perspiring from the three-block walk in the hot August sun back to his office from the meeting he had just been to at Rich's Department Store. At the meeting, he had been told that Rich's, the newspaper's largest advertiser, wanted to test the effectiveness of TV and radio advertising versus newspaper advertising for its upcoming Harvest Sale. He had promised to make his suggestions for the research plan in 48 hours and felt he had much work to do in that short time. He wondered what recommendations he should make for the study and was concerned that the research design and questionnaire be developed so the study would represent fairly the effectiveness of *The Atlanta Journal* and the *Atlanta Constitution.* As he began to review his notes from the meeting, he picked up the phone to call his wife and tell her he would be home very late that evening.

Background

The Atlanta Journal and the *Atlanta Constitution* are a union of two of the largest-circulation newspapers in the South. The *Atlanta Constitution,* winner of four Pulitzer Prizes for its efforts in the area of social reform, was founded June 16, 1868. *The Atlanta Journal,* founded February 24, 1883, became the largest daily newspaper in Georgia by 1889. Also a winner of the Pulitzer Prize, *The Journal* is the Southeast's largest afternoon newspaper.

In 1950, *The Atlanta Journal* and the *Atlanta Constitution* were combined into Atlanta Newspapers, Inc., a privately held company. The two newspapers maintained independent editorial staffs, and there was very little overlap of readers. Exhibits 1 through 4 present data concerning the adult readership of the newspapers, the gross reader impressions, reach and frequency, and readership over five weekdays and four Sundays.

---

*This case was written by Kenneth L. Bernhardt. Copyright © 1996 by Kenneth L. Bernhardt.

EXHIBIT 1 Gross readership impressions, reach, and frequency of *The Atlanta Journal* and *Constitution*

Gross reader impressions

The Atlanta Journal and *Constitution* in 15-county metro Atlanta:

During any five weekdays, 864,500 adults read *The Atlanta Journal* or *Constitution* an average of 3.5 times for a total of 3,025,800 weekday gross reader impressions.

During any four Sundays, 907,600 adults read *The Atlanta Journal* and *Constitution* for an average of 3.4 times for a total of 3,085,800 Sunday gross reader impressions.

These newspapers deliver 3,933,400 adult gross reader impressions when one Sunday is added to five weekdays.

Reach and frequency of newspaper reading

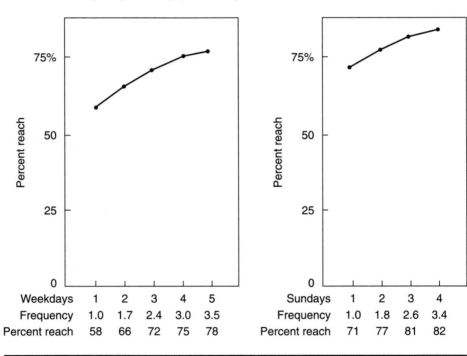

Weekdays	1	2	3	4	5
Frequency	1.0	1.7	2.4	3.0	3.5
Percent reach	58	66	72	75	78

Sundays	1	2	3	4
Frequency	1.0	1.8	2.6	3.4
Percent reach	71	77	81	82

EXHIBIT 2   *The Atlanta Journal* and *Constitution* readership information

78 percent of all daily circulation and 66 percent of all Sunday circulation
is within 15-county metro Atlanta.

Of all metro Atlanta
adults, 644,400 read
The Atlanta Journal
or *Constitution* on the
average weekday. Of
this total, 412,700
read *The Journal* and
366,100 read the
Constitution. 134,400
adults read both. On
the average Sunday,
782,200 metro Atlanta
adults read *The Atlanta
Journal* and *Constitution*.

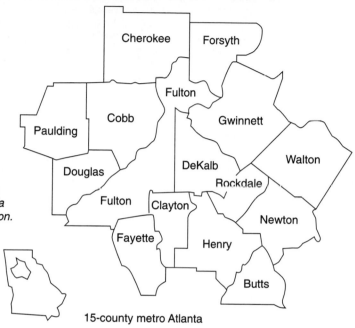

15-county metro Atlanta

Adult readers of *The Atlanta Journal* and *Constitution* in a 15-county metro Atlanta

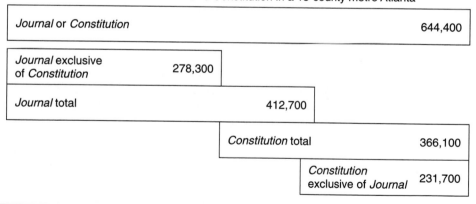

Journal or *Constitution*	644,400
Journal exclusive of *Constitution*	278,300
Journal total	412,700
Constitution total	366,100
Constitution exclusive of *Journal*	231,700

EXHIBIT 3   Readership of *The Atlanta Journal* and *Constitution* over five weekdays

644,400, or 58 percent, of all metro Atlanta adults read *The Atlanta Journal* or *Constitution* on the average weekday. Over five weekdays these newspapers deliver 864,900, or 78 percent, of all metro-area adults with an average frequency of 3.5 days.

	Total metro area adults	Average 1-day readership		Cumulative 5-weekday readership		
		Number	Percent	Number	Percent	Frequency
Total adults	1,105,500	644,400	58%	864,900	78%	3.5
Sex						
Female	588,500	331,700	56	447,600	76	3.5
Male	517,000	312,700	61	416,800	81	3.5
Household income						
$25,000 and over	104,200	85,900	82	102,700	99	4.2
$15,000–24,999	195,300	146,400	75	181,900	93	4.0
$10,000–14,999	241,900	152,800	63	203,900	84	3.7
$5,000–9,999	334,200	170,600	51	241,800	72	3.5
Under $5,000	229,900	88,500	39	133,000	58	3.3
Age						
18–34	470,500	234,500	50	345,200	73	3.4
35–49	305,600	197,200	65	250,300	82	3.9
50–64	211,900	145,800	69	184,600	87	3.9
65 and over	116,500	66,700	57	84,700	73	3.9
Race						
White	872,800	528,800	61	685,100	78	3.9
Nonwhite	232,700	115,600	50	180,100	77	3.2
Education						
College graduate	173,500	138,000	80	172,600	99	4.0
Part college	194,700	137,600	71	174,100	89	4.0
High school graduate	360,500	225,000	62	302,900	84	3.7
Part high school or less	365,600	137,000	38	202,200	55	3.4

To provide the advertisers and potential advertisers with information necessary to help them make their advertising media decisions, the newspaper does a considerable amount of research, often approaching $25,000 in a year. Most of the research is designed to be used in selling advertising to a wide range of advertisers, and includes data on retail trading areas, shopping patterns, product usage, and newspaper coverage patterns. In addition to Mr. Rood, the research department had two other trained market researchers and one secretary.

Although there are nine daily newspapers in the Atlanta trading area, all but *The Journal* and the *Constitution* have very small circulations. The principal competition for large advertisers is with radio and TV stations. Exhibit 5 presents information on the circulation of the print media in the Atlanta area. Exhibit 6 contains information on the broadcast media in Atlanta. Although there were 40 radio stations, 28 AM and 12 FM, and 6 TV stations, WSB Radio and TV dominated the market. WSB Radio, for example, was consistently rated among the top six stations in the nation and had a greater Atlanta audience than the next four stations

EXHIBIT 4   Readership of *The Atlanta Journal* and *Constitution* over four Sundays

782,200, or 71 percent, of all metro Atlanta adults read *The Atlanta Journal* and *Constitution* on the average Sunday. Over four Sundays, these newspapers deliver 907,300, or 82 percent, of all metro-area adults with an average frequency of 3.4 Sundays.

	Total metro area adults	Average 1-Sunday readership	Cumulative 4-Sunday readership	Number of Sundays frequency
Total adults	1,105,500	782,200	907,300	3.4
Sex				
Female	588,500	418,800	477,800	3.5
Male	517,000	363,400	429,500	3.4
Household income				
$25,000 and over	104,200	89,100	97,200	3.7
$15,000–24,999	195,300	168,800	180,700	3.7
$10,000–14,999	241,900	190,100	216,400	3.5
$5,000–9,999	334,400	215,600	267,300	3.2
Under $5,000	229,900	118,500	145,600	3.3
Age				
18–34	470,500	313,000	390,000	3.2
35–49	305,600	221,300	248,500	3.6
50–64	211,900	167,000	179,900	3.7
65 and over	116,500	80,600	88,500	3.6
Race				
White	872,800	633,100	727,900	3.5
Nonwhite	232,700	149,100	179,100	3.3
Education				
College graduate	173,500	150,200	163,700	3.7
Part college	194,700	157,300	180,200	3.5
High school graduate	360,500	273,900	313,500	3.5
Part high school or less	365,600	192,300	240,000	3.2

combined. WSB-TV and WSB Radio, both affiliated with the NBC Network, were owned by Cox Broadcasting Corporation, which also owns television stations in Charlotte, Dayton, Pittsburgh, and San Francisco and radio stations in Charlotte, Dayton, and Miami. Cox Broadcasting and WSB-TV and Radio stations shared corporate headquarters in Atlanta.

WSB Radio was founded in 1922 by *The Atlanta Journal* newspaper. In 1939, former Democratic presidential nominee and Governor of Ohio James M. Cox acquired the newspaper-radio combine. In 1948, WSB-TV was founded, and two years later the newspapers and broadcast media were separated when Atlanta Newspapers, Inc., was established. Today, there is no relationship between the newspapers and WSB Radio and TV.

Rich's Department Store was the largest advertiser for *The Journal* and the *Constitution,* accounting for almost 5 percent of their advertising revenue, and was WSB's largest local advertiser. Founded in 1867, Rich's by 1970 had grown to a company with seven stores distributed throughout Atlanta, as shown in Exhibit 7. Sales were approximately $200 million per year with

EXHIBIT 5   Circulation of print media in Atlanta

Metro Atlanta newspapers	Edition	Total circulation
Dailies		
Atlanta Constitution	Morning	216,624
Atlanta Journal	Evening	259,721
Journal-Constitution	Sunday	585,532
Gwinnett Daily News	Evening (except Sat.)	10,111
Gwinnett Daily News	Sunday	10,100
Marietta Daily Journal	Evening (except Sat.)	24,750
Marietta Daily Journal	Sunday	25,456
Fulton County Daily Report	Evening (Mon.–Fri.)	1,600
Atlanta Daily World	Morning	19,000
Atlanta Daily World	Sunday	22,000
The Wall Street Journal	Morning (Mon.–Fri.)	16,180
Jonesboro News Daily	Evening (Mon.–Fri.)	9,100
North Fulton Today	Evening (Mon.–Fri.)	2,300
South Cobb Today	Evening (Mon.–Fri.)	2,400
New York Times	Morning (Mon.–Sat.)	500
New York Times	Sunday	3,100
Weekly newspapers		
Atlanta Inquirer		30,000
Atlanta Voice		37,500
DeKalb New Era		16,400
Atlanta's Suburban Reporter		3,900
Lithonia Observer		2,765
Northside News		8,000
Georgia Business News		4,900
Southern Israelite		4,300
Decatur-DeKalb News		73,000
Southside Sun (East Point)		37,700
Tucker Star		10,000
Alpharetta, Roswell Neighbor		6,800
Austell, Mableton, Powder Springs Neighbor		12,123
Acworth, Kennesaw-Woodstock Neighbor		3,242
Northside, Sandy Springs, Vinings Neighbor		20,836
Smyrna Neighbor		6,872
College Park, East Point, Hapeville, South Side, West End Neighbor		18,813
Chamblee, Doraville, Dunwoody, North Atlanta Neighbor		14,963
Clarkston, Stone Mountain, Tucker Neighbor		15,074
The Journal of Labor (Atlanta)		17,500
Austell Enterprise		1,911
The Cherokee Tribune (Canton)		7,100
Rockdale Citizen		6,031
The Covington News		6,000
The Forsyth County News		4,800
Dallas New Era		4,075
Douglas County Sentinel		7,350
South Fulton Recorder (Fairburn)		4,000
Fayette County News		4,500
Jackson Progress Argus		2,635
The Weekly Advertiser (McDonough)		5,650
The Walton Tribune (Monroe)		5,102
Liburn Recorder		5,000
Lawrenceville Home Weekly		2,000
The Great Speckled Bird (Atlanta)		7,925
The Georgia Bulletin		14,000

(continued)

EXHIBIT 5 *(concluded)*

Metro Atlanta newspapers	Total circulation
The Covington News (Tues. & Thurs.)	6,200
Creative Loafing in Atlanta	30,000
Atlanta area newspapers*	
Cobb	28,000
North Fulton	36,000
North DeKalb-Gwinnett	45,000
South DeKalb	44,000
South Fulton-Clayton	53,000
Major magazines in Georgia	
American Home	70,485
Better Homes and Gardens	145,962
Good Housekeeping	114,045
McCall's	139,728
Ladies' Home Journal	128,331
Family Circle	106,245
Woman's Day	100,566
Redbook	86,354
National Geographic	103,941
Reader's Digest	331,240
Newsweek	41,070
Time	60,438
U.S. News & World Report	40,417
TV Guide	345,871
Playboy	98,389
Sports Illustrated	38,263
Outdoor Life	25,918
True	18,244
Southern Living	95,000
Progressive Farmer	70,000
Cosmopolitan	25,075
Calendar Atlanta	50,000

*These are supplements to *The Atlanta Journal,* and circulation is to *The Atlanta Journal* subscribers only.
Source: WSB Research Department.

earnings after taxes of almost 5 percent of sales. The company was classified as a general merchandise retailer, and carried a very wide line of products including clothing, furniture, appliances, housewares, and items for the home. Rich's dominated the Atlanta market, with close to 40 percent of department store sales and approximately 25 percent of all the sales of general merchandise. The merchandising highlight of the year was the annual Harvest Sale, first held in October 1925. The sale typically ran for two weeks and had become a yearly tradition at Rich's.

Background on the Media Effectiveness Study

Before preparing his proposal to Rich's for the media effectiveness study, Mr. Rood reflected upon the events of the past 24 hours. The day before, he had received a phone call from the vice president and sales promotion director from Rich's, inviting him to the meeting at Rich's the next day. Having been

EXHIBIT 6   Broadcast media in Atlanta

Location	Station/network	Established	Frequency	Power	Channel	Network
Metro Atlanta AM radio stations						
Atlanta	WSB (NBC)	1922	750 khz	50 kw		
	WAOK	1954	1380 khz	5 kw		
	WGKA (ABC)	1955	1190 khz	1 kw day		
	WGST (ABC-E)	1922	920 khz	5 kw day		
				1 kw night		
	WIGO (ABC-C)	1946	1340 khz	1 kw day		
				250 w night		
	WIIN (MBS)	1949	970 khz	5 kw day		
	WPLO	1937	590 khz	5 kw		
	WQXI	1948	790 khz	5 kw day		
				1 kw night		
	WXAP	1948	860 khz	1 kw		
	WYZE (MBS)	1956	1480 khz	5 kw day		
Decatur	WAVO	1958	1420 khz	1 kw day		
	WGUN	1947	1010 khz	50 kw day		
	WQAK	1964	1310 khz	500 w		
N. Atlanta	WRNG (CBS)	1967	680 khz	25 kw day		
Morrow	WSSA	1959	1570 khz	1 kw day		
East Point	WTJH	1949	1260 khz	5 kw day		
Smyrna	WYNX	1962	1550 khz	10 kw day		
Buford	WDYX	1956	1460 khz	5 kw day		
Austell	WACX	1968	1600 khz	1 kw		
Lawrenceville	WLAW	1959	1360 khz	1 kw		
Marietta	WCOB	1955	1080 khz	10 kw day		
	WFOM	1946	1230 khz	1 kw day		
				250 w night		
Canton	WCHK (GA)	1957	1290 khz	1 kw day		
Covington	WGFS	1953	1430 khz	1 kw day		
Cumming	WSNE	1961	1170 khz	1 kw		
Douglasville	WDGL	1964	1527 khz	1 kw		
Jackson	WJGA	1967	1540 khz	1 kw day		
Monroe	WMRE	1954	1490 khz	1 kw		
Metro Atlanta FM radio stations						
	WSB-FM	1934	98.5 mhz	100 kw		
	WPLO-FM	1948	103.3 mhz	50 kw		
	WZGC-FM	1955	92.9 mhz	100 kw		
	WKLS-FM	1960	96.1 mhz	100 kw		
	WQXI-FM	1962	94.1 mhz	100 kw		
	WBIE-FM	1959	101.5 mhz	100 kw		
	WLTA-FM	1963	99.7 mhz	100 kw		
	WJGA-FM	1968	92.1 mhz	3 kw		
	WCHK-FM	1964	105.5 mhz	3 kw		
	WGCO-FM	1969	102.3 mhz	100 kw		
	WABE-FM	1948	90.0 mhz	10.5 kw		
	WREK-FM	1968	91.1 mhz	40 kw		
Metro Atlanta television stations						
	WSB-TV	9/29/48			2	NBC
	WAGA-TV	3/8/49			5	CBS
	WXIA-TV	9/30/51			11	ABC
	WTCG-TV	9/1/67			17	IND
	WETV	1958			30	NET
	WGTV	1960			8	NET

Source: WSB Research Department.

EXHIBIT 7   Map of Atlanta and seven Rich's stores

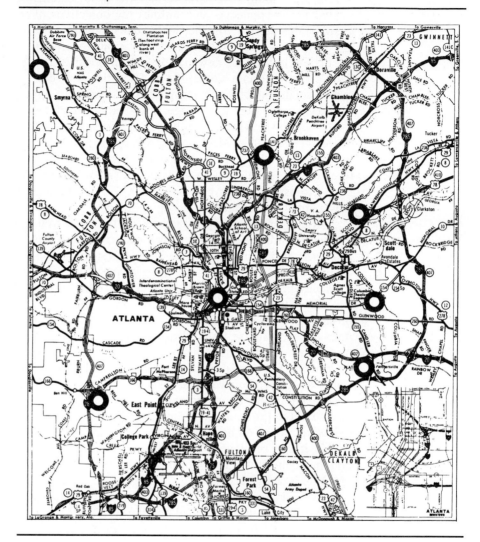

told that Rich's research director and the research director of WSB-TV and Radio would also be there, Mr. Rood had been a little apprehensive before going. At the start of the meeting, he was asked if the Atlanta newspapers would be interested in participating in a cooperative research study aimed at measuring the effectiveness of various advertising media during Rich's September Harvest Sale, their largest annual sales event. It became immediately apparent that the research director from WSB, Jim Landon, had met with the Rich's people the week before, and was undoubtedly the source of the idea to conduct the study. A document was then passed out that had been prepared by WSB and was entitled "Suggestions for Rich's Media Research." This document is included in the appendix, and outlines the objectives of the study and a suggested methodology, together with a questionnaire.

The suggested objectives for the project were: (1) to measure the ability of TV, radio, and newspapers to sell specific items of merchandise in Rich's seven Atlanta stores; (2) to determine how each advertising medium complements the others in terms of additional units sold to various segments of the customer population (age, sex, charge account ownership, and so on); (3) to determine what each advertising medium contributed in regard to additional store traffic. Mr. Rood's broadcasting counterpart stated at the meeting that "If Rich's is interested in conducting research to measure the effectiveness of various advertising media, WSB-TV and WSB Radio will be happy to assist." Rood had no choice, so he volunteered the support of the newspapers to the study.

Rich's research manager then asked if the media would participate financially in the study. Mr. Rood suggested that each of the three media participate equally and committed the newspapers to $500 for a study that he figured should cost between $2,500 and $3,000 for interviewing. Mr. Landon indicated that Cox Broadcasting would be willing to put in $500 each for TV and radio.

They then discussed how the research could be conducted. The WSB proposal suggested in-store surveys, with a separate survey conducted for each item of merchandise tested. The survey would be conducted by Rich's employees working overtime in appropriate store locations during the peak shopping hours. The tabulation of the results could be handled by the broadcast station's computer. Care was to be taken to ensure that the TV, radio, or newspaper advertising for the individual items not be "stacked" in favor of one particular medium. The questions in the proposed questionnaire (see the appendix) included questions on how the respondents happened to buy the merchandise at Rich's, if they recalled seeing TV, newspaper, or radio advertising, and if they bought anything else. Questions were also asked concerning age and ownership of a Rich's charge account.

Mr. Landon stated that WSB was not trying to take business away from the newspapers and that Rood had nothing to fear. His recommendation was that Rich's not take anything away from the newspaper advertising budget. He suggested that the amount of space purchased in the newspapers be the same as the previous year, with additional monies being committed to the broadcast media. The Rich's sales promotion director then discussed some of his thoughts concerning the study. He indicated that Rich's had been sending 400,000 direct mail pieces to announce the Harvest Sale; this year they would send 200,000, diverting the other money to broadcast. This would make $7,600 available for broadcast, and another $12,000 to $15,000 would be made available to purchase broadcast time.

The Harvest Sale was to open with courtesy days on Monday and Tuesday, September 21–22, with the sale beginning the evening of the 22nd and running for 13 days. While decisions concerning which sales items were to be included in the study and the media schedules to be used were not yet available, some progress had been made. Approximately 10 items were to be researched, and the newspaper ads on Sunday, September 20, would include all or most of the 10 items. Newspaper ads for the items would be repeated Monday and Tuesday with emphasis on *The Journal.* The interviews were to be conducted Monday through Wednesday.

On Sunday and Monday, with a possible spillover to Tuesday due to availability, Rich's would run 120 30-second TV commercials on all commercial stations except Channel 17. During the same time, they would run 120 radio 30-second commercials on a list of stations which had not yet been determined. With both TV and radio, WSB was to get the lion's share if availability could be arranged. Mr. Rood felt certain, in view of the client and the research, that WSB would manage to come up with several prime-time commercial openings even if it meant bumping some high-paying national advertisers.

Eleven items were mentioned as possible subjects for the research. The 10 final items selected would come mostly from this list, although one or two other items might be chosen. The items mentioned included: (1) color TV console at $499; (2) custom-made draperies; (3) Stearns & Foster mattress at $44; (4) carpeting at $6.99 per square yard; (5) Gant shirts at $5; (6) Van Heusen shirts and Arrow shirts at two for $11; (7) women's handbags at $9.99; (8) Johannsen's shoes; (9) pants suits; (10) Hoover upright vacuum cleaner; and (11) GE refrigerator.

Mr. Rood, who had not said very much at the meeting, then asked for 48 hours to review the proposal. Everyone agreed to this, and Mr. Rood promised to present a counterproposal at that time.

Even though it had been rather obvious who initiated the idea for the study and that he at first felt that newspapers were being "set up" by WSB, it had been basically a friendly and relaxed meeting among friends. Mr. Landon and Mr. Rood had worked together in the Atlanta Chapter of the American Marketing Association and had a great deal of mutual respect. Mr. Rood thought Landon was a tough competitor, and understood that he had been successful using awareness-type studies in Cox Broadcastings' other markets to gain additional advertising for broadcast.

When he returned to his office, Rood pulled out some of his files on Rich's. He noticed that the amount of advertising had been fairly constant, approximately 40 pages over the two-week period, during the past three Harvest Sales, and that basically the same products had been promoted. A typical Harvest Sale ad is included in Exhibit 8. He also pulled from the files rate schedules for *The Atlanta Journal* and *Constitution* and WSB (see Exhibits 9 and 10), even though he realized that the exact media schedule would be developed by Rich's advertising agency. Approximately $100,000 would be spent promoting the Harvest Sale, with perhaps a third of this amount being devoted to the sale items.

EXHIBIT 8 Typical Rich's Harvest Sale ad

EXHIBIT 9   *The Atlanta Journal* and the *Atlanta Constitution* retail display rates

Open rate per column inch:*

Constitution	$8.15
Journal	$11.27
Combination	$14.83
Sunday	$15.56

Yearly bulk space rates:

Inches per year	Cost per inch			
	Constitution	*Journal*	*Combined*	*Sunday*
100	$6.21	$8.43	$11.09	$11.65
250	6.16	8.35	11.00	11.55
500	6.10	8.28	10.90	11.45
1,000	6.05	8.21	10.81	11.35
2,500	5.99	8.13	10.70	11.24
5,000	5.93	8.05	10.59	11.12
7,500	5.90	8.01	10.54	11.07
10,000	5.87	7.97	10.48	11.01
12,500	5.85	7.93	10.43	10.96
15,000	5.82	7.89	10.38	10.90
25,000	5.70	7.73	10.17	10.68
50,000	5.61	7.69	10.05	10.61
75,000	5.51	7.65	9.93	10.53
100,000	5.41	7.61	9.81	10.46
150,000	5.21	7.51	9.56	10.31
200,000	5.01	7.41	9.32	10.15
250,000	4.81	7.31	9.08	9.99

*There are 8 columns by 21 inches or 168 column inches on a full page.

EXHIBIT 10   WSB radio and TV advertising rates

	One minute	*20/30 seconds*	*10 seconds*
WSB-AM radio: Spot announcements— package plans*			
12 per week	$40.00	$34.00	$24.00
18 per week	38.00	30.00	21.00
24 per week	32.00	26.00	19.00
30 per week	28.00	24.00	17.00
48 per week	26.00	20.00	15.00
WSB-FM radio: Package plan—52 weeks[†]	16.00	14.00	
WSB-TV			
Daytime rates			
60 seconds	$75–235 depending on program		
30 seconds	40–140 depending on program		
Prime-time rates			
60 seconds‡	$540–660 depending on program		
30 seconds	390–725 depending on program		

*Available 5:00–6:00 A.M., 10:00 A.M.–3:30 P.M., and 7:30 P.M.–midnight Monday–Saturday; and 5:00 A.M.–midnight Sunday. Best available positions in applicable times—no guaranteed placement.
[†]Quantity discounts available. For example, 18 times per week for 52 weeks is one half the above rates.
[‡]Very few available.

Mr. Rood decided that he would have to assume confidence in the effectiveness of the newspapers. He felt if the study were done right he would get his share of media exposure and influence. The other decision he quickly made was that, in preparing his comments on the proposed research, he would take Rich's point of view rather than that of *The Atlanta Journal* and *Constitution.* He then began to review the events of the day and the WSB proposal in light of what he felt Rich's needed to know. He also knew that whatever he proposed would have to be acceptable to Mr. Landon. Noting the lateness in the day, he began work on the counterproposal.

Appendix Suggestions for Rich's Media Research

Objectives

If Rich's is interested in conducting research to measure the effectiveness of various advertising media, WSB-TV and WSB-Radio will be happy to assist. As a basis for discussion, here are suggested objectives for this project:

1. Measure the ability of TV, radio, and newspapers to sell specific items of merchandise in Rich's seven Atlanta metro stores.
2. Determine how each advertising medium complements the others in terms of additional units sold to various segments of the customer population (age, sex, charge account ownership, etc.).
3. Determine what each advertising medium contributes in regard to additional store traffic.

How the Research Could Be Conducted

The project could consist of a series of in-store surveys. A separate survey would be conducted for each item of merchandise tested. The more items tested, the more reliable the results of the overall research project.

If possible, all seven Rich's stores in the Atlanta metro area should participate in the research.

Each survey could be conducted by placing interviewers (Rich's personnel working overtime) in appropriate store locations during "peak" shopping hours with instructions to complete *brief* questionnaires with customers purchasing the item being tested. (See accompanying questionnaire.)

The interview could cover how the customer got the idea to buy the item, other planned purchases in the store during the same visit, charge account ownership, and any other pertinent data. Each interview would last less than a minute and would not bother the customers.

The sample size would vary, depending upon the number of stores participating, the type of merchandise, and the sales volume. Interviewers would strive to include all customers purchasing the items during peak hours. Tabulation of the results could be handled by the WSB computer.

Careful Attention to Items and Media Schedules

In order to make the research valid and meaningful, the items to be tested must be selected carefully. In addition, care should be taken to ensure that the TV, radio, or newspaper advertising for these items is not "stacked" in favor of one particular medium. Close attention to the items being tested and the media schedule for each is necessary.

Questionnaire

The proposed questionnaire follows:

(All customers purchasing the item advertised are interviewed.)

1. *How* did you happen to buy this merchandise at Rich's?

Saw on TV	( )
Heard on radio	( )
Saw in newspaper	( )
TV and radio	( )
TV and newspaper	( )
TV, radio, and newspaper	( )
Saw on display	( )
Other: _____	( )

ASKED OF CUSTOMERS NOT MENTIONING A MEDIUM: (2, 3, 4)

2. Do you recall seeing this merchandise advertised on the TV?

Yes	( )
No	( )

3. Do you recall seeing this merchandise advertised in the newspaper?

Yes	( )
No	( )

4. Do you recall hearing this merchandise advertised on the radio?

Yes	( )
No	( )

5. Are you buying *anything* else at Rich's today?

Yes	( )
No	( )
Maybe	( )
Don't know	( )

6. Do you have a charge account at *Rich's*?

Yes	( )
No	( )

7. In which group does your age fall?

Under 25	( )
25–34	( )
35–49	( )
50 and over	( )

Store _____

Time of Interview _____

Case 6

Greenwood Federal Savings and Loan*

In early October, Jenny Harris was reviewing the results of the latest research that had been conducted by Greenwood Federal Savings and Loan Association and its advertising agency. Harris had been asked by the chairman of the board, Paul Robinson, to prepare a strategic marketing plan for Greenwood Federal. Annual marketing plans had been prepared in previous years, but these tended to be tactical in nature. Many changes had taken place in the previous year, necessitating a longer-term look at the organization's marketing planning. Ms. Harris grabbed several items off her bookshelf, including new research study results, last year's marketing plan, and the latest financial reports available documenting Greenwood's recent performance. She then reached for the phone to call her husband to tell him that she would be home very late that evening.

Background

Greenwood Federal Savings (GFS) is one of the nation's larger savings and loan associations. It was founded in 1927 in the largest milk-producing county south of Wisconsin. At the time, the county was beginning to emerge from an agricultural economy into a semi-urban economy oriented toward a major fast-growing city, Sunbelt City, located six miles to the west. The founder was an attorney, state legislator, and business and community leader who was president of the Chamber of Commerce and many civic and charitable groups. The board of directors consisted of a number of leading citizens in the community, and their goal was to make the city the finest residential city in the region. To ease unemployment and provide some new homes during the Depression, the Association pioneered in making construction loans. To ensure the quality of the homes built, the officers of Greenwood developed a code of minimum specifications and named an inspector to see that the homes complied with it.

---

*This case was prepared by Kenneth L. Bernhardt for the purpose of class discussion. Names and selected data have been disguised. Copyright © 1996 by Kenneth L. Bernhardt.

From the beginning, those who directed the policies of Greenwood Federal were concerned with people and the environment in which members of the Association lived. A commitment was made to serve all citizens without prejudice. The first loan to a black citizen was made in 1928. A close relationship with builders and developers was established and has been maintained throughout the years. In the early years, movies and slide presentations of land developments in other parts of the country kept the community's builders abreast of the latest developments. The first branch was established in 1952, when assets had grown to more than $25 million. During the 1960s, the Association expanded its services, adding college education loans, home improvement loans, and FHA and VA loans. The officers were concerned that people in moderate- and low-income categories should have adequate housing.

Greenwood was seeking to help the people of the community achieve "the good life," including the privilege of home ownership. Over the years, Greenwood was always in the forefront as an ethical, caring organization. For example, it was the last financial institution in the area to raise rates on loan assumptions. All employees were trained and continually reminded that their role was to satisfy customers. Greenwood had a strong corporate creed outlining its commitment to excellence. The officers and employees of Greenwood believed in the creed, which is reproduced in Exhibit 1.

EXHIBIT 1   Corporate creed

GREENWOOD FEDERAL
SAVINGS & LOAN ASSOCIATION

Commitment to Excellence: A Corporate Creed

Greenwood Federal Is Committed:

- To the pursuit of a leadership position in the delivery of financial services and to the belief that quality is more important than size.
- To be innovative in all that we do, including products we design and support services we render.
- To understanding the value of customer confidence and realizing that achieving this goal is only outweighed by the need to maintain it.
- To the setting of sound financial policies that protect the future while enhancing the present.
- To be human, open, friendly, and sincere and to recognize that results should never be achieved at the expense of human dignity.
- To specialize in product areas where the future appears strongest and the Association is best able to excel.
- To our employees by rewarding merit, by providing an environment for growth, by creating a team spirit by encouraging open, two-way communications, and by enabling them to feel pride in the products and services we provide.
- To honest, fair, and enduring relationships with suppliers and associates.
- To the concept of corporate social responsibility to our local communities through individual and company participation.

To all of these precepts because they are not only intrinsically right but also happen to be good business.

Greenwood Federal Savings grew rapidly during the 1970s and 1980s, mirroring the growth of the city of Greenwood and the metropolis of Sunbelt City. In 1972, the first branch outside the city of Greenwood was opened, representing the Association's 10th office. During the mid- and late 1970s, savings offices were opened in four regional malls, and by the end of the decade Greenwood had offices in five counties throughout the metropolitan area. In the 1980s, Greenwood moved statewide through a series of mergers. Faced with severe losses, the board of directors decided to concentrate on the Sunbelt City metropolitan area and the northern part of the state, and sold off some of the offices purchased earlier.

An organization chart is shown in Exhibit 2. Jenny Harris reported directly to the chairman of the board and CEO and was responsible for all aspects of marketing, advertising, and product management. Since her arrival from a major packaged goods company several years earlier, Greenwood had introduced automated teller machines, discount brokerage services, homeowner's and personal lines of credit, automobile loans, credit cards, and checking accounts.

Competitive Environment

Many changes took place in the competitive environment for GFS. Recently, the U.S. Supreme Court handed down a decision upholding regional banking. During the next several months, the major banks in Sunbelt City all merged with or acquired other large banks in surrounding states, resulting in the creation of "super banks." Other regulations resulted in a blurring of the distinction between banks and savings and loan institutions. In addition, large national organizations such as Sears, CitiCorp, Merrill Lynch, and several major insurance companies all expanded their financial service offerings and entered the Sunbelt City market in a big way.

Like most savings and loan associations, GFS concentrated on the "middle market," which comprised the bulk of its deposits and loans. GFS did not get much patronage from very high-income consumers or from low-income consumers. Competition for this retail middle market had become intense in recent years. There were 20 S&Ls in the Sunbelt City metropolitan area, and most of these, especially the major competitors, concentrated on the middle market. In addition, two of the three largest banks in town concentrated on this market, as did many of the national organizations that had recently entered the market. Jenny Harris recognized the problems created by the intense competition for this middle market and knew that it would be important for GFS to segment the market even more finely than it had in the past. The key, she thought, was to identify target markets where GFS could do a better job than competitors in meeting consumer needs.

EXHIBIT 2   Greenwood's organization chart

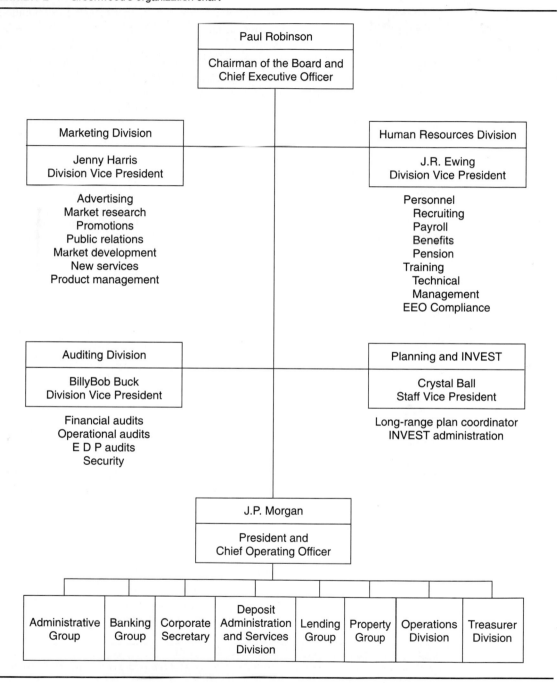

Exhibit 3 shows GFS's market share and the shares for each of the major competitors. The data in Exhibit 3 comes from a study that GFS had conducted among residents living within three miles of each of its branches. The results show that about one quarter of the people living near its branches have one or more accounts with GFS. Only 9 percent of the residents, however, indicate that GFS is their primary financial institution. Information on each of the major competitors is presented in Exhibit 4. GFS's growth in assets, advertising expenditures, and number of branches are all below those of the major competitors, with the exception of Home Federal.

GFS was a major factor in construction lending due to its long-term strong relationship with builders and its excellent image in the construction community. GFS did not have the lowest interest rates, and over the years had been very conservative in its appraisals and the amount of its loans. It worked with the cream of the builders, catering to them and to the realtors in the community, who recognized that there would be fewer hassles in working with GFS. The organization was very "loan oriented," and almost all the senior management had come from the loan side of the Association.

GFS became profitable again, following four straight years of losses. The reserve ratio (net worth/total assets) had deteriorated from 6.3 percent 3 years ago to 2.7 percent last year. It had increased to 3 percent by the end of the current year. Most of GFS's savings and loan competitors had converted to stock organizations or were in the process of converting as a result of the Federal Home Loan Bank Board Regulations raising the required reserve ratio from 3 percent to 6 percent over the next five years. The easiest way to comply with this regulation would be to sell stock, thus raising a substantial amount of equity. GFS management be-

EXHIBIT 3   Market share analysis by competitor

	Percent who have relationship with institution	Percent indicating primary institution	"Primary" as a percent of "have relationship"
City National Bank	32%	19%	59%
First National Bank	28	10	36
Greenwood Federal	24	9	38
Heritage Trust	24	15	63
Sunbelt Federal	13	5	38
Home Federal	8	3	38
Credit unions	24	7	29
All others	NA*	32	NA*
		100%	

Note: Table is interpreted as follows: 32 percent of the population living within three miles of Greenwood branches have a relationship with City National Bank; 59 percent of those with a relationship with City National (19 percent of the population) indicate City National is their primary financial institution.
*NA = not available.

EXHIBIT 4   Information on major competitors ($ in billions)

	Greenwood Federal Savings & Loan	Sunbelt Federal Savings & Loan	First National Bank	Heritage Trust Bank	City National Bank	Home Federal Savings & Loan
Total assets 12/31/85	$1.3	$2.0	$12.7	$13.9	$9.8	$1.4
Percent growth in assets 1985 versus 1984	4.0%	20.6%	12.7%	22.9%	15.3%	5.4%
Total deposits 12/31/85	$1.1	$1.5	$9.1	$10.6	$6.9	$1.3
Percent growth in deposits 1985 versus 1984	6.9%	4.0%	13.2%	15.1%	9.3%	4.6%
Net worth/assets 12/31/85	3.0%	6.2%	5.8%	5.6%	5.9%	1.9%
Return on assets, 1985	.6%	1.0%	1.2%	1.0%	1.0%	(loss)
1985 advertising expenditures ($ millions)	$0.7	$1.4	$1.5	$1.6	$1.4	*
Number of branches in Sunbelt City area	19	30	55	41	63	15

*Figure not available.

lieved that they could achieve the required ratio if they concentrated on increasing the profitability of the organization. Top management was concerned that, if they converted to stock ownership, it would not be clear how stockholders would fit in versus employees and customers. They feared they would lose flexibility in marketing and would need to direct a great deal of attention to investor relations and the stockbroker community.

Detailed financial information for Greenwood Federal, its number of accounts, and the structure for its savings and its loans are presented in Exhibit 5. Comments on the competitive situation for each of the major product categories follow.

Savings Certificates

The primary competitors for savings certificates are local banks, savings and loans, and credit unions. In the last year, First National Bank and several of the smaller banks and savings and loans have been particularly aggressive in their pricing. Banks especially are able to pay higher rates on certificates because of their greater ability to match assets and liabilities. Brokerage firms and insurance companies must also be considered competitors for these savings dollars. GFS has always been a leader in the savings certificate product area with high awareness levels. Recent strategy has been to replace 91-day and six-month certificates with long-term certificates in the portfolio.

EXHIBIT 5 GFS financial data and savings structure, July 31, 1986 (year to date)

Total assets . . . . $1.34 billion
Total savings deposits . . . . $1.18 billion
Number of savings accounts 140,144
Total loans . . . . $1.14 billion
  Number of first mortgage loans 27,387
  First mortgage loans (average yield 10.0 percent) . . . . $1.07 billion
  Second mortgage loans, including home equity loans (home equity yield
    10.5 percent) . . . . $24.5 million
  Education loans (average yield 10.1 percent). . . . . $11.1 million
  Consumer loans (average yield 13.0 percent on unsecured and 11.6 percent
    on secured) . . . . $19.7 million
  Savings account loans . . . . $8.4 million
  Other loans . . . . $10.0 million
Operating income as percent of assets 11.75%
Average cost of all funds—July 8.2%
Average cost of new funds acquired—July. 6.4%
Operating expenses 2.6%
Return on assets 6%

Savings structure	Dollars (millions)	Percent of total
Passbook savings	$ 61.2	5.2%
NOW accounts.	37.9	3.3
Super NOW accounts	112.0	9.5
Money market accounts.	202.7	17.0
Certificates:		
Jumbo	12.8	1.1
3-month	12.6	1.1
6-month	108.2	9.2
12–24-month	145.9	12.5
25–36-month	170.0	14.4
Greater than 36-month.	234.7	20.0
Retirement accounts	78.6	6.7
	$1,176.6	100.0%

Checking Accounts

Commercial banks, savings and loans, and credit unions are also direct competitors for both regular checking and NOW accounts. The source of business for checking accounts has been commercial banks, and Sunbelt Federal has been particularly aggressive in its marketing of checking accounts. The banks have a definite convenience advantage, and they possess the majority of checking accounts. Many, however, are demarketing the smaller-deposit checking accounts through the use of high service fees. Harris felt there was opportunity to attract new checking accounts, with pricing as an important part of the strategy.

Money Market Accounts

Competitors for money market deposit accounts (MMDA) include commercial banks, savings and loans, money market funds, and bond and equity funds. For a large number of consumers, the MMDA has actually replaced the passbook as the primary savings relationship. Harris thought that, with its large base of savings customers, GFS had some competitive advantage here, but marketing of the MMDA had not been very aggressive since its introduction. Competitors in the Sunbelt City market were not actively marketing these accounts.

Credit Lines

Commercial banks, savings and loans, mortgage bankers, and brokerage firms have all marketed home equity and personal credit lines aggressively during the past two years. GFS introduced its homeowners line of credit (HOLOC) two years ago, and a personal line of credit product was introduced last year. Jenny Harris felt that GFS had a tremendous marketing opportunity with the home equity product because of GFS's large pool of mortgage loan customers and because of changes in the federal tax laws expected to occur in the next year.

Residential Mortgage Loans

GFS is the leader among mortgage bankers, savings and loans, and commercial banks in the mortgage loan market. The market has changed dramatically in the past few years, with a large number of new competitors in the local market. Harris believed the tradition of good service and market leadership at GFS, together with its entrenched position with the real estate professional target market, provided excellent opportunities for continued success for GFS.

Consumer Loans

GFS has a weak competitive position in the consumer loan product area. Commercial banks have much greater experience with consumer loans and higher awareness. Finance companies, credit unions, and other savings and loans also compete for loan volume. GFS has tried in a modest way to build awareness of the availability of the consumer loan product. Harris thought there were opportunities to build this volume by differentiation based on product features rather than on the interest rate. None of the major competitors had developed an aggressive, innovative way to market consumer loans.

Brokerage Services

GFS was an equity partner in INVEST, a discount brokerage service. The service became profitable for GFS in the past year, with over 2,000 new accounts and $43 million in sales. INVEST was not an exclusive service, and several savings and loans in the area, including Sunbelt Federal, offered the service. The competition for this service included traditional brokerage firms, discount brokers, insurance companies, and depository institutions.

Strategies of Major Competitors

The major competitors employed different strategies and tactics, depending on the product involved. Harris's perceptions of some selected competitors are discussed below.

Sunbelt Federal Savings operated almost 60 offices in 20 communities, with 30 of the offices in the Sunbelt City metropolitan area. Most of its recent marketing effort focused on checking accounts and consumer loans. It has priced its checking account lower than most competitors and is actively seeking younger checking account customers. Focus groups conducted by GFS showed that consumers perceived Sunbelt Federal as dynamic, progressive, friendly, having low service charges, and a good place for savings.

Harris felt that First National Bank had earned the reputation as an innovative retail bank and had begun in earnest to cultivate a position as a rate leader. The bank has experienced dramatic growth in consumer deposits during the past year, at the expense of lower interest margins. A major strength is its extensive branching network, with over 75 offices (55 in the Sunbelt City metropolitan area). Its current advertising campaign, "If your bank isn't First, you should have second thoughts," is more aggressive than previous campaigns. In two television commercials, First National Bank compares its performance on investment products with that of Heritage Trust and City National Bank. First National aggressively markets VISA cards throughout the South and is among the top 10 VISA banks in the country. Key image attributes for First National Bank mentioned by the participants in the focus groups include efficient, innovative, flashy, colorful, and convenient.

Heritage Trust had successfully positioned itself as the bank for upwardly mobile people, according to Harris. Its advertising had enjoyed high awareness levels and had served as an umbrella for product advertising, stressing how well the bank suits the needs of its customers. Heritage Trust had aggressively attracted newcomers to the market through strong corporate relationships. Its upscale banking program had been in operation for years and was considered by Harris as one of the best in the region. Attributes for Heritage Trust identified by the focus group respondents included "pinstriped," educated, professional, confident, successful, convenient, and smart.

City National Bank is the largest commercial bank in the state and has a very strong retail presence through over 75 offices (63 in the Sunbelt City metropolitan area). City National had traditionally been a strong consumer lender and had recently been directing its advertising at the baby boom generation with its campaign, "Think of your future with City National." Product advertising had stressed simple interest loans, discount brokerage services, and Ready Equity (their equity-based credit line). City National's image as profiled by focus group respondents included convenience, but also some negative attributes such as "bully," impersonal, and greedy.

The image of GFS, as perceived by the attendees at the focus group sessions, is "established," conservative, friendly, and older. GFS had, in fact, attracted a market somewhat older than that of the banks.

Exhibit 6 presents data on the importance of various features to consumers, together with the ratings of GFS and four competitors on each of the features. The consumers in the study were asked to rate the importance of each of the features using a scale of 0–10. They were then asked to give a rating to each financial institution on each feature, again using a scale of 0–10 (with 0 being poor and 10 extremely good). Overall, the most important features for a financial institution include:

Seldom make mistakes.

Do a good job overall.

Statements are clear and easy to understand.

Open at convenient hours during the week.

Personnel are polite and courteous.

Long history of financial stability.

Offer all the services I need.

Sufficient tellers to avoid long lines.

GFS is not rated the best on any of these factors, although it is rated better than Sunbelt Federal Savings on six of the eight. It is also rated higher than City National Bank on four of the eight. GFS is rated lower than First National Bank on all eight and lower than Heritage on six of the eight. The biggest "gap" for GFS is in providing consumers with all the services they need. Harris wondered whether this perception could be changed by increasing the promotion of many of the services currently available at GFS.

Consumer Research

To learn more about what consumers wanted in financial services and how the overall market could be segmented better, Harris had commissioned, in cooperation with the GFS advertising agency, a major consumer segmentation study. The research was designed to provide several clusters of consumers (segments) based on activities, interests, and opinions rather than on conventional demographic characteristics such as age, sex, or income. Harris wanted to use the results of the study to help develop a market niche for GFS, to identify appropriate target markets, to evaluate existing and new products, and to improve marketing communications for GFS.

National Family Opinion (NFO), one of the nation's largest marketing research firms, was used to conduct the study. NFO maintains a nationally representative consumer panel of 150,000 households, with over 3,000 in the Sunbelt City metropolitan area. NFO mailed out 1,250 questionnaires, and 57 percent,

EXHIBIT 6   Importance of features and comparative ratings

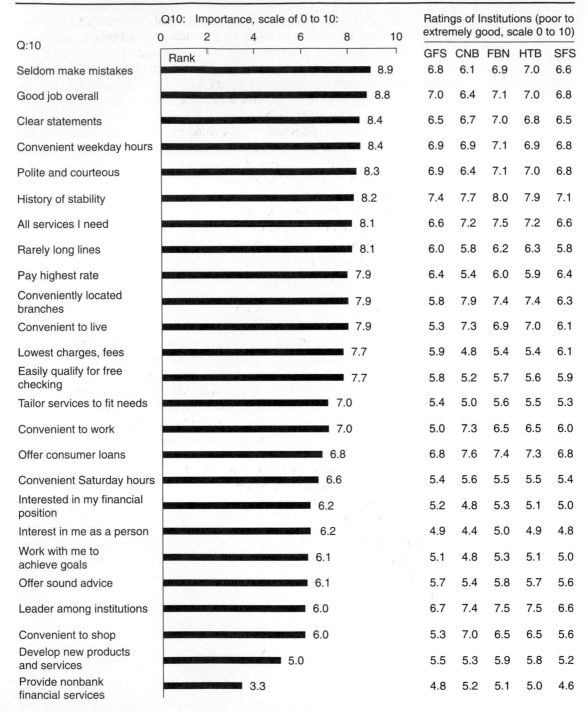

Q:10	Q10: Importance, scale of 0 to 10:	Ratings of Institutions (poor to extremely good, scale 0 to 10)				
	Rank	GFS	CNB	FBN	HTB	SFS
Seldom make mistakes	8.9	6.8	6.1	6.9	7.0	6.6
Good job overall	8.8	7.0	6.4	7.1	7.0	6.8
Clear statements	8.4	6.5	6.7	7.0	6.8	6.5
Convenient weekday hours	8.4	6.9	6.9	7.1	6.9	6.8
Polite and courteous	8.3	6.9	6.4	7.1	7.0	6.8
History of stability	8.2	7.4	7.7	8.0	7.9	7.1
All services I need	8.1	6.6	7.2	7.5	7.2	6.6
Rarely long lines	8.1	6.0	5.8	6.2	6.3	5.8
Pay highest rate	7.9	6.4	5.4	6.0	5.9	6.4
Conveniently located branches	7.9	5.8	7.9	7.4	7.4	6.3
Convenient to live	7.9	5.3	7.3	6.9	7.0	6.1
Lowest charges, fees	7.7	5.9	4.8	5.4	5.4	6.1
Easily qualify for free checking	7.7	5.8	5.2	5.7	5.6	5.9
Tailor services to fit needs	7.0	5.4	5.0	5.6	5.5	5.3
Convenient to work	7.0	5.0	7.3	6.5	6.5	6.0
Offer consumer loans	6.8	6.8	7.6	7.4	7.3	6.8
Convenient Saturday hours	6.6	5.4	5.6	5.5	5.5	5.4
Interested in my financial position	6.2	5.2	4.8	5.3	5.1	5.0
Interest in me as a person	6.2	4.9	4.4	5.0	4.9	4.8
Work with me to achieve goals	6.1	5.1	4.8	5.3	5.1	5.0
Offer sound advice	6.1	5.7	5.4	5.8	5.7	5.6
Leader among institutions	6.0	6.7	7.4	7.5	7.5	6.6
Convenient to shop	6.0	5.3	7.0	6.5	6.5	5.6
Develop new products and services	5.0	5.5	5.3	5.9	5.8	5.2
Provide nonbank financial services	3.3	4.8	5.2	5.1	5.0	4.6

Key: GFS = Greenwood Federal;   CNB = City National Bank;   FNB = First National Bank;
HTB = Heritage Trust Bank;   SFS = Sunbelt Federal Savings.

712, were returned. In addition, a supplemental sample of 122 GFS customers also completed the questionnaire. The study included results only from persons primarily responsible for household financial decisions (approximately half male and half female). The median age was just under 45 years old. The proportion classified as "working preferred," that is, employed and reporting a minimum of $5,000 savings, was 40 percent, a level considered normal based on previous studies conducted by GFS.

Slightly over half, 57 percent, used a commercial bank as the main financial institution, 23 percent used a savings and loan, 12 percent used a credit union, and 18 percent listed all other types of institutions. GFS's market share for the main study was 15 percent (having any account, not "primary" institution).

The questionnaire presented 100 opportunities for each respondent to record his or her attitudes or opinions about financial matters and about his or her banking habits and preferences. Examples of questions include "I like to pay cash for almost everything I buy," "I'm always looking for a way to make more interest on my money," and "I need very little advice when making decisions about the types of financial services I should use." In addition, each person was presented with 25 questions concerning the importance to them of individual banking practices and services, together with questions concerning the rating of the individual financial institutions.

A large mainframe computer then was used to perform advanced statistical analysis of the questionnaire data. The objective was to cluster or group the 712 respondents into meaningful segments based on commonality of their attitudes rather than into groups based on age, income, or other demographic characteristics. The computer program identified five clusters or segments similar enough in their attitudes to be classified as distinct survey segments. These segments were then given names to help describe them. Most segmentation studies of this type attempt to group people according to lifestyles, thus ending up with such groupings as "yuppies," "young suburbia," or "gray power." Here the groupings were based on the way the respondents think and act about money, credit, banking, and financial services. Five clusters were identified and named:

Secure Steve (self-confident and self-assured).

Retiring Richard (72 percent employed, but the highest proportion of retirees).

Fast Lane Phil (overspending, undersaving youth).

Minimal Martha (highest proportion of females, but not necessarily female; users of a minimum of products and services).

Single-Minded Sam (desire for one-stop banking at a full-service convenient institution).

Exhibits 7 through 10 present data from the two samples concerning the five segments, including size of the segments, demographics, amount of savings, and financial attitudes. Exhibits 11 through 13 present data from the study concerning each

EXHIBIT 7 Descriptions and size of each segment

	GFS customers 100%	Total segmentation study 100%	Percent of segmentation that were W.P. * 40%
High assets, high checking Wants single account, single interest Wants security, personal attention Organized, disciplined Budgets, saves High TV and radio, high newspaper	Singleminded Sam 7%	Singleminded Sam 11%	32%
Oldest, most affluent High assets Well managed, highly organized Wants security, does not shop No ATM Uses many services Low checking, high savings High newspaper, high magazine	Retiring Richard 17%	Retiring Richard 13%	47%
Middle aged, well educated Good income Technical/Sales/Administrative Undisciplined, uninvolved, wife handles Has difficulty managing, overspends Low assets, low savings High TV, moderate other media	Fastlane Phil 15%	Fastlane Phil 19%	28%
Middle aged Married Likely male Educated Managerial/Professional High income, high savings High investments Self-confident Uses ATM Shops for rate Actively involved in managing finances Low checking balance Likely S & L Customer Ages 25 – 49 Low TV and radio, high magazine	Secure Steve 30%	Secure Steve 22%	44%
Decision maker — female Pays cash, avoids credit Distrustful Low ATM usage Offices not convenient Lowest income (51% under 25K) Lowest savings Low education Blue collar Daytime TV, low radio, low news Age 25 – 55	Minimal Martha 30%	Minimal Martha 33%	28%
Base	106	712	†
Percent of total	15%	100%	†

*Note: W.P. means working preferred, those employed with at least $5,000 in savings.
†Each segment total.

EXHIBIT 8   Demographics of the segmentation study

Sex of the Segments

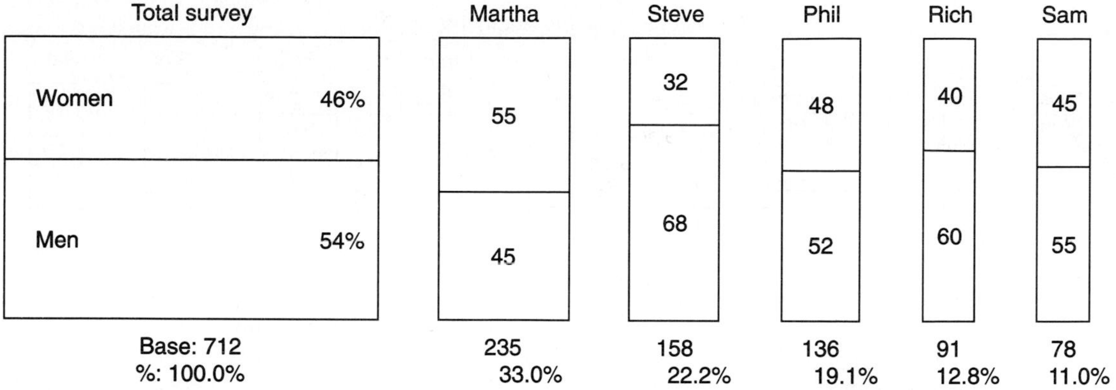

Total survey		Martha	Steve	Phil	Rich	Sam
Women	46%	55	32	48	40	45
Men	54%	45	68	52	60	55
Base: 712		235	158	136	91	78
%: 100.0%		33.0%	22.2%	19.1%	12.8%	11.0%

Age of the Segments

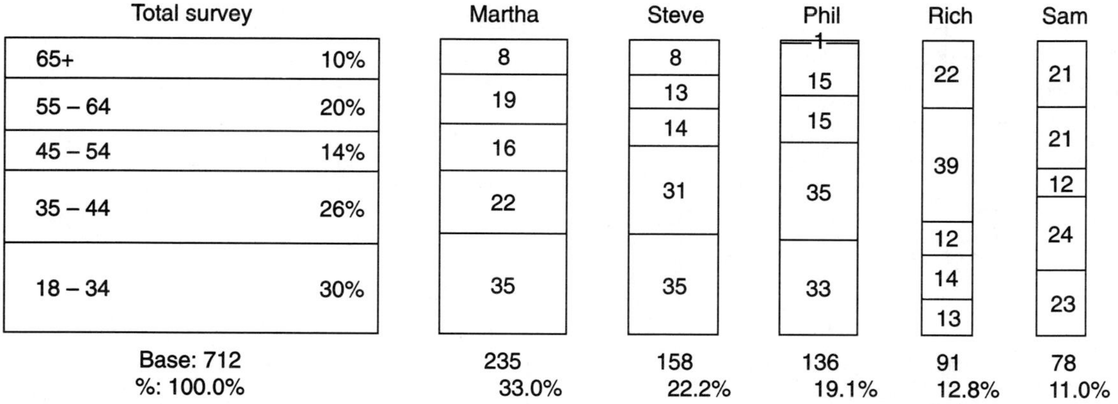

Total survey		Martha	Steve	Phil	Rich	Sam
65+	10%	8	8	1	22	21
55 – 64	20%	19	13	15		21
45 – 54	14%	16	14	15	39	12
35 – 44	26%	22	31	35	12	24
18 – 34	30%	35	35	33	14 / 13	23
Base: 712		235	158	136	91	78
%: 100.0%		33.0%	22.2%	19.1%	12.8%	11.0%

Household Income of the Segments

Total survey		Martha	Steve	Phil	Rich	Sam
$50 +	15%	7	25	12	17	18
$35 – 49.9	23%	22		23	31	18
$25 – 34.9	21%	20	22	23		12
$10 – 24.9	41%	51	26 / 27	42	21 / 31	53
Base: 712		235	158	136	91	78
%: 100.0%		33.0%	22.2%	19.1%	12.8%	11.0%

(continued)

EXHIBIT 8   *(concluded)*

Occupation of the Segments

Total survey		Martha	Steve	Phil	Rich	Sam
Retired	11%	7	8	4	27	19
Other	11%	13	11	8		
Blue collar	14%	23	7	12	11	10
					6	13
White collar	64%	57	74	76	56	58

	Base: 712	235	158	136	91	78
	%: 100.0%	33.0%	22.2%	19.1%	12.8%	11.0%

Savings of the Segments

Total survey		Martha	Steve	Phil	Rich	Sam
$25,000+	22%	13	24	8	53	31
$5,000 – 24,999	29%	30	33	25	33	25
Under $5,000	49%	57	43	67	14	44

	Base: 712	235	158	136	91	78
	%: 100.0%	33.0%	22.2%	19.1%	12.8%	11.0%

Working Preferred Status

Total survey		Martha	Steve	Phil	Rich	Sam
All other	60%	72	56	72	53	68
W.P.	40	28	44	28	47	32

	Base: 712	235	158	136	91	78
	%: 100.0%	33.0%	22.2%	19.1%	12.8%	11.0%

EXHIBIT 9   Average amount of savings (by study segments)

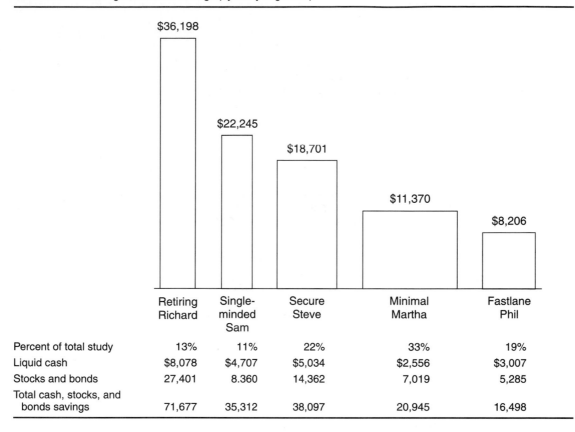

	Retiring Richard	Single-minded Sam	Secure Steve	Minimal Martha	Fastlane Phil
Percent of total study	13%	11%	22%	33%	19%
Liquid cash	$8,078	$4,707	$5,034	$2,556	$3,007
Stocks and bonds	27,401	8.360	14,362	7,019	5,285
Total cash, stocks, and bonds savings	71,677	35,312	38,097	20,945	16,498

segment's rating of Greenwood Federal and usage of various products and services. The share of market for GFS and its major competitors by segment is included in Exhibit 14. Selected findings for each segment are discussed below.

Minimal Martha

This segment was the largest identified, with one-third of all consumers and 30 percent of GFS customers included. Minimal Martha had the least usage of financial products and institutions among the five segments. This was the only segment where the financial decision maker was most often female and the banking chores were also handled most often by the female head of household. Minimal Martha generally manages her personal finances by paying cash, keeping funds in separate accounts, and avoiding credit. She is less comfortable and trusting of financial institutions. The convenience of a financial institution is probably the major determinant in its selection. Martha has a low income, less education, and is more likely to be married with a larger household and a blue-collar husband than other segments.

EXHIBIT 10   Agreement with various attitudinal statements

		Mean, Scale 1–7
When it comes to services such as checking accounts, I shop around to find the least expensive provider.	Total — 49 GFS = 57	4.3
	Martha — 56	4.7
	Steve — 73	5.1
	Phil — 35	3.9
	Richard — 24	3.3
	Sam — 31	3.3
I like to try new and different things.	Total — 62 GFS = 65	4.9
	Martha — 63	4.9
	Steve — 77	5.4
	Phil — 59	4.7
	Richard — 45	4.2
	Sam — 59	4.7
I would rather have one place for all my financial needs.	Total — 59 GFS = 49	4.9
	Martha — 67	5.2
	Steve — 50	4.5
	Phil — 67	5.1
	Richard — 26	3.6
	Sam — 78	5.8
It's more important to live well now than to save money for the future.	Total — 13 GFS = 10	2.4
	Martha — 11	2.3
	Steve — 15	2.5
	Phil — 11	2.6
	Richard — 11	2.3
	Sam — 24	2.7
It's important that my financial institution is conveniently located near home.	Total — 80 GFS = 84	5.6
	Martha — 86	5.9
	Steve — 74	5.3
	Phil — 83	5.7
	Richard — 70	5.2
	Sam — 86	5.8

(continued)

Secure Steve

The second-largest segment is Secure Steve, who is upscale (managerial, professional, well educated, high income, high savings, high investment) and innovative. Secure Steve shops for low charges and high interest with self-confidence. He rejects frills and is unwilling to pay to get personal attention. Typically, Secure Steve is in the prime of his career, aged 25–49, married, with a confident, ambitious outlook. He maintains the minimum in checking, shops for the best terms, and is willing to try new products. He actively shops around for the "best" financial products and is more willing to change institutions to get the best deal. He represents 22 percent of the sample and 30 percent of GFS customers.

EXHIBIT 10   *(concluded)*

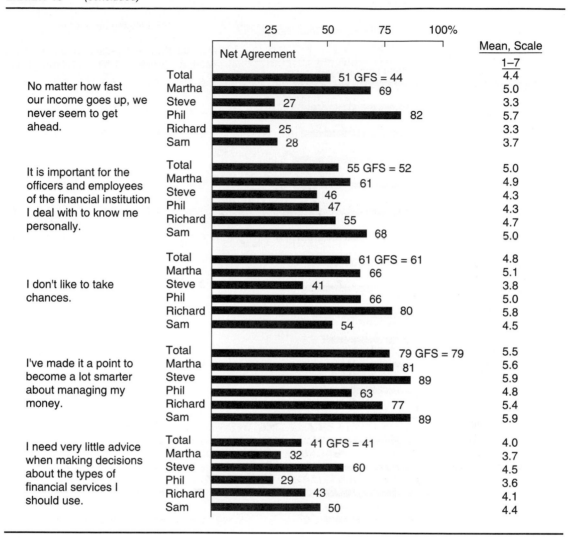

		Net Agreement	Mean, Scale 1–7
No matter how fast our income goes up, we never seem to get ahead.	Total	51 GFS = 44	4.4
	Martha	69	5.0
	Steve	27	3.3
	Phil	82	5.7
	Richard	25	3.3
	Sam	28	3.7
It is important for the officers and employees of the financial institution I deal with to know me personally.	Total	55 GFS = 52	5.0
	Martha	61	4.9
	Steve	46	4.3
	Phil	47	4.3
	Richard	55	4.7
	Sam	68	5.0
I don't like to take chances.	Total	61 GFS = 61	4.8
	Martha	66	5.1
	Steve	41	3.8
	Phil	66	5.0
	Richard	80	5.8
	Sam	54	4.5
I've made it a point to become a lot smarter about managing my money.	Total	79 GFS = 79	5.5
	Martha	81	5.6
	Steve	89	5.9
	Phil	63	4.8
	Richard	77	5.4
	Sam	89	5.9
I need very little advice when making decisions about the types of financial services I should use.	Total	41 GFS = 41	4.0
	Martha	32	3.7
	Steve	60	4.5
	Phil	29	3.6
	Richard	43	4.1
	Sam	50	4.4

Fast Lane Phil

Phil likely can be found in the fast lane at Household Finance Corporation, but is not found among the jet set in the fast lane at the airport. The segment is undisciplined, and they are poor managers of financial affairs. Three out of four in this segment report less than $5,000 in savings. Phil frequently overspends with credit cards and often makes purchases with personal installment loans. He has the highest usage of checking accounts *without* interest and passbook accounts, but the lowest usage of other savings or investment products. This segment represents 19 percent of the total sample and 15 percent of GFS customers.

EXHIBIT 11   Rating of Greenwood Federal Savings (poor to extremely good; scale of 0 to 10)

	GFS Rating: Total Study	GFS Rating by Segment				
	Rank (importance) 0 2 4 6 8 10	Minimal Martha	Secure Steve	Fastlane Phil	Retiring Richard	Single Sam
Seldom make mistakes	6.8	6.3	7.2	6.7	7.2	6.6
Good job overall	7.0	7.0	7.0	6.8	7.5	7.1
Clear statements	6.5	6.4	6.5	6.3	6.9	6.7
Convenient weekday hours	6.9	7.1	6.6	6.6	7.5	7.1
Polite and courteous	6.9	6.6	7.3	6.5	7.2	6.9
History of stability	7.4	7.5	7.2	6.9	8.3	7.8
All services I need	6.6	6.8	6.9	6.2	6.5	6.4
Rarely long lines	6.0	5.7	6.1	6.0	6.3	6.0
Pay highest rate	6.4	6.4	6.5	6.1	6.5	6.8
Conveniently located branches	5.8	5.7	5.8	5.5	6.5	5.8
Convenient to live	5.3	5.0	5.6	5.2	6.1	5.1
Lowest charges, fees	5.9	5.9	6.0	5.6	5.8	5.9
Easily qualify for free checking	5.8	5.4	6.3	5.3	6.3	6.2
Tailor services to fit needs	5.4	5.6	5.2	5.3	5.4	5.4
Convenient to work	5.0	5.1	4.8	4.7	5.8	4.6
Offer consumer loans	6.8	6.9	6.9	6.6	6.6	7.1
Convenient Saturday hours	5.4	5.3	5.8	4.9	5.3	5.8
Interested in my financial position	5.2	5.3	4.8	5.2	5.4	5.3
Interest in me as a person	4.9	4.9	4.5	4.9	5.1	5.5
Work with me to achieve goals	5.1	5.2	4.9	4.9	5.1	5.5
Offer sound advice	5.7	5.8	5.5	5.7	5.5	5.8
Leader among institutions	6.7	6.7	6.4	6.3	7.3	7.2
Convenient to shop	5.3	5.1	5.4	5.1	5.7	5.4
Develop new products and services	5.5	5.6	5.5	5.1	5.9	5.6
Provide nonbank financial services	4.8	4.9	4.9	4.3	5.0	5.2

EXHIBIT 12   Product usage: Segmentation study: January 25–March 18, 1985

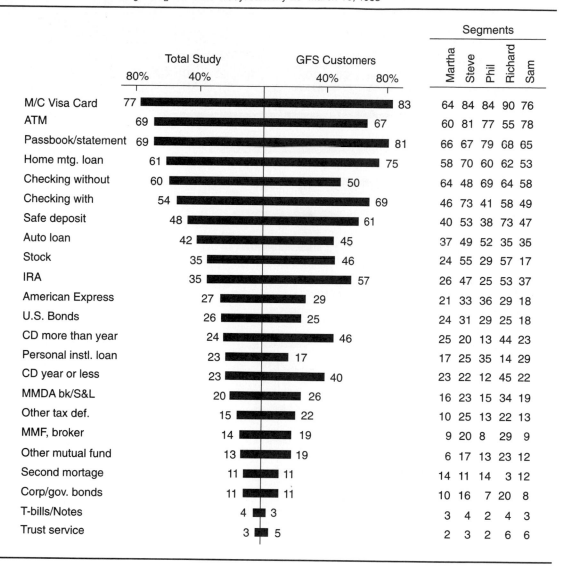

	Total Study	GFS Customers	Martha	Steve	Phil	Richard	Sam
M/C Visa Card	77	83	64	84	84	90	76
ATM	69	67	60	81	77	55	78
Passbook/statement	69	81	66	67	79	68	65
Home mtg. loan	61	75	58	70	60	62	53
Checking without	60	50	64	48	69	64	58
Checking with	54	69	46	73	41	58	49
Safe deposit	48	61	40	53	38	73	47
Auto loan	42	45	37	49	52	35	35
Stock	35	46	24	55	29	57	17
IRA	35	57	26	47	25	53	37
American Express	27	29	21	33	36	29	18
U.S. Bonds	26	25	24	31	29	25	18
CD more than year	24	46	25	20	13	44	23
Personal instl. loan	23	17	17	25	35	14	29
CD year or less	23	40	23	22	12	45	22
MMDA bk/S&L	20	26	16	23	15	34	19
Other tax def.	15	22	10	25	13	22	13
MMF, broker	14	19	9	20	8	29	9
Other mutual fund	13	19	6	17	13	23	12
Second mortage	11	11	14	11	14	3	12
Corp/gov. bonds	11	11	10	16	7	20	8
T-bills/Notes	4	3	3	4	2	4	3
Trust service	3	5	2	3	2	6	6

Retiring Richard

This segment has by far the highest savings. They prefer low risk to high interest and like personal attention. The Richard segment contains the highest proportion of retirees, 28 percent, more than double the average for the total sample. His financial affairs are well established, and he is somewhat resistant to changing them. Retiring Richard has the highest usage of most financial products and is the oldest and most married of the five segments. The segment represents 13 percent of the total sample and 17 percent of GFS customers.

EXHIBIT 13   Service usage

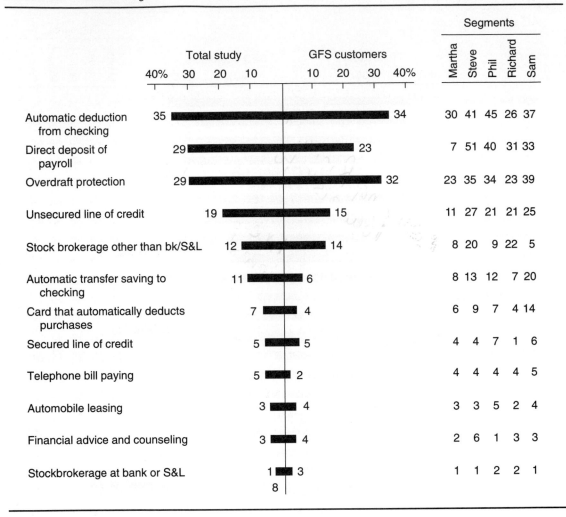

	Total study	GFS customers	Segments: Martha	Steve	Phil	Richard	Sam
Automatic deduction from checking	35	34	30	41	45	26	37
Direct deposit of payroll	29	23	7	51	40	31	33
Overdraft protection	29	32	23	35	34	23	39
Unsecured line of credit	19	15	11	27	21	21	25
Stock brokerage other than bk/S&L	12	14	8	20	9	22	5
Automatic transfer saving to checking	11	6	8	13	12	7	20
Card that automatically deducts purchases	7	4	6	9	7	4	14
Secured line of credit	5	5	4	4	7	1	6
Telephone bill paying	5	2	4	4	4	4	5
Automobile leasing	3	4	3	3	5	2	4
Financial advice and counseling	3	4	2	6	1	3	3
Stockbrokerage at bank or S&L	1	3	1	1	2	2	1

8

Single-Minded Sam

This segment, representing 11 percent of the sample and 7 percent of GFS customers, has the strongest preference for a single integrated account with one financial institution. This segment likes the security of a big institution, especially banks, and personal attention is very important. One-stop banking is more important than low fees or a high interest rate on savings. Sam is the second oldest and the most divorced, widowed, or separated of the segments.

Harris felt that the key to finding a niche for GFS and for differentiating it from the competition could be found in Exhibits 7 through 14. She planned to spend considerable time interpreting the meaning of this data.

EXHIBIT 14   Share of market (by study segments)

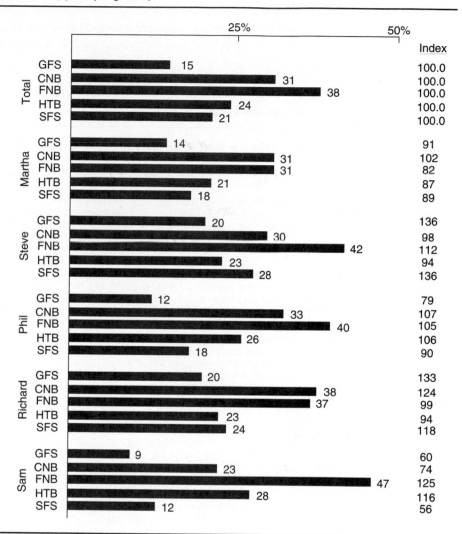

		Index
Total GFS	15	100.0
CNB	31	100.0
FNB	38	100.0
HTB	24	100.0
SFS	21	100.0
Martha GFS	14	91
CNB	31	102
FNB	31	82
HTB	21	87
SFS	18	89
Steve GFS	20	136
CNB	30	98
FNB	42	112
HTB	23	94
SFS	28	136
Phil GFS	12	79
CNB	33	107
FNB	40	105
HTB	26	106
SFS	18	90
Richard GFS	20	133
CNB	38	124
FNB	37	99
HTB	23	94
SFS	24	118
Sam GFS	9	60
CNB	23	74
FNB	47	125
HTB	28	116
SFS	12	56

Marketing Strategy Considerations

The senior management of Greenwood Federal had recently developed a mission statement. It read, "The mission of Greenwood Federal is to discover and provide needed financial services to consumers in a manner consistent with their reasonable expectations and consistent with the achievement of reasonable earnings." Given the change in regulations that had taken place in the past year and the mission statement, Harris felt that she should develop a strategic marketing plan to provide "controlled growth orchestrated to the beat of profitability, protecting assets and net worth while directing a positive course of profits." The Association had always used conservative policies, and loan delinquencies over the years had been consistently low because of the relatively strict loan underwriting standards. She felt it was important to maintain a conservative posture, but still felt there was considerable opportunity to increase consumer lending with new products,

EXHIBIT 15   Payment Shrinker ad copy

Payment Shrinker Auto Financing Cuts Monthly Payments Up to 49 Percent
Now you can afford to drive the automobile you really want. GFS Federal makes it possible with Payment Shrinker, the auto loan that can reduce your monthly payments by 25 to 49 percent.

Here's How Payment Shrinker Reduces Monthly Payments
GFS Federal Payment Shrinker combines the lower monthly payment advantages of auto leasing with the ownership and tax benefits offered by conventional car loans.

Depending on your choice of terms, your monthly payments will extend over 24, 36, or 48 months. The final payment amount will be determined at the time you make the loan and will be based on the residual value of the car* at the end of the loan.

Interest is computed on the full amount of the loan, but your monthly payments are lower because the residual car value is subtracted from the purchase price. The monthly principal payments are based upon the difference.

The interest that is charged on the full amount of the loan is tax deductible, as well as any sales tax you pay. This tax benefit is not available for personal automobile leases.

Four Options at End of Loan Term
At the end of the loan term, you'll have a choice of four options regarding your final payment: If you wish to keep your car, you may (1) pay off the residual car value amount figured in with the last monthly payment or (2) refinance the residual. If you would like another car, you may (3) sell or trade your car and keep the profit you make over and above the residual value or (4) return the car in good working condition (subject to condition and mileage requirements) to GFS Federal with no further obligation except to pay a nominal return fee.

Example of How Payment Shrinker Auto Loan Works

Purchase price of the car you want	$13,528
Less: Down payment (10%)	1,353
Amount to be financed over 36 months at	
13 3/4%[†] annual percentage rate.	$12,175
Residual value of car at end of 36-month loan term.	$ 6,935
Monthly payments are composed of two parts:	
1. Principal and interest payable on $5,240	
($12,175 minus the $6,935 residual value)	$178.44
2. Interest payments on the $6,935 residual car value	$ 79.46
Total monthly payment	$257.90
Monthly payment with conventional auto loan at	
12 1/4%[†] annual percentage rate	$405.86
Monthly payment with Payment Shrinker	$257.90
Amount saved per month	$147.96

[†]This is an example. Actual rate may vary.

	Compare Monthly Payments— Payment Shrinker versus Conventional Financing	
Amount financed	Conventional auto loan (monthly)	Payment Shrinker auto loan (monthly)
$24,000		
24 months	$1,132.58	$712.24
36 months	$ 800.01	$573.31
48 months	$ 634.96	$501.72
$16,000	—	—
24 months	$ 755.05	$474.82
36 months	$ 533.34	$382.21
48 months	$ 423.31	$334.48
$8,000	—	—
24 months	$ 377.52	$237.41
36 months	$ 266.67	$191.11
48 months	$ 211.65	$167.24

*The residual value of the automobile is determined by *Automotive Lease Guide,* a published residual value book, in effect at the time the loan is originated. The residual value represents the estimated value of the vehicle after the 24- to 48-month loan is completed.

Note: The monthly payment chart shown is based on the following assumptions: Payment Shrinker auto loan: **13.75% annual percentage rate;** Conventional auto loan: **12.25% annual percentage rate.** Assume residual value is 50% of sticker price for 24 months, 45% of sticker price for 36 months, 40% of sticker price for 48 months. Amount financed is 90% of purchase price.

such as the homeowner's line of credit, the personal credit line, and a new type of auto loan, the "Payment Shrinker." Exhibit 15 contains copy the ad agency had developed for a brochure to explain how the Payment Shrinker auto loan works.

To help determine the relative importance of the various products offered by GFS, Ms. Harris had developed a product hierarchy ranking matrix. This is presented in Exhibit 16, together with the key used to give the ratings. According to her analysis, money market deposit accounts, certificates of deposit, IRAs, mortgage loans, and regular savings accounts were the products that should receive the highest priority. Harris was very uncomfortable with what she had done and wondered whether the results were accurate. For example, she had weighted each of the factors equally and was now having some second thoughts about this decision. She vowed to take another look at the product hierarchy rankings as she started to develop the strategic marketing plan.

The advertising agency had recommended several new campaigns for her consideration. The "25K Account" proposal is included in Exhibit 17. The goal of this ad is to attract larger accounts, and the campaign would use the tag line "your partner."

Exhibit 18 contains an ad the agency had developed to attract more consumer loans. This ad made use of the proposed alternative tag line, "Experience the Partnership." Finally, Exhibit 19 contains the third proposal from the ad agency, "For the Good Life." This ad was designed to attract high dollar volumes for longer periods of time through the use of attractive premiums. These new certificates of

EXHIBIT 16   Product hierarchy

	WP* usage	WP hot button	Comp. opp.†	GFS position	Profit	Commitment	Total
MMDA	3	3	3	2	3	2	16
CDs	3	3	2	2	3	3	16
IRA	3	3	1	2	2	3	14
Mortgage loans	3	2	1	3	2	3	14
Regular savings	3	1	3	2	3	2	14
Checking	3	2	2	1	1	3	13
HOLOC	1	3	1	3	3	1	12
INVEST	3	3	1	2	1	2	12
Consumer loans	2	3	2	1	1	3	12
Super NOW	1	2	3	2	2	1	11
Safe deposit	3	2	3	1	2	1	11
Credit card	3	2	1	1	2	1	10
Travel company	1	1	3	1	1	2	9

Product Hierarchy Key

Working Preferred Usage:
    1 = Less than 30 percent use the product.
    2 = 30–50 percent use the product.
    3 = More than 50 percent use the product.
Working Preferred Hot Button:
    1 = Low priority—not likely to move or open account.
    2 = Medium priority—might move or open if offer is strong.
    3 = High priority—will move or open if offer is strong.
Competitive Opportunity:
    1 = Competitors are actively marketing the product.
    2 = Some competitive activity.
    3 = No competitive activity.
Greenwood Federal's Position:
    1 = Weak position.
    2 = Potential for unique position.
    3 = Strong position.
Profitability:
    1 = Significant losses on product.
    2 = Product is losing money but has potential.
    3 = Product is profitable.
Commitment:
    1 = Little or no resources have been committed in the past.
    2 = Some resources have been committed in the past.
    3 = Major resources have been committed in the past.

*WP = Working preferred (employed and savings of $5,000 and up).
†Comp. Opp. = Competitive opportunity.

deposit were to be priced 35 basis points below comparable three-, five-, and six-year certificates, with interest to be paid and compounded annually rather than quarterly. The agency proposed that advertising previously scheduled for high-interest checking be switched to this premium promotion and that newspaper ads and radio also be used.

EXHIBIT 17   Proposed campaign for 25K Account

Greenwood Federal Announces
A Golden Opportunity.

THE 25K ACCOUNT.

Take a moment to review your investments. If you aren't currently earning a preferred rate on any amount of $25,000 or more, you should consider investing in Greenwood Federal's 25K Account. With 25K you'll earn our highest money market account rate. A fiercely competitive figure you'll rarely find bested. One that changes with market conditions to keep you head and shoulders above the crowd.

Your 25K Account is easily accessible every seven days. And federal insurance makes it as safe as, well, money in the bank.

The 25K Account. It's designed for those who are already experienced in recognizing golden opportunities. And for those interested in smaller investments, we offer competitive rates on a regular money market account with a minimum balance of $2,500. We invite you to come in to any Greenwood Federal office and seize the opportunity today.

your partner

GREENWOOD FEDERAL

Substantial Penalty for early withdrawal.

EXHIBIT 18   Ad designed to attract more loans

AFFORDABLE LOANS. ACADILLACABLE LOANS. APONTIACABLE LOANS. APOOLABLE LOANS. ANEWPORCHABLE LOANS. AVACATIONABLE LOANS. ACOLLEGEABLE LOANS. ASPEEDBOATABLE LOANS.

Available loans. We've got plenty. Everything from auto loans, boat loans, home improvement loans, lines of credit, and of course, mortgage loans. In fact, we've always been a leader in mortgage lending. And that leadership carries over into all the other loans you need.

Agreeable loans. We're there to make it easier for you. With

convenient terms, a variety of services, quick responses, simple interest, no prepayment penalties and service with a smile.

Affordable loans. Don't worry. We'll make sure your monthly payments are well within your reach.

A whatever-you-wantable loans. You'll find all you need at Greenwood Federal.

GREENWOOD FEDERAL

Experience The Partnership.

Member F.S.L.I.C.

EXHIBIT 19   "For the Good Life" ad proposal

Gifts for the Good Life.

Get a special bonus now with your new Greenwood Federal savings certificate ... you'll still get interest later.

RCA 20" ColorTrak TV w/Remote.

Sony 8mm Camera w/Recorder.

Pearl Grandfather Clock w/Chimes.

Apple Macintosh Personal Computer.

Litton Space Saving Microwave.

Cannon Typewriter.

Fisher Deluxe VCR.

Lawn-Boy Self-Propelled Mower.

CERTIFICATE TERMS AND DEPOSIT LEVELS			
GIFT DESCRIPTION	7 Years	5 Years	3½ Years
Toshiba Gourmet Coffee Maker, OR Pulsar Quartz Watch—Men's/Ladies'	$2,500	$3,500	$5,000
Cannon Typewriter w/Adaptor, OR Litton Space-Saving Microwave	$4,000	$5,000	$8,000
GE 13" Portable Color TV	$5,000	$6,500	$10,000
Zenith 13" Color TV w/Remote, OR Magic Chef Deluxe Microwave w/Turntable	$7,000	$9,500	$15,000
RCA 20" ColorTrak TV w/Remote, OR GE VCR w/Wireless Remote	$9,500	$13,000	$20,000
Lawn-Boy Deluxe Self-Propelled Mower, OR Fisher Deluxe VCR w/MTS Stereo	$11,500	$16,000	$25,000
RCA 26" ColorTrak Console TV w/Remote	$14,500	$20,000	$30,000
Pearl Grandfather Clock w/Westminster Chimes	$19,000	$25,500	$40,000
Fisher Stereo Home Entertainment Center	$23,000	$32,500	$50,000
Sony 27" Console TV w/Stereo	$28,000	$38,000	$60,000
Sony 8mm Handycam Camera/Recorder	$32,500	$45,000	$70,000
Apple Macintosh Personal Computer	$35,000	$50,000	$80,000

Greenwood Federal announces a new, special kind of savings certificate. It pays you part of your interest income now, in the form of a luxury gift. You'll receive one or more of the gifts listed here, for yourself or to give as a gift. And your money will still earn interest compounded annually. For current rates, call 373-SAVE. So if you have money to invest, come to Greenwood Federal where your investment is rewarded handsomely ... and immediately.

Offer limited. Interest rates, qualifying deposit levels, and items of merchandise subject to change without notice. • Items of merchandise represent interest; therefore, the value of the merchandise will be reported as interest earned in the year received. • Allow minimum of 4 weeks for delivery. • This offer not applicable to IRA or KEOGH accounts. • A substantial penalty, which will include the value of merchandise received, may be imposed for early withdrawal of certificate funds.

GREENWOOD FEDERAL

FOR THE GOOD LIFE

"Why don't you get your grandson a TV set?"   "I'm giving him the Apple computer."

EXHIBIT 20 Types of accounts held by GFS customers

Account type	Percent of GFS households	Average number of GFS products per household
Savings only	28%	
Mortgage only	18	
Checking only	7	
Consumer loan only	3	
Total one product type	56	1.4*
Checking and savings	16	
Mortgage and savings	5	
Consumer loan and savings	3	
Consumer loan and checking	2	
Consumer loan and mortgage	2	
Checking and mortgage	0	
Total two product types	28	3.1
Checking, savings, and mortgage	5	
Checking, savings, and consumer loan	3	
Savings, mortgage, and consumer loan	3	
Checking, mortgage, and consumer loan	1	
Total three product types	12	4.6
All four types	4	6.8
	100	2.5
Any savings	67	
Any checking	39	
Any mortgage	38	
Any consumer loan	21	
Any deposit	83	
Any loan	46	

*This number is greater than 1.0 because many households had more than one account (although all were the same type of account).

As shown in Exhibit 20, the majority of GFS customers used only one type of product from among the offerings available, although a number of households had more than one account within the type (two or more savings accounts in the household, for example). Harris thought that there was great opportunity to "cross sell more services to more households." GFS had recently established a small telemarketing operation, and she wondered if this might be used for this purpose. She wondered how to direct mail to customers or prospects, and if advertising might work to increase cross-selling opportunities. To determine what had happened recently with some of the newer products, she pulled out the report in Exhibit 21 which contained information on new loan production and consumer loans outstanding as of July (the latest report available).

Lots of things were popping into Harris's mind. She was concerned about how much attention she should pay to the short run versus the long run. For example, she knew that for GFS to devote strong emphasis to increase its penetration in the small business market would take a long time, given the lack

EXHIBIT 21   Banking group monthly report for July

Consumer loans production:

	Number	*Total dollar amount*
Real estate loans		
Second mortgages	19	$ 358,800.00
Equity line	39	1,145,100.00
Total	58	$1,503,900.00
Installment and single-pay loans		
Payment Shrinker	10	118,763.86
Auto	184	1,239,500.10
Personal, secured and unsecured	291	2,145,839.73
Personal LOC	80	760,100.00
Total	565	4,264,203.69
Total production for July	623	$5,768,103.69

Consumer loans outstanding:	*Total available credit*	*Number*	*Total dollar amount*
Unsecured		1,234	$ 3,280,607.34
Secured other		704	3,718,010.66
Auto		3,106	15,147,248.45
Payment Shrinker		106	1,409,657.19
Subtotal		5,150	23,555,523.64
Equity line	12,493,481.68	1,086	17,383,580.59
Personal LOC	5,348,844.40	760	2,552,124.24
Total		6,996	43,491,228.47

	Number	*Total*
2nd mortgages	795	9,219,720.55
Less participated 2nds	419	−4,956,014.39
Total 2nd mortgages	376	4,263,706.16
Grand total	7,372	$47,754,934.63
Second mortgages maintained on mortgage loan system	726	$12,488,112.80

Credit life insurance—Net income for July: $8,374.52.

Delinquencies:	*Over 30 days*		*Over 60 days*	
Real estate	11		4	
Other	60		27	
Total	71	.8%	31	.3%

Charge-offs in July—$11,382.62.   Recoveries—$198.00.

---

of history in marketing to this segment. Likewise, a strong commitment to home banking using personal computers would be a long-run effort. On the other hand, increasing the emphasis on the Payment Shrinker auto loan, the homeowners line of credit (HOLOC), personal line of credit, or consumer loans would be easy to accomplish in the short run, given that the products had already been developed.

She wondered how much emphasis to put on INVEST, the discount brokerage service. A recent study GFS had conducted showed that 77 percent of the money invested through INVEST came out of other sources and that 23 percent came from GFS accounts. Some of the management at GFS felt that the money pulled out of the accounts would have been invested in stock or bonds anyway, so that at least with INVEST some fees were generated. Also, heavy promotion of INVEST, which had just recently become profitable, could reduce the asset base for the Association while generating some fees, enabling a rise in the reserve ratio. Other GFS managers were more skeptical about this happening.

Harris had seen potential in the segmentation study for high-interest checking products with several of the segments. She also thought that the proposed tax law, which would remove deductions for consumer loans, could have a big impact on her strategic planning. Did it mean, for example, that emphasis should not be put on automobile loans (even the Payment Shrinker) and other consumer loans? Did it mean that homeowner equity loans were the wave of the future? She had seen Internal Revenue Service data indicating that only 38 percent of all taxpayers itemized deductions on their returns. Did this suggest that consumers simply will not care enough about tax savings to establish a home equity credit line when they are ready to buy a car? Homeowner equity lines typically cost $500–$700 in closing cost alone. She had heard rumors that several of the Sunbelt City banks were considering waiving the fees, and wondered how GFS should respond if this in fact happened in the near future. She also had heard rumors that one or more of the banks might lower the rates, currently two percentage points above prime, to prime or even below for several months to attract new accounts with home equity loans.

Finally, Harris thought about the advertising agency. It had been bugging her for some time to give it more direction. Did GFS intend to become a full-service financial institution in the mold of a traditional commercial bank, or did it plan to continue to specialize in the consumer savings and mortgage lending areas? Which niche would be appropriate for GFS to seek relative to other financial institutions? What competitive differences could be used to set GFS apart from the competition? She wondered whether it might just be simpler to become a stock company, which would be the quickest and easiest way to raise the net worth/total assets ratio to 6 percent.

Case 7

AGT, Inc.*

AGT, Inc., is a marketing research company located in the city of Karachi, Pakistan. Jeff Sons Trading Company (JST) has approached it to look at the potential market for an amusement park in Karachi. As the city is very crowded and real estate costs are very high, it will be difficult to find a large enough piece of land to locate such a facility. Even if there is some land available it will be very expensive, and that will have a detrimental effect on the overall costs of the project. JST wants to know the potential of this type of investment. They want the market research to identify if a need for the amusement park exists, and, if so, what is the public's attitude toward that type of recreational facility. If a need is found and support is sufficient, then they want to know what type of amusement park is required by the potential customers. JST will make its investment decision based on the results of this study.

Background

Pakistan is a country which qualifies as a Less Developed Country (LDC). It is a typical developing country of the Third World faced with the usual problems of rapidly increasing population, sizable government deficit, and heavy dependence on foreign aid. The economy of Pakistan has grown rapidly in the last decade, with GDP expanding at 6.7 percent annually, more than twice the population growth. Like any other LDC, it has dualism in its economic system. For example, the cities have all the facilities of modern times, whereas the smaller towns have some or none. Such is also true for income distribution patterns. Real per capita GDP is Rupees 10,000, or $400 annually. There is a small wealthy class (1 to 3 percent) and a middle class consisting of another 20 percent, while the remainder of the population is poor. Half of the population lives below the poverty line. Most of the middle class is an urban working class. Only 24 percent of the population is literate.

---

*This case was written by Professor William J. Carner, University of Texas, Austin. Copyright 1993 by William J. Carner, Ph.D. All rights reserved. Used with permission.

Karachi, the largest city with a very dense population of over 6 million, has been chosen for the first large-scale amusement park in Pakistan. The recreational facilities in Karachi are very small, including a poorly maintained zoo, and people with families avoid visiting most facilities due to the crowds. There are other small parks but not enough to cater to such a large population. The main place people go for recreation is the beach. The beaches are not well developed and are regularly polluted by oil slicks from the nearby port. There seems to be a growing need for recreational activity for people to spend their leisure time. It is also true that many of the people in the higher social classes take vacations with their families and spend money on recreational activities abroad. To see that there is a true need for this type of recreational facility, we propose to conduct a marketing research study of its feasibility. Other potential problems facing the project include:

- Communication system is very poor.
- Only a small percentage of the people own their own transportation.
- Public and private systems of transportation are not efficient.
- Law and order is a problem, described as similar to Los Angeles.

Research Objectives

In order to make an investment decision, JST outlined its research objectives necessary to design a marketing strategy that would accomplish the desired return-on-investment goals. These objectives are as follows:

1. Identify the potential demand for this project.
2. Identify the primary target market and what they expect in an amusement area.

Information Needs

To fulfill our objectives, we will need the following information:

1. Market:
   a. Is there a need for this project in this market?
   b. How large is the potential market?
   c. Is this market sufficient to be profitable?
2. Consumer:
   a. Are the potential customers satisfied with the existing facilities in the city?
   b. Will these potential consumers utilize an amusement park?
   c. Which segment of population is most interested in this type of facility?
   d. Is the population ready to support this type of project?
   e. What media could be used to get the message across successfully to the potential customers?
3. Location:
   a. Where should this project be built to attract the most visitors?

    b. How will the consumer's existing attitudes on location influence the viability and cost of this project?

    c. Will the company have to arrange for the transportation to and from the facility if location is outside the city area?

    d. Is security a factor in location of the facility?

4. Recreation Facilities:

    a. What type of attractions should the company provide at the park to attract customers?

    b. Should there be some overnight facility within the park?

    c. Should the facility be available only to certain segments of the population or be open to all?

Proposal

With the objectives outlined above in mind, AGT, Inc., presented the following proposal:

The city of Karachi's population has its different economic clusters scattered haphazardly throughout the city. To conduct the marketing research in this type of city and get accurate results will be very difficult. We recommend an extensive study to make sure we have an adequate sampling of the opinion of the target market. Given the parameters above, we recommend that the target market be defined as follows:

Desired Respondent Characteristics

The desired respondent characteristics are:

- Upper class 1 percent (around 60,000).
- Middle class 15 to 20 percent (around 900,000 to 1,200,000).
- Male and female.
- Age: 15 to 50 years (for survey; market includes all age groups).
- Income level: Rs 25,000 and above per year (Rs: 2000 per month).
- Household size—with family will be better for sample.
- Involved in entertainment activities.
- Involved in recreational activities.
- Actively participates in social activities.
- Members of different clubs.
- Involved in outdoor activities.

To obtain accurate information regarding respondent's characteristics, we have to approach the market very carefully because of the prevailing circumstances and existing cultural practices (the country is 97 percent Muslim). People have little or no knowledge of market surveys. Getting their cooperation, even without the cultural barriers, through a phone or mail survey will be very difficult. In the following paragraphs, we will be discussing negative and positive points of all types of surveys and select the appropriate form for our study.

The first, and possibly best, method to conduct the survey under these circumstances will be through the mail, which will not only be cheaper but can also cover all the clusters of population easily. We cannot rely totally on a mail survey, as the mail system in Pakistan is unreliable and inefficient. We can go through courier services or registered mail, but it will skyrocket the cost. It will not be wise to conduct a mail survey alone.

The other option is to conduct the survey through telephone. In the city of 6 million there are around 200,000 working telephones (1 per 152 people). Most of the telephones are in businesses or in government offices. It is not that the people cannot afford a telephone, but that they cannot get one because of short supply. Another problem with a telephone survey is cultural; it is not considered polite to call someone and start asking questions. It is even more of a problem if a male survey team member were to reach a female household member. People are not familiar with marketing surveys and would not be willing to volunteer the information we require on the telephone. The positive point in a telephone survey is that most of the upperclass women do not work and can be reached easily. However, we must use a female survey staff. Overall, the chances of cooperation through a telephone survey are very low.

A mall/bazaar intercept could also be used. Again, however, we will face some cultural problems. It's not considered ethical for a male to approach a female in the mall. The only people willing to talk in public are likely to be the males and we will miss female opinion.

To gather respondent data by survey in a country such as Pakistan, we will have to tailor our existing data collecting methods and make them fit accordingly to the circumstances and cultural practices of the marketplace. As a company based in Pakistan with the experience of living under these cultural practices, we propose the following design for the study and questionnaire.

Design of the Study

Our study's design will be such that it will have a mixture of three different types of surveys. Each survey will focus on a different method. The following are the types of surveys we recommend, tailored to fit in the prevailing circumstances:

1. Mail survey. We plan to modify this type of survey to fit into existing circumstances and to be more efficient. The changes made are to counter the inefficient postal system and to generate a better percentage of response. We plan to deliver the surveys to the respondent through the newspapermen. We know that average circulations of the various newspapers are 50,000 to 200,000 per day. The two dailies chosen have the largest circulations in the city.

A questionnaire will be placed in each newspaper and delivered to the respondent. This will assure that the questionnaire has reached its destination.

This questionnaire will introduce us to the respondent and ask for his cooperation. The questionnaire will have return postage and the firm's address. This will give the respondents some confidence that they are not volunteering information to someone unknown. A small promotional gift will be promised on returning the completed survey. Since respondents who will claim the gift will give us their address, this will help us maintain a list of respondents for future surveys. Delivery through newspapermen will also allow us to easily focus on specific clusters.

We accept some loss in return mail because there is no acceptable way to get the questionnaires back except through the government postal system. We plan to deliver 5,000 questionnaires to the respondents to counter the loss in return mail. The cost of this survey will be less than it would be if we mailed the questionnaires. As this will be the first exposure for many respondents which allows them to give their views about a nonexisting product, we do not have any return percentage on which to base our survey response expectations. In fact, this may well be the base for future studies.

2. Door-to-door interviews. We will have to tailor the mall/bazaar intercept, as we did in mail survey, to get the highest possible response percentage. Instead of intercepting at malls, it will be better to send surveyors from door to door. This can generate a better percentage of responses and we can be sure who the respondent is. To conduct this survey, we will solicit the cooperation of the local business schools. By using these young students, we stand a better chance of generating a higher response. Also, we plan to hire some additional personnel, mostly females, and train them to conduct this survey.

3. Additional mail survey. We are planning to conduct this part of the survey to identify different groups of people already involved in similar types of activity. There are 8 to 10 exclusive clubs in the city of Karachi. A few of them focus solely on some outdoor activity such as yachting and boating, golf, etc. Their membership numbers vary from three to five thousand. High membership cost and monthly fees have made these clubs restricted to the upper middle class and the wealthy. We can safely say that the people using these clubs belong to the 90th percentile of income level. We propose to visit these clubs and personally ask for the members' cooperation. We also plan to get the member lists and have the questionnaire delivered to them. They will be asked to return the completed questionnaire to the club office or to mail it in the postage-paid reply envelope. We believe that this group will cooperate and give us a quality feedback.

The second delivered survey will be to local schools. With the schools' cooperation, we will ask that this questionnaire be delivered by their pupils to the parents. The cover letter will request that the parents fill out the questionnaire and return it to school. This will provide a good sample of people who want outdoor activities for their children. We hope to generate a substantial response through this method.

Questionnaire Design

The type of questions asked should help our client make the decision of whether to invest in the project. Through the survey questionnaires we should answer the question, "Is the population ready for this project and are they willing to support it?" The questionnaire (see the Appendix) will be a mixture of both open-ended and close-ended questions. It will answer the following questions:

- Is there a market for this type of project?
- Is the market substantial?
- Is the market profitable?
- Will this project fill a real need?
- Will this project be only a momentary fad?
- Is the market evenly distributed in all segments/clusters or is there a high demand in some segments?
- Is the population geared towards and willing to spend money on this type of entertainment facility? If so, how much?
- What is the best location for this project?
- Are people willing to travel some distance to reach this type of facility? Or do they want it within city limits?
- What types of entertainment/rides do people want to see in this amusement park?
- Through what type of media or promotion can the prospective customers best be reached?

Discussion Questions

1. Does the survey satisfy the objectives of the research project?
2. How do the elements of culture affect the research design, collection of data, and analysis? Contrast this with the design, collection of data, and analysis of a similar survey project in the United States, Japan, or Western Europe.
3. What alternative data collection methods, such as personal interviews at current recreational areas, might be acceptable?

Appendix   Questionnaire

Please check the appropriate box. Thank you.

1. Are there adequate recreational facilities in the city?

   Yes ☐   No ☐

2. How satisfied are you with the present recreational facilities? (Please rate at 0 to 10 degrees.)

   0—1—2—3—4—5—6—7—8—9—10
   Poor   Excellent

3. How often do you visit the present recreational facilities? (Please check)

Weekly ☐
Fortnightly ☐
Monthly ☐
Once in two months ☐
Yearly ☐
More (indicate number) ☐
Not at all ☐

4. Do you visit recreational areas with your family?

Yes ☐   No ☐
If No, *why?*
Security ☐
Distance ☐
Expense ☐
Crowd (not family type) ☐
Poor service ☐
Other (please specify) _____
_____

4a. Do you stay overnight?

Yes ☐   No ☐

If yes, how long? _____
(Please indicate number of days.)

4b. If No, would you have stayed if provided the right circumstances or facilities?

Yes ☐   No ☐

5. Have you ever visited an amusement park?
(Here in Pakistan ☐   Abroad ☐)

Yes ☐   (Please, go to question 5b)
No ☐   (Please, go to question 5a)

5a. If No, *why?*

Security ☐
Distance ☐
Expense ☐
Crowd (not family type) ☐
Poor service ☐
Other (please specify) _____
_____

5b. If Yes, when did you last visit an amusement park?

Last month ☐
Last six months ☐
Within a year ☐
More (specify number) ☐
Where? _____

6. What did you enjoy the most in that park?

Roller coasters ☐
Water slides ☐
Children's play areas ☐
Shows ☐
Games ☐
Simulators ☐
Other _____

6a. How much did you spend in that park? (approximately)

Rs. 50 or Less ☐
51 to 100 ☐
101 to 150 ☐
151 to 200 ☐
More than 200 ☐
Where? _____

6b. How would you rate the value received? (Please rate at 0 - 10 degrees).

0—1—2—3—4—5—6—7—8—9—10
Poor   Excellent

7. Would you utilize an amusement park if one was built locally?

Yes ☐   No ☐

8. What would you like to see in an amusement park?
(Please give us your six best choices)

a. _____   d. _____
b. _____   e. _____
c. _____   f. _____

(continued)

9. Where would you like its location to be?

Within city area ☐
Beach area ☐
Suburbs ☐
Outskirts of city ☐
Indifferent ☐

10. How many kilometers will you be willing to travel to the park?

Under 10 kms ☐
11 to 20 ☐
21 to 35 ☐
35 to 55 ☐
55 to 65 ☐
More than 65 ☐

11. How often do you take vacations for recreation purpose?

None ☐
Once a year ☐
Twice a year ☐
More (please specify) _____

Please tell us about yourself:

12. Please indicate your age.

Under 15 years ☐
16 to 21 ☐
22 to 29 ☐
30 to 49 ☐
50 to 60 ☐
Over 60 ☐

13. Please indicate your gender.

Male ☐   Female ☐

14. Are you married?

Yes ☐   No ☐

15. How many children do you have?

Please indicate number _____

16. Please indicate your total family income (yearly).

Under Rs. 12,000 ☐
Over 12,000 to 15,000 ☐
Over 15,000 to 20,000 ☐
Over 20,000 to 25,000 ☐
Over 25,000 to 40,000 ☐
Over 40,000 to 60,000 ☐
Over 60,000 to 80,000 ☐
Over 80,000 ☐

17. Do you own a transport?

Yes ☐   No ☐

18. Any other comments?
(If you need more space, please attach additional sheet)

_____
_____
_____
_____
_____
_____
_____

Thank you, we appreciate your time.

Important:

If you *want* us to contact you again in later stages of this project or will be interested in its results, give us your name and address. We will be glad to keep you informed. Thank you.

_____
_____
_____
_____

Case 8

Modern Plastics (A)*

Institutional sales manager Jim Clayton had spent most of Monday morning planning for the rest of the month. It was early July and Jim knew that an extremely busy time was coming with the preparation of the following year's sales plan.

Since starting his current job less than a month ago, Jim had been involved in learning the requirements of the job and making his initial territory visits. Now that he was getting settled, Jim was trying to plan his activities according to priorities. The need for planning had been instilled in him during his college days. As a result of his three years' field sales experience and development of time management skills, he felt prepared for the challenge of the sales manager's job.

While sitting at his desk, Jim recalled a conversation that he had a week ago with Bill Hanson, the former manager, who had been promoted to another division. Bill told him that the sales forecast (annual and monthly) for plastic trash bags in the Southeast region would be due soon as an initial step toward developing the sales plan for the next year. Bill had laughed as he told Jim, "Boy, you ought to have a ball doing the forecast, being a rookie sales manager!"

When Jim had asked what Bill meant, he explained by saying that the forecast was often "winged" because the headquarters in New York already knew what they wanted and would change the forecast to meet their figures, particularly if the forecast was for an increase of less than 10 percent. The experienced sales manager could throw numbers together in a short time that would pass as a serious forecast and ultimately be adjusted to fit the plans of headquarters. However, an inexperienced manager would have a difficult time "winging" a credible forecast.

Bill had also told Jim that the other alternative meant gathering mountains of data and putting together a forecast that could be sold to the various levels of Modern Plastics management. This alternative would prove to be time-consuming and could still be changed anywhere along the chain of command before final approval.

*This case was written by Kenneth L. Bernhardt, Professor Tom Ingram, University of Memphis, and Professor Danny N. Bellenger, Georgia State University. Copyright © 1996 by the authors.

Clayton started reviewing pricing and sales volume history (see Exhibit 1). He also looked at the key account performance for the past two and a half years (see Exhibit 2). During the past month Clayton had visited many of the key accounts, and on the average they had indicated that their purchases from Modern would probably increase about 15–20 percent in the coming year.

EXHIBIT 1   Plastic trashbags—sales and pricing history, 1993–1995

	Pricing dollars per case			Sales volume in cases			Sales volume in dollars		
	1993	1994	1995	1993	1994	1995	1993	1994	1995
January	$6.88	$7.70	$15.40	33,000	46,500	36,500	$227,000	$358,000	$562,000
February	6.82	7.70	14.30	32,500	52,500	23,000	221,500	404,000	329,000
March	6.90	8.39	13.48	32,000	42,000	22,000	221,000	353,000	296,500
April	6.88	10.18	12.24	45,500	42,500	46,500	313,000	432,500	569,000
May	6.85	12.38	11.58	49,000	41,500	45,500	335,500	514,000	527,000
June	6.85	12.65	10.31	47,500	47,000	42,000	325,500	594,500	433,000
July	7.42	13.48	9.90*	40,000	43,500	47,500*	297,000	586,500	470,000*
August	6.90	13.48	10.18*	48,500	63,500	43,500*	334,500	856,000	443,000*
September	7.70	14.30	10.31*	43,000	49,000	47,500*	331,000	700,500	489,500*
October	7.56	15.12	10.31*	52,500	50,000	51,000*	397,000	756,000	526,000*
November	7.15	15.68	10.72*	62,000	61,500	47,500*	443,500	964,500	509,000*
December	7.42	15.43	10.59*	49,000	29,000	51,000*	363,500	447,500	540,000*
Total	$7.13	$12.25	$11.30*	534,500	568,500	503,500*	$3,810,000	$6,967,000	$5,694,000*

*July–December 1995 figures are forecast of sales manager J. A. Clayton, and other data comes from historical sales information.

EXHIBIT 2   1995 key account sales history (in cases)

				Monthly average			
Customer	1993	1994	First six months 1995	1993	1994	First half 1995	First quarter 1995
Transco Paper Company	125,774	134,217	44,970	10,481	11,185	7,495	5,823
Callaway Paper	44,509	46,049	12,114	3,709	3,837	2,019	472
Florida Janitorial Supply	34,746	36,609	20,076	2,896	3,051	3,346	2,359
Jefferson	30,698	34,692	25,044	2,558	2,891	4,174	1,919
Cobb Paper	13,259	23,343	6,414	1,105	1,945	1,069	611
Miami Paper	10,779	22,287	10,938	900	1,857	1,823	745
Milne Surgical Company	23,399	21,930	—	1,950	1,828	—	—
Graham	8,792	15,331	1,691	733	1,278	281	267
Crawford Paper	7,776	14,132	6,102	648	1,178	1,017	1,322
John Steele	8,634	13,277	6,663	720	1,106	1,110	1,517
Henderson Paper	9,185	8,850	2,574	765	738	429	275
Durant Surgical	—	7,766	4,356	—	647	726	953
Master Paper	4,221	5,634	600	352	470	100	—
D.T.A.	—	—	2,895	—	—	482	—
Crane Paper	4,520	5,524	3,400	377	460	566	565
Janitorial Service	3,292	5,361	2,722	274	447	453	117
Georgia Paper	5,466	5,053	2,917	456	421	486	297
Paper Supplies, Inc.	5,117	5,119	1,509	426	427	251	97
Southern Supply	1,649	3,932	531	137	328	88	78
Horizon Hospital Supply	4,181	4,101	618	348	342	103	206
Total cases	346,007	413,217	156,134	28,835	34,436	26,018	17,623

Schedule for Preparing the Forecast

Jim had received a memo recently from Robert Baxter, the regional marketing manager, detailing the plans for completing the 1996 forecast. The key dates in the memo began in only three weeks:

August 1	Presentation of forecast to regional marketing manager.
August 10	Joint presentation with marketing manager to regional general manager.
September 1	Regional general manager presents forecast to division vice president.
September 1–September 30	Review of forecast by staff of division vice president.
October 1	Review forecast with corporate staff.
October 1–October 15	Revision as necessary.
October 15	Final forecast forwarded to division vice president from regional general manager.

Company Background

The plastics division of Modern Chemical Company was founded in 1975 when Modern Chemical purchased Cordco, a small plastics manufacturer with national sales of $15 million. At that time, the key products of the plastics division were sandwich bags, plastic tablecloths, trash cans, and plastic-coated clothesline.

Since 1975, the plastics division has grown to a sales level exceeding $200 million with five regional profit centers covering the United States. Each regional center has manufacturing facilities and a regional sales force. There are four product groups in each region:

1. Food packaging: Styrofoam meat and produce trays; plastic bags for various food products.
2. Egg cartons: Styrofoam egg cartons sold to egg packers and supermarket chains.
3. Institutional: Plastic trash bags and disposable tableware (plates, bowls, etc.).
4. Industrial: Plastic packaging for the laundry and dry cleaning market; plastic film for use in pallet overwrap systems.

Each product group is supervised jointly by a product manager and a district sales manager, both of whom report to the regional marketing manager. The sales representatives report directly to the district sales manager, but also work closely with the product manager on matters concerning pricing and product specifications.

The five regional general managers report to J. R. Hughes, vice president of the plastics division. Hughes is located in New York. Although Modern Chemical is owned by a multinational oil company, the plastics division has been able to operate in a virtually independent manner since its establishment in 1975. The reasons for this include:

1. Limited knowledge of the plastics industry on the part of the oil company management.
2. Excellent growth by the plastics division, which has been possible without management supervision from the oil company.
3. Profitability of the plastics division, which has consistently been higher than that of other divisions of the chemical company.

The Institutional Trash Bag Market

The institutional trash bag is a polyethylene bag used to collect and transfer refuse to its final disposition point. There are different sizes and colors available to fit the various uses of the bag. For example, a small bag for desk wastebaskets is available, as well as a heavier bag for large containers such as a 55-gallon drum. There are 25 sizes in the Modern line, with 13 of those sizes being available in three colors—white, buff, and clear. Customers typically buy several different items on an order to cover all their needs.

The institutional trash bag is a separate product from the consumer-grade trash bag, which is typically sold to homeowners through retail outlets. The institutional trash bag is sold primarily through paper wholesalers, hospital supply companies, and janitorial supply companies to a variety of end users. Since trash bags are used on such a wide scale, the list of end users could include almost any business or institution. The segments include hospitals, hotels, schools, office buildings, transportation facilities, and restaurants.

Based on historical data and a current survey of key wholesalers and end users in the Southeast, the annual market for institutional trash bags in the region was estimated to be 55 million pounds. Translated into cases, the market potential was close to 2 million cases. During the past five years, the market for trash bags has grown at an average rate of 8.9 percent per year. Now a mature product, future market growth is expected to parallel overall growth in the economy. The 1996 real growth in GNP is forecast to be 4.5 percent.

General Market Conditions

The current market is characterized by a distressing trend. The market is in a position of oversupply with approximately 20 manufacturers competing for the business in the Southeast. Prices have been on the decline for several months but are expected to level out during the last six months of the year.

This problem arose after a record year in 1994 for Modern Plastics. During 1994, supply was very tight due to raw materials shortages. Unlike many of its competitors, Modern had only minor problems securing adequate raw materials supplies. As a result, the competitors were few in 1994, and all who remained in business were prosperous. By early 1995, raw materials were plentiful, and prices began to drop as new competitors tried to buy their way into the market. During the first quarter of 1991, Modern Plastics learned the hard way that a competitive price was a necessity in the current market. Volume fell off drastically in February and March as customers shifted orders to new suppliers when Modern chose to maintain a slightly higher-than-market price on trash bags.

With the market becoming extremely price competitive and profits declining, the overall quality has dropped to a point of minimum standard. Most suppliers now make a bag "barely good enough to get the job done." This quality level is acceptable to most buyers who do not demand high quality for this type of product.

Modern Plastics versus Competition

A recent study of Modern versus its competition had been conducted by an outside consultant to see how well Modern measured up in several key areas. Each area was weighted according to its importance in the purchase decision, and Modern was compared to its key competitors in each area and on an overall basis. The key factors and their weights are shown below:

	Weight
1. Pricing	.50
2. Quality	.15
3. Breadth of line	.10
4. Sales coverage	.10
5. Packaging	.05
6. Service	.10
Total	1.00

As shown in Exhibit 3, Modern compared favorably with its key competitors on an overall basis. None of the other suppliers were as strong as Modern in breadth of line, nor did any competitor offer as good sales coverage as that provided by Modern. Clayton knew that sales coverage would be even better next year since the Florida and North Carolina territories had grown enough to add two salespeople to the institutional group by January 1, 1996.

Pricing, quality, and packaging seemed to be neither an advantage nor a disadvantage. However, service was a problem area. The main cause for this, Clayton was told, was temporary out-of-stock situations which occurred occasionally, primarily due to the wide variety of trash bags offered by Modern.

During the past two years, Modern Plastics had maintained its market share at approximately 27 percent of the market. Some new competitors had entered the market since 1993 while others had left the market (see Exhibit 4). The previous district sales manager, Bill Hanson, had left Clayton some comments regarding the major competitors. These are reproduced in Exhibit 5.

EXHIBIT 3   Competitive factors ratings (by competitor*)

Weight	Factor	Modern	National Film	Bonanza	South- eastern	PBI	BAGCO	South- west Bag	Sun Plastics	East Coast Bag Co.
.50	Price	2	3	2	2	2	2	2	2	3
.15	Quality	3	2	3	4	3	2	3	3	4
.10	Breadth	1	2	2	3	3	3	3	3	3
.10	Sales coverage	1	3	3	3	4	3	3	4	3
.05	Packaging	3	3	2	3	3	1	3	3	3
.10	Service	4	3	3	2	2	2	3	4	3

Overall weighted ranking[†]

1. BAGCO	2.15		6. Southeastern	2.55
2. Modern	2.20		7. Florida Plastics	2.60
3. Bonanza	2.25		8. National Film	2.65
4. Southwest Bag (Tie)	2.50		9. East Coast Bag Co.	3.15
5. PBI (Tie)	2.50			

*Ratings on a 1-to-5 scale, with 1 being the best rating and 5 the worst.
[†]The weighted ranking is the sum of each rank times its weight. The lower the number, the better the overall rating.

EXHIBIT 4   Market share by supplier, 1993 and 1995

Supplier	Percent of market 1993	Percent of market 1995
National Film	11	12
Bertram	16	0*
Bonanza	11	12
Southeastern	5	6
Bay	9	0*
Johnson Graham	8	0*
PBI	2	5
Lewis	2	0*
BAGCO	—	6
Southwest Bag	—	2
Florida Plastics	—	4
East Coast Bag Co.	—	4
Miscellaneous and unknown	8	22
Modern	28	27
	100	100

*Out of business in 1995.
Source: This information was developed from a field survey conducted by Modern Plastics.

Developing the Sales Forecast

After a careful study of trade journals, government statistics, and surveys conducted by Modern marketing research personnel, projections for growth potential were formulated by segment and are shown in Exhibit 6. This data was compiled by Bill Hanson just before he had been promoted.

Jim looked back at Baxter's memo giving the time schedule for the forecast and knew he had to get started. As he left the office at 7:15, he wrote himself a large note and pinned it on his wall—"Get Started on the Sales Forecast!"

EXHIBIT 5   Characteristics of competitors

National Film	Broadest product line in the industry. Quality a definite advantage. Good service. Sales coverage adequate, but not an advantage. Not as aggressive as most suppliers on price. Strong competitor.
Bonanza	Well-established tough competitor. Very aggressive on pricing. Good packaging, quality okay.
Southeastern	Extremely price competitive in southern Florida. Dominates Miami market. Limited product line. Not a threat outside of Florida.
PBI	Extremely aggressive on price. Have made inroads into Transco Paper Company. Good service but poor sales coverage.
BAGCO	New competitor. Very impressive with a high-quality product, excellent service, and strong sales coverage. A real threat, particularly in Florida.
Southwest Bag	A factor in Louisiana and Mississippi. Their strategy is simple—an acceptable product at a rock bottom price.
Sun Plastics	Active when market is at a profitable level with price cutting. When market declines to a low profit range, Sun manufactures other types of plastic packaging and stays out of the trash bag market. Poor reputation as a reliable supplier, but can still "spot-sell" at low prices.
East Coast Bag Co.	Most of their business is from a state bid which began in 1993 for a two-year period. Not much of a threat to Modern's business in the Southeast as most of their volume is north of Washington, D.C.

EXHIBIT 6   1996 real growth projections by segment

Total industry	+5.0%
Commercial	+5.4%
Restaurant	+6.8%
Hotel/motel	+2.0%
Transportation	+1.9%
Office users	+5.0%
Other	+4.2%
Noncommercial	+4.1%
Hospitals	+3.9%
Nursing homes	+4.8%
Colleges/universities	+2.4%
Schools	+7.8%
Employee feeding	+4.3%
Other	+3.9%

Source: Developed from several trade journals.

Part 4

Product and Brand Management Decisions

The six cases concerned with product strategy decisions in this section involve a number of different kinds of decisions. Many marketers believe that product decisions are the most critical of the marketing mix variables because of their importance to consumers in their decision-making process, and because product decisions, once made, are not quickly or easily reversed or changed. Promotion and pricing changes, for example, can be made much more quickly and with greater ease. Furthermore, most product changes usually require changes in the rest of the marketing strategy—changes in promotion, pricing, and sometimes distribution.

Before examining the various issues in the product strategy area, the concept of what a product is should first be understood. A product is "anything that can be offered to a market for attention, acquisition, or consumption; it includes physical objects, services, personalities, places, organizations, and ideas."[1] A product is thus much more than its physical properties and is everything a consumer buys when he or she makes a purchase. It is a set of want-satisfying attributes. It is important to understand this definition because what the consumer is buying is not necessarily what the company thought it was marketing. So marketers must be aware of consumer attitudes, values, needs, and wants with respect to their products.

The major decisions related to product strategy are:

1. What new products should be developed?
2. What changes are needed in current products?
3. What products should be added or dropped?
4. What positioning should the product occupy?
5. What should the branding strategy be?

---

[1]Philip Kotler, *Marketing Management: Analysis, Planning and Control,* 3rd ed. (Englewood Cliffs, N.J.: Prentice Hall, 1976), p. 183.

A brief discussion of some of the concepts related to each of these decisions follows.

New Product Development

The sales and profits of a product category tend to change over time. The pattern a product category typically follows is called the product life cycle. It is defined to have the introductory, growth, maturity, and decline stages. Because most products reach the maturity and decline stages eventually, a marketer must continually seek out new products which can go through the introductory and growth stages in order to maintain and increase the total profits of the firm. But what new products should be introduced?

To answer this question, a marketer must consider the objectives of the firm, the resources available, the target markets the firm is trying to satisfy, and how the new product would fit in with other products offered by the company and the competition.

To successfully develop new products, the organization will have to set up formalized strategies for generating new product ideas, means for screening these ideas, product and market testing procedures, and, finally, commercialization. The objective is to obtain products which are differentiated from those of its competitors and which meet the needs of a large enough segment of the market to be profitable.

Changes in Current Products

The needs, wants, attitudes, and behavior of consumers change over time, and a company must change its products also or risk losing these consumers to a competitor who more quickly responds to these changes in the marketplace.

Should new features be added to the product? Should the warranty be extended? Should the packaging be changed? Should new services be offered? The marketer must continually monitor its target market and the competition to be able to answer such questions.

What Products Should Be Added or Dropped

A marketer must make decisions concerning the product mix or composite of products the firm will offer for sale. This requires decisions concerning the width and depth of products. Width refers to the number of product lines marketed by the firm. For example, General Electric has many lines while Kellogg's has concentrated on breakfast foods. The depth of the product mix is the number of items offered for sale within each product line. Kellogg's, for example, would have a very deep product line with many different alternatives offered for sale.

Whether a product line should be extended or reduced depends on a number of factors, including financial criteria, market factors, production considerations, and organizational factors. The marketer, in making these decisions, must examine the potential profit contributions, return on investment, impact on market share, fit with consumers' needs, fit with the needs of the channels of distribution, and the expected reactions of competitors. The production and organizational considerations include impact on capacity for other products, and on the goals and objectives of the firm, both in the short and long run.

Product Positioning

Product positioning is defined as that idea that is put into the consumers' minds by telling them how our product differs from its competitors. The position we strive to occupy will depend on the different market segments available, the attributes of our product compared to the needs of each segment, and the positions occupied by our competitors against each market segment.

Branding Strategy

The basic decisions here are whether or not to put brand names on the organization's products, whether the brands should be manufacturers' or distributors' brands, and whether individual or family brands should be used.

These decisions depend on the company's resources, objectives, the competition, and consumer choice behavior. For example, a small firm with few resources and much competition in a product category where consumers perceived small differences in the brands available would probably choose to market its product using private distributors' brands. Family brands such as General Electric and Campbell's are used when the marketer wants the consumer to generalize to the new products all those attributes he associates with the family brand name. The time and money required to establish the brand's name is much lower with this strategy, but it does not allow the marketer to establish a separate image for the new product.

Case 9 _____

Machine Vision International®*

Our industry is very much like a newly found gold mine. Each vein in the mine is a different market opportunity. We're entering the main mine shaft, digging first in the directions our research shows will contain the largest ore deposits, those in the automotive and electronics industries. We'll use the knowledge we gain in those shafts of the mine to tunnel to other veins, finding gold deposits in other markets. This is our approach.

> Richard P. Eidswick
> *Chairman and CEO, MVI*

As 1985 came to a close, Machine Vision International (MVI) was completing its third year of operations. Only two years earlier, MVI had had only 37 employees. By the end of 1985, MVI had expanded greatly. The company now had three sales divisions and was selling products for very diverse applications in many varied industries. However, the financial results for 1985 showed that MVI was not yet making a profit. The question being asked was whether MVI had expanded into too many markets too quickly for a company in a fast-growing, quickly changing industry.

The Machine Vision Industry—A Definition

A machine vision product is a high-technology, computer-based image processing system enabling a machine or other device to "see." The use of this technology permits automation of industrial tasks involving the interpretation of the work scene or the controlling of work activity.

_____

*This case was prepared by Constance M. Kinnear, Research Associate, with the assistance of Thomas C. Kinnear, Professor of Marketing, both at the Graduate School of Business Administration, The University of Michigan. Copyright © 1986 by the authors. This abridged version was prepared, with permission of the authors, by Adrian B. Ryans and Terry Deutscher, faculty at Western Business School, University of Western Ontario.

Machine vision may be understood by way of analogy to human vision. A human eye captures an image, which is then transmitted to the brain via the optic nerve. The brain processes those parts of the image most important to the situation; it ignores parts of the image which are irrelevant. The brain then tells other parts of the body what actions to take. In machine vision, the camera (eye) captures an image and transmits it to the controller (brain) via a coaxial cable (optic nerve). The controller sorts relevant from irrelevant data and instructs the machine tool, conveyor, or robot what action to take.

MVI's Prospectus
September 18, 1985

There were many potential application areas for machine vision in the industrial workplace. Data received by a computer from television cameras viewing an assembly area could be almost instantaneously analyzed so that task performance guidance commands could be sent to a robot. Vision systems could be used in quality control processes to check work in process against required product parameters, which were stored in the system's computer. A vision system could, therefore, check during production for the proper dimensions and shape of the product, for the presence of all features or parts, and for its general condition including surface flaws. Deviations from acceptable parameters could be brought to the attention of supervisory staff before they caused a substandard product to be produced. Because vision systems could recognize different shapes or identifying markings, production parts could be sorted, facilitating the movement, processing, or assembly of parts. The goals in the use of vision systems were to increase product quality, increase product rates and industrial efficiency, and provide labour savings.

The Market for Machine Vision Products

The machine vision industry did not exist in 1980. In 1981, total industry sales were $7 million. Between 1981 and 1984, sales more than doubled each year, so that by 1984 industry sales totalled $80 million. A compound average growth rate of 60 percent per year had been estimated for the industry as a whole for the period from 1984 to 1990. Estimated sales for 1985 were $125 million. For 1990, the total market was estimated to reach between $750 and $800 million.

Despite all the optimistic estimates for growth in the market, not one competitor in machine vision had consistently made a profit by 1985. Between 70 and 100 competitors were vying for the industry's total sales of $125 million in that year, in literally thousands of different applications. The bulk of this revenue was shared among 20 companies. The major competitors in the industry and their sales for the period 1983–85 are shown in Exhibit 1. In 1984, none of these competitors made a profit in this industry.

Analysts of the machine vision industry were hard pressed to pick which companies would survive the early growth years. For one thing, the technologies in the industry were not yet perfected. There were many technologies applicable to vision applications, and these technologies were still very much in

EXHIBIT 1   Competitive sales figures (millions)—1983–85

Company	1983 Sales	1984 Sales	Expected 1985 sales	Type of financing
Applied Intelligent Systems, Inc. (1976)	$0.4	$1.4	$5.0	Private
Automatix	6.3	17.3	27.0	Public
Cognex Corp.	2.0	5.0	6.0	Private
Diffracto Ltd. (1973)	3.7	5.1	7.3	Private
International Robomation/Intelligence	1.0	2.3	8.0	Public
Itran Corp. (1982)	0.2	1.1	2.2	Private
Machine Vision International	0.5	4.0	10.0	Public
Perceptron, Inc. (1981)	1.0	5.5	15.0	Private
Robotic Vision Systems, Inc. (1977)	1.0	5.1	10.0	Public
View Engineering (1976)	7.5	15.0	19.0	Private
All others	11.4	18.2	15.5	
Total market	$35.0	$80.0	$125.0	

the developmental stage. Possible applications of machine vision could be found in almost any industrial setting where part inspection, part identification, or automated assembly processes were used. These usually came from large-volume sales or repeatably manufacturable products. The market was often uneducated or unrealistic about the true capabilities of machine vision. Competitors were finding it very difficult to determine all the variables that had to be satisfied and solved to make the products work in an actual, operating industrial environment.

One development with great potential impact on the machine vision industry was the involvement of General Motors. GM became very interested in production automation. This interest was spurred by the results of several automobile industry studies, which found that the Japanese had a sizable cost advantage, ranging between $1,500 and $1,800 per car, over U.S. producers in 1985. Also, it was estimated that it took approximately three times as many labour-hours for U.S. automobile manufacturers to produce a car than it did their Japanese competitors. Studies predicted that U.S. car manufacturers would have to reduce their costs by about 25 percent between 1985 and 1990 to remain competitive in the industry. Of possible automation alternatives, it was determined that the use of robotics and machine vision was key strategy to solve the problem. Forty-four thousand machine vision applications were identified within GM alone by GM analysts.

Taking action on these findings, GM entered into a joint venture with Fanuc Ltd. of Japan, forming GMF, a highly respected robotics firm. To back its belief that vision was also key to automation, GM invested in five machine vision companies in 1983 and 1984. These were Applied Intelligent Systems (AIS), Automatix, Diffracto Ltd., Robotic Vision Systems (RVS), and View Engineering. The full impact of these investments on the machine vision industry was yet unknown.

The Customers for Machine Vision Products

Though the machine vision market was very fragmented and very new, some information about the buyers of these products was provided by a study entitled *Vision Systems Survey of End Users,* conducted by Prudential-Bache Securities and published on February 6, 1985.

The report showed several interesting characteristics of present and potential machine vision customers. Sixty-seven percent of the companies surveyed achieved annual gross revenues of greater than $1 billion. Eighty-four percent of the companies had annual gross revenues of greater than $100 million. Fifty-seven percent of the companies interested in vision were located in the Midwest. Another 19 percent were located in the Northeast, with 9 percent on the West Coast. The end users surveyed were in the following industries:

Industry	Percentage of study
Automotive	35%
Electrical/electronics	35
Aerospace	12
Construction	3
Pharmaceutical	1
Other*	14

*Ranges from paper products to metal fabricators.

Ninety-seven percent of the end users surveyed indicated that vision was an important factor in the overall manufacturing process. Sixty-four percent had an actual capital budget for vision system purchases.

Decision makers in the purchasing of vision systems were located in many different levels of the companies surveyed. Sixteen percent responded that the purchase decision was made at the corporate level only, while 29 percent said that the decision was made at the division level. Another 37 percent responded that vision system purchase decisions were made at the department level, with the remaining 17 percent of those surveyed answering that the decision involved more than one level within the company.

The lengths of present and anticipated future buying cycles for vision systems were as follows:

Buying cycles	Present	Future
Less than 3 months	13%	31%
6–9 months	47	41
9–12 months	23	18
Over a year	8	6

Many customers believed that machine vision systems would not only be installed for production work applications but also for internal development work on automation processes. Nineteen percent of respondents had installed vision systems for development work only, while 54 percent said that they had or planned to install vision systems for both production work and development work.

Fifty-nine percent of survey respondents purchased their vision systems through the direct salesforces of the suppliers. Twenty percent used only OEMs, while 8 percent purchased through distributors. The remaining 13 percent used more than one channel for their purchases.

Vision companies most often mentioned as possible suppliers were Automatix, View Engineering, Machine Vision International, and Perception. The factors most important to purchasers of vision systems, in their order of importance, were technology, service and support, applications engineering, user friendliness, reputation of vendor, expendability, and price.

The end users were also asked to list areas of application of vision systems in both the present and the future. The responses were:

Applications	Present	Future
Inspection	84%	93%
Gauging	44	60
Sorting	21	35
Process control	37	63
Robot guidance	40	45

The Technologies Employed in Machine Vision

There were four main technologies employed in machine vision systems. These were signal processing, mathematical morphology, statistical pattern recognition, and artificial intelligence. These four and the significant characteristics of each are displayed in Exhibit 2.

EXHIBIT 2   Vision systems technologies and their characteristics

	Image based	Object based	
How is the processing done?	**Signal processing** High speed Simple discrimination Requires special hardware	**Statistical pattern recognition** Low speed Simple discrimination No special hardware required	Arithmetic computations
	Mathematical morphology High speed Complex discrimination High hardware requirements	**Artificial intelligence** Low speed Very complex discrimination Can require special hardware	Logical computations
	What is being processed?		

To more fully understand these technologies, it is useful to see how each is used in a given application. MVI had a 3-D robot guidance product in which vision was used to direct the robot's placement of windshields in a car moving along an assembly line at the pace of 60 cars per hour. All four technologies were employed in this application. Lighting was used to produce a very sharp, mirror-like image of the car as it came into the work area. The bouncing of the light off the car surface to produce this image employed signal processing, a technology developed from radar technology. However, this light reflected off more than just the edge of the car body needed to be seen to perform the window insertion task; mathematical morphology allowed the computer control to extract from the image reflected only the part of the image needed for the task, and eliminated the rest from consideration. That was done through complex computer programs that directed the computer to search the image for the exact shape needed for analysis. Statistical pattern recognition was used to take measurements of window position and orientation, since the actual opening size and the position of the car body on the assembly line could vary slightly from car to car. Thus, this technology made use of another set of computer algorithms to take statistical measurements of the pertinent areas of the problem in question. Artificial intelligence software was used to answer such questions as "Is the window opening the right shape for the windshield that is here?" and "Can the robot reach the opening from its present position?" These questions could all be answered logically; they were either true or false. If corrections were necessary, the computer controls could command the robot to move and change position before actual insertion commands were given.

Exhibit 3 takes the example given above one step further, showing which technologies were necessary to perform the most common applications of vision systems currently on the market. Many applications required the use of only one of the technologies available, while others required multiple technologies. It was estimated that between 50 percent and 60 percent of the applications in the market in 1985 used signal processing. Between 20 percent and 30 percent of applications made use of statistical pattern recognition. The remaining 15 percent of the applications relied on mathematical morphology to perform the desired task.

Exhibit 4 shows how many of the current competitors in the vision systems market were positioned along technology lines. Most competitors used only one technology. MVI was unique in the employment of all four technologies. MVI began as a mathematical morphology company; then it consciously developed the use of the other three technologies in order to be able to handle more difficult industrial problems and to give itself a technology edge over its competition. This was explained in the company's prospectus, as follows:

> The company specializes in mathematical morphology, which it believes is the most suitable technology for application in machine vision. Moreover, the company is complementing its capabilities in mathematical morphology by establishing capabilities in pattern recognition, signal processing, and artificial intelligence, and believes that the combination of these technologies will enhance the applications of the company's systems. It is the advanced application of

EXHIBIT 3   Technologies used in machine vision applications

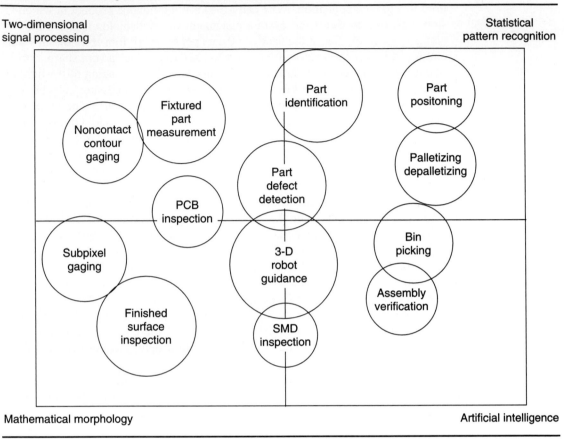

Two-dimensional
signal processing

Statistical
pattern recognition

Mathematical morphology

Artificial intelligence

mathematical morphology and the move toward a combination of technologies to complement mathematical morphology that the company believes differentiates it significantly from its competitors.

Dr. Sternberg explained why it is important to use all the available technologies. He said:

> You can force a solution using just one tool, but you end up working 10 times harder than if you use the right tool for the right part of the job. You can find a way to change the spark plugs on your car with just a hammer, but it will take you a lot longer to do it this way than if you had all the right tools for the job.

Machine Vision International—History

MVI was founded in June 1981 by Dr. Stanley R. Sternberg. Dr. Sternberg had previously worked at the Environmental Research Institute of Michigan, where he was instrumental in the development of the technology of mathematical mor-

EXHIBIT 4   Industry competitors' technology positions

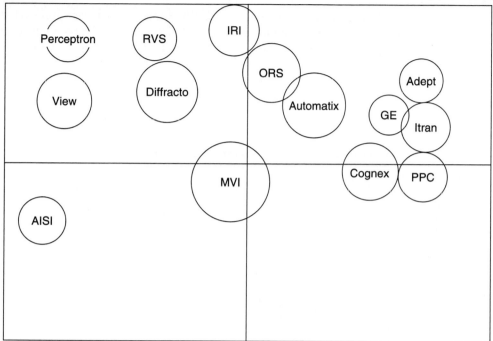

Two-dimensional
signal processing

Statistical
pattern recognition

Perceptron

RVS

IRI

ORS

Adept

View

Diffracto

Automatix

GE

Itran

MVI

Cognex

PPC

AISI

Mathematical morphology

Artificial intelligence

phology. Dr. Sternberg's idea was to develop products based on this technology that could be used for measurement, inspection, and control in manufacturing processes. In the fall of 1982, Dr. Sternberg joined with Richard P. Eidswick to develop strategy to bring this technology to market. Prior to joining MVI, Mr. Eidswick was senior vice president and director of Comshare, Inc., an international computer services company.

To fund the company, nearly $9.5 million of equity capital was raised through private offerings of MVI securities. Approximately $5 million of these funds were raised through the sales of common stock to Safeguard Scientifics, Inc. As of November 5, 1985, MVI was a public company, with its shares traded in the over-the-counter market.

As its strategy in the vision industry, MVI chose to focus on three business areas and three specific applications of machine vision. The business areas were automotive, electronics, and general industrial. The applications were three-dimensional robot guidance, surface inspection, and surface-mounted electronic component inspection. The principal component of all systems sold by MVI was the image flow computer (IFC), an image processing computer that used MVI's proprietary operating software, BLIX, to perform the mathematical calculations necessary for image analysis.

MVI marketed its products primarily through direct sales groups dedicated to end users in the three business areas. It also marketed its products to original equipment manufacturers (OEMs) who specified MVI products in their systems, and through certain specialized sales representatives. Through September 1985, MVI had manufactured and sold approximately 100 machine vision systems for an aggregate sales price of nearly $12 million. Financial statements for MVI are presented in Exhibits 5 and 6.

EXHIBIT 5   Machine Vision International Corporation—statements of operations

			First six months	
	June 25, 1981– Dec. 31, 1983	Jan. 1– Dec. 31, 1984	1984	1985
Net sales	$ 541,058	$ 4,011,730	$ 760,807	$ 4,481,476
Cost of sales	338,921	2,536,398	555,891	2,021,068
Gross profit	$ 202,137	$ 1,475,332	$ 204,916	$ 2,460,408
Operating expenses:				
Product development	$ 318,961	$ 1,733,667	$ 610,836	1,354,943
Selling	360,601	1,979,102	652,364	2,011,329
General and administration	542,101	904,272	420,356	365,184
Total operating expenses	$ 1,221,663	$ 4,617,041	$ 1,683,556	$ 3,731,456
Loss from operations	$(1,019,526)	$(3,141,709)	$(1,478,640)	$(1,271,048)
Other income (expense):				
Interest expense	$ (5,076)	$ (105,089)	$ (15,697)	$ (116,207)
Other	23,342	67,895	64,858	19,410
Total other income (expense)	$ 18,266	$ (37,194)	$ 49,161	$ (96,797)
Net loss	$(1,001,260)	$(3,178,903)	$(1,429,479)	$(1,367,845)
Loss per share	$(.41)	$(.56)	$(.28)	$(.18)
Weighted average number of shares	2,458,495	5,714,391	5,164,775	7,457,460

Market Approach

An organizational chart for MVI is shown in Exhibit 7. The sales function within MVI was divided along market segment lines. The three current sales divisions— automated systems, electronic systems, and manufacturing technology—mirrored those markets pointed out by the Prudential-Bache survey as the major customers interested in machine vision products.

The Automated Systems Division (ASD)

MVI began its search for applications in the automotive industry, where executives were already talking about putting resources into finding vision solutions to solve automation problems. Mr. Jake Jeppesen, who joined MVI in

EXHIBIT 6   Machine Vision International Corporation—balance sheet

| | December 31 | | |
	1983	1984	June 30, 1985 (unaudited)
Assets			
Current assets:			
Cash and cash equivalents	$ 104,117	$ 191,361	$ 151,601
Receivables	272,945	2,095,875	3,255,081
Inventories	238,772	1,964,951	3,749,191
Prepaid expenses and deposits	8,689	34,961	34,228
Total current assets	$ 624,523	$4,287,148	$7,190,101
Property and equipment			
Computer and other equipment	$ 221,274	$ 972,614	$1,213,574
Office furniture and equipment	91,436	171,737	249,738
Leasehold improvements	6,520	91,665	102,232
	$ 319,230	$1,236,016	$1,565,544
Less: accumulated depreciation	31,154	275,087	470,087
Net property and equipment	$ 288,076	$ 960,929	$1,095,457
	$ 912,599	$5,248,077	$8,285,558
Liabilities and shareholders' equity			
Current liabilities:			
Current portion of long-term debt	$ 42,500	$ 74,823	$ 118,000
Note payable	—	675,000	500,000
Accounts payable	246,058	993,292	1,887,677
Accrued liabilities	104,540	407,842	633,709
Total current liabilities	$ 393,098	$2,150,957	$3,139,386
Long-term debt, less current portion above	$ 118,365	$1,671,775	$1,205,073
Shareholders' equity			
Common stock, no par value, stated value $.001	$ 4,018	$ 6,509	$ 8,214
Paid-in capital	1,398,378	5,598,999	9,480,893
Accumulated deficit	(1,001,260)	(4,180,163)	(5,548,008)
Total shareholders' equity	$ 401,136	$1,425,345	$3,941,099
	$ 912,599	$5,248,077	$8,285,558

June 1983 to head the Automated Systems Division, found a group at GM that had been talking for two years to various vision companies about the possibility of using vision to automate auto glass insertion. The other companies had failed to develop a product that worked. Mr. Jeppesen convinced them to try again with the mathematical morphology technology that MVI offered. The first order for the window insertion product was received by MVI in December 1983. A prototype was working in a GM lab in March 1984, and the first plant installation was made in June 1984. See Exhibit 8 for a representation of how this product worked.

Even though the first vision applications taken on by MVI showed themselves to be successful working projects within the automotive industry, the sales process for ASD remained a very complicated one. The division maintained an ongoing educational sales effort, selling everyone from the executive level to plant production people on who MVI was and what the company and machine vision were capable of doing. Automotive executives and manufacturing research staff person-

EXHIBIT 7 Corporate organization chart

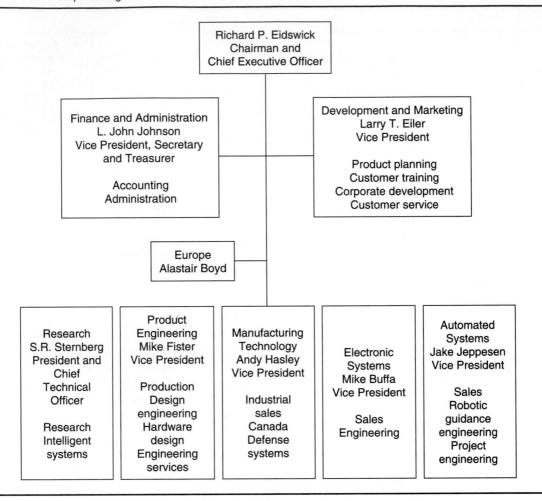

nel were interested in the technology involved and its advantages over existing or alternative assembly automation techniques. However, manufacturing staff were interested in finding ways in which higher-quality cars could be built better, cheaper, and faster. Plant production staff were generally interested in improvements in product quality, but were mainly concerned with production speed so that their quotas could be met. To this group, a product's reliability on the assembly line was of the utmost importance. Since orders within automotive companies came most often from the manufacturing staff or the plant production people, it was the goal of the sales process to give these people confidence that MVI's product "will do what we say it's going to do forever, first time every time, and never fail," as Jeppesen put it. These groups were not interested in machine vision for its technology; they wanted their task performed in the most reliable, fastest way possible.

EXHIBIT 8   Representation of MVI's window insertion system

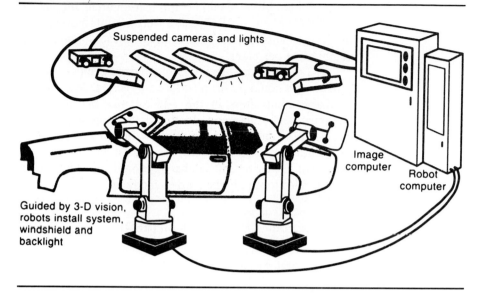

Suspended cameras and lights

Image computer

Robot computer

Guided by 3-D vision, robots install system, windshield and backlight

Since this sales effort was so educational in nature, the decision was made to approach the market on a direct basis; MVI did not want to entrust this type of basic technology and company-image selling to a third party. The ASD was currently selling products for two applications in the automotive industry. These were 3-D robot guidance for window insertion and other applications, and surface paint inspection.

The window insertion product had a selling price of approximately $450,000 per installation. It was only a part of an entire window insertion system that included robots, body handling equipment, material handling equipment, and controls supplied by other vendors. This total system cost in the neighborhood of $5 million. The surface paint inspection product was currently used only to inspect finished paint surfaces; it sold for approximately $500,000 per system. MVI had received seven orders for window insertion systems and one for a paint inspection system.

Though relatively few orders for these products had been received to date, the markets for these products were very large. Jeppesen saw many potential application areas for both MVI's 3-D robot guidance and paint surface inspection products. 3-D robot guidance could also be employed to automate such tasks as automobile wheel and cockpit loading, to apply paint stripes, and to control many fluid fill operations. Although paint inspection systems were currently used only for finished product inspection, the market could be expanded to include inspection of bare metal after frameup, phosphate coating before priming, primer coats, and other checkpoints during automobile production. In total, Jeppesen currently foresaw 10 application possibilities for 3-D robot guidance and 6 application areas for surface inspection in each automobile plant. In 1985, there were 73 automobile assembly plants operating in the United States, and many of these operated with more than one assembly line per plant.

At the time, no other vision company even claimed to be able to supply a product that could perform surface inspection. Jeppesen listed three companies as major competitors in the 3-D robotics business: GMF Robotics, ASEA Robotics, and Automatix. In this area, Jeppesen said that many companies claimed to be able to perform this task, but they really did not have the necessary capabilities. As a result, there was a great amount of confusion in the marketplace, but Jeppesen believed that this confusion would soon be dispelled as competitors tried to supply the market and failed.

The Electronics Sales Division (ESD)

The electronics market was very different from the automotive area. Therefore, the sales strategy and marketing positioning employed in the electronics market were unique to it. The sales process for the ESD began with marketing research to find out the vision needs in the electronics industry, and was subsequently combined with a concerted effort to get to know the decision makers within that industry. In this effort, MVI marketing personnel attended electronics industry meetings, where they got to know the technology leaders within the industry. Thus they gained firsthand knowledge of the industry's technology trends as well as the strategies of the major electronics firms.

In 1985, the U.S. electronics industry was currently undergoing a great change in production procedures. Ninety percent of electronics assembly was being done on lead-through boards. However, overseas, and especially in Japan, nearly 95 percent of electronics assembly was being done on higher-quality, more reliable surface-mounted boards. It was believed that U.S. production would shift to surface-mounted boards very rapidly. This type of production would be highly compatible with automated assembly techniques since the components on surface-mounted boards were much smaller and required greater production sensitivity than lead-through boards.[1]

The total market for surface-mounted inspection systems was divided into three segments by MVI's market researchers. The two in which MVI thought it could successfully compete were (1) low-speed, high-precision inspection of a

---

[1]Surface mount technology (SMT) was an electronic manufacturing method in which miniaturized, prepackaged components were assembled on the top (hence surface) of a circuit. In lead-through assembly, the components had conductors or leads that were inserted through holes that are drilled or punched through the board. These leads were folded or clinched on the back of the board to provide mechanical component attachment. In SMT manufacturing, the components were placed on the board by an automatic mechanism and then soldered in place.

broad range of components, and (2) high-volume, low-precision inspection of a limited range of components. For these areas, MVI made the following total market size projections.

Year	Segment 1 total number of vision systems	Segment 1 total dollar market (in millions)	Segment 2 total number of vision systems	Segment 2 total dollar market (in millions)
1984	30	$3.6	7	$1.05
1985	65	7.8	20	3.0
1986	90	10.8	130	19.5
1987	125	15.0	340	51.0
1988	350	42.0	525	78.75

MVI had spent two years developing a product that could use vision to control the assembly process and provide inspection for this automated production. MVI believed that the contrast and complexity of the components used in this process required the capabilities of the company's mathematical morphology technology. An effective product for this market had to be able to perform three tasks: (1) determine if the correct component (chip, diode, resistor, or capacitor) was present; (2) determine if each part was in the correct position relative to the other components; and (3) check the solder used to attach parts to the board for voids and excess solder material. MVI's vision technology was capable of solving the first two tasks. The third task required a low-level X-ray capability, which MVI did not currently have but was working to achieve.

Unlike ASD sales, ESD sales were technology sales. ESD's personnel talked to technical processing engineers, not the traditional purchasing departments within the electronics firms. MVI people talked to these technical people to determine their automation needs and to educate them as to the capabilities of MVI's product. The goal was to get to know the people who would use the system and get their support before there was a quotation request made on the part of the electronics firm.

By the end of the third quarter of 1985, MVI had three working surface-mounted inspection systems in the field. The company expected to make deliveries on nine or ten more orders before the end of the year. Prices on these systems ranged from $80,000 to $200,000. The hardware used in these systems was priced to match closely the prices of MVI's competition. The software used was specific to each application and, therefore, was priced to be the profit margin producer for the company.

Competitors in this market were View Engineering, International Robomation/Intelligence (IRI), and Automatix. IRI was specifically mentioned as an aggressive price competitor. IRI's system that competed with MVI was priced between $75,000 and $125,000.

The Manufacturing Technology Division (MTD)

MVI's Manufacturing Technology Division comprised two sales groups, the Industrial Sales Group (ISG) and the Aerospace Sales Group (ASG). This division had as its goal finding new markets for the products developed by the other sales divisions. Manufacturing technology sales groups were to take on applications that required extensions of existing technology or new combinations of what had already been developed by MVI's R&D and engineering personnel. The MTD was headed by Andrew Hasley.

Industrial sales group. MVI received between 250 and 300 inquiries each month through its marketing work, by its presence in several vision shows, and through references from its present customers. Many of these inquiries did not come from people within the automotive or electronics industries. Leads from these other nonspecialized industries were turned over to the Industrial Sales Group, which was under the direction of John Kufchock.

Kufchock used three initial criteria to determine whether MVI would pursue these inquiries. The lead had to come from a Fortune 500 company; thus, the company would have considerable funds to spend on capital investments. The application being pursued had to involve the use of technology already developed by MVI; thus, sales of the ISG were meant to produce a multiplier effect on sales for MVI. Furthermore, the inquiry had to come from a company that had an established engineering group capable of understanding both the technology involved and the advantages of MVI's technology over competitors.

The ISG had made sales in many industries, all of surface inspection products that performed very diversified tasks. For example, in the food industry, surface inspection was used to identify foreign objects in produce coming from the fields as well as produce of less than acceptable grade, so that these could be eliminated from further processing. In the lumber industry, surface inspection was used to check plywood as it was produced so that its grade and sales quality could be determined. In the rubber industry, tires were checked for flaws. By the end of 1985, the ISG had placed more than 20 systems in the industrial workplace. Kufchock expected to have nearly 50 more systems on the market in the first six months of 1986. He predicted that ISG could sell over 100 systems per year from a total of only 20 different customer corporations.

The sales process for the ISG usually began with an inquiry from a prospective customer. Qualified leads were turned over to one of Kufchock's two sales-oriented application engineers. Through talking with and visiting the prospect, the application engineer studied the customer's vision needs to determine whether MVI's technology could meet the requirements of the task. The application engineer also identified the right people to deal with in the customer's organization. These included those who would understand the technology, those who would use the product, and those who would actually make the purchase decision. All those involved in the decision process had to be "put on the team" if the sales process was to be successful. When this had been completed, a test of MVI's product on the prospect's material would be made at ISG's own lab. When the test was successful, the application engineer contacted the customer, asking that they send people to see the test results. Then, a trip was made to the customer's business to determine the actual conditions under which the system had to perform and to talk to all the decision makers involved, getting their input on a preliminary sales proposal. Then a final proposal was drawn up and sent to the purchasing department of the customer. This entire selling process took between three and nine months.

The ISG also sold its products to other firms that needed vision to make their large automation systems work for their customers. MVI called these firms strategic partners because often significant development work had been done by MVI's engineering staff to make the vision products work successfully for this partner. These strategic partners had market knowledge that MVI did not possess. Often, the vision portion of the systems sold by these partners comprised less than 20 percent of the entire system's selling price.

Prices on vision systems sold through the ISG ranged from $45,000 to $75,000 each. These prices included the hardware and software necessary for the application plus training. Fees for engineering services at the customer's plant to get the system up and running were charged separately at an established per diem rate. In the first applications, it was common for MVI to find this engineering support taking more time than expected. This resulted in profit margins less than what had been predicted.

Aerospace Sales Group (ASG). The Aerospace Sales Group was established in mid-1985. It was spun off from the ISG when it was believed that there was enough business in this area alone to support a dedicated sales effort. The first sales made in the aerospace industry were made by the ISG group.

This group sold products for many different applications involving the different technologies developed by the ASD and ESD. These included 3-D robot guidance systems, small parts inspection systems, surface inspection products, and combinations of small parts inspection and 3-D robot guidance in which the system would recognize, inspect, and control the handling of parts. Current applications included turbine blade inspection, surface-coating inspections on space shuttle booster rockets, and 3-D robot guidance used for assembling wiring harnesses in aircraft.

The defense supply industry had different requirements for vision products than did the other industries MVI sold to. Here speed was of less concern than it was in other industrial environments. What was important here was the complexity of the parts to be inspected or assembled. As a result, the systems sold by the ASG were complicated and averaged in price from $400,000 to $500,000.

Major competitors were Robotic Vision Systems, IRI, and View Engineering. As in the automotive industry, no other competitor even claimed to be able to perform surface inspection. Also, MVI believed there was little competition in the area of parts inspection. In discussing the competitive environment, Hasley, director of the Manufacturing Technology Division, said,

> In a lot of cases, we don't find we're competing directly with anybody. We still make a lot of cold calls. Selling here is a market development problem really. It's just getting the application defined. Can you do this? Can you do that? It involves a lot of education on what vision can do.

Commonalities of Sales Approach

Though each of MVI's three divisions sold to different markets and to different groups of people within customer firms, each application's real bottom-line sales approach was similar. What MVI was really selling was improved return on investment (ROI). In some sales, MVI's salespeople were showing how their product could reduce warranty claim costs. This was especially true in automobile paint inspection, since paint flaws were the industry's fourth-largest warranty claim cost. Thus, improving paint finish quality was a paramount goal for these firms. In others, it was improved product quality that resulted from the use of vision equipment. For yet other applications, the main purpose of the vision equipment was to reduce the costs of inspection. For example, Kufchock pointed out that the plywood inspection system in one facility replaced the use of eight inspectors, each earning $21 per hour.

Production

For each first-time application, MVI built whatever hardware and software were needed to make the project work for the customer. For further similar applications, MVI looked for a supplier for the necessary components of the system. Thus, for all of MVI's multiple applications, it purchased the optics, hardware, circuit boards, cables, communications devices, and other material handling equipment from outside suppliers. The role of production then became that of packaging the optical equipment, the hardware, the software, and the communications materials so that the application worked for the customer.

The Future Goals for MVI

Richard Eidswick, MVI's chairman and CEO, established the company's goal of being a dominant supplier in the machine vision industry. This goal translated into obtaining a 15 percent share of this market within five years and then sustaining that 15 percent share.

Eidswick also set achievement goals for each sales division. The ASD and the ESD were to be specialized divisions and, as such, technology and market share leaders within their industries. Here, there would be a continuing effort to take on new projects that had a strategic purpose. The groups within the Manufacturing Technology Division were to have multiplier strategies; their sales were to come from extensions of products developed by the ASD and ESD. The MTD groups were also to seek out strategic partners, finding companies who needed vision in their products and who already had market knowledge and a strong customer base. For this type of customer, MVI would sell its products at a discount from the prices quoted to direct end users since the strategic partners would take over much of the selling process for MVI.

Eidswick prepared sales expense breakdowns for the company's two types of sales, those direct to end users and those made through strategic partners.

These expense breakdowns, expressed as percentages of sales revenue, are shown below. The third column shows the breakdown of expenses as percentages of sales for MVI's sales for the first half of 1985.

	End user	Strategic partner	First six months of 1985
Revenue	100%	100%	100%
Cost of goods sold	35	55	45
Gross margin	65	45	55
Selling expense	25	9	45
R&D and engineering	10	10	30
Corporate expenses	10	6	8
Total expenses	45	25	83
Profit before taxes	20	20	(28)

MVI had not made a profit to date; however, no competitor in the vision industry had been consistently profitable. MVI had bid each project, even the first one for each of its applications, at a price that the company thought would be profitable. However, the number of engineering, selling, and application development hours that these early applications needed to achieve systems capable of or working in real industrial environments and to educate customers on the use of the products had been hard to estimate. These problems led to the higher-than-desired selling, R&D, and engineering expenses to date. Eidswick was most concerned about the high selling-expense figure. He was not so concerned about the R&D and engineering expense, since this was to be expected in a new, high-technology industry. MVI needed, as Eidswick saw it, to find ways to reduce its selling expense.

The Question of Focus

Some vision companies have chosen to be very specialized. They believe that an emerging company cannot afford to spread itself too thin. It must establish a market niche, exploit that niche, make some money, and then go out and spread itself. Others say that this is a new market. No one understands it. What may be a niche one day might just disappear. Some competitors are very specialized. Others are all over the place. Some of each have failed. Why? For the specialized firms, perhaps the market never appeared or the task they chose proved too difficult. For those who were in all markets, each project was different and they had no repeat sales.

Dr. Sternberg

Multiple orders of the same kind of things, that's the kind of result we want to have. We want more repeat orders for the same product, the same application . . . less customization. That way we don't have to keep reinventing the wheel, inventing new technology, and engineering new software for every order that we get.

Larry Eiler

Eidswick believed that the fact that MVI had "so much going on, in so many markets, with so many different applications" was the company's biggest problem. But he explained that "we have to do this if we want to find the applications that will provide repeat business, applications that will establish us as an industry leader."

Eiler pointed out that the company had purposefully chosen only very difficult applications, a strategic approach he called "a tough jobs positioning." That product positioning, along with what Kufchock called the company's credo that "There is no unhappy customer," was designed to build a strong company image for MVI as "the company that makes products that work," as Eiler put it.

MVI had not found that it was easy to get a vision application job, even after another competitor had failed to provide a product that worked. Often customers who had spent thousands and thousands of dollars on vision equipment wanted to protect that investment by giving their supplier another chance to succeed. Other customers turned away from vision after initial system failures, waiting for the technology to mature and for the market winners to appear rather than give another company a chance at that time.

The prospectus published by MVI at the time of its stock offering to Safeguard Scientifics shareholders stated that MVI focused on three applications. These were three-dimensional robot guidance, surface inspection, and surface-mounted electronic component inspection. Dr. Sternberg believed that, in looking at the company, one should be careful not to confuse its technological diversity with its market position. He said, "MVI is focused; we are working toward three standardized products."

Case 10

Voice Mail Around the World*

On July 19, 1994, as CEO Burt Mason reviewed his company's spectacular performance during the last quarter of FY 1994, a big question loomed in his mind. International operations were becoming an increasing source of revenue, and the potential for growth in these overseas markets was immense. Further expansion in these markets was essential for the future success of the company, especially since the domestic market was becoming more mature. Although its existing international operations were successful, the company had not yet developed a comprehensive international strategy—which markets/countries to enter, in what order, what entry strategy to use for these markets, and how to further develop the markets. The company had so far used an ad hoc "shotgun" approach. How well would this approach work in the future? As Burt pondered further on this issue, he realized that a discussion with Harry Embry, the VP of international operations, was imperative. After all, his company, Tyrix Communications Corporation, was the worldwide leader in the voice mail industry, and it was his number one goal that it maintain its position. He immediately fired off an urgent voice mail message to Embry summoning him for a meeting that afternoon.

However, international expansion was not the only issue on Burt's mind at this time; he was also grappling with a major challenge on the domestic front. Trends emerging in the U.S. market, where different communication services such as phone, fax, cellular, and computer networks were merging, were seriously threatening the company's position. He had to figure out how to effectively respond to them.

---

*This case was prepared by Pranati Kapadia, MBA '95, and Professor David B. Montgomery, Stanford University Graduate School of Business, as the basis for class discussion rather than to illustrate either effective or ineffective handling of an administrative situation. The names of all independent voice mail companies, their employees, and their products have been disguised in order to protect confidential information. Reprinted with permission of Stanford University, Graduate School of Business, Copyright © 1995 by the Board of Trustees of The Leland Stanford Junior University.

The Voice Mail Industry

Voice mail (or voice messaging) is a means of storing, forwarding, and retrieving messages via codes entered on a touch-tone telephone. The technology for facilitating voice mail originated more than 20 years ago, when it used analog tape recordings. In 1980, digital voice messaging was initiated by means of microprocessor-based voice-processing systems.

Voice mail operates through a voice-processing computer that integrates its functions with a telephone system to provide voice messaging service. The computer first records the human voice message, and then synthesizes it by converting it from an analog to a digital format. A reverse converter can then replay the digitized message. The voice message is stored on magnetic disk, and can be manipulated like other disk-stored data.

In its early days, voice mail provided just the basic store, forward, and retrieve functions, whereas today's "voice mail," if one could still call it that, encompasses an enormous number of features, driven by new developments in technology as well as competitive pressures. Some of these new features include interactive voice response, call answering, informational audiotex where voice messages are displayed on a PC monitor or computer terminal, and integration of voice with facsimile and electronic mail, as well as the transformation of the telephone into a multimedia communications terminal.

Voice processing systems can also provide links with electronic mail, electronic bulletin boards, and computer databases or information services. Here the user can tap into broadcast news services, retrieve and update computer database records, initiate or receive facsimile and electronic mail messages, and even have them read by a computer-generated voice—all from the lowly telephone.

Benefits of Voice Messaging

Voice messaging provides many benefits to both the business and the residential customer. It serves to eliminate errors that occur when a live message taker misunderstands the caller, ensures that important calls are not missed, and improves time management.

For residential customers, it adds greater reliability and additional features than its substitute product, the answering machine. Answering machines can break down, run out of recording tape, accidentally erase messages, or not take any messages during a power outage. Unlike answering machines, a voice mail system picks up calls even when the line is engaged. Another substitute product that is now becoming popular is the personal computer equipped with a special board that provides a number of communication facilities, such as voice mail, fax mail, and electronic mail. This substitute product also suffers from the same problems as the answering machine.

The greatest benefits of voice mail are often to large national or multinational companies, where callers operate in different time zones. Communication is more effective, and productivity increases. In the United States voice mail is viewed primarily as a productivity tool, especially among the many companies that are "downsizing" and cutting support staff. With its broadcast feature, voice messaging eliminates the use of paper for sending memos to a large number of people. Perhaps the biggest advantage of voice mail is that it eliminates "telephone tag." If the other party is on the phone or away from his desk, it is always possible to leave a message.

One might claim that electronic mail also provides all the benefits listed above, and question the real utility of voice mail. The answer to that is that voice mail is simpler, easier, and quicker to access than electronic mail. This is further detailed in Exhibit 1.

EXHIBIT 1   Comparison of voice mail with electronic mail

Voice mail	*Electronic mail*
Voice is the foundation	Text is the foundation
Simple addressing scheme (recipient's phone number)	Complex or difficult-to-discern addressing scheme
Easy to use since there is a uniform and simple interface—the telephone key pad	Harder to use since different E-mail systems have different interfaces
Easy and quick access since it only needs a telephone	Needs a computer
External mechanism (blinking light or stutter dial tone) to indicate that a new message has arrived	No external mechanism to indicate that a new message has arrived. User needs to log into computer to find out

---

Industry Segments

Although the end user of voice mail services cannot really distinguish between the two, the voice mail industry is segmented according to the providers of voice mail services, as described below and in Exhibit 2. The customer, here, is defined as the entity that owns the voice processing system and provides voice mail services to the end user.

1. In the customer premises equipment (CPE) segment, the customers are mainly corporations and academic and government institutions. Here, the system is located behind the private branch exchange (PBX) owned by the customer. PBXs became popular for two reasons. First, it was less expensive to route a call internally than through the central office of the local phone company and back to the customer. Second, it was far quicker and easier for the customer to make changes to its system, such as changing the extension assignments when personnel were moved throughout a building. Customers in this segment provide voice mail services to internal end users, e.g., employees of the corporate and government customer, and faculty, staff, and students of the academic customer.

2. In the voice information service (VIS) provider segment, the customer is a service bureau that sells voice mail services to external end users. Several companies, including Tyrix and Lemocom, who make voice processing

EXHIBIT 2 Overview of the voice mail industry

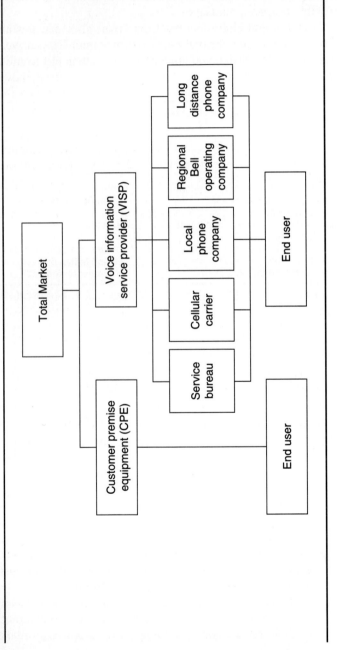

systems for the CPE segment, also manufacture such systems for VIS providers. This segment provides an alternative to corporations where they can outsource their voice mail services, instead of maintaining the voice processing system in-house, which would be required for the CPE solution. This segment, which used to be dominated by independent service bureaus, is now beginning to experience the entry of phone companies and cellular carriers. By offering voice mail services, cellular carriers are able to generate additional revenue for themselves, since incoming calls not completed over the wireless medium due to problems in the cellular network can be completed through the voice mail system. Hence, these incoming calls can be charged to the cellular phone user. The forecast is that phone companies will take over this segment, especially in the residential market, because they provide greater convenience (one-stop shopping) to end users.

This is a highly competitive industry. The two major industry segments, described above, also compete with each other, especially for large corporate accounts. The principal competitive factors are voice-messaging features, technology, robustness, and the ability to tailor the system to the different characteristics of the different customer markets (e.g., large, medium-sized, and small businesses, and residential customers).

Emerging Market Trends[1]

With over 60 million users, including almost 97 percent of all large corporations, the United States has the largest voice mail market. In the U.S., voice mail is viewed as an efficient—if somewhat irritating and impersonal—means of communication, used primarily as a productivity tool. It is a technology that Americans love to hate, but are using in ever-increasing numbers. In the U.S., the market is maturing, particularly in the business world, and voice mail is becoming a commodity product. To differentiate their products and services, major players in this market are bundling voice mail with other communication services, such as paging, electronic mail, fax, long distance, and calling card services, e.g., Lemocom offers computerized text-to-speech conversion, and Tyrix offers features that turn touch-tone keys on the telephone keypad into a kind of keyboard to type fax messages, select news or traffic reports, and post electronic messages. Although voice processing systems manufacturers claim that their products are complementary to computer network systems, it seems certain that the two industry segments will eventually collide, or preferably converge.

In other parts of the world, sales of voice messaging systems have been slower to take off, primarily because there is more resistance to talking to machines. In Europe, there are also regulatory hurdles. It takes about six months and

---

[1]Frost & Sullivan, "World Voice Processing Markets," 1994.

costs U.S. $500,000 to obtain approval from a European PTT (national telephone company) to connect a voice messaging system to the phone network. Yet as voice messaging system manufacturers step up their international marketing efforts, voice mail appears set to become more widely accepted.

Refer to Exhibit 3 for U.S. and international market voice mail revenue forecasts.

EXHIBIT 3   U.S. and international revenue forecasts for voice mail

U.S. forecasts ($ million)*

	Revenues	Growth Percent
1992	$1,318.6	—
1993	1,479.3	12.2%
1994	1,667.5	12.7
1995	1,882.3	12.9
1996	2,163.5	14.9
1997	2,514.0	16.2
1998	2,894.1	15.1
1999	3,329.3	15.0

International forecasts ($ millions)†

	1992	1993	1994	1995	1996	1997	1998	1999
European markets								
France	$332.7	$370.8	$419.0	$479.8	$566.1	$679.3	$828.8	$1,036.0
Germany	250.0	278.6	312.6	357.9	415.2	489.9	585.4	708.4
Italy	233.2	259.8	290.7	326.2	371.8	429.5	504.6	603.1
Switzerland	136.0	151.6	171.3	196.1	229.5	273.1	330.4	406.4
UK	44.8	49.9	56.4	64.6	76.2	91.4	111.5	139.4
Rest of Western Europe	538.1	599.7	684.7	795.1	969.2	1,201.7	1,513.4	1,884.0
Eastern Europe	157.3	175.2	196.0	220.0	250.8	289.6	340.3	406.7
Europe (Total)	1,692.1	1,885.6	2,130.7	2,439.7	2,878.8	3,454.6	4,214.6	5,184.0
Asia/Pacific markets								
Japan	485.0	540.5	610.8	699.3	825.2	990.2	1,208.1	1,510.1
S. Korea	114.5	127.6	144.2	165.1	194.8	233.8	285.2	356.5
Rest of Asia/Pacific	369.4	411.6	460.6	520.5	595.9	691.3	819.2	983.0
Asia/Pacific (Total)	968.9	1,079.7	1,215.5	1,384.9	1,615.9	1,915.3	2,312.5	2,849.6
Latin America	294.7	328.4	367.8	417.5	480.1	556.9	659.9	798.5
Middle East	116.2	129.5	146.3	167.6	197.7	237.3	289.5	361.8

*Frost & Sullivan, "US Voice Messaging Services," 1994.
†Frost & Sullivan, "World Voice Processing Markets," 1994.

Tyrix Communications Corporation

Tyrix was founded in 1982 by Burt Mason and Tim Coleman. It was incorporated in 1984, and became a public corporation in 1988. Since its incorporation, Tyrix has performed remarkably well, and has never experienced negative income.

Today, Tyrix has not only expanded into every existing segment in the industry, but also created new segments with innovative solutions like the "virtual telephone." Its goal is to become a major force in the telecommunications market by providing better, faster, and more affordable products and services.

Success Factors

Tyrix's superior position in the industry as compared to its competitors' can be attributed to the following factors:

1. Its CEO, Burt Mason, a true visionary, is the company's most significant success factor. He has a keen understanding of the voice messaging market, and the ability to accurately forecast changes and growth opportunities in each segment of the market. He is able to specifically identify potential competitors as well as competing/substitute technology that is likely to be introduced in the near future, and then steer the company to meet these challenges, e.g., his prediction that PC-based voice processing systems would start serving small businesses was absolutely on the mark, and when the first PC-based products entered the market, Tyrix already had a competing solution.
2. It has developed a core voice processing technology that can be used repeatedly for different applications. This creates a high degree of flexibility, allowing the company to quickly adapt to different environments, e.g., to different vendor-specific PBXs, as well as to rapidly develop new products.
3. Its management has the ability to make synergistic, mutually value-creating acquisitions and mergers. With its most recent acquisition, BMY Inc., the company has the potential to extend its lead even further. BMY brings significant value to Tyrix—access to 21 European markets, as well as software applications for personal computers based on newly developed standards. Refer to Exhibit 4 for details of companies acquired by Tyrix.
4. It provides excellent high-quality customer support services, including full product integration, strong pre- and post-sale support, and worldwide regional sales offices.
5. Other success factors include:
   a. A wide range of product features and applications that meet the requirements of almost every market segment.
   b. Longer time experience in the industry that allows it to rapidly develop new products and respond to changing market trends.
   c. A dual-channel distribution system which consists of both independent distributors as well as a direct salesforce. The "Manufacturing and Distribution" section below provides more details on this topic.

Products, Customers, and Competitors

Tyrix prides itself on developing high-quality (99.97 percent reliable) products, with the goal of protecting the customer's investment. By using the core voice-processing technology that it has developed, Tyrix is able to make products that

EXHIBIT 4 Companies acquired by Tyrix

BMY

The acquisition of BMY, a major player in the CPE segment, brought with it a host of software that integrates voice-related products and technologies, such as voice mail, audiotex, text-to-speech, speech recognition, fax, and computer networks. BMY's technology will help Tyrix to respond faster to emerging market trends which call for the integration of different communication services. Also with BMY, Tyrix's international competitive position has benefited significantly, since this acquisition brought with it access to 21 countries in Europe, as well as distribution alliances with major organizations such as Siemens, Bull S.A., Ericsson, Toshiba, and Hitachi. BMY, in turn, benefited by gaining access to the U.S. market and the chance to work with Tyrix's prestigious corporate customers. Moreover, several BMY senior managers became senior managers at Tyrix.

Firefox

With the acquisition of Firefox, an independent service bureau, Tyrix became the owner of the world's largest voice mail network. Firefox, in turn, has benefited from being purchased by Tyrix because it can now offer off-site management of Tyrix equipment, project management, and other telecommunications consulting and management services to Tyrix's customers.

PCVoice

With the acquisition of PCVoice, a small, financially weak company in Massachusetts, Tyrix added a PC-based voice processing product line to its existing product portfolio. PCVoice also brought with it an extensive dealer network. PCVoice, in turn, returned to financial stability with a greatly expanded customer base.

---

are essentially global in that they have a common, standardized core with the ability to be customized for different market environments. Its customer base includes businesses of all sizes, as well as telephone companies and wireless operators in the VISP segment. It has an installed base of 45,000 systems in more than 40 countries, representing a total of over 19 million mailboxes. The top five customers average 260 systems each; the top 25 customers average 118 systems each. CPE customers include 35 companies in the Fortune 50 industrial group, as well as Coca-Cola, McDonald's, General Electric, Hewlett Packard, New York Life, Stanford University, and McCaw Cellular. VISP customers include all seven regional Bell operating companies, and all the major telephone companies in Canada, as well as Leicester Cable (U.S.), Cable Corporation (U.S.), SIP (Italy), and Mannesmann Mobilfunk (Germany).

In the CPE segment, the company markets its flagship Vocall, Magnatel, as well as PC-based products for small businesses. These products have the ability to communicate with one another over a network, thus allowing for the integration of all the geographically distributed sites of a company. One of the factors of the company's success in this segment is the provision of excellent customer services, where the company works closely with customers to understand their requirements and ensure that they are met, even if it requires additional expenditures on its part. Customers in this segment are now demanding applications beyond basic voicemail, like audio-tex, interactive voice response, and fax. The company's products already provide these features, which gives it additional competitive advantage.

Tyrix competes with two types of companies in the CPE segment:

1. PBX manufacturers, including AT&T, Northern Telecom, and ROLM Systems. These companies have considerably greater financial, technical,

marketing, and sales resources, and may have a competitive advantage when customers are purchasing a voice mail system at the same time that they are purchasing a new PBX.

2. Independent voice mail systems manufacturers, such as Lemocom.

With the acquisition of Firefox, the company created its Tyrix Network Services (TNS) division which acts as a service bureau, providing complete voice processing services to corporate customers that prefer to outsource their voice mail capabilities. With TNS, the company currently maintains the world's largest voice messaging network. TNS also provides network management and other services to CPE customers. The major competitors in this area are Telovoch, a company that offers voice mail through franchises in the United States, Puerto Rico, and Canada, and Comavic, a private company. TNS controls about 42 percent of the U.S. independent service bureau market; the market shares of Telovoch and Comavic are 30 percent and 25 percent, respectively.

In the VIS provider segment, the company sells its Nelli product line to OEMs, primarily telephone companies and, increasingly, wireless operators and independent service bureaus, who then resell voice mail services to end customers. VIS providers demand products that are flexible in size and compatible across different telephone switching systems (PBXs) from different manufacturers. Tyrix has been successful in this segment primarily because its products are geared to satisfy the above-mentioned requirements of VIS providers.

Competitors in the VIS provider segment include ClearVoice, Digicom, Lemocom, and Vocitech. Refer to Exhibit 5 for financial details of Tyrix's competitors in both the CPE and VISP segments.

EXHIBIT 5   Profiles of competitors (independent voice mail system manufacturers)

(all amounts are in $ millions)

	Tyrix			Lemocom			Clearvoice		
	1994	*1993*	*1992*	*1994*	*1993*	*1992*	*1994*	*1993*	*1992*
Total revenues	$406.2	$338.5	$262.7	$80.0	$60.0	$44.7	$70.3	$49.5	$36.4
Net income	32.3	29.6	13.5	6.2	5.2	4.1	6.7	3.1	−2.4
Working capital	132.7	147.0	162.1	35.4	25.7	19.4	31.3	22.3	15.2
Total assets	346.1	297.3	252.0	62.3	48.0	34.0	65.3	41.3	32.3
Long-term debt	1.4	2.0	0.4	235.0	217.0	320.0	1.0	0.2	0.3
Stockholders' equity	256.2	229.7	202.3	38.6	32.1	23.8	40.8	31.6	25.0

	Digicom			Vocitech		
	1994	*1993*	*1992*	*1994*	*1993*	*1992*
Total revenues	$98.8	$70.4	$38.4	$28.4	$23.3	$34.3
Net income	11.8	12.7	5.7	1.5	−5.7	2.2
Working capital	144.7	137.1	NA	25.4	23.4	28.0
Total assets	187.7	169.1	NA	37.5	36.5	42.8
Long-term debt	NA	NA	NA	NA	NA	NA
Stockholders' equity	102.7	90.5	NA	31.2	29.2	34.5

Additionally, Tyrix has invented a unique voice mail solution—the "virtual telephone"—for international markets, such as China and India, where private phone lines are difficult and costly to obtain. Here, Tyrix partners with the local phone company that then offers voice mail services by selling voice mail boxes, which are accessible via any public phone. This allows a voice mail subscriber to receive and send voice messages to others without ever having to own a telephone or obtain a phone line. An added benefit is that each voice mail box is able to service multiple users, e.g., members of a family.

Manufacturing and Distribution

Tyrix's manufacturing operations consist primarily of final assembly and quality testing of materials, components, and subassemblies.

Tyrix sells and supports its products through both independent distributors and direct sales with over 60 domestic and 11 international offices. The majority of its sales are conducted by distributors. Each distributor enters a contract with the company that grants it the nonexclusive right to sell the company's products in a designated territory. Distributors are responsible for sales, installation, support, service, and maintaining a supply of spare parts. Tyrix invests heavily in training its distributors and in providing support. It maintains sales, customer support, and technical service personnel around the U.S. and in Canada for the sole purpose of supporting the distributor organizations, including training, making joint sales calls, and assisting in servicing and customer support.

Tyrix's International Efforts

Tyrix currently operates in 48 countries outside the United States, spanning all the continents, with countries as diverse as Bahrain and Australia. Exhibit 6 lists all the international markets that Tyrix has entered so far. It is actively seeking entry into the South Asian market, starting with India. Its international revenues, as a percentage of total revenues, are increasing; in FY 1994 they represented 25 percent ($102M) of total revenues (31 percent of total revenues in the 4th quarter, 94), as compared to 23 percent and 22 percent in FY 1993 and 1992, respectively.

Past Entry Strategy and Market Development

CPE segment. For the CPE segment, the company chose to first solicit sales orders from one or more large multinational corporations before approaching a potential distributor in any given country. These lucrative sales orders, which only needed to be filled, along with the allocation of exclusive sales territory, were good incentives for potential distributors to carry Tyrix's product line. The company sought foreign distributors who were financially secure,

EXHIBIT 6   Tyrix's international expansion: Country list

1.	Argentina	25.	Ireland
2.	Australia	26.	Italy
3.	Austria	27.	Japan
4.	Bahrain	28.	Korea
5.	Belgium	29.	Luxembourg
6.	Bolivia	30.	Malaysia
7.	Brazil	31.	Mexico
8.	Bulgaria	32.	Netherlands
9.	Canada	33.	New Zealand
10.	Chile	34.	Norway
11.	China	35.	Philippines
12.	Colombia	36.	Poland
13.	Costa Rica	37.	Portugal
14.	Croatia	38.	Puerto Rico
15.	Denmark	39.	Saudi Arabia
16.	El Salvador	40.	Singapore
17.	Finland	41.	Spain
18.	France	42.	Sweden
19.	Germany	43.	Switzerland
20.	Greece	44.	Taiwan
21.	Hong Kong	45.	Thailand
22.	Hungary	46.	Turkey
23.	Indonesia	47.	U.K.
24.	Iran	48.	Venezuela

carried a line of PBX equipment, and thus had an understanding of the marketplace. Once they were established, the distributors were responsible for post-sale support for existing customers, and also for generating their own business for selling voice processing systems in the CPE market, relying on Tyrix only for technical support.

In the next phase, Tyrix typically targeted large local businesses and institutions, such as government agencies and universities. As the foreign markets matured, this segment comprised a growing share of the business. For example, in countries that Tyrix has operated in for a few years, such as Australia and Singapore, about 80 percent of the CPE business originated from local companies, with less reliance on large multinationals. Tyrix has been so successful in penetrating the Australian market that the word "Vocall," the name of its CPE product line, has become both a noun and a verb associated with voice messages.

VISP segment. For the VISP segment, Tyrix generally established a partnership with U.S. cellular carriers or phone companies who partially owned foreign phone companies or cellular providers. This provided an easier method of entry into the overseas market than attempting to venture on its own. Here, Tyrix's biggest challenge was to localize its systems quickly enough to fill this demand.

In developing countries, Tyrix targeted the residential market with its "Virtual Telephone" solution, described earlier. Experiences to date indicate that there is a significant demand for the service.

Table 1 below shows the three different entry strategies in the two market segments, voice information service provider (VISP) and customer premise equipment (CPE), that Tyrix has used so far. Although they are numbered I, II, and III, they do not indicate a specific sequence in which an international market was entered and developed. In most countries, Tyrix started with VISP I, gaining entry into the country via a cellular carrier that used Tyrix's VISP products, and then moved to VISP II, where it provided the virtual phone solution through the country's PTT (post, telephone, and telegraph)—the state-owned phone company. However, in Taiwan and Indonesia, the company started with CPE I, where it entered the country by providing a CPE solution to a multinational company, and then went to VISP I. In China, it started with VISP II. In Europe, much of Tyrix's CPE business has been initially driven by large multinational companies who use their own private branch exchanges (PBX).

Barriers to International Market Entry

Entry into overseas markets has not been problem free for Tyrix. Discussed below are the kinds of barriers that it faces in its international ventures.

Regulations. Granting licenses to operate on a country's telephone network is often a matter of national security. In Europe, each nation maintains its own PTT organization that strictly regulates access, technology standards, etc. The French have the most stringent set of specifications for telephone hardware. It encompasses electromagnetic interference (EMI) shielding, electrical isolation, and other limits to control the volume of any voice, including the Tyrix product's voice, over the network. In Asia and Latin America, many national phone companies are controlled by highly bureaucratic governments, which results in long delays for obtaining licenses and/or permits to operate in the country.

However, many countries are currently in the process of deregulating parts of the telecommunication industry, although the national phone service may still be under government control. This deregulation creates competition

TABLE 1   Market entry strategies

Market Segment	Entry strategy		
	I	*II*	*III*
VISP	Cellular	Virtual phone	PTTs
CPE	U.S. multinationals	Institutions and local companies	Open to all customers

Legend:	VISP:	voice information service provider.
	CPE:	customer premise equipment.
	PTT:	post, telephone, and telegraph.

in the market, which in turn creates a strong requirement for the previously un-interested state-owned phone company to provide additional services like voice mail so that it can compete effectively in the changing environments. Such countries represent a high growth opportunity for voice mail companies like Tyrix.

Technology. To operate effectively, Tyrix's products require dual tone mul-tifrequency (DTMF) tones generated by the user's phone to provide voice mail services. However, currently only half of the world's phone systems support DTMF signals. Moreover, many developing countries have installed this tech-nology only in parts of the country, not all over. Voice recognition, if adequately robust, could potentially overcome this technological barrier to growth, although it will take considerable time (more than five years) to perfect and implement this technology. However, what is encouraging for voice mail companies is that tele-com equipment providers are trying to overcome this limitation by providing tone generators as intermediaries between mechanical switches and peripheral equip-ment such as voice processing systems. Tyrix, in fact, already uses tone generat-ing devices for its operations in Brazil.

Culture. In many countries, one of the biggest cultural barriers is that peo-ple are very reluctant to talk to a machine. Also, in several developing countries where the joint family system prevails, someone is always likely to be at home, which provides a cheaper and more personal alternative to voice mail. Hence, it appears that the demand for voice mail would be low here. However, in these same countries, the virtual phone solution is a great benefit since many people do not have a personal phone line.

Language is another major barrier in some countries, making product de-velopment and customization an almost prohibitively lengthy and troublesome experience. Issues such as translation, syntax, context, pronunciation, and the availability of a proper "voice" for the voice systems are ones that need to be dealt with in many countries. There are many opportunities for miscommunications and misunderstandings which cause Tyrix to shy away from market opportunities that require extensive language modifications.

The user interface of voice information systems is the Touch-Tone telephone keypad, which enables a user to navigate through a series of menu choices. Although these menu choices and informative notices are in the form of sentences, they are actually recorded as over 2,000 phrases and words, which are then con-catenated together to form sentences. For instance, the sentence "You have four new messages" is actually the string of words "you have"/"four"/"new"/"mes-sages." This is done in an effort to conserve space on the data storage disk, which is one of the most expensive and volatile components of the system.

This phrase-based architecture can make customization easier and more flexible. When operating a VISP system within a Malaysian company, for in-stance, users may want to operate this interface in one of five languages. While the word for "four" may change from language to language, the syntax, or order of the words, is also subject to change. In some languages, the sentence in the previous example would be spoken "four" /"new" /"messages" /"you have." The system must know the preferences of each individual user, and know how to piece together the appropriate words for that language.

However, this phrase-based architecture can also be a liability, in that the meanings of certain words may change depending upon the context in which they are used. Although it is difficult to translate over 2,000 phrases into a new language, it is nearly impossible to verify that each new sentence, or permutation of those phrases, makes sense. With over 2,000 words and phrases in a VISP system that yield tens of thousands of permutations, the Tyrix development teams are never completely sure that a system has been localized correctly. However, the rapid development of high-density, low-cost disk drives will hopefully enable them to record full sentences, rather than having to patch together words and phrases. This will not only help ensure that words are being used in proper context, but it will eliminate problems they have had in syntax, or the order in which words appear in sentences.

It is often difficult to customize a system for use in another country, even an English-speaking country, due to the many different regional dialects in use. For example, there is no "pound" key on a telephone in England or Australia. They have a "hash" key. And telephone calls are not "routed" (where the "ou" in "routed" is pronounced as the "ou" in "out"), but they are "routed" (where the "ou" in "routed" is pronounced as the "oo" in "boot"). When developing systems for Latin America, they desperately tried to develop a common system. In Spanish, there is no common proper term for "mailbox," but they ended up choosing "casita" which translates to "little house." After over a year of selling systems in Latin America, they discovered, upon entering the Puerto Rican market, that in that country, a casita is a "little house" built over a septic system in areas without sewers. They have decided that the Puerto Rican market is not large enough to warrant customized products at this time.

The time-consuming process that the company currently uses to translate the "system voice" into the native language of their customers suffers from several sources of potential error and misunderstanding. There are often teams of marketers, engineers, vocal "talent," customers, and third-party translators involved in the process, each of which have their own subjective opinions as to what phrases are appropriate. The correct grammar and pronunciation of Mandarin differs in Taiwan, Malaysia, and China. It is difficult to qualify an appropriate translator because knowledge of all three languages is required. While working across long distances and fax lines, translations are often performed on paper; in some languages, the way a sentence would be written is often different from the way it would be spoken.

In addition to language modifications, it is important for Tyrix to find appropriate "talent" to record the voice, which will become the "soul" of the operating system. From a technical perspective, it is important that the voice, especially if it is a woman's, not have a "voice print" or wave pattern that resembles that of a dual-tone multifrequency (DTMF) tone. It is not uncommon for women, while leaving a voice-mail message, to be interrupted by the system voice, scolding "six is not a valid option."

More important than the technical implications of the talent's voice are the social implications. Employees, suppliers, and customers will all interact with the system voice, which personifies the company that uses a VISP system. It is important that the voice not be too offensive, aggressive, pushy, meek, friendly, sexy, or aloof. Focus groups spend hours listening to and evaluating subtle voice qualities. While western nations have come to expect a female voice to personify a phone system, in nations where women commonly do not work, such as the Arab Emirates, this is not appropriate.

Localization. Aside from just changing the language of the system voice, customers often demand that the system manager's software interface, and all the related documentation, manuals, and training materials, also be localized to one or more foreign languages. This can be a very time-consuming and expensive undertaking, especially since there are so few units over which to spread the costs.

In many cases, Tyrix asks its distributors in foreign countries to help bear the cost or responsibility for the translations. Typically, it tries to create situations where customers are willing to use documentation and system management software in English.

Customization of systems can be even more difficult in foreign markets, where different perceptions of how phones should be used prevail. Often, customers want to customize user interfaces and defaults for deferring unanswered calls to a mailbox, another extension, or to an automated screening process that requests the name of the caller. Although Tyrix's voice processing systems are very flexible at the back end for interfacing with different types of PBXs, etc., the end-user interface is not that flexible. Currently, the costs of modifying the end-user interface vary from $6,000 to $30,000, depending on the number and complexity of changes that need to be made. The company is in the process of developing a more user-friendly, flexible end-user interface that will allow customers to configure it to their taste.

The Asia-Pacific Market

Table 2 indicates that the Asia-Pacific market provides a huge opportunity for development for telephone companies and other telecommunication vendors (assuming that one takes an optimistic attitude towards the figures). Even so, each region has its own peculiarities, which makes it difficult for voice mail companies such as Tyrix to expand their operations there.

Customer requirements. To enter these markets, it is imperative to meet customers' language requirements, mailbox features (e.g., a keypad on the receiver is perceived to be awkward), and specific criteria for the acceptance of voice processing applications. People in this part of the world prefer to have live conversations, rather than leaving detailed messages behind on machines.

TABLE 2   Telephones per 100 people*

Hong Kong	64
Japan	50
Thailand	9
China	3
India	2
Indonesia	2
U.S.	60
E.C.	54

*Frost & Sullivan, "World Telecommunication Services Database," 1994.

Therefore, the basic voice processing services may not be very popular, but other applications like interactive voice response (IVR) and fax store and forward may have higher appeal.

In Asian cellular companies, the power in the organization resides in the engineering departments. Therefore, Tyrix will have to take measures to help make sure that its engineers can easily collaborate with their counterparts in Asia.

In addition to developing the VISP market, Tyrix should consider entry into the CPE segment, the segment in which they have been historically strong. By concentrating only on VISP, Tyrix will stand the risk of moving into a new market with a new product (new-new combination), a strategy that has often turned out to be detrimental for similar product-oriented companies.

China. Among all Asian countries, China has the largest potential for growth in this industry. China is now investing tens of billions of dollars into laying millions of phone lines by the year 2000. The government controls the telecommunication market through its Strategic Planning Committee (SPC). A major problem is the lack of strategic planning and the nonexistence of marketing departments in Chinese telephone companies. The lack of a marketing department is due to the fact that marketing is still perceived as "begging for money" and therefore not honorable.

Tyrix is currently taking a two-pronged approach in China: (1) seeking opportunities in an unstructured manner and accepting anything that is likely to work out, and (2) approaching SPC chiefs to discuss implementation of the virtual phone solution. Tyrix has experienced hard sells to phone companies in China, whose systems are so underdeveloped that they have an endless line of people waiting in line for their service. With this kind of backlog of realizable revenues, these companies see no need to diversify and offer additional services.

India. Due to the common use of the English language in business and its large population, India is a fairly attractive market for Tyrix. The barriers of localization are minimal, because of India's long-time exposure to Western culture. However, the language barriers, if required to adapt the system voice to any of the numerous native languages, could be a monumental task. But the most formidable barriers to doing business in India are the technology infrastructure, which to a large extent is old fashioned, and the government's regulatory structure, which grants licenses through a slow bureaucratic process. Tyrix is still waiting for its license from the ministry of Telecom. An alternate way of entering the Indian market would be to ride on the strong tide of foreign investment pouring into India, as major U.S. corporations, including Hewlett Packard, Coca-Cola, and Morgan Stanley, set up shop here.

Eastern Asia. In Eastern Asia, people have slowly been adopting voice mail services.

In the Japanese business environment, people are accustomed to working in groups, typically sharing a phone or appointing someone to answer it. Consequently, when you call a company, a human almost always answers the phone. They have been accustomed to personal service over the phone and are often insulted if a machine answers and tries to serve them with a series of menus. A positive trend that has recently started is that all cordless phones sold in Japan have answering machines built into them, and their culture is becoming accustomed to using them in a home setting.

The telecommunication markets in many countries in this area have been controlled by governments, and are not open to competition. Although the Japanese market was deregulated in mid-1985, it wasn't until 1987 that competitors to the giant NTT (Nippon Telegraph and Telecommunications) emerged.[2] Moreover, foreign telecommunication manufacturers were barred from entering the Japanese market, which resulted in a stymied growth of the cellular market. In South Korea, the telecommunication market was opened to competition in September, 1993,[3] whereas Hong Kong, which has been preparing for deregulation for over two years now, has not yet opened up its market for competition. Deregulation is now scheduled for 1995.[4]

However, the cellular base in each of these markets has been increasing rapidly. This increase will consequently create a larger demand for voice messaging, and voice mail services will take off with this growth in the cellular market. The close interrelation between cellular and voice processing services is exemplified by the continuously growing number of collaborations between cellular and voice processing companies in the Pacific Rim. Tyrix is predicted to obtain a 22 percent market share ($24 million) in this market by 1996, second only to ClearVoice.

The Latin American Market

To date, Tyrix has targeted some Latin American markets, but has predominantly concentrated on Brazil. Many of the problems in Brazil are ones that occur in other emerging markets, too. Brazil's infrastructure has not been equipped for

---

[2]*Telephony* (July 1987).

[3] *Telecommunications Policy* (September/October 1993).

[4] *Business Asia* (August 1993).

DTMF usage yet, so Tyrix needs to sell DTMF-rotary dialing interfaces. In addition, several important features, such as call forwarding, have not yet been implemented on Brazil Telecom's switches. Since Tyrix's voice processing systems provide these services, the company sees this as another opportunity for growth in this market.

Tyrix has identified three ways of providing its voice mail services in the Latin American market, and is working on all of them: (1) cellular service, (2) residential/individual business phone service, and (3) the virtual phone. In order to enter these markets, Tyrix is in the process of establishing partnerships with foreign cellular companies and other telephone companies in order to help them to educate end users about how to use voice services. This kind of "pre-marketing" partnership has often benefited Tyrix in Asia, and is likely to do so in Latin America.

The European Market

In Europe, there are major regulatory hurdles. It takes about six months and costs about U.S. $500,000 to obtain approval from a European PTT (national post, telegraph, and telephone agencies) to connect a voice messaging system to the phone network. As European nations are undergoing processes of deregulation, the PTTs of Germany, The Netherlands, Sweden, Switzerland, Italy, and Spain are being privatized. As a result, they will gradually also lose their monopoly position, making it easier for competitors to offer phone service in those countries. As they compete, they will seek ways to differentiate their services, making it easier for equipment providers such as Tyrix to enter the market.

France has especially formidable regulatory barriers to overcome. They have strict guidelines for all goods purchased by the government. Specifically, the French government must first try to purchase the product from a local vendor. If a local vendor cannot be found, the second preference is a vendor from within the E.C. Only if no vendor can be found within the E.C. can the government consider purchasing from other countries like the United States or Japan.[5] Hence, Tyrix is at a major disadvantage here, since all its products are made in the U.S. Also, the French government's nationalistic attitude precludes buying equipment from nonnative suppliers. An additional critical barrier to entry for Tyrix in the CPE market in France was the need to meet French Telecom's technical standards and gain regulatory approvals. The technical changes to the products were not trivial. They involved modifying aspects such as frequency ranges (the 450Hz used in the U.S. is not a worldwide standard), busy tones and DTMF tone matching.

Further product changes were required to meet customer expectations. While the U.K. (through British Telecom and Mercury Communications) and

---

[5] Telecommunication Department, International Trade Association, U.S. Department of Commerce, 1995.

Germany (through Deutsche BundesPost) were rapidly adopting voice mail-boxes, French customers wanted an unanswered call to be routed to a secretary, with the use of a voice mailbox as a backup.

In 1990, the E.C. settled on a new digital standard of cellular communications called Groupe Standard Mobile (GSM) that covers all of Europe, enabling the cellular phone user to seamlessly operate across country borders. Tapping into the GSM market is attractive, due to its size (it covers 270 million out of the 350 million E.C. people), but challenging, due to the sophisticated product modifications that Tyrix needs to make.

Mercury Personal Communications (MPC), a division within Mercury Communications, is one of the largest cellular providers in this yet-to-be-regulated industry. It currently has 25 percent of the U.K. market of 300,000, and is forecasted to grow rapidly and expand its operations all over Europe. Tyrix was the first to sell voice messaging services to it, which gave a voice mailbox to all of its subscribers. This product was very attractive to MPC because it boosted its revenues almost overnight. In the past, every time a call was not completed on its network, no revenues were realized. Now, however, a caller can leave a voice-mail message, and MPC can charge for the call.

Now that the PTTs are being privatized, Tyrix needs to convince them that it is in their best interest to preemptively add these services now, by offering VIS for businesses and residences. One thing that is helping Tyrix to convince them is a deregulation of the cable television industry. The cable companies have begun selling bandwidth to cellular companies, competing with the PTTs for residential telephony.

Issues in the International Arena

When Tyrix first expanded into international markets, the field sales representatives led the charge. No corporate marketing group existed for the purpose of charting international strategies. The field personnel used their own strategies to enter these markets, and have since developed significant expertise in their respective areas and, in this sense, gained power. Now, however, with the domestic market maturing, the company's emphasis on international operations is becoming stronger. The marketing managers at corporate headquarters want to centralize international marketing now. They feel that field personnel, who have short-term perspectives on local markets, are not qualified to develop what is required now—longer-term strategies that take into account all potential international opportunities. Although each new international venture will require decentralized implementation, resources for customization are limited. These resources need to be deployed only toward those opportunities that are likely to yield the greatest returns.

Field personnel, on the other hand, are resisting the centralization effort and do not want to yield control. They believe that, since they are closest to the markets, they are the most able to respond to changes in the market environment. Tensions between corporate headquarters and the field are building up.

Case 11

Schweppes Raspberry Ginger Ale*

As Sam Johnson stood looking out from the window of his luxurious office, he wondered how he should go about evaluating the performance of his division's new product—Schweppes Raspberry Ginger Ale—during the first half of 1991, as compared to his expectations at the beginning of the year when the product was first introduced to the market. Further, he wondered if, in fact, the product would take his division into the mainstream soft drink market as he had hoped.

Company Background

Cadbury Schweppes Public Limited Company was one of the largest British-owned confectionery and soft drink companies, with marketing operations in more than 100 countries around the world. In 1989, the company recorded total sales of £2,843.2 million and a before-tax profit of £251 million.[1] The company managed its beverage operations in North America through Cadbury Beverages North America (CBNA). CBNA was organized into several subdivisions, each handling projects under a specific brand, namely, Schweppes, Canada Dry, Sunkist, Crush, Hires, and Mott's. Although divisions of one company, they operated independently and competed freely in the market. A product director and an associate product manager, Sam Johnson, managed the Schweppes subdivision for the whole of North America. Exhibit 1 presents the organization structure of Cadbury Schweppes Public Limited Company.

*This case was prepared by Shreekant G. Joag as a basis for class discussion rather than to illustrate either effective or ineffective handling of an administrative situation. Used with permission from Shreekant G. Joag.

[1] £ 1 = U.S. $1.70.

EXHIBIT 1   Organization structure of Cadbury Schweppes Public Limited Company

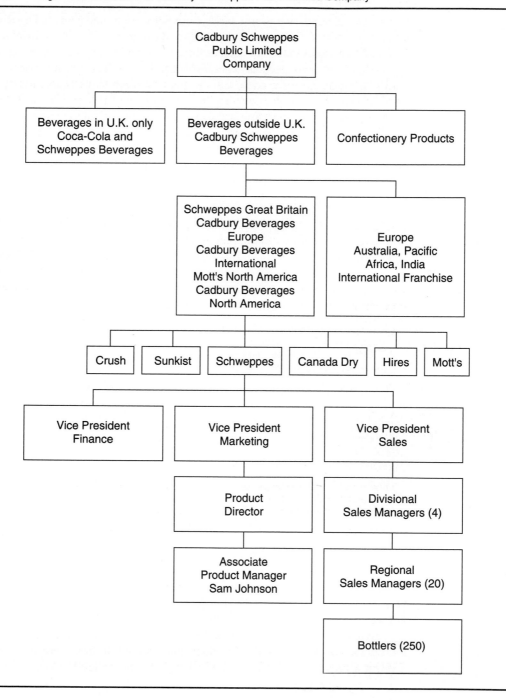

The Adult Soft Drink Business

Of the several subdivisions of CBNA, both Schweppes and Canada Dry divisions marketed products that came under the broad category of adult soft drinks. These included beverages that were used as mixers with alcoholic beverages, as well as others that were consumed as general soft drinks. Adult soft drinks consisted primarily of ginger ale, club soda, tonic water, bitter lemon, unsweetened manufactured and natural sparkling waters, and sweetened sparkling waters. By composition, the sweetened sparkling waters were in fact identical to regular soft drinks, even though they were marketed as waters. Exhibit 2 presents some basic information about adult soft drinks and the alcoholic beverages with which they are mixed. There were four leading brands in the adult soft drink market: Schweppes,

EXHIBIT 2   Basic information about adult soft drinks

Soft drink	Composition	Used as a mixer with	Percentage consumed as a	
			Mixer	Soft drink
Ginger ale	Carbonated water, sugar syrup, ginger flavor	Bourbon, rye	5%	95%
Club soda	Carbonated water, sodium carbonate (soda), common salt (sodium)	Whiskey	50	50
Tonic water	Carbonated water, quinine, sugar	Gin, vodka, rum	85	15
Bitter lemon	Carbonated water, quinine, sugar, lemon flavor	Gin, vodka	95	5
Unsweetened sparkling manufactured/ seltzer/seltzer water	Purified water, carbonation	Used by itself for digestion	5	95
Natural	Carbonated water from natural springs	Used by itself for digestion	5	95
Sweetened sparkling waters	Soft drinks marketed as waters	Used by itself	5	95
Bottled still waters manufactured	Purified natural lake or spring water	Used by itself for drinking	0	100
Natural	Lake or spring water as available in nature	Used by itself for drinking	0	100

Source: Schweppes, CBNA.

Canada Dry, Seagrams, and Polar. Many brands sold flavored and unflavored versions of sparkling water. Exhibit 3 presents the adult soft drinks marketed by Schweppes and major competing brands.

Although these four brands dominated the adult soft drink market, numerous small local brands together contributed a large portion of sales. Exhibit 4 presents the sales of the leading brands, collective sales of all other

EXHIBIT 3   Competing brands of adult soft drinks

Adult soft drink	Schweppes (SP)	Canada Dry (CD)	Seagrams (SG)	Polar (PR)
Ginger ale	SP ginger ale	CD ginger ale	SG ginger ale	PR ginger ale
	SP diet ginger ale	CD diet ginger ale	SG diet ginger ale	PR diet ginger ale
Club soda	SP club soda	CD club soda	SG club soda	PR club soda
	SP sodium-free club soda			
Tonic water	SP tonic water	CD tonic water	SG tonic water	PR tonic water
	SP diet tonic water	CD diet tonic water	SG diet tonic water	PR diet tonic water
Bitter lemon	SP bitter lemon	CD bitter lemon		
Unsweetened sparking waters				
Manufactured— unflavored	SP unsweetened, unflavored sparkling water	CD unsweetened, unflavored sparkling water	SG unsweetened, unflavored sparkling water	PR unsweetened, unflavored sparkling water
Manufactured— flavored	SP unsweetened, flavored sparkling water	CD unsweetened, flavored sparkling water	SG unsweetened, flavored sparkling water	PR unsweetened, flavored sparkling water

Source: Schweppes, CBNA.

EXHIBIT 4   Sales and market shares of major brands of adult soft drinks in 1990 (in thousands of cases)

						Industry total	
Adult soft drink	Schweppes	Canada Dry	Seagrams	Polar	Others	Cases	Percentage of Industry
Ginger ale	23,820	55,580	9,600	700	69,100	158,800	2.0%
Club soda	6,350	23,820	1,400	100	90	31,760	0.4
Tonic water	19,850	15,880	2,500	450	8,960	47,640	0.6
Sparkling waters	1,240	—	—	—	316,360	317,600	4.0
Others	—	17,845	2,980	—	177,675	198,500	2.5
Total adult soft drinks	51,260	113,125	16,480	1,250	572,185	754,300	9.5
Other CBNA products							
Sunkist		56,000					
Diet Sunkist		3,500					
Total soft drinks	51,260	172,625	16,480	1,250		7,940,000	100.0

Source: Estimates based on *Beverage Industry Annual Manual 90–91* (New York: Edgell Communications Inc., 1990); Scanner Data, Schweppes, CBNA.

small brands, and total industry sales of each type of adult soft drink in 1990. In the soft drink industry, general soft drinks constituted the bulk of the market. The share of adult drinks in the total soft drink market had increased modestly, from 6 percent in 1980 to 7 percent in 1990. Exhibit 5 presents the trends in market shares of various soft drink flavors, and the leading marketers within each flavor for the period 1980 to 1990.

EXHIBIT 5   Soft drink market trends in the United States by flavor

	1980	1985	1990
Cola	63.0%	67.5%	70.0%
Coca-Cola Company	30.0	33.0	33.0
PepsiCo	25.0	25.0	26.0
Royal Crown Company	3.0	3.0	3.0
Others	5.0	6.5	8.0
Lemon-lime	13.0	12.2	10.0
Coca-Cola Company	4.0	4.0	5.0
Seven-Up Company	5.0	5.0	4.0
Others	4.0	3.2	1.0
Pepper	6.0	4.9	5.0
Juice added	—	3.9	—
Root beer	3.0	2.7	3.0
Orange	6.0	4.7	2.5
Sunkist			0.8
Others			1.7
*All other flavors**	9.0	8.0	9.5
Total all flavors together	100.0	100.0	100.0

All other flavors in 1990	9.5 %
Ginger ale	2.0
Schweppes	0.3
Canada Dry	0.7
Other	1.0
Club soda	0.4
Schweppes	0.08
Canada Dry	0.3
Other	0.02
Tonic Water	0.6
Schweppes	0.25
Canada Dry	0.20
Other	0.15
Sparkling waters	4.0
All remaining flavors	2.5

*All figures are rounded up.

Source: Estimates based on *Beverage Industry Annual Manual 90–91* (New York: Edgell Communications, Inc., 1990).

The soft drink industry as a whole competed with all other hot and cold beverages and liquids for a share of the consumer's stomach. In the period between 1965 and 1990, the soft drink share of the average per capita consumption of all liquids increased from 17.8 gallons to 48.0 gallons per year. The total U.S. population increased from 194 million to 250 million in the same period, resulting in the increase in total soft drink sales/consumption from 2,490 million cases per year to 7,940 million cases per year. Exhibit 6 presents the market trends in terms of per capita consumption of various liquids in the United States from 1965 to 1990. The exhibit reports all liquid consumption figures based on the assumption that the consumer, on average, consumes 182.5 gallons of liquids in a year. The exhibit also presents the U.S. population figures and actual total sales of all soft drinks for comparison.

Because of their popular image and use as mixers, adult soft drinks were primarily sold in 1-liter polyethylene (PET) bottles rather than 12-ounce cans and

2-liter PET bottles, which were popular packages for all other soft drinks. Exhibit 7 presents U.S. market trends in packaging for the industry. Exhibit 8 presents similar market trends in the diet versus regular versions.

EXHIBIT 6   Liquid market trends in the United States

	U.S. per capita liquids consumption, in gallons						
	1965	*1970*	*1975*	*1980*	*1985*	*1989*	*1990*
Soft drinks	17.8	22.7	26.3	34.2	40.8	46.6	48.0
Coffee	37.8	35.7	33.0	27.4	25.8	24.7	23.6
Beer	15.9	18.5	21.6	24.3	23.8	23.3	23.0
Milk	24.0	23.1	22.5	20.8	20.2	20.9	20.5
Tea	3.8	5.2	7.3	7.3	7.3	7.3	7.3
Bottled water	—	—	1.2	2.7	4.5	7.1	12.0
Juices	3.8	5.2	6.7	6.8	7.0	6.8	7.0
Powdered drinks	—	—	4.8	6.0	6.2	4.8	5.0
Wine	1.0	1.9	1.7	2.1	2.4	2.2	2.4
Distilled spirits	1.5	1.8	2.0	2.0	1.8	1.4	1.3
Subtotal	105.6	113.5	127.1	133.6	139.8	145.2	150.0
Imported tap water	76.9	69.0	55.4	48.9	42.7	37.3	32.5
Total	182.5	182.5	182.5	182.5	182.5	182.5	182.5
U.S. population (in millions)	194.0	205.0	216.0	223.0	238.0	247.0	250.0
Soft drink consumption (192-oz. cases, in millions)	2,490	3,090	3,780	5,180	6,500	7,710	7,940

Source: *Beverage Industry Annual Manual 90–91* (New York: Edgell Communications, Inc., 1990); figures estimated by extrapolation; and *Current Population Reports: Population Estimates and Projections* (Washington, D.C.: U.S. Bureau of the Census, various years).

EXHIBIT 7   Soft drink packaging trends in the United States— percentage of soft drinks using each

Packaging	*1980*	*1985*	*1990*
Cans	40.0%	40.8%	50.0%
Polyethylene (PET) bottles	30.0	30.6	30.0
Nonrecycled glass	14.0	13.0	12.0
Recycled glass	16.0	15.6	8.9
Total	100.0%	100.0%	100.0%

EXHIBIT 8   Soft drink market trends in the United States—diet versus regular

		1980	*1985*	*1990*
Diet	M Cases	770.0	1,500.2	2,223.0
	%	15.0	23.1	28.0
Regular	M Cases	4,403.0	4,999.8	5,717.0
	%	85.0	76.9	72.0
Total	M Cases	5,180.0	6,500.0	7,940.0
	%	100.0	100.0	100.0

Manufacturing of Schweppes Adult Soft Drinks

Both Schweppes and Canada Dry were primarily marketing companies. They imported the concentrate for tonic water from Great Britain. Concentrates for all other Schweppes soft drinks and most Canada Dry soft drinks were manufactured by the Dr Pepper Company in the United States. Both Schweppes and Canada Dry sold the concentrate to their separate bottlers under a licensing agreement. Each bottler was assigned a territory on an exclusive basis.

Historically, colas dominated the U.S. soft drink market (70 percent market share in 1990), as did, to a much lesser extent, lemon-limes (10 percent market share in 1990). Further, the cola market was dominated by Coca-Cola or PepsiCo brands. Therefore, most major bottlers had exclusive agreements with either Coca-Cola or PepsiCo to market their colas as the primary product line.

Because of their heavy dependence on the cola giants, the bottlers were under great pressure to bottle and market the other soft drink products produced by the cola companies. Many medium-sized bottlers had exclusive agreements with the Seven-Up Company and depended on 7-Up as their principal product. The remaining bottlers were mostly small local companies dependent on other smaller soft drink brands. Once the principal product line was established by an exclusive agreement, the bottlers widened their product assortment by marketing other noncompeting adult soft drinks such as ginger ale, tonic water, sodas, and bottled waters and general soft drinks such as the peppers, oranges, and root beers. Thus a typical product line of a medium- to large-sized bottler would consist of one of the following three combinations:

1. Coca-Cola, Fanta, Sprite, and Schweppes or Canada Dry (but not both).
2. Pepsi Cola, Slice, Mountain Dew, and Schweppes or Canada Dry (but not both).
3. 7-Up, 7-Up Gold, a noncompeting cola, and Schweppes or Canada Dry (but not both).

Fortunately for Schweppes and Canada Dry, Coca-Cola, Pepsi, and Seven-Up did not have their own brands of adult soft drinks. Therefore, the products marketed by Schweppes and Canada Dry complemented the general soft drinks of the cola and the lemon-lime giants. This made it relatively easy for them to convince major bottlers to accept adult soft drinks as complementary to their main product lines. Thus, though rigidly defined by factors beyond their control, Schweppes and Canada Dry found the market structure to be excellent. In some territories, Schweppes had exclusive agreements with Coca-Cola bottlers to market its adult soft drinks and Canada Dry had exclusive agreements with Pepsi bottlers. In some other territories, Schweppes went with Pepsi bottlers while Canada Dry went with Coca-Cola bottlers. Thus, Schweppes and Canada Dry both marketed their products through Coca-Cola as well as PepsiCo bottlers. However, in no territory did Schweppes and Canada Dry use a common bottler. The competition between Schweppes and Canada Dry was carried out in earnest in every aspect of the business.

In addition, historically, Canada Dry had developed a network of exclusive Canada Dry bottlers. Though totally committed to Canada Dry, their strength and importance in the market as well as to Canada Dry had gradually been reduced because of their limited product line. The total volume of soft drink business handled by each bottler ranged from 500 thousand cases to 50 million cases per year, with 3 million cases per year as the typical size.

Distribution of Adult Soft Drinks

The exclusive agreements made the bottlers solely responsible for distributing the soft drinks of their principals in the assigned territories. Armed with the exclusive distributorship of a full range of products, each bottler competed with the others to market its products through the various channels available. Depending on its relative influence, each bottler obtained its share of the space in supermarkets, drug stores, retail chains, convenience stores, gas stations, vending machines, and other outlets for soft drinks.

Marketers commonly classified store space as shelf space or display space. Shelf space was the regular space allocated to a product on the shelves in the aisles. Display space was the space on the shelves located at the end of the aisles that faced outward toward the periphery of the store. Over half of all shoppers invariably circled the store to buy daily necessities such as meats, vegetables, dairy products, and bakery products, which the stores positioned along the periphery. The customers entered the aisles only when they needed specific items located there. As such, the end-of-aisle displays received the maximum consumer exposure and served to remind consumers of the items they might need. Thus, the shelf space and the display space each had its unique role in generating sales. Both were very precious to retailers, bottlers, and the soft drink companies alike. Naturally, there was great competition to acquire an adequate share of the limited store space.

Once a bottler had negotiated the store space with the retailers, management had to determine how to allocate it optimally among the various soft drink brands so as to offer a complete assortment to the consumers and maximize sales and profits. Conventionally, the bottlers displayed the general soft drinks, adult soft drinks, and the bottled waters in separate groups, though in close proximity to one another. Typically, the colas and the lemon-limes accounted for most of the business of a bottler, with the adult soft drinks constituting an important but very small portion of the business. Invariably, the cola and the lemon-lime companies were able to dictate their terms in deciding the allocation of the total store space available to a bottler. As such, the colas and the lemon-limes dominated all prime display space and a large portion of the shelf space as well. In comparison, adult soft drinks had to fight hard for adequate shelf space. Fortunately, the dominant position of Canada Dry and Schweppes in the adult soft drink group and the noncompeting nature of their product lines made the task of obtaining shelf space slightly less difficult. Adult soft drinks accounted for 1 to 15 percent of the total business of Schweppes' bottlers, with 3.3 percent as the typical proportion. Generally, a store carried an average inventory of six cases of each soft drink product that turned over 25 times in a year. The relatively low bargaining power of even large bottlers of adult soft drinks made the marketing of adult soft drinks one of the toughest and most challenging tasks. Convincing the bottlers to allocate adequate space to adult soft drink brands became the primary focus of Schweppes' marketing efforts. Johnson described the task: "Our bottlers spill more Coke or Pepsi than the ginger ale they sell. We have no illusions here. Although we make an important contribution to their profits, it is only a small contribution. They do not really depend on us. We need them far more than they need us."

Schweppes's Ginger Ale Product Line

Ginger ale consists of carbonated water, sugar syrup, and ginger flavor. Both Schweppes and Canada Dry marketed their own brands of ginger ale in regular and diet varieties. A much larger quantity of ginger ale was consumed when used as a soft drink than as a mixer. Therefore, in regions where both applications were popular, the consumption as a soft drink invariably generated the bulk of the sales volume. The relative consumption of the product for these two purposes varied in different regions of the United States. In the Northeast, ginger ale was equally popular as a soft drink or as a mixer. In the West, it was primarily consumed as a mixer with alcohol. Because the sales of both Schweppes and Canada Dry were heavily concentrated in the Northeast, a very large proportion of the total ginger ale marketed by the two divisions was consumed as a soft drink.

It was fair to assume that the various brands of ginger ale competed among themselves for the market segment preferring ginger ale flavor. However, in a general sense, they also competed with all other adult soft drinks as well as all general soft drinks, and even all hot and cold beverages. Canada Dry was the largest marketer of ginger ale in North America, controlling 33.5 percent of the U.S. ginger ale market. Schweppes was the second-largest marketer with 16.6 percent share of the market. The third competitor, Seagrams, had only 3.1 percent of the market.

Consumer Image of Ginger Ale

Despite the predominant use of ginger ale as a soft drink, most consumers did not think of ginger ale as a soft drink. Several unaided recall tests among users and nonusers of ginger ale had shown that very few people remembered or considered ginger ale to be a general soft drink. Most people primarily considered it either as a mixer or as a soft drink for special occasions such as adult social gatherings when alcohol was being consumed. There were many possible explanations for this phenomenon.

As mentioned previously, a person tended to consume a much larger quantity of ginger ale as a soft drink as compared to the quantity consumed as a mixer. Although the bulk of the ginger ale was consumed as a soft drink, only a small number of consumers were involved in generating that volume, with each person consuming a relatively large quantity. In contrast, a relatively larger number of consumers were involved in generating a relatively smaller sales volume of ginger ale as a mixer, with each person consuming a small quantity of the soft drink. Such consumption was often in an adult setting where at least some people were consuming alcohol. This further confirmed the association of ginger ale with alcohol in the consumers' perceptions.

In addition, the small market share of ginger ale compared to all soft drinks suggested that a large proportion of individuals were nonusers of the product. The image of ginger ale in the minds of such consumers was based on where they saw it being consumed and what they heard about it. On both these accounts, the probability was far greater that the nonusers encountered the ginger ale as a mixer rather than as a soft drink.

The bottlers also perceived ginger ale primarily as a mixer; therefore, they distributed it mainly in 1-liter PET bottles and promoted it as a mixer. This further confirmed and perpetuated the consumer image of ginger ale as a mixer. The only exception was in the Northeast, where the product was widely available in popular soft drink packaging of 12-ounce cans and 2-liter PET bottles.

Interestingly, surveys showed that even those who consumed ginger ale as a soft drink considered it primarily a mixer. Johnson was always puzzled by this apparent contradiction in the use of the product and its image. Further, he often felt that such a distorted image prevented ginger ale from exploiting its full potential as a tasty, refreshing general-purpose soft drink for all occasions. He wondered what he could possibly do to change the image of the product and reposition it in the consumer's mind as a mainstream general soft drink.

Schweppes Raspberry Ginger Ale

In May 1988, one of the Schweppes's leading bottlers conceived the idea of marketing raspberry-flavored ginger ale as a general soft drink for all occasions. After obtaining initial clearance to explore the concept further, Johnson spent considerable time perfecting the product ingredients and conducting laboratory and field tests. The tests indicated that the product had a unique, appealing taste, and many of those who tried it felt that it was a fascinating new soft drink. By October 1990, the product was fully developed and Schweppes had to make the final decision about its commercial introduction. Johnson realized that product development was perhaps the easiest part of the whole process. The real challenge was to analyze the feasibility of the idea and prepare a new product proposal to convince top management to proceed with the product's introduction. Once that decision was made, Johnson would have to convince the bottlers to adopt the product and obtain their commitment to make it available in retail outlets by January 1991.

Johnson was really excited about Schweppes Raspberry Ginger Ale (SRGA). He had always felt that, for some unknown reason, all Schweppes adult soft drinks, and especially ginger ale, had been locked in the upscale mixer image that limited their growth potential and isolated them from the volume business of the mainstream general soft drinks. However, he was confident that the SRGA had a unique and distinct personality that was powerful enough to make a clear break from the ginger ale's traditional image and present itself as a legitimate general soft drink before the bottlers as well as the ultimate consumers. He felt that this product could launch the company on a totally new course to become a major player in the soft drink industry in time to come. This was an ideal way to bridge the gap between the company's image as a marketer of mixers and its desire to be a mainstream soft drink company.

In principle, the idea of creating new flavored versions of established soft drinks was not totally new. Other leading soft drink manufacturers had introduced different flavored soft drinks. Some of these products, such as Cherry Coke and Cherry 7-Up, had achieved limited success in the market, whereas others, such as 7-Up Gold, had failed and had to be withdrawn. Although the moderately successful products had created small segments of loyal consumers, they had been tried and rejected by many others. These consumers may be less enthusiastic about trying such new product versions the next time. Thus, despite the support of a major bottler, the product's unique refreshing taste, and strong consumer appeal, the company feared that it might face strong consumer resistance or disinterest. Moreover, Schweppes had always taken pride in its upscale image, if not its snob appeal. The new product concept aimed at the mass market might not fit this image as well.

Another area of uncertainty was the effect SRGA would have on other Schweppes products, as well as on Canada Dry and other CBNA divisions. Johnson felt that his immediate concern was to estimate the extent to which SRGA would cannibalize Schweppes's own ginger ale business. As a conservative estimate, he felt that initially about 20 percent of all SRGA sales would come from ginger ale. The cannibalized volume of Schweppes ginger ale would peak at 2 million cases per year and level off. However, he had no idea how the new product would impact various other brands of CBNA and other competitors in the market.

Johnson realized that he would have to modify the strategy he developed to convince his top management for them to convince the bottlers. In turn, he would have to help the bottlers convince the retailers to adopt the product. His major thrust would have to be on the new business generated by SRGA and the increase in total profits earned by each channel member.

In order to analyze the feasibility of SRGA, Johnson had compiled all relevant information. He estimated that ginger ale sold at an average price of $10 per 192-ounce case to the ultimate consumer. SRGA would be sold at about the same price. The retailers expected a margin of 20 percent on their sales revenue. Similarly, bottlers expected a margin of 25 percent on their sales to the retailers. The cost of each case to the bottler was $1 for the ginger ale concentrate paid to Schweppes, $2 for other variable materials, and $3 for all other variable costs. In Johnson's opinion, the channel members earned similar margins on all other major competing brands. Schweppes would have to sell SRGA concentrate to the bottlers at the same price as that of ginger ale concentrate.

For Schweppes, the cost of buying the ginger ale concentrate from its supplier was 15 percent of its sales revenue. In addition, Schweppes spent 45 percent of its sales revenue for marketing expenses. The SRGA concentrate would cost Schweppes 20 percent of sales and its marketing costs would be 50 percent of sales. In addition, $990,000 would have to be spent on introductory promotions.

Johnson realized that his first task would be to analyze how consumers were likely to perceive the new product in comparison with Schweppes ginger ale. Such an analysis would help him to understand what efforts he had to make to successfully position SRGA as a mainstream soft drink. On the basis of his previous experience with new products and considering the fact that SRGA was to be introduced as a mainstream soft drink, Johnson's conservative forecast of SRGA sales in the first five years was 2, 5, 8, 10, and 14 million cases. Using these figures as the basis, Johnson now had to establish SRGA's feasibility for Schweppes, its bottlers, and its retailers. He would also have to estimate the likely consumer response to the new product. He realized that he would have to prepare his new product proposal shortly so that there was sufficient time to approach the bottlers and actually introduce the product by January 1991.

Market Introduction of Schweppes Raspberry Ginger Ale

In January 1991, Schweppes Raspberry Ginger Ale was introduced nationally in the United States with full fanfare, spending a total of $1 million on introductory promotions. By the end of June, the company had surpassed all sales forecasts and sold 2 million cases of SRGA. When management compared the performance of various Schweppes product lines in the first six months of 1991 with the same period of 1990, they observed that Schweppes ginger ale sales had stayed at 15.6 million cases, although all other Schweppes products had recorded an increase of 4 percent, the same as the growth rate of the soft drink industry.

In an attempt to understand what impact SRGA had made on the other brands, the company conducted a consumer survey. Using a consumer panel, the study compared actual purchases of various brands during the first six months of 1990 compared to the first six months of 1991. The data were analyzed to determine what percentage of total SRGA sales had been generated at the cost of various other brands. The results of the study are summarized in Exhibit 9. Johnson realized that he had only a few days to analyze the SRGA's sales performance and the results of the survey. By the following week, he would have to present his findings before CBNA's top management and recommend a future course of action.

EXHIBIT 9   Percentage of SRGA sales sourced from various competing brands

Soft drink types	Schweppes	Canada Dry	Other CBNA	Total CBNA	Other competitors	Total
Colas					22%	22%
Lemon-lime					10	10
Peppers					1	1
Root beer					5	5
Orange			3%	3%	11	14
All other flavors	4%	23%		27	21	48
Total	4	23	3	30	70	100
All other flavors						
Ginger ales	3	23		26	10	36
Club soda + tonic water	1	0		1	0	1
Bottled waters					1	1
Other					10	10

Source: Schweppes, CBNA Consumer Study, January–June 1991.

Case 12

Electrohome (A): Projection Systems Division*

On Monday morning, September 25, 1989, in Kitchener, Canada, the department heads of the Projection Systems Division of Electrohome Limited met to discuss what, if anything, could or should be done in light of the Sony Corporation's launch of a new, high-end projector that outperformed all other projectors on the market. Kenneth Mitchell, manager of the Projection Systems Division (Electrohome), had called the meeting with Terry Schmidt, advanced development engineer; Lloyd Wilson, director of sales; Alan Caskey, North American sales manager; Gerry Zinger, manufacturing manager; and Tom Sutherland, marketing manager.

Sony had surprised the electronic projection system industry in August by unveiling its new Sony 1270 "superdata" projector at the Siggraph trade show in Boston. The Sony 1270 captured first place at the show as the industry's highest-performing projector. Placing even more pressure on Electrohome was the rumour that the 1270 was going to be priced 20–40 percent below the established market price for high-end projectors. Most of the industry saw this as an attempt to widen the market through low prices. Because Electrohome was a relatively small batch manufacturer, such a combination of high performance and low price posed a major threat.

The 1270's introduction was timed to prevent substantial competitive response. The most important trade show to the industry, Infocomm, was scheduled to take place in January, 1990, in the United States. Industry analysts, dealers, and large customers would be there and top product performance typically translated into increased sales. Sony had a product with superior picture quality, and it was

*Neil Miller prepared this case under the supervision of Adrian Ryans and Mark Vandenbosch solely to provide material for class discussion. The case is not intended to illustrate either effective or ineffective handling of a managerial situation. Certain names and other identifying information may have been disguised to protect confidentiality. Some of the material in this case was drawn from the Barco Projection Systems (A) case (HBS 9-591-133) prepared by Research Associate Krista McQuade under the supervision of Professor Rowland T. Moriarty. Any form of reproduction, storage, or transmittal of this material is prohibited without written permission from Western Business School. Copyright © 1995 The University of Western Ontario.

favored to capture first place as the top-performing projector at Infocomm. The management team at Electrohome now had to decide how they would respond to Sony's new product.

Electrohome

Electrohome Limited was formed in 1907 by the efforts and drive of Arthur B. Pollock. A bookkeeper, clerk, and salesperson by trade, Pollock found himself in New York City at the turn of the century, looking for success. While there, he discovered phonographs with the horns concealed in a cabinet. After many discussions with the designers and manufacturers, Arthur felt such a machine would be successful in Canada.

From assembling imported parts to make Canada's first hornless phonograph, Electrohome progressed to designing, engineering, and manufacturing a wide array of products, including televisions, high-fidelity entertainment centers, phonographs, radios, high-style occasional wooden, metal, and upholstered furniture, electric fans, heaters, air circulators, fractional-horsepower motors, humidifiers, can openers, and industrial electronic devices. Through all of this, Electrohome remained a Canadian-owned company, with John Pollock, a third-generation member of the family, acting as chairman and CEO in 1989.

In 1973, Electrohome was largely a consumer product manufacturer. The firm was producing 800 color television sets and 1,200 black and white monitors per day. At that time, Electrohome was experiencing a small decline in TV sales. This slump in sales was due to the lack of replacement business, as Electrohome televisions lasted much longer than any other manufacturer's, and the competition from Japanese manufacturers, who were emerging as a major force in North America with their low-cost products. In contrast, monitor sales were picking up, with businesses making up the bulk of the customer base. By 1982, Electrohome was no longer manufacturing consumer television sets.

In 1975, Electrohome entered into a 5-year contract with Advent Corporation, which was based in Cambridge, Massachusetts. Advent was the pioneer in manufacturing large-screen (6 feet diagonal) projection TV sets. Electrohome was chosen by Advent to manufacture the electronics chassis for the TV. Advent had a vision of putting one in every home in North America, and, over the next five years, 130,000 units were sold. However, in 1980, sales slowed down. The product was too big and expensive ($4,000 U.S.) for every home.

Throughout the 1980s, Electrohome remained committed to providing quality products and services that conformed to specified customer requirements. By 1988, with the sale of the firm's furniture interests and consumer product servicing division, Electrohome had effectively removed itself from the consumer market. This led to the firm's mission statement:

> To provide creative and technological solutions through the marketing and manufacturing of products and services for selected world communication and industrial markets.

Electronics Group

Until 1984, the Electronics Group was a centralized entity within Electrohome. In 1984, the group decentralized and split into six individually managed profit centers. In 1987, the group was reorganized into four divisions:

1. Projection Systems
2. Display Systems
3. Digital Video Systems
4. Operations Services.

The Projection Systems Division designed, manufactured, and marketed industrial projectors (see Exhibit 1). Unlike movie projectors that shone white light through film, these projectors recreated the image electronically. Electrohome's projectors could be connected to cameras, VCRs, or computers. The main use of these projectors was to project images and information onto large screens for large audience viewing.

Display Systems developed and manufactured monitors and other display equipment for a wide array of applications. The Digital Video Systems division produced technology that would display data and information on top of, or "over," video segments (video special effects). Operations Services carried out metal stamping operations and manufactured printed circuit boards for Electrohome's products as well as for sale to third-party customers.

Each division had its own marketing, development, and sales personnel. Electrohome Projection Systems was the firm's largest business unit, with 1988 sales of $30.7 million (Canadian), 15 percent of the company's total sales (see Exhibit 2). Electrohome competed in a global market and had a strong commitment to timely introductions of new, innovative products based on R&D efforts. The Electronics Group's R&D expenditures totalled $6.3 million in 1988.

Kenneth Mitchell had a small but effective management team for the Projection System Division (see Exhibit 3). Lloyd Wilson, who had just joined the division, was the sales manager. Reporting to him was Alan Caskey, the North American sales manager. The marketing manager was Tom Sutherland.

Evolution of Electrohome's Projection Systems' Product Line

In 1978, Electrohome was the supplier of monitors used at the IBM training center in Toronto, Canada. IBM wanted to have the ability to display computer-generated training material to large audiences and was trying to hook up computers to existing projection televisions. The problem was that consumer products, such as TVs and basic monitors, would not work with the computer-generated data. The TV's circuits were just not compatible with the computer's. IBM had Sony attempt to interface the two technologies to no avail.

EXHIBIT 1   Projector system

Electrohome became aware of IBM's need and attempted to find a technological solution. Electrohome had considerable technological expertise in monitor design, including a number of patents on its own proprietary design. By separating the scanning circuits, the technicians were able to increase the scanning frequency, allowing the computer source to interface with the monitor. This development led to Electrohome entering the monochrome computer projection market.

EXHIBIT 2 Projection Systems Division operating statements ($ millions)

	1988	1989
Sales	$30.7	$36.2
Gross contribution	13.5	17.7
Division expenses		
Marketing and sales	6.6	7.3
Administration	1.3	1.4
Other	0.3	0.5
Development	2.3	2.3
Total expenses	10.5	11.5
Division profit contribution	3.0	6.2
Corporate administration	0.6	0.7
Finance charges	0.4	0.6
Pretax income	$2.0	$4.9

EXHIBIT 3 Projection Systems Division

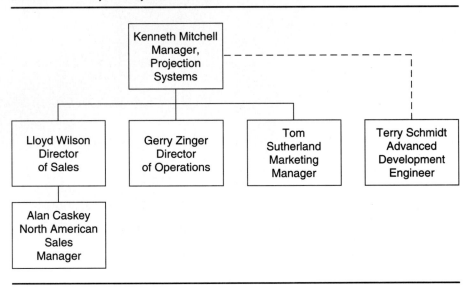

Electrohome then took a rough prototype of this new product to a trade show to gauge the response and potential demand for such a product. Even though they only had the prototype, Electrohome sales representatives at the trade show ended up taking 17 orders for the product. That response far exceeded Electrohome's expectations. Following some further research, Electrohome decided to go ahead and produce this new type of product. Electrohome delivered its first monochrome cathode ray tube (CRT) data projection system in 1979. This was the first of several engineering firsts in Electrohome's projector business.

In 1983, Electrohome introduced the first CRT-based single-lens color data/graphics projection system with variable scanning and auto lock. The variable scanning frequency allowed the projection system to interface with a variety of different input sources, such as VCRs and computers, which had different scan rates. By 1985, this technology had advanced enough to be able to handle ultra-high-resolution CAD/CAM systems (30–71 kHz).

With its commitment to user-friendly products, the engineering division developed the first three-lens projector system with digital convergence, microprocessor memory, remote control, and adjustable image size (5–25') in 1987. The microprocessor was incorporated to allow the end user to select certain predetermined focus settings. This meant that if the machine was moved from one room to another or from video to data applications, the end user would only have to go through the complex procedure of setting it up once. The microprocessor would then save the settings and, when needed, could recall them and automatically set up the machine. When Sony later introduced a machine with similar capabilities, everyone at Electrohome felt vindicated in their decision to develop this technology. From then on, Electrohome concentrated on the development of three-lens projectors.

Electrohome Products in 1989

Electrohome's projectors were comprised of tubes (three), lenses (three), and electronic controls, which represented 15 percent, 20 percent, and 50 percent, respectively, of a projector's cost structure. All of Electrohome's projector designs in 1989 used 7" tubes and lenses. Electrohome's particular strength was in the electronic systems that affected quality, reliability, and user-friendliness. Since 1983, all tubes used in Electrohome products were purchased from the Components Division of Sony Corporation. This was a totally separate division from Sony's Projectors Division. Organizationally, the reporting structure of the two divisions only came together at the chairman of the Sony Corporation. Not everyone at Electrohome was in agreement with the decision to buy one of the most important components of the end product from a major competitor. The end result, however, was a better-quality picture, because no other tubes on the market could match the quality of the Sony tube. In 1989, all the major manufacturers of video projection systems were using Sony tubes, and Electrohome alone was spending over $1 million per year on Sony tubes.

The main characteristic that distinguished the various products in the market was scan rate, or scanning frequency. This was a measure of the speed at which a projector could read and process incoming electronic signals. Customers were categorized as commercial, government, educational, and other, regardless of the particular application for which they were using the projector. Video projectors were designed to scan at a rate of 15 kHz, which was compatible with TV and VCR technology. Data projectors scanned at a rate of 15–36 kHz and were used to display material from computers. The most powerful projectors, with scan rates of 15–70 kHz, were the graphics projectors. These were used to display information from computer-aided design and manufacturing (CAD/CAM) systems.

Scan rate was an important basis of competition at the high end of the projection system market. Once an adequate scan rate was achieved, firms had to find other ways of differentiating themselves. The main differentiating features of the products were "picture quality" (a combination of brightness, image quality, and resolution), reliability, user-friendliness, and price. Given Electrohome's small size, relative to some of its competitors, management knew that it was not the low-cost producer in the industry. Combining this with another competitor's commitment to be at the technological forefront of the industry, Electrohome management had to carve its own niche in the industry to remain competitive. Electrohome differentiated its products on the basis of reliability and user-friendliness. While its picture quality was generally not the best in the industry, it was more than acceptable to most customers. In an industry that was notorious for poor reliability and very complex machines, Electrohome's reliability and user-friendliness were valued by many customers.

The end users of projectors made their purchase decisions partly on the basis of a series of "head-to-head" comparisons. The "shoot-out" at trade shows, where all the competitors would bring their best products and line them up side by side for comparison, was one way major customers and dealers could compare all of the products. A more common scenario was for the purchaser to narrow her or his choice down to two manufacturers, and have the chosen firms come to the purchaser's own premises and demonstrate the machines. These two buying processes were the driving forces behind Electrohome's commitment to user-friendliness.

With the customer watching the machines being set up and operated at a shoot-out or a private demonstration, Electrohome felt that it could not afford to have any problems. If it did have a technical problem, Electrohome wanted to be assured that it could be easily and quickly fixed. At on-site demonstrations, most manufacturers would allow as much time as possible to set up and prepare the projector. Electrohome sales staff would purposely arrive with only a few minutes to spare to illustrate how easy Electrohome projectors were to set up and operate.

By 1989, Electrohome had three product lines and was well established in the data and graphics markets. Scanning rates were available up to 80 kHz. User-friendly features included microprocessor memory, automatic digital convergence, remote control, and adjustable image size. The three projectors in the Electrohome line were the ECP 2000, 3000, and 4000, respectively (see Exhibit 4). The ECP 2000 projector was a simple, easy-to-use, single-lens projector that was being phased out. The ECP 2000 sold to a very small segment of the market and accounted for only 5 percent of Electrohome's sales.

The ECP 3000 and 4000 were three-lens projectors with very respectable picture quality and ease of use. The 3000 projector was targeted at the training and conference room segments of the market, where the signal sources for the projectors were personal computers and VCRs. The 3000 was also very popular with corporate boardroom displays and presentations. Many companies found the ECP 3000 so easy to use that anyone at the presentation could operate it with limited technical support personnel.

EXHIBIT 4   Product comparisons*

Manufacturer	Model	Scan rate (kHz)	Light output (lumens)	Resolution (# of lines)	Ease to use (reputation)	Price ($U.S.)
Barco	BD600	16–45	600	1,600	Extremely complex	12,000
	BG400	16–72	400	2,000	Extremely complex	24,000
Electrohome	ECP2000	16–36	400	1,280	Very easy	8,600
	ECP3000	16–50	650	1,280	Very easy	14,500
	ECP4000	16–70	650	1,280	Very easy	24,000
Sony	VPH1031	16–35	300	1,100	Moderate	10,500
NEC	DP1200	16–35	475	800	Moderate	10,500
	GP3000	16–54	600	1,100	Moderate	16,000

*Adapted from Barco Projection Systems (A) case (HBS 9-591-133) prepared by Research Associate Krista McQuade under the supervision of Professor Rowland T. Moriarty.

The ECP 4000 was targeted at the engineering (CAD/CAM) and status display/mapping system segments. An example of such a segment customer would be a utility or a railroad company that required the status of the firm's entire system to be displayed or mapped out on large screens. Through a computer interface, the projectors would display what was happening in the system at that point in time. The majority of this segment required the higher resolution that the 4000 provided. The ECP 3000 and 4000 represented 60 percent and 35 percent of Electrohome's sales, respectively.

Projector Markets

Growth for the worldwide projector market through 1994 was expected to be 6.1 percent per year. However, expected growth rates for the different types of projectors varied widely (see Table 1).

TABLE 1   The worldwide market for industrial projectors, 1988*

	Percent of units	Predicted growth 1989–1994[†]	Price range ($U.S.)
Video	63%	0.8%	$ 5,000–$ 7,000
Data	33	12.3	$ 8,000–$15,000
Graphics	4	40.2	$20,000–$24,000
Total	**100%**	**6.1%**	**$ 5,000–$24,000**

*Estimated average annual growth.
[†] Adapted from Barco Projection Systems (A) case (HBS 9-591-133), prepared by Research Associate Krista McQuade under the supervision of Professor Rowland T. Moriarty.

For industrial projectors, the largest market in 1989 was estimated to be North America, with 50 percent of total unit sales. The expected annual growth for North America over the next five years was 3 percent. Estimated to be second in total unit sales was Western Europe, with 36 percent and a five-year annual growth rate predicted to be 8 percent. The Far Eastern market followed with 12 percent of 1989 unit sales and with an expected annual growth rate of 15 percent through 1994. Total worldwide sales in 1988 were just over 30,000 units.

Distribution System

In the industrial projector industry, dealers ranged from "box" dealers to "system" dealers. The box dealer sold projectors on the basis of cost alone. Normally found in large cities, box dealers would carry a large selection of audio/video equipment from a variety of manufacturers, would provide little consultative selling, and had limited service capabilities. System dealers had the expertise and knowledge to design and install integrated packages of equipment according to the end user's specifications and needs. Often, these systems involved more than one type of equipment. System dealers were attracted to Electrohome's products because of their reliability, ease of installation and set up, and margin. Surveys conducted by Electrohome showed Electrohome products to be the most profitable line for its dealers.

Almost all of Electrohome's dealers were system dealers. Electrohome had close to 100 dealers in the United States, each serving a limited geographical area. At any point in time, only 30–40 dealers were active and effective. Electrohome had a reputation for taking care of its dealers better than any other manufacturer in the industry. This close relationship was very beneficial to Electrohome, because the dealers became an invaluable source of feedback on the customers' needs and problems. The firm had sales representatives throughout the U.S. and one in Canada. Electrohome was also represented to a lesser extent in Europe and the Far East (about 50 dealers in total). The representatives were responsible for training and retaining the attention and loyalty of the dealers. It was common practice for Electrohome representatives to accompany the dealer on sales calls in order to provide technical and sales support. Electrohome's marketing and sales expenses typically ranged from 20 to 23 percent of sales.

It was also common for members of the engineering department to spend time in the field, witnessing first hand how end users used the projectors and what they liked and disliked about them. This knowledge was then used to further develop and upgrade Electrohome's product line.

Electrohome utilized a simple two-tier pricing structure based on volume, but with a low hurdle. Dealers who sold nine or more units per year were offered a larger discount than those dealers selling less than 9 units per year. This simple, two-step price discount structure tended to attract and retain the loyalty of small to medium-sized system dealers, since there was no large-volume discount that high-volume box dealers could take advantage of. Large-volume discounts would have attracted box dealers, who would then have been able to undercut the prices of the smaller system dealers.

	Margin
Electrohome	48% gross margin
Dealer	35% margin on list price

Projector dealers usually carried two or three different manufacturers' projectors, selecting lines for the low-, mid-, and high-end markets with some overlap. These dealers also carried other audio-visual equipment such as overhead projectors, screens, lighting, etc. A typical dealer in the U.S. would have annual sales around $3 million, of which about 10 percent came from after-sales service.

Price competition among dealers could be quite intense. A dealer's nominal margin of 35 percent could sometimes be cut to 5 percent in order for the dealer to capture a customer in a highly competitive situation. Dealer overheads were usually higher than 5 percent. Margins on services were larger, usually ranging from 25 percent to 35 percent, but occasionally reaching as high as 70 percent.

Competition

Electrohome had three main competitors in the data and graphics segment of the industrial projectors market: Sony, NEC, and Barco (see Exhibit 4 for product comparisons). Several other firms competed in the video and low-scanning frequency segments. These firms included large companies such as Mitsubishi, Panasonic, and General Electric. Although these firms were very large relative to Electrohome, they were not considered to be major competitors as they confined their activities to the video projection segment in which Electrohome did not actively compete. Sony held the largest market share in data projection, while Barco held the largest share of the graphics segment (see Table 2).

TABLE 2   Market share of the major competitors in 1988 (units sold)*

		Electrohome	Sony	Barco	NEC	Other
Europe	Data	8%[†]	35%	35%	6%	16%
	Graphics	43	—	55	—	2
North America	Data	14	62	16	8	—
	Graphics	40	—	60	—	—
Far East	Data	7	30	15	23	25
	Graphics	80	—	15	—	5
Gen. Total	Data	11	49	23	9	8
	Graphics	44	—	55	—	1
	Total[‡]	14	45	25	8	8

*Adapted from Barco Projection Systems (A) case (HBS 9-591-133), prepared by Research Associate Krista McQuade under the supervision of Professor Rowland T. Moriarty.

[†]All percentages are read horizontally, i.e., Electrohome had an 8 percent share of the data projector market in Europe.

[‡]Omits video projectors.

Sony

Sony was one of the largest and most diversified electronics corporations in the world, with 1988 sales of $11.5 billion. Sony Projectors Division, which accounted for 1 percent of total company sales, manufactured Sony's industrial projectors. Sony dominated both the video and data segments of the market with almost a 50 percent share in each segment. Until August 1989, its fastest projector was the 1031, with a maximum scanning rate of only 35 kHz. In 1988, of the

15,000 units sold by Sony, 66 percent were video and 34 percent data. Sony hadn't had the best-quality projector on the market in terms of scan rate, brightness, image quality, and resolution. It consistently priced its products 15 percent below the prices of the industry leaders in every projector category.

Sony sold its projectors through its captive commercial video distributors worldwide. These distributors had access to 1,500 dealers around the world. About 50 percent of Sony's dealers were box dealers. This extensive network of dealers, 500 in the U.S. alone, contributed to low street prices for Sony projectors. In general, dealers sold a high volume of Sony products. Few dealers could survive without the Sony volume, and about 80–90 percent of dealers worldwide carried Sony video equipment. Sony had a reputation among the dealers as having reliable projectors at a low price. Despite this reputation, Sony did not promote the reliability of the projectors to the end users.

Barco

Headquartered in Kuurne, Belgium, Barco N.V. entered the industrial projector market in the early 1980s to take advantage of the emerging technology in video projection. From Barco's early years in radio broadcast receiver production, to TV manufacturing, to industrial projectors, Barco had established a strong reputation on the basis of a commitment to R&D and product quality. Barco developed a leadership position in a variety of niche markets through its technological expertise and R&D efforts.

Barco's Projection Systems Division had 1988 sales of $35 million, which represented 23 percent of the company's revenues. The company used a two-step distribution system, with 45 distributors and approximately 400 dealers worldwide. Box dealers represented about 20 percent of the distribution network and were normally located in large urban centers. Since Barco was Electrohome's only competitor in the graphics market, few dealers carried both manufacturers' lines. Barco competed in all segments. However, their 8 percent share of the video segment was much smaller than their share of the high-end segments. Barco had a reputation for manufacturing very complex projectors that delivered very high picture quality.

NEC

A major Japanese manufacturer of electronics, NEC had 1988 sales of $21.9 billion. NEC Projection Systems focused on video and data projectors, with sales split almost evenly between the two lines. NEC pioneered digital convergence technology in 1987, which made it easier for the user to adjust the focus of the projector.

NEC's market share had never been as high as expected. This was due in part to its ineffective distribution system. The projectors were originally distributed through their well-established network of computer dealers, who carried the very successful Multisync line of NEC computer monitors. These dealers were strongly encouraged by NEC to carry the projectors. After disappointing results, NEC signed an OEM distribution agreement with General Electric. In 1988, NEC sold about 1,800 units through its own network and 1,200 through General Electric.

The Sony 1270 Introduction

Sony's announcement of its 1270 projector brought back memories to Electrohome's top management. In 1985, Electrohome's dealers informed the company of the upcoming Sony 720. There was a lot of talk in the industry that the projector was going to revolutionize the industry with its superior quality. Ultimately, the product was never as successful as expected, but it did provide Electrohome and the rest of the industry with its first Sony scare.

The Sony 1270 used a new Sony 8″ projection tube. The engineering department at Electrohome had been notified of, and inspected, the new tube earlier in 1989 and concluded that it could provide high-quality images. However, Electrohome decided not to begin developing an 8″ projector with the new tube for several reasons. The tube was new and untested, and its adoption would require a major redesign of the projector to adapt to the square 8″ tube rather than the rectangular 7″ tubes Electrohome was then using. This change would represent a significant engineering challenge and would result in a significant increase in unit manufacturing costs due to the larger lens and housing. Also, unlike Barco, Electrohome was not committed to industry leadership in picture quality.

Electrohome was proud not only of its relationships with its dealers, but also of its relationships with its suppliers. Sony Components Division had a very good working relationship with Electrohome. When the Sony representative presented the Sony 8″ tube to Electrohome, he acknowledged the fact that the tube was ". . . not what you guys (Electrohome) are looking for," and that the new tube was not a viable component for the architecture and design of Electrohome products at that time.

Electrohome expected that it would have to provide an 8″ projector as part of its product line at some point in the future, but it did not see the need to introduce it immediately. Electrohome's engineers were focused more on improving the quality and ease of use of the existing product line.

In August 1989, Terry Schmidt received a package from one of Electrohome's sales representatives. The package contained a copy of a technical paper on the Sony 1270, provided to dealers worldwide, and the preliminary marketing literature for the product. Terry realized from this information that the 1270 represented a large improvement in quality for Sony. However, the product still had a lot of shortcomings. Terry saw that the 1270 would be 30 pounds heavier and bulkier than the ECP line. He reasoned that customers and system dealers would prefer more compact and lighter projectors, which were easier to install and move. In addition, Terry found that the scan rate and bandwidth capabilities of the projector were not in sync. Bandwidth was the measure of how fast a projector can turn on and off the pixels used to project the image. The higher the bandwidth, the sharper and brighter the picture was. Electrohome, and most of the competition, had a scan rate to bandwidth ratio of 1 kHz to 1 MHz. The 1270 was Sony's first projector with a high scan rate (75 kHz). The problem was that the maximum bandwidth was only 40 MHz. Though the 1270 had displayed superior picture quality at Siggraph with the new 8″ tube, Terry believed that if a high scan rate was used for a particular graphics application, the bandwidth would not be sufficient to maintain the "superior" picture quality. However, he was uncertain whether customers would recognize this potential flaw during the buying process.

The Situation in September 1989

The aggressive entrance into the high-end projector market by Sony led the management team at Electrohome to review their options. Kenneth Mitchell, Terry Schmidt, Lloyd Wilson, and Alan Caskey reviewed all of the information they could gather from their departments and had brought two main options to the table for discussion.

Development Options

Several R&D projects were at different stages of completion. One major project that was well underway dealt with building automatic convergence (focusing) into the projector. This feature would automatically focus the image for the user. Electrohome felt that the earliest it could have the feature ready for the market was mid-1990. Other than that, the engineering department had nothing to introduce quickly, let alone by the end of the year.

Pricing Options

Management also had the option of changing the prices of the three main products (ECP 2000, 3000, and 4000). Their concerns revolved around how customers and dealers would respond to this new, high-end projector at mid-range prices from Sony. The Projection Systems Division was the most profitable business unit at Electrohome Limited and enjoyed a respectable gross margin. Lloyd Wilson and Alan Caskey had to estimate how the dealers would react to a reduction in the 35 percent discount they received off the list price. This would reduce "street" prices while maintaining Electrohome's margin. If the Sony 1270 did enter the market 20–40 percent below established market prices, and dealers refused to reduce their margins, Electrohome would have to consider lowering its prices, effectively eliminating much of its margin, in order to remain competitive with Sony.

If the Electrohome team decided to lower prices, it had to determine how much and when they should be lowered. If they lowered the prices immediately, before Sony's formal launch, they might be able to thwart some of Sony's efforts and retain customers. However, if the 1270 was eventually priced high or did not meet expectations, Electrohome would be leaving money on the table. If Electrohome reduced prices after the 1270 launch, there might be a backlash from current customers who could claim that Electrohome had been charging excessively high prices.

With Infocomm rapidly approaching, Kenneth knew he had to make a decision about how to respond. Electrohome needed to do something for Infocomm in order to keep itself visible to its dealers and customers.

Part 5

Distribution Decisions

Marketers must make decisions on how to present the products they produce to their ultimate purchasers. Most producers do not present their products to end consumers themselves. They tend to make use of wholesalers and retailers.

The marketing decision maker has a number of decisions to make with respect to the distribution of a product. These include:

1. The types of wholesale and retail intermediaries to use.
2. The number of wholesale and retail intermediaries to use of each type.
3. The number of levels in the channel (degree of directness).
4. The ways to motivate existing channel members to perform effectively.

The first cases in this section deal with these issues. Beyond these decisions are a series of decisions concerning the physical distribution of the product. These include customer service level, inventory size, order quantities, reorder points, warehouse locations, and transportation.

The next sections of this introduction are short reminders of some of the concepts related to each of these decision points.

Types of Intermediaries

There are many different types of wholesale and retail intermediaries. They vary on the types of products they carry and the services that they are able to perform. The decision on which types of intermediaries to utilize is related to the services that a firm desires to have performed. This is in turn related to the resources and skills of the firm and the needs and behavior of the ultimate consumer.

The Number of Intermediaries

The firm must decide whether to have intensive, selective, or exclusive distribution at the wholesale and retail levels. This decision is related to the quality of support these intermediaries will give in each situation, the ability of the firm to service the intermediaries, and the behavior of the ultimate consumer. For example, a wholesaler whom you want may only be willing to carry your products on an exclusive basis, or you may not be able to afford to contact all the retailers of a particular type. Alternatively, consumers may demand that your product be available at all outlets. This may force you into an intensive distribution situation.

Number of Channel Levels

The decision on how direct a channel from producer to ultimate consumer should be is related to the cost of alternative channels, the service and control provided, the characteristics of the end consumer in terms of their numbers and geographic location, the perishability and bulkiness of the product, plus the characteristics of the firm, and competitive activity.

Motivation

Once a channel is selected, motivating its members to perform effectively is an important activity. Motivating vehicles include monetary things such as margins, allowances, and cooperative programs; service activities such as training and technical advice, inventory taking, and display management; and provision of physical items such as racks. Also important here are the interpersonal relationships among the people in the intermediaries and in your firm.

Physical Distribution Management

Physical distribution management is a complex area where management science techniques have become important. In simple terms, the decision maker sets a customer service level (for example, deliver 95 percent of all orders within seven days) and then makes inventory, warehousing, and transportation decisions to reach this service level at minimum cost. The customer service level is set by considering costs, consumer behavior, and competitive activity.

Case 13

Chaebol Electronics Company, U.S.*

In mid-1984, Park Sung-Il, grandson of the founder of Chaebol Industries, Inc., and president of Chaebol Electronics Company, U.S., was deciding how his company should enter the U.S. videocassette recorder (VCR) market. As of March 1985, the agreement signed by his company—which gave it access to the proprietary technology of the Japanese company Japan Victor Corporation (JVC) for the manufacture of VCRs but limited sales to only the domestic Korean market—would expire. After that date, Chaebol was free to market VCRs worldwide. The decision had already been made to begin selling Chaebol VCRs in the United States as soon as possible. The decision Park faced was that of marketing his company's VCRs as it was already selling its televisions, or positioning this new product line differently, selling it through different channels of distribution.

History of Chaebol Industries, Inc.

Chaebol Industries, Inc., had its beginnings with a small construction firm started by Park Kyung-Yung in 1945. After gaining several large port construction projects following the Korean War, Park expanded the firm into shipbuilding, and through this into the exporting business. While Chaebol was growing in these areas, other large Korean conglomerates, such as Lucky-Goldstar, Samsung, and Hyundai, diversified their corporations into such fields as chemicals, oil refining, textiles, appliance manufacture, and electronics manufacturing. Each of these firms developed its own foreign distribution capabilities and became very successful in worldwide markets. As a result, these other Korean firms began to become strong competitors for Chaebol's exporting business.

In 1965, Park Kyung-Yung retired, and his son, Park Taik-Cha, became president of Chaebol. Looking at the successes of his competitors and their

* This case was prepared by Constance M. Kinnear, Research Associate, with the assistance of Thomas C. Kinnear, Professor of Marketing, both at the Graduate School of Business Administration, The University of Michigan. Copyright © 1986 by the authors.

impact on Chaebol's business, Park decided in 1966 that the time had come for Chaebol to expand its areas of operation into the electronics field. In 1967, Chaebol Electronics Company was established, and began producing black-and-white televisions. Room air conditioners, washing machines, refrigerators, and electric typewriters were added to Chaebol's list of products by 1970. As each new product was added to the Chaebol line, it was marketed only in Korea. However, the Korean market consisted of only 41 million people, with a per capita income of just under $2,000 per year. Faced with intense competition from the other large Korean conglomerates for its domestic market, Park soon became aware that his company would have to begin exporting its products to gain economies of scale in their manufacture.

Park hoped that Chaebol's long experience in exporting would give it a competitive advantage in foreign markets. To build on this experience, Chaebol first marketed its black-and-white TVs in the United States in 1975 through Johnson Importers of Atlanta, Georgia, the importer that had handled the export goods the company had transported for years. Since this importer was used to handling only low-cost items carried mainly by discounters, Chaebol offered only its lower-cost, lower-priced 12-inch and 19-inch black-and-white models for export. Johnson Importers found a market for 25,000 Chaebol sets in 1975, sold under the PKY brand name, in discount stores in Georgia, Alabama, and Florida. These stores on average priced the 12-inch sets at $105 and the 19-inch sets at $120 each. These stores included a 20 percent margin in these prices. Johnson Importers made a 15 percent margin on its sales of TVs to these outlets. Chaebol priced its 12-inch sets at $71.50 and its 19-inch sets at $81.50 each. Encouraged by this acceptance, Chaebol increased its production capacity in late 1975 from 300,000 to 400,000 sets per year.

In 1976, Johnson Importers was able to increase the sale of PKY sets to a total of 60,000 sets throughout the South. Park believed that similar success in the sale of Chaebol's TVs could be found in discount chains in other parts of the country. To achieve this, Park sent two Chaebol sales representatives to establish a sales office and arrange for warehousing facilities in Atlanta. These sales representatives received $25,000 in salary each, and it was budgeted that their sales expenses would come to another $15,000 each per year. These direct Chaebol employees contacted several large discount chains in the Northeast and Midwest. In 1977, sales to these chains, all employing private labels, were 50,000 units, increasing total company sales that year to 115,000 units. In 1978, Chaebol's salespeople were able to land the sale of 100,000 sets to Kmart Corporation under Kmart's KC brand name. As part of the arrangement for these sales, Chaebol agreed to open a service center to which sets could be sent by the retailer for repair. This center was located in Atlanta. As a result, total sales in 1978 jumped to 240,000 sets. Korean production capacity was increased to 600,000 units per year to handle these sales. In 1979, sales reached 275,000 units. In 1980, with additional private label sales to discounters in the West and constantly increasing sales to previous customers, Chaebol sold 375,000 units.

In 1981, Chaebol increased its number of U.S. sales representatives to five and opened a second sales office, warehouse facility, and service center in Chicago. These sales representatives were now being paid a salary of $37,000 per year and had $20,000 a year in expenses each. Chaebol's salespeople began approaching large department store chains, such as Sears and Montgomery Ward, to increase sales. Again, the TVs sold to these accounts carried the retailers' own labels. 1981 total sales were 450,000 units. Of this total, only 100,000 sets carried the PKY brand name, and these were sold primarily to independent discounters who operated only a few stores each in regional areas.

In 1979, Park had directed Chaebol to begin manufacturing color TVs. As with Chaebol's previous products, these were first marketed only in Korea. By 1981, Park was ready to bring three color models, 9-inch, 13-inch, and 19-inch sets, to the United States. The decision to introduce color sets was brought on by a shift in sales patterns in the U.S. marketplace. By 1980, annual total sales of black-and-white TVs was dropping by an average of 6 percent per year. Along with this drop in total sales, black-and-white set prices were dropping steadily, causing profit margins on the products to fall. Nineteen-inch black-and-white models were no longer desired in the market; buyers preferred to spend their money on a smaller color set than on a large black-and-white set. Furthermore, the color TV market was growing steadily, with growth rates of nearly 15 percent per year. Half of Chaebol's capacity was shifted to color TV production, and within black-and-white sets, 19-inch sets were dropped while small, portable 9-inch sets were added to the line. Cost information on Chaebol's export TV product line in 1981 is shown in Exhibit 1.

EXHIBIT 1   Cost information on 1981 export television sets

	Black-and-white		Color		
	9-inch	12-inch	9-inch	13-inch	19-inch
Direct material	$57.85	$32.70	$102.30	$121.35	$147.05
Labor	1.40	1.00	2.40	2.95	3.45
Overhead	2.50	1.40	4.00	5.00	5.80
Transportation	5.10	6.25	5.20	6.30	6.85
Duty	3.15	1.90	5.35	6.40	7.70
Total costs	$70.00	$43.25	$119.25	$142.00	$170.85
Chaebol's selling price to channel	$100.00	$60.00	$195.50	$232.00	$280.00
Average retail selling price of Chaebol sets	$125.00	$75.00	$230.00	$290.00	$350.00
Retail price of leading domestic brand	$156.00	$95.00	$271.50	$345.00	$415.00

Chaebol marketed its color TVs through the same discount channels it was using for its black-and-white models. However, with color, Chaebol's U.S. salespeople were able to have its sets sold using the PKY label at Kmart and two other large discounters. Color TV sales began with 100,000 units in 1981 and grew to

EXHIBIT 2   Black-and-white TV market—retail brand shares and market size, 1981–1984

	1981	*1982*	*1983*	*1984*
Domestic manufacturers				
RCA	16.3	16.3	15.5	12.5
Zenith	15.5	15.4	13.6	10.2
General Electric	8.9	8.2	8.4	7.5
North American Phillips	5.8	6.9	8.2	10.3
Other domestic	2.6	2.0	2.7	2.7
Total domestic	49.1	48.8	48.4	43.2
Japanese				
Panasonic	6.0	5.9	7.0	8.1
Sony	4.4	3.9	3.5	5.3
Sanyo	3.6	3.2	3.3	3.2
Hitachi	1.3	0.9	0.7	0.5
Sharp	1.0	1.6	1.0	1.4
Toshiba	0.5	0.6	0.2	0.4
Other Japanese	1.0	1.4	0.8	0.4
Total Japanese	17.8	17.5	16.5	19.3
Far East				
Samsung (Korea)	2.1	2.4	2.9	3.5
Goldstar (Korea)	1.8	1.9	2.3	2.5
Chaebol (Korea)	1.7	1.9	2.5	3.3
Other Far East	0.5	0.6	0.9	1.2
Total Far East	6.1	6.8	8.6	10.5
Private label				
(Sears, JC Penney, Montgomery Ward, Kmart, etc.)	20.2	20.0	18.5	17.5
All other	6.8	6.9	8.0	9.5
Market size in units (000)	5,806	5,597	5,488	4,717

300,000 units in 1982. Forty percent of these color sets carried the PKY label. (See Exhibits 2 and 3 for competitive market shares).

In late 1982, Chaebol drastically changed its approach to the U.S. TV market. Great pressure in the press was being brought upon Korean TV producers, with many accusations of TV dumping by these companies within the U.S. market. In accusing them of dumping, it was being alleged that Korean manufacturers were selling TVs in the United States for prices below those charged for the same product in the domestic market. Park decided not to wait for the decision from the U.S. International Trade Commission on the dumping charges. He began construction in November 1982 of TV assembly and production facilities in Marietta, Georgia. Initial capacity of 100,000 units per year came online in June 1983. An additional 200,000 units of capacity was scheduled for 1985. Cost figures for 1983 production of 13-inch color TV sets in the United States as compared to in Korea was as shown in Exhibit 4.

Even though Chaebol's costs were higher when TVs were produced in the United States, management believed these U.S. costs were approximately 10 percent below those of domestic TV producers.

EXHIBIT 3   Color TV market—retail brand shares and market size, 1981–1984

	1981	1982	1983	1984
Domestic manufacturers				
RCA	20.0%	20.1%	18.9%	18.1%
Zenith	18.7	18.9	16.8	16.2
General Electric	8.0	7.8	7.6	6.4
North American Phillips	12.4	11.8	10.5	10.2
Other domestic	4.7	3.8	3.9	3.5
Total domestic	64.0	62.4	57.7	54.4
Japanese				
Sony	7.7	6.9	7.5	6.7
Panasonic	2.6	3.7	4.0	3.9
Sharp	1.4	2.0	2.4	3.1
Hitachi	2.5	2.8	2.8	3.0
Sanyo	1.2	1.2	1.7	1.5
Other Japanese	3.1	3.0	3.0	4.2
Total Japanese	18.5	19.6	21.4	22.4
Far East				
Samsung (Korea)	0.2	0.5	1.6	1.6
Goldstar (Korea)	0.5	0.7	0.8	0.9
Chaebol (Korea)	0.7	1.1	1.3	1.7
Other Far East	0.5	0.8	0.7	0.8
Total Far East	1.9	3.1	4.4	5.0
Private label				
(Sears, JC Penney, Montgomery				
Ward, Kmart, etc.)	13.4	12.7	13.2	12.9
All other	2.2	2.2	3.3	5.3
Market size				
in units (000)	10,641	11,567	13,608	15,646

EXHIBIT 4   Production costs for 13-inch color TV sets

	Korean production	U.S. production
Direct material	$101.20	$113.40
Labor	2.40	5.25
Overhead	4.25	5.85
Transportation	5.85	
Duty	5.35	
Total cost	$119.05	$124.50

In conjunction with the establishment of U.S. production facilities, Park established Chaebol Electronics Company, U.S., and sent his son, Park Sung-Il, to the United States to head the company. The younger Park hired six new American sales representatives to work in three new sales offices in Denver, Los Angeles, and New York. Warehouse facilities and service centers were also established in these cities. Chaebol's five warehouses cost an average of $250,000 per year each. Service costs were one-quarter percent of sales in 1984. Park's goal was to expand TV sales into new markets. In late 1983,

Chaebol U.S. succeeded in gaining contracts to sell its TVs in 9-inch black-and-white and 13-inch color to two major catalog showroom companies. These sets were all to carry the PKY label.

Chaebol's sales revenue in 1981 from sales of black-and-white TVs was $36.2 million. In 1983, sales revenue from black-and-white sets was $39.2 million, while sales of color sets brought in $83.75 million. Profit on these 1983 sales was $4.91 million.

The Electronics Market in 1984

Exhibit 5 shows the types of retail stores that sold electronic products in 1975 and 1984. It also shows the number of each type of store and the percentage of total electronic products sold in the United States in that year by that type of store. As the exhibit shows, there has been a significant increase not only in the total number of outlets selling electronic products but also in the variety of store types that carry this kind of product.

Although Exhibit 5 shows that the total number of radio/TV/appliance stores has greatly decreased since 1975, the importance of this type of outlet within the electronics market grew to the point where radio/TV/appliance stores sold more of these products than all the other outlet types combined. The key characteristics of this type of store were wide selection, low price, and high volume. The major appliance stores stocked virtually every model of every major mass market line. It was common to find up to 150 different TV models and 100 VCRs. The stores advertised low prices and often guaranteed that they would meet any price offered by a competitor in their market area. The salespeople were usually quite knowledgeable and were paid on commission. Thus, they were aggressive in selling their higher-margin models. Price cutting was a necessity, and dealers often bought in large quantity lots, watching for deals, damaged-model sales, and other ways to cut costs. The average margin for this type of outlet was about 22 percent. These stores commonly had extensive service departments.

EXHIBIT 5 Types of electronics products sales outlets; number and percent of electronics market sales by type

Type of outlet	1975		1984	
	No. of stores	Percent sales	No. of stores	Percent sales
Radio/TV/appliance	50,152	31.4%	30,004	54.1%
Discount chains	17,887	25.0	5,764	12.4
Department stores	11,240	19.7	4,217	9.3
Furniture stores	38,732	15.9	29,609	3.7
Catalog/mail order	7,671	4.8	16,347	11.8
Auto/home supply	—	—	40,729	3.6
Drug/variety	—	—	60,516	3.3
Home centers	—	—	24,837	1.2
Hardware stores	—	—	19,870	0.6
Other	9,874	3.2	—	—
Total	135,556	100%	231,893	100%

Discount chains, such as Kmart stores, had been handling electronic products for 15 years. They bought in large quantity at lowest possible cost. The manufacturers were usually willing to cut prices in order to obtain large volume orders. Some of the larger chains also engaged in private branding, from which they were able to gain very favorable terms from manufacturers. For example, a U.S. manufacturer who engaged in private branding for one of the large chains obtained an average margin of 19 percent versus 34 percent for national brand sales. Chains usually required the customer to contact the company or independent service facility for warranty service. Some stores supported "service centers," which would simply accept the set and send it on to the manufacturer for repairs. With low overhead and low margins (18 percent), the salespeople were usually few in number and rarely informed about electronics or the differences in major lines. These stores also carried very small lines of a few manufacturers, concentrating for the most part on the low end of the model line.

Department stores carried a limited variety of brands and models of electronic products. They usually did not carry either the lowest- nor the highest-priced models, but concentrated on the largest sales models of well-known brand names. The salespeople were quite knowledgeable, and engaged in a fair amount of trying to get the customer to "trade up." Prices were sometimes discounted, particularly in larger chains. The department stores usually got about a 30 percent margin. In addition, they were eager to seek "deals" on quantity buys, closeouts, and so on. Only the national department store chains, such as Sears, JC Penney, and Montgomery Ward, had their own service facilities or carried their own private brands.

Furniture stores were involved only in the sales of console model TVs. Their salespeople were well informed about cabinetry and styling, but usually not too knowledgeable about electronics. These outlets usually sold at suggested retail price, and thus gained about a 37 percent margin on their sales. Furniture stores offered no in-store service facilities. With the introduction of the wide variety of electronic products since 1975, the importance of this type of outlet to the total sales of these products had decreased greatly.

Catalog/mail-order sales outlets usually sold a limited range of models from well-known brands. Unlike department stores, the range of models offered by catalog/mail-order stores went from the lower- to mid-priced models. It was also common for catalogs to offer lesser-known brands that could be priced at a significantly lower price than national brands as long as they offered high quality for that price. Catalog/mail-order outlets usually had a 15 percent margin on sales. Little selling at point of purchase was available. No repair services were offered. This type of sales outlet was of increasing importance for electronic product categories that had reached the point of mass acceptance in the marketplace.

Auto/home supply stores tended to carry only specialty products to fit the needs of small segments of the electronics market. Therefore, models and brands offered were limited, and prices and margins were relatively high. Salespeople were very knowledgeable, and these stores often offered repair services.

Drug/variety, home centers, and hardware stores had many characteristics in common. They all carried lower-priced, basic models of electronic products that were commonly purchased only through "special deals" so that low prices were possible. The variety of products and models sold by any given outlet in this group varied greatly from time to time, but usually they carried only radios, small black-and-white TVs, and accessory items like stereo speakers. The salespeople at these outlets had little knowledge of electronics. Margins for this group averaged 25 percent. No service facilities were offered on these products.

The VCR Market in 1984

The VCR market in the United States had grown very quickly from the time of the product's introduction in 1979. In 1981, 1.7 million units were sold. This number grew to 2.0 million units in 1982, 3.75 million units in 1983, and nearly 7.5 million units in 1984. The market shares of the major firms selling VCRs in 1984 are shown in the first part of Exhibit 6. The second part of the exhibit shows the num-

EXHIBIT 6   U.S. videocassette recorder market—retail brand shares, 1984

	1984 share
Domestic manufacturers	
RCA (VHS)	15.1%
General Electric (VHS)	6.2
Quasar (VHS)	5.1
Magnavox (VHS)	4.1
Zenith (VHS/Beta)	3.2
Sylvania (VHS)	1.4
Curtis-Mathes (VHS)	1.3
Total domestic	36.4%
Japanese	
Panasonic (VHS)	12.8
Sony (Beta)	6.8
Sanyo (Beta)	6.3
Sharp (VHS)	4.6
Hitachi (VHS)	3.7
MGA (VHS)	2.7
JVC (VHS)	4.1
Toshiba (Beta)	1.6
Total Japanese	42.6%
Private label	9.5%
Other	11.1%

VCR market—Number of brands and models and price ranges by type of outlet

Type of outlet	No. of brands offered	No. of models offered	Price range
Radio/TV/appliance	12	60	$259–$1,100
Discount chains	5	7	$257–$459
Department stores			
National chains	3	11	$269–$599
Regionals and independents	6	12	$399–$799
Catalog/mail-order stores	6	9	$278–$650

ber of brands and models of VCRs sold at each type of electronics outlet and the range of prices charged at each kind of store in 1984. Of the units sold in 1984, 48 percent sold for under $500, 20 percent for between $501 and $600, 17 percent for between $601 and $800, 13 percent for between $801 and $1,000, and only 2 percent for more than $1,000. The average price of VCRs sold in the United States had dropped by over $550 since their introduction in 1979. Typical features offered on low-, medium-, and high-priced VCRs in 1984 are shown in Exhibit 7.

EXHIBIT 7   Features offered on VCRs in 1984

Low-priced models (under $400)	Medium-priced models ($400–$750)	High-priced models (over $750)
2 video heads	2 video heads	4 video heads
1 audio head	1 audio head	2 audio heads—stereo, hi-fi
Varactor tuner (preset 12–14 channels)	Varactor tuner (preset 80–99 channels)	Direct access quartz tuner
1-event/7-day programmability	4-event/14-day programmability	8-event/1-year programmability
8-hour/3-speed recording	8-hour/3-speed recording	8-hour/3-speed recording
8-function remote (many wired)	10-function wireless remote	13–17-function wireless remote
Not cable ready	107-channel cable capability	133-channel cable capability

The total U.S. market for VCRs in 1985 was expected to be between 11 and 12 million units. With this level of sales, VCRs will have succeeded in penetrating 25 percent of the product's total market potential (households with televisions) by the end of 1985. Because of the quickness with which VCR sales reached this sales level, industry analysts did not foresee much future growth for the product line, although they did predict sales levels maintaining a 10 million to 11 million unit-per-year pace for the next five years.

The quick growth of VCR sales has had long-reaching effects on the development of the market for these products. After only five years on the market, the demographics of VCR buyers were already broadening. Originally, VCRs were most commonly purchased by upper-income (over $32,000), well-educated, married heads of household between the ages of 35 and 49. In 1984, 27 percent of VCR units were purchased by 18-to-24-year-old singles with average income between $27,000 and $32,000. The amazing sales growth of VCRs attracted many new entrants to the market each year, so that by 1984 there were over 70 VCR brands available. Many brands offered extensive VCR lines. For example, RCA, the market share leader, offered 25 VCR models ranging in suggested retail price from $330 to $1,300. The more entrants there were to the market, the stronger price competition became. This led to progressively lower and lower margins and profitability for both manufacturers and retailers. This margin loss was greatest on the lower-price-range products. To counteract this, many manufacturers were adding VCRs with greater features and capabilities to their lines—VCRs that were higher priced but also more profitable.

In late 1984, market analysts expressed the belief that Korean VCR manufacturers would enter the U.S. market using the same strategy that had gained them market share in TV sales: that of offering low-priced products that would allow them to take advantage of their lower labor costs. Thus, their expectations were that Korean VCRs would be priced $50 to $75 below the 1984 $400 mid-priced Japanese units with the same features. Furthermore, analysts believed that this kind of price differential would require retailers to pick up the Korean models. However, many analysts felt retailers would only carry these models as advertising draws and would often try to get customers to buy up from these low-priced VCRs to more profitable models.

Chaebol's Decision

Park Sung-Il had narrowed down Chaebol's VCR entry strategy to between one of two alternatives.

Strategy I

The first entry strategy alternative involved using distribution channels and retail outlets for VCRs similar to those Chaebol had employed for TV sales. For VCRs, Park wanted to limit distribution to only high-volume buyers. Thus, if this strategy was employed, Chaebol would only seek sales to large discount chains and catalog/mail-order retailers. Park planned to produce three models for these outlets. All would be two video head, one audio head models, with varactor tuning allowing 12 stations to be preset. The lowest-cost model, Model CHA, would also feature one-event/one-week programmability, wired remote, auto rewind, and would not be cable ready. Model CHA would cost Chaebol $143.50 to produce. The next step up in Chaebol's offerings would be Model CHB, which would have 1-event/14-day programmability, an eight-function wireless remote, auto rewind, and be cable ready. Model CHB would cost $201 to manufacture. Model CHC, the highest-priced model offered under this strategy, would feature 1-event/14-day programmability, 12-function remote control, auto rewind, frame advance, a sharpness control, and would be cable ready. Model CHC would cost Chaebol $247.90. Park believed Chaebol's costs on these products would allow its customers to price these models 15 percent below similar VCRs on the market.

Since Chaebol salespeople were already calling on these customers, Park believed this alternative would have few additional costs over Chaebol's present expenses. Additional warehouse space and service personnel would have to be acquired, but no new sales offices would be needed. Park believed that most of these sales would be low-priced, private brand VCRs, although he hoped that those customers who were purchasing PKY brand TVs would purchase PKY brand name VCRs. Park estimated he could sell 225,000 VCRs in 1985 with this strategy, 70,000 carrying the PKY name. He believed private label sales would carry a 27 percent gross margin for Chaebol, while the PKY brand sales would bring a 34 percent gross margin.

Strategy II

Park's alternative to the above strategy was to use Chaebol's cost advantage, arising from lower labor costs than either U.S. or Japanese competitors, to gain admission to the TV/radio/appliance outlets that had the largest share of VCR sales and sold only brand name products. Park believed Chaebol's cost advantage would allow it to produce VCRs that carried more features than competitors' products at each price point in the market. Selling VCRs in this channel would enable Chaebol's products to be distinguished from the 50 or more brands of low-cost, low-priced VCRs, and firmly establish the PKY brand name. In the future, he hoped to move Chaebol TVs into this channel where there were higher margins for producers and retailers. His dream was to have the PKY brand obtain the same quality reputation that Sony and Panasonic had achieved.

The models Chaebol would offer under this strategy are shown in Exhibit 8.

EXHIBIT 8   Chaebol's VCR models under Strategy II

Model	Chaebol cost	Features
CHC	$247.90	Two video heads, 1 audio head, 1-event/14-day programmability, varactor tuning for 12 preset stations, 12-function wireless remote, auto rewind, frame advance, sharpness control.
CH1A	$286.15	Two video heads, 2 audio heads, stereo, 5-event/14-day programmability, varactor tuning for 50 preset stations, 14-function wireless remote, auto rewind, tape memory, memory backup, time-remaining indicator, 107-channel cable ready.
CH1B	$367.90	Four video heads, 2 audio heads, stereo/hi-fi/Dolby, 8-event/1-year programmability, quartz tuning, 133-channel cable ready, 17-function wireless remote, auto rewind, tape memory, time-remaining indicator, one-touch recording, slow motion, frame advance, video dub, audio dub, sharpness control.
CH1P	$388.30	All of the features of the CH1B Model plus portable.

Park estimated that these models would sell at retail for considerably less than competitive products with similar features. On Model CH1B, he believed the retail price difference could be as much as $350. With this kind of differential, Park believed he would find many TV/radio/appliance store-owners eager to take on his products since they would allow the retailer to gain larger margins than other brands. Chaebol expected to make nearly a 44 percent gross margin on models sold to this type of outlet.

Park was considering two approaches to getting his company's VCRs in TV/radio/appliance outlets. The first was to sell directly to the owners of these stores. This approach would require a significant expansion of Chaebol's marketing organization. Since the number of TV/radio/appliance stores to be reached was large and geographically dispersed, new sales offices would have to be established in Boston, Indianapolis, Dallas, St. Louis, and Seattle. Each sales office would have three salespeople. In addition, three regional sales managers would have to be hired to help organize the now diverse and large sales function of the company. Furthermore, the establishment of a high recognition for Chaebol's PKY brand name would have to come from extensive advertising. Park estimated that the expenditure of $6 million on advertising in 1985 would be minimal to achieve the results he desired.

As an alternative, Park knew this market could also be approached through the employment of distributors who were already selling the VCRs of other manufacturers to TV/radio/appliance stores. Under this plan, no new sales offices would need to be opened, but one new salesperson would be added to the staff of each existing office. These five salespeople would be charged with maintaining relationships with the 10 geographically dispersed consumer electronics distributors that Chaebol's head office would choose to carry its VCRs. These distributors would work first on getting PKY brand VCRs into the largest regional and national TV/radio/appliance chains. Chaebol's salespeople would also call on PKY retailers in their areas, working on incentive programs with outlet salespeople, solving any problems that might arise, and checking that the services expected from the distributors were being adequately performed. Using distributors would cost Chaebol 11 percent of its margin; that is, the distributors would get an 11 percent margin on sales while Chaebol's margin would drop to approximately 33 percent on these sales. Under this approach, no additional warehouses over those proposed under Strategy I would be required. However, since this approach required the establishment of the PKY brand name, the advertising cost of $6 million would still be necessary.

Park believed Chaebol could achieve sales of 120,000 VCRs in 1985 using the direct approach and 150,000 VCRs using distributors. Though these figures were lower than the initial sales that could be achieved under the first strategy, Park believed the long-term strength of the company was better served by the firm establishment of a brand name and a strong position in TV/radio/appliance outlets.

A comparison of the costs involved in the plans considered by Park is shown in Exhibit 9.

EXHIBIT 9   Costs involved in Chaebol's sales plans

| | | | Strategy II | |
Expense area	Cost of each new unit	Strategy I	Direct	Distributors
Sales offices	$ 25,000/yr	—	5	—
Salespeople	$ 42,000/yr. salary $ 23,000/yr. expenses	—	18	5
Warehouses	$300,000/yr.	3	5	3
Service facilities		.25% sales	.33% sales	.33% sales
Average margins		27%, 34%	44%	33%
Advertising		$1.5 million	$6 million	$6 million

As Park worked on estimating the relative costs of these alternatives, he wondered if there was another approach to the market that might lead to success both now and in the future for Chaebol Electronics Company, U.S.

Case 14

Ito-Yokado Company*

In mid-March 1991, Masanori Takahashi, a senior strategy analyst for Ito-Yokado Company, was preparing to depart for Dallas, Texas. Once there, he would be leading a team of Japanese and American managers responsible for establishing transitional and long-term strategies for the Southland Corporation. After nearly an entire year of intense bargaining and negotiation with Southland and its creditors, Ito-Yokado acquired Southland on March 5, 1991.

Takahashi began working with Ito-Yokado in 1972 as an assistant manager of one of the company's superstores. He had advanced to the position of regional manager by 1979. In early 1981, Ito-Yokado's Operation Reform Project was conceived, and Takahashi was asked to be a member of the team leading the project.

During the first few months on the team, Takahashi quickly understood certain crucial aspects of the new project, most notably the use of point-of-sale (POS) systems. Since implementation of the project advanced most rapidly in Ito-Yokado's 7-Eleven Japan subsidiary, he also had become familiar with the operating environment of convenience stores in Japan.

As Takahashi left his Tokyo office, he could not help but feel both excitement and apprehension regarding his new position. He had gained confidence while involved with the successful Operation Reform Project at Ito-Yokado's superstores and 7-Eleven Japan convenience stores. But this experience might or might not prove to be useful in respect to Southland.

Company Background

Ito-Yokado's founder, Masatoshi Ito, was born in 1924 and graduated from a commercial high school in Yokohama. He worked briefly at Mitsubishi Heavy Industries before joining Japan's war effort in 1944. After World War II, he

* This case was written from public sources by M. Edgar Barrett and Christopher D. Buehler as a basis for class discussion rather than to illustrate either effective or ineffective handling of an administrative situation. Copyright © 1991 by M. Edgar Barrett. Used with permission from M. Edgar Barrett.

worked with his mother and elder brother at the family's 66-square-foot clothing store in Tokyo.[1] The store was incorporated as Kabushiki Kaisha Yokado in 1958. By 1960, Ito was in sole control of the family business. During that same year he made his first visit to the United States.

In 1960, Ito visited National Cash Register (NCR) in Dayton, Ohio.[2] While in the United States, Ito was introduced to terms such as *supermarkets* and *chain stores* by NCR, which was interested in selling cash registers to Japanese retailers. In Japan, retailing was dominated by mom-and-pop stores and a handful of venerable department stores, with few types of retail outlets in between. At this time, Ito began to see the possible role of mass merchandisers in a society becoming "mass-oriented."

Ito soon opened a small chain of superstores in the Tokyo area. These stores carried a large selection of household goods, food, and clothing of generally lesser quality and lower price than either the mom-and-pop or department stores.[3] By 1965, Ito had opened eight superstores. In the same year, the name of the chain was changed to Ito-Yokado.

The Growth of Ito-Yokado as a Superstore

Ito's concept for the superstores was centered on having the rough equivalent of several types of retail stores contained within one multistory superstore. The initial stores were located near population centers and railroad stations in the Tokyo area.[4] Often, several stores were located in close proximity in order to achieve "regional dominance."[5] The results were high name recognition, reduced distribution costs, and the effective squeezing out of competition.

Ito soon realized that social changes in Japan could create new opportunities for his retailing ideas. Younger and more mobile Japanese appeared to be less willing to spend a great deal of time shopping at numerous mom-and-pop stores. Also, Japanese society was experiencing increased suburbanization. Ito decided to locate stores in suburban prefectures. There are 47 prefectures (provinces) in Japan.

One reason for locating stores in suburban areas was the lower cost of real estate. This allowed Ito-Yokado to open larger stores with more parking spaces than competitors located in congested urban areas. Ito continued to use a strategy of "regional dominance" with these new openings, most of which were concen-

---

[1]Andrew Tanzer, "A Form of Flattery," *Forbes* (June 2, 1986).

[2]Jim Mitchell, "Southland Suitor Ito Learned from the Best," *Dallas Morning News* (April 1, 1990).

[3]Ito was not the first to open this type of retail outlet. Isao Nakauchi opened the first Daiei superstore in the Osaka area a few years before the first Ito-Yokado store was opened. In 1990, Daiei was Japan's largest retailer in terms of gross sales.

[4]Mitchell, "Southland Suitor."

[5]Hiroshi Uchida, *First Boston/CSFB Report on Ito-Yokado, Ltd.* (April 20, 1988), p. 7.

trated in the greater Kanto district, which consists of the Tokyo metropolitan area and surrounding cities. By the early 1970s, Ito-Yokado stores were opening at the rate of four or five per year. By the late 1970s, 9 or 10 new stores were opened annually.[6] In early 1987, 101 of 127 Ito-Yokado superstores were located in the greater Kanto district.

Ito also adopted a strategy of leasing some properties for new stores. As of the mid-1980s, over 87 percent of Ito-Yokado's aggregate sales floor space, 10 of the company's 11 distribution centers, and the company headquarters in Tokyo were all leased.[7] Often, property prices were astronomical, or the owners of well-located sites would not part with their property for any price.

Constraints on Growth

The initial success of Ito-Yokado and the other superstores soon resulted in re-taliatory action by a powerful competitor: the mom-and-pop store owners. These small retailers were said to "pull the strings of Liberal Democratic Party politicians at the local level."[8] The action initiated by the small retailers re-sulted in the 1974 Large Store Restriction Act, which was subsequently strengthened in 1979. The original act restricted the opening of stores with sales areas of over 1,500 square meters (16,500 square feet). In addition, the act restricted the hours of operation of new and existing large stores. A series of changes in 1979 added restrictions on stores with sales areas greater than 500 square meters (5,500 square feet). A Commerce Coordination Committee was established in each area in order to set policy regarding large-store open-ings and hours of operation. The committees were effectively controlled by the small retailers. By the early 1980s, Ito-Yokado was opening only four or five new stores annually.[9]

Factors other than the Large Store Restriction Act adversely affected Ito-Yokado. Japanese consumers' real disposable income decreased by a little over 1 percent during 1980–1981.[10] Japan experienced a general economic downturn in the early 1980s, as did the rest of the world, again serving to limit consumer pur-chasing power. Net income for Ito-Yokado—which had grown almost 30 percent per year between 1976 and 1981—grew by 9.7 percent in 1982 and by 0.9 per-cent in 1983.[11] The legal restrictions imposed on large stores, when combined with the economic downturn, led to both lower current earnings and a projection of reduced rates of growth in future earnings.

---

[6]Ibid., p. 6.
[7]Ibid., p. 7.
[8]Tanzer, "A Form of Flattery."
[9]Uchida, *First Boston,* pp. 7–8.
[10]Ibid.
[11]Ibid., p. 8.

Ito-Yokado as a Parent Company

During the early 1970s, Ito began pursuing new retailing interests. In 1972, he approached Dallas-based Southland Corporation in an attempt to secure a license to operate 7-Eleven stores in Japan. He was rebuffed.[12] He made a similar attempt in 1973 with the aid of a Japanese trading company, C. Itoh and Company, and was successful in obtaining the license. Concurrently, Ito was pursuing another U.S. firm, Denny's Restaurants, in an attempt to obtain rights for opening Denny's Restaurants in Japan. Both subsidiaries, Denny's Japan and 7-Eleven Japan (originally called York Seven but renamed 7-Eleven Japan in 1978), were established in 1973. The first 7-Eleven and the initial Denny's in Japan were both opened in 1974. Stock for each of the two majority-owned subsidiaries was traded independently on the Tokyo Stock Exchange. Both subsidiaries became profitable around 1977.[13]

Ito-Yokado in the 1980s

The Ito-Yokado group consisted of three business segments: Superstores and Other Retail Operations, Restaurant Operations, and Convenience Store Operations. The Convenience Store Operations segment was made up of 7-Eleven Japan. The Restaurant Operations segment consisted of Denny's and Famil Restaurants. Ito-Yokado superstores, Daikuma discount stores, two supermarket chains (York Mart and York-Benimaru), Robinson's Department Stores, and Oshman's Sporting Goods Store made up the Superstores and Other Retail Operations segment. Ito-Yokado's financial statements are shown in Exhibits 1 through 3.

Superstores and Other Retail Operations

York Mart and York-Benimaru

York Mart was a 100 percent owned subsidiary established in 1975. In 1990, it operated 40 supermarkets located primarily in the Tokyo area.[14] These stores sold mainly fresh foods and packaged goods, and competition was high in this geographic and retail area. Ito-Yokado's Operation Reform Program was implemented by York Mart in 1986 as a means to boost efficiency and profits. By 1990, sales were increasing at 6 percent per year.[15]

York-Benimaru was a 29-percent-owned affiliate of Ito-Yokado, and was an independently managed regional supermarket chain. York-Benimaru operated 51 stores as of 1988. The stores were located in the Fukushima prefecture

---

[12]Mitchell, "Southland Suitor."
[13]Uchida, *First Boston,* p. 8.
[14]Ibid., p. 8; and *Moody's Industrial Manual* 1, 1990, p. 1275.
[15]Ibid.

EXHIBIT 1   Ito-Yokado Company, Ltd., consolidated balance sheet (in millions of yen)

	As of February 28				
	1986	*1987*	*1988*	*1989*	*1990*
Assets					
Cash	¥26,188	¥25,596	¥32,527	¥31,566	¥32,529
Time deposits	32,708	64,894	55,631	125,809	163,524
Marketable securities	33,882	33,635	75,924	63,938	60,905
Notes and accounts receivable	16,570	16,582	19,042	26,949	24,195
Inventories	48,813	48,163	49,372	56,519	56,168
Other current assets	13,014	13,951	13,655	15,156	17,892
Total current assets	171,175	202,821	246,151	319,937	355,213
Investments and advertisement	18,097	21,642	24,352	25,589	33,779
Gross property and equipment	465,049	505,450	544,752	600,815	663,263
Less accumulated depreciation	160,409	183,185	207,561	237,079	262,958
Net property and equipment	304,640	322,265	337,191	363,736	400,305
Leasehold deposits	81,500	88,386	93,358	98,639	114,678
Total Assets	¥575,412	¥635,114	¥701,052	¥807,901	¥903,975
Liabilities and owners' equity					
Short term	¥23,577	¥22,425	¥17,815	¥20,090	¥20,140
Debt due	13,450	8,396	5,689	3,964	6,815
Accounts and notes payable	105,790	103,519	119,982	135,516	153,551
Accrued liability	40,892	45,217	53,654	61,077	65,941
Other current liability	12,777	13,523	17,297	20,458	25,404
Total current liabilities	196,486	193,080	214,437	241,105	271,851
Long-term debt	86,802	109,563	99,961	93,720	85,265
Accrued sev. indemnity	1,201	1,248	1,319	1,227	1,297
Deferred income taxes	1,912	2,036	969	0	2,150
Minority interests	45,011	51,974	60,619	83,102	95,920
Owners' Equity					
Common stock	17,364	18,184	22,462	28,913	33,328
Capital surplus	78,202	82,070	88,139	95,817	100,230
Other capital	9,292	9,292	9,292	16,210	16,210
Legal reserve	4,029	4,837	5,715	6,741	7,858
Retained earnings	135,307	163,042	198,351	241,078	290,078
Owner's equity	244,194	277,425	323,959	388,759	447,704
Less treasury stock	(212)	(212)	(1,423)	(212)	(212)
Net owners' equity	575,394	277,213	322,536	388,547	447,492
Total liabilities and owners' equity	¥243,982	¥635,114	¥701,052	¥807,701	¥903,975

Source: *Moody's Industrial Manual* 1, 1990.

EXHIBIT 2   Ito-Yokado Company, Ltd., consolidated income statement (in millions of yen)

	As of February 28				
	1986	*1987*	*1988*	*1989*	*1990*
Net sales	¥1,201,347	¥1,281,203	¥1,371,960	¥1,524,947	¥1,664,390
Cost of goods sold	829,077	875,343	923,771	1,025,839	1,113,659
Gross margin	372,270	405,860	448,189	499,108	550,731
Depreciation and amortization	27,328	31,106	32,064	33,777	37,695
Selling, general, and administrative expense	252,355	271,204	294,208	324,295	354,321
Operating income	92,587	103,550	121,917	141,036	158,715
Interest income	6,585	5,827	7,173	8,662	12,838
Interest expense	6,982	5,962	4,755	3,400	3,751
Foreign currency gains	2,089	488	74	—	—
Income before taxes	94,279	103,903	124,409	146,298	167,802
Income taxes					
Current	54,452	61,005	72,191	84,930	91,561
Deferred	1,153	106	(1,400)	(2,498)	3,183
Total income taxes	55,605	61,111	70,791	82,432	94,744
Minority interests	7,471	8,862	11,058	13,338	15,777
Equity in affiliated earnings	618	829	951	1,058	984
Net income	¥31,821	¥34,759	¥43,511	¥51,586	¥58,265
Opening retained earnings	¥109,717	¥135,307	¥163,042	¥198,351	¥241,078
Cash dividends	5,570	6,216	7,324	7,833	8,348
Transfer to legal reserves	664	808	878	1,026	1,117
Closing retained earnings	¥135,304	¥163,042	¥198,351	¥241,078	¥289,878
Per common share					
Net income	¥81.44	¥88.05	¥108.40	¥127.35	¥143.71
Cash dividends	¥15.70	¥18.18	¥19.55	¥20.00	¥23.00
Average number of shares	396,798	400,449	406,554	408,037	408,770

Source: *Moody's Industrial Manual* 1, 1990.

of Koriyama-city in northern Japan.[16] Like York Mart, York-Benimaru operated with a higher profit margin than the supermarket industry as a whole. York-Benimaru's earnings growth rate of 13 percent per year was expected to last into the 1990s, and Ito-Yokado's share of this profit was the major contribution to the "equity in earnings of affiliates" portion of Ito-Yokado's income statement (see Exhibit 2).[17]

Daikuma

Daikuma discount stores were consolidated into the Ito-Yokado group in 1986, when Ito-Yokado's ownership of Daikuma increased from 47.6 percent to 79.5

---

[16]Ibid.
[17]Ibid.

EXHIBIT 3   Ito-Yokado Company, Ltd., statement of cash flows (in millions of yen)

	As of February 28			
	1987	*1988*	*1989*	*1990*
Cash flow from operations				
Net income	¥ 34,759	¥ 43,511	¥ 51,586	¥ 58,465
Adjustments				
Depreciation and amortization	31,106	32,064	33,777	37,695
Minority interest	8,862	11,058	13,338	15,577
Undistributed earnings of affiliates	(603)	(719)	(811)	(732)
Deferred income tax and other	985	1,328	1,641	5,677
Increase in accounts and notes receivable, less allowance	(12)	(2,140)	(10,675)	58
Decrease (increase) in inventory	650	(1,196)	(6,049)	740
Decrease (increase) in prepaid expenses	(2,194)	734	(1,109)	(8,875)
Increase in accounts and notes payable and accrued liability	2,054	24,740	22,296	22,388
Increase in other liability	718	3,744	2,945	4,815
Net cash provided by operations	¥ 76,325	¥112,854	¥106,939	¥135,808
Cash flow from investing				
Increase in property and equipment	¥ (50,832)	¥ (50,075)	¥ (55,802)	¥ (72,927)
Increase in investments and advertising	(3,492)	(3,260)	(1,706)	(6,339)
Proceeds from disposal of property and equipment	1,460	731	1,991	1,442
Other	(6,206)	(5,629)	(5,878)	(13,888)
Net cash used by investing	¥ (58,620)	¥ (58,233)	¥ (61,395)	¥ (91,742)
Cash flow from financing				
Issue of long-term debt	¥ 37,859	¥7,692	¥ 9,755	¥ 10,135
Repayment of long-term debt	(15,331)	(9,321)	(6,472)	(7,112)
Proceeds from issuance of common stock by subs	0	0	18,554	0
Dividends paid	(6,216)	(7,324)	(7,833)	(8,834)
Other	(2,670)	(5,711)	(2,317)	(3,096)
Net cash provided by financing	¥ 13,642	¥ (14,664)	¥ 11,687	¥ (8,421)
Net change in cash equivalent	¥ 31,347	¥ 39,957	¥ 57,231	¥ 35,645
Cash equivalent at start of year	92,778	124,125	164,082	221,313
Cash equivalent at end of year	¥124,125	¥164,082	¥221,313	¥256,958

Source: *Moody's Industrial Manual* 1, 1990 and 1989.

percent.[18] In 1990, Daikuma was one of the largest discount store chains in Japan with 14 stores. While Daikuma was popular among young Japanese consumers, the discount stores attracted the critical attention of competing small retailers. Because the discount stores were regulated by the Large Store Regulation Act, intensive effort was required to open new stores. Despite these circumstances and increasing competition, Daikuma opened two discount stores in 1989.[19]

---

[18]Ibid.
[19]*Moody's Industrial Manual,* p. 1275.

Robinson's Department Stores

In 1984, the Robinson's Japan Company was established to open Robinson's Department Stores in Japan. The Robinson's name was used under the terms of a license granted by the U.S. store of the same name. The Japanese company was 100 percent owned by Ito-Yokado, and the first Robinson's Department Store in Japan was opened in November 1985 in Kasukabe City of Saitama Prefecture.[20] This was a residential community north of Tokyo and was a rapidly growing area. Although an Ito-Yokado superstore was located nearby, Ito-Yokado's management believed that a niche existed for a slightly more upscale retail store. Ito-Yokado had "shattered traditional wisdom by opening up a department store in the suburbs, not in the center of Tokyo."[21] The location was expected to serve a population area of over 600,000 residents and to offer a broad selection of consumer goods at prices higher than superstores yet lower than the downtown Tokyo department stores.

Many of the strategies employed by Ito-Yokado in opening its Robinson's Department Store followed similar strategies employed in its superstores. The land was leased (in a suburb). Instead of purchasing goods on a consignment basis, as most other department stores did, Robinson's managers were made responsible for the outright purchase of goods from suppliers. This allowed Robinson's to purchase goods at a significantly reduced price. Robinson's reported its first profit in fiscal 1989, approximately four years after opening.[22] In contrast, most Japanese department stores operate approximately 10 years before reporting a profit.[23] The single Robinson's location grossed about ¥28 billion (U.S.$220 million) in fiscal 1989.[24] The second Robinson's Department Store opened in late 1990 in Utsunomiya, about 100 kilometers (60 miles) north of Tokyo.

Oshman's Sporting Goods

Ito-Yokado licensed the Oshman's Sporting Goods name from the Houston, Texas, parent company in 1985. That year, two stores were opened. One of the stores was located inside the original Robinson's Department Store.

Restaurant Operations

Famil

The Famil Restaurant chain was started in 1979 as an in-store restaurant to serve customers at Ito-Yokado superstores. It had, however, expanded to 251 locations by 1988.[25] The Famil chain did not record its first positive earnings until 1986.

---

[20]Uchida, *First Boston,* p. 10.
[21]Ibid.
[22]*Moody's Industrial Manual,* p. 1275.
[23]Uchida, *First Boston,* p. 10.
[24]*Moody's Industrial Manual,* p. 1275.
[25]Uchida, *First Boston,* p. 12.

In Famil's attempts to expand operations, the company had emphasized its cater-ing business.[26] By 1990, the in-store operations (those located in Ito-Yokado su-perstores) accounted for 45 percent of Famil's sales, the catering business ac-counted for 32 percent of sales, and free-standing stores accounted for 23 percent of sales.[27]

Denny's Japan

Ito-Yokado opened the initial Denny's (Japan) Restaurant in 1974 with a license from Denny's of La Mirada, California. Ito-Yokado tailored the U.S. family restaurant to the Japanese market, and Denny's Japan became profitable around 1977. By 1981, 100 Denny's Japan restaurants had been established,[28] and in 1990 there were 320 such restaurants operated by Ito-Yokado.[29] In 1990, Ito-Yokado controlled 51 percent of Denny's Japan stock. In the early 1980s, Ito-Yokado decided that Denny's Japan should purchase all rights to the Denny's name in Japan. The purchase was made in 1984, and royalty payments to the U.S. parent were thereby discontinued.[30]

For the fiscal year 1990 (March 1989 to February 1990), Denny's Japan reported a net annual sales increase of 10.9 percent, as compared to the 4.9 percent Japanese restaurant industry sales increase for the same period.[31] Exhibits 4 and 5 contain financial statements for Denny's Japan. In 1988, Denny's Japan began using an electronic order-entry system, which allowed managers of individual restaurants to quickly order food supplies based on trends in their own restaurant. It also allowed for the periodic updating of menus to reflect new food items.

Convenience Store Operations

7-Eleven Japan

Since the opening of the first 7-Eleven store in 1974, the chain had grown to over 4,300 stores located in virtually all parts of Japan by February 1990.[32] At that time, about 300 new stores were being opened annually.[33] Ito-Yokado owned ap-proximately 50.3 percent of 7-Eleven Japan in 1990.

---

[26]Ibid.

[27]*Moody's Industrial Manual,* p. 1275.

[28]Ibid.

[29]Yumiko Ono, "Japanese Chain Stores Prosper by Milking American Concepts," *Asian Wall Street Journal* (April 2, 1990).

[30]Ibid.

[31]*Moody's Industrial Manual*, pp. 1275–76.

[32]James Sterngold, "New Japanese Lesson: Running a 7-11," *New York Times* (May 9, 1991), p. C1.

[33]Ono, "Japanese Chain Stores Prosper."

EXHIBIT 4   Denny's Japan Company, Ltd., consolidated balance sheet (in millions of yen)

	As of February 28		
	1988	*1989*	*1990*
Assets			
Cash	¥ 1,436	¥ 1,686	¥ 1,516
Time deposits	4,430	4,930	13,340
Marketable securities	104	0	14
Notes and accounts receivable	76	87	111
Inventories	562	569	617
Prepaid expenses	529	610	758
Short-term loans	4,527	6,241	5
Short-term leasehold deposits	267	286	300
Other current assets	414	233	341
Total current assets	12,345	14,643	17,092
Investments and advances	2,452	2,133	2,273
Gross property and equipment	18,894	21,291	23,739
Less: accumulated depreciation	9,108	10,397	11,937
Net property and equipment	9,786	10,894	11,802
Fixed leasehold deposits	5,177	5,334	5,496
Deferred charges other assets	4,449	3,940	3,380
Total assets	¥34,209	¥36,944	¥40,043
Liabilities and owners' equity			
Accounts payable	¥ 3,728	¥ 3,865	¥ 3,932
Accrued expenses	1,560	1,743	1,837
Income tax	2,009	2,210	2,140
Consumption tax withhold	328	0	653
Other current liabilities	0	383	299
Total current liabilities	7,625	8,201	8,861
Common stock	7,125	7,125	7,125
Additional paid-in capital	9,533	9,785	9,785
Legal reserves	233	286	345
Closing retained earnings	9,724	11,547	13,927
Owners' equity	26,584	28,743	31,182
Total liabilities and owners' equity	¥34,209	¥36,944	¥40,043

Source: *Moody's International Manual* 1, 1989, 1990.

Originally, young urban workers represented the primary customer base. As 7-Eleven penetrated the Japanese market, however, almost everyone became a potential customer. In Tokyo, for example, utility bills could be paid at the chain's stores.[34]

The 7-Eleven stores were small enough, with an average of only 1,000 square feet, to effectively avoid regulation under the Large Store Regulation Act. This allowed 7-Eleven to compete with the mom-and-pop retailers on the basis of longer hours of operation and lower prices. Faced with this competition, many of the small retailers joined the ranks of 7-Eleven. By converting

---

[34]Ibid.

EXHIBIT 5   Denny's Japan Company, Ltd., consolidated income statement (in millions of yen)

	As of February 28		
	1988	*1989*	*1990*
Net sales	¥58,241	¥64,604	¥70,454
Interest income	317	434	650
Other revenue, net	223	236	290
Total revenue	58,781	65,274	71,394
Cost of sales	20,196	22,233	23,952
Gross margin	38,585	43,041	47,442
Selling, administrative, and general expenses	32,444	35,990	40,177
Interest expense	19	9	17
Loss on sale of property	73	153	119
Income before taxes	6,049	6,889	7,129
Income taxes	3,521	3,894	4,074
Net income	¥ 2,528	¥ 2,995	¥ 3,055
Opening retained earnings	¥ 7,755	¥ 9,152	¥11,547
Cash dividends	508	535	588
Transfers to legal reserves	51	53	59
Closing retained earnings	¥ 9,724	¥11,559	¥13,955
Earnings per share (based on 26,741,000 weighted average shares)	¥94.50	¥112.40	¥114.20

Source: *Moody's International Manual* 1, 1989, 1990. The data are presented here as shown in Moody's. Some minor math errors exist.

small retailers to 7-Eleven stores, Ito-Yokado was able to expand rapidly and blanket the country.[35]

7-Eleven Japan pursued a strategy of franchising stores instead of owning them. The franchise commission for 7-Eleven stores was approximately 45 percent of the gross profit of the store (the commission was 43 percent for 24-hour stores). Ito-Yokado provided most of the ancillary functions for each store (e.g., administration, accounting, advertising, and 80 percent of utility costs). In 1987, 92 percent of all 7-Eleven stores in Japan were franchised,[36] and by 1990, only 2 percent of the 7-Elevens were corporate owned.[37]

Within the Ito-Yokado group, 7-Eleven contributed 6.8 percent of revenues in 1990. With this relatively small portion of overall corporate revenues, however, 7-Eleven Japan contributed over 35 percent of the group's profit. Under its licensing agreement, 7-Eleven Japan paid royalties of 0.6 percent of gross sales to the Southland Corporation. In 1989 and 1990, 7-Eleven Japan paid royalties of

---

[35]Tanzer, "A Form of Flattery."
[36]Uchida, *First Boston,* p. 13.
[37]*Moody's Industrial Manual,* p. 1276.

EXHIBIT 6   7-Eleven Japan consolidated balance sheet (in millions of yen)

	As of February 28		
	1988	1989	1990
Assets			
Cash	¥ 11,868	¥ 15,739	¥ 14,373
Time deposits	23,440	31,090	65,510
Short-term loans	26,169	52,228	29,136
Notes and accounts receivable	2,343	2,517	2,582
Inventory	247	285	222
Prepaid expenses	223	285	124
Less: allowance for other debts	1,990	320	180
Other current assets	351	651	369
Total current assets	66,631	102,315	112,136
Investments and advances	3,534	3,382	9,355
Gross property and equipment	94,703	108,319	123,871
Less: accumulated depreciation	25,665	30,316	35,010
Net property and equipment	69,038	78,003	88,861
Fixed leasehold deposits	4,351	6,501	7,725
Other assets	1,460	2,213	8,248
Total assets	¥145,014	¥192,417	¥226,325
Liabilities and owners' equity			
Accounts payable	¥ 40,498	¥ 46,678	¥ 52,912
Accrued expenses	1,427	1,487	1,738
Advances	685	778	718
Income taxes	14,818	17,341	20,068
Other current liabilities	867	552	3,289
Total current liabilities	58,295	66,836	78,725
Long-term debt	1,612	1,781	1,933
Common stock	5,902	17,145	17,145
Additional paid-in capital	13,073	24,619	24,589
Legal reserves	1,142	1,491	1,919
Retained earnings	65,233	80,545	101,984
Owners' equity	85,107	123,800	145,667
Total liabilities and owners' equity	¥145,014	¥192,417	¥226,325

Source: *Moody's International Manual* 1, 1989, 1990.

about $4.1 million and $4.7 million, respectively. The financial statements for 7-Eleven Japan for the years 1986 to 1990 are shown in Exhibits 6 and 7.

Operation Reform Project

Ito-Yokado implemented the Operation Reform Project in late 1981 in a retail industry environment punctuated by reduced consumer spending and decreasing margins. The goals of the project were to increase efficiency and boost profitability by increasing the inventory turn while avoiding empty stores shelves. The plan was originally implemented in the Ito-Yokado superstores and the 7-Eleven Japan convenience stores.

EXHIBIT 7   7-Eleven Japan consolidated income statement (in millions of yen)

	As of February 28		
	1988	*1989*	*1990*
Revenue	¥96,236	¥102,314	¥118,490
Cost of goods sold	13,484	8,702	9,249
Gross margin	82,752	93,612	109,241
Selling, administrative, and general expenses	39,672	42,491	49,185
Loss on sale of property	232	(66)	(230)
Income before taxes	42,848	51,187	59,826
Tax expenses	23,911	28,882	33,599
Net income	¥18,937	¥ 22,305	¥ 26,227
Opening retained earnings	¥49,646	¥ 62,139	¥ 80,545
Dividends	3,054	3,495	4,280
Transfers to legal reserves	306	350	428
Officers' bonus	0	54	80
Closing retained earnings	¥65,223	¥ 80,545	¥101,984
Earnings per share (based on 179,569,000 weighted average shares)	¥ 129.1	¥ 126.7	¥ 146.1

Note: "Cost of goods sold" represents primarily the cost of merchandise sold in the 152 company-owned stores.
Source: *Moody's International Manual* 1, 1989, 1990.

The implementation of the project involved a coordinated effort of catering to rapidly changing consumer preferences while, simultaneously, monitoring merchandise flow more closely. This coordination was accomplished by making individual store managers more responsible for such decisions as what merchandise was to be stocked on store shelves, thus allowing managers to tailor merchandise selection in their individual stores to local preferences. Top Ito-Yokado regional managers held weekly meetings with store managers to monitor the implementation of the project. As late as 1988, these meetings were still held on a weekly basis.[38]

In order to avoid depletion of store stocks, Ito-Yokado established an on-line ordering system with vendors. In 1982, the ordering system reached only 400 vendors. By 1988, however, the system linked Ito-Yokado with 1,860 vendors.[39]

---

[38] Hiroaki Komatsu, *Nomura Securities Report on Ito-Yokado Co., Ltd.* (June 7, 1988), p. 4.
[39] Ibid.

Point-of-Sale System[40]

As implementation of the Operation Reform Project began, Ito-Yokado paid increased attention to the importance of obtaining information regarding the flow of merchandise through individual stores. The tool chosen to accomplish this task was the point-of-sale (POS) system. POS system usage was increasing in the United States in the early 1980s, but the systems were used primarily to increase productivity at the cash register.[41] In contrast, Ito-Yokado used similar systems as a part of the project by monitoring specific merchandise flow. As of the late 1980s, many retailers in the United States had begun utilizing POS in similar capacities, and some had begun to use POS to track the purchases of individual consumers.[42]

The first use of POS systems in Japan came in 1982, when 7-Eleven Japan began installing them in its stores. By 1986, every 7-Eleven store in Japan was equipped with such a system.[43] The systems available were sophisticated enough to monitor the entire stock of merchandise in a typical convenience store having about 3,000 items.[44] The systems could monitor the flow of every item of merchandise through the purchase, inventory, sale, and restocking stages.

In late 1984, Ito-Yokado decided to install POS systems in the superstores. The sophistication of those systems installed in convenience stores, however, was not adequate to handle the merchandise flow of a superstore, which could stock up to 500,000 items.[45] New POS systems were developed in a coordinated effort by Ito-Yokado, Nippon Electric, and Nomura Computer Services.

---

[40]POS systems are computer-based merchandise control systems. They can provide a variety of functions such as inventory monitoring, price identification and registering, and —in some circumstances—merchandise ordering.

The implementation of POS systems became a reality in the early 1970s, when IBM announced the creation of a merchandise system that later became the Universal Product Code (UPC). In 1974, Marsh Supermarkets became the first retail store to utilize UPC-based POS systems. Also in 1974, the European Article Number (EAN) system, which is virtually a superset of the UPC, was introduced in Europe. The EAN system was adopted by 12 European nations in 1977. In 1978, Japan joined the EAN association (EANA). By 1989, 40 countries were members of the EANA.

The Japanese domestic market utilizes the same bar-code system used in the United States and Europe for product marking under the EAN guidelines for product marking. The Japanese coding system for consumer goods is called Japanese Article Numbering (JAN). A similar system for product marking used by wholesalers and distributors in Japan is the value-added network (VAN). The first product utilizing the JAN code was introduced in Japan in 1978.

Source: Ryosuke Assano "Networks Raise Efficiency," *Business Japan* (October 1989), pp. 45–52; Radack et al., "Automation in the Marketplace" (March 1978); "Pointing Out Differences in Point-of-Sale," *Chain Store Age Executive* (October 1990), pp. 16B–17B.

[41]Tanzer, "A Form of Flattery."

[42]For an example of one such application, see Blake Ives, et al., *The Tom Thumb Promise Club,* Edwin L. Cox School of Business, Southern Methodist University, 1989.

[43]Hiroaki Komatsu, *Nomura Securities Report on 7-Eleven Japan* (March 15, 1988), p. 4.

[44]Uchida, *First Boston,* p. 13.

[45]Ibid.

The installation of POS systems in the existing superstores was completed in November 1985, with over 8,000 POS registers installed in 121 stores.[46] With 138 stores in 1990, Ito-Yokado had an estimated 9,000 POS registers in the superstores alone. In 1986, after the systems had been installed in all superstores and 7-Elevens, Ito-Yokado accounted for about 70 percent of the POS systems in use in Japan.[47] As of 1988, 7-Eleven Japan was the only major convenience store chain in Japan to have installed POS systems.[48] By August 31, 1989, Japan had 119,137 POS scanner-equipped registers in 42,880 stores, making it the country with the most POS systems in use.[49]

The POS systems used by 7-Eleven Japan and Ito-Yokado superstores were upgraded in 1986 to add a new dimension to Ito-Yokado's Operation Reform Project.[50] The upgraded systems allowed for bidirectional communication with the company headquarters. This feature essentially allowed information to flow not only from individual stores to a central location, but also from the central location back to individual stores. By linking the central system to other computer systems, more information than just sales of retail items could be transmitted. This capability allowed Ito-Yokado to increase the efficiency of deliveries by centralizing some orders. By increasing the total size of orders, Ito-Yokado increased its bargaining position with distributors. One result of this bargaining strength was more frequent deliveries of smaller volume. From 1987 to 1988, deliveries increased from one to three per week for stores in many regions of Japan, notably the Tokyo, Hokkaido, and Kyushu areas.

Using the POS systems, 7-Eleven began to offer customers door-to-door parcel delivery in conjunction with Nippon Express. In addition, some POS terminals were being used to issue prepaid telephone credit cards.[51] Since October 1987, Tokyo-area customers had been able to pay their electric bills at 7-Eleven; since March 1988, they had also been able to pay their gas bills.[52] Since women traditionally manage household finances in Japan, these services were designed to attract more women customers to the convenience stores.

Results

For the Ito-Yokado superstores alone, average days of inventory decreased from 25.8 in 1982 to 17.3 in 1987. By 1990, it was estimated to be 13 days.[53] The effect on operating margins and net income for the entire Ito-Yokado cor-

---

[46]*Moody's Industrial Manual,* p. 1275.
[47]Tanzer, "A Form of Flattery."
[48]Komatsu, *Nomura Securities Report,* p. 4.
[49]*Business Japan* (October 1989), p. 51.
[50]Komatsu, *Nomura Securities Report,* p. 5.
[51]Ibid.
[52]Ibid.
[53]Uchida, *First Boston,* pp. 12, 22; and *Moody's Industrial Manual,* p. 1276.

EXHIBIT 8   Daiei, Inc., consolidated balance sheet (in millions of yen)

	As of February 28		
	1988	*1989*	*1990*
Assets			
Cash	¥ 60,409	¥ 61,096	¥ 55,529
Time deposits	89,090	61,866	85,713
Marketable securities	18,919	18,762	20,022
Net receivables	100,214	98,449	103,455
Inventories	95,924	90,203	108,241
Prepaid expenses and deferred income tax	7,784	11,149	15,338
Total current assets	372,340	341,525	388,298
Gross property and equipment	284,007	358,443	410,870
Less accumulated depreciation	108,540	120,955	141,172
Net property and equipment	175,467	237,488	269,698
Lease depreciation and loans to lessors	231,996	245,139	266,474
Investment and long-term receivables	118,009	170,676	164,853
Other assets	13,689	16,540	21,306
Total assets	¥911,501	¥1,011,368	¥1,110,629
Liabilities and owners' equity			
Short-term borrowings	¥256,539	¥ 338,188	¥ 350,274
Debt due	51,488	47,816	34,667
Notes and accounts payable	176,450	186,390	221,815
Accruals	18,370	18,274	21,256
Income taxes	7,872	7,284	8,445
Total current liabilities	510,719	597,952	636,457
Long-term debt	199,616	187,625	216,763
Lease deposits	52,656	56,750	60,489
Estimated retirement and term allowance	10,002	9,437	9,789
Reserve for investment losses	35,903	35,293	37,151
Deferred income	7,423	7,343	7,425
Other liabilities	1,636	4,604	7,314
Translation adjustment	2,179	1,979	1,754
Minority interests	663	692	2,794
Common stock (¥50)	18,144	25,649	33,783
Additional paid-in capital	82,748	92,426	100,664
Legal reserves	3,875	4,481	5,108
Deficit	(14,063)	(12,863)	(8,862)
Owners' equity	90,704	109,693	130,693
Total liabilities and owners' equity	¥911,501	¥1,011,368	¥1,110,629

Source: *Moody's International Manual* 1, 1990 and 1989.

poration was equally dramatic. In 1982, the company's operating margin stood at 5.1 percent. It had increased to 8.1 percent by 1987. By 1990, the operating margin had climbed to 10.5 percent. Net income for the corporation increased from ¥14,662 million in 1982 to ¥34,649 million in 1987, and ¥58,465 million in 1990.[54]

---

[54]Ibid.

EXHIBIT 9   Daiei, Inc., consolidated income statement (in millions of yen except earnings per share)

	As of February 28		
	1988	*1989*	*1990*
Net sales	¥1,718,886	¥1,880,825	¥2,114,909
Real estate revenue	0	21,235	22,790
Other revenue	45,588	37,623	55,171
Total operating revenue	1,764,474	1,939,683	2,192,870
Cost of goods sold	1,327,618	1,460,007	1,626,850
Gross margin	436,856	479,676	566,020
Selling, general, and administrative expenses	392,914	432,269	510,469
Operating income	43,942	47,407	55,551
Net interest expenditures	16,942	19,115	21,312
Other expenses	1,760	1,283	3,401
Income before taxes	25,240	27,009	30,838
Income tax	13,405	14,868	17,101
Minority interests	50	32	730
Equity losses	7,204	4,229	3,504
Translation adjustment	211	134	(46)
Net income	¥ 4,792	¥ 8,014	¥ 9,457
Opening retained earnings	¥ (13,929)	¥ (14,063)	¥ (12,863)
Decrease due to merger of chain store operations	0	0	1,497
Cash dividends	5,083	6,059	6,269
Transfer to legal reserves	73	606	627
Bonuses	114	141	143
Translation adjustment	(344)	8	(86)
Closing retained earnings	¥ (14,063)	¥ (12,863)	¥ (8,862)
Earnings per share	¥ 14.27	¥ 21.67	¥ 24.72
Shares outstanding	n/a	369,871,000	382,499,000

Source: *Moody's International Manual* 1, 1990 and 1989.

7-Eleven Japan recorded similar increases in operating margins and net income during the same period. In 1982, 7-Eleven Japan's operating margin was 20.7 percent. It had increased to 34.6 percent by 1987. Net income from the 7-Eleven operations increased from ¥7,837 million in 1982 to ¥33,000 million in 1987.[55]

As of 1990, the Ito-Yokado corporation was the second-largest retailer in Japan, with ¥1,664,390 million of annual gross sales. The leading retailer was Daiei, with ¥2,114,909 million of revenues. Ito-Yokado was, however, the most profitable retailer in Japan, with net income of ¥58,465 million. In comparison, Daiei recorded net income of only ¥9,457 million for 1990. Financial statements for Daiei are shown as Exhibits 8 and 9.

---

[55]Ibid.

The Southland Corporation[56]

The Southland Corporation began in Dallas, Texas, in 1927 when Claude S. Dawley consolidated several small Texas ice companies into the Southland Ice Company. This new company was under the direction of 26-year-old Joe C. Thompson, Sr. Under Thompson's guidance, Southland began to use its retail outlets (curb service docks) to sell products in addition to ice, such as watermelon, milk, bread, eggs, and cigarettes. With the addition of these products, the concept of the convenience store was born.

During the Great Depression and the 1940s, Southland's convenience store business added several more products, including gasoline, frozen foods, beauty products, fresh fruit and vegetables, and picnic supplies. Because the store opened at 7 A.M. and remained open till 11 P.M., the store name 7-Eleven was adopted during this time.

The 1950s were a period of substantial growth in terms of the number of stores and of 7-Eleven's geographical coverage. The first stores located outside of Texas were opened in Florida in 1954. During the same year, 7-Eleven's operating profit surpassed the $1 million mark for the first time. By 1959, the entire 7-Eleven empire constituted 425 stores in Texas, Louisiana, Florida, and several other East Coast states.

John Thompson became president of Southland when his father, Jodie Thompson, died in 1961. During the 1960s, a population migration toward the suburbs and changing lifestyles presented Southland with new growth opportunities. John Thompson led Southland on the path of expansion, and over 3,000 stores were opened in the decade. The product line of 7-Eleven also grew during this time to include prepared foods, rental items, and some self-service gasoline pumps.

The 1970s were also a period of achievement for Southland. In 1971, the $1 billion sales mark was surpassed. Southland stock began trading on the New York Stock Exchange in 1972, and the 5,000th store was opened in 1974. It was at this time that Masatoshi Ito approached Southland with the prospect of franchising 7-Eleven stores in Japan.

During the 1970s and early 1980s, Southland's activities became more diversified. In 1986, the company had four operating groups: the Stores Group, the Dairies Group, the Special Operations Group, and the Gasoline Supply Division.

The Stores Group represented the largest of the operating groups in terms of sales through the 1980s. The Stores Group was responsible for the operating and franchising of convenience stores. At the end of 1985, there were 7,519 7-Eleven stores in most of the United States and five provinces of Canada. This group was also responsible for 84 Gristede's and Charles & Company food stores, 38 Super-

---

[56]A more detailed history of Southland can be found in cases written by M. Edgar Barrett, of the American Graduate School of International Business: *The Southland Corporation (A)*, 1983, and *The Southland Corporation (B)*, 1990.

7 outlets, and 7-Eleven stores operated under area licensees in the United States, Canada, and several Pacific Rim countries, including Japan.

The Dairies Group was one of the nation's largest dairy processors in 1986, and served primarily the Stores Group, although aggressive marketing in the 1980s targeted service to institutional dairy needs. This group operated in all of the United States and parts of Canada. The Special Operations Group consisted of Chief Auto Parts (acquired in 1979); Pate Foods (a snack food company); Reddy Ice (the world's largest ice company); and Tidel Systems (a manufacturer of cash dispensing units and other retailer equipment). The Gasoline Supply Division was formed in 1981 to serve the gasoline requirements of the over 2,800 7-Eleven stores handling gasoline. This division's history was punctuated by the 1983 acquisition of Cities Service Refining, Marketing, and Transportation businesses (CITGO) from Occidental Petroleum.

Southland's Recent Activities[57]

Southland's dramatic growth and diversification during the 1970s and early 1980s resulted in 7-Eleven having a dominant position in the convenience store industry. Despite this position, circumstances since the mid-1980s had greatly eroded 7-Eleven and Southland's strengths.

The oil price collapse of early 1986 was the sharpest drop of crude oil prices in history. The instability of crude oil and wholesale refined products, coupled with CITGO's inventory methods and various write-downs, resulted in only modest income for a previously very profitable company. The volatility of CITGO's financial position greatly affected Southland's earnings. Southland's equity interest in CITGO contributed to a $52 million loss for the entire corporation in 1986. In order to reduce the impact of an unstable crude oil market and the accompanying volatility of CITGO's earnings, Southland entered into a joint venture with Petroleos de Venezuela (PDVSA) in late 1986.

The joint venture with PDVSA had several components. Southland sold a half-interest in CITGO to a subsidiary of PDVSA for $290 million. In addition, PDVSA agreed to both supply CITGO with a minimum of 130,000 barrels of crude oil per day and provide its share of CITGO's working capital requirements.

A takeover attempt of Southland occurred in April 1987. Canadian financier Samuel Belzberg approached the Southland board of directors with an offer of $65 per share of common stock. Unwilling to relinquish control of Southland, the Thompson family tendered $77 per share for two-thirds of the outstanding shares in July 1987. The other third of the shares would be purchased at $61 per share (plus $16 per share of new preferred shares) by the would-be private Southland Corporation.

Financing for this acquisition came from $2 billion in loans from a group of banks and a $600 million bridge loan from Goldman, Sachs and Salomon

---

[57]Barrett, *The Southland Corporation (B),* offers more detailed information.

Brothers. An additional $1.5 billion was generated by the issue of subordinated debentures (junk bonds) in November 1987. This occurred after the stock and junk bond markets crashed in October 1987. Southland's investment bankers had to sell the bonds at a blended rate of almost 17 percent, instead of the anticipated rate of 14.67 percent. The Thompson family emerged from the buyout owning 71 percent of Southland at a total cost of $4.9 billion.

Paying the High Costs of a Leveraged Buyout

After Southland had been taken private through the leveraged buyout (LBO), significant changes occurred in both Southland and 7-Eleven operations. Southland was restructured, with the elimination of two levels of middle managers. During this time, Southland began selling more 7-Eleven stores than it opened in the United States and Canada. Due to the increased number of licensees opening stores overseas, however, the total number of stores worldwide continued to increase. 7-Eleven Japan was primarily responsible for this increase, with the opening of 340 stores in 1988 and 349 stores in 1989. Southland also divested itself of many large assets in the 1988 to 1990 period (see Exhibit 10). Significant in this group of divestments were the entire Dairy Group, over 100 7-Eleven stores in the continental United States, Southland's remaining interest in CITGO (sold to PDVSA), and 7-Eleven Hawaii (purchased by 7-Eleven Japan).

In November 1989, 7-Eleven Japan purchased 58 stores and additional properties from Southland. These properties and stores, which were located in Hawaii, were exchanged for $75 million in cash. The 58 convenience stores were organized as 7-Eleven Hawaii which was established as a subsidiary of 7-Eleven Japan.

As of December 31, 1990, Southland operated 6,455 7-Eleven convenience stores in the United States and Canada, 187 High's Dairy Stores, and 63 Quick Mart and Super-7 Stores. Southland owned 1,802 properties on which 7-Eleven stores were located. Another 4,643 7-Eleven stores in the United States and Canada were leased. In addition, the company possessed 234 store properties held for sale, of which 109 were unimproved, 77 were closed stores, and 48 were excess properties adjoining store locations.[58]

Three of Southland's four food processing facilities were owned (the other was leased). The company owned six properties in the United States on which distribution centers were located. Five of the six distribution centers were company owned. The company also owned its corporate headquarters (called Cityplace) located near downtown Dallas.[59] Financial statements for Southland Corporation are shown in Exhibits 11 and 12.

---

[58]Southland Corporation 1990 Form 10-K, pp. 21–23.
[59]Ibid.

EXHIBIT 10   Asset divestitures of Southland, 1988–1990

Date announced	Asset	Buyer	Amount
January 1988	Tidel Systems	D.H. Monnick Corp.	Undisclosed
February 1988	Chief Auto Parts	Management & Shearson Lehman	$130 million
March 1988	Movie Quik	Cevax U.S. Corp.	$51 million
March 1988	Reddy Ice	Reddy Ice	$23 million
April 1988	402 properties including 270 Houston-area 7-Elevens	National Convenience Stores	$67 million plus $13 million for related inventories
April 1988	473 7-Eleven stores in 10 states	Circle-K	$147 million
April 1988	Southland Dairy Group	Morningstar Foods	$242.5 million
July 1988	Snack Food Division	Undisclosed	$15 million
November 1988	79 San Antonio-area 7-Elevens	National Convenience Stores	Undisclosed
July 1989	184 7-Elevens in three states	Ashland Oil et al.	Undisclosed
October 1989	50% of CITGO	Petroleos de Venezuela S.A. (PDVSA)	$661.5 million
November 1989	58 7-Elevens in Hawaii, plus other properties	7-Eleven Japan	$75 million
April 1990	56 Memphis-area 7-Elevens	Undisclosed	$12.9 million
August 1990	28 7-Elevens in Florida, plus other properties	Undisclosed	$7.5 million
December 1990	Cityplace in Dallas	Oak Creek Partners	$24 million

Source: *Dallas Morning News* (November 15, 1989), p. D-1; *Dallas Morning News* (October 10, 1988), p. D-1; *Automotive News* (February 8, 1988), p. 108; *The Wall Street Journal* (February 19, 1988); *The Wall Street Journal* (January 28, 1988); *The Wall Street Journal* (March 4, 1988); *New York Times* (March 4, 1988); Southland Corporation, 1990 Form 10-K.

The Proposed Purchase of Southland by Ito-Yokado

The divestments of 1988, 1989, and 1990 constituted attempts by Southland to generate sufficient cash to service the massive debt incurred from the LBO of 1987. By early 1990, however, it was apparent that the cash generated from these divestments and Southland's operations was not sufficient to cover its interest expense. Some experts estimated that Southland's cash shortfalls would reach $89 million in 1990 and over $270 million in 1991.[60] Southland's long-term debt still totaled about $3.7 billion, and interest expense alone in the first three quarters of 1989 was almost $430 million.[61] In March of 1990, Southland announced that it was seeking "rescue" by Ito-Yokado.[62]

---

[60]Linda Sandler, "Southland's Junk Bonds Face Trouble," *The Wall Street Journal* (September 7, 1989).

[61]Richard Alm, "Southland Seeks Rescue by Japanese Firm," *Dallas Morning News* (March 23, 1990).

[62]Ibid.

EXHIBIT 11   Southland Corporation consolidated balance sheet (in thousands of dollars)

	As of December 31			
	1988	*1989*	*1990*	*1990**
Assets				
Cash and short-term inventory	$ 21,783	$ 8,045	$ 108,294	$ 351,678
Accounts and notes receivable	208,686	188,251	161,778	161,778
Inventories	428,098	276,112	301,756	301,756
Deposits and prepaid expenditures	25,929	25,483	64,075	44,889
Investment in CITGO	—	469,687	—	—
Total current assets	684,496	958,578	635,903	860,101
Property, plant, and equipment	2,632,060	2,620,137	2,504,090	2,504,090
Less depreciation	416,822	624,807	788,589	788,589
Net property, plant, and equipment	2,215,238	1,995,330	1,715,501	1,715,501
Investment in CITGO	440,777	—	—	—
Excess acquisition costs	986,356	—	—	—
Other assets	534,644	484,847	447,638	397,349
Total assets	$4,861,511	$3,438,755	$2,799,042	$2,972,951
Liabilities and owners' equity				
Debt due	$ 527,174	$ 692,508	$3,522,647	$ 647,512
Accounts payable	692,596	723,694	647,512	9,145
Income taxes payable	377	139	9,145	171,729
Total current liabilities	1,220,147	1,416,341	4,298,119	828,386
Deferred credits	96,359	115,334	142,315	142,315
Long-term debt	3,787,578	3,457,015	182,536	3,118,797
Redeemable preferred stock	118,850	139,740	148,496	—
Redeemable common stock purchase warrants	26,136	26,136	26,136	26,136
Common stock	2,050	2,050	2,050	41
Additional paid-in capital	18,318	18,318	20,364	594,146
Deficit	(407,927)	(1,736,179)	(2,018,926)	(1,736,870)
Total owners' equity	(387,559)	(1,715,811)	(1,998,560)	(1,142,683)
Total liabilities and owners' equity	$4,861,511	$3,438,755	$2,799,042	$2,972,951

*This depicts the balance sheet for Southland on December 31, 1990, as if the later buyout by Ito-Yokado had been completed.
Source: Southland Corporation 1990 and 1989 Forms 10-K.

Proposed Acquisition of Southland by Ito-Yokado

Southland had "looked at possibilities of receiving assistance from other U.S. companies, but decided that . . . Ito-Yokado was the best potential partner."[63] The original proposal would have resulted in Ito-Yokado receiving 75 percent ownership of Southland for $400 million. This proportion of Southland would be split between Ito-Yokado and 7-Eleven Japan, with 7-Eleven Japan obtaining two-thirds of the 75 percent share.

---

[63]Karen Blumenthal et al., "Japanese Group Agrees to Buy Southland Corporation," *The Wall Street Journal* (March 23, 1990).

EXHIBIT 12   Southland Corporation consolidated income statement (in thousands of dollars)

	As of December 31		
	1988	*1989*	*1990*
Net sales	$7,950,284	$ 8,274,921	$ 8,347,681
Other income	40,213	76,962	62,375
Total revenues	7,990,497	8,351,883	8,410,056
Cost of sales	6,268,854	6,544,237	6,661,273
Gross margin	1,721,643	1,807,646	1,748,783
Selling, administrative expenses	1,543,090	1,607,312	1,664,586
Loss on assets sold	—	—	41,000
Write-off acquired assets	—	946,974	—
Interest expense	560,268	572,248	459,500
Employee benefits, etc.	15,416	13,372	13,653
Net before taxes	(397,132)	(1,332,260)	(429,956)
Income taxes	(111,900)	(11,984)	(128,459)
Loss from continuing operations	(285,232)	(1,320,276)	(301,497)
Discontinued operations			
Equity, CITGO	69,001	70,480	—
Loss, equity disposition	—	1,070	—
Loss before extraordinary charges	(216,231)	(1,250,866)	(301,497)
Extraordinary charges	—	(56,047)	52,040
Effect of account change of medical benefits	(27,163)	—	(27,163)
Net income	$ (216,231)	$(1,306,913)	$ (276,620)
Opening retained earnings	$ (166,998)	$ (407,927)	$(1,736,179)
Dividends paid, redeemable preferred stock	(20,856)	(12,634)	(1,011)
Accretion	(6,706)	(8,257)	(7,744)
Currency translation adjustment	2,864	(488)	(2,628)
Deficit	$ (407,927)	$(1,736,179)	$(2,018,926)
Earnings per share data			
Loss, before extraordinary charges	$ (15.63)	$ (62.02)	$ (15.14)
Effect of extraordinary charges	—	(2.74)	2.54
Net loss	$ (12.19)	$ (64.76)	$ (13.93)
Year-end common shares (000)	205,042	205,042	205,042

Source: Southland Corporation 1990 and 1989 Form 10-K.

The deal was contingent on Southland's ability to swap its outstanding publicly traded debt for stock and zero-coupon (non-interest-bearing) bonds. The publicly traded debt amounted to approximately $1.8 billion. There were five classes of public debt, ranging in type and interest paid. The interest rate of the bonds varied from 13.5 percent to 18 percent. Ito-Yokado's offer was also contingent on 95 percent of all bondholders of each public debt issue accepting the swap. Under this original proposal, the Thompson family would retain a 15 percent stake in Southland, and the remaining 10 percent of the company would be held by bondholders.

The original proposal had a deadline of June 14, 1990, at which time either Ito-Yokado or Southland could cancel the agreement. Neither party indicated that such action would be taken, even though Southland's bondholders balked at the swap proposal. A bigger problem was facing the two companies: a rapidly approaching interest payment due on June 15, 1990. Southland's failure to pay the $69 million payment would result in Southland having a 30-day grace period in which to compensate bondholders. At the end of the 30-day period, unpaid bondholders could try to force Southland into bankruptcy court.[64]

Revisions to the Proposed Buyout

Southland did not make its scheduled interest payment that was due on June 15, 1990. Bondholders, meanwhile, had shown little regard for the original deal struck between Ito-Yokado and Southland.

Three more revisions of the proposed debt restructuring and terms for the buyout were submitted between mid-June and mid-July 1990. In each revision, either Ito-Yokado's or the Thompson family's stake in Southland was reduced and the share of Southland stock offered to bondholders increased. With each revision came increased bondholder support, yet this support was far short of either the two-thirds majority (as required in Chapter 11 restructuring cases) or the 95 percent acceptance rate dictated by Ito-Yokado. As revisions were submitted, the expiration dates of the debt restructuring and stock purchase by Ito-Yokado were extended.

On July 16, a bondholder filed suit against Southland for failure to pay interest on June 15, because on July 15 Southland's grace period had expired.[65] By September 12, a majority of bondholders had tendered their notes.[66] This majority was still far short, however, of the 95 percent swap requirement dictated by Ito-Yokado. The deadlines were extended to September 25 for both the debt swap offer by Southland and the stock purchase offer by Ito-Yokado.[67] As Southland was apparently headed for involuntary bankruptcy filing under Chapter 11, the proposal again seemed in jeopardy.

Acceptance of the Proposed Buyout

The deadline for Southland's debt swap offer was again extended. Bondholder approval was finally obtained in late October. Ito-Yokado's offer to buy out Southland was extended to March 15, 1991, pending court approval of the prepackaged bankruptcy deal.[68] The bankruptcy-court petition for approval of the prepackaged debt restructuring was filed on October 24, 1990.[69]

---

[64]Karen Blumenthal, "Southland Approaches 2 Crucial Dates in Plan to Rearrange $1.8 Billion in Debt," *The Wall Street Journal* (April 12, 1990).

[65]Ibid.

[66]Kevin Helliker, "Southland May Be Considering Seeking Chapter 11 Status, Thus Risking Bailout," *The Wall Street Journal* (September 14, 1990).

[67]Ibid.

[68]Kevin Helliker, "Southland Says Reorganization Clears Hurdle," *The Wall Street Journal* (October 24, 1990).

[69]"Southland Chapter 11 Plan Needs Approval from SEC," *The Wall Street Journal* (December 6, 1990).

Although Southland did not have sufficient bondholder approval as dictated by Ito-Yokado, the bankruptcy court proceedings were swift. The last few bondholders who held out were placated in January when the Thompsons relinquished warrants for half of their 5 percent stake of Southland's stock.[70] On February 21, 1991, the U.S. bankruptcy court in Dallas approved the reorganization of Southland.[71] At that time, at least 93 percent of the holders of each class of debt issued by Southland had approved the reorganization.[72] On March 5, 1991, Ito-Yokado purchased 71 percent of Southland's stock for $430 million.[73] Two-thirds of this stock was purchased by 7-Eleven Japan, and the other third purchased directly by Ito-Yokado. The terms of the accepted debt-restructuring agreement between Southland and its bondholders are shown in Exhibit 13.

EXHIBIT 13   Southland Corporation debt restructuring terms for $1,000 principal debt of various classes as accepted by bondholders on February 21, 1991

	13.5% Senior notes	15.75% Senior notes	16.5% Senior notes	16.75% notes	18% Junior notes
Principal retained	$450	$300	$255	$200	$95
Interest rate of new debt received	12%	5%	5%	4.5%	4%
Number of shares of common stock received	86.5	40.5	35	28	11
Number of stock warrants received	1	7.5	6.5	6	6

Notes:
- "Principal retained" was in the form of newly issued bonds bearing interest as shown.
- Holders of 13.5% senior notes also received $57 cash per $1,000 principal of old debt.
- Holders of 16.5% notes may have received $250 of 12% notes with no stock warrants instead of $200 of 4.5% and 6 stock warrants (per $1,000 principal of old debt). In either case, the holder would have been entitled to 28 shares of common stock.
- Stock warrants gave the holder the option to purchase one share of common stock per warrant for $1.75 per share from June 5, 1991, to February 23, 1996.

Source: Southland Corporation 1990 Form 10-K.

The Convenience Store Industry in the United States

The convenience store industry in the United States changed dramatically during the decade of the 1980s. The number of convenience stores in the United States, the gross sales of these stores, and the gross margins all increased during this time period. The net income of convenience stores, however, decreased significantly. This outcome was largely the result of the rapid expansion of several chains of convenience stores and the increased number of convenience stores opened by oil companies.

---

[70]David LaGeese, "Judge Approves Southland's Reorganization," *Dallas Morning News* (February 22, 1991), p. 1D.
[71]Ibid.
[72]Ibid.
[73]"Southland Sells 70 Percent Stake, Completing Reorganization," *The Wall Street Journal* (March 6, 1991), p. A2.

Aggregate Measures of the Industry

The number of convenience stores grew from about 39,000 in 1982 to over 70,000 in 1989. From 1985 to 1989, industry sales increased from $51.4 billion to $67.7 billion, an increase of 6.3 percent per year. Gross margins increased from 22.8 percent in 1985 to 26.2 percent by 1988. Despite such growth, convenience store operations experienced a decrease in net profit in the late 1980s. The total industry pretax profit peaked in 1986 at $1.4 billion, fell to $1.16 billion in 1988, and plummeted to $271 million in 1989. Some trends are shown in Exhibit 14.[74]

The expansion of convenience stores in the 1980s was led by large convenience store chains and oil companies. In addition to the growth experienced by the Southland Corporation's 7-Eleven, Circle-K, a Phoenix-based convenience store chain, expanded from 1,200 stores in 1980 to 4,700 stores in 1990.

EXHIBIT 14   Industrywide convenience store performance, 1985–1989

	1985	1986	1987	1988	1989
Number of stores	61,000	64,000	67,500	69,200	70,200
Gross revenue (in billions)	$51.4	$53.9	$59.6	$61.2	$67.7
Net income (in billions)	$1.39	$1.40	$1.31	$1.16	$0.27
Average per-store profit before tax (in thousands)	$22.8	$21.9	$19.2	$16.8	$3.9

Source: National Association of Convenience Stores, *1990 State of the Convenience Store Industry.*

The Role of the Oil Companies

The impact of oil companies on the convenience store industry has been significant. Virtually all of the major U.S. oil companies began combining convenience store operations with gasoline stations in order to boost profits. In 1984, Exxon opened its first combination convenience store and gas station. By 1989, it had 500. Texaco operated 950 Food Marts in the same year. From 1984 to 1989, the number of convenience stores operated by oil companies increased from 16,000 to 30,000.[75]

Since gasoline sold at a lower margin (about 6 percent in 1984) than nongasoline convenience store products (32 percent in the same year), the sale of convenience store items presented an opportunity for those gas stations with good locations (i.e., street corners) to increase profits. In order to capitalize on the potential for higher profits in retailing, the major oil companies boosted their marketing expenditures. In 1979, the petroleum industry spent about $2.2 billion for their marketing efforts. By 1988, these expenditures were almost $5 billion.[76]

---

[74]This information is drawn largely from National Association of Convenience Stores (NACS), *1990 State of the Convenience Store Industry* (1990).

[75]Claudia H. Deutsch, "Rethinking the Convenience Store," *New York Times* (October 8, 1989).

[76]National Association of Convenience Stores, *Challenges for the Convenience Store Industry in the 1990s: A Future Study,* p. 194.

The convenience stores operated by oil companies were growing in both number and size. In 1986, only about 20 percent of the oil company convenience stores were 1,800 or more square feet in size (the size of about 90 percent of traditional convenience stores). By 1990, however, over 50 percent of the oil company convenience stores were between 1,800 and 3,000 square feet in size.[77]

Merchandise Trends for Convenience Stores

Because of the intensified retailing efforts of oil companies and large convenience store chains, some trends (other than those mentioned above) evolved. In 1985, gasoline accounted for 35.4 percent of convenience store sales. By 1989, gasoline accounted for 40 percent of sales.[78] The gross profit margin for gasoline sales had increased from 7.3 percent to 11.7 percent over the same period.[79] Of the 61,000 convenience stores in the United States in 1985, 55 percent sold gasoline, and in 1989, 65 percent of 70,200 convenience stores sold gasoline. In 1989, 75 percent of the new convenience stores built were equipped to sell gasoline.[80]

Although gasoline sales and margins became an increasingly significant contributor to convenience store revenues, contributions of revenue from other merchandise stagnated. In 1985, merchandise (other than gasoline) sales for the convenience store industry amounted to $33.2 billion. In 1989, sales reached $40.6 billion.[81] This increase in merchandise sales, however, was offset by the large number of store openings. In 1985, the average yearly merchandise sales per store was $544,000. This number increased to only $578,000 in 1989.[82]

The Setting

While flying from Japan to the United States, Takahashi reflected on the success that both Ito-Yokado and 7-Eleven Japan had enjoyed over the course of many years. These achievements were the result of long-term strategies that were carefully tailored to the Japanese market. Could these same, or similar, strategies be the foundation for making Southland financially successful again? He realized that the convenience store industry in the United States was vastly different from that of Japan. Nevertheless, he was confident that, through careful and thorough planning, the goal of making Southland profitable could be achieved.

---

[77]Ibid., p. 198.
[78]NACS, *1990 State of the Convenience Store Industry,* p. 14.
[79]Ibid., p. 16.
[80]Ibid., pp. 25–26.
[81]Ibid., p. 14.
[82]Ibid., p. 16.

Case 15

Levi Strauss Japan K.K.*

In May 1993, A. John Chappell, president and representative director, Levi Strauss Japan K.K. (LSJ), was contemplating a conversation he just had with the national sales manager and managing director, Masafumi Ohki. They had been discussing the most recent information regarding the size of the jeans market in Japan. It appeared that after two years of market shrinkage in 1990 and 1991, the market contracted further in 1992. Although LSJ was still increasing its share of the market, Mr. Chappell was disturbed by this trend and wondered what new strategies, if any, LSJ should pursue.

In addition, Mr. Ohki had brought up the issue of selection criteria for retailers and sales agents. The distribution channel was undergoing structural changes, and Ohki believed that LSJ needed to evaluate and possibly revise their distribution strategy. LSJ was very selective in choosing its retailers and had historically focused their distribution on traditional urban jeans specialty shops. However, there were many new, large stores opening in the suburbs which were carrying jeans, amongst other items. Although LSJ did sell their jeans in some of these new stores, they had not pursued this new channel as aggressively as some of their competitors. As a result, their largest competitor, Edwin, was currently represented in twice as many stores as LSJ.

Mr. Chappell realized that increasing the number of stores would improve LSJ's reach and possibly help to stimulate the overall market. However, this could have a serious impact on LSJ's image. LSJ had spent years developing a premium product image which had catapulted them to market leader. Besides their product and advertising strategies, this image had also been cultivated by their selectivity in choosing retail outlets and sales agents. Not only did this ensure that LEVI'S would have a good image with the consumer, but it also was the only way LSJ could influence the retail price. Mr. Chappell feared that a decision

*This case was prepared by Elizabeth Carducci and Akiko Horikawa, second year MBA students, and Professor David B. Montgomery, Stanford University Graduate School of Business, as the basis for class discussion rather than to illustrate either effective or ineffective handling of an administrative situation. The authors gratefully acknowledge the cooperation and assistance of A. John Chappell and Masafumi Ohki of Levi Strauss Japan, and David Schmidt and S. Lindsay Webbe of Levi Strauss International. Reprinted with permission of Stanford University, Graduate School of Business, Copyright © 1994 by the Board of Trustees of the Leland Stanford Junior University.

to expand the number of retail outlets would have a negative impact on LEVI'S prices and might even result in discounting. This could seriously affect the premium product image LSJ had worked hard to foster over the years.

Mr. Chappell wondered what new strategies he should pursue to deal with these issues, or whether he should continue with the strategy that had made LEVI'S the number one jeans brand in Japan.

Levi Strauss Associates

Overview

Levi Strauss invented jeans in San Francisco in the middle of the 19th century gold rush. At that time, Levi Strauss made pants for the gold miners that would not rip apart when miners filled their pockets with gold. Since then, the company bearing the founder's name has been faithful to the guiding principle—"Quality Never Goes Out of Style"—and has built a strong reputation and broad customer base.

Today, Levi Strauss Associates (Levi Strauss) designs, manufactures, and markets apparel for men, women, and children, including jeans, slacks, jackets, and skirts. Most of its products are marketed under the LEVI'S® and DOCKERS® trademarks and are sold in the United States and throughout North and South America, Europe, Asia, and Australia. In 1992, Levi Strauss was the world's largest brand name apparel manufacturer. Sales of jeans-related products accounted for 73 percent of its revenues in 1991.

Levi Strauss International

Levi Strauss International (LSI), which markets jeans and related apparel outside the United States, is organized along geographic lines consisting of the Europe, Asia Pacific, Canada, and Latin America divisions. In terms of sales and profits, Europe is the largest international division. Asia Pacific is the second largest, particularly due to the strong performance of its Japanese and Australian operations. Sales growth in LSI is faster than in the domestic division. Exhibit 1 gives the breakdown of domestic and international sales for the recent years.

Organization and products. In 1991, LSI was more profitable than the domestic operations on a per-unit basis. LSI was generally organized by country. Each country's operations within the European division are generally responsible for sales, distribution, finance, and marketing activities. With few exceptions,

EXHIBIT 1   Levi Strauss domestic and international sales ($ millions)

	1989		1990		1991	
Domestic	$2,395	66.0%	$2,560	60.3%	$2,997	61.1%
LSI	1,233	34.0	1,686	39.7	1,906	38.9
Total	$3,628	100.0%	$4,247	100.0%	$4,903	100.0%

Canada, Latin America, and the Asia Pacific divisions are staffed with their own merchandising, production, sales, and finance personnel.

LSI's sales are derived primarily from basic lines of jeans, shirts, and jackets. LSI resells directly to retailers in its established markets, although other distribution agreements are made elsewhere in the world. Retail accounts are currently serviced by approximately 310 sales representatives. LSI's manufacturing and distribution activities are independent of domestic operations. However, in 1991, LSI purchased $117.7 million of jeans products from the domestic division.

The markets, competition, and strategy. The nature and strength of the jeans market varies from region to region and from country to country. Demand for jeans outside of the U.S. is affected by a variety of factors, each of varying importance in different countries, including general economic conditions such as unemployment, recession, inflation, and consumer spending rates. The non-U.S. jeans markets are more sensitive to fashion trends, as well as being more volatile than the U.S. market. In many countries, jeans are generally perceived as a fashion item, rather than a basic functional product, and are higher priced relative to the U.S. Sales in Japan have increased in recent years due primarily to increased consumer spending and population growth. Internationally, LSI maintains advertising programs similar to the domestic programs, modified as required by market conditions and applicable laws. Advertising expenditures for LSI were $108.4 million (5.7 percent of total sales) in 1991, a 21 percent increase from 1990.

Industry. The worldwide apparel market is affected by demographic changes in the consumer population, frequent shifts in prevailing fashions and styles, international trade and economic developments, and retailer practices. With the maturation of "the baby boomer" generation, the target market, a company's success will become more dependent on its ability to quickly and effectively respond to changes in fashion and other customer preferences.

Japanese Jeans Industry Environment and Trends

Jeans Market

Jeans were introduced into the Japanese market before World War II. Yet, the first market boom occurred right after the war, when U.S. forces brought a large supply of jeans into the country. The second growth spurt in the market for jeans was in the mid-1970s, concurrent with the United States bicentennial. During this time, being American was in vogue, greatly enhancing the demand for American culture and products. The third boom, in 1986, was fueled by the increasing popularity of the casual fashion look among Japanese youth. This fashion trend, along with more leisure time, has greatly increased the market for jeans, resulting in a doubling of output from 26 million pairs in 1985 to more than 50 million pairs in 1990[1] (compound annual growth rate of 14 percent). However, the trend is towards slower growth, and the market actually shrunk in 1991. The growth in total production of jeans from 1987 to 1991 is given in Exhibit 2.

The financial results of major jeans manufacturers in 1992 indicates that the market continued to shrink following 1991. Yet, towards the end of 1992, some companies started to see the market revive. After the last couple years of market contraction, the jeans industry seems to be revitalized due to the development of new dyeing techniques (such as antique-look jeans), as well as the development of jeans made of new fabrics such as light-ounce denim and rayon. In addition, some of the smaller jeans manufacturers which have concentrated on the women's market are experiencing double-digit growth in sales.

Competitive Environment

During this period of rapid expansion, LSJ grew 35 percent annually, more than twice as fast as the market.[2] As a result, LSJ currently enjoys the highest share of any single brand, at 16 percent of total market sales. Still, there is fierce competition for market share with the five other large brands in the jeans market: Lee, Wrangler, Edwin, Big John, and Bobson, due to the fact that all of the brands market similar product lines (emphasizing basic blue denim jeans, followed by other basic jeans, fashion jeans, and chino pants) targeted at essentially the same customer segment. Also, all the American brands market their products by emphasizing the image of Americana.

Sales figures for the six largest jeans manufacturers are given in Exhibit 3. These figures show that the market share of the three large domestic Japanese brands, Edwin, Big John, and Bobson, is currently declining. LSJ, however, moved up from fifth position in 1986 to second position following Edwin in 1990 with a market share of almost 13 percent, and in 1991 LSJ became the top-selling brand with approximately 15 percent of total jeans sales.

Following is a brief description of each of LSJ's major competitors.

> **Edwin**—In addition to marketing its own brand of jeans, Edwin, the largest domestic manufacturer, also markets Lee jeans under a license agreement with VF Corporation, the U.S. company which owns the Lee brand. Edwin wants to increase market share of its original brand; however, Lee is important for them to compete with Levi's. This is a dilemma for Edwin, since the Lee brand seems to be cannibalizing the Edwin brand. In 1992, for the first time, LSJ exceeded Edwin in the total sales amount, as shown in Exhibit 3. The figures for Edwin include revenues from Lee and Liberto brands. Edwin is also planning to sell a new Italian brand called Fiorucci beginning in the autumn of 1992.
>
> **Big John**—Sales and net income are expected to increase after two consecutive years of decrease. This is due to the success of their new product

---

[1]"Fashions Come and Go, but Blue Jeans Never Fade," *The Nikkei Weekly*, August 17, 1991.
[2]"Fundamentals Lend More-than-Casual Look," *The Nikkei Weekly*, September 14, 1991.

EXHIBIT 2   Size of the Japanese jeans market

Units of total jeans production

	Blue jeans		Color jeans		Total jeans	
	Units	*Growth*	*Units*	*Growth*	*Units*	*Growth*
1987	36,924		15,186		52,110	
1988	43,274	17.2%	12,904	(15.0)%	56,178	7.8%
1989	45,614	5.4	13,310	3.2	58,924	4.9
1990	45,401	(0.4)	13,238	(0.5)	58,639	(0.5)
1991	43,864	(3.4)	12,946	(2.2)	56,810	(3.1)

Source: Japanese Jeans Manufacturing Association (JJMA).

Notes: These numbers include imports; but not exports, thus are an appropriate proxy for market size. Also, these production quantities are more than LSJ estimates based on annual consumer surveys. For example, in 1991, LSJ estimates the total market size to be 45 million pairs, while the JJMA indicates 25 percent more. As JJMA's figure is based on self-reporting by each of the jeans manufacturers, it is likely to be inflated over the actual sales quantity.

Total jeans production in yen

(¥ millions)

	Blue jeans	Color jeans	Total
1988	90,660	27,273	117,933
1989	95,562	28,124	123,686
1990	95,115	27,972	123,087
1991	86,992	24,774	111,766

Source: Yano Institute.

Jeans production by type

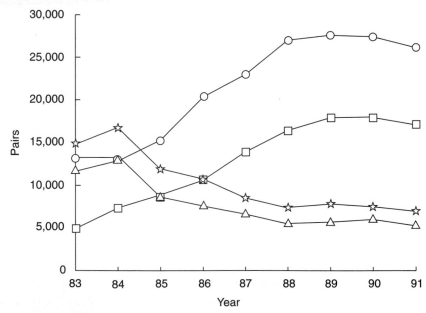

○ Male Blue Jeans   □ Female Blue Jeans   ☆ Male Color Jeans
△ Female Color Jeans

Source: Yano Institute.

EXHIBIT 3   Sales and income data for jeans manufacturers

Sales of top six jeans brands* (¥ million)

	1988	1989	1990	1991	1992	1993[§]
LEVI'S	¥15,425	¥21,508	¥28,855	¥35,056	¥37,626	¥38,600
Edwin (incl. Lee)	30,342	33,579	38,250	38,534	37,099	
Lee			5,000‡	6,300‡	6,500‡	10,000
Wrangler	11,715	13,550	15,367	16,972	17,847	
Big John	13,939	16,472	18,163	17,684	17,421	18,400
Bobson[†]	13,190	15,578	18,187	18,277	16,403	
Other	90,439	98,674	103,689	108,363	111,327	
Total	¥175,050	¥199,361	¥222,511	¥234,886	¥237,723	

Net income of top five jeans manufacturers (¥ million)

	1988	1989	1990	1991	1992	1993[§]
LEVI'S	¥3,585	¥4,421	¥6,124	¥7,058	¥6,532	¥6,280
Edwin (incl. Lee)	2,592	3,445	3,365	3,045	3,039	
Wrangler	596	631	1,118	1,127	802	
Big John	881	1,358	827	781	346	1,250
Bobson	531	812	1,413	883	925	
Other	1,814	3,023	2,380	2,416	3,141	
Total	¥9,999	¥13,690	¥15,227	¥15,310	¥14,785	

Return on sales of top five jeans manufacturers (percent)

	1988	1989	1990	1991	1992	1993[§]
LEVI'S	23.2%	20.6%	21.2%	20.1%	17.4%	16.3%
Edwin (incl. Lee)	8.5	10.3	8.8	7.9	8.2	
Wrangler	5.1	4.7	7.3	6.6	4.5	
Big John	6.3	8.2	4.6	4.4	2.0	6.8
Bobson	4.0	5.2	7.8	4.8	5.6	
Other	2.0	3.1	2.3	2.2	2.8	
Total	5.7%	6.9%	6.8%	6.5%	6.2%	

* Includes sales of jeans and tops.

[†] Bobson merged its sales affiliate in 1990, therefore, the financial statement has not been publicized since then. The figures since 1990 are taken from a report by the Yano Institute.

‡ Since Edwin does not break out sales of Lee brand. Lee sales numbers are estimates provided by LSJ.
§ 1993 estimates for LEVI'S and Lee provided by LSJ. 1993 Big John figures estimated by Big John.

Source: Company financial statements. Yano Institute.

line, the "antique collection." The company expects the blue jeans market will grow again in 1993. Since blue jeans is Big John's major product line, the company believes it is well positioned for growth in 1993. In May 1993, the company will begin construction of a new headquarters which will enable it to effectively concentrate the cutting, distribution, trading, and kids clothes sections into one location.

Wrangler Japan—Wrangler, also a jeans brand of VF Corporation, is produced and sold through a license agreement with Wrangler Japan, a joint venture between Mitsubishi and Toyo Boseki. Sales have begun to pick up in September 1992, especially in the women's jeans market which is growing at double-digit rates.

Bobson—Bobson's sales target for 1993 is ¥20,000 million. The company has been incredibly successful in the women's jeans market. As a result, from October 1992 to January 1993, sales in that segment have increased 40 percent over the same period of the previous year. The company expects 1993 to be a growth year.

It is interesting to note that, up to this point, Levi Strauss' U.S. competitor, VF Corporation, has chosen to operate in Japan solely under licensing arrangements. However, there is speculation that VF Corporation is planning to shift its marketing strategy from licensing to direct sales. This could drastically change the competitive market in the near future. Market experts predict that the Japanese jeans market will eventually be dominated by the three major American brands: Levi's, Lee, and Wrangler.

New Emerging Markets

In 1990, Wrangler Japan Inc. tried to reinforce their traditional image by marketing "revival jeans," which feature natural dye extracted from the indigo plant. These indigo blue jeans, named Vintage Wrangler, are made of 100 percent denim and are hand dyed. They are priced at ¥30,000 (approximately $240.00), but are selling well.[3] LSJ also introduced reproductions of its 5033BSXX and 701SXX styles, popular in the 1950s and 1960s, which are priced at ¥48,000 ($384.00) in September 1991. Yet, it is reported that LSJ cannot make these jeans fast enough to satisfy the demand.[4]

On the other hand, well-preserved second-hand jeans are in high demand, some of which are being sold for more than ¥500,000 ($4,000.00). About 30 to 40 stores have opened which specialize in selling used jeans from the United States made in the 1940s, 1950s, and 1960s. One store says that the most popular items are priced slightly below ¥100,000 ($800.00).[5] However, the slowing growth in demand seems to indicate that oversupply is becoming a problem and that the market is close to saturation. According to the national sales manager of LSJ, this trend is supported primarily by jeans enthusiasts and may not last long.

Sales of women's blue jeans registered a phenomenal 109 percent growth between 1985 and 1989, increasing from 8.5 million to 17.8 million pairs a year. With the forecast that the young men's market is stabilizing, all the companies are looking at the potential in the market for women's jeans, creating fierce competition in that category.[6]

---

[3]"Fashions Come and Go, but Blue Jeans Never Fade," *The Nikkei Weekly,* August 17, 1991.
[4]"Vintage American Products Attract Japanese Rebels," *The Nikkei Weekly,* December 7, 1991.
[5]Ibid.
[6]"Fashions Come and Go, but Blue Jeans Never Fade," *The Nikkei Weekly,* August 17, 1991.

Changing Distribution Channel

Unlike the United States, Europe, and other countries in Southeast Asia, jeans sales in Japan are still predominately through jeans specialty stores. In other countries, jeans specialty stores have already lost market share to large national chains (such as Sears and JCPenney's) and to discounters (such as Walmart and Kmart). The successful specialty stores in the U.S. are those which have been able to develop their own brands, such as The Gap and The Limited.

Although there has not been a similar shift in the Japanese market (from specialty stores to national chains), the shift is occurring within the jeans specialty shop channel. The structure of this channel seems to be changing with the emergence of a new type of jeans shop. Traditionally, jeans shops were located in urban areas and sold only jeans (both factors placing a constraint on store size). Recently, new chain stores have been built in the suburbs which are usually five to seven times larger and may carry other products besides jeans. These jeans stores have proliferated, increasing their revenue at the expense of the smaller jeans stores. Their success is partly a result of their emphasis on sales promotions, ability to stock a full line of products, and the unique store designs. Two such chains, Marutomi and Chiyoda (the two largest shoe store chains), entered the jeans retail market four to five years ago and now boast retail stores in excess of 200 each. This emergence of jeans specialty store chains has saved this category from losing market share following those in other countries.

In 1992, approximately 250 new stores were opened, most of which are large-scale suburban stores of the type described above. Even though the peak is over, an additional 230 stores are likely to open in 1993. This consists mainly of Chiyoda's 75 to 85 "Mac House" stores and Marutomi's 100 "From USA" stores. In some suburban areas, the increasing number of stores has started to stimulate competition for local market share. For example, at the city of Tsukuba, a growing suburban area outside of Tokyo, 10 jeans stores (including those under construction) ranging in size up to 4,500 square feet are clustered in 3.1 square miles. Many retailers, therefore, are attempting to differentiate themselves by increasing customer service and being more selective in what product lines they will carry. Yet, with the slowing down in the jeans market, compounded by the recession, the excessive increase in jeans retail space is worsening the inventory turnover, leading to inventory surpluses.

Given this new retail situation, the ability to develop an effective inventory control system and low-cost operations is an important competitive advantage. Jeans manufacturers and retailers are entering a new era of competition where capital strength and efficient inventory management and distribution systems will have a significant impact on the success of the company. Moreover, in order to provide extensive customer service, the recruiting and training of employees are becoming increasingly important points of differentiation. In the U.S., Canada, and Europe, the shift in jeans distribution towards the discount stores negatively affected the overall image of jeans. Thus, jeans manufacturers have had to invest heavily in order to revive the former image. The destiny of the

Japanese jeans industry will depend on how manufacturers, retailers, and customers react to the changes that are occurring in the retail environment.

Potential impact on pricing. Thus far, most of the distribution channels, including jeans specialty stores, department stores, and even national chain stores, have maintained the suggested retail price. National chain stores such as Daiei and Ito-Yokado have discount stores as their affiliates, yet these discount stores have different supply routes and sell different products. This enables Daiei and Ito-Yokado to maintain the retail price suggested by jeans manufacturers.

A similar change in channel structure has occurred in the distribution of business suits, where sales of department stores and specialty stores in the cities have suffered due to the emergence of larger men's shops in the suburbs. In this case, price competition is increasing between the discount stores (the "category killer"), but not between the national chain stores as has occurred in the past. National chain stores have not entered the price war but are stuck in the middle between the discount stores (at the low end) and the specialty and department stores (at the high end).

If this holds true in the jeans industry, national chain stores are not likely to begin competing on price. Also, department stores and traditional jeans specialty stores (with few stores) are unlikely to discount. However, the new jeans specialty stores with many outlets, giving them strong purchasing power against manufacturers, may begin competing on price. These stores, which have expanded rapidly, are experiencing increasing competition and inventory surpluses, creating a ripe environment for price competition. The eventual outcome depends somewhat on how jeans manufacturers will react to discounting, should it occur, and on the sales policies of traditional jeans specialty stores.

Levi Strauss Japan K.K

Overview[7]

Levi Strauss entered Japan with the opening of a branch office of Levi Strauss (Far East) Limited (Hong Kong) in April of 1971. Prior to this, its presence was limited to a minimal level of sales generated by importers. The Hiratsuka Distribution Center was opened in November of 1973, and in June 1974, Levi Strauss began domestic production of jeans products.

In December of 1975, Levi Strauss began selling through wholesale agencies, in addition to its direct sales to retailers. Levi Strauss also began importing products from the U.S. in 1978. In the same year, the reporting line of the Japanese office was changed from Hong Kong to LSI headquarters in San Francisco.

---

[7]For more extensive background, see the Appendix, "Levi Strauss Japan K.K. Company Brochure."

In 1982, Levi Strauss Japan K.K. (LSJ) was established as an independent operating company. Another important milestone occurred in June of 1989, when 4.1 million shares of LSJ were listed on the Tokyo OTC market in an initial public offering. This sale brought in $80 million, while still leaving Levi Strauss with an 85 percent share of the Japanese company's equity.

LSJ's strategy has been to maintain consistency and a long-term view. With a heavy emphasis on advertising, constant new product introduction in addition to traditional styles, systems development, good relationships with suppliers, contractors, wholesalers, and retailers, and personnel training, LSJ has successfully built its position in Japan. (See the following sections for elaboration on LSJ operations.)

This position is largely due to LSJ's marketing strategy described below.

1. Target young male customers and advertise extensively through TV commercials and men's magazines, creating the image that LEVI'S jeans is cool American casual wear.
2. In order to have extensive accessibility, contract with various kinds of sales outlets, from small specialty jeans shops, mainly located in urban areas, to national chain stores which have larger sales space, mainly located in suburbs.
3. Provide not only the traditional jeans imported from the United States, but also new jeans which are in line with current fashion and sewn to fit Japanese physical features.

Performance

LSJ experienced sluggish sales until around 1984. Since then, year-on-year sales have been increasing by approximately 35 percent every year until they slowed down to 20 percent in 1991. The company expects this slower level of growth to continue in the short term. In 1991, LSJ sales were ¥35.056 billion, with profits of ¥7.058 billion. LSJ is planning to raise its market share to over 20 percent by fiscal 1995.

LSJ experienced a decrease in profit in 1992 due to an increase in indirect marketing costs, including depreciation from investment on the distribution center and system development. Yet, LSJ still posted an impressive 17.4 percent return on sales, far higher than its competitors, and nearly three times the industry average. In 1993, the company expects sales growth to be moderate. Therefore it expects a further decrease in net income.

Employing the strategy described above, LSJ has successfully increased sales volume through stimulating the jeans market. It enjoys constant demand not subject to the whims of fashion or the changing season. LSJ has been successful in establishing the reputation of high-quality products and brand image, allowing them to sell higher-end products than their competitors. This high-quality, premium product strategy was successful since it capitalizes on the Japanese economy (with one of the highest GNP per capita and significant growth).

On the cost side, LSJ is very efficient in the sense that it does not have ꞁ tory requiring huge capital expenditure, but instead, contracts out all its pr in Japan. As a result, it does not have to worry about potential costs associated with downtime, equipment improvement, and workers compensation both in monetary and nonmonetary terms. Moreover, LSJ has a very small sales force to cover all of Japan. As a result, LSJ's sales-to-employee ratio is ¥180 million ($1.4 million), which is roughly three times the average of its rivals.[8] Another strength of LSJ is its no-debt strategy to alleviate risk due to interest rate fluctuations. Since its IPO on the Tokyo Stock Exchange, the stock price has been constantly increasing to the current P/E ratio of 50.[9]

Products

Product lines sold by LSJ consist of tops (shirts, jackets, and sweatshirts), men's and women's basic jeans, other basic jeans, and fashion jeans. There are approximately 18 kinds of men's basic jeans (excluding multiple colors), 10 kinds of women's basic jeans, 20 kinds of other basic jeans (including 5 for women), and several fashion jeans. Other basic jeans consist of trendy jeans products, and fashion jeans consist of cotton (nondenim) pants. The sales breakdown is as follows: 20 percent from tops, 20 percent from women's jeans, 40 percent from basic men's jeans, and 20 percent from the remainder.

Belts, accessories, shoes, socks, bags, and kid's jeans are sold by another company under a license agreement. In addition, apart from traditional styles, product managers in LSJ design new styles which are in line with the fashion at the time. New products are introduced twice a year, in spring and in autumn. Occasionally, product innovations developed for the Japanese market are later introduced into other markets. This was the case for "stone-washed" denim jeans and the DOCKERS line, which were successfully introduced in the U.S. after being developed and introduced in Japan.[10]

Organization

LSJ currently employs approximately 500 people spread throughout its headquarters, sales offices, and distribution center. The company's headquarters is in Tokyo, while additional sales offices are located in big cities such as Osaka, Nagoya, and Fukuoka. The company operates a large distribution center in Hiratsuka, outside Tokyo, in order to store the finished products and to distribute based on orders. Among the 500 employees, 160 people work at the department stores as sales personnel, 150 people work at the distribution center, and the remainder are employed at the headquarters. An organization chart for LSJ is shown in Exhibit 4.

---

[8]"Fundamentals Lend More-than-Casual Look," *The Nikkei Weekly,* September 14, 1991.
[9]Ibid.
[10]Geoffrey Duin, "Levi's Won't Fade in the Japanese Market," *Tokyo Business Today,* April 1990, p. 46.

EXHIBIT 4   LSJ organizational structure

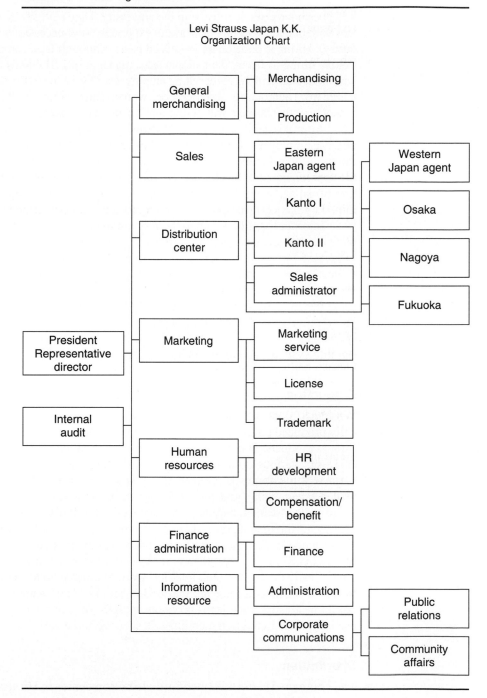

Levi Strauss Japan K.K.
Organization Chart

Human Resources

LSJ does not recruit directly from the university. They tend to hire university graduates with one to two years of working experience (not necessarily in the apparel industry). Hiring is done on an as-needed basis. Although U.S. companies often have trouble hiring in Japan, the national sales manager of LSJ claims that the company has not had difficulties in recruiting employees. This is due to the fact that LSJ tends to hire from nontraditional sources, i.e., women and experienced hires, therefore they do not directly compete with traditional Japanese companies for labor resources.

Approximately 300 of the 500 employees work under contract to LSJ. Most of these employees work in the distribution center. Although this is not typical of the traditional Japanese system of lifetime employment, it is not uncommon in the apparel industry. In addition, compensation is not determined according to the traditional Japanese system based on seniority. Rather, compensation is determined by the job description covering the activities performed by the employee.

In order to build company loyalty among employees, LSJ provides a complete educational system. The company recognizes training to be one of the most important factors contributing to the overall success of the company in Japan. Education provided by the company ranges from educating new employees on the importance of the customer to developing management skills. Many of the programs are designed to upgrade the skills of each employee. There are five major training systems: a training system for newly entered employees, a correspondence education system, an English education system, various objective training systems, and an overseas training system.

Production

While LSJ does not own its own production facilities in Japan, all its domestically produced clothing is made by contracted factories which produce only Levi Strauss products. These contractors sew jeans products from denim purchased by LSJ from various domestic textile manufacturers and from trading companies. Currently, the domestic production accounts for 50 percent of the total products sold in Japan, while 30 percent is imported from the United States and 20 percent from Southeast Asia, mainly from factories in the Philippines.

It is interesting that, until 1978, the company sold only domestic- and Asian-made jeans products in Japan. Then, realizing the importance of having the original U.S.-made jeans, the company started to sell some U.S.-made products (specifically the 501 product line) in Japan. According to Mr. Ohki, it was crucial to send customers a message that LSJ is selling "real" American products. Yet, the domestically made jeans products actually fit Japanese bodies better, which partially contributed to the company's success in the early years.

Distribution

The company first established its distribution center in Hiratsuka, Kanagawa, in November 1973, two years after establishing operations in Japan.

However, LSJ recently reconstructed its distribution center in order to enhance customer service by improving the quality and quantity of warehouse and shipping facilities. In October 1990, it completed the first stage of reconstruction, including installation of the computer-controlled warehouse system named AS/RS (automated storage and retrieval system). Automation of picking and shipping areas, which are controlled along with the automated warehouse, was completed in May 1991. These renovations greatly improved the storage capacity and more than doubled the daily shipping capability. They also enabled the company to handle small-quantity, frequent, short-term-delivery orders. In addition, LSJ has installed automated ordering systems at some of the national chain stores, allowing for better inventory control and quicker response.

The company has two distribution channels. One is direct sales by sales personnel, and the other is wholesale by sales agencies. Currently, 53 percent of total sales comes from direct sales made by 40 LSJ sales personnel located in the four sales offices. Using 1991 sales data to calculate the revenue generated by the direct sales force, the average salesperson generated ¥464.5 million (approximately $3.7 million) of revenue in that year. This demonstrates the extraordinary productivity of LSJ's sales force. The remaining 43 percent comes from 13 domestic sales agencies.

Sales of LSJ products occur through four kinds of sales outlets. LSJ's sales personnel and sales agencies both have contact with these key sales outlets consisting of: (1) major nationwide jeans shops such as Big American and Eiko; (2) major nationwide department stores, from the prestigious Mitsukoshi Department Store to Marui, a department store specifically targeted to the younger generation; (3) national chain stores such as Daiei, Ito-Yokado, and Seiyu; and (4) nationwide men's shops such as Iseya. Most of LSJ's sales occur in jeans shops (70 percent), with the remaining sales fairly evenly split among department stores (12 percent), national chain stores (10 percent), and other stores (8 percent). A listing of LSJ's major sales outlets, as well as suppliers and sales agencies, is given in Exhibit 5.

Currently, LEVI'S are sold at fewer sales outlets than some of their domestic competitors. For example, 5,000 stores carry the LEVI'S brand, while more than 10,000 stores sell the Edwin brand. Although LSJ receives a higher percentage of its sales through traditional jeans shops (70 percent) than the market overall (60 percent), there is very little difference between LSJ distribution patterns and that of the other top brands.

LSJ's effort to be a Japanese company can be observed from its strategy of building good relationships with its sales outlets. LSJ provides various services to each outlet store, from giving advice on product displays and in-store arrangements to organizing seminars and handing out sales manuals. Japanese department stores rely heavily on the manufacturers to provide sales staff, forcing LSJ to place 160 employees in department stores as sales clerks. However, this necessity allows LSJ, and other Japanese manufacturing companies, to gather information regarding customer preferences.

EXHIBIT 5   Key sales agencies, suppliers, and sales outlets

Sales agencies	Key sales outlets
K.K. Daiman Shoten	*Jeans shops:*
Daimaru K.K.	Big American
Daiwa K.K.	Blue mate
Eiko Shoji K.K.	Eiko
Igarashi K.K.	Goshibo
Ishida Sangyo K.K.	IB Shoji
Maruhon K.K.	Joint
Mori Iroy K.K.	Kyushu Sanshin Group
Morimen K.K.	Marukawa Hachioji
K.K. Ohno Iryo	Marukawa Ogawa
Sanwa Iryo K.K.	Sun Village
Takaya Shoji K.K.	Taro's House
K.K. Yamakatsu	US Sanshin

Key suppliers	National chain stores:
	Daiei
C. Itoh & Co., Ltd.	Ito-Yokado
Ihara Kogyo K.K.	Jusco
K.K. Kasuya Shokai	Nichii
K.K. Kisugi Sewing Center	Seiyu
K.K. Kurabo Apparel	Uni
Kurashiki Boseki K.K.	
Levi Strauss & Co. (USA)	*Department stores:*
Levi Strauss (Far East) Ltd.	Daimaru
Nagao Shoji K.K.	Hankyu
Nishie Denim Co., Ltd.	Hanshin
Nisshin Bouseki K.K.	Isetan
Scovill Japan Co., Ltd.	Kintestu
Sundia K.K.	Matsuya
Takahata Co., Ltd.	Matsuzakaya
Tentak K.K.	Maruei
	Marui
	Mitsukoshi
	Odsakyu
	Seibu
	Sogo
	Takashimaya
	Tokyu
	Men's shops:
	Iseya
	Roughox

Pricing

Historically, LSJ was positioned as a price leader, charging 15 to 20 percent higher than competitors for similar jeans products. However, about 10 years ago, competitors raised their prices to match LEVI'S (pricing of LEVI'S remained flat), allowing LSJ to greatly increase their market share. Today, compared to competitive brands such as Edwin, Lee, and Wrangler, LSJ has a similar price range for its jeans products. Even so, the average product price which LSJ's customers pay (¥7,900 = approximately $63.20) is about 5 to 10 percent higher than the average price received by competitors. This is due to the fact that LSJ customers are willing to buy more expensive types of jeans.

Wholesale price varies by distributor due to the rebate scheme. However, the average price charged to sales outlets is 55 percent of retail, while sales agents pay about 50 percent of retail on average. LSJ charges a higher wholesale price to the department stores in order to offset the cost of LSJ employees who work as sales personnel in those stores. However, there is no significant difference in retail price across the various distribution channels, since retail outlets so far have maintained the suggested retail price.

Advertising and Promotion

Similar to the strategy employed by Levi Strauss in the U.S., LSJ emphasizes a pull strategy, spending heavily on advertising to increase demand. Since 1976, LSJ has been spending approximately 6 percent of total sales on advertising (TV and print) compared to an industry average of 4 percent.[11] It uses James Dean as an advertising character in order to establish the image of the young, active American. Its target customer has traditionally been young men, aged 16 to 29, who have grown up with, and maintain a good image towards, American products.

When LSJ first launched its campaign in 1984 with the slogan "Heroes Wear LEVI'S," its main purpose was to increase the awareness of the LEVI'S brand. The ads showed movie scenes in which James Dean, John Wayne, Steve McQueen, and Marilyn Monroe wore jeans, while a famous movie announcer, Haruo Mizuno, read the slogan. In 1985, the slogan was changed to "*My Mind, LEVI'S,*" and, in 1987, to "*The Original LEVI'S,*" both of which were intended to project traditional American values and a pioneering spirit with a more familiar nuance. The current slogan, "*Re-Origin,*" was launched in 1989 to emphasize the revival of traditional jeans. Since the very beginning, the company has recognized the Japanese purchase mentality towards imported goods—Japanese are willing to choose imports and even pay more for these goods—and has been maximizing its marketing by appealing to this psychology.

LSJ focuses on TV commercials and magazine advertisements, which account for 65 percent of the total promotional budget (see Exhibit 6). Of this advertising expense, approximately 70 percent is used for TV commercials and 30 percent for magazine advertisements. The company uses mass media effectively based on differences in features. For TV commercials, LSJ uses an advertising agency in order to maximize reach and communicate the company's image to a larger audience. In contrast, the company creates its magazine advertisements mostly in house, since the goal of the magazine ads is to increase consumers' understanding of its products and to appeal strongly to certain target customer segments (see Exhibit 7). In terms of cooperative advertising with sales outlets, LSJ is consistent with other Japanese manufacturing companies, which tend not to use this method as much as U.S. companies.

---

[11]"Fundamentals Lend More-than-Casual Look," *The Nikkei Weekly,* September 14, 1991.

EXHIBIT 6 LSJ promotional expenditures

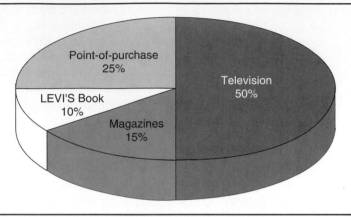

EXHIBIT 7 LSJ magazine advertising 1991 and 1992

1991 LSJ magazine advertisements			
Magazine	*Type*	*Readership profile*	*Number of LSJ ads, 1/91–12/91*
Popeye	Fashion	Young males, 18–23	22
H D Press	Fashion	Young males, 18–23	24
Men's Non No	Fashion	Young males, 18–23	20
Fineboys	Fashion	Young males, 18–23	15

1992 LSJ magazine advertisements			
Magazine	*Type*	*Readership profile*	*Number of LSJ Ads, 1/92–10/92*
Popeye	Fashion	Young males, 18–23	18
H D Press	Fashion	Young males, 18–23	17
Men's Non No	Fashion	Young males, 18–23	17
Fineboys	Fashion	Young males, 18–23	11
Asahi Weekly	News	White collar males, all ages	1
Shincho Weekly	News	White collar males, all ages	1
Bunshun Weekly	News	White collar males, all ages	1
Bart	News	Young, white collar males	1
Non No	Fashion	Young single females	1
Pia	Entertainment	Young males/females, <35	1
Dime	New product intro	Affluent males, 30–40	1
Sarai	Housekeeping	Married females, 25–35	1
Number	Sports	Males, all ages	1

LSJ also publishes seasonal product catalogs named "LEVI'S Book," and places them in outlet stores in order to introduce new products. Two million copies of this catalog are produced twice a year, accounting for 10 percent of LSJ's promotional expenditures. The remaining 25 percent of promotional expense is used for direct communication with customers at the point of purchase. By these consistent advertising and promotional activities, the company is trying to increase (1) awareness of the LEVI'S brand, (2) understanding of its products, and (3) the willingness to buy.

Future Challenges

LSJ's major challenges, resulting from the changing market and retail environment, are:

- How to continue to grow faced with a contracting market;
- How to respond to the changing structure of the distribution channel; and
- How to develop and implement a pricing strategy given the current retail environment.

First, the traditional market for jeans in Japan has peaked and will likely continue to shrink or remain flat. The number of young people is decreasing due to the lower birth rate, shifting the demographics to an older population. For the last 12 years, the birth rate each year has been the lowest ever recorded, a trend which is expected to continue.[12] Also, the average frequency of jeans purchase per person per year in Japan is a meager 0.5, compared to the 1.5 in the U.S.[13] This is due to the fact that high schools in Japan require students to wear uniforms, so there is significantly less time and chance to wear jeans. These trends will further impact the market size of the young male segment, the traditional market which jeans manufacturers (including LSJ) have targeted.

Second, the development of a new type of jeans specialty store has presented some interesting issues for LSJ. The rapid expansion requires LSJ to develop a strategy for how many and what types of stores (i.e., jeans specialty, department, national chain, etc.) should distribute the LEVI'S brand. Once a strategy is decided on, selection criteria for retailers and sales agents need to be determined. In addition, servicing a growing number of retailers creates challenges in delivery and inventory systems (described in the distribution section), production capacity, and sales force expansion.

Finally, with increased competition between both the manufacturers and the retailers, the possibility of discounting cannot be ignored. Price competition may be initiated by manufacturers, or certain retail channels may elect not to maintain the suggested retail price. A feasible strategy must address the fact that LSJ has little direct control over retail pricing due to antitrust laws. Government intervention is also a concern in that, as part of an international company, LSJ must be sensitive to trade policies regarding pricing. In addition, operating in various countries requires a pricing policy which limits the potential for a gray market. Thus, the pricing strategy will significantly impact LSJ's future, since price discounting could negatively affect the premium product image that LSJ has established.

Mr. Chappell wondered how he should deal with these important strategic and marketing issues to ensure LSJ's continued success.

---

[12]*1992 Statistics Handbook*. Statistics Bureau, Management and Coordination Agency; Ministry of Health and Welfare.

[13]"Fundamentals Lend More-than-Casual Look," *The Nikkei Weekly,* September 14, 1991.

Appendix   Levi Strauss Japan K.K. Company Brochure

Levi Strauss Japan K.K. continues its business by maintaining consistency and a long-term view.

Greetings

Levi Strauss invented jeans in San Francisco in the middle of the 19th century. At that time he was asked by the gold miners to make some pants that would not rip apart when they filled their pockets with gold. Since then, LEVI'S® brand has been faithful to our simple guiding principle: "Quality Never Goes Out of Style," and as such has built a strong reputation among our consumers for more than 140 years.

Levi Strauss Japan K.K. was established in 1971 as a branch of Levi Strauss (Far East) Ltd., and later was incorporated as Kabushiki Kaisha in 1982. Having just marked the 21st anniversary, we see a number of new challenges facing Levi Strauss Japan K.K.

One of those challenges is the current environment of a slowdown in the nation's entire economy. This, however, represents an opportunity for Levi Strauss Japan K.K. We will use this breathing space, after years of rapid growth, to strengthen our business foundations and prepare for future growth. We will do this by continuing to develop new programs, particularly those addressing customer services, and by consolidating recent investments and new development such as our new automated distribution center in Hiratsuka.

The future outlook is one of opportunity. The market will continue to grow as more leisure time and a more casually dressed outlook become widespread. Continuing expansion of retail outlets will make our products available to an increased number of consumers, and will maintain consumers' interest in the jeans category at a high level. As the Japanese jeans market grows—not as dramatically as in the past few years but now more steadily over an extended period of time—Levi Strauss Japan K.K. will continue to grow on the traditions we have inherited and on the foundations we have built.

Our strategy will be to maintain consistency and a long-term view. In other words, we will continue to carry out our existing strategies, with a heavy emphasis on consumer advertising, constant product improvement, systems development, constant customer service improvement, and personnel training.

These strategies should enable us to increase our share of the growing jeans market while maintaining a healthy and profitable business.

We appreciate the strong partnership which we have with our suppliers and our customers, and look forward to continuing to work with them for the future to meet the needs of the Japanese jeans consumers.

Sincerely yours,
May, 1992
A. John Chappell
President
Levi Strauss Japan K.K.

Company Profile

Company Name:
Levi Strauss Japan K.K.
Head Office:
Sumitomoseimei Aoyama Building
1–30, Minamiaoyama 3-chome, Minato-ku, Tokyo 107
Tel. 03-5410-8700
Head Office Annex:
Minamiaoyama City Building
2–5, Minamiaoyama 3-chome, Minato-ku, Tokyo 107
Tel. 03-5411-6300
President and Representative Director:
A. John Chappell
Capital:
¥5,213,600,000
Establishment:
November, 1982
Levi Strauss Japan K.K. established
[April, 1971, Levi Strauss (Far East) Limited Japan
Branch Office established]
Line of Business:
Import, manufacture, and sales of jeans, jackets, and
shirts
Employees:
Approximately 500
Work Hours:
9:30–18:00
Workdays:
Mon.–Fri., 5 days a week

Holidays:
Paid holidays, congratulation and condolence, year
end/new year, and other special holidays
Sales Offices:
• Osaka Sales Office
Kurabo Annex Building
4–11, Kyutaro-cho 2-chome, Chuo-ku, Osaka-shi,
Osaka 541
Tel. 06-261-9500
• Nagoya Sales Office
Nakakuyakusho Asahiseimei Building
1–8, Sakae 4-chome, Naka-ku, Nagoya-shi, Aichi 460
Tel. 052-243-1341
• Fukuoka Sales Office
Sumitomoseimei Hakata Building
2–8, Hakataekimae 3-chome, Hakata-ku, Fukuoka-
shi, Fukuoka 810
Tel. 092-441-5688
Distribution Center:
Hiratsuka Distribution Center
2576 Ohkami, Hiratsuka-shi, Kanagawa 254
Tel. 0463-53-0711
Main Banks:
Mitsubishi bank, Aoyama branch
Sakura Bank, Akasaka branch
Sumitomo Bank, Aoyama branch

Directors and Auditors

A. John Chappell	President, Representative Director
Masafumi Ohki	Managing Director, National Sales Manager
Robert C. Hopkins	Director, Finance & Administration
Hajime Tanaka	Director, General Merchandising Manager
Shunsuke Fujiwara	Director, Human Resources Manager
Takayasu Funabiki	Director, Controller
S. Lindsay Webbe	Director
Toshio Tonomura	Statutory Auditor
Alan Gregson	Auditor

Sales & Recurring Profit

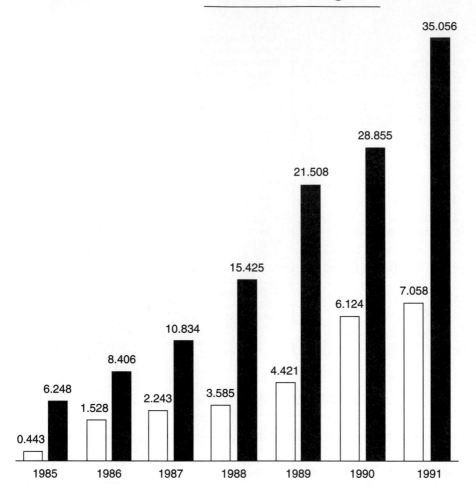

Levi Strauss Japan K.K. leading the Japanese jeans
market with "LEVI'S," the traditional brand.

History

1971 April 1971	Established Levi Strauss (Far East) Limited Japan Branch Office. Principal sum of ¥351M.	1988 Aug. 1988	Renovation of Hiratsuka Distribution Center.
1973 Nov. 1973	Established Hiratsuka Distribution Center.	1989 Jun. 1989	Listed on OTC, first public stock offering. Capital ¥5,213.6M.
1974 Jun. 1974	Began domestic production of jeans.	1990 Oct. 1990	Completed first stage of reconstruction of Hiratsuka Distribution Center.
1975 Dec. 1975	Commenced selling through wholesale agencies in addition to direct sales.	1991 May 1991	Completed second stage of reconstruction of Hiratsuka Distribution Center.
1978 May 1978	Began sales of U.S. imported products.	1991 Jul. 1991	Established Tokyo Head Office Annex Building. Moved Merchandising Dept., Production
1978 Dec. 1978	Began "Heroes Wear LEVI'S®" campaign.		Dept., East Japan Agency Dept., Kanto Sales Dept. Div. I, Kanto
1980 Aug. 1980	Moved Head Office to Sumitomo Seimei Aoyama Building, Minami Aoyama 3–1–30, Minato-ku, Tokyo.		Sales Dept. Div. II, Marketing Services Dept., and License Dept.
1982 Nov. 1982	Established Levi Strauss Japan K.K. Capital ¥3,780M.	1991 Sept. 1991	Moved Nagoya Sales Office to Sakae, Naka-ku, Nagoya.
1988 Mar. 1988	Moved Fukuoka Sales Office to Hakata Ekimae, Hakata-ku, Fukuoka.	1992 Apr. 1992	Moved Osaka Sales Office to Kyutaro-cho, Chuo-ku, Osaka.

Organization Structure Chart

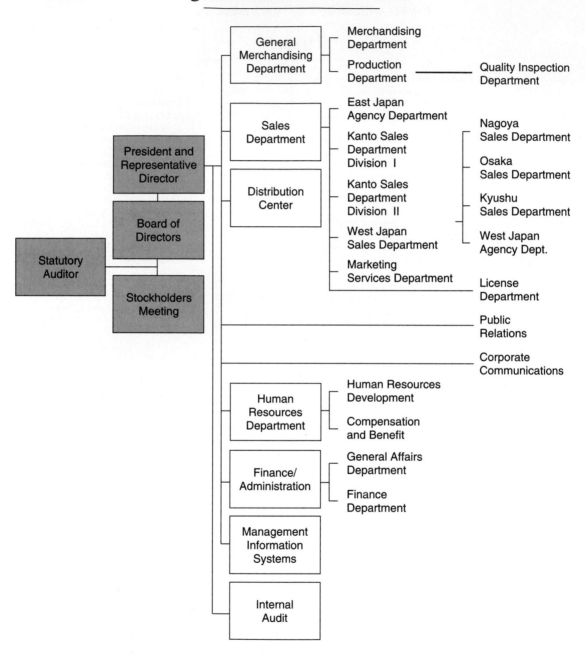

Employee Education System

In order to cope with a changing society and to do business appropriately, the company provides a complete and efficient educational system. Educating people is one of the most important tasks for the company. From training new employees to specialized training for acquiring various qualifications and licenses, many systems are facilitated for upgrading the skills of each employee. Every effort is put in from the education of developing skills of management to the education of the younger generation who will be taking on responsibilities in the future.

- Training system for newly entered employees.
- Correspondence education system.
- English education system.
- Various objective training systems.
- Overseas training system.

Welfare Facilities

For every employee to produce quality work everyday with a feeling of ease, the company also pays full attention to its facilities. Efforts are made to create the best working atmosphere, which ensures satisfaction and warm human contacts with our complete benefits.

- Group life insurance, accident insurance.
- Family travel support.
- Employee's childrens' scholarship system.
- Long-term employee commendation system.
- Company trips.
- Club activities.

CIT

CIT, "Community Involvement Team," signifies LEVI'S® corporate social responsibility which is our commitment to our employees and to our communities. This is the company's volunteer group in which the employees participate voluntarily and its aim is to contribute to the community.

- Volunteer activities.
- Donations funded by Levi Strauss Foundation to social welfare activities.
- Awareness activities for the employees.

LEVI'S® created the original product called "jeans." The history of jeans is therefore the history of LEVI'S.®

LEVI'S® Jeans

Styling and details of jeans were almost all created by LEVI'S®. LEVI'S® is today the origin of the clothing called "jeans" and is also the model for creating products. Since pants with rivets were developed for the first time in the world and for over a century, the product concept has been unchanged and has always been in the pursuit of high-quality merchandise of strength and comfort. The trend of the times has always been considered in the design, fit, material, and color, and LEVI'S® has constantly kept its tradition and yet a refreshing "American Face." The speciality of jeans is therefore the idea of LEVI'S®.

Special Features and Definition of Jeans

Jeans, which are a representative of casual clothing, can be worn by any age or sex all year round. To define jeans is to reflect on the specifications developed by LEVI'S®. In other words, it is the key features that consists of patch pockets, reinforcement using rivets, stitching by sewing machine, no lining, and various parts which have the brand name on. These specifications make mass production possible from the manufacturing process, and from the users point of view, it is durable and easy to care for.

The History of LEVI'S® Jeans

1850–70s

America, which was in the midst of the frontier era in the mid-1850s, was looking for strong work clothing. At that time, Levi Strauss made durable pants from canvas material used in tents and later from genova material that became the origin of the word "jeans." However, he was continuously trying to improve the durability and it was at that time that tailor Davis came up with using rivets to reinforce the pockets.

1873

Levi Strauss, along with tailor Jacob Davis, who brought in the idea of rivets for reinforcement, applied for the patents of the "Method of metal rivet usage in reinforcing outfit" and these were received on May 20, 1873. This is the reason for LEVI'S® jeans being called "Original riveted clothing." This historical day was designed onto the leather patch and is still used today. 17 years after the patent, LEVI'S® riveted outfit became LEVI'S® original merchandise.

1873–80s

In the year that the patents for the rivets were granted, the double arcuate pattern on the back pocket, "Arcuate stitch," began to be used. This was registered as one of the LEVI'S® trademarks which is used today and considered to be one of the oldest trademarks of clothing. The leather patch was created several years after 1873 and the basic details of jeans are reflected in today's 501 jean.

1906

A great earthquake hit San Francisco, the home of LEVI'S®. The damage was big, destroying the company's headquarters and its factory. But LEVI'S® had grown into a strong company and within several weeks it was able to begin production again. The Valencia factory with modern equipment was completed five months after the earthquake. The Valencia factory even now produces 501 jeans, the original model of LEVI'S®.

1915

LEVI'S® began production using the assembly line, the first such attempt in the apparel industry. The idea originated from the Ford Automobile Factory and attracted a lot of attention at that time in the United States.

1940s

Only soldiers or those that were directly related to the war effort could purchase LEVI'S®. One of the trademarks, the "arcuate stitch" thread, was considered a waste and paint was used to represent the arcuate pattern. This was the most difficult time for LEVI'S® which was always pursuing top quality products.

1945

Still considered the "clothing of the West," however, during and after the War, the LEVI'S® name and reputation for quality spread among the soldiers to the East and Europe.

1954

The two heroes that looked good in jeans, James Dean and Marlon Brando, appeared, which made LEVI'S® popularity grow rapidly.

1950–60s

In the late 1950s, there was a big boom in jeans. LEVI'S® grew rapidly and the number of factories increased to thirty. This is also the time that jeans became clothing not only for Americans but for the young worldwide. LEVI'S® not only produced blue but also produced products in white and corduroy, etc. All turned out to be best sellers and this was when the complete current line-up of basic jeans was established. In the 60s, LEVI'S® became a symbol of the counterculture.

First Half of 1970s

The Japan branch was inaugurated in 1971. LEVI'S® started its activities in the Japanese market in which it was a key factor of the jeans fashion. "The LEVI'S® Denim Art Contest" in which the world of arts was transformed onto jeans was held on a worldwide scale and attracted a lot of attention.

Latter Half of 70s–Present

Over 2.5 billion jeans have been produced since the birth of LEVI'S®. This astronomical number is still rapidly increasing. 501 jeans are included in the collection at the Smithsonian Institute in Washington, D.C. The history of LEVI'S® is a part of the history of United States.

The New Hiratsuka Distribution Center

Consistent efforts are being made to reinforce the foundation for a business system with enriched customer service and future prosperity.

The New Hiratsuka Distribution Center was established to respond to the rapidly growing demand for LEVI'S® products in the Japanese market and to enhance customer service by improving quality and quantity of warehouse and shipping capacities. The first stage of construction was completed in October, 1990 on the computer-controlled warehouse, AS/RS (automated storage and retrieval system). The second stage of construction was completed in May, 1991, that made the automation of picking and shipping areas controlled along with the automated warehouse. This greatly improved the storage capacity, and the daily shipping capability became more than double. This not only increased the storage capacity and distribution efficiency but made it possible to handle small-quantity, frequent, short-term-delivery orders. It also improved the working environment of the employees.

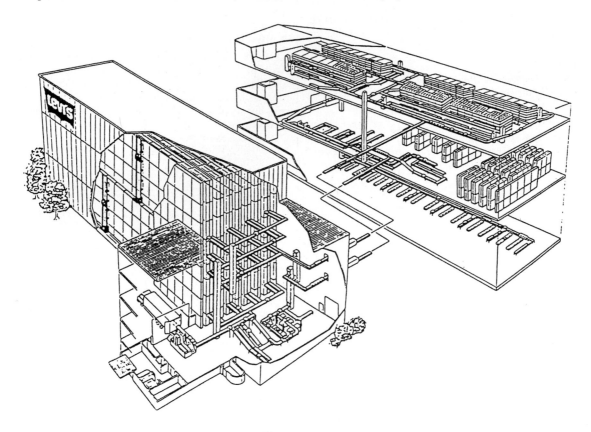

LEVI'S® and Its Outlets

The Japanese jeans market consists of various brands. Within this environment, LEVI'S® has been able to attain today's success because of the many sales outlets which appreciate the true value of LEVI'S® products. We believe that LEVI'S® are recommended to consumers because the sales people trust LEVI'S® brand and products. We also give advice on product displays and in-store arrangement. Levi Strauss Japan K.K.'s basic posture is that mutual development can only be achieved when a close bond exists between LEVI'S® and the sales outlets.

Advertising and Sales Promotional Activities

We have formed and executed efficient advertising and promotional activities over the past ten years towards the Japanese jeans market. James Dean has been used as an advertising character and the seasonal product catalog "LEVI'S® Book" has been published.

Consumers know all about such advertisements of important products seen on magazines. These consistent advertising and promotional activities increase the awareness and brand image of LEVI'S® in the Japanese market.

Sales Agencies

K.K. Daiman Shoten
Daimaru K.K.
Daiwa K.K.
Eiko Shoji K.K.
Igarashi K.K.
Ishida Sangyo K.K.
Maruhon K.K.
Mori Iryo K.K.
Morimen K.K.
K.K. Ohno Iryo
Sanwa Iryo K.K.
Takaya Shoji K.K.
K.K. Yamakatsu

Key Suppliers

C. Itoh & Co.,Ltd.
Ihara Kogyo K.K.
K.K. Kasuya Shokai
K.K. Kisugi Sewing Center
K.K. Kurabo Apparel
Kurashiki Boseki K.K.
Levi Strauss & Co. (U.S.A.)
Levi Strauss (Far East) Ltd.
Nagao Shoji K.K.
Nishie Denim Co.,Ltd.
Nisshin Bouseki K.K.
Scovill Japan Co.,Ltd.
Sundia K.K.
Takahata Co.,Ltd.
Tentak K.K.

Key Sales Outlets

Jeans shops
Big American
Blue Mate
Eiko
Goshibo
IB Shoji
Joint
Kyushu Sanshin Group
Marukawa Hachioji
Marukawa Ogawa
Sun Village
Taro's House
US Sanshin
Other major nation-wide jeans shops

Department Stores
Daimaru
Hankyu
Hanshin
Isetan
Kintetsu
Matsuya
Matsuzakaya

Maruei
Marui
Mitsukoshi
Odakyu
Seibu
Sogo
Takashimaya
Tokyu
Other major nation-wide department stores

National chain stores
Daiei
Ito-Yokado
Jusco
Nichii
Seiyu
Uni
Other national chain stores

Men's shops
Iseya
Roughox
Other major nation-wide men's shops

LEVI'S® World Network

LEVI'S®, the most famous brand in the world of jeans! The guiding principle of "Quality Never Goes Out Of Style" has been recognized all over the world.

Levi Strauss Japan K.K., which imports, manufactures, and sells the "LEVI'S®" brand in Japan, is a member of Levi Strauss & Co. in San Francisco, U.S.A., which is the birthplace of "jeans." The Levi's® group now has production facilities around the world and holds a very high share of the market in many regions. Staff from key fashion stations such as America, Europe, and Japan exchange ideas in developing new products. Such business activities became possible because Levi's® is the world's largest apparel manufacturer.

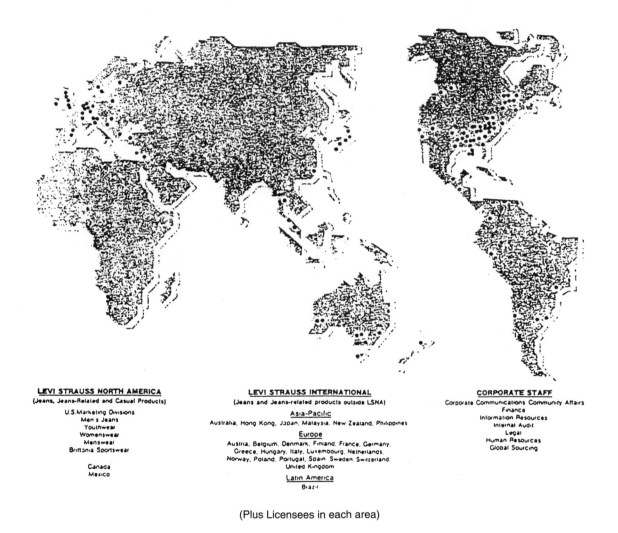

LEVI STRAUSS NORTH AMERICA
(Jeans, Jeans-Related and Casual Products)

U.S.Marketing Divisions
Men's Jeans
Youthwear
Womenswear
Menswear
Brittania Sportswear

Canada
Mexico

LEVI STRAUSS INTERNATIONAL
(Jeans and Jeans-related products outside LSNA)

Asia-Pacific
Australia, Hong Kong, Japan, Malaysia, New Zealand, Philippines

Europe
Austria, Belgium, Denmark, Finland, France, Germany,
Greece, Hungary, Italy, Luxembourg, Netherlands,
Norway, Poland, Portugal, Spain, Sweden, Switzerland,
United Kingdom

Latin America
Brazil

CORPORATE STAFF
Corporate Communications Community Affairs
Finance
Information Resources
Internal Audit
Legal
Human Resources
Global Sourcing

(Plus Licensees in each area)

Mission Statement

The mission of Levi Strauss & Co. is to sustain profitable and responsible commercial success by marketing jeans and selected casual apparel under the LEVI'S® brand.

We must balance goals of superior profitability and return on investment, leadership market positions, and superior products and service. We will conduct our business ethically and demonstrate leadership in satisfying our responsibilities to our communities and to society. Our work environment will be safe and productive and characterized by fair treatment, teamwork, open communications, personal accountability, and opportunities for growth and development.

Aspiration Statement

We all want a Company that our people are proud of and committed to, where all employees have an opportunity to contribute, learn, grow, and advance based on merit, not politics or background. We want our people to feel respected, treated fairly, listened to, and involved. Above all, we want satisfaction from accomplishments and friendships, balanced personal and professional lives, and to have fun in our endeavors.

When we describe the kind of LS & CO. we want in the future, what we are talking about is building on the foundation we have inherited: affirming the best of our Company's traditions, closing gaps that may exist between principles and practices, and updating some of our values to reflect contemporary circumstances.

What Type of Leadership Is Necessary to Make Our Aspirations a Reality?

New behaviors: Leadership that exemplifies directness, openness to influence, commitment to the success of others, willingness to acknowledge our own contributions to problems, personal accountability, teamwork, and trust. Not only must we model these behaviors, but we must coach others to adopt them.

Diversity: Leadership that values a diverse workforce (age, sex, ethnic group, etc.) at all levels of the organization, diversity in experience, and a diversity in perspectives. We have committed to taking full advantage of the rich backgrounds and abilities of all our people and to promote a greater diversity in positions of influence. Differing points of view will be sought; diversity will be valued and honesty rewarded, not suppressed.

Recognition: Leadership that provides greater recognition—both financial and psychic—for individuals and teams that contribute to our success. Recognition must be given to all who contribute: those who create and innovate and also those who continually support the day-to-day business requirements.

Ethical management practices: Leadership that epitomizes the stated standards of ethical behavior. We must provide clarity about our expectations and must enforce these standards through the corporation.

Communications: Leadership that is clear about Company, unit, and individual goals and performance. People must know what is expected of them and receive timely, honest feedback on their performance and career aspirations.

Empowerment: Leadership that increases the authority and responsibility of those closest to our products and customers. By actively pushing responsibility, trust, and recognition into the organization, we can harness and release the capabilities of all our people.

Case 16

American Airlines: SABRE Reservation System in Europe*

Toward the end of 1985, American Airlines decided to enter the European market with its computer reservation system (CRS). Three years before that, it had introduced its first flight to the Old World since September 1950, when American's president C. R. Smith had sold the subsidiary "American Overseas Airlines" to its only direct competitor, Pan American World Airways. Within three years, American offered flights to London, Paris, and Frankfurt. As European airline officials were beginning to talk about the liberalization of their skies, Robert Crandall, the newly elected CEO of the company, looked to gain a foothold in Europe by acquiring landing rights in as many cities as possible. By connecting European travel agents to SABRE, he also hoped to increase the airline's awareness overseas. This case shows the complexity of the CRS business in the rapidly changing airline industry.

The Early Years of American Airlines[1]

The birth of the commercial airline industry in the United States can be attributed in great part to the Kelly Act, which was passed by Congress in 1925. The act turned the airline business over from the Post Office Department to the private sector by requiring contractors to bid for each route. Until then, the U.S. Post Office Department was by far the biggest civil user of airplanes. It had hired 40 pilots in 1919 to fly its mail around the country. (Thirty-one of them had died in crashes by 1925.) There was also a handful of passenger airlines. One private shuttle flew Ford employees between Detroit and Chicago, while a sightseeing airline was run by the brother of Charlie Chaplin. But the number of airlines

---

*This case was written with the cooperation of American Airlines by Martin Schreiber under the supervision of Thomas C. Kinnear. Copyright © 1990 by Thomas C. Kinnear.
[1]Historical data were found in Robert I. Sterling, *Eagle—The Story of American Airlines* (New York: St. Martin's Press, 1985).

boomed after the Kelly Act was passed. Within weeks, the federal government received several hundred applications.

One of the successful applications belonged to Robertson Aircraft Corporation. The company was awarded the route between St. Louis and Chicago (by way of Springfield and Peoria) and began its service April 15, 1926. In an old DH–4 biplane, The Lone Eagle—better known as Charles A. Lindbergh—made what became the first regularly scheduled flight of American Airlines.

American Airlines owes its existence to Sherman Fairchild, head of the Fairchild Airplane Manufacturing Company. In 1929, fearing the loss of a good customer to the competition, he tried to convince his board of directors to help the airline finance the acquisition of additional airplanes to service a recently awarded air mail route. The board of directors went much further: On March 1, 1929, a financing company, The Aviation Corporation (AVCO) was incorporated in Delaware; they sold 2 million shares at $17.50 each, raising $35 million.

Within one year, AVCO acquired majority interests in more than 80 companies: 5 airlines consisting of 13 carriers (one of them being the Robertson Aircraft Corporation of Charles Lindbergh), flying schools, aircraft and engine manufacturers, two airports, one motor bus line, even one broadcasting station. In 1930, AVCO's president, Frederic G. Coburn, consolidated all the domestic air transportation lines into a new corporation: American Airways. Realizing the dependency of the airline on the mail service (75 percent of its revenues), Coburn also helped develop a passenger plane. The airline, nevertheless, was losing about $1 million every year. The situation deteriorated even more when President Franklin D. Roosevelt cancelled all domestic air mail contracts in February 1934, when a federal investigation discovered that larger airlines had secretly been favored for air mail routes. But six months after the army had been assigned to fly the mail—and 66 of its planes had crashed causing 12 casualties—Congress quickly passed legislation returning the air mail business to the private sector. The Airmail Act, however, reduced the fares to be paid by the Post Office Department from 42.6 cents to 25.3 cents per flown mile. It also included two provisions: first, that airlines had to sell off their aircraft manufacturing subsidiaries; and second, no company involved in prior bidding was allowed to apply for the new air mail contracts. While sounding rather radical, the second provision was easily bypassed by the airlines: American Airways came back to the bidding table as American Airlines, United Aircraft & Transport as United Airlines, Eastern Air Transport as Eastern Airlines, and TWA with Incorporated added to its name.

If nothing else, the carriers had discovered the danger in their heavy dependency on government contracts. American Airlines was losing almost $2.5 million in 1934 and was looking for a strong leader to turn the business around. On October 26, 1934, a Texan was appointed as the new president of the company: Cyrus Rowlett Smith. Except for a period during World War II, he would remain president until 1963, when he became chairman and CEO, a position he held for five years.

C. R. Smith was committed to changing the airline into a passenger transportation business. His strategy consisted of:

• Targeting the business travelers.
• Improving service.
• Replacing old equipment with better and safer equipment.
• Excelling in marketing.

He began by training his employees in what he called esprit de corps. Realizing the importance of the flight attendants, he started a training program designed for stewardesses. In 1936, he convinced Donald Douglas, Sr., to design the DC–3, which became the first profitable all-passenger airplane. In the same year, he offered the first sleeper flights between New York and Los Angeles (via Memphis, Dallas, and Tucson) and introduced the industry to air traffic control systems. He even entered the catering business by opening several restaurants in airports. The strategy paid off: the airline showed its first profit after only two years, and within three years, the revenue from mail service decreased from 71 percent to 31 percent of total revenue (Table 1). In 1938, Smith moved American's headquarters from the Chicago Midway Airport to the newly built LaGuardia Airport in New York City. There, he founded the first Admirals Club and opened a reservation school. By then, American's largest reservation office in New York was booking an average of 250 passengers a day.

TABLE 1	American Airways turns into a passenger airline	
	Mail revenue	*Passenger revenue*
1933	$4,728,000	$1,885,000
1937	2,980,000	6,598,000

After serving in the Air Transport Command during World War II, Smith returned to American. He soon dazzled his competitors when he successfully offered the first family fares in the industry. On a 50-acre piece of land in Dallas that he won in a gin rummy game, he built a new learning center, where stewardesses went through a 20-day training program. On January 25, 1959, he introduced the first jetliner, a Boeing 707; seven years later, he retired American's last piston plane.

The Development of SABRE

Until 1946, reservation offices used large display boards, which listed entries and space availability. During the 50s, American introduced the Magnetronic Reservisor to keep track of seat inventories on all flights and to electronically format and send teletype messages to other airlines. This process required that reservations be routed to a keypunch operator, run through a sorting machine, and then processed by another machine which cut the paper tape in order to send the teletype message (prior to being filed).

During a flight in 1953, C. R. Smith met an IBM senior sales representative, R. Blair Smith. As C. R. Smith described the capacity and speed constraints American was encountering with their reservation system, Blair Smith quickly saw a wonderful business opportunity. In November of 1959, American Airlines and IBM announced a joint development project called Semi-Automated Business Research Environment, or in short form, SABRE. Introduced first in 1962 and expanded systemwide two years later, SABRE became the largest electronic data processing system designed for business use. Its computer center was located in Briarcliff Manor, New York. In one day the system could process:

85,000   phone calls.

30,000   requests for fare quotations.

40,000   confirmed passenger reservations.

30,000   queries to and from other airlines regarding seat space.

20,000   ticket sales.

The initial research, development, and installation was estimated at $40 million, the price of four Boeing 707 aircraft.

In the late 1960s, two other airlines came up with their own reservation systems. United introduced APOLLO, while TWA Inc. operated PARS.

Bob Crandall Improves SABRE

By 1974, C. R. Smith had been replaced as president and chairman of American Airlines by Albert V. Casey, a business school graduate with limited prior airline experience. "There are only four jobs in any company, regardless of what kind of business you're in," he once said. "You have one guy in charge of making the product, someone in charge of selling it, the third one's a bean counter who keeps score, and then there's the boss." In June of 1974, he placed Robert Crandall in charge of selling the product by appointing him senior vice president of marketing.

Bob Crandall was determined to utilize American's reservation system as a marketing tool for the airline. He ordered a new and improved SABRE to help analyze collected flight and booking data. American Airlines' yield management system emerged, which could predict booking trends on specific flights and monitor the effectiveness of various marketing strategies. SABRE also introduced new functions such as baggage tracing, crew management, inventory management, and financial analysis.

Together with American's chief of data processing, Max Hopper, Crandall introduced the concept of a joint industry computerized reservation system (JICRS). Travel agents would be able to subscribe to the system and thus quickly access information about any carrier. There had already been several separate efforts to set up an industry system (Table 2). The major purpose was to eliminate continued duplication of investments and to reduce the reservations and sales cost by shifting the sales efforts from high-cost internal reservation offices to commission-paid travel agencies. Furthermore, before deregulation, all companies

TABLE 2 Failed attempts to standardize the CRS industry

1967	Donnelly Official Airline Reservation System (DOARS)
1970	Automatic Travel Agency Reservation (ATARS)
1974	Joint Industry Computer Reservation System (JICRS)
1976	United, then American, pulls out of JICRS to market their own reservation systems
1976	Multi-Access Agent Reservation System (MAARS)
1980	American Express makes last major effort to establish an industry system

charged the same fare for the same service, and it took years to change prices and service. None of the attempts succeeded, however, for lack of capital, lack of agreement, or fear of government suspicions that a joint system would be anti-competitive within the industry. The JICRS concept would die as well, as United started to sell its own system to travel agents. American immediately followed suit and in May of 1976 installed its first SABRE terminal in a travel agency. Other airlines were allowed to offer their services through SABRE and were charged about 35 cents for ticketing through a competitor's system.

Strategically, the distribution of CRSs to travel agents proved to be a very successful move. Not only were airlines gaining increased sales exposure, they also enjoyed high entry barriers against competitors due to travel agency investments in hardware and training, as well as to certain restrictive contract terms.

Although successful, it was not until 1978, when legislation ordered the deregulation of the airline industry, that the reservation systems achieved the importance they enjoy today.

Deregulation

The Airline Deregulation Act of 1978 provided for a phased abolition of regulation on route entry and tariffs. Until then, both of these were issued under the authority of the Civil Aeronautics Board (CAB). However, during its 40-year reign, the CAB had allowed no new major passenger carrier (called a trunk carrier) to enter the industry. Only domestic local service air carriers, commonly called feeder airlines, had been allowed to enter minor markets, as they became uneconomical for trunk carriers to service with their larger planes. Before deregulation, most routes had been served by only one carrier. Prices were set for airlines to obtain a defined industry margin.

As the CAB gradually relinquished authority, the Department of Transportation (DOT) temporarily took over the remaining functions. (The public interest in airline operations was to pass to the Justice Department only in 1989.) New carriers were now allowed to enter the market, not on the basis of "convenience and public necessity," but if they were "fit, willing and able to perform air transportation." In addition, airlines could set their own prices according to supply and demand.

The cooperative attitude prevailing until 1981 quickly disappeared. Many former interline partners went into direct competition with each other. During the

FIGURE 1   The effect of deregulation on airline ticket prices

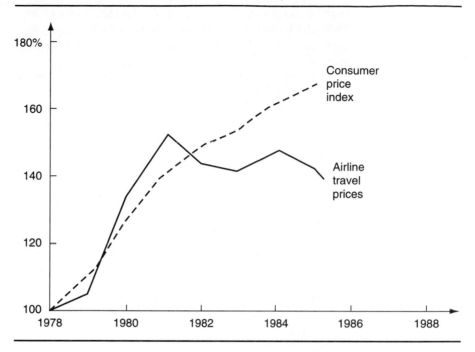

four years following deregulation, 119 new carriers entered the industry. As they began offering lower fares, a fierce price competition was launched, which ultimately lowered the average ticket price (Figure 1). In 1982, 80 percent of all tickets were sold at discount fares and the looming question became, who would survive the price war?

The impact of deregulation on airline operation was as far reaching as it was diverse.

Increase in Productivity

Increased competition forced established carriers to improve their productivity. Using larger, more fuel-efficient jets, they increased their average domestic route length. The incentive to replace their old aircraft with more fuel-efficient planes became even more pressing when fuel prices began to rise at the turn of the decade. Some of the used planes were put on the market and sold to smaller airlines seeking to increase the reach of their networks. Others were simply grounded. Sure enough, when oil prices dropped again, these older aircraft were put back into service.

As smaller, fuel-efficient planes were developed, productivity became less dependent on aircraft size than on maximum aircraft utilization, higher load factors, lower labor cost, and less-restrictive work rules.

Lowering of Labor Cost

In order to survive, the large trunk carriers had to cut costs, and fast. With wages being the largest cost component (Figure 2), managers looked for ways to trim the high prederegulation salaries down to market rates and to allow for more flexible work rules.

The most common practice was to engage in negotiations with unions. In March of 1983, Robert Crandall of American Airlines first reached an agreement with his employees in a deal that became the basis for negotiations at other carriers. (This is described in a later section.) Other airlines seeking concessions through negotiation were United, TWA, Delta, and Northwest. Pan American and Eastern, which were in more serious financial difficulties, were obliged to offer equity shares (10 percent and 25 percent) to their employees in exchange for wage and work rule concessions.

Two smaller airlines, Texas International and Frontier, tried to bypass the unions by starting their own low-cost nonunion subsidiary. Although initially successful, they were both later acquired by Texas Air Corp. shortly before being forced into Chapter 11 bankruptcy.

Finally, two other airlines, Braniff and Continental, chose the most extreme path to revise their labor costs. Braniff filed for bankruptcy in 1982 and Continental in 1983. In addition to restructuring their debt, both airlines defaulted on their labor contracts and started their operations again as nonunion companies.

FIGURE 2   American Airline's cost structure during 1985

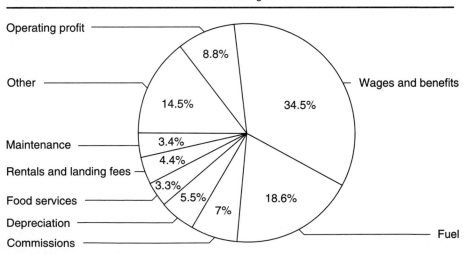

Bankruptcies/Mergers

Originally, deregulation was intended to increase competition, but six years after the deregulation act, 75 carriers remained in the market, down from 105. The number contracted due to bankruptcies, mergers, and liquidations. The avalanche of mergers was facilitated by the fact that all regulatory authority had been given to the Department of Transportation, which in several cases overruled objections raised by the Department of Justice.

Pan Am and National were the first airlines to merge. The deal allowed Pan Am, which had been restricted to international air service prior to deregulation, to compete domestically.

Republic resulted from the second major postderegulation merger. The airline consisted of North Central, Southern, and Hughes Airwest. Republic later merged with Northwest Airlines. Other mergers followed, and in 1985, the trend did not seem to have an end.

Hub and Spoke

As airplanes became more fuel efficient, the load factor became the most crucial variable for an airline's success. To increase the number of passengers per flight, airlines started to expand their hub airport utilization. Hub airports, operating as a central connecting point between city pairs (spokes) offered a competitive alternative to direct flights (Figure 3). By combining passenger traffic from different origins and with different destinations, the airline could increase the number of city pairs served, as well as the average number of passengers and corresponding revenue per flight. For flights to be attractive to customers, the connecting time at the hub had to be as short as possible. Airplanes would land in clusters and wait for all or most of the connecting passengers before taking off. As hubs grew in size and traffic (Table 3), passengers soon faced increasing delays.

FIGURE 3   The use of hub

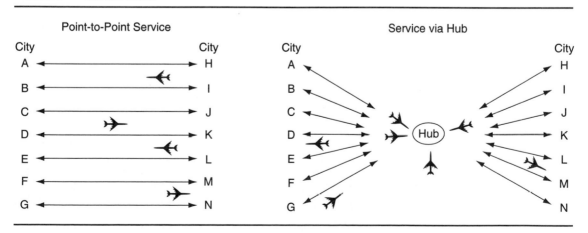

TABLE 3   Increased use of hub airports

Airline	Leading hub city in 1983	Percent of airline's domestic departures at hub	
		1978	1983
American	Dallas-Ft. Worth	11.2%	28.6%
Continental	Houston	12.8	22.9
Delta	Atlanta	18.3	21.4
Eastern	Atlanta	18.3	21.0
Northwest	Minneapolis-St. Paul	16.1	20.7
Pan American	New York	12.3	22.4
TWA	St. Louis	11.9	33.0
United	Chicago	16.0	18.9

International Growth—American Airlines' Response to Deregulation

Robert Crandall was named American's president in 1980, three years after he had successfully introduced the Super Saver fares. Even so, as deregulation approached, many analysts predicted the end of American Airlines' existence. In his biography about American Airlines, Robert Serling wrote: "It was like assuming command of the Titanic the day she sailed." Albert V. Casey had tried to limit the damages by moving American's headquarters from New York to the Dallas/Ft. Worth area, but in 1980 the airline reeled under a $111.1 million loss (Table 4).

Crandall's strategy was to "grow a new, low-cost airline inside the old one." He started to lower American's labor cost. Through hard negotiations with unions, Crandall obtained concessions for a two-tiered wage scale, by which American would pay newly hired employees only 50 percent of what present employees received. In return, Crandall guaranteed that there would be no layoffs and no pay cuts. His hard negotiating style earned him a reputation of "eating nails for breakfast." With the money saved, Crandall decided to expand the airline dramatically. "The faster we grow, the lower our average cost will be," he argued. Within four years, he bought almost 100 new planes, increasing American's old fleet by 41 percent. American started to build hubs in Dallas/Ft. Worth and Chicago. Both airports accounted for 80 percent of the airline's departures in 1983. The small, semiautonomous commuter airline, American Eagle, operated as a feeder airline funneling passengers from smaller outlying areas into American's route systems.

In 1983, while incorporated under AMR Corp., American began service to Europe with a flight from DFW to London (Braniff left the route open after filing for bankruptcy). By 1985, it had added flights to Paris and Frankfurt. Crandall also consolidated by selling off subsidiaries worth $60.3 million, which included its 45-year-old Sky-Chefs catering company and its AMR Energy Corp. In 1982, American lost $18.2 million, but one year later it registered an operating profit of $249.5 million. By 1985, American was credited with the largest market share (Table 5).

TABLE 4   American Airlines' income summary

	1978	1979	1980	1981	1982	1983	1984	1985
Operating results (in millions)								
Revenues								
Passengers	$2,329.5	$2,753.0	$3,154.4	$3,377.0	$3,414.2	$3,885.3	$4,335.8	$4,985.5
Other	406.0	499.5	551.7	546.6	563.0	647.1	751.6	873.8
Total operating revenues	$2,735.5	$3,252.5	$3,706.1	$3,923.6	$3,977.2	$4,532.4	$5,087.4	$5,859.3
Expenses								
Wages, salaries, and benefits	$1,083.4	$1,248.5	$1,372.7	$1,417.4	$1,472.9	$1,601.2	$1,748.7	$1,951.9
Aircraft fuel	514.7	801.5	1,114.8	1,115.7	1,115.7	1,038.6	1,091.8	1,141.8
Other	1,018.5	1,197.6	1,329.7	1,346.5	1,346.5	1,643.1	1,907.8	2,259.1
Total operating expenses	$2,616.6	$3,247.6	$3,817.2	$3,879.6	$3,935.1	$4,282.9	$4,748.3	$5,352.8
Operating income (loss)	$ 118.9	$ 4.9	$ (111.1)	$ 44.0	$ 42.1	$ 249.5	$ 339.1	$ 506.5
Operating statistics								
Revenue yield per passenger mile	7.96¢	8.17¢	11.12¢	12.13¢	11.04¢	11.39¢	11.81¢	11.30¢
Revenue passenger miles (in millions)	29,987	33,364	28,178	27,798	30,900	34,099	36,702	44,138
Passenger load factor	63.7%	67.4%	60.4%	61.4%	63.3%	65.0%	62.6%	64.6%
Number of operating aircraft at year-end	251	263	242	232	231	244	260	291

TABLE 5   1985 Market shares in passenger miles

Airline	Market share in revenue passenger miles
American	13.1%
United	12.4
Eastern	9.9
TWA	9.5
Delta	9.0
Pan American	8.1
Northwest	6.7
Continental	4.9
People Express	3.3
Republic	3.2
Western	3.1
USAir	2.9
Piedmont	2.4
Southwest	1.6
Others	9.9

Frequent Flier Programs

Deregulation cannot be discussed without mentioning the frequent flier programs. Designed to entice loyalty to one carrier, they would reward passengers with bonuses (usually a free trip) based on mileage flown and/or fares paid. Obviously, such programs were especially attractive with larger airlines serving many cities. American initiated the frequent flier wars when it introduced its AAdvantage program. The entire service was run through SABRE. Two years after its introduction, American's competition developed similar programs of their own.

Increased Importance of the CRS Market

With deregulation, the number and complexity of airline fares increased, making reservation systems with their large databases more of a competitive tool. In 1977, before deregulation, travel agencies had booked only 38 percent of all tickets; in 1985, the percentage had jumped to 90 percent. As travel agents booked an increasing share of ticket sales, airlines doubled their efforts to place their CRS terminals with as many agents, particularly business travel specialists, as possible. The commission from ticket sales, which represented the agent's largest revenue source, jumped to 10 percent, even 13 percent in 1985, up from the CAB specified 7 percent. During the same time, the percentage of agencies automated with CRS terminals shot up from 5 percent to 90 percent (Table 6).

These five CRSs competed for market share (Figure 4):

SABRE of American Airlines. SABRE accounted for one third of American Airlines' $506 million in net earnings in 1985. However, as Robert Crandall testified before the Senate Aviation Subcommittee in March of the same

TABLE 6   Automatization of travel agencies

Year	Agents	Percent automated with CRS
1976	12,262	*
1977	13,454	5%
1978	14,804	*
1979	16,112	24
1980	17,339	*
1981	19,203	59
1982	20,962	75
1983	23,058	85
1984	25,748	*
1985	27,193	90

* Not available.

FIGURE 4   1985 market share of the major CRS vendors' installations

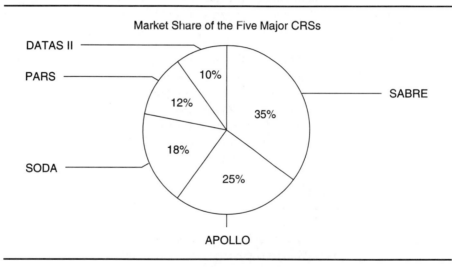

Market Share of the Five Major CRSs

year, SABRE had been profitable only since 1983 (Table 7). The accumulated investment in the CRS was estimated at $350 million.

APOLLO of United Airlines. With a 25 percent market share, APOLLO was the second-largest system in the country. Along with SABRE, it was the most sophisticated CRS in the market. At the end of 1983, United's total investment in APOLLO was estimated at $250 million.

PARS of TWA. TWA had unveiled its reservation system to travel agents shortly after American and United had started selling their CRS service in 1976. A decade later, 12 percent of all 32,000 U.S. travel agency terminals were connected to PARS.

TABLE 7   Estimated operating results of SABRE (millions)

Year	Revenue	Expenses	Operating income (loss)
1976	$0.3	$4.4	$(4.1)
1977	2.4	12.7	(10.3)
1978	6.0	24.5	(18.5)
1979	15.6	41.7	(26.1)
1980	32.0	56.6	(24.6)
1981	53.6	68.3	(14.7)
1982	82.9	92.4	(9.5)
1983	124.3	118.8	5.5
1984	179.0	136.2	42.8
1985	483.0	367.0	116.0

SODA of Eastern Airlines. Eastern Airlines had introduced SODA (System One Direct Access) shortly after Congress had passed the deregulation act. Thanks to Eastern's position as the third-largest domestic carrier, SODA's market share rose to an impressive 18 percent by 1985.

DATAS II of Delta Air Lines. In 1979, Delta and United entered into an arrangement that allowed Delta to market the APOLLO system using its own name. Delta called its system DATAS. As the advantages of owning a CRS became apparent, Delta developed its own system and called it DATAS II. Its market share in 1985 was 10 percent.

Some other carriers, such as Alaska Air Lines, Pan Am, or USAir also maintained small CRS networks.

Prices charged to travel agents included three components: a one-time installation charge, a monthly hardware fee, and a monthly maintenance charge. To entice travel agents to join their networks, airlines offered financing and booking incentives (free hardware, software, or communication lines when processing a certain level of bookings through the system). Airlines were basing their efforts on the fact that an agent who had opted for their system would find it hard to switch to another system.

With travel agents selling most of the tickets, it became increasingly important for airlines to be listed on other airlines' CRS terminals. CRS vendors quickly raised their fees to about $1.75, up from the preregulation fee of 35 cents. Charges were even higher around hubs of a CRS vendor due to the carrier's—and thus the reservation system's—monopoly position. (Travel agents would subscribe to the CRS that offered the most flights.) Other, mostly new carriers were facing difficulties in obtaining cohost status. Frontier Airlines, for instance, had to wait two years before having its flight information displayed on APOLLO. As travel agents demanded access to all other airlines' flight schedules through their system, CRS vendors were forced to comply.

They soon faced yet another charge: display bias. With many flights available, a standard terminal could not display all of them on one screen. The order by which flights were listed was defined by an algorithm written by the CRS vendor. Usually, nonstop and direct flights were listed first, followed by in-line and then off-line connecting flights.[2] Within each category, systems commonly would give priority to the flights of the CRS vendor. SABRE, for instance, listed the flights alphabetically, putting American with its acronym "AA" at the top of the list. Makes good business sense? Not for subscribing airlines. According to a survey, 90 percent of all travel agents' bookings were made from the first screen. In fact, 50 percent were made from the first line.

To get a more favorable screen display, certain non-CRS carriers offered to pay higher fees to the system operators, contributing to the discriminatory pricing in placement. Other carriers decided they could no longer wait for government regulations or the outcome of lawsuits and started to invest heavily in their own CRS systems. But as they tried to sell their systems to agencies, they faced restrictive contracts prohibiting travel agents from installing more than one system. The only way to gain market share was to convince agencies to change systems. As new systems encroached on their territory, established CRS vendors began to include liquidated damage clauses in the contracts, and sue for damages in case of breach.

In November 1984, six weeks before closing its doors, the CAB issued a final ruling over computer reservation systems.

- The regulation banned both explicit and indirect bias in search routines. CRS vendors were ordered to disclose their algorithms.
- CRS vendors were forbidden to tie travel agents for more than five years. They also were not allowed to force travel agents to book most of their tickets on the CRS's airline.
- Charges to participating airlines could not be "unfair or discriminatory."

In spite of these rules, cohost airlines still faced another bias called the halo effect: Travel agents, who were heavily dependent on the CRS vendor for training and maintenance, seemed to favor flights of the CRS vendor over non-vendor flights by a margin of about 10 percent.

The most common algorithms now listed the flights according to flight duration. To be on the top of the list, some airlines published unrealistic flight times, while others focused on shortening connecting times in hubs, causing an inadvertent flood of delays.

Trying to expand their system, CRS vendors enticed hotels and car-rental companies to offer their services through the reservation system. They also added "backoffice" software packages that would automate agents' billing and accounting procedures. The airline's task was to create a virtual circle. The more products it could put on its system for people to reserve, the more people would want to hook their terminals to the network. Conversely, the more people on the system, the more economically feasible it would be to offer a diversity of services (e.g., hotel and car reservation). Every new service also increased the dependency of travel agents on their CRS system.

---

[2]In-line connections refer to two flights of the same airline. Off-line connections refer to two flights of different airlines.

With the increased demand for PCs, dumb terminals were replaced with intelligent workstations. To make the CRS compatible with PCs, connectivity and compatibility problems had to be resolved.

Marketing finally became an integral part of the CRS business. Government agencies and larger agency chains, for instance, were discovered to be very profitable market niches. Both, because of their size, were highly attractive to CRS vendors. On the other hand, they also enjoyed a strong negotiating position.

International Consequences of Deregulation

The international passenger service accounts for a large share of aggregate airline revenue. While the numbers vary among airlines, all U.S. carriers combined have transported roughly 50 percent of all passengers traveling to and from the United States during the last 10 years. An estimated 46.6 million passengers have traveled between the United States and foreign countries (excluding Canada); 40.7 percent of these were crossing the North Atlantic (Table 8).

TABLE 8   International traffic

Region	Passengers (millions)	Share percent
All countries	46.6	100.0%
Central America and Mexico	6.8	14.6
Caribbean	8.8	18.9
South America	2.4	5.2
Europe	19.0	40.7
Africa/Middle East	1.1	2.4
Far East	7.0	15.0
Oceania	1.5	3.2

Bilateral Agreements

In the early days of the airline industry, carriers had to negotiate directly with foreign governments in order to obtain landing rights and to offer services between the United States and a foreign country. It was not until 1943 that the U.S. government took over the responsibility of negotiating bilateral treaties with foreign countries for common air routes. A year later, government representatives from 52 countries tried to define a standard framework for international air service. Because they failed to agree on a multilateral transport agreement, bilateral negotiations between the governments of two countries remained the only way for airlines to obtain the rights to provide service to a foreign country. A typical bilateral agreement would define:

- The right of each government to designate the airline to serve the foreign country.

- The destinations available to the designated airlines.
- The type of traffic the designated airlines are allowed to carry (Table 9).
- The capacity allowed for the designated airlines.
- The pricing of international services.
- Provisions concerning profit repatriation, access to local distribution (CRS) channels, ground handling, airport charges, aviation safety, and other ancillary issues.

TABLE 9   The freedoms of the air

1. The right to use the airspace of another country without landing.
2. The right to land in another country for servicing and other noncommercial purposes.
3. The right to discharge in a foreign country passengers and cargo coming from the home country.
4. The right to pick up in another country passengers and cargo bound for the home country.
5. The right to pick up passengers and cargo in a foreign country and convey them to yet another country.
6. The right to transport passengers and cargo from one to another foreign country by routing through the home country.

Early agreements between the United States and European countries were rather favorable to the United States. One reason lay in the technical superiority of U.S. carriers, which had the capacity to fly more passengers than their European counterparts. Another reason could be found in the large geographical size of the United States. While American airliners could fly to every smaller country with which their government had an agreement, each European carrier was restricted to only a limited number of American gateways.

In an effort to extend deregulation to international air service, the U.S. government in 1978 urged far more liberal agreements. It offered access to new American cities in exchange for fifth-freedom rights. With these rights, American carriers could enter in direct competition with European carriers on inter-European routes. As transatlantic flights were offering high margins, the short flights between foreign gateways would count only as marginal revenue, putting the airline in a position to offer relatively low fares. To no one's surprise, many European airlines opposed the exchange of these rights and instead demanded cabotage rights in the United States (i.e., rights to fly passengers and cargo within the United States). These rights were strongly protected in most countries. Some voices in the EC argued that the European Community was to be regarded as one country, which would change fifth-freedom rights to cabotage rights. But in 1985, a united European transportation system was far from being established.

European Air Transportation

Geographically speaking, Europe consists of 34 countries, each having its own language, currency, and laws. Only 22 of these are listed as members of the European Civil Aviation Conference (ECAC) (Table 10). West Germany, France,

TABLE 10 ECAC and AEA membership

ECAC members	AEA members
Austria	Austrian
Belgium	Sabena
Cyprus	
Denmark	SAS
Finland	Finnair
France	Air France
	UTA
Greece	Olympic
Iceland	Icelandair
Ireland	Air Lingus
Italy	Alitalia
Luxemburg	Luxair
Malta	
Netherlands	KLM
Norway	
Portugal	TAP
Spain	Iberia
Sweden	
Switzerland	Swissair
Turkey	
United Kingdom	British Airways
	British Caledonian
West Germany	Lufthansa
Yugoslavia	Jugoslav

and Great Britain represent the largest economies; accordingly, they are also registering the largest demand for scheduled flights. From these countries, most of the tourists travel to the hot spots of Italy, France, and Spain.

Route Length

While the average route length in the United States is over 800 miles, the European average is a mere 465 miles. The longest European route (between London and Athens) is only two-thirds the distance between New York and Los Angeles. European carriers thus have a higher percentage of smaller planes than their American counterparts. They also pay a higher percentage for landing fees and are subject to airspace usage charges throughout the Continent. With these constraints, European airliners are estimated to have operating costs 20 percent higher than U.S. carriers. This is not enough, however, to account for the ticket price difference. During the 1980s, the average ticket price in Europe was 35–40 percent more expensive than in the United States for a comparable stretch.

Government Ownership

In 1985, most European airlines were completely or partially owned by their respective governments and received financial subsidies. In return, they were bound to provide a public transportation service. This service included connecting a country's cities, even when demand would not justify it. Government ownership goes back to when operating an airline was thought to add international prestige to the country. Airlines were long considered the commercial ambassadors of their country. This attitude was still predominant during the first half of the 1980s, although some governments, such as Great Britain, were starting to talk about selling a share of their ownership.

Partly because of their relationship with the government, European airlines were heavily unionized. In addition, many countries had strict rules regarding layoffs. In France, for instance, the newly elected socialist government recently passed a law making any firing in the country dependent on governmental approval.

Charter Flights

Passengers in Europe had three options to avoid paying regular fares:

1. Buy a discount ticket offered by regular carriers (Table 11).
2. Buy a ticket in the gray market, consisting of second-hand and stand-by tickets.
3. Fly with a deregulated, nonscheduled carrier (charters).

TABLE 11   The importance of discount fares in Europe and the United States

	Discount fares issued as a percent of total traffic	Average discount below full fare
Europe	57%	40%
United States	85	56

Charters offered complete tours, which included flight and accommodations. Since they were excluded from bilateral agreements, they escaped many price regulations. Unlike in the United States, nonscheduled travel (charter) plays a very important role in Europe. In the United States, the market share of charter service dropped from 27 percent in 1977 to 8 percent in 1985. In Europe, by contrast, 43 percent of all passengers flying within the Continent during 1985 took charters for 55 percent of the total passenger miles. Spain and Greece registered particularly heavy charter traffic. During 1984, 19.9 million passengers used nonscheduled services to visit Spain, while only 4.4 million passengers used scheduled services.

Once scheduled carriers realized the vast opportunity that charter operations could offer, they began buying shares of existing charter carriers. The result was a complicated network of ownership.

Rail Transportation

Europe's air transportation is also exposed to fierce competition from the rail system, particularly over shorter distances. While the U.S. rail system accounts for only 0.5 percent of domestic traffic, European trains carry about 13 percent of all passenger traffic. Like the airlines, the rail systems are regarded as a public utility and, thus, are heavily subsidized by their respective governments. Traveling by train is usually cheaper but takes more time than air travel. With the development of faster trains, rail systems have increasingly been able to compete on longer routes. Probably the most prominent high-speed train is the French TGV ("train à grande vitesse") that, at a speed of over 170 mph, connects Paris and Lyon within three and a half hours.

Bilateral Agreements

European bilaterals on scheduled services were relatively rigid:

- Only one airline from each country was usually permitted to service a route.
- The two selected airlines were allowed to offer no more than a designated percentage of the total capacity. Usually, carriers had to share the capacity 50–50; a more liberal bilateral between France and Great Britain allowed for capacity shares between 45 percent and 55 percent.
- The two selected airlines were to share the revenue in proportion to the capacity allocated to them.
- Fares had to be accepted by the regulatory body of both countries.

Liberalization—The role of the EEC

The European Economic Community (EEC) has its origin in the Treaty of Rome, signed in 1957. During the fall of that year, government representatives of 12 countries agreed to work toward economic integration. The community was to establish conditions which would ensure fair competition among businesses of different countries by eliminating state boundaries for businesses. Without directly naming the airline industry, the treaty nevertheless included provisions that applied to any kind of business, like an article guaranteeing the freedom to supply services in any of the given countries. The community also was to establish a common transportation policy. Finally, Articles 85–90 prohibited cartels and anticompetitive practices.

Until 1985, however, the treaty had been mostly overlooked by airline authorities. Most carriers held that the treaty did not address the airline industry. Articles 85–90 applied specifically to acts of enterprises. Carriers, on the other hand, were owned by autonomous governments. Even if the carriers wished to deregulate Europe's skies, they had no authority to do so. The Treaty of Rome had assigned the power of decision over air transportation to a Council of Ministers and not to the AEA. Lastly, deregulation did not make much sense as long as governments were subsidizing their airlines.

Nevertheless, as of 1985, most European carriers agreed to the idea of liberalization, while remaining undecided about the pace by which this liberalization should come about.

The CRS Market in Europe

During the 70s, European airlines had discovered the use of computerized reservation systems. Each carrier had developed its own system, offering diverse functions. A 1983 survey on the world's largest reservation systems (Table 12) clearly showed that European CRSs were not as sophisticated as American ones. Backoffice systems, for instance, were not offered by any of the European airlines.

Although travel agents accounted for the majority of ticket sales, not all of the airlines offered their systems to travel agents. The airlines that did, did so only to agencies within their respective countries, since the systems generally displayed only flights for the domestic airline. Travel agents wishing to book a reservation on a foreign carrier had to call the other airline's reservation office, ask for seat availability, and if available, ask to have the ticket sent.

TABLE 12   Survey of major CRSs

	Air France	British Airways	Finnair	Icelandair	KLM	Lufthansa	Sabena	SAS	Swissair	TAP-Air Portugal	American Airlines
Reservations	I	I	I	I	I	I	C	I	I	C	I
Check-in	I	I	C	—	I	I	C	I	I	C	I
Ticketing	I	I	I	I	I	I	C	I	I	—	I
Fare quote	I	I	—	—	I	I	C	—	I	—	I
Hotel reservations	I	I	I	—	I	I	C	—	I	—	I
Car rental	I	C	—	—	I	—	C	—	—	—	I
Baggage trace	I	C	C	—	C	C	C	I	C	—	I
Scheduling	I	I	—	—	I	I	—	I	I	—	I
Crew management	I	I	I	I	I	I	I	I	I	I	I
Flight planning	I	I	I	—	I	I	I	I	C	—	I
Weight and balance	I	I	C	—	I	I	I	I	I	C	I
Inventory management	I	I	I	I	I	I	I	I	I	I	I
Maintenance schedule	I	I	I	I	I	I	I	I	I	I	I
Performance analysis	I	I	—	I	I	I	I	I	I	I	I
Financial	I	I	I	I	I	I	I	I	I	I	I
Cargo control	I	I	I	I	I	I	I	I	I	I	I
Management information	I	I	I	I	I	I	I	I	I	I	I

I = In-house.
C = Contracted.
— = Not available.

SABRE's 1986 European Marketing Plan

Having a 35 percent share of the nearly saturated U.S. travel agency market in 1985, American decided to expand further and to "focus its attention on sales and service of its SABRE system internationally."[3] The 1986 marketing plan for sales and service outlined the strategic steps to successfully enter foreign markets. Besides offering additional revenue generated by new subscribers, the expansion into foreign markets would lead to increased visibility for American Airlines and would generate useful data for yield management concerning international flights.

At American, the foreign network was divided into three areas:

Area I: Central America, South America, and Caribbean.

Area II: Europe, Africa, and the Middle East.

Area III: Australia, New Zealand, Pacific, and South East Asia.

Although trying to expand worldwide, the early phases of the plan concentrated on Europe. Accordingly, we will focus only on the marketing plan as it relates to Europe.

The introduction to the plan also stated the following:

> A most effective premise upon which this entire plan is built relates to positive interaction with the International Passenger Sales Division of American Airlines . . . so that, hand in hand, both organizations may identify new opportunities leading to worldwide SABRE distribution.

Competitive Environment

SABRE faced competition from both local systems and CRSs of U.S. carriers. Furthermore, the European market was practically unaware of SABRE. "They may have heard the name, but in their own minds, they do not differentiate its functionality from APOLLO or any other U.S. system."

The marketing plan went on describing several competitive advantages of local systems over SABRE:

- Unlike SABRE, all local systems could issue tickets. Most of them did so through a Bank Settlement Plan (BSP).[4] American was in the process of receiving BSP specifications from each country that offered such a procedure. In non-BSP countries such as France, ticketing capability was administrated through the national carrier.
- Local systems were able to quote fares more accurately than SABRE. To quote fares through SABRE, reliable sources for fare information had to be determined and the information continually updated.

---

[3]This and the following quotes are taken from the SABRE 1986 Marketing Plan.

[4]The Bank Settlement Plan (BSP) is a unified procedure by which travel agents give the coupons of the tickets they sold to an organization, which manages for a fee the money transfer to the different airlines. In certain cases, a travel agent can strike a deal with an airline and pay the ticket revenue (minus commission) directly to that airline, therefore avoiding the BSP fee.

- Most local systems had booking and ticketing capabilities for national rail services. American had just started to negotiate with its first rail participants—the French SNCF and Swiss Rail.
- Local systems maintained nationalistic arguments to promote the use of their systems. They were also backed by the national flag carriers, which objected to the use of foreign CRSs.

Special attention was lavished upon reservation systems in the United Kingdom, Germany, and France, because of the large size of their market (Table 13). In Scandinavia, the reservation system of SAS (Scandinavian Airlines System) represented the major competitor of SABRE. Unknown to American at that time were the operating procedures in Switzerland, Austria, Spain, Belgium, the Netherlands, and Italy.

TABLE 13   Major European CRS competitors

Country	United Kingdom	Germany	France	Scandinavia
CRS	TRAVICOM	START	ESTEREL	
BSP	Yes	Yes	No	No
Special features	Comprehensive fares and quoting capabilities, telex capabilities	Ticketing capabilities for rail system, backoffice system	Ticketing capabilities for rail system	

Other U.S. CRS vendors had already entered the European market (Table 14). United Airlines was by far the most aggressive vendor. Promoting APOLLO, United had placed sales representatives throughout Europe and built a large demonstration facility in Paris. It also offered free installation, several months of free equipment rental, and special override commissions for flight segments booked on United.

TABLE 14   Position of major U.S. CRSs in Europe

CRS	APOLLO	DATAS II	PARS
Airline	United/Covia	Delta Airlines	TWA
Main location	Paris	Germany	London
Comments	Aggressive marketing and pricing	Services U.S. military bases	

Objectives and Goals

While never expressively stated, the objectives were obvious: first, to acquire significant international market share to become the worldwide leader in the distribution of travel information; second, to collect through SABRE market information about competitors' operations and pricing, enabling American Airlines to increase its presence on international routes.

The key is to get SABRE's "foot in the door." As we establish our distribution and enhance functionality, bookings will increase. Optimum revenue potential to American will be long term in nature. Significant booking fee revenue potential exists once the system eases into the role of a primary system and additional CRTs are installed.[5]

The goal was to install SABRE in 310 European locations by the end of 1986 and to achieve a penetration of 4 percent in the worldwide IATA travel agency market (Table 15).[6]

The focus of the initial sales effort will concentrate primarily on IATA locations. Depending on the particular sensitivities which are present from one country to another, a decision may be reached to automate non-IATA locations as well.

TABLE 15 SABRE's objectives in Europe

	SABRE locations	IATA agencies	Percent
United Kingdom	65	3,155	2.1%
Norway	25	233	10.7
Sweden	25	262	9.5
Denmark	20	150	13.3
Finland	24	300	8.0
Germany	40	1,342	2.9
France	30	1,200	2.5
Switzerland	17	355	5.0
Belgium	14	180	3.0
Holland	20	250	8.0
Other Europe	30	300	10.0
	310	7,727	4.0

Global Strategies

Until SABRE could offer ticketing capabilities and cater to local travel habits, it could be promoted and sold only as a secondary system. Subscribers could only book flight segments in the United States and order tickets to be sent by mail.[7] While the system would be gradually upgraded to meet the requirements for a primary system, sales were to focus on the technological superiority of the product and price the system at a level competitive with existing U.S. systems.

---

[5] Cathode-ray tube; commonly used to design computer workstations.

[6] The International Air Transport Association (IATA) is the airlines' own trade association. Until 1984, among other duties, it assumed the jobs of determining equitable fares and controlling the distribution part of the business. It still is assigned to the latter duty. Under its Standard Agency Agreement of 1952, travel agents accredited under the agreement (i.e., those meeting the necessary criteria of competence, financial soundness, and suitable premises) get the right to issue IATA's interlinable air tickets plus the opportunity (if available in their country) to participate in its Bank Settlement Plan (BSP).

[7] Subscribers, such as travel agents, are customers who are using SABRE to process reservations.

American was considering two ways to enter the local markets: first by getting local travel agents to connect to SABRE, and second, by licensing the sophisticated SABRE software to national carriers. Thus, while advertising the system as a competitive alternative to local CRS systems, the sales and service departments also had to consider every opportunity to make SABRE the CRS standard in each country.

> It should be noted that direct sales activity will be supplemented by ongoing Prime Host discussions with key selected carriers. In the event that a Prime Host opportunity is successful, direct sales of SABRE to locations with the national carrier system will cease.

During this early stage, product development was to focus its efforts on:

- Expanding ticketing capabilities.
- Permitting booking and ticketing capabilities for rail and small regional air services.
- Adapting travel agency backoffice accounting software to national standards.
- Offering billing in foreign currencies.

SABRE specialists were scheduled to visit travel agents in order to help them increase their bookings. Agents were also to be offered repeated training and invited to various workshops. Agency sales were also to induce European hotel chains, car rental companies, and other local travel firms to become associates and list their services through SABRE for a fee.[8]

Once all necessary enhancements would be customized for a single-country market, SABRE would finally be promotable as a primary system to compete directly with local CRSs.

Configuration Strategy

Two major competitive disadvantages for SABRE were its high communication costs and its long response time. With the mainframe in Tulsa, Oklahoma, long distances had to be traversed when processing a booking in Europe. The low efficiency was especially evident when an incorrect command was sent by a European travel agent to the mainframe only to be answered, after a long delay, with an error message. It also was very inefficient to have a service used mainly by Europeans (e.g., Swissair shuttle between Zurich and München) being listed and managed in Tulsa. To avoid wasteful communication costs, a European mini-mainframe could be designed to filter the messages and send to Tulsa only those which it could not process by itself. Such a system, however, was not feasible in the near future and a study of different alternatives continued.

---

[8]Associates, such as hotel chains, are customers who are offering their services through the reservation system to the subscriber.

Initial Research

In March of 1986, three senior analysts were to be hired to conduct a three-month marketing study to determine the potential subscriber base in each region and country. The research would also provide specific country-by-country information about:

- Current operating methods and procedures for travel agencies.
- Import/export regulations and other documentation requirements.
- Cultural and business practices.
- Communication requirements, and installation and maintenance procedures.
- Language requirements to develop a comprehensive sales, marketing, and installation program.
- Legal ramifications for operations.

The research was also expected to indicate recommendations for:

- Staffing and sales representation.
- Time frames for implementing the sales and installation efforts.
- Training requirements.
- SABRE functional enhancements.
- Promotion strategies.

Sales Staffing

New personnel would be added to headquarters as well as to the overseas staff. Each of the three foreign regions would be controlled by a regional manager. The regional manager of Europe would be based in London and report to the vice president of automation at headquarters. Four country managers would report to the regional manager (Figure 5). They would be responsible for the United Kingdom, France, Germany, and Scandinavia, and oversee one sales and one product specialist as well as one marketing service representative. Further recruiting would be necessary for the product development and training areas (eight analysts) and for the finance department (eight analysts).

Training and HELP Desk

Comprehensive training for travel agents would be crucial for the success of SABRE in Europe. The training had to not only be comprehensive in nature but also be offered in the native languages of travel agents. While located first in Dallas, the training was later to take place in London. Immediate assistance would be available through Help desks, consisting of two SABRE specialists located in London, Paris, and Frankfurt. The desks could be contacted by phone or electronic mail. "During the third quarter, an in-depth evaluation will be undertaken to determine the feasibility of adding additional Help desks in the cities of Paris, Frankfurt, and Stockholm."

FIGURE 5   Organization chart of European SABRE operations

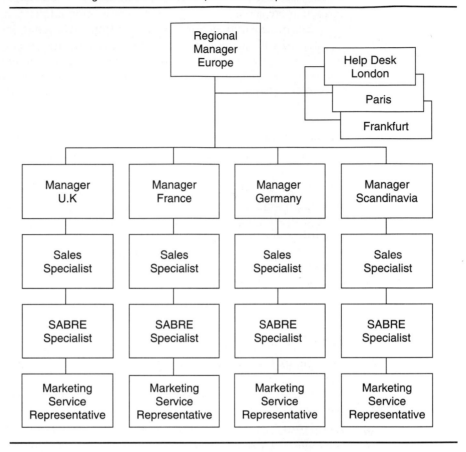

For internal training, regional meetings between the regional manager and all SABRE field personnel would be held on a quarterly basis. "The meetings will be a forum for discussion of current corporate objectives, analysis of results, planning of strategies, and solicitation of feedback and input relating to the international marketplace."

A training session for international passenger sales would also be conducted quarterly to increase awareness and confidence among the sales force.

Advertising and Promotion

New brochures and a video presentation were being developed to highlight the international functionality and the broad features of SABRE for potential subscribers. SABRE was also represented at various air, travel, and computer trade shows throughout Europe. Additionally, the SABRE subscriber conference, which was held in the United States annually, would target international subscribers more actively and highlight its new international enhancements.

During the third quarter, an analyst from advertising and promotion would be charged with the development of international advertising and sales promotion. "This analyst will address the individual customs, cultures, and language requirements of each respective country and coordinate these efforts with the local advertising agency."

Legal Issues

The contract administration department of American Airlines faced working around many different contract laws and government regulations in Europe. In conjunction with the legal, financial controls, and international SABRE sales and service departments, it had to ensure the administration of highly comprehensive and enforceable agreements in each country. As SABRE's presence grew in the European market, contract administration would be required to move into each foreign location in order to address the local legal issues more effectively.

The legal and financial control departments were facing yet another issue: foreign currency billing.

Pricing

As noted earlier, SABRE would be priced at a competitive level. The rates of competing U.S. systems had to be matched immediately.

Conclusion

As American prepared itself to relive SABRE's success story in Europe, many questions remained unanswered. Many of them addressed the local marketplace, others were more concerned with global issues. In particular,

- How long would it take SABRE to reach the status of a primary system in each country?
- On which strategy should American focus its efforts, direct sales to travel agents or software licensing to national carriers?
- How would the competition react to SABRE's entry?
- How would the liberalization movements in EEC countries impact SABRE's attempt to become a major CRS in Europe?

"*Alea iacta sunt.*" Like Caesar when he crossed the Rubicon, Crandall had thrown the dice in the air; now only the future would tell whether his plans would end successfully.

Part 6

Promotion Decisions

A. Advertising Decisions

Advertising is the most visible and controversial activity carried on in marketing. The first seven cases in this section focus their attention on this function.

Advertising is defined as all paid, nonpersonal forms of communication that are identified with a specific sponsor. It, therefore, includes expenditures on radio, television, newspaper, magazines, and outdoor billboards, plus the Yellow Pages. The largest absolute dollar spenders on advertising tend to be big consumer products companies, like Procter & Gamble, General Foods, and General Motors. The industries that spend the highest percentage of their sales on advertising are the drug and cosmetic companies, followed closely by packaged food products and soaps.

The marketing decision maker has a number of decisions to make with respect to advertising for a product. These include:

1. Setting advertising objectives.
2. Determining the advertising budget.
3. Deciding on what creative presentation should be used.
4. Selecting what media vehicles to use.
5. Selecting what scheduling pattern should be used.
6. Deciding how the advertising should be evaluated.

In the cases that follow in this section, the reader will work to make decisions in most of these areas. The next section of this note is a short reminder of some of the concepts related to each of these decision points.

Advertising Objectives

Advertising objectives should be stated in qualified terms with a specific time period designed for a specific market target. The objective may be in terms of profits, sales, or communications measures such as awareness, interest, and preference. The objective "increase brand awareness" is obviously not as good a statement as "increase brand awareness to 85 percent of all women 18–40, in the next six months."

Advertising Budgets

Advertising budgets are difficult to set. That is why companies have fallen into using rule-of-thumb methods such as (1) the "all we can afford" method, (2) the percentage of sales method, and (3) the matching competitors method. We would prefer decision makers to proceed by defining the task they hope to accomplish and then have them calculate the cost of doing this. This is called the task approach. To do this method, the advertiser must understand the functional relationship between his or her task and advertising expenditures.

Creative Development

Creative activity is usually done by an advertising agency. The final product is usually the result of much copy testing on dimensions such as attention getting and persuasiveness.

Media Decision

Media decisions are of two types. The first is the selection of broad classes of media to be considered for future analysis. This is done by matching the media characteristics with the needs of the advertiser. For example, television allows for good visual demonstration. This may be a desired characteristic for the campaign at hand.

The second stage involves the selection of specific media vehicles, for example, the NFL football game versus "All in the Family" versus a page in *Fortune*. The procedures for doing this are complex. Simply stated, vehicles are compared on the basis of their cost per thousand (CPM) target audience persons reached. The vehicle with the lowest CPM is selected. Audience sizes are then adjusted to allow for duplication between vehicles, and new CPMs are calculated. Then the lowest CPM vehicle at that point is selected. This process continues until the budget is used up. A number of computer algorithms have been developed to handle the many calculations made in this process.

Scheduling Patterns

The advertisers must decide whether to (1) spend their budget continuously throughout the period; (2) concentrate it at a short interval; or (3) spend it intermittently throughout the period. There are no good rules of thumb to answer this question. The advertisers must experiment to find out which pattern makes the most sense for their products.

Evaluating Advertising

If the advertiser has specified quantitative objectives, one is then in a position to measure to see if the objectives were met. The procedure used should be specifically designed to fit the type of objective stated.

B. Sales Management Decisions

The last three cases in this section of the book deal with the management of the personal selling function. Personal selling is defined as all paid, personal forms of communication that are identified with a specific organization.

Organizations in the United States spend over one and one-half times as much money on personal selling as they do on advertising. Effective management of personal selling activity is thus very important.

The marketing decision maker has a number of decisions to make with respect to personal selling for a product. These include:

1. Defining the selling job to be performed.
2. Establishing the desired characteristics of the salespersons who will do this job.
3. Determining the size of the sales force.
4. Recruiting and selecting salespersons.
5. Training salespersons.
6. Organizing the sales force.
7. Designing sales territories.
8. Assigning salespersons to territories.
9. Motivating salespersons.
10. Compensating salespersons.
11. Evaluating salespersons.

In the three sales management cases that are in this section, the reader will work to make decisions in most of these areas. Again, the next section of this note is a short reminder of some of the concepts related to each of these decisions.

Definition of the Selling Job

The beginning point of all sales management decisions is the definition of the selling job to be performed. For example, is the job basically just order taking or are there complex engineering presentations involved? In defining a particular selling job, one must keep in mind the role of personal selling in the overall marketing strategy and understand well the needs of the buyer or buyers involved. The competitive and physical environments of the job are also important considerations.

Desired Characteristics for Salespersons

Out of the definition of the selling job, the manager is able to establish a set of criteria for determining the type of person who should perform the selling job. One should list the personal background and individual skills and qualifications that are necessary to effectively perform the defined job. For example, in selling complex electrical equipment, the criteria might include the holding of a degree in electrical engineering, with strong oral communications skills to make presentations to customers.

Sales Force Size

Determining the necessary size of a sales force involves determining the effort level capabilities of an average salesperson and dividing that into a measure of the total selling job to be done. In doing so, judgments must be made on how many total accounts to serve, how often to call on them, and how many accounts an average salesperson can effectively handle.

Recruiting and Selecting Salespersons

The selection of the right salespersons basically involves generating a pool of prospects and evaluating those prospects using the criteria established for the selling job. Information is collected on prospects using application forms, personal interviews, and psychological tests.

Training

The basic objective of training is to bring a salesperson up to the required level of competence in those areas of the defined selling job that were deficient upon hiring. These might include product knowledge, oral presentation skills, field procedures, and so on. Decisions must be made as to who should do the training and where it should be done. Do we let current salespersons do the training in the field or have special people to do it at the office, or some combination?

Organizing the Sales Force

The sales force may be organized on a geographical, product, market, or some combination of these factors basis. If a salesperson can effectively handle all the company's products in a given geographic area, then the geographical structure probably makes the most sense. Otherwise, the product or market basis seem appropriate. The selection between these two approaches depends on whether product or market knowledge is the most important.

Case 17

South-West Pharmaceutical Company*

In August, Frank Van Huesen, vice president of the New Orleans-based advertising agency, Advertising Associates, was sitting in his skyscraper office contemplating a meeting scheduled for the next week. At that time, he was to meet with Lewis Spring, president of South-West Pharmaceutical Company (S.W.P. Company), to discuss agency recommendations for Gentle Care advertising for the next year. Although advertising expenditures for Gentle Care, a skin conditioner for pregnant women, were relatively small, the client was an important account for Advertising Associates, with about $700,000 in billings. Even though the number of pregnant women had been declining, Gentle Care had been experiencing a sudden, unexpected surge in sales. Therefore, planning its future strategy posed a definite challenge to Van Huesen's marketing and advertising expertise. Before the meeting, he had to come up with sound answers to such questions as: "How much to spend for advertising?"; "What media mix to employ?"; and "What to say in messages for Gentle Care?"

Company Background

The S.W.P. Company of New Orleans, Louisiana, is the oldest manufacturer of proprietary medicine products in the United States. It all began in Iberville, Louisiana, in 1826 when Captain N. L. Denard obtained the "formula" for a tonic from the Choctaw Indians. Formulation took place on south Louisiana plantations for many years until 1860 when Charles Thomas Spring, a pharmacist, bought the formula for $25 and started making and selling bottles of the tonic for $5. The company was moved to New Orleans in 1874 because of the city's better transportation facilities, and growth continued in a sporadic way. In 1955, the Stanfield Company was absorbed and with it another unique product, Gentle Care, joined the S.W.P. product line.

---

*This case was prepared by Kenneth L. Bernhardt and John S. Wright, Professor of Marketing, Georgia State University. Copyright © 1996 by Kenneth L. Bernhardt.

EXHIBIT 1 Product and price list for S.W.P. Company

Wholesale discounts: 18 percent on net billing	Quantity: 150-pound minimum prepaid shipment. Any assortment of S.W.P. Company products in original case lots can be combined to meet these shipping requirements.		Resale to retailers. At list less applicable wholesaler's cash discount when earned. Terms: 2 percent if paid within 30 days from date of invoice. Net and due after discount period.	
Product	Unit size	List dozen	List	Packed case	Case weight
Gentle Care liquid	3 oz.	$29.60	$3.70	3 doz.	9½ lbs.
Gentle Care cream	2 oz.	29.60	3.70	1 doz.	3 lbs.

The company now manufactures and sells three principal products: Spring's Tonic, Ease Eye Drops, and Gentle Care. Exhibit 1 shows a partial product list which includes package sizes, prices charged to retailers per dozen items, suggested "list" prices to be charged customers by retailers, as well as case sizes and weights. Wholesalers selling the products receive an 18 percent discount for performing their functions. Sales volume for the company was at an annual rate of less than $5 million, and had been growing about 10 percent per year.

The firm's products have traditionally been sold in retail drugstores, which received the merchandise through drug and specialty wholesalers. The company employs one salesman who calls upon present and prospective customers, primarily in the Southwest. Mr. Spring is active in several trade associations and spends much time traveling to cement trade relations. Management is keenly aware that customer buying patterns are changing and, therefore, efforts are being made to have company products stocked in discount stores, supermarkets, and chain drugstores. Consequently, many "direct" sales are made to large retailers and to rack jobbers. Of its 3,000 active accounts, 500 are large retail chains, and the remaining 2,500 are to a variety of middlemen including wholesale grocers, rack jobbers, and specialty jobbers.

The Product and Its Market

Gentle Care is also very old as products go, having been first sold in 1869. The product, which is a skin conditioner especially formulated for use during pregnancy to relieve tight, dry skin, was originally provided in liquid form. When massaged on the skin, it has a very soothing and relaxing effect on the muscles. Gentle Care's basic ingredients include winter-pressed cottonseed oil, soft-liquid soap, camphor, and menthol.

In 1967, a line extension of the product was devised in the form of Gentle Care cream, whose ingredients include cottonseed oil, laury, myrestyl, cetyl, stearyl in absorption base, glycerin, sorbitol, perfume, and color. Currently the cream form comprises a small but growing percentage of Gentle Care sales.

Van Huesen describes the industry as "body lotions and creams for use during pregnancy." Exhibit 2 shows the few other companies in the industry, along with the pricing they employ. It should be noted that the other brands are very small in comparison to Gentle Care, are sold primarily through maternity shops, and have only regional or local distribution. None advertises, nor do the brands pose a competitive threat to Gentle Care, which is believed to have better distribution for its sales volume than any other drug product in the United States. By its very nature, the product is a "slow-mover" at the store level, and smaller outlets order the product in half-dozen lots. No deals have been made available to the middlemen in the past; however, an experiment was planned for the fall when retailers would be offered a "one free in five" package deal.

EXHIBIT 2   Industry and pricing structure—body lotions and creams for use during pregnancy

Company	Product	Size	Retail price	Wholesale price per dozen
S.W.P. Company, New Orleans, La.	Gentle Care (liquid)	3 oz.	$3.70	$25.60
	Gentle Care (cream)	2 oz.	3.70	25.60
Leading Lady Foundations, Inc., Cleveland, Ohio	Anne Alt Body Lotion	8 oz.	3.00	n.a.
Mothers Beautiful, Miami Beach, Fla.	Mothers Beautiful Body Lotion	8 oz.	2.50	n.a.
Shannon Manufacturing Co., North Hollywood, Calif.	Mary Jane Maternity Lotion	8 oz.	3.00	n.a.
Maternity Modes, Niles, Ill.	Maternity Modes Protein Body Creme	4 oz.	3.00	n.a.

n.a. = not available.

Isolating the target market for Gentle Care may appear to be an obvious exercise—it consists of all pregnant women. Within that category of womankind, however, Van Huesen thought the prime target for such lotions and creams should be the first-time mother-to-be. If she decides to use such a product at that time, it is quite likely she will again use it during succeeding pregnancies. What role is played by "influencers" (the expectant mother's mother, older mothers in the neighborhood, aunts, nurses, maternity shop personnel, and so forth) in the purchase and use decision is not known.

Birthrates in the United States have been declining precipitously, and the United States is approaching a state of zero population growth, a point where deaths and births are in balance. Reference to Exhibit 3 shows, nevertheless, that one woman in seven in the 20–24 age range does have a baby in a given year.

Little is known about the consumer decision to use these lotions and creams during pregnancy. How do women learn about such products? Are influencers important to the decision, or does advertising inform the expectant mother of the product's availability? In the absence of specific research into this area of consumer behavior, it was assumed by both Mr. Spring and Mr. Van Huesen that advertising

EXHIBIT 3 Birthrate by age of mother and color, United States

Age (years)	Nonwhite			White		
	Ten years ago	Now	Percent change	Ten years ago	Now	Percent change
15–19	15.3%*	12.9%	−16%	7.9%	5.4%	−32%
20–24	29.3	18.5	−37	24.8	14.5	−42
25–29	22.2	13.6	−39	19.4	13.5	−30
30–34	13.6	8.0	−41	11.0	6.6	−45
35–39	7.5	4.0	−47	5.3	2.7	−49
40–44	2.2	1.2	−45	1.5	0.6	−60

* Table is read as follows: Ten years ago, of all nonwhite women between 15 and 19 years of age, 15.3 percent gave birth.

plays a significant, if not *the* critical, role. The product recently had been experiencing large increases in sales, with this year's sales expected to be about 50 percent greater than the level of two years earlier, in spite of a decline in the market potential for the product category. Exhibit 4 gives the sales of Gentle Care for the previous seven years, as well as the advertising-to-sales ratio for that period. The large sales increases were being achieved by both the liquid and cream forms of Gentle Care.

EXHIBIT 4 Gentle Care—advertising-to-sales ratios

	Sales	Advertising	A/S ratio
Seven years ago	$189,578	$140,512	0.74
Six years ago	195,664	82,092	0.42
Five years ago	205,102	69,390	0.34
Four years ago	250,314	69,050	0.28
Three years ago	253,818	40,902	0.16
Two years ago	264,286	68,176	0.26
Last year	315,918	65,706	0.21
Current year	400,000 (projected)	75,000	0.19

Marketing Strategy

The marketing strategies employed by S.W.P. Company are reflections of the marketing philosophy of its president, Lewis Spring. Before joining the firm, Spring worked in promotional jobs in the petroleum and entertainment industries and he views promotion as an important part of his job. Technical people are hired to handle the manufacturing and physical distribution sides of the business, while Spring concentrates on the marketing-sales-advertising operations.

This circumstance simplifies Van Huesen's job. There are no layers of bureaucratic approval of S.W.P. Company. Once Van Huesen and Spring agreed on a strategy to be followed, it was implemented. The process involved a combination of Spring's ideas on how proprietary drugs should be promoted and Van Huesen's understanding of how advertising can be used to achieve the company's goals.

For a long time, Spring has maintained great faith in the importance of package design to the sales success of the kind of products manufactured by his company. The company once changed advertising agencies over this issue; Spring thought the Gentle Care package needed changing, while agency personnel felt that such a change would destroy the product's "image with the consumer."

Another of Spring's marketing guidelines is that the smaller company "must find the one single most important use for the product" and build the promotional program around that point. Closely related is another philosophical belief, namely that the firm "should do what the competition is not doing," whether it is in the area of media selection, creative strategy, or other promotional concerns.

The Advertising Budget

The company management does not have any "cut-and-dried" formula for arriving at the advertising budget. Advertising's importance to the sales of company products is recognized by Lewis Spring; nevertheless, as Exhibit 4 reveals, the advertising-to-sales ratio has been declining over the past decade without a consequent decline in sales. The relatively large budget seven years ago was due to the simultaneous introduction of the cream and a change in package design, which was accompanied by an increased budget to help secure greater distribution. The drastic cutback in advertising expenditures three years ago was due to an unsuccessful diversification into the cosmetic business that necessitated a recoupment of financial resources. The relative cutbacks this year and last year were in response to tight money conditions at the time and to a management decision to "make this year a year of profit." Spring believes, however, that such cutbacks can be only a temporary phenomenon; in respect to advertising, he holds that "you must be everlastingly at it."

Media Strategy

As has been characteristic of the proprietary drug industry for generations, Gentle Care was traditionally advertised by means of small space ads placed in newspapers. Twenty years ago it was realized that, for a product whose market is as highly segmented as that for Gentle Care, this media strategy resulted in a great deal of "wasted circulation" of the advertising message; thereafter, advertising for the product was concentrated solely in magazines.

As shown in Exhibit 5, there exists an appreciable number of magazines which can be characterized as "baby oriented." Of course, within the category, those read during the prenatal stage are desired by the producers of pregnancy body skin conditioners. Once the child is born, the product is no longer needed, although it is possible that the woman will continue to use the product for other skin care purposes.

For many years, Gentle Care was featured in smaller-sized ads (one-sixth page to one-half page) in 8 or 10 magazines, one or two insertions per year. In other words, the emphasis was placed on the *reach* strategy—trying to get the message before as many different prospects as possible for a given expenditure of advertising dollars. This strategy was replaced with one aiming at greater *frequency;* fewer publications were used with more insertions in each magazine over the year. The

EXHIBIT 5 Baby-oriented magazines

Magazine	Frequency of publication	Circulation	CPM (B/W)	Page rate (B/W) one insertion
American Baby	Monthly	1,108,700	$8.92	$ 9,890
Baby Care	Quarterly	575,785	7.49	4,310
Baby Talk	Monthly	1,021,693	8.28	8,460
Congratulations	Annually	2,624,120*	n.a.[†]	20,670
Expecting	Quarterly	855,013	9.11	7,790
Good Housekeeping	Monthly	5,703,732	3.94	22,765
Modern Romances	Monthly	752,339	3.48	2,645
Mothers' Manual	Bimonthly	913,085	8.77	8,010
Parents' Magazine and				
Better Family Living	Monthly	2,017,029	6.52	13,565
Redbook's Young Mother	Annually	1,519,888	4.77	19,345

*Distributed to specific places; CPM not determinable.
[†]n.a. = not available.
Source: SRDS *Consumer Magazines and Farm Publications.*

EXHIBIT 6 Gentle Care—current advertising plan

Magazine	Size ad	Cost per ad	Number ads	Total cost
Expecting	1/2 page	$6,620	2	$13,240
	(2 1/4 × 6 15/16 inches)			
American Baby	1 col.	3,640	3	10,920
	(2 3/8 × 5 inches)			
Mothers' Manual	1/3 page	3,600	2	7,200
	(4 9/16 × 5 inches)			
Parents' Magazine	1 col.	5,330	2	10,660
	(2 1/4 × 5 inches)			
McFadden's Group	1/3 page	6,082	4	24,328
True Story	(2 1/4 × 5 1/16 inches)			
Photoplay				
TV-Radio Mirror				
True Confessions				
Motion Picture				
True Romance				
True Experience				
True Love				
Redbook				
Reserve for special				
regional				
availabilities				4,000
				$70,348
Estimated production				4,652
				$75,000

rationale behind this change was based on the fact that there is no seasonality in the product's use; women become pregnant throughout the 12 months.

The current advertising schedule for Gentle Care is shown in Exhibit 6. One key change made last year was switching out of *Redbook,* where the product had been advertised every other month adjacent to the magazine's "expectant mother's" column. To ensure that position, larger space had to be purchased, so for the same amount of money, the entire McFadden Group of eight magazines was available, although for small-sized ads. The agency's media department felt that the McFadden Group would be a better match with the target market for Gentle Care than would *Redbook. Parents' Magazine* was included in the media schedule primarily to allow the company to use the seal of approval in Gentle Care advertising, even though its impact on sales was undetermined.

Creative Strategy

Before Advertising Associates took over the account five years earlier, Gentle Care was advertised through ads which featured the product jar. A typical ad, as created by the former agency, is shown in Exhibit 7. This ad shows an attractive woman's head with her hand apparently rubbing her shoulder. The headline is very general in content; it is not until the reader sees the subheading does she

EXHIBIT 7   Pre-Advertising Associates ad for Gentle Care

learn that Gentle Care is for use during pregnancy. Seals of approval from two well-known certification agencies were also featured, which meant that advertisements had to be placed in *Good Housekeeping* and *Parents' Magazine*. Exhibit 8 shows the first advertisement in company history which prominently displays that the product is for use during pregnancy.

EXHIBIT 8   First Gentle Care ad prominently featuring use during pregnancy

The new campaign inaugurated by Advertising Associates, an example of which is shown in Exhibit 9, was more direct; the reader could readily determine who used the product and for what purpose. One seal of approval, that of *Good Housekeeping* magazine, was dropped in the belief that the magazine's audience was much older than the target market for Gentle Care. The decision was discussed at length because the role of older women in the purchase and use of the product was not known.

Changing standards and values in our society are reflected in the current campaign as shown in Exhibit 10. Here a nude model is seen actually applying the product as it would be done by the purchaser. Furthermore, the headline is direct and to the point. The *Parents' Magazine* seal is again featured, and the product package is illustrated in a subordinate position.

EXHIBIT 9   First ad in the Advertising Associates campaign

Make Yourself Comfortable.

Treat your skin to a soothing beauty massage with GENTLE CARE. It's the body skin conditioner that's especially recommended during pregnancy. The rich, lubricating liquid helps tight, dry skin stay soft and supple. It brings you ease and comfort while you wait. Look for GENTLE CARE at your drug counter.

Gentle Care

The New Advertising Plan

In mulling over the advertising history of his client, Van Huesen jotted down several questions which he felt needed answering before he could design the new advertising plan for Gentle Care:

1. What level of advertising should be recommended for next year?
2. What changes, if any, should be made in media strategy? Are specialized magazines the best media choice for Gentle Care? If so, are "baby-oriented" publications the best choice?

EXHIBIT 10   Example of current advertising for Gentle Care

Don't let your tummy get out of shape while you're pregnant.

Give your tight, dry skin a soothing massage with Gentle Care. Its special formula will help relieve the taut feeling and minimize itching. And it will help your skin stay soft and supple. So make yourself comfortable. Look for Gentle Care in cream or liquid form at your drug counter.

3. Is the frequency rather than the reach strategy to be continued for Gentle Care advertising next year?
4. Should the *Parents' Magazine* seal be retained?
5. What changes, if any, should Van Huesen recommend in the creative strategy for the product?

Once these questions were answered, Mr. Van Huesen felt he was ready to meet with Mr. Spring to present his recommendations for the Gentle Care advertising. Van Huesen knew from past experience that he could anticipate some probing questions from Mr. Spring concerning how the effectiveness of the advertising for Gentle Care could be measured.

Case 18

Suburban CableVision*

Kim Harrison had joined Communications Industries, Inc., six months ago, following her graduation from a well-known midwestern business school. Now, in late 1986, she had been promoted to marketing manager for Suburban Cable-Vision, a New England subsidiary of Communications Industries (CI), with the responsibility for marketing cable services in four suburban communities. Suburban CableVision had just been acquired, and a new management team had been put in place.

Harrison had been assigned the task of developing a marketing plan for 1987. Given that the new year was only a few weeks away, she realized that she did not have much time. The problem was complicated by the regulatory changes that were due to take place on January 1. The new regulations allowed considerably greater flexibility in packaging and pricing cable TV services. As she began to review the marketing files left by her predecessor, she realized that this holiday season was going to be very busy for her and very different than the previous few years when she was on Christmas break from her university studies.

Background on the Cable TV Industry

The cable television industry was born in 1948. At that time, Ed Parsons of Astoria, Oregon, lived at the foot of a mountain. The mountain was between his home, which contained a TV set with nothing but snow on the screen, and the transmitters for the television stations he wanted to watch. Parsons climbed the mountain with antenna in hand, secured it at the top, and strung a wire all the way back down to his TV set. As the only person in town with good picture quality, he soon had friends and neighbors at his house all of the time. When neighbors asked him if he would hook up their sets to his wire, he quickly agreed, allowing him and his wife to have time alone together for the first time since he had climbed the mountain.

*This case was prepared by Kenneth L. Bernhardt and James Novo. Copyright © 1987 by Kenneth L. Bernhardt.

After this birth of cable television, the industry grew very slowly. In areas where TV reception was poor, people put up towers and ran cable to those households willing to pay for better reception. By 1975, only about 10 percent of U.S. television households were cable subscribers. RCA launched the first communications satellite, SATCOM I, in 1975. Programs from the East Coast could now be received by the West Coast instantaneously. Home Box Office became the first company to provide programming specifically aimed at cable subscribers. Others followed, and today there are over 150 programming sources. The rapid increase in programming led to a rapid growth in the number of cable subscribers.

Consumers were expected to spend more than $10 billion on cable television in 1986, more than they spend on going to the movies or renting home video programs. More than 77,000 people were employed by cable systems. The number of subscribers had doubled during the previous five years, and now totaled 42 million. More than three fourths of all TV households now had cable available to them, but only about 60 percent of those households able to receive cable actually chose to buy it.

The number of subscribers had grown at a compound annual growth rate of 14.2 percent between 1980 and 1985. This rate was expected to slow to under 5 percent between 1986 and 1990. An Arthur D. Little study indicated that spending on new cable systems would decline from a peak of $1.4 billion in 1982 to $160 million by 1990. Ms. Harrison recognized that the future of the industry lay in increasing the number of subscribers and revenue from existing systems rather than from laying new cable in areas that previously did not have cable TV available.

Planning for 1987 was complicated by the Cable Communications Policy Act of 1984 (CCPA). The act took away the power of state and local authorities to regulate the rates that cable companies charge subscribers for basic cable service. At the same time, the Federal Communications Commission was phasing out such regulations as the requirement that local cable systems carry all available local channels. Thus, starting January 1, 1987, local systems were free to raise rates and to put whatever programming they wanted on the channels.

The amount of money the average U.S. subscriber paid for cable TV services nearly doubled between 1980 and 1986, to $21 per month. One leading cable TV analyst recently estimated that the average monthly fee would grow to $28 in 1990 and $39 by 1995. Others in the industry were afraid that higher prices could drive away potential new subscribers and cause some existing subscribers to drop cable. A number of premium channels—such as Home Box Office (HBO), Showtime, and The Movie Channel—were already experiencing a slowing in their growth patterns as consumers appeared to be rejecting expensive cable bills that included multiple premium services.

Background on Communications Industries and Suburban CableVision

Communications Industries (CI) owned and operated four cable television systems servicing 43 cities in the states of Delaware, Connecticut, Rhode Island, and Massachusetts. The four systems had cable passing 315,000 homes, 196,000 of which subscribed to basic cable programming services. More than 113,000 (62 percent) also subscribed to premium programming services, such as movie channels or pay sports channels. CI was the 35th largest cable company but was very small compared to the larger firms in the industry (see Exhibit 1). Total revenues for CI were in excess of $100 million from four television stations, six radio stations, and outdoor advertising services in addition to the cable TV revenues.

EXHIBIT 1   1985 Statistics on Communications Industries, Suburban CableVision, and 10 largest cable companies

Rank	Company	Basic subscriptions (million)	Pay units (million)	Homes passed (million)	Percent basic /Homes passed*	Percent premium /Basic†
1	Tel-Communications	3.7	2.7	6.4	57	73
2	ATC (Time Inc.)	2.6	2.3	4.6	56	91
3	Group W	2.0	1.6	3.9	53	76
4	Cox Communications	1.5	1.5	2.7	57	97
5	Storer	1.5	1.5	2.7	56	95
6	Warner-Amex	1.2	.9	2.7	45	75
7	Times-Mirror	1.0	.8	2.0	49	87
8	Continental	1.0	1.1	1.8	54	114
9	Newhouse	.9	1.0	1.5	62	107
10	Viacom	.8	.6	1.5	54	78
35	Communications Industries	.2	.2	.3	62	83
NA	Suburban CableVision	.01	.02	.02	64	119

*Basic penetration $= \dfrac{\text{Basic subscribers}}{\text{Homes passed (those with access to cable)}}$

†Premium-to-basic ratio $= \dfrac{\text{Premium services subscribed to}}{\text{Basic subscribers}}$

Suburban CableVision marketed cable services in four communities. As described in Exhibit 2, the communities had very different profiles. Downing was a blue-collar, industrial town. Suburban had penetrated 75 percent of the homes in Downing with access to cable, which was the highest penetration of any of the cities in the area. However, the number of premium service subscriptions was lower than in the other areas. Some of the Suburban managers attributed this to the lower incomes of Downing's households—many could not afford basic plus several pay channels. They felt that the basic penetration was high because TV was a major form of entertainment for these people, and they were willing to pay for basic cable service.

The town of Anderson had a high percentage of the population employed in white-collar and managerial jobs. There was also a large elderly population. Suburban managers felt that these people would drive some distance to attend plays and the opera, so TV was less important to them. Those who did subscribe to basic cable, however, were likely to buy more pay services because of their relatively high incomes.

The towns of North Lexington and Middletown were rural, farm areas just beginning to be developed. Although these suburbs were relatively far from the downtown metropolitan area, a number of subdivisions were being created and

EXHIBIT 2   Profile of four towns

	Downing	Anderson	North Lexington–Middletown	
Basic penetration*	75%	58%	61%	
Premium-to-basic ratio[†]	1.00	1.26	1.26	
Proportion of total households	one-third	one-third	one-third	
Demographics	Blue-collar, industrial	Very white-collar, managerial, elderly	Rural, farm areas rapidly being developed into far-out suburban subdivisions; young families; mixed demographics.	
Number of years system in operation	5	4	3	2

*Basic penetration $= \dfrac{\text{Basic subscribers}}{\text{Homes passed (those with access to cable)}}$

[†]Premium-to-basic ratio $= \dfrac{\text{Premium services subscribed to}}{\text{Basic subscribers}}$

many young families were moving into the area. The basic penetration and purchase of premium services were similar to the rates experienced in Anderson.

Although the population in Suburban's market area was growing relatively slowly, the company had experienced rapid growth. During 1985–86 the number of households with access to cable increased by only 1.4 percent. The system as a whole comprised 22,675 households, and 14,600 (64 percent) of these were basic cable subscribers. Although the number of basic subscribers had grown by 7.8 percent in the previous year, the number of pay channel subscriptions, 17,200, was up only 2 percent over the previous year.

Channels 2 through 42 contained a wide variety of basic cable programming. Included were several news channels, network and independent broadcast stations, and specialized channels devoted to local programming, movies, children's programs, and music and culture (see Exhibit 3). On channels 44 through 52, a number of premium channels were available for an extra charge above the basic cable service.

Pricing

Suburban's pricing structure was very complex (see Exhibit 4). Basic service was broken down into five tiers. The lowest level of service generally available, basic service, consisted of tiers 1 and 2 (channels 2 through 29). Subscribers signing up for this basic service were charged $7.25 per month. The three other tiers available had options to add super stations (tier 3, $2.05 per month), family stations (tier 4, $3.10), and sports stations (tier 5, $2.35). In addition, eight premium channels were available at prices ranging from $7.95 per month to $11 per month.

EXHIBIT 3   Guide to the satellite and premium channels

Channel	Title	Description
2	Local origination	Programming produced locally for all subscribers.
3	Eternal Word	"Inspirational programming"; Catholic Cable Network.
4	Lifetime	Women-oriented programming; many subscriber call-in shows; exercise, lifestyles, star interviews.
5 and 6 (seen on 55 and 56)	Reuters News & Sports	(5 and 6 are a "channel lock," which keeps other channels in tune.) News and financial reports.
7	The Weather Channel	Local and world weather reports.
8	CNN (Cable News Network)	Live coverage of national and world news.
9	CNN Headline	"Around the world in 30 minutes"; for the busy news viewer.
10	C-SPAN (Cable Satellite Public Affairs Network)	Senate and House committee meetings from start to finish; viewer call-in programs.
11	Public access	"Your community channel"; Suburban CableVision supplies the equipment and training free of charge to anyone in the community who wishes to produce and cablecast a television show or event for the community.
12	Educational access	Channel reserved for use by the school system of the community.
13	Middletown College	Channel reserved for use by local college.
14–29		These channels are the network and independent broadcast stations in the area.
30	WOR 9, New York	Movie classics and television programming from the late 60s and 70s; New York news and sports with Knicks, Rangers, Islanders, Devils, Jets, and Mets.
31	CKSH 9, Canada	Canadian television station; broadcasting in French; programming similar to U.S. network stations.
32	WTBS (Turner Broadcast System)	Movie classics and TV programming from the late 60s and 70s.
34	CBN (Cable Broadcast Network)	Family programming; specializes in movies and early television shows from the 50s and 60s.
35	Nickelodeon	Cable channel for kids of all ages; quality non-violent entertainment.
37	SPN	From movies to music to international entertainment.
38	Nashville Network	Sports, comedy, dance, and news about country-western favorites.
39	MTV–Music Television	Video music, music news, interviews with the stars.
40	Arts & Entertainment	Cultural programming.
41	USA Network	TV series from the 70s no longer seen on broadcast television.
42	ESPN	The total sports network.
44	Sports Channel	The best of Eastern sports; all home Celtics games live.
45	Bravo	International award-winning films; exciting theater productions featuring the world's best performers; opera, symphony, and ballet.
46	Showtime	Latest box office hits.
47	HBO	Hollywood blockbusters; original HBO premier films.
48	Cinemax	More movies than HBO and Showtime; late-night, adult-only films.
49	TMC (The Movie Channel)	More movies than HBO and Showtime.
50	HTN (Home Theatre Network)	Family programming; the movie channel that doesn't have sex and violence.
51	Disney	Disney movies and classic cartoons.
52	NESN	New England's Sports Network; exclusive live coverage of Bruins and Red Sox.

EXHIBIT 4 Pricing structure

Basic tiers/premium channels	Channels	Service	Cost/month
Tiers 1 and 2	2–29	Basic service	$ 7.25
Tier 3	30–32	Super stations	2.05
Tier 4	34–40	Family stations	3.10
Tier 5	41, 42	Sports stations	2.35
Sports Channel	44	Celtics and eastern sports	6.95
Bravo/HBO/Showtime/			
Movie Channel/Cinemax	45–49	Movie channels	11.00 each
HTN	50	Family movies	7.95
Disney	51	Disney movies and cartoons	11.00
NESN	52	Bruins and Red Sox	7.95

Note: If subscribers order basic tiers 1–4, they get a $1 discount off of all $11 services (movie channels plus Disney) and HTN. If subscribers order any three premium channels, they get Bravo free.

Exhibit 5 shows a breakdown by level of service. Only 1,000 subscribers, 6.9 percent, subscribed to tiers 1 and 2 only. Ms. Harrison believed that the current system was much too complicated and caused problems in the development of advertising copy. In addition, it was difficult for Suburban's telephone sales representatives to explain the system to potential new subscribers. Thus, she felt that it was important to create a new system now that the company had the ability to change rates without having to get approval from each city council. She wondered whether she should include tier 3 as part of a basic subscriber package and felt that there was a marketing opportunity to simplify the system into basic and super basic (consisting of all five tiers). Other systems typically charged between $5 and $15 for basic service and anywhere from $7 to $12 for premium channels.

Ms. Harrison believed that Suburban made more money on basic service than on premium channels. The cost to Suburban for most of the premium movie channels was about $4 per subscriber per month, some being slightly more and some slightly less. The premium sports channels cost about $3. Many of the basic channels did not cost Suburban anything, and most of the others only cost about 25 cents per subscriber per month. Counting all costs for billing, maintaining subscriber records, and programming costs, the average variable cost per month for basic subscribers (tiers 1 through 5) was about $5.

EXHIBIT 5 Breakdown by level of basic service

	Number of subscribers	Percent of subscribers
Tiers 1 and 2 only	1,000	6.9%
Tiers 1, 2, and 3 only	4,550	31.1
Tiers 1, 2, and 4 only	100	.7
Tiers 1, 2, 3, and 4 only	2,950	20.2
Tiers 1, 2, 4, and 5 only	300	2.1
Tiers 1, 2, 3, and 5 only	150	1.0
Tiers 1, 2, 3, 4, 5	5,550	38.0
	14,600	100.0%

Some cable executives believed that "basic subscriptions pay for the costs of the system, and you make your profit from premium channel sal̩ Others felt that subscribers perceived more value in the basic channels and th̩ premium channels were already priced about as high as they could be. In fact, many felt that if basic channel rates were raised, then premium channel rates should be decreased to prevent pricing people out of the cable market. These managers believed that instead of downgrading their service (for example, having one of the premium channels disconnected), many people would simply have the total cable service disconnected. Ms. Harrison had heard that some systems had substantially increased sales of the Disney channel by lowering the price to $7.95. Ms. Harrison knew that she would have to give considerable thought to the issue of how she packaged the channels together and how she priced them.

Advertising

Exhibit 6 contains a copy of the newspaper advertising that Suburban had been running. The campaign had been only moderately successful, and Harrison wondered whether newspaper advertising was just not effective or whether it was the copy itself that caused the poor results.

Suburban had been experimenting recently with the use of direct mail in cooperation with premium channel programming suppliers. For example, it had recently completed a test of a promotion with the Disney channel. The promotion, run in September, was centered around a free preview weekend. Direct mail and print ads informed consumers that they could preview the Disney channel for free, and if they decided to sign up, a 50 percent discount ($5) was given toward the $10 installation charge. While she had not had time to fully evaluate the promotion, she felt that it had been a success. The advertising and mailing costs had been $2,160, but the Disney co-op rebate had covered $783 of this. The Suburban customer service representatives were given 50 cents per new Disney subscriber as their commission. The gross margin (revenue less cost of programming) was $6 per subscriber per month. In addition, Suburban received the $5 installation fee per new subscriber to the Disney channel and incurred only about 25 cents in actual costs for the installation. Over the course of the promotion, 188 subscribers took advantage of the offer and added the Disney channel to their service. This represented a 14 percent increase in the number of people subscribing to the Disney channel.

A similar offer from HBO and Cinemax was far less successful. This promotion was communicated to subscribers via print advertising only. Only 12 subscribers added HBO as a result of the offer, and nobody added Cinemax.

During the fall, Suburban also tested a heavy newspaper advertising campaign for adding The Movie Channel. New subscribers were given an AM/FM radio premium. Only 18 sales were attributable to the campaign, and Harrison thus had questions about the effectiveness of newspaper advertising and premiums.

A second direct mail campaign was tested, promoting the Sports Channel and the New England Sports Network. Sales of these two premium channels

...he difference between these two pictures?

Cable Channels 2 - 29

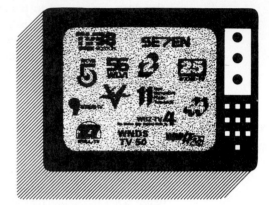

SUBURBAN CABLEVISION

All area stations, *and MORE*

Less than 24¢ per day.

Including wireless remote control and monthly cable guide.

---

increased 25 percent and 17 percent, respectively, at a cost per new subscriber of $2.58. No discounts or premiums were used.

As a result of the successes with the premium channel direct mail promotions, Harrison decided to test targeted direct mail for basic subscriber acquisition. Eleven hundred mailers were sent to apartment addresses that had never had cable service. The mailers cost 25 cents each, and 3 percent of those receiving them signed up. In addition, the mailer was sent to 321 homes where cable had been disconnected because the residents were moving. These homes represented 30 percent of the moves; the other 70 percent had been reconnected when the new residents moved in. One sixth of those receiving the mailing signed up for cable. Harrison thought that there might be potential with direct mail targeted to subsegments of the nonsubscriber base, including the elderly, educators, managers, and those who disliked network TV.

In the early days of cable, there were a number of "truck chasers"—consumers who would actually chase after the cable television truck when it was in their neighborhood laying cable. They would beg to get hooked up immediately, and direct salespeople were used extensively to make door-to-door sales calls in neighborhoods where cable was being laid. With changing demographics, two-income families, and increased customer sophistication, Harrison doubted whether door-to-door salespeople would be effective today, but she wondered whether it would be worth testing. A good salesperson would probably cost $25,000, including benefits.

She also wondered whether it might make sense to use public relations to help sell cable subscriptions. She was aware of Toys For Tots campaigns in various cities. In return for bringing in a toy for an orphan, the installation fee for new subscribers would be waived.

Harrison's predecessor had recommended a public relations program shortly before he left, but a decision had not been made on the program. He had recommended that Suburban sponsor a telethon in North Lexington in support of raising money for the renovation of the local library. There were 1,200 households in North Lexington that had never subscribed to cable, and anyone from these households who donated $25 or more to the telethon would be given free cable installation. Harrison made a note to review this plan to see whether by changing or keeping its present form it would be a good promotional vehicle for the coming year.

Other Potential Segments

Harrison was unsure about exactly which segments should be targeted. Much emphasis in the industry had been devoted to increasing the amount of revenue per cable household. Adopting this as a goal would mean that efforts should be directed at increasing the number of services to each current subscriber household, thus increasing the total revenue.

One industry leader believed instead that it's easier to acquire a nonsubscriber than to get someone who is already paying $20 a month to pay $30. This person recommended that cable systems target the "Young and Busies," conveying the message that cable provides a sense of control over one's viewing habits. He also recommended going after TV lovers already predisposed to the product category and promoting cable's variety and choices.

Still another target market recommended by others in the industry was videocassette recorder (VCR) owners. A recent study had shown a relationship between VCR ownership and cable subscriptions. Only 18.5 percent of nonsubscribers owned a VCR versus 27 percent for basic-only subscribers. The percent owning a VCR increased to 33 percent for those who subscribed to one premium service, and to 34 percent for those who subscribed to two services.

Another recent study indicated that VCR ownership was related to cable subscriber behavior, depending on the degree to which the VCR owner rented tapes. As shown in Exhibit 7, light renters of VCR tapes were more likely than average to upgrade (add premium services), and much less likely than average to downgrade (cancel premium channels) or disconnect the cable service. Harrison had read in a trade journal about one leading cable company that had been testing a strategy of positioning itself as an expert consultant on video electronics. This cable company promoted a $15 VCR hookup kit, and even offered to come out and hook up a subscriber's VCR for a fee. The company offered technical assistance over the telephone to its subscribers, and had begun selling GE VCRs in several markets. The trade journal article reported that the company had sold 389 VCRs in one and one-half months in a four-market test. Special discounts were offered, tied to a pay channel upgrade campaign. Given that industry projections indicated that 50 percent of the population would soon have VCRs, she wondered whether Suburban should target VCR owners in its advertising and promotional efforts.

EXHIBIT 7   Impact of VCR ownership on subscriber behavior (indexed against all cable subscribers)

	All cable subscribers	Non-VCR owners	VCR owners	Heavy renters	Light renters
Downgrade rate	100	100	100	115	50
Disconnect rate	100	105	89	114	55
Upgrade rate	100	112	88	54	132

Source: *Cable Television Administrative and Marketing Society Newsletter* 1, no. 3 (1985).

Another potential market that she thought should be given some consideration was former subscribers. She thought a direct mail campaign targeted toward these households might have a high payoff. Many in the industry were concerned about "churn." Churn was a result of households downgrading their service or having it totally disconnected, and was computed by dividing the number downgrading or disconnecting each month by the total number of subscribers at the beginning of the month. Depending on the season (it was higher in the summer and lower in the winter), the churn percentage for Suburban had been running between 2 and 3 percent for basic service, and between 4 and 6 percent for premium channels. If she chose to concentrate on increasing retention of subscribers (thus reducing churn), there were a number of promotional techniques that could be used. Some cable systems had experienced success in mailing letters to new subscribers that explained all aspects of cable. Thus these better-educated people were able to get more out of their subscriptions. She felt that it would be important to beef up customer service, since some people disconnected in frustration after having trouble getting billing and reception problems taken care of promptly and competently. Finally, she had heard that some cable systems had had some success in reducing churn by using advertising to inform people about programs on cable channels. Apparently, bringing these programs to the attention of subscribers through advertising made them appreciate the service more, and thus they were less likely to downgrade or disconnect. Suburban's churn rate was about average for the industry, and she wondered whether it made any sense to use her promotional budget to reduce churn.

Other Considerations

Suburban's system used the latest technology and was an "addressable" system. This meant that the subscriber's service could be changed by merely pushing a button at the central office. It also allowed the use of pay-per-view (PPV) television. Basically, PPV is just what the name implies—cable TV customers call their cable company and order a particular movie (or other program, such as a sports event) at one of the times it is offered. The cable company transmits the movie and bills the customer accordingly. This means that cable companies can offer subscribers the ability to watch a movie at home without having to pay a full month's price for such services as Home Box Office or Showtime. It is also more convenient than renting a videotape: You don't have to have a VCR, and you don't have to leave your house.

One leading industry consultant estimated that by the end of 1986, 2.6 million households will have PPV available, and industry revenues are projected to reach $70 million. The same consultant predicts that by the end of the decade, PPV will reach nearly 10 million cable subscribers and generate revenues of more than $350 million. The typical price of a PPV movie is $4.50 (ranging from $3.95 to $4.95, depending on the particular movie).

Currently, movies are shown first in the movie theaters and then are released on videotape to the tape rental stores. Finally, they become available on premium movie channels, such as HBO. With PPV it is sometimes shown on cable TV before it is released on videotape for rental. Suburban's technology would allow the introduction of PPV movies, and Harrison wondered whether that was the direction in which to go.

Thinking about all of the available alternatives, Harrison recognized the challenging opportunity in front of her. She realized that putting together the marketing plan for the new management team would be quite a job, and thought that she had better get started.

Case 19

Rich's Department Store*

The Executive Committee meeting had been a lengthy session, lasting through most of the morning, but Dick Mills, vice president and sales promotion director of Rich's Department Store, had returned to his office knowing that a major advertising decision was still not ready to be made. And Mills realized that it would be his responsibility to submit a final recommendation on media strategy at the next meeting.

Mr. Mills stared at the two neatly bound research reports that he had placed side by side on his desk. The pair of documents represented summaries of the two presentations that had been made to the Rich's Executive Committee that morning. These studies had been based on exactly the same data, drawn from the same in-store survey of Rich's customers. Each report had been prepared by an experienced and professional marketing researcher. Mills had expected the strong self-interests of the researchers to be reflected in their presentations and interpretations of the survey results, but he was confident that neither person would misrepresent the actual facts.

Mr. Mills had to admit to himself that he had been very surprised at the apparent major contradictions between the two presentations that he had heard earlier that morning. Mr. Mills and the research director of Rich's, who had also attended the morning presentations by the two outside researchers, had discussed the situation briefly after the meeting. The two had decided to separately review the written reports and, then, to meet later in the afternoon to decide what additional steps to take.

Before rereading the reports, Mr. Mills thought back over the events of the past three months that had eventually led to this situation.

Rich's Department Store was both the largest merchant and the largest single advertiser in Atlanta, Georgia. The store had been founded in 1867 and had grown to an annual sales volume of approximately $200 million through its downtown store and six branch stores located in major suburban shopping cen-

---

*This case was prepared by Kenneth L. Bernhardt. Copyright © 1990 Kenneth L. Bernhardt.

ters. The Rich's market share was 40 percent of department store sales in Atlanta and 25 percent of all general merchandise sales.

The Rich's advertising strategy in the past had been to emphasize newspaper advertising for specific sales items and to utilize broadcast media primarily for image purposes. Newspaper was also used for some image-oriented advertising, with occasional direct mailings used to promote specific sales items of merchandise. Rich's is the largest local advertiser in both print and broadcast media.

The two principal daily newspapers in Atlanta are *The Atlanta Journal* (evenings) and the *Atlanta Constitution* (mornings). These are two of the largest circulation newspapers in the South, and both have distinguished journalism traditions, including Pulitzer Prizes. Although both newspapers are owned by the same company, Atlanta Newspapers, Inc., there is little overlap of readership except for the combined Sunday morning edition.

There are 6 TV stations and 40 radio stations in the Atlanta market. However, broadcast media are dominated by WSB-TV and WSB Radio, both of which are owned by Cox Broadcasting Corporation.

Mills recalled that several months earlier, executives of Cox Broadcasting and of their two local stations had met with key executives of Rich's. One topic discussed at that meeting had been possible use of broadcast media to promote individual sales items. WSB had offered to participate with Rich's in a market test to determine the abilities of different media to sell specific items of merchandise.

As a result of these discussions, Mills had held a series of meetings with Jim Landon, research director of WSB-TV and Radio, and Ferguson Rood, research director of the Atlanta Newspapers, Inc., to design the market test. It was eventually decided to conduct the test during Rich's annual Harvest Sale, which has been the merchandising highlight of the year since 1925. This sale runs for two weeks each fall. The test was to center on 10 specific items of merchandise which would be advertised in both print and broadcast media during the first three days of the sale. During this same period, in-store interviews would be conducted by professional interviewers, with all purchasers of these 10 items in three representative stores (see appendixes for detailed survey design, sample questionnaire, and media plan).

At the conclusion of the survey period, the Research Departments of both Atlanta Newspapers, Inc., and WSB were furnished duplicate computer card decks by Rich's containing survey data. It was this data that served as the basis for the presentations that Jim Landon and Ferguson Rood had made to the Rich's Executive Committee. Excerpts from *The Atlanta Journal* and *Constitution* report are in Appendix A, and excerpts from the WSB report are presented in Appendix B.

These were the two presentations that Mills would have to reconcile to arrive at a decision about future media strategy for Rich's. Mills knew that a decision would have to be made quickly, in view of TV production lead times, if any change in media mix were to be considered for the upcoming Christmas sales season.

Appendix A An Analysis of a Rich's In-Store Study of Advertising Effectiveness on Specific Purchase Decisions*

Foreword

This report is the result of an innovative research study conducted by Rich's Department Store in partnership with Atlanta Newspapers, Inc., and Cox Broadcasting Corporation.

The study was designed to measure:

1. The relative performance of newspapers, television, and radio as a source of influence on shoppers' decisions to purchase specific items.
2. Shoppers' exposure to specific item advertising messages.

The advertising period covered in this study consisted of three days (beginning Sunday, September 20) prior to Rich's annual Harvest Sale.

A total of 2,176 interviews were made on Monday and Tuesday, September 21 and 22. The interviews were made in three of Rich's seven stores—Downtown, Lenox Square, and Greenbriar, and focused on the 10 departments in each store where the advertised items were sold.

An Atlanta interviewing firm was employed by Rich's to interview shoppers in each department immediately after they made their purchase. To qualify for the survey, shoppers had to purchase the specific advertised item or a directly related item.

Summary and Interpretation

More than 9 out of 10 shoppers covered in this survey had the specific purchase in mind before going to Rich's, or knew it was *on special.*

Three-fourths of all shoppers recalled being recently exposed to advertising messages for specific items.

More than half of all shoppers' decisions to purchase specific items were attributed to advertising.

Attributions to newspapers were more than twice those of television and radio combined in influencing specific item purchase decisions (71 percent versus 33 percent).

Dollar for dollar . . . newspapers delivered more than three times the influence on specific item purchase decisions than television and radio combined.

The advertising schedule placed in newspapers . . . was conspicuously more effective and more efficient . . . in influencing specific purchase decisions . . . than the saturation schedule placed on television and radio.

---

*Presented by *The Atlanta Journal* and *Constitution* Research & Marketing Department.

See Exhibits A–1 through A–16.

EXHIBIT A–1   Newspaper advertising schedule*

	Sunday Journal and Constitution (inches)	A.M. Constitution (inches)	P.M. Journal (inches)
Sunday	1,064		
Monday		172	247
Tuesday	_____	0	505
Total	1,064	172	752

*1,989 column inches, the equivalent of 11.6 pages, made up the newspaper schedule covered in this survey.

EXHIBIT A–2   Broadcast schedule*

	Television			Radio		
	Sunday	Monday	Tuesday	Sunday	Monday	Tuesday
6 A.M.		X			X	X
7		X			X	X
8		X	X		X	X
9		X	X	X	X	X
10		X		X	X	X
11		X			X	X
12		X	X	X	X	X
1 P.M.	X	X	X	X	X	X
2	X	X	X	X	X	X
3	X	X	X	X	X	X
4	X	X	X	X	X	X
5	X	X	X	X	X	X
6	X	X		X	X	
7	X	X		X	X	
8	X	X				
9	X	X				
10	X	X				
11	X	X				
Total spots	42	86	49	53	121	87
Average number per schedule hour	3.8	4.8	6.1	5.3	8.6	7.2

*438 30-second spots were scheduled to run on five television and five radio stations, for an average of 8 spots per hour, between 6 A.M. and 11 P.M., over the three-day period.

EXHIBIT A–3   Comparison of advertising schedule and budget

	Broadcast spots			Newspaper space
	TV	Radio	Total	(inches)
Hard goods:				
Mattress	12	19	31	35
Carpeting	12	23	35	150
Draperies	16	26	42	407
Vacuum sweeper	15	22	37	172
Color television*	0	0	0	150
Soft goods:				
Handbags	15	27	42	189
Girdles[†]	15	27	42	0
Shoes	15	27	42	398
Shirts*	56	64	120	86
Pant suits	21	26	47	400
Total 10 departments:				
Sunday	42	53	95	1,064
Monday	86	121	207	420
Tuesday	49	87	136	505
Total	177	261	438	1,989
Budget			$27,158	$16,910

*The original broadcast schedule included 20 TV and 24 radio spots for the color television sets to run Tuesday. Since all the sets were sold on Monday, this commercial time was switched to shirts.
[†]While no Playtex girdle ads were scheduled to run in newspapers, other foundation advertising during the test period supported the influence.

EXHIBIT A–4   Interviews

	Number	Percent
Total	2,175	100%
Women	1,764	81
Men	380	18
Couples	31	1
Under 35	963	44
35–49	817	44
50 and older	394	18
White	1,966	90
Nonwhite	209	10
Hard goods	527	24
Mattress	71	3
Carpeting	45	2
Draperies	123	6
Vacuum sweeper	134	6
Color television	154	7
Soft goods	1,649	75
Handbags	284	13
Girdles	249	11
Shoes	393	18
Shirts	483	22
Pant suits	240	11
Distribution of interviews by store		
Downtown	683	31
Lenox Square	848	39
Greenbriar	645	30

EXHIBIT A–5

"Before coming to Rich's today, did you have in mind buying this specific brand/item, or did you decide after you came into the store?"

63 percent of all shoppers had the specific purchase in mind before going to Rich's.

These shoppers described the following as sources of influence on their buying decision when asked: "What was it that gave you the idea to buy this brand/item?"

Advertising	52%
Needed or wanted it	23
Past experience with it	16
Outside source suggestion	6
Other	7

EXHIBIT A–6

"Was the store having a special on this specific brand/item today, or were they selling at the regular price?"

84 percent of all shoppers said the brand/item was on special.

These shoppers gave the following sources when asked: "Where did you learn about that?"

Advertising	63%
Store display/crowds	27
Outside source	6
Other	4

EXHIBIT A–7   Advertising influence

55 percent of all shoppers attributed their specific purchase decision to advertising. Of these, 71 percent attributed their purchase to newspapers, 33 percent to broadcasts (28 percent to television and 9 percent to radio), and 9 percent to mail circulars.

Newspapers and broadcast accounted for 94 percent of all advertising influence. 61 percent of these influences were attributed to newspapers exclusive of broadcast. 23 percent were attributed to broadcast exclusive of newspapers, and 10 percent were attributed to both.

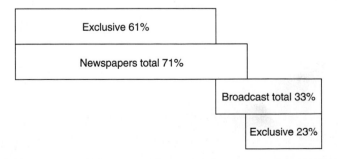

Exclusive 61%

Newspapers total 71%

Broadcast total 33%

Exclusive 23%

EXHIBIT A–8   Advertising influence

Newspapers and television accounted for 90 percent of all advertising influence. 62 percent of these influences were attributed to newspapers exclusive of television. 19 percent were attributed to television exclusive of newspapers, and 9 percent were attributed to both.

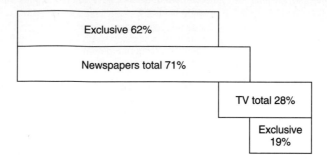

Newspapers and radio accounted for 77 percent of all advertising influence. 68 percent of these influences were attributed to newspapers exclusive of radio. 6 percent were attributed to radio exclusive of newspapers, and 3 percent were attributed to both.

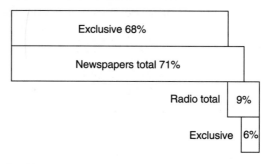

EXHIBIT A–9   Advertising influence—by shopper demographics (among the 55 percent of all shoppers who were influenced by advertising)

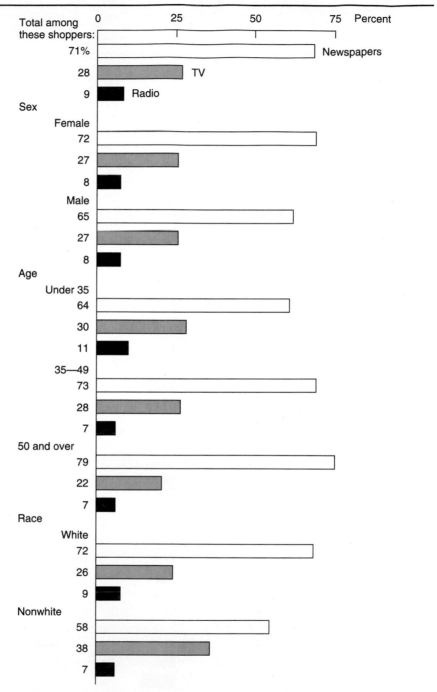

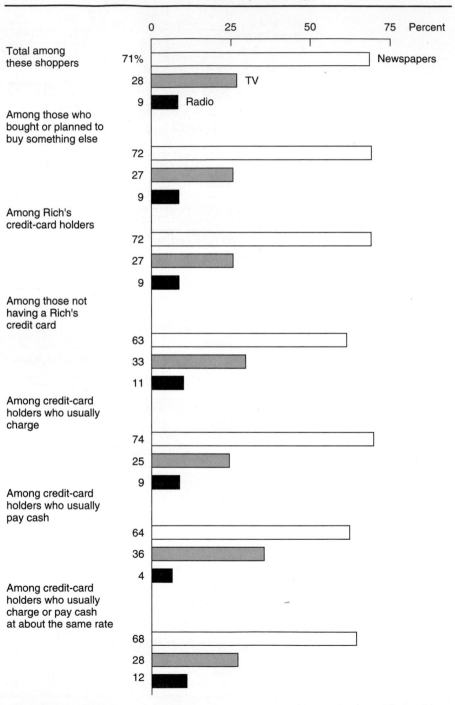

EXHIBIT A–10 Advertising influence—by shopping patterns (among the 55 percent of all shoppers who were influenced by advertising)

EXHIBIT A–11   Share of budget versus share of influence

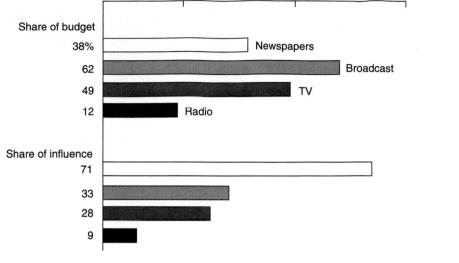

EXHIBIT A–12   Newspapers/broadcast—share of influence versus share of budget by departments

	Newspapers		Broadcast	
	Share of influence	Share of budget	Share of influence	Share of budget
Total	71%	38%	33%	62%
Hard goods	77	45	30	55
Mattress	43	11	69	89
Carpeting	83	39	23	61
Draperies	83	56	22	44
Vacuum sweeper	70	25	45	75
Color TV	99	100	1	—
Soft goods	68	34	34	66
Handbags	68	41	27	59
Girdles	28	—	74	100
Shoes	87	54	25	46
Shirts	63	12	36	88
Pant suits	82	53	16	47

EXHIBIT A–13 Comparison of advertising schedule/budget/shopper influence*

| | Total 10 departments | | | | |
| | Broadcast spots | | Newspaper space | | |
Schedule	TV	Radio	Journal–Constitution	Constitution	Journal
Sunday	42	53	1,064		
Monday	86	121		172	248
Tuesday	49	87		0	505
	177	261	1,064	172	753

*438 broadcast spots versus 1,989 inches; budget—$27,158 for broadcast spots versus $16,910 for newspaper space; and shopper influence—33 percent for broadcast spots versus 71 percent for newspaper space.

EXHIBIT A–14 Advertising exposure

74 percent of all shoppers recalled being exposed to specific advertising messages within the past day or two. Of these, 79 percent recalled newspapers, 53 percent recalled broadcasts (46 percent television, 18 percent radio), and 24 percent recalled mail circulars.

Newspapers and broadcast accounted for 96 percent of all advertising messages. 43 percent recalled newspapers exclusive of broadcast. 17 percent recalled broadcast exclusive of newspapers, and 36 percent recalled both.

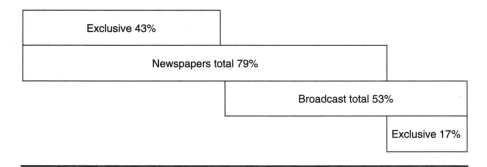

EXHIBIT A–15   Advertising exposure

Newspapers and television accounted for 93 percent of all advertising messages. 47 percent recalled newspapers exclusive of television. 14 percent recalled television exclusive of newspapers, and 32 percent recalled both.

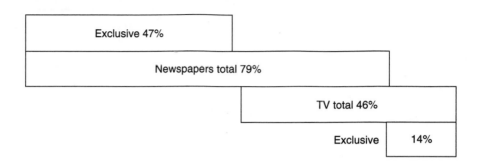

Newspapers and radio accounted for 85 percent of all advertising messages. 67 percent recalled newspapers exclusive of radio. 6 percent recalled radio exclusive of newspapers, and 12 percent recalled both.

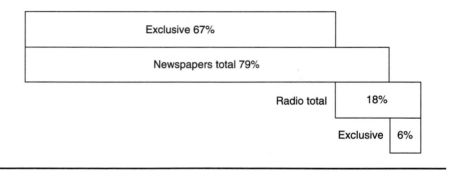

EXHIBIT A–16

Questionnaire   HARVEST SALE IN-STORE CUSTOMER SURVEY

Interviewer Name: _____ (1–2)   STORE: . . . . . . Downtown . . . . . Lenox . . . . . Greenbriar   (3)
                                                                      1   2   3

DATE: M   T   W   TIME OF INTERVIEW: _____ DEPARTMENT: _____   (6)
        1   2   3   (4)   (5)

Hello. We're conducting a short survey among RICH'S customers:

1.   What did you happen to buy in this department today? _____
                                                  (PROBE, BRAND, STYLE)   (7–8)

2.   Before coming to RICH'S today, did you have in mind buying this specific brand/item, or did you decide after you came into the store?

       HAD IN MIND . . . . ( )1   DECIDED IN STORE . . . . . ( )2   SKIP TO Q. #3   (9)

       What was it that gave you the
       idea to buy this brand/item? _____

       (IF APPROPRIATE, ASK: Where did you learn about that?) _____

       _____   (10–11)

3.   Was the store having a special on this specific brand/item today, or were they selling at the regular price?

       SPECIAL . . . . ( )1   REGULAR PRICE . . . . ( )2   SKIP TO Q. #4   (12)

       Where did you learn about that? _____

       _____   (13–14)

4.   Do you recall seeing or hearing any advertising within the past day or two on radio or television or in the newspapers or in a
mail circular that may have reminded you or helped you decide to buy this _____ today?

       YES . . . . ( )1   NO . . . . ( )2   SKIP TO Q. #5   (15)

       a. Where did you see or hear it? _____   (16)

	4a. UNAIDED RECALL	5. AIDED RECALL	
		YES	NO, DK
RADIO	1	1	2	(17)
NEWSPAPERS	2	1	2	(18)
TELEVISION	3	1	2	(19)
MAIL CIRCULAR	4	1	2	(20)
OTHER, DON'T KNOW	5			

ASK FOR EACH MEDIUM NOT CHECKED IN Q. #4a.

5.   Did you happen to see or hear any of the following within the past day or two:
A radio commercial for this specific _____? A newspaper ad for this
specific _____? A television commercial for this specific _____?
A mail circular for this specific _____? _____

6.   Have you bought anything else at RICH'S today, or do you plan to buy anything else at RICH'S today?

       YES . . . . ( )1   NO . . . . ( )2

7.   Do you (or your wife/husband) have a RICH'S credit card?   (21)

       YES . . . . ( )1   NO . . . . ( )2   (22)

       a. Do you usually charge or pay cash for most of your purchases at RICH'S?

       CHARGE . . . . ( )1   CASH . . . . ( )2   SAME . . . . . ( )3   (23)

8.   What is the name of the county where you live? _____ OUT-OF-STATE . . ( )   (24–25–26)

ESTIMATE AGE: UNDER 35 YEARS . . ( )1   SEX: FEMALE . . . ( )1   RACE: WHITE . . . . . ( )1   (27)
              35 – 49 . . . . ( )2   MALE . . . . . ( )2   NON WHITE . ( )2   (28)
              50+ . . . . ( )3   (29)

Appendix B Analysis of Rich's In-Store Survey*

Introduction

First, we would like to state that WSB television and radio were pleased to have the opportunity to participate in this research effort with Rich's. We have one basic characteristic in common with Rich's—both WSB-TV and WSB Radio, like Rich's, are dominant in the Atlanta market. Like Rich's, we are an Atlanta institution and have enjoyed dominance since our origination.

In this presentation, we will not attempt to interpret the results of your research from a marketing standpoint. You have your own market research department, and we are sure that they have done a capable job of analyzing and interpreting the results of the study from that aspect. Instead, we will concentrate on interpreting the results from a media standpoint, which is our particular area of experience.

The following pages contain our detailed analysis of this research for Rich's management.

Pre-Harvest Sale Advertising Weight

Rich's Pre-Harvest Sale was heavily promoted with a "mix" of three media: radio, TV, and newspaper.

On the broadcast side, Rich's ran 261 radio spots on five stations and 177 TV spots on five stations promoting 10 different items during a three-day period. It can be estimated that the total radio campaign reached about 90 percent of the Atlanta adult metro population, with the average listener exposed to seven commercial announcements (all products combined). The total television campaign also reached an estimated 90 percent of the Atlanta adult population, with the average viewer exposed to 10 commercial announcements.

The newspaper campaign consisted of 13 ads for the specific items and 11 ads for related[1] items, or a total of 24 ads representing 1,987 inches of space in the *Journal* and *Constitution*. Rich's also ran 6,140 inches of other newspaper advertising during the three-day period. We have no way of estimating the reach and frequency of the newspaper ads.

Pre-Harvest Sale a Success

Rich's total advertising effort helped make the store's pre-Harvest Sale a tremendous success.

Monday, September 21, and Tuesday, September 22, were two of Rich's biggest days of the year according to traffic and sales volume. As far as we know,

---

*Presented by WSB-TV, WSB Radio, and Cox Broadcasting Research.
[1]Same item but different price than in the radio and TV commercial.

the departments participating in the test were all up considerably in sales volume compared to a year ago.

Unfortunately, sales results for the *specific items* tested were not available. However, it is our understanding that the departmentwide sales results reflected the success of the individual items in those departments that were tested.

The advertising effort for the pre-Harvest Sale represented one of the few times that Rich's has used a media-mix for *item selling.* Radio and TV have been used extensively by Rich's for institutional advertising and to announce sale events, but item selling has been limited in the past primarily to newspaper and direct mail. *The media-mix for item selling worked from a sales results standpoint.*

Summary of Media Recall Findings

After analyzing the results of the survey, we found the following to be the most significant findings:

1. Because of the confusion and particularly the conditioning factor regarding newspaper, the three media cannot be completely compared in recall.
2. Recall for both radio and TV was significantly higher on Tuesday versus Monday, indicating that the broadcast media were building in impact on customers. Sales results were also generally better on Tuesday versus Monday.
3. Both radio and TV did *best* in recall (compared to newspaper) for items having the *least* amount of newspaper advertising. Radio and TV did *poorest* for items having the *greatest* amount of newspaper advertising.
4. In general, items where radio and TV did *best* in recall (compared to newspaper) had better sales results than items where radio and TV did poorest.
5. All three media performed better among high-priced items and for items where customers decided to buy before coming into the store.
6. Radio and TV balanced newspaper quite well by reaching younger adults than the print medium.

See Exhibits B–1 through B–3.

Three Types of Media Recall in the Study

The questionnaire used in Rich's in-store survey obtained information about customers' recall of advertising media in three areas:

1. Idea to Buy

For customers purchasing the item being tested, those that indicated having in mind buying that specific merchandise before coming to the store were asked *what gave them the idea to buy the item.* In this question, answers involving media came from top-of-mind recall (not aided). Nonmedia answers to this question, such as "needed" item, "wanted" item, or "had past experience" with item were accepted.

EXHIBIT B–1   Summary of newspaper recall

Item	Budget	Day/ads	Got idea	Learned of special	Direct recall
Draperies	$4,412	Sun.–2, Tues.–2	48%	68%	81%
Pant suits	3,359	Sun.–2, Mon.–1, Tues.–3	50	56	63
Shoes	2,834	Sun.–1, Mon.–2, Tues.–1	48	55	72
Handbags	1,670	Sun.–1, Tues.–1	30	30	60
Carpeting	1,503	Sun.–1	61	63	80
Color TV	1,503	Sun.–1	62	68	66
Dress shirts	859	Sun.–1	40	40	54
Vacuum cleaner	780	Mon.–4	36	62	64
Mattresses	260	Tues.–1	30	37	54
Career shirts	—	—	19	27	45
Girdles	—	—	12	15	16
Averages, all items*			42	51	64

*Excludes girdles (no ads), but includes career shirts because of ads for dress shirts, a related item.

EXHIBIT B–2   Summary of television recall

Item	Budget	Adult audience (000)	Got idea	Learned of special	Direct recall
Career shirts	$2,998	1,373.4	15%	16%	27%
Draperies	2,714	776.5	11	15	37
Pant suits	2,494	885.4	8	9	39
Playtex girdles	2,364	752.1	25	34	32
Dress shirts	2,028	824.8	16	16	29
Handbags	1,922	649.2	10	10	34
Shoes	1,909	724.7	11	14	41
Vacuum cleaner	1,867	627.4	19	36	42
Carpeting	1,790	624.5	8	12	29
Mattresses	1,627	691.9	40	48	49
Color TV	—	—	0	0	5
Averages, all items*			16	21	36

*Excludes color TV (no commercials).

EXHIBIT B–3   Summary of radio recall

Item	Budget	Adult audience (000)	Got idea	Learned of special	Direct recall
Career shirts	$903	489.1	2%	6%	17%
Draperies	560	654.3	1	2	8
Shoes	544	566.8	5	6	14
Pant suits	539	633.9	1	2	12
Carpeting	513	590.9	8	7	24
Dress shirts	498	496.4	4	5	12
Girdles	482	553.0	6	9	11
Mattresses	477	527.6	11	23	29
Handbags	476	475.1	2	3	20
Vacuum cleaner	453	482.1	7	8	10
Color TV	—	374.2	—	1	2
Averages, all items*			5	7	16

*Excludes color TV (no commercials).

2. Learned of Special

Those customers who were aware of the store having a special on the specific item purchased were asked *where they learned about it.* In this question, answers involving media also came from top-of-mind recall and nonmedia responses such as "saw on display" or "friend told me" were accepted.

3. Direct Recall

Customers were also asked if they recalled seeing or hearing any advertising that may have reminded them or helped them decide to buy the specific item. If they answered in the affirmative, they were then asked *where they saw or heard it.* If radio, newspaper, TV, or mail circular were not mentioned by the respondent, they were also asked if they happened to hear a radio commercial, see a newspaper ad, and so on (aided recall). For purposes of analyzing the results, the unaided and aided answers to direct recall have been combined in this question.

Effect of Confusion and "Conditioning"

First, we would like to emphasize three points that should be taken into consideration when evaluating each advertising medium's performance based on the recall results of the study:

1. Because of the heavy amount of Rich's advertising activity in all media during the three-day period of interviewing, there was a certain amount of confusion that occurred among the customer-respondents regarding where they saw or heard advertising. This fact will be documented in the pages to follow.
2. Because Rich's traditionally has done the vast majority of its *item* advertising in newspaper, customers are "conditioned" to this particular medium; i.e., more inclined to think of Rich's merchandise being advertised in a newspaper.
3. During the three-day period of the study, *other department stores* were also running *newspaper* ads for items similar to Rich's items being tested. Some newspaper ad recall in this study could have been due to confusion with other stores' ads.

These points can all be substantiated by the following results.

Only Slight Confusion for Radio Commercials

There were *no* radio commercials for color TV sets, since the spots were canceled before they were scheduled to run on Tuesday afternoon.

0%	Claimed they got the idea to buy a color TV set from radio commercials.
1%	Thought they learned of color TV sets being on sale from radio commercials.
2%	Said they recalled hearing radio commercials for color TV sets.

Only Slight Confusion for TV Commercials

There were *no* TV commercials for color TV sets, since the spots were canceled before they were scheduled to run on Tuesday afternoon.

0%	Claimed that they got the idea to buy a color TV set from TV commercials.
0%	Thought they learned of color TV sets on sale from TV commercials.
5%	Said they recalled seeing TV commercials for color TV sets.

Some Confusion and "Conditioning" for Mail Circular

In the mail circular that Rich's distributed to its customers the week prior to the survey, there were *no* ads for any specific items, yet among the total sample of customer-respondents purchasing any of the 11 items tested:

3%	Claimed they got the idea to buy the specific item from a mail circular.
5%	Thought they learned of the specific item being on sale from a mail circular.
18%	Said they recalled seeing a mail circular for the specific item.

Greater Confusion and "Conditioning" for Newspaper Ads

There were *no* Rich's newspaper ads for Playtex girdles, yet:

12%	Claimed they got the idea to buy girdles from newspaper ads.
15%	Thought they learned of girdles being on sale from newspaper ads.
16%	Said they recalled seeing newspaper ads for girdles.

There were *no* Rich's newspaper ads for mattresses on either Sunday or Monday of the survey, yet among customers interviewed on Monday:

27%	Claimed they got the idea to buy a mattress from newspaper ads.
30%	Thought they learned of the mattress being on sale from newspaper ads.
49%	Said they recalled seeing newspaper ads for mattresses.

Caution in Comparing Media by Recall!

As you can see, the extent of erroneous recall of newspaper advertising ranged from a low of 12 percent to a high of 49 percent. For this important reason, it is impossible to derive any accurate yardstick for measuring the separate value of each medium, dollar for dollar. In addition, these results cannot be converted to any type of advertising-to-sales ratio.

Radio May Have Been Higher with More WSB Spots

Due to the problem created by trying to find enough availabilities on WSB only in morning and evening drive time (because of the agency's buying criteria) to handle commercials for 11 different items in three days, Atlanta's dominant radio station was not able to contribute as much weight as it should have to most of the media schedules. As a result, a higher proportion of spots ran on WQXI (primarily teens), WAOK (primarily ethnic), WRNG (primarily 50+ listeners), and WPLO (lower socioeconomic level). A brief analysis of the number of radio commercials that ran for each item, showing the light proportion of WSB spots, is shown in the accompanying table.

	Total spots	WSB spots	WSB morning drive spots*
Career shirts	48	10	0
Carpeting	23	6	3
Color TV	—	—	—
Draperies	26	7	2
Dress shirts	15	6	2
Girdles	27	5	1
Handbags	27	5	1
Mattresses	19	6	2
Pant suits	26	8	2
Shoes	27	6	2
Vacuum cleaner	22	5	2
Total	260	64	17

*Monday or Tuesday.

Television versus Newspaper

While TV budgets were fairly even, newspaper budgets ranged from $260 for mattresses up to $4,412 for draperies. TV versus newspaper performance in all types of recall showed a good relationship to the amount of money spent in newspaper. The smaller the newspaper budget versus TV, the better TV performed versus newspaper in recall, and vice versa:

1. TV did *best* in all types of recall *compared to newspaper* for mattresses, career shirts, and vacuum cleaners. These items had the *smallest amount* of advertising space in the newspaper compared to the others.
2. TV did *poorest* in all types of recall *compared to newspaper* for draperies, pant suits, shoes, and carpeting. These items had the *greater amount* of advertising space in the newspaper.

Radio versus Newspaper

Again, radio budgets were fairly even compared to the wide range in newspaper budgets. Radio versus newspaper performance in all types of recall also showed a fairly strong relationship to the amount of money spent in newspaper. The smaller the newspaper budget versus radio, the better radio performed versus newspaper in recall, and vice versa:

1. Radio did *best* in all types of recall *compared to newspaper* for mattresses, vacuum cleaners, and career shirts. These items generally had the least newspaper space.
2. Radio did *poorest* in all types of recall *compared to newspaper* for draperies, pant suits, and handbags. These items generally had the greatest newspaper space.

Less Newspaper Space—No Harm to Sales Volume

We have just indicated that, as newspaper space was reduced, both radio and TV did better in recall.

How about Rich's Sales Volume?

There appeared to be little, if any, correlation between the amount of newspaper space and sales volume as measured by department sales increases. If anything, the reverse occurred:

	Monday	Tuesday
TV and radio did best (least newspaper space):		
Girdles	+7%	+92%
Career shirts	+151	+349
Mattresses	+43	+76
Vacuum cleaners	+98	+222
TV and radio did poorest (most newspaper space):		
Draperies	−0	+9
Pant suits	+17	+46
Shoes	−19	+14
Carpeting	−9	+526

Idea to Buy versus Direct Recall

One probable indication of the "conditioning" of Rich's customers to newspaper advertising comes from comparing initial "idea to buy" recall, where media responses came purely from top of mind, to the direct recall that came later in the interview, concentrating on each medium. All three media gained in regard to the proportion of customers recalling (from idea to buy to direct recall), but newspaper, having been recalled more from top of mind, gained the least, while TV and especially radio, in the background during top of mind "idea to buy," came to the surface more in the direct recall.

	Average recall, all items*		
	Idea to buy	Direct recall	Percent increase
Newspaper	42%	64%	+52%
TV	16	36	+125
Radio	5	16	+220

*Girdles were eliminated for newspaper and color TV sets were eliminated for radio and TV because of no advertising.

First Day versus Second Day Recall

Analysis of the direct recall results by day of interview produced an interesting fact. The impact of newspaper was initial, while both radio and TV performed significantly better on the second day. This is probably due to the nature of the broadcast media, which gain impact and effectiveness with *increased frequency* (as listeners and viewers are exposed to more commercials). In addition, sales results for all items were generally better on Tuesday than on Monday, compared to a year ago. This also indicates that, if spots had been spread more evenly over Sunday, Monday, and Tuesday (rather than concentrated on Sunday and Monday in most cases), and if interviewing had been extended through Wednesday, both radio and TV would have performed better in recall, at no increase in budget for either medium.

	Average recall, all items*		
	Monday	Tuesday	Tuesday percent difference
Newspaper	66%	62%	−6%
TV	33	38	+15
Radio	13	18	+38

*Mattresses were eliminated for newspaper as an invalid comparison, since there were no ads on Sunday or Monday. However, even though there were no radio or TV commercials for career shirts on Sunday or Monday, and no newspaper ads at all, this item was included in this comparison because there was advertising for dress shirts, a related item. Also girdles were eliminated for newspaper and color TV for radio and TV because of no advertising.

High-Priced versus Low-Priced Items

In order to analyze media performance by item *price range,* the items were divided into either a high-price (carpeting, color TV, draperies, mattresses, and vacuum cleaners) or a low-price (career shirts, dress shirts, girdles, handbags, pant suits, and shoes) group. All three media performed better among high-priced items compared to low-priced merchandise, especially radio and TV. However, the differences were greater regarding "idea to buy" recall and "learned of special" recall than with the direct recall. Customers who had made up their minds to buy a large-ticket item were apparently more persuaded by advertising than those coming to Rich's for lower-priced merchandise. However, whether in the market for high- or low-priced items, both type customers were exposed to advertising, as indicated in the direct recall.

	High-priced items	Low-priced items	High-priced percent difference
Idea to buy:			
Newspaper	47%	37%	+27%
TV	20	14	+43
Radio	7	3	+133
Learned of special:			
Newspaper	60	42	+43
TV	28	16	+75
Radio	10	5	+100
Direct recall:			
Newspaper	69	59	+17
TV	39	34	+15
Radio	18	14	+29

"Had in Mind" versus "Decided in Store"

In order to analyze media performance by the extent to which customers had in mind to buy the item before coming to the store, the items were divided into two groups: "had in mind" and "decided in store," based on results to the question covering this aspect of purchasing. The four items where roughly half of the customers indicated deciding in the store (pant suits, dress shirts, career shirts, and handbags) were placed in the "decided in store" group. The other seven items, where significantly less customers indicated deciding in store, were placed in the "had in mind" group. All three media performed significantly better among items in the "had in mind" group, that is, for items where a greater proportion of customers made their decision in advance. The differences were greater regarding "idea to buy" and "learned of special" recall than with the direct recall.

	"Had in mind" items	"Decided in store" items	"Had in-mind" percent difference
Idea to buy:			
Newspaper	48%	35%	+37%
TV	19	12	+58
Radio	6	2	+200
Learned of special:			
Newspaper	59	38	+55
TV	26	13	+100
Radio	9	4	+125
Direct recall:			
Newspaper	70	56	+25
TV	38	32	+19
Radio	16	15	+7

Broadcast Media Recall Reflected Younger Adults

By analyzing media recall by age of customer, it was determined that radio and TV balanced newspaper quite well by reaching younger adults. In all three types of recall, the under-35 age group was proportionately higher for broadcast, especially radio, than for newspaper. These figures are based on all items combined.

Age	Radio	TV	Newspaper
Got idea:			
Under 35	56%	44%	36%
35–49	31	38	44
50 and over	13	18	20
Learned of special:			
Under 35	50	43	36
35–49	34	41	41
50 and over	16	16	23
Direct recall:			
Under 35	49	44	41
35–49	33	38	41
50 and over	18	18	18

Note: Read table: Of those customers indicating that they "got the idea" to buy an item from radio commercials, 56 percent were in the under 35 age group.

Rich's Dominant Position in Atlanta

In concluding this presentation, we would like to announce the results of separate research that we have just completed that indicates the extent to which Rich's dominates the department store market in Atlanta, a domination that we feel is due to:

Outstanding management.

Quality of merchandise.

Attention to customer service and satisfaction.

Efficient use of advertising and promotion, *especially the use of a media-mix.*

Presentation Summary

1. With use of media-mix for item selling, the pre-Harvest Sale was a success. All departments participating in the test were up in sales volume.
2. Because of confusion and conditioning factors, recall results are not completely comparable between media.
3. In general, as the amount of newspaper space was reduced, the proportion of recall for both TV and radio was increased, and sales results were generally more favorable.
4. Sales volume was up significantly on Tuesday versus Monday in all departments, indicating a relationship with broadcast media recall, also up significantly on Tuesday as frequency increased.
5. All media had higher recall for higher-priced items and items where customers generally decided in advance.
6. Separate research confirms Rich's dominance of the Atlanta market, especially versus Davison's. Rich's uses radio and TV effectively, Davison's uses very little broadcast media.

Case 20

Exercise in Print Advertising Assessment*

One of the most important and most difficult marketing decisions is the choice of creative executions in advertising. The purpose of this exercise is to help you develop skills in determining what is a good and a bad creative execution.

In preparation for your class session using this exercise, we would like you to spend time looking at *print* advertising (newspaper and magazine advertising). We would like you to select what you think is the "best ad" you have seen and the "worst ad" you have seen. To aid you in this task you might ask yourself the following questions:

1. What is the sponsor's apparent target segment(s)?
2. What are the objectives of the ad?
3. Are the basic appeal, theme, and copy approach appropriate for these purposes?

To the bottom of each ad you selected, attach a small piece of paper containing the following information:

1. Sponsor of the ad.
2. Publication in which the ad appeared.
3. Publication date.
4. Your reason(s) for selecting that ad as the best or worst.
5. Your name.

Staple or tape this information to the bottom of the ad but don't obscure any of the ad. Turn in your ads to your professor as required. In the class session you will get a chance to compare your choice of ads with those of your classmates.

Case 21

The Customer-Focus Challenges of Integrated Marketing Communication at CCH*

Introduction

Only 33 years old, Oakleigh Thorne had just been put in charge of saving his great-great-grandfather's company. On a quiet day in 1991, Thorne sat at his desk in the modern Riverwoods, Illinois, structure which houses Commerce Clearing House (CCH). Its ample, open workspaces and high, wide windows reveal surrounding woodland from which animals, including deer, occasionally peer. CCH had always been a quiet company which sold printed products through a network of 1,000 field representatives with territories across the United States.

But the company's prospects were disquieting: net income had slid from $53 million in 1987 to $31 million in 1991 ("CCH sets up home page," 1995). CCH had enjoyed high profits and little, if any, competitive threat until the 1990s. Then, with the advent of alternative media, including CD-format products, online information services, and other nonprint products, CCH began to lose market share and profitability quickly. The company's stock had lost half its value, knocking it off The Forbes Four Hundred. Thorne faced an attitude of "Let's do things the way we've always done them." But it was clear to Thorne that CCH did not have a divine decree to make money. To let the troops know there was no such decree, in a disquieting move, Thorne fired 1,200 of the 7,000 workers on the CCH payroll.

---

*This case was prepared by Carla Johnson, assistant professor, Communications Department, Saint Mary's College (Notre Dame, IN), and Tony Hughes, president, Letterperfect Marketing Communications. All product names and trademarks used in this report are registered properties of CCH Incorporated. Reproduction of any material in this document without written permission is strictly prohibited. Copyright 1996 © by Carla Johnson and Tony Hughes.

Although he cut his sales force by nearly two-thirds, Thorne's vision was of a more customer-focused CCH through the implementation of a new theory, *integrated marketing communication.* His IMC toolbox, including direct marketing and the latest technologies, should have increased CCH's intimacy with its customer base, or so the IMC textbooks would suggest. In reality, the swiftness of Thorne's reengineering and the downsizing of the field sales force created many new customer service challenges. How could CCH utilize the tools of integrated marketing communication—direct marketing, database, and other new, interactive technologies—to reestablish the close, personal customer relationships for which it had been known?

A Columbia University M.B.A., Thorne "knew a wall of inertia when he saw it." ("CCH sets up home page," 1995). "We used to be a company that was very much product-focused," Thorne reflected. "We produced this product and then sold to whoever wanted it." He knew CCH had to become "a company that looks at who its customers really are, and then backs into whatever product we want to produce" ("Thorne leads push to customer focus at CCH," 1995).

The company and its subsidiaries track, explain, and analyze tax and related law, producing publications for accounting, legal, human resources, securities, and health care professionals. Clearly, CCH could not afford to lose the successful customer relations that it once enjoyed and that helped make it a leading provider of tax and business law information, software, and related services. Thorne saw weak customer service and a culture that failed to encourage serving the customer. He recently observed, "We've managed to change the culture and the attitude. But in 1995, we've got to implement new phone systems and new computer systems that will give our employees the power to really assist our customers with their problems." Four years after reengineering and the introduction of the tenets of customer-focused integrated marketing theory, the Riverwoods campus is still disquiet.

CCH Corporate History

In 1892, Oakleigh Thorne bought Corporation Trust Co., the predecessor to today's CCH. The foundation of the company's current business was established in 1913, the year the U.S. federal income tax was created. As a result, CCH has long been one of the most respected company names among accountants and lawyers. As government grew and new generations of Thornes took over the company, so did CCH's bottom line.

Keeping a low profile, the company established intimate relationships with their customers. As a large part of its sales came from subscriptions and renewals of those subscriptions, CCH accomplished this through a large network of field representatives. "But the predictable happened. Later generations of Thornes were less committed to the business than the first. Oakleigh B. Thorne began spending less time at the firm, and more time at his 800-acre horse farm in Millbrook, N.Y. Thus, the company was adrift in the late 1980s, when accounting and law firms ran into hard times and began cutting back on subscriptions to services like CCH's once-popular *Standard Federal Tax Reporter,* at $1,215 a pop. Meanwhile, aggressive competitors like Research Institute of America moved in and competed for CCH's business in a shrinking market ("CCH sets up home page," 1995). Most critical, CCH failed to embrace the various technologies that were changing the publishing industry as well as the way its customers worked.

Fortunately, a fourth-generation Thorne, also named Oakleigh, had inherited his great-great-grandfather's energy and commercial instincts. After working in various divisions, the younger Thorne was put in charge of the company by his father (and chairman) Oakleigh B. Thorne. The younger Thorne served as president of CCH's Legal Information Services, then became an executive vice president in 1991 ("CCH names Thorne as as Massie's replacement," 1994). On April 1, 1995, Thorne was named to the positions of president and chief executive officer as 64-year-old Edward L. "Pete" Massie retired.

Today, CCH annually produces approximately 600 publications in print and electronic form.

CCH Enters the '90s

As CCH entered the 1990s, change had caught up with them in publishing and, particularly, in their mainframe tax processing business. Overall, revenue had dropped from $716.1 million in 1990 to $578 million in 1993. At the same time, computer tax processing revenue dropped from a peak of $223.3 million to $84.4 million. The company took a $50 million charge in 1992 to pay for its switch away from its service bureaus. At the same time, Legal Information Services (LIS) grew from $93.5 million to $102.5 million. Publishing revenue fell from a peak of $411 million in 1992 to $391 million in 1994 (see Exhibit 1).

Exhibit 1   Financial Data, 1988–1994

	1994	1993	1992	1991	1990	1989	1988
Revenues							
Publishing	$384,782	$391,018	$411,017	$410,636	$398,354	$374,280	$350,977
Computer processing	77,400	84,441	151,220	197,580	224,260	215,783	177,575
LIS	116,594	102,536	97,171	96,009	93,474	87,389	83,842
	$578,776	$577,995	$659,408	$704,225	$716,088	$677,452	$612,394
Operating earnings (loss)							
Publishing	$(8,792)	$(9,388)	$29,472	$28,999	$39,649	$41,046	$41,657
Computer processing	21,560	(3,452)	(49,816)	10,158	4,487	3,712	14,511
LIS	12,596	(2,528)	619	5,459	7,689	3,745	13,078
Subtotal	25,364	(15,368)	(19,725)	44,616	51,825	48,503	69,246
Other income, net	7,065	23,969	7,977	9,339	18,846	14,732	12,743
Earnings*	32,429	8,601	(11,748)	53,955	70,671	63,235	81,989
Income taxes	13,500	2,160	1,900	22,930	30,000	28,900	32,500
Earnings[†]	18,929	6,441	(13,648)	31,025	40,671	34,335	49,489
Benefits[‡]	—	—	(51,675)	—	—	—	—
Income Taxes	—	—	1,173	—	—	—	—
Net earnings (loss)	$18,929	$6,441	$(64,150)	$31,025	$40,671	$34,335	$49,489

*Earnings (loss) before income taxes and cumulative effect of accounting changes.
[†]Earnings (loss) before cumulative effect of accounting changes.
[‡]Postemployment and postretirement benefits other than pensions.

Facing increasing competitive threats and the migration to electronic products, CCH implemented a massive reengineering program in 1992. CCH consolidated the staff of two separate sales forces, reducing the total number of sales people from 800 to 360. To add to customer confusion, CCH introduced 33 new products between 1993 and 1994. In comparison, the company had only introduced 33 new products during the years between its founding and 1993. To augment its streamlined sales force, CCH implemented a comprehensive direct marketing program using direct mail, telemarketing, and on-line systems (see Exhibit 2).

Acknowledging the new customer focus, the company "set out on a mission to build CCH into a provider of powerful decision-making tools for professionals, a company that delivers products that increase profitability and improve productivity. This mission was established in response to our customers' growing need to contain costs and in response to rapid changes in the technology to deliver and use information. To achieve this mission, we knew we needed to produce truly innovative products, to deliver top-notch customer service, and to beat the competition to the market with applications that joined new technologies to our traditional content." (1994 Annual Report)

Exhibit 2   CCH organization chart

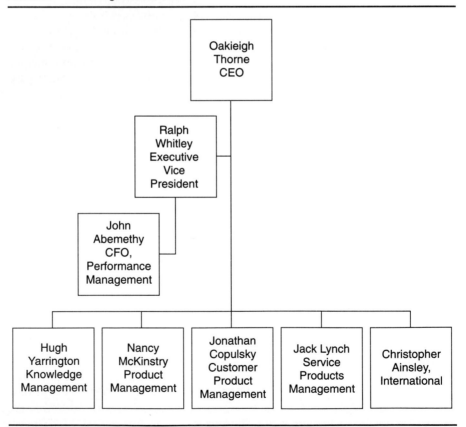

Thorne's vision paid off. After four years of reengineering, a new, more innovative CCH entered a definitive agreement for the sale of the company to Wolters Kluwer NV, an international publisher of print and electronic information for professionals and business. The sale price—$1.9 billion—represented a generous three times anticipated revenues of $600 million for 1995, and served as a validation of the success of CCH's reengineering effort.

"The advantages (of the sale) for CCH are many," commented Thorne, "particularly when we look at the long-term growth opportunities. CCH is firmly established as the leader in our core market segments and will achieve substantial earnings growth in future years. Now, in combination with Wolters Kluwer, new opportunities for long-term growth in new markets are clearly within reach."

However, while restoring its competitive footing, CCH's reengineering has put some distance between CCH and its customers.

CCH Products

CCH markets approximately 600 products for the U.S. market. Many are subscription publications that are updated daily, monthly, or annually. Information is provided via a variety of media in order to meet the needs of a diverse customer base. These media include loose-leaf publications, CD-ROM, soft books and booklets, newsletters, on-line database, computer disk, audio cassette, Lotus Notes™ database application, and the Microsoft Network.

Markets for its products include accountants, lawyers, tax professionals, government, corporate, and small office/home office (SOHO) professionals. CCH's flagship product is *The Standard Federal Tax Reporter.* Other major publications for which the company is known include *The U.S. Master Tax Guide, CCH Federal Tax Guide, Human Resources Management,* and *CCH Medicare and Medicaid Guide.* The company sells most of its print and electronic products through a recently downsized 360-person sales force.

CCH Business Structure

CCH operates three primary businesses.

CCH Publishing. CCH Publishing develops and sells print and electronic publications and software to meet a wide range of tax and business law needs. The company built its reputation for editorial excellence and authoritative products in tax and business law upon this unit. For more than 80 years, CCH Publishing has set the standard for tax research and compliance tools for accountants, attorneys, government agencies, educators, and others who use legal information references and software.

CCH's Publishing unit makes up the largest percentage of the company's business, with 1994 revenues of approximately $385 million.

CCH products provide professionals with different degrees of information and knowledge, from the simple, printed text of Congressional legislation to sophisticated practice system software. Company editors and analysts draw information from a vast database to develop and provide interactive software for research, planning, and compliance; professional analyses; summaries and explanations; tax and business-related legislation, rulings, and decisions; and forms.

CCH also publishes a number of consumer and client marketing publications. These low-cost, soft-cover booklets provide easy-to-read information for taxpayers on topics from home office deductions to tax implications for high-income individuals to year-end tax planning.

When it comes to accounting, CCH is the leader in the print, CD-ROM, and practice system market with approximately 150 products. Its flagship product is the *Standard Federal Tax Reporter,* a subscription service available in a 22-volume, 40,000-page print format, on CD-ROM, or through an on-line service. Its other tax publications cover a full range of topics including corporate, individual, and specialized tax laws and issues; court rulings; IRS decisions; forms; and gift and estate, state, and real estate taxes.

In 1994, CCH developed a new generation of "knowledge" software for human resources and tax professionals. Tax Assistant practice systems, for federal and state tax topics, guide and support tax professionals with research, analysis, and compliance, all in one product. CCH HR Assistant, Payroll Assistant, and Safety Compliance Assistant provide a line of innovative, PC-based, interactive systems that focus on specific areas and make decision-making a snap.

CCH publishes a wide range of publications across the broad spectrum of business law. *Federal Securities Law Reports, Blue Sky Reports,* and *Guides* for all of the major U.S. exchanges are among its best-known publications. It also publishes on specialized business law topics such as aviation, energy, the environment, and computers.

Human resources professionals depend on CCH publications and computer software to ensure compliance with federal and state employment laws, guarantee worker safety, and provide tools and information for making effective management decisions. Print and CD-ROM publications cover topics including human resources management and law pertaining to such issues as employee benefits, payroll, and workers' compensation. HR Assistant, an interactive software system that draws on CCH's vast database to help human resources professionals conduct research, create policies, and ensure legal compliance, was named one of the best products of 1994 by *Human Resources Executive* magazine.

CCH publishes a wide range of health and medical information in print, on-line, and CD-ROM formats. The company utilizes its substantial experience in tracking and analyzing the legislative process to report of health care reform actions in Washington, D.C., and at the state level. It is a leading provider of Medicare and Medicaid information.

CCH also publishes a number of publications for business planning and financial services. *Capital Changes Daily* is the company's first product offered via Lotus Notes.

ProSystem fx. ProSystem fx provides computer software and services for processing tax returns. Compliance software allows the tax professional to service a client from client interview to completed and filed tax return. Compliance software generated 1994 revenues of $77,400,000. In recent years, CCH has repositioned this business area, moving away from service bureau processing. CCH also operates two tax processing service bureaus, in New Jersey and California, to provide mainframe-based return processing for tax professionals.

Legal Information Services (LIS). Legal Information Services (LIS), New York City, is a group of companies that offer a variety of services to assist attorneys and businesses in handling corporate, securities, credit, and intellectual property matters. LIS provides services to over 75 percent of the Fortune 500 companies. LIS is the first CCH company to develop and market electronic knowledge products such as Blue Sky Advantage, CT Advantage, and CT Corporate Profile.

The companies that comprise LIS are CT Corporation System, Washington Service Bureau (WSB), Trademark Research Corporation, and McCord Company. CT Corporation, now 102 years old, was the first company to provide corporate services to attorneys. It acts as Registered Agent for over 220,000 corporations and manages over 400,000 service-of-process transactions each year. WSB provides a full range of SEC information services for securities law professionals. It pioneered the development of SEC research services and document retrieval.

Trademark Research Corporation has provided intellectual property information and services for over 40 years. "Trademark ACCESS," a CD-ROM-based personal search system for in-house use, provides unlimited access to over one million complete, current records and associated images of the U.S. Patent and Trademark Office. "Vigilance Watching Service," a customized monitoring system, monitors trademarks in the U.S. and 140 countries around the world.

McCord Company, a division of CT Corporation, provides Uniform Commercial Code (UCC) and related services to legal, lending, and business professionals at state and county levels, covering 3,100 jurisdictions nationwide.

Small Office/Home Office (SOHO) Products

According to *Accounting Today,* CCH has expanded its move into small business services with plans to offer information on the AT&T Business Network. The move follows closely on the heels of CCH's announced plans for its "Business Owner's Toolkit," a small office/home office offering for the new Microsoft Network.

For CCH, the move to the SOHO area represents diversification from its traditional professional business offerings. Target businesses for the SOHO offerings include those with 10 employees or less. (Oct. 9, 1995, v 9 n 18 p 26)

SOHO content is developed by CCH's in-house reporters, editors, and analysts. The "Toolkit" includes several topic areas, with content updated and expanded on a timely basis. "SOHO Information and Tools" follow the life cycle of a small business, i.e., startup, marketing, office equipment, tax control. "News to Use" offers selective, daily reporting and analysis of legislative, regulatory, and business news affecting small businesses and their owners. "Download Zone" provides access to a wide range of forms and documents such as business, tax, banking, employment, and other business forms. "Business Owners BBS" facilitates online dialog, networking, and information exchange for small business owners and their advisors.

International Subsidiaries

In addition to its U.S. operations, the company operates international subsidiaries in Canada, Europe, Asia, Australia, and New Zealand.

CCH Personnel

Oakleigh Thorne, President & CEO. After serving three years on the executive committee, Thorne was named president and CEO in April 1995. It was Thorne's vision and drive which conceived and guided CCH through its reengineering effort. Thorne is the fourth generation of his family to be associated with CCH. His great-great-grandfather established the Thorne family's 103-year commitment to CCH. He is also a board member of Wolters Kluwer U.S.

Working with executive committee members Ralph C. Whitley and Edward L. Massie, Thorne had a major hand in reshaping the services provided by CCH as it has shed its mainframe tax processing business in favor of producing software in house. As it grapples with change, CCH has also cut facilities and jobs in its publishing and legal information services.

"This kind of change has some sad impact as well," Thorne said in an interview. "There were a lot of people who were dedicated to the company, who worked here for a long time, and now, don't work here any more. But if we didn't make those changes, we'd be on the road to extinction. We do have a different kind of profile now in the company. We have more of a technology focus. You have to be current with technology to work here" ("Thorne leads push to customer focus at CCH," 1995). Thorne sees technology as helping CCH become more responsive, delivering information to where people can best use it.

Oakleigh Thorne worries about reputation, not lifestyle. "If CCH dies, everyone is going to point the finger at me and say, 'Oh look, his dad let him run the company and he screwed it up' " ("CCH sets up home page," 1995).

The Integrated Marketing Management Team. CCH's reengineering effort reflected Thorne's commitment to the principles of integrated marketing communication. Reengineering necessitated reorganization which would integrate what had been autonomous departments (see Exhibits 2, 3, and 4). Thorne's vision of a more customer-focused and responsive CCH meant that the company had to speak with one voice. The installation of a new management team was a first step in that direction. The Integrated Marketing team would have to lead the company toward customer-focused goals in the areas of software development, direct marketing applications, and database management. Following is a description of the CCH Integrated Management team which Thorne installed.

Exhibit 3   Product management organization chart

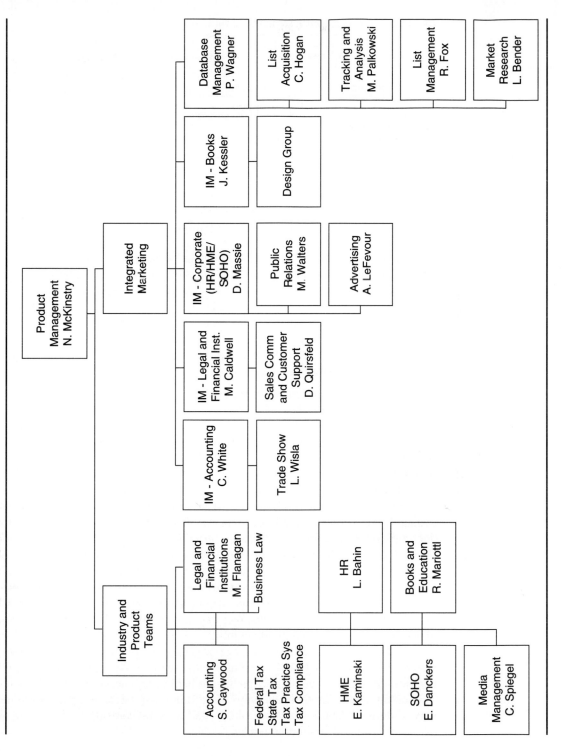

Exhibit 4   Pre-engineering organization chart

Vice President, Marketing *(now Product Management)*

Sales Promotion	Trade Shows	Advertising	Customer Service
	Conferences	Direct Mail	
(now sales comm & customer support)	*(same)*	*(now IM)*	*(now a sales function)*

Jeffrey H. Kessler, Integrated Marketing Manager: Books & Internet & Corporate Design. "Oakleigh has taken the visionary role," Kessler says. "He's constantly looking at the new media for getting information to the markets CCH serves." (See Exhibit 3.)

Kessler notes that "there's still so much that has to be done. How do we assimilate the multiple databases we have out there into one single, usable source? How do we anticipate the needs we'll have next month, next year, or five years from now? How do we structure a database to meet the myriad demands on it? How do we structure a database to retrieve data ranging from market segmentation to appending new customer information? We're committed to technology and to editorial excellence in all our products. We need to use new media" to communicate interactively with customers.

Diane M. Massie, Integrated Marketing Manager: Health Care, Human Resources, Emerging Technologies, Advertising & Public Relations, Sales Communications. Massie believes that "a lot of companies fail in their reengineering efforts. One reason is because they didn't reengineer the entire company but just parts of it. I don't think that approach could work with CCH. We had a group of fresh-thinking people who were excited about the job of reengineering CCH. The hardest part was instilling a new corporate culture to replace the established one."

Massie described the challenges of reengineering: "Some people were very resistant. We went from a 35-hour work week to a 40-hour work week—not an uncommon feature of most companies doing business today. But we met a lot of resistance. We heard things like 'We want a pay raise if we're working more hours.' CCH, as a company, and the people who were still working here, had to make a shift to the new way of doing business—a change that had to be made if we were going to be successful. It was one thing to reengineer CCH to a new way of doing business. A lot of the changes came from the top down. It was a matter of 'do it the new way or find a new job.'

"More difficult was the challenge of getting people to embrace the new vision of the future for CCH. This culture had to be accepted and implemented by people—from the inside out. People had to believe and accept the new 'technology' culture, abandon their old ways of working, and become a part of the new way of doing business. It couldn't be forced by management, but had to be understood, accepted, and implemented."

As Massie notes, internal relations problems have further complicated the mission of creating a customer-responsive company.

Carol White: Manager, Integrated Marketing Manager: Accounting & Business Law, Trade Shows. As head of Integrated Marketing for CCH's Accounting and Business Law groups, White coordinated advertising and communications for CCH's Los Angeles-based tax compliance subsidiary prior to transferring to corporate headquarters in 1992. White's responsibilities also include management of CCH's trade show activities. Since reengineering, White has been at the forefront of the customer relationship challenge. Her concerns involve development of CCH's customer relationships, use of telemarketing for mass market retention, testing elements of CCH's direct mail programs, and educating customers on CCH changes.

"We went through so many changes so fast," she said. "We had to tear down an entire corporation and reassemble it in a way that would work. There were unpleasant times involved with layoffs and instilling a new corporate culture with the remaining personnel. We now need to figure out how we can use direct marketing technology to get back in touch with our customers. We have a tremendous amount of resources at our disposal—people, direct marketing tools, and extensive distribution channels. The question is 'how do we integrate these resources to achieve our goals?' "

Paul R. Wagner, Manager: Database Management. "We're still a case in progress," Wagner said. "We were forced by competition and the marketplace to change. With a dramatic increase in new product introductions, a large reduction of the field sales force, an expansion of alternative channels of distribution, and an overhaul of the company's technology infrastructure, we completely changed the way we did business. Since it has all happened within a relatively short period of time, we are simultaneously evaluating our results while fine-tuning the reengineering model.

"We have multiple and independent customer databases which don't 'talk' to one another. Unfortunately, the same customer can exist in more than one database. CCH's immediate challenges, especially until all customer databases can be integrated into one, are:

- How do we effectively manage our channels of distribution?
- How can integrated marketing help strengthen our customer relationships?
- How can we make it easier for our customers to do business with us?
- How can we provide meaningful and accurate information to the sales, marketing, accounting, and operations departments?

Commenting on CCH's reengineering and the integration of direct marketing programs, Wagner said, "We have shifted from a rather unsophisticated, non-technology-driven operation, to one which is the antithesis of that. We know that our database marketing programs can only be as strong as the database itself. Cleaning and enhancing existing databases, coordinating customers from multiple databases, coordinating new data from multiple sources (e.g., the field, customer service, telemarketing), and developing a broad range of marketing reports, have put huge demands on the responsiveness, flexibility, and logistical capabilities of CCH's Technology Departments."

Integrated Marketing at CCH

What is integrated marketing? "Simply put, traditional marketing is the process of developing relationships with customers around a particular product. Frequently, this is accomplished by communicating to a mass (and sometimes segmented mass) audience. According to Ingall, "Integrated marketing communications (IMC) is the process of developing and maintaining relationships with customers around customer behavior and needs. IMC is about creating a dialogue between an organization and its customers." As with Thorne's vision of a customer-focused rather than product-focused CCH, IMC theory reverses traditional inside-out marketing to outside-in.

White defines CCH's integrated marketing management (IMM) as "the art and science of managing diverse marketing media (advertising, direct mail, telemarketing, field sales, etc.) deployed with a unified goal and message, using sophisticated database methodologies to identify high-potential prospects." IM managers work with field sales representatives (FSR) on calls, and keep them apprised of upcoming direct mail campaigns. FSRs have also served on task force projects, including a welcome kit, retention program, and renewal incentive programs. Each product team has a FSR liaison so there is open communication between corporate marketing and field and sales personnel.

IM tools: Direct marketing. Prior to reengineering, CCH's sales force developed and maintained one-on-one customer relationships. With the drastic downsizing of that department, CCH has faced some disintegration of these relationships. According to White, "In building customer relations, we've always had the field representative. For instance, a customer might tell a rep that he wasn't interested in a particular product until June. The FSR would make a note: 'See Joe in June.' The FSR knew when the customer's birthday was, whether he played golf or not." CCH now employs alternative means to dialogue with customers, such as telemarketing and interactive on-line services.

Direct marketing has provided a new avenue for customer communication. Customers can get more information from CCH more often via direct mail campaigns. Direct marketing also gives the client more choice—the customer can deal with CCH via FSR, mail, or telephone, whichever feels most comfortable.

One IM goal is to provide an FSR/direct marketing mix to mutually benefit both CCH and CCH clients by producing better client profiles and selling to the client through appropriate channels. Client contact preference (FSR or direct marketing) and lifetime value of the customer (how much the customer spends) greatly influence which channel is most appropriate. A low-value customer may want to see an FSR every week, but that may not be economically viable. On the other hand, a high-lifetime-value customer may not want to see the FSR as often. CCH intends to track this information, and design its sales mix to meet both the customer's preferences and CCH's lifetime value parameters.

Prior to reengineering, CCH's sales force spent, on average, 70 percent of its time on customer service and renewal and only 30 percent on new sales. Today, CCH's integrated marketing team stresses the need to maintain a high level of customer service, but strives to do it through direct marketing channels. Loss of field representatives especially impacted Health Care products, which went "cold turkey" with no field reps at all for one year.

Telemarketing. CCH conducts both inbound and outbound telemarketing programs—executed by internal telephone marketing associates (TMAs) working with 5–10 FSRs each, and by outside service providers. Leads generated by these programs are sent to FSRs via E-mail, but the program has its drawbacks. "Our database is filled with leads which the FSRs haven't been able to respond to yet," Wagner said. "It's an area we need to work on."

CCH also provides customer service personnel to answer customer's questions and take orders called in from direct mail and other sales generation programs. An ACD voice response system distributes calls and prompts customer service representatives with source codes, which are then entered into the customer's order.

Direct marketing is also used in the renewal process. CCH has segmented customers so that the high-value customers are contacted directly by FSRs. Others are solicited by mail and the TMAs. The letters contain a renewal certificate which provides a complete list of CCH products in a customer's portfolio. The customer can amend the list and sign at the bottom to assure receipt of the desired products for the current year—all without the inconvenience and the cost of an FSR visit. Direct mail channels account for 30 percent of CCH's order renewals.

CCH's IM team feels that direct marketing has allowed CCH to tailor the level of service to client needs and wants. Direct marketing also has given the client at least three contact points—FSR, TMA, and telemarketing customer service—to communicate with CCH. Customer service can be reached at an 800 number from 6 A.M. to 6 P.M., making CCH more accessible and easier to reach.

CCH on the Internet. Kessler has pioneered CCH's use of the Internet to enhance customer service. The Internet allows for the crucial two-way communication required for relationship marketing dialog. Further, many of CCH's customers "feed off of the financial markets. Lawyers, accountants, analysts, and the like," commented Kessler.

CCH has put the Internet to use in its attempt to bridge the customer relations gap. Its WorldWide Web Home Page on the Internet includes corporate and product press releases, new product information, basic subscription information on each product, a full books catalog, and corporate information.

Product demonstrations may be downloaded, helping to replace demonstrations previously performed by field representatives or requested by mail. Customers can call, write, and order on line without human intervention.

Through a CCH home page on the Internet's WorldWide Web (WWW), clients have an open line of communication with CCH. Customers can order missing product pages; soon they will be able to order complete new product lines. This channel feeds directly into the CCH's Lotus Notes system and promptly fulfills and ships requested customer information. Customer service uses tracking systems provided by UPS and Federal Express to provide status of shipments via these carriers to customers.

Customer service plans to add other Internet capabilities. These include input of simple address changes; access to commonly asked questions on products, processes, etc., maintained by Customer Service and offered as a 24-hour service; access to trouble-shooting information regarding electronic products, networks, etc., including a library of documents that customers can view, download, or request on FAX; and an inbound channel for any type of question.

CCH plans to expand customer service functions by developing a secure method for Internet users to place account or credit card orders; developing cancellation request and general inquiry forms; developing a menu of frequently asked questions that would include a product use and platform functionality section; and publishing an on-line newsletter.

CCH has been able to improve customer service without recourse to the previous number of FSRs. Nevertheless, some customer information was lost in the reengineering transition, and some customers remain confused by rapid personnel and product changes.

IM tools: Database management. In addition to direct marketing, the database—which facilitates collection and analysis of customer information—often provides an effective tool for customer-focused, integrated marketing goals.

According to Schultz/Tannebaum/Lauterborn (1995), IMC requires two-way communication, which is often referred to as "relationship marketing." The database is the "most successful way to establish two-way relationship communications." Marketers send information to customers "through a variety of distribution forms" including "a direct mail piece, a telephone call, a purchase warranty card, or other direct response form through which the consumer then responds. Response information is then stored in the database." Marketers may use these methods to communicate with prospects as well as established customers.

CCH's databases are viewed as tools to help build customer relationships. Commented Wagner, "In 1995, a large task force was created to build a marketing-driven database. Among the task force's objectives was to build a series of predictive models which would be used to 'score' customers and assist in segmenting customers for future mail and telemarketing campaigns." By mid-1995, with most of its objectives met, the task force was dissolved.

Exhibit 5   CCH Enterprise architecture components

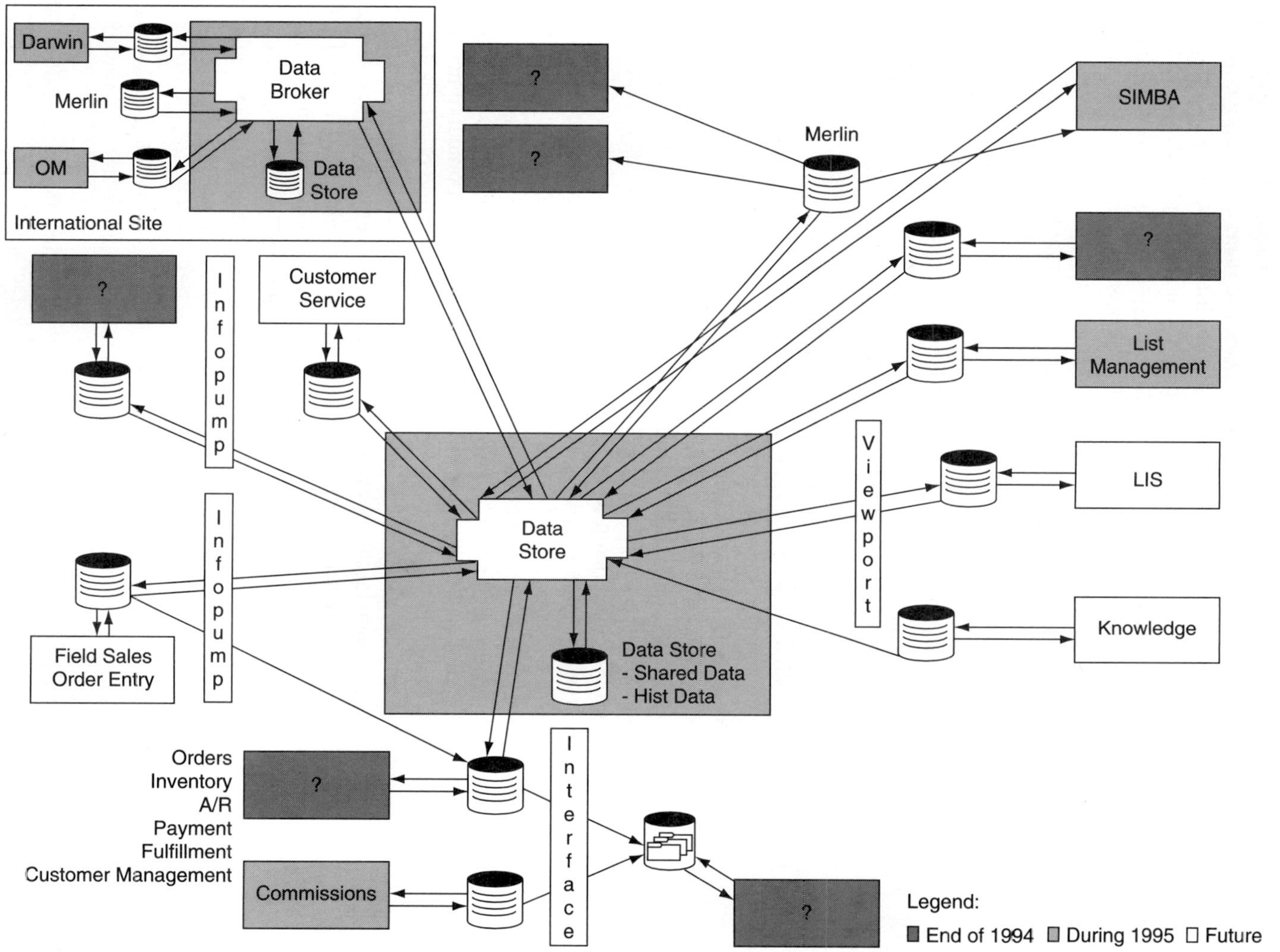

Legend:
■ End of 1994   ▨ During 1995   □ Future

409

Wagner notes that CCH could use the database for customer retention: if a customer cancels an order, the field sales force could be notified and react quickly to counter the customer's objections. CCH also plans to track buyer behavior and use that information to determine customer lifetime value.

Wagner faces numerous challenges, among them "how to service a wide variety of database users, who often have unique data and reporting requirements, while the database infrastructure is still in transition." Even though numerous activities are under way to build for the future—data cleanup, consolidation of duplicate accounts, enhancing the database with demographic information, and providing improved reports—we cannot forget that the database users need to focus on running their businesses today.

CCH's customer database consists of both transactional information and demographic information which has been purchased from an outside provider (see Exhibit 5).

In 1995, senior management created a task force to coordinate and prioritize CCH's efforts in correcting and enhancing its new relational database. The task force consists of a representative from each of the major functional areas of CCH, along with the key members from each of CCH's various technology departments.

In an effort to solve existing problems, the task force developed a process where system users registered problems through a "defects" database. A "defects" response mechanism allowed the individual to send the task force a notification that a database shortcoming had been found (e.g., Customer Service may not be able to retrieve a particular piece of needed customer data, or the information which had been retrieved was incorrect). The task force would combine these requests, along with its own recommendations for enhancements, and prioritize the requests, assign resources, track progress, and notify users when corrections and enhancements were completed.

Wagner is the Product Management Organization's representative for this task force. This participation helps coordinate the development of new integrated marketing goals—such as improved statistical measuring of orders, leads, "stick rates," and back-end analyses—while also benchmarking levels for future direct marketing campaigns. Working together, the integrated marketing managers, along with various members of the Database Management group, need to develop strategies and tactics for future direct marketing programs, while also ensuring that the programs can be tracked against prior efforts.

Questions for Consideration

1. How can CCH further use integrated marketing technologies and direct marketing channels to reestablish the personal contact it enjoyed with the field sales force?
2. How can its multiple data sources be assimilated into one usable database?
3. How can CCH measure customer satisfaction?
4. How can CCH determine exactly what its customers want?

5. How can CCH plan for the inevitable change in future database demands by its sales, marketing, customer service, and IMM departments?
6. How might internal relations problems impact the relationship CCH has with its customer? How should CCH address personnel concerns, i.e., employee morale, brought on by technological changes?
7. Should CCH consider alternative distribution channels, i.e., retail?
8. Should CCH continue to outsource telemarketing to a professional telemarketing firm?

References

CCH names Thorne as Massie's replacement. (1994, August 22). *Accounting Today,* 2.

CCH sets up home page (on Internet World Wide Web). (1995, August 21). *Accounting Today,* 20.

Ingall, Tina. "A Stamp of Approval: Integrated Marketing and the United States Postal System." Unpublished, 1995, pp. 2–3.

Schultz, Don E., Tannenbaum, Stanley I., & Lauterborn, Robert E. (1995) *Integrated Marketing Communication.* Chicago: NTC Business Books, 52–53.

Thorne leads push to customer focus at CCH. (1995, Jan. 16). *Accounting Today,* 24.

Exhibit 6   Direct marketing resources

Group	Number of people	Programs	Annual budget
Paul Wagner	16	—	
Jeff Kessler	9	75	
Carol White	6	15	
Diane Massie	13	35	
In-house sales	33		
Telemarketing	2		
DM operations	8		

Case 22

Allied Food Distributors*

In April 1996, Elizabeth Ramsey, the district sales manager for the upper Midwest district of Allied Food Distributors, was preparing to hire a new salesperson for the southwest Indiana sales territory. The current salesperson in this territory was leaving the company at the end of June. Ramsey had narrowed the list of potential candidates to three. She wondered which of these applicants she should select.

Company Background

Allied Food Distributors was one of the largest food wholesalers in the United States. The company carried hundreds of different packaged food items (fruits, vegetables, cake mixes, cookies, powdered soft drinks, and so on) for sales to supermarkets and grocery stores. Allied carried items in two different circumstances. First, some small food companies had Allied carry their entire line in all areas of the United States. Allied was in essence their sales force. Second, some large food companies had Allied carry their lines in less-populated parts of the country. These areas were not large enough to sustain a salesperson for each food company.

Allied operated in all 50 states. The country was divided into 20 sales districts. Ms. Ramsey's sales district included Michigan, Indiana, and Illinois. Each district was divided into a number of sales territories. A salesperson was assigned to each territory.

The Southwest Indiana Territory

The sales territory for which Ms. Ramsey was seeking a salesperson was located in the southwest corner of Indiana. Exhibit 1 presents a map of the territory. It was bordered on the south by the Ohio River and the state of Kentucky, on the west by the Wabash River and the state of Illinois, and on the east by the Hoosier

---

*This case was written by Thomas C. Kinnear. Copyright © 1996 by Thomas C. Kinnear.

Exhibit 1   A map of the southwest Indiana territory

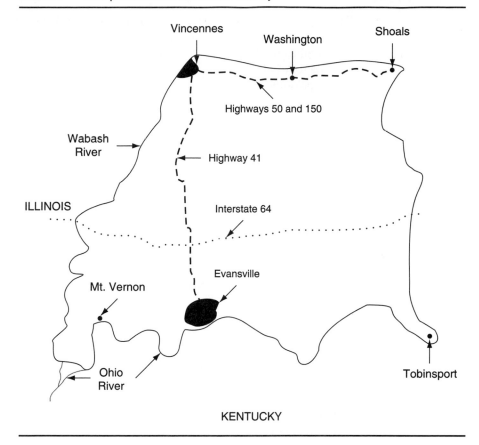

National Forest. The northern boundary ran a few miles north of Highways 50 and 150 that ran from Vincennes in the west through Washington to Shoals in the east. Evansville was the largest city in the area with a population of about 140,000. The salesperson for the territory was expected to live in Evansville, but would spend about three nights a week on the road. The only other reasonably large population concentration was in Vincennes with a population of about 20,000. Vincennes was located about 55 miles straight north of Evansville on Highway 41. Interstate Highway 64 ran the 80 miles east-west through the territory about 15 miles north of Evansville. Evansville was 165 miles southwest of Indianapolis, 170 miles east of St. Louis, Missouri, and 115 miles northwest of Louisville, Kentucky. The territory was very rural in character with agriculture being the dominant industry. The terrain was quite hilly, with poor soil. As a result, the farms in the area tended to be economically weak. There were many small towns and villages located throughout this basically rural environment.

The Choices

On the basis of application forms and personal interviews, Ms. Ramsey had narrowed the field of applicants down to three. A summary of the information on their application forms, along with the comments she had written to herself, are contained in Exhibits 2, 3, and 4. She wondered which person she should select for the position.

Exhibit 2 Information on Michael Gehringer

Personal information

Born July 15, 1954; married; three children ages 14, 16, and 19; height 5 feet, 10 inches; weight 205; excellent health; born and raised in Indianapolis.

Education

High school graduate; played football; no extracurricular activities of note.

Employment record

　　1. Currently employed by Allied Food Distributors in the warehouse in Indianapolis; two years with Allied; job responsibilities include processing orders from the field and expediting rush orders; current salary $3,600 per month.
　　2. In 1992–93 employed by Hoosier Van Lines in Indianapolis as a sales agent; terminating salary was $1,100 per month; left due to limits placed on salary and lack of challenge in the job.
　　3. In 1990–92 employed by Main Street Clothiers of Indianapolis as a retail salesperson in the men's department; terminating salary $2,000 per month; left due to boring nature of this type of selling.
　　4. Between 1980 and 1990 held six other clerical and sales-type jobs, all in Indianapolis.

Applicant's statement

I feel that my true employment interest lies in selling in a situation where I can be my own boss. This job seems just right.

Ramsey's comments

　　Seems very interested in job as a career.
　　Well recommended by his current boss.
　　Reasonably intelligent.
　　Good appearance.
　　Moderately aggressive.

The Selling Task

Allied maintained 75 active retail accounts in the southwest Indiana territory. About 10 of these accounts were medium- to large-sized independent supermarkets located in Evansville and Vincennes. The rest of the accounts were small, independent general food stores located throughout the territory.

　　The salesperson was expected to call on these accounts about every three weeks. The salesperson's duties included: checking displays and inventory levels for

Exhibit 3   Information on Carley Tobias

Personal information

Born February 12, 1967; married; two children ages 1 and 4; height 6 feet, 2 inches; weight 170; excellent health; born in San Francisco; raised in Cleveland, Ohio.

Education

High school and Community College graduate in business administration; student council president at Community College; plus belonged to a number of other clubs.

Employment record

1.   Currently employed by The Drug Trading Company in Cincinnati as a salesperson; job responsibility involves selling to retail drugstores; seven years with Drug Trading; current salary $3,300 per month.
2.   In 1987–90 U.S. Army private; did one tour of duty in Germany.

Applicant's statement

I am seeking a new position because of the limited earning potential at Drug Trading, plus my family's desire to live in a less populated city.

Other information

He is very active in civic and church organizations in Cincinnati; he is currently president of the Sales and Marketing Executives of Cincinnati.

Ms. Ramsey's comments

Very personable.
Reasonably intelligent.
Good appearance.
He seems to like Cincinnati a lot.
Good experience.

---

items already carried, obtaining orders on these items, informing retailers about new items, attempting to gain sales orders on these items, setting up special displays, and generally servicing the retailers' needs. Often, the salesperson would check the level of inventory on an item, make out an order, and present it to the retailer to be signed. The salesperson generally knew the store owner on a first name basis. The ordered goods were sent directly to the retailer from a warehouse located in Indianapolis.

The Selection Process

The responsibility for recruiting salespersons for the territories within a district was given to the district sales manager. The process consisted of the following steps:

1.   An advertisement for the job was placed in newspapers in the state in question.
2.   Those responding to the ad were sent job application forms.
3.   The returned application forms were examined and certain applicants were asked to come to the district sales office for a full day of interviews.
4.   The selection was then made by the district sales manager, or all applicants were rejected and the process started again.

Exhibit 4   Information on Arthur Woodhead

Personal information

Born May 26, 1974, single; height 6 feet; weight 180; excellent health; born and raised in Chicago.

Education

Will graduate in May 1996 from the University of Illinois, Chicago, with a B.B.A. Active in intramural athletics and student government.

Employment record

Summer jobs only; did house painting and gardening work for his own company. Earned $1,600 per month in summer of 1995.

Applicant's statement

I really like to run my own affairs, and selling seems like a good position to reach this objective.

Ms. Ramsey's comments

Well dressed and groomed.
Very intelligent.
Management potential, not career salesperson.
Not very aggressive.

Training

Allied did all its salesperson training on the job. The salesperson on the territory to which a new person would be assigned was given the task of training. Basically, this involved having the new person travel the territory to meet the retailers and to be shown how to obtain and send in orders. The district sales manager usually assisted in this process by traveling with the new salesperson for a few days.

Compensation

The current salesperson on the southwest Indiana sales territory was earning a straight salary of about $43,000 per year plus fringe benefits. Ms. Ramsey indicated that she was willing to pay between $25,000 and $50,000 for a new person depending on the qualifications presented.

Case 23

Outdoor Sporting Products, Inc.*

The annual sales volume of Outdoor Sporting Products, Inc., for the past six years had ranged between $6.2 million and $6.8 million. Although profits continued to be satisfactory, Hudson McDonald, president and chief operating officer, was concerned because sales had not increased appreciably from year to year. Consequently, he asked a consultant in New York City and the officers of the company to submit proposals for improving the salespeople's compensation plan, which he believed was the basic weakness in the firm's marketing operations.

Outdoor's factory and warehouse were located in Albany, New York, where the company manufactured and distributed sporting equipment, clothing, and accessories. Hudson McDonald, who managed the company, organized it in 1956 when he envisioned a growing market for sporting goods resulting from the predicted increase in leisure time and the rising levels of income in the United States.

Products of the company, numbering approximately 700 items, were grouped into three lines: (1) fishing supplies, (2) hunting supplies, and (3) accessories. The fishing supplies line, which accounted for approximately 40 percent of the company's annual sales, included nearly every item a fisherman would need such as fishing jackets, vests, caps, rods and reels of all types, lines, flies, lures, landing nets, and creels. Thirty percent of annual sales were in the hunting supplies line, which consisted of hunting clothing of all types including insulated and thermal underwear, safety garments, shell holders, whistles, calls, and gun cases. The accessories line, which made up the balance of the company's annual sales volume, included items such as compasses, cooking kits, lanterns, hunting and fishing knives, hand warmers, and novelty gifts.

While the sales of the hunting and fishing lines were very seasonal, they tended to complement one another. The January–April period accounted for the bulk of the company's annual volume in fishing items, and most sales of hunting

---

*Adapted from a case written by Zarrel V. Lambert, Auburn University, and Fred W. Kniffin, University of Connecticut, Stamford. Used with permission.

supplies were made during the months of May through August. Typically, the company's sales of all products reached their lows for the year during the month of December.

Outdoor's sales volume was $6.57 million in the current year, with self-manufactured products accounting for 35 percent of this total. Fifty percent of the company's volume consisted of imported products, which came principally from Japan. Items manufactured by other domestic producers and distributed by Outdoor accounted for the remaining 15 percent of total sales.

Mr. McDonald reported that wholesale prices to retailers were established by adding a markup of 50 to 100 percent to Outdoor's cost for the item. This rule was followed on self-manufactured products as well as for items purchased from other manufacturers. The resulting average markup across all products was 70 percent on cost.

Outdoor's market area consisted of the New England states, New York, Pennsylvania, Ohio, Michigan, Wisconsin, Indiana, Illinois, Kentucky, Tennessee, West Virginia, Virginia, Maryland, Delaware, and New Jersey. The area over which Outdoor could effectively compete was limited to some extent by shipping costs, since all orders were shipped from the factory and warehouse in Albany.

Outdoor's salespeople sold to approximately 6,000 retail stores in small- and medium-sized cities in its market area. Analysis of sales records showed that the firm's customer coverage was very poor in the large metropolitan areas. Typically, each account was a one- or two-store operation. Mr. McDonald stated that he knew for a fact that Outdoor's share of the market was very low, perhaps 2 to 3 percent; and for all practical purposes, he felt the company's sales potential was unlimited.

Mr. McDonald believed that, with few exceptions, Outdoor's customers had little or no brand preference, and in the vast majority of cases they bought hunting and fishing supplies from several suppliers.

It was McDonald's opinion that the pattern of retail distribution for hunting and fishing products had been changing during the past 10 years as a result of the growth of discount stores. He thought that the proportion of retail sales for hunting and fishing supplies made by small- and medium-sized sporting goods outlets had been declining compared to the percent sold by discounters and chain stores. An analysis of company records revealed Outdoor had not developed business among the discounters with the exception of a few small discount stores. Some of Outdoor's executives felt that the lack of business with discounters might have been due in part to the company's pricing policy and in part to the pressures which current customers had exerted on company salespeople to keep them from calling on the discounters.

Outdoor's Sales Force

The company's sales force played the major role in its marketing efforts since Outdoor did not use magazine, newspaper, or radio advertising to reach either the retail trade or consumers. One advertising piece that supplemented the work of the salespeople was Outdoor's merchandise catalog. It contained a complete listing of all the company's products and was mailed to all retailers who were either current accounts or prospective accounts. Typically, store buyers used the catalog for purposes of reordering.

Most accounts were contacted by a salesperson two or three times a year. The salespeople planned their activities so that each store would be called upon at the beginning of the fishing season and again prior to the hunting season. Certain key accounts of some salespeople were contacted more often than two or three times a year.

Management believed that product knowledge was the major ingredient of a successful sales call. Consequently, Mr. McDonald had developed a "selling formula," which each salesperson was required to learn before taking over a territory. The "formula" contained five parts: (1) the name and catalog number of each item sold by the company; (2) the sizes and colors in which each item was available; (3) the wholesale price of each item; (4) the suggested retail price of each item; and (5) the primary selling features of each item. After a new salesperson had mastered the product knowledge specified by this "formula," he or she began working in the assigned territory and was usually accompanied by McDonald for several weeks.

Managing the sales force consumed approximately one-third of Mr. McDonald's efforts. The remaining two-thirds of his time was spent purchasing products for resale and in general administrative duties as the company's chief operating officer.

Mr. McDonald held semiannual sales meetings, had weekly telephone conversations with each salesperson, and had mimeographed bulletins containing information on products, prices, and special promotional deals mailed to all salespeople each week. Daily call reports and attendance at the semiannual sales meetings were required of all salespeople. One meeting was held the first week in January to introduce the spring line of fishing supplies. The hunting line was presented at the second meeting, which was scheduled in May. Each of these sales meetings spanned four to five days so the salespeople were able to study the new products being introduced and any changes in sales and company policies. The production manager and comptroller attended these sales meetings to answer questions and to discuss problems which the salespeople might have concerning deliveries and credit.

On a predetermined schedule, each salesperson telephoned Mr. McDonald every Monday morning to learn of changes in prices, special promotional offers, and delivery schedules of unshipped orders. At this time, the salesperson's activities for the week were discussed, and sometimes the salesperson was asked by Mr. McDonald to collect past due accounts in the territory. In addition, the salespeople submitted daily call reports, which listed the name of each account contacted and the results of the call. Generally, the salespeople planned their own itineraries in terms of the accounts and prospects that were to be contacted and the amount of time to be spent on each call.

Outdoor's sales force during the current year totaled 11 full-time employees. Their ages ranged from 23 to 67 years, and their tenure with the company

Exhibit 1 Salespeople: Age, years of service, territory, and sales

				Sales	
				Previous	Current
Salespeople	Age	Years of service	Territory	year	year
Allen	45	2	Illinois and Indiana	$ 330,264	$ 329,216
Campbell	62	10	Pennsylvania	1,192,192	1,380,240
Duvall	23	1	New England	—	414,656
Edwards	39	1	Michigan	—	419,416
Gatewood	63	5	West Virginia	358,528	358,552
Hammond	54	2	Virginia	414,936	414,728
Logan	37	1	Kentucky and Tennessee	—	447,720
Mason	57	2	Delaware and Maryland	645,032	825,088
O'Bryan	59	4	Ohio	343,928	372,392
Samuels	42	3	New York and New Jersey	737,024	824,472
Wates	67	5	Wisconsin	370,712	342,200
Salespeople terminated in previous year				1,828,816	—
House account				257,384	244,480
Total				$6,478,816	$6,374,816

ranged from 1 to 10 years. Salespeople, territories, and sales volumes for the previous year and the current year are shown in Exhibit 1.

Compensation of Salespeople

The salespeople were paid straight commissions on their dollar sales volume for the calendar year. The commission rate was 5 percent on the first $300,000, 6 percent on the next $200,000 in volume, and 7 percent on all sales over $500,000 for the year. Each week, a salesperson could draw all or a portion of his or her accumulated commissions. McDonald encouraged the salespeople to draw commissions as they accumulated since he felt that they were motivated to work harder when they had a very small or zero balance in their commission accounts. These accounts were closed at the end of the year so each salesperson began the new year with nothing in the account.

The salespeople provided their own automobiles and paid their traveling expenses, of which all or a portion were reimbursed by per diem. Under the per diem plan, each salesperson received $70 per day for Monday through Thursday and $42 for Friday, or a total of $322 for the normal workweek. No per diem was paid for Saturday, but a salesperson received an additional $70 if he or she spent Saturday and Sunday nights in the territory.

In addition to the commission and per diem, a salesperson could earn cash awards under two sales incentive plans that were installed two years ago. Under the Annual Sales Increase Awards Plan, a total of $10,400 was paid to the five salespeople having the largest percentage increase in dollar sales volume over the previous year. To be eligible for these awards, a salesperson had to show a sales increase over the previous year. These awards were made at the January sales

Exhibit 2   Salespeople's earnings and incentive awards in the current year

| Salespeople | Sales | | Annual sales increase awards | | Weekly sales increase awards (total accrued) | Earnings* |
	Previous year	Current year	Increase in sales (percent)	Award		
Allen	$ 330,264	$ 329,216	(0.3%)	—	$1,012	$30,000†
Campbell	1,192,192	1,380,240	15.8	$3,000 (2d)	2,244	88,617
Duvall	—	414,656	—	—	—	30,000†
Edwards	—	419,416	—	—	—	30,000†
Gatewood	358,528	358,552	(0.1)	400 (5th)	1,104	18,513
Hammond	414,936	414,728	—	—	420	30,000†
Logan	—	447,720	—	—	—	30,000†
Mason	645,032	825,088	27.9	4,000 (1st)	3,444	49,756
O'Bryan	343,928	372,392	8.3	1,000 (4th)	1,512	19,344
Samuels	737,024	824,472	11.9	2,000 (3d)	1,300	49,713
Wates	370,712	342,200	(7.7)	—	612	17,532

*Exclusive of incentive awards and per diem.
†Guarantee of $600 per week or $30,000 per year.

meeting, and the winners were determined by dividing the dollar amount of each salesperson's increase by his or her volume for the previous year, with the percentage increases ranked in descending order. The salespeople's earnings under this plan for the current year are shown in Exhibit 2.

Under the second incentive plan, each salesperson could win a Weekly Sales Increase Award for each week in which his or her dollar volume in the current year exceeded sales for the corresponding week in the previous year. Beginning with an award of $4 for the first week, the amount of the award increased by $4 for each week in which the salesperson surpassed his or her sales for the comparable week in the previous year. If a salesperson produced higher sales during each of the 50 weeks in the current year, he or she received $4 for the 1st week, $8 for the 2d week, and $200 for the 50th week, or a total of $4,100 for the year. The salesperson had to be employed by the company during the previous year to be eligible for these awards. A check for the total amount of the awards accrued during the year was presented to the salesperson at the sales meeting held in January. Earnings of the salespeople under this plan for the current year are shown in Exhibit 2.

The company frequently used "spiffs" to promote the sales of special items. The salesperson was paid a spiff, which usually was $4, for each order obtained for the designated items in the promotion.

For the past three years in recruiting salespeople, Mr. McDonald had guaranteed the more qualified applicants a weekly income while they learned the business and developed their respective territories. During the current year, five salespeople, Allen, Duvall, Edwards, Hammond, and Logan, had a guarantee of $600 a week, which they drew against their commissions. If the year's cumulative commissions for any of these salespeople were less than their cumulative weekly drawing accounts, they received no commissions. The commission and drawing accounts were closed on December 31 so each salesperson began the new year with a zero balance in each account.

The company did not have a stated or written policy specifying the maximum length of time a salesperson could receive a guarantee if commissions continued to be less than his or her draw. Mr. McDonald held the opinion that the five salespeople who currently had guarantees would quit if these guarantees were withdrawn before their commissions reached $30,000 per year.

Mr. McDonald stated that he was convinced the annual earnings of Outdoor's salespeople had fallen behind earnings for comparable selling positions, particularly in the past six years. As a result, he felt that the company's ability to attract and hold high-caliber professional salespeople was being adversely affected. He strongly expressed the opinion that each salesperson should be earning $50,000 annually.

Compensation Plan Proposals

In December of the current year, Mr. McDonald met with his comptroller and production manager, who were the only other executives of the company, and solicited their ideas concerning changes in the company's compensation plan for salespeople.

The comptroller pointed out that the salespeople having guarantees were not producing the sales that had been expected from their territories. He was concerned that the annual commissions earned by four of the five salespeople on guarantees were approximately half or less than their drawing accounts.

Furthermore, according to the comptroller, several of the salespeople who did not have guarantees were producing a relatively low volume of sales year after year. For example, annual sales remained at relatively low levels for Gatewood, O'Bryan, and Wates, who had been working four to five years in their respective territories.

The comptroller proposed that guarantees be reduced to $250 per week plus commissions at the regular rate on all sales. The $250 would not be drawn against commissions as was the case under the existing plan, but would be in addition to any commissions earned. In the comptroller's opinion, this plan would motivate the salespeople to increase sales rapidly since their incomes would rise directly with their sales. The comptroller presented Exhibit 3, which showed the incomes of the five salespeople having guarantees in the current year as compared with the incomes they would have received under his plan.

From a sample check of recent shipments, the production manager had concluded that the salespeople tended to overwork accounts located within a 50-mile radius of their homes. Sales coverage was extremely light in a 60- to 100-mile radius of the salespeople's homes, with somewhat better coverage beyond 100 miles. He argued that this pattern of sales coverage seemed to result from a desire by the salespeople to spend most evenings during the week at home with their families.

Exhibit 3   Comparison of earnings in current year under existing guarantee plan with earnings under the comptroller's plan*

Salespeople	Sales	Existing plan			Comptroller's plan		
		Commissions	Guarantee	Earnings	Commissions	Guarantee	Earnings
Allen	$329,216	$16,753	$30,000	$30,000	$16,753	$12,500	$29,253
Duvall	414,656	21,879	30,000	30,000	21,879	12,500	34,379
Edwards	419,416	22,165	30,000	30,000	22,165	12,500	34,665
Hammond	358,552	18,513	30,000	30,000	18,513	12,500	31,013
Logan	447,720	23,863	30,000	30,000	23,863	12,500	36,363

*Exclusive of incentive awards and per diem.

He proposed that the per diem be increased from $70 to $90 per day for Monday through Thursday, $42 for Friday, and $90 for Sunday if the salesperson spent Sunday evening away from home. He reasoned that the per diem of $90 for Sunday would act as a strong incentive for the salespeople to drive to the perimeters of their territories on Sunday evenings rather than use Monday morning for traveling. Further, he believed that the increase in per diem would encourage the salespeople to spend more evenings away from their homes, which would result in a more uniform coverage of the sales territories and an overall increase in sales volume.

The consultant from New York City recommended that the guarantees and per diem be retained on the present basis and proposed that Outdoor adopt what he called a "Ten Percent Self-Improvement Plan." Under the consultant's plan, each salesperson would be paid, in addition to the regular commission, a monthly bonus commission of 10 percent on all dollar volume over his or her sales in the comparable month of the previous year. For example, if a salesperson sold $40,000 worth of merchandise in January of the current year and $36,000 in January of the previous year, he or she would receive a $400 bonus check in February. For salespeople on guarantees, bonuses would be in addition to earnings. The consultant reasoned that the bonus commission would motivate the salespeople, both those with and without guarantees, to increase their sales.

He further recommended the discontinuation of the two sales incentive plans currently in effect. He felt the savings from these plans would nearly cover the costs of his proposal.

Following a discussion of these proposals with the management group, Mr. McDonald was undecided on which proposal to adopt, if any. Further, he wondered if any change in the compensation of salespeople would alleviate all of the present problems.

Part 7

Pricing Decisions

The cases in the pricing section of this book involve several different kinds of decisions. A firm's pricing strategy is extremely important because of the quickness with which a change can be implemented, because of the importance of price to consumers in their purchase decisions, and because of the direct impact of prices on profits.

The first important consideration in establishing a price for a product is the firm's pricing objectives. A firm striving for growth may utilize a totally different strategy from one who is seeking to discourage others from cutting prices or to desensitize consumers to price. Firms with objectives oriented around maximizing long-run profits may utilize different strategies than firms who are seeking to maximize short-run profits. Thus, the first step in establishing a price should be to clearly identify what the objectives are.

Two alternative strategies often utilized are skimming and penetration. A skimming strategy is one in which a high initial price is set, and the product is sold to all those consumers willing to pay this price. The price is then lowered somewhat, and the product is sold to those consumers willing to pay that price. This process continues for some time, "skimming the cream" off the top of the market with each price change. For example, when electronic calculators were first introduced, they were priced at more than $300. A number of scientific and engineering-related organizations were willing to purchase the product at this price. The price was then lowered to the neighborhood of $150 to $200, and a number of other organizations were willing to purchase the product. Later, the price was reduced to the $50 to $100 range, and very many more buyers entered the market. Eventually, the price was lowered still further, and many more consumers entered the market.

A skimming strategy is appropriate when there are no close substitutes for the product and the demand is inelastic with respect to price. It is a very conservative policy allowing the marketer to recover as much of the costs as possible quickly in the event that demand is not that great. It also allows the marketer to accumulate money for aggressive penetration later when competition enters the market. A skimming strategy is an effective way to segment the market, as in the calculator example and in the case of the book market where a skimming strategy is used for hardcover books, and the paperback edition is later introduced using a penetration strategy.

A penetration strategy utilizes a low initial price in the hopes of penetrating a large proportion of the market in a short period of time. This strategy would be used when one or more of the following conditions existed:

a. High short-run price elasticity (for example, the low price of the Model-T Ford allowed many people to purchase a car for the first time).
b. Large economies of scale in production.
c. The probability of quick public acceptance.
d. The probability of quick competitive imitation.

The specific pricing decisions that have to be made include the price level to set, price variation including discount structure and geographic price differences, margins to be given to various intermediaries in the channels of distribution, and the determination of when to change the price structure.

A number of different pricing methods are utilized by organizations. Some use the cost-plus method, whereby a certain percentage is added to the firm's costs to establish their pricing. This method is often used by industrial marketers and by wholesalers and retailers. Other organizations use break-even analysis, marginal cost analysis, and/or marginal revenue analysis to determine their pricing structure. Still other organizations are price followers and use a strategy of meeting the prices of competitors.

The ideal way to determine the price that should be charged involves analyzing a number of variables before actually setting the price. Included would be:

1. *Consumer buying patterns.* What price would consumers expect to pay for this type of product? What are the important price points or price lines that different segments of the market desire?
2. *Product differentiation.* In what ways is the company's product different from the others on the market? What advantages does the product offer the consumer?
3. *What is the competitive structure* of the industry, and what stage of the product life cycle is the product in?
4. *How price sensitive* is total industry demand, and how price sensitive is demand for the individual firm's product? What is the size of the total market and what is the likelihood of economies of scale?
5. *What is the economic climate forecast,* and how sensitive is the demand of the product to changes in the economic climate?

6. *Legal and social considerations.* New interpretations of the Robinson-Patman Act (prohibiting price discrimination) and various state laws governing pricing must be taken into consideration.

7. *Cost structure of the firm.* The relationship between fixed costs and variable costs is extremely important in pricing decisions, as is the cost structure of the firm compared to competitors' pricing structure. Pricing strategy for a hotel, with a very low variable cost ratio, will of necessity be quite different than pricing strategy for a clothing manufacturer, which has a very high variable cost ratio.

8. *The overall marketing strategy for the product.* It is important to recognize that the pricing strategy must be consistent with all the other elements of the firm's marketing strategy.

Case 24

Royale Suites*

"It's a great day for sitting high above the inner harbor eating crab cakes." Bill Abbott and his New Property Planning Team were enjoying a lunch break on a sunny day in January 1993. After lunch, they would return to developing a marketing plan for the new Royale Suites Baltimore Hotel. The 11-story, 325-room hotel, opening in 12 months, was located within blocks of the financial district and Inner Harbor tourist sites. Although only a few rooms would have an Inner Harbor view, they expected to capitalize on the already successful Royale Suites concept. "We've only got two days to bring our plan together before we present it to Corporate Planning. Where do we stand now?"

The Royale Suites Concept

Royale Suites was one of the early entries into the all-suite hotel segment. Recognizing the increasing demand by business people to conduct small meetings in their hotel rooms and families' desires for larger and more private hotel rooms, Royale Suites opened their first property in the early 1980s. Additional units had been opened in most of the largest cities in the United States. Baltimore was one of the few prime locations remaining to Royale Suites. Royale Suites Real Estate staff had been fortunate to locate and acquire an outstanding site.

The typical Royale Suite property is from 8 to 12 stories high, including from 225 to 350 two-room suites. A typical floor plan is shown in Exhibit 1. Kitchen facilities are not included since they are believed to be of little interest to business people and create significant additional equipment and cleaning costs.

Interior decorations are adapted to specific markets, and local, classical themes are encouraged. The Baltimore Royale Suite would have two meeting rooms seating 60 persons in each. They can be combined into a larger room seating 100 and used for meals.

Exhibit 1   Typical room layout

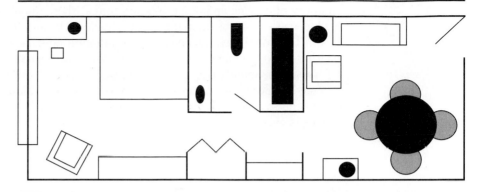

The New Properties Planning Team

Royale Suites uses a New Properties Planning Team to plan the opening of all new properties. This team consisted of planning managers for each of the major departments in the hotel (Exhibit 2). Often those on the planning team continue on as the operating managers for the site.

The team was headquartered in a building overlooking Baltimore's Inner Harbor. They were charged with developing the marketing plan for the hotel opening and the first year of service.

Exhibit 2   New Properties Planning Team

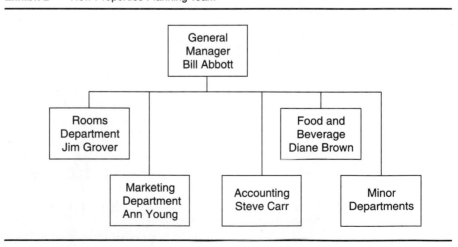

Competition

A minority of downtown hotel rooms are suites. These are either in local hotels or included as part of the room inventory of national chains (Table 1). As a result, suites in Baltimore have received little promotion both locally and nationally. This is a relatively untapped product in the downtown market area.

Serving as mainly upscale rooms within nonsuite hotels, suites are generally priced higher than standard rooms in these hotels. Although the occupancy rate for suites was not known, the planning team estimated that downtown occupancy rates averaged 60 percent for the past two years.

TABLE 1   Competitor room rates*

Major hotels in Baltimore	Number of employees	Number of rooms	Number of suites	Low single room rate	High single room rate
Omni	500	702	17	$129	$149
Stouffer	620	622	46	175	220
Marriott	400	525	12	129	195
Hyatt	500	489	26	155	173
Radisson	200	440	28	119	134
Holiday Inn	140	375	2	69	119
Sheraton	275	339	20	145	160
Tremont Suite	150	290	290	115	140
Days Inn	100	250	8	70	90
Harbor Court	300	203	25	155	210
Comfort Inn	50	200	5	59	125
All suite outside Baltimore					
Guest Quarters BWI	153	251	251	109	139
Embassy Suites Hunt Valley	120	223	223	109	119

*Rates as of June 19, 1992. Price increases of 5 percent per year are expected.
Source: *Baltimore Business Journal,* (July 3–9, 1992), p. 9.

Consumer Behavior

Ann Young noted that reservations were made in several ways:

- *Pure transient:* Tourist or business travelers who either dropped in or made reservations direct to the Baltimore site. This group paid the rack rate (published rate charge).
- *Computer reservations:* Customers who made reservations through Royale Suites national toll-free number.
- *Government:* Government employees on relatively low per diem.
- *Bus tours:* Contracts with travel agents for tour groups at negotiated rates.

- *Corporate groups:* Corporation and association meetings. These consisted of very small groups that could meet in the suites and larger groups that attended meetings in the Convention Center or in other hotels.
- *Airlines:* Contracts with airlines as a part of a vacation plan and also with flight crews.
- *Weekend packages:* Two-night weekend plans, including some special services to make them attractive.

A customer survey was available to the planning team that suggested parity between major all-suite hotels (Table 2). However, this data did not break down quality perceptions for specific market segments. It was not clear what attributes were most important to these segments and how the chains compared in the minds of these segments.

TABLE 2   Relative quality evaluations (last year)*

	Residence Inn	Embassy Suites	Royale Suites
Sample size	209	243	256
Overall satisfaction			
Very satisfied	42%	40%	38%
Satisfied	53	56	57
Dissatisfied	5	4	5
*Specific attributes * (5 = COMPLETELY SATISFIED 1 = COMPLETELY DISSATISFIED)*			
Staff	4.1	3.2	4.5
Food	N/A	2.9	3.3
Room Quality:			
Cleanliness	4.2	3.8	4.1
Size	4.8	4.7	4.6
Bed comfort	2.9	3.1	2.9
Climate	3.1	2.8	3.2
Noise	3.3	3.4	3.1
Amenities	2.8	3.1	2.8

*Attributes scale: 5 = completely satisfied, 1 = completely dissatisfied.

A second survey provided some overall insights into service attributes that were important to business people (Table 3). Ann felt that this might provide some guidance in positioning Royale Suites.

The Marketing Mix

Product

The physical product was fixed by corporate architectural and planning standards as adapted to the specific Baltimore site. There were a number of possible services that could be offered.

TABLE 3 Importance of hotel service attributes and perceived performance by managers and executives

Hotel service attribute	Importance to customer	Consumer belief of actual performance
Billing accuracy	91%*	83%*
Efficient check-in	80	55
Reliable message and wake-up service	79	76
Cares about the consumer	77	54
Competitive room rates	72	52
Reasonable charge for in-room phone	72	37
Express checkouts	68	63
Attractive and generously sized rooms	59	55
Fast breakfast service	54	48
Well-lighted and ample work space	48	51
Availability of no-smoking rooms	47	49
Quality frequent-traveler program	41	34
Multiple dining and lounge facilities	36	54
Late evening room service	24	38

*Scores: Percent who answer 8, 9, or 10 on a 1-to-10 scale.
Source: Opinion Research Corporation Executive Travel Tracking Service, 1990.

Although most Royale Suites offered free breakfasts and happy hours, this was no longer a standard corporate policy or included in corporate advertising. Diane Brown estimated the cost of breakfast to average $4.00 per occupied room and a happy hour at $1.00 per occupied room.

Diane favored these services. "Although happy hours and breakfasts have become pretty standard through the all-suite industry, this is not yet the standard in Baltimore. If we introduce this as a standard feature we can be a pace setter here and avoid playing catch-up if others introduce these later."

Ann Young replied, "It's a great marketing feature, however, will it lead to us charging noncompetitive room rates? Our consumers are sensitive about prices and there are plenty of alternatives for breakfast and booze downtown. I'm also concerned about our restaurant; its services may be very important to our customers."

Restaurant policy. Royale Suites had a flexible policy on restaurants. Throughout the chain they are both owned and leased. "We have built a reputation for having restaurants with a little local flair. We don't just 'cookie-cut' our food services, they are adapted to each site either by opening our own facility or leasing our space to a local restaurant with a good reputation." Diane Brown felt that the contribution to profits would be about the same either owning or leasing the restaurant and the primary concern must be to design food services that enhanced the image of the Baltimore Royale Suites with its customers. Brown also believed that, although hotel restaurants traditionally were mainly used by guests, careful design and positioning had increased their potential to attract customers from outside the hotel.

Prices

"We pay 1½ percent of room revenues into the corporate computer system," Steve commented. "This would seem to be a lot just to book rooms; however, it provides us an opportunity. As you know, we can implement a yield management pricing system using the corporate computer (see Appendix A for a description of yield management). The information system permits us to do much more than we could last year. We can develop a set of pricing rules and update them in just a minute or two. If we make all our advance, group, and transient booking through corporate's computer, we can fully implement a yield management pricing program.

"Let me give you some background on this. When we opened our first units, we stressed a single price policy nationwide. This made a lot of sense to the consumer and it made a lot of sense to us. However, as competition got tougher, we all learned that each city is a unique, local market with different costs and competition. Market pricing became a necessity. This made accountants into marketers and marketers into accountants—probably a good idea. Our computer has turned us into an airline in a pricing sense. If we were clever enough, every room would be booked and profits would be maximized. Of course, every room might have a different price. We have to start somewhere, so let's develop a fairly simple set of pricing rules.

"To simplify this, let's develop rules that give us average prices and occupancy rates for Monday to Thursday, Friday, Saturday, and Sunday. These can be used in our pro forma. We can make use of competitor's prices (Table 1) and some of our historic prices and occupancy rates (Table 4). Let me propose a starting point. There are 52 Sundays with 16,900 rooms available. Perhaps 25 percent of these will be sold at rack rate. How do we price and sell the remaining rooms?"

Advertising, Sales, and Public Relations

Corporate charges each Royale Suites two percent of room revenues for national advertising. This is used to position Royale Suites, provide information about its features and locations, and promote the toll-free reservations number. Media include

TABLE 4 Royal Suites occupancy rates, 1992 (selected sites)

	Average room rate*	August		September		Annual	
City		M–R	F–S	M–R	F–S	M–R	F–S
Chicago	$115.00	56.1%	51.1%	63.4%	61.7%	62.3%	56.8%
Dallas	$120.00	55.5	57.4	63.2	58.7	60.2	58.1
Denver	$120.00	61.5	57.4	67.8	59.2	63.5	58.8
Detroit	$120.00	68.4	61.5	70.2	60.2	69.3	61.4
New Orleans	$120.00	68.4	56.4	71.4	62.4	70.4	58.8
Phoenix	$115.00	68.4	47.7	73.2	51.4	71.2	49.2
San Francisco	$125.00	75.2	76.0	80.2	73.5	78.2	75.5
Average		64.8	58.2	69.9	61.0	67.9	59.8
Weekly Avg.—7 sites		62.9		67.4		65.6	
Weekly Avg.—all sites		61.5		64.7		63.7	

Average occupancy rate spans the August, September, and Annual M–R/F–S columns.

*Room rate increases of about 5 percent per year are expected.

TABLE 5 Media rates and circulation

Magazine	Rate*	Circulation	CPM†
Time—National	$120,130	4,339,029	$ 27.69
Time—Eastern	63,290	1,457,910	43.41
Time—National Business	73,500	1,679,998	43.75
Newsweek—National	100,980	3,180,011	31.75
Newsweek—Eastern	39,278	951,000	41.30
Newsweek—National Business	42,460	753,043	56.38
New Yorker	32,275	622,123	51.88
Business Week—National	56,700	889,535	63.74
Business Week—Northeast	21,210	199,316	106.41
Business Week—Mid Atlantic	14,380	131,813	109.09
Fortune—National	40,900	668,972	61.14
Fortune—Northeast	19,360	160,135	120.90
Fortune—Mid Atlantic	11,500	85,175	135.02
Forbes	45,550	743,533	61.26
Baltimore Magazine	4,760	55,442	85.86
Newspaper			
Wall Street Jour.—National	$99,384	1,835,713	$54.14
Wall Street Jour.—Eastern	43,956	757,483	58.03
Baltimore Sun—Morning	11,241	238,533	47.13

*Rates: Magazine—color, full-page ads, one insertion. Newspaper—black-and-white, full-page ads, one insertion.
†Cost per 1,000 circulation.

national TV, consumer and business magazines, airline flight magazines, and travel trade publications.

Each Royale Suite location is responsible for any national or local advertising featuring its specific property. Media rates for magazines and newspapers under consideration are given in Table 5. Ann addressed her concerns about advertising: "We have to develop a plan that creates a favorable awareness in the minds of our target market segments. An opening kick-off is a must, and then we must sustain interest and expand awareness through the rest of the year. Our budget is limited so we should be very creative with our public relations for the opening. It's important that we're noticed among all the other attractions here.

"I'm also concerned about our sales effort. Salary and expenses will average $50,000 per salesperson. This includes a car and quite a bit of travel. We should be able to trade some travel with the airlines. However, we must be much more specific about our target market segments before we allocate our budget between advertising and salespersons. Are we a business hotel or are we aggressively going after other segments? Help me to define the targets and I'll define the promotional plan."

Financial Analysis and Final Marketing Plan

Steve had produced a first cut at an income statement based on these initial ideas of the market situation and marketing mix (Table 6). "This just isn't good enough. Most other units are averaging over 10 percent profits as a percent of revenues, and several are at 15 percent. I've used the room prices proposed by corporate headquarters.

TABLE 6   Pro forma income statement for new Baltimore Royale Suites hotel

Summary					
Average daily rate		$113.59	←calculated		
Pre-tax income		$813,864	←calculated		
Percent of revenues		5.6%	←calculated		
Occupancy rate		62.6%	←calculated		
Number of rooms		325			

	Mon.-Thr.	Fri.	Sat.	Sun.	Average
Average daily rate*	$120.00	$105.00	$105.00	$105.00	$113.59
Percent change occ. per $1 price[†]	0.50%	1.00%	1.25%	1.25%	
Occupancy rate (est.)*	66.0%	58.0%	58.0%	58.0%	62.57%
Days	209	52	52	52	365

Variable costs		
Housekeeping	$30.00	per room per day
Breakfast[‡]	$4.00	per room per day
Happy hour[§]	$1.00	per room per day
Advertising charge	2.0%	of room revenues
Computer charge	1.5%	of room revenues

Revenues	Percent of revenue	Annual total
Rooms	58.7%	$8,465,939
Food	25.0	3,605,596
Beverages	10.0	1,442,238
Other (telephone, gifts, newspapers, etc.)	6.3	908,610
Total	100.0%	$14,422,383
Expenses		
Rooms		
Variable costs		
Housekeeping	15.4%	$2,226,738
Advertising charge	1.2	169,319
Computer charge	0.9	126,989
Food & Bev.		
Fixed costs	16.6	2,400,000
Variable costs (varies directly as		
% of total revenue)	10.5	1,514,350
Breakf. and/or happy hour	2.6	371,123
Undistributed expenses		
Administration	10.4	1,500,000
Marketing[‖] (do not set less than $200,000)	3.5	500,000
Operations/maint.	10.4%	$1,500,000
Other (telephone, property tax, etc.)	9.0%	$1,300,000
Depreciation	13.9%	$2,000,000
Total	94.4%	$13,608,519
Income before taxes	5.6%	$813,864

Notes: Those rows marked with footnotes can be revised.

*Average daily rates and Occupancy rates are weighted average of all available rates.

[†]Price elasticity: For Mon.–Thr., as rates change by $1, occupancy rate moves in the opposite direction by the percent shown. For Fri., Sat., and Sun., a change in price of $1 results in an opposite change in occupancy rate as given. Elasticities are expected to hold within a $30 range. Price elasticities can be changed if services offered are either decreased or increased.

[‡, §]Breakfast and Happy hour costs must include all expected costs. These rows can also be used to include any other variable costs in your market plan. Specify these to the right of your cost.

[‖]Includes all advertising and salesforce costs. This row can also be used to include any other fixed costs in your market plan. Specify these to the right of the cost.

We have the authority to change these to meet local conditions. I've estimated the effects of price changes on our occupancy rates and included these in the pro forma."

Bill concurred. "I know we've done a lot of work on this project and now we have to concentrate and focus our efforts on a specific marketing plan that provides a realistic, reasonable return to Royale Suites. This is a good location and I know we can build a top performer. Let's see how we can improve this."

Appendix A Yield Management Pricing

Airline deregulation, coupled with large computer reservations systems, encouraged the development of the first computerized yield management systems. The principle of yield management is recognition of the price sensitivities of specific market segments. Ideally as many full-fare seats as possible are sold, and then unfilled seats are sold at decreasingly lower prices until occupancy approaches 100 percent and profits are maximized. Competition assures that full fares will seldom be achieved for 100 percent of capacity. Therefore a block of lower-fare seats can be made available for advance purchase. Seat inventory is monitored to expand or reduce this block of seats before the advance reservations deadline or to open them again closer to flight time. This requires computers to manage the seat as a perishable commodity. Some large airlines make over 30,000 fare changes daily.

The yield management system must have specific rules to match prices to the demands of different segments. These can include services provided, time of day for the flight, day of week, length of stay, how far in advance the ticket is purchased, and other factors. Penalties are often required to minimize high-price segments' use of low-price tickets. These are generally advance payment and loss of all or part of the fare when canceling.

Airlines, like many services, have low variable costs. Any seat priced above variable costs contributes to fixed costs or profits. Empty seats are lost contribution. Low variable costs permit significant added contribution, even from deeply discounted seats. Frequent flyer awards only cost an airline the variable cost of the seat, provided the awards do not displace a paying fare. Thus, travel restrictions are placed on free seat awards.

Yield management pricing has been adopted by communications companies, banks, car rental companies, hotels, and other service firms.

Hotel Room Yield Management

Relihan[1] describes yield management applied to hotel rooms. Hotel guests can be grouped into a wide variety of market segments. At the most general level, business and leisure segments must be served. The leisure segment tend to plan

---

[1]Walter J. Relihan, "The Yield-Management Approach to Hotel-Room Pricing," *The Cornell Hotel and Restaurant Administration Quarterly* (May 1989), pp. 40–45.

ahead, booking earlier than the business segment, and are more price sensitive. Business consumers often are unable to book ahead and are more concerned with availability of a room than price. The hotel must accurately forecast demand to maximize the contribution produced by these segments. The basis for this is accurate reservations history information.

Reservations history can provide the occupancy rate as a function of the average room rate for the total property and for specific market segments. An example of occupancy rate as a function of average room rate is given in Exhibit A–1. Occupancy rates and average room rates can be entered into an income statement to estimate the expected total contribution as shown in Exhibit A–1. In this example, contribution is maximized at an average room rate of $120 with an expected occupancy rate of 65 percent. Break-even occurs at any rate between $100 and $140; however, profits are very sensitive to room rates at this hotel and decline rapidly at rates other than $120. Lower rates produce low unit contribution margins, and higher rates drive away too many consumers.

Exhibit A–1   Revenues and occupancy as a function of average room rate

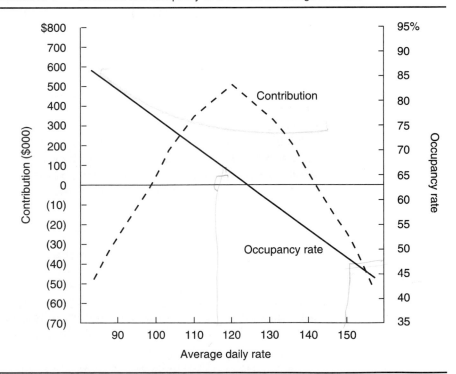

Note: This is not the data for Royale Suites–Baltimore.

Case 25

Techtronics Limited*

In late 1993, the FCC is expected to decide on the broadcast standard for high-definition television (HDTV) in the United States. Subsequently, manufacturers of HDTV sets expect the first consumer sets to be available about two years later. Mark Leeds, the founder and president of Techtronics Limited (TL), has committed a significant amount of time and resources to TL's new HDTV product and is now faced with a major pricing decision with respect to it. "Based on the new technologies developed in our labs, I believe Techtronics Limited is in a strong position to compete in the market. However, I haven't been able to develop an effective pricing strategy," Mr. Leeds exclaimed.

Company History

Techtronics Limited was founded in White Plains, New York, in 1970 by Mr. Leeds. Mr. Leeds, an electrical engineer, founded TL to manufacture and market products that incorporated inventions he had developed while earning his Ph.D. at Columbia University. In recent years, TL's revenues have been mostly derived from sales to the military of video screen televisions, having screen sizes from 8 to 10 feet diagonally. Sales revenues grew from $250,000 in 1970 to $35 million in 1992. Profits in 1992 were $4.7 million.

HDTV Project

The end of the Cold War has brought about a reduction in military spending. As a result, Mr. Leeds is looking for ways to diversify to ensure future viability, and he believes HDTV set production is one such way. Because Techtronics Limited has been producing video screen TVs for a number of years, it finds itself in a strong position to make the transition to HDTV set production. Additionally, TL

---

*This case was written by Brian Murray and Thomas C. Kinnear. Copyright © 1993 by Thomas C. Kinnear.

has been experimenting with various digital data compression techniques in order to enhance the speed and quality of its fax machines. Leeds expects the new technology to be very similar in its application. Since the company's inception, TL has prided itself on technological innovation for the high-end video market. Mr. Leeds expounded on the new patented innovation that he feels will give TL an initial competitive edge:

> Our lab, in conjunction with Columbia University, has developed a breakthrough in eliminating the edge effect. Presently, reception worsens the farther away from the broadcast tower the set is located. The edge effect refers to the digital signal limitation of getting a crystal-clear picture or no picture at all depending on the strength of the signal. Where the signal cuts out also depends partly on the weather. Thus, sets in outlying areas may suddenly go blank. This work will allow our sets to be marketed to consumers in rural areas or areas with volatile weather patterns.

High-Definition Television

Under the present analog system, a wave is converted to 525 horizontal lines, which comprise the picture. Due to inefficiencies inherent with this process, broadcasters are forced to lower the resolution to about 350 lines in order to produce a continuous picture. These inefficiencies also produce the ghosts or double images that sometimes appear. Conversely, the new HDTV system is all digital. A series of 1s and 0s are transmitted to sets equipped to interpret this code. Additionally, over 1,000 horizontal lines per screen are going to be transmitted 30 or 60 times per second (the standard has not yet been set) for increased definition equivalent to 35 mm film. Moreover, the new HDTV format enables manufacturers to employ a greater screen aspect ratio (the ratio of the screen's width to its height). The new ratio of 16:9, as compared to the previous standard's 4:3, removes the box perception of the current television and allows standard 35 mm movies to be viewed uncropped. Thus, a viewer will see more of the picture at a clarity level of more than twice what is currently offered. By employing a digital signal, the sound quality will be akin to that of a compact disc. Overall, the viewer will ultimately feel more a part of the program. This is especially true for sporting events.

It should be noted that detractors of HDTV technology point out that in order to appreciate the enhanced definition, sets must be at least 32 inches across. Moreover, studies have concluded that the average viewer cannot notice the effects of HDTV from 9 feet away, a typical viewing distance.

This new technology will soon be replacing the existing system, and the FCC has mandated the eventual extinction of our present system. By 2008, broadcasters will be switched to a completely digital signal. Until then, broadcasters will broadcast in both digital and analog, with a greater percentage of programs produced for HDTV as sets become widely available. Consumers unwilling or unable to purchase HDTV sets will be able to purchase a converter box, at a nominal price, which will allow their old sets to receive the digital signals.

Consequently, television manufacturers will eventually convert or be forced out. Presently, major television manufacturers like Sony, Mitsubishi, Thompson, and Zenith are among the best positioned to enter the U.S. HDTV market, due to the fact that they already make high-definition televisions for the Japanese market. This market, however, uses a different standard for the HDTV signal. Thus, the manufacturers are still required to make major adjustments in production for the U.S. market. TL, being a small company with related technological and production experience, can quickly move into set production without incurring the large switching costs a larger manufacturer may face. Moreover, it is expected that other low-cost manufacturers, such as Korean manufacturers, will enter the market as HDTV becomes more affordable to the consumer.

Costs

Mr. Leeds expects that TL's direct manufacturing costs will vary depending on the volume produced. Specifically, he believes direct labor costs will fall at higher production levels because of increased automation of the process and improved worker skills. Likewise, less waste is expected due to automation and will lower material costs. Exhibit 1 presents the estimates. The equipment costs necessary to automate the product process are $90,000 to produce between 0 and 5,000 units, an additional $120,000 to produce 5,001 to 10,000 units, and an additional $170,000 to produce between 10,001 and 20,000 units. The useful life of the equipment is set at five years. Moreover, R&D expenses are estimated at one to two million dollars per year. Because other competitors have begun compensating for edge effects in a less-cost-effective manner, Mr. Leeds is confident that TL's production costs are substantially below current competitors. Mr. Leeds is unwilling to produce over 20,000 units per year in the first few years due to the limited cash resources of the company to support inventories.

Exhibit 1   Estimated production costs of TL's HDTV sets*

Volume	0–5,000	5,000–10,000	10,001–20,000
Raw materials	$480	$460	$410
Direct labor	540	320	115
Total direct costs	$1,020	$780	$525

*R&D is estimated at $1–2 million.

Market Studies

Despite the fact that Mr. Leeds believes that the initial market for HDTVs is going to be in the commercial sector, especially bars and hotels, he feels that establishing a long-term position in the consumer market will afford a much greater potential. With this in mind, Mr. Leeds has hired a small economic research consulting firm to perform a consumer study on the likely reactions to alternative retail prices for the set. After extensively interviewing potential HDTV purchasers and examining the sales and pricing histories of similar products, the consultants have concluded that TL's sets would be highly price elastic across the range of prices from $500 to $5,000, both in the primary and secondary senses. They also reported the estimated price elasticity of demand in the range to be between 4.0 and 6.5.

Pricing

Mr. Leeds relates the following situation facing him: "In the Japanese market, only a few thousand were sold in the first year. Manufacturers have been forced, due to this lack of sales, to cut prices from the $30,000–$40,000 range to the $5,000–$10,000 range. I believe that when HDTV sets are introduced into the U.S. market, the initial median price will be around $3,000." Experts feel that by the late 1990s the price will come down to around $1,000, at which price the general public will begin to purchase HDTV sets.

In terms of numbers, Zenith projects one million sets could be sold in the first two years of production. Other, more conservative, estimates predict HDTV set makers won't sell their millionth set until seven or eight years after introduction. This 1 percent of the market benchmark will then be reached in about the same amount of time it took color television. The long-term outlook projects that HDTV sets will have penetrated between 25 and 56 percent of the consumer market by 2008.

Furthermore, Mr. Leeds figures that about 50 percent of the suggested retail selling price will go to wholesaler and retail margins. Subsequently, he is considering a number of different pricing options to ensure profitability. "My marketing staff has given me valid arguments for pricing anywhere from above Sony to below the impending Korean products," he says.

Case 26

Big Sky of Montana, Inc.*

Introduction

Karen Tracy could feel the pressure on her as she sat at her desk late that April afternoon. Two weeks from today she would be called on to present her recommendations concerning next year's winter season pricing policies for the Big Sky of Montana, Inc.—room rates for the resort's accommodation facilities as well as decisions in the skiing and food service areas. The presentation would be made to a top management team from the parent company, Boyne U.S.A., which operated out of Michigan.

"As sales and public relations manager, Karen, your accuracy in decision making is extremely important," her boss had said in his usual tone. "Because we spend most of our time in Michigan, we'll need a well-based and involved opinion."

It'll be the shortest two weeks of my life, she thought.

Background: Big Sky and Boyne U.S.A.

Big Sky of Montana, Inc., was a medium-sized destination resort[1] located in southwestern Montana, 45 miles south of Bozeman and 43 miles north of the west entrance to Yellowstone National Park. Big Sky was conceived in the early 1970s and had begun operation in November 1974.

The 11,000-acre, 2,000-bed resort was separated into two main areas: Meadow and Mountain Villages. The Meadow Village (elevation 6,300 feet) was located 2 miles east of the resort's main entrance on U.S. 191 and 7 miles

---

*This case was prepared by Anne Senausky and Professor James E. Nelson for educational purposes only. It is designed for classroom purposes and not for purposes of research nor to illustrate either effective or ineffective handling of administrative problems. Some data are disguised. Copyright © 1978 by the Endowment and Research Foundation at Montana State University. Used with permission.

[1] Destination resorts were characterized by on-the-hill lodging and eating facilities, a national market, and national advertising.

from the ski area. The Meadow Village had an 800-bed capacity in the form of four condominium complexes (ranging from studios to three-bedroom units) and a 40-room hostel for economy lodging. Additional facilities included an 18-hole golf course, 6 tennis courts, a restaurant, post office, a convention center with meeting space for up to 200 people, and a small lodge serving as a pro shop for the golf course in the summer and cross-country skiing in the winter.

The Mountain Village (elevation 7,500 feet) was the center of winter activity, located at the base of the ski area. In this complex was the 204-room Huntley Lodge offering hotel accommodations, three condominium complexes (unit size ranged from studio to three-bedroom), and an 88-room hostel, for a total of 1,200 beds. The Mountain Mall was also located here, next to the Huntley Lodge and within a five-minute walk of two of the three condominium complexes in the Mountain Village. It housed ticket sales, an equipment rental shop, a skier's cafeteria, two large meeting rooms for a maximum of 700 persons (regularly used as sack lunch areas for skiers), two offices, a ski school desk, and ski patrol room, all of which were operated by Boyne. Also in this building were a delicatessen, drug store/gift shop, sporting goods store/rental shop, restaurant, outdoor clothing store, jewelry shop, a T-shirt shop, two bars, and a child day-care center. Each of these independent operations held leases, due to expire in two to three years.

The closest airport to Big Sky was located just outside Bozeman. It was served by Northwest Orient and Frontier Airlines with connections to other major airlines out of Denver and Salt Lake City. Greyhound and Amtrak also operated bus and train service into Bozeman. Yellowstone Park Lines provided Big Sky with three buses daily to and from the airport and Bozeman bus station (cost was $4.40 one way, $8.40 round trip), as well as an hourly shuttle around the two Big Sky villages. Avis, Hertz, National, and Budget offered rent-a-car service in Bozeman with a drop-off service available at Big Sky.

In July 1976, Boyne U.S.A., a privately owned, Michigan-based operation, purchased the Huntley Lodge, Mountain Mall, ski lifts and terrain, golf course, and tennis courts for approximately $8 million. The company subsequently invested an additional $3 million into Big Sky. Boyne also owned and operated four Michigan resort ski areas.

Big Sky's top management consisted of a lodge manager (in charge of operations within the Huntley Lodge), a sales and public relations manager (Karen), a food and beverage manager, and an area manager (overseeing operations external to the lodge, including the mall and all recreational facilities). These four positions were occupied by persons trained with the parent company; a fifth manager, the comptroller, had worked for pre-Boyne ownership.

Business figures were reported to the company's home office on a daily basis and major decisions concerning Big Sky operations were discussed and approved by "Michigan." Boyne's top management visited Big Sky an average of five times annually, and all major decisions such as pricing and advertising were approved by the parent for all operations.

The Skiing

Big Sky's winter season usually began in late November and continued until the middle of April, with a yearly snowfall of approximately 450 inches. The area had 18 slopes between elevations of 7,500 and 9,900 feet. Terrain breakdown was as follows: 25 percent novice, 55 percent intermediate, and 20 percent advanced. (Although opinions varied, industry guidelines recommended a terrain breakdown of 20 percent, 60 percent, and 20 percent for novice, intermediate, and advanced skiers, respectively.) The longest run was approximately three miles in length; temperatures (highs) ranged from 15 to 30 degrees Fahrenheit throughout the season.

Lift facilities at Big Sky included two double chairlifts, a triple chair, and a four-passenger gondola. Lift capacity was estimated at 4,000 skiers per day. This figure was considered adequate by the area manager, at least until the 1980–81 season.

Karen felt that the facilities, snow conditions, and grooming compared favorably with those of other destination resorts of the Rockies. "In fact, our only real drawback right now," she thought, "is our position in the national market. We need more skiers who are sold on Big Sky. And that is in the making."

The Consumers

Karen knew from previous dealings that Big Sky, like most destination areas, attracted three distinct skier segments: local day skiers (living within driving distance and not utilizing lodging in the area); individual destination skiers (living out of state and using accommodations in the Big Sky area); and groups of destination skiers (clubs, professional organizations, and the like).

The first category was comprised typically of Montana residents, with a relatively small number from Wyoming and Idaho. (Distances from selected population centers to Big Sky are presented in Exhibit 1.) A 1973 study of four Montana ski areas performed by the advertising unit of the Montana department of highways characterized Montana skiers as:

1. In their early 20s and males (60 percent).
2. Living within 75 miles of a ski area.
3. From a household with two skiers in it.
4. Averaging $13,000 in household income.
5. An intermediate to advanced ability skier.
6. Skiing five hours per ski day, 20 days per season locally.
7. Skiing four days away from local areas.
8. Taking no lessons in the past five years.

Karen was also aware that a significant number of day skiers, particularly on the weekends, were college students.

Exhibit 1

(a) Population centers in proximity to Big Sky (distance and population)

City	Distance from Big Sky (miles)	Population (U.S. 1970 Census)
Bozeman, Montana	45	18,670
Butte, Montana	126	23,368
Helena, Montana	144	22,730
Billings, Montana	174	61,581
Great Falls, Montana	225	60,091
Missoula, Montana	243	29,497
Pocatello, Idaho	186	40,036
Idaho Falls, Idaho	148	35,776

(b) Approximate distance of selected major U.S. population centers to Big Sky (in air miles)

City	Distance to Big Sky*
Chicago	1,275
Minneapolis	975
Fargo	750
Salt Lake City	375
Dallas	1,500
Houston	1,725
Los Angeles	975
San Francisco	925
New York	2,025
Atlanta	1,950
New Orleans	1,750
Denver	750

*Per passenger air fare could be approximated at 20 cents per mile (round trip, coach rates).

Destination, or nonresident skiers, were labeled in the same study as typically:

1. At least in their mid-20s and males (55 percent).
2. Living in a household of three or more skiers.
3. Averaging near $19,000 in household income.
4. More an intermediate skier.
5. Spending about six hours per day skiing.
6. Skiing 11–14 days per season with 3–8 days away from home.
7. Taking ski school lessons.

Through data taken from reservation records, Karen learned that individual destination skiers accounted for half of last year's usage based on skier days.[2] Geographic segments were approximately as follows:

---

[2] A skier day is defined as one skier using the facility for one day of operation.

Upper Midwest (Minnesota, Michigan, North Dakota)	30 percent
Florida	20 percent
California	17 percent
Washington, Oregon, Montana	15 percent
Texas, Oklahoma	8 percent
Other	10 percent

Reservation records indicated that the average length of stay for individual destination skiers was about six or seven days.

It was the individual destination skier who was most likely to buy a lodging/lift package; 30 percent made commitments for these advertised packages when making reservations for 1977–78. Even though there was no discount involved in this manner of buying lift tickets, Karen knew that they were fairly popular because it saved the purchaser a trip to the ticket window every morning. Approximately half of the individual business came through travel agents, who received a 10 percent commission.

The third skier segment, the destination group, accounted for a substantial 20 percent of Big Sky's skier day usage. The larger portion of the group business came through medical and other professional organizations holding meetings at the resort, as this was a way to "combine business with pleasure." These groups were typically comprised of couples and individuals between the ages of 30 and 50. Ski clubs made up the remainder with a number coming from the southern states of Florida, Texas, and Georgia. During the 1977–78 season, Big Sky drew 30 ski clubs with membership averaging 55 skiers. The average length of stay for all group destination skiers was about four or five days.

A portion of these group bookings were made through travel agents, but the majority dealt directly with Karen. The coordinator of the professional meetings or the president of the ski club typically contacted the Big Sky sales office to make initial reservation dates, negotiate prices, and work out the details of their stay.

The Competition

In Karen's mind, Big Sky faced two types of competition, that for local day skiers and that for out-of-state (i.e., destination) skiers.

Bridger Bowl was virtually the only area competing for local day skiers. Bridger was a "nonfrills," nonprofit, and smaller ski area located some 16 miles northeast of Bozeman. It received the majority of local skiers including students at Montana State University, which was located in Bozeman. The area was labeled as having terrain more difficult than that of Big Sky and was thus more appealing to the local expert skiers. However, it also had much longer lift lines than Big Sky and had recently lost some of its weekend business to them.

Karen had found through experience that most Bridger skiers usually "tried" Big Sky once or twice a season. Season passes for the two areas were mutually honored at the half-day rate for an all-day ticket, and Big Sky occasionally ran newspaper ads offering discounts on lifts to obtain more Bozeman business.

For out-of-state skiers, Big Sky considered its competition to be mainly the destination resorts of Colorado, Utah, and Wyoming. (Selected data on competing resorts is presented in Exhibit 2.) Because Big Sky was smaller and newer than the majority of these areas, Karen reasoned, it was necessary to follow an aggressive strategy aimed at increasing its national market share.

Exhibit 2   Competitors' 1977–1978 package plan rates,* number of lifts, and lift rates

	Lodge double (2)[†]	Two bedroom condo (4)	Three bedroom condo (6)	Number of lifts	Daily lift rates
Aspen, Colo.	$242	$242	$220	19	$13
Steamboat, Colo.	230	230	198	15	12
Jackson, Wyo.	230	242	210	5	14
Vail, Colo.	230	242	220	15	14
Snowbird, Utah	208	none	none	6	11
Bridger Bowl, Mont.	(No lodging available at Bridger Bowl)			3	8

*Package plan rates are per person and include seven nights lodging, six lift tickets (high season rates).
[†]Number in parentheses denotes occupancy of unit on which price is based.

Present Policies

Lift Rates

It was common knowledge that there existed some local resentment concerning Big Sky's lift rate policy. Although comparable to rates at Vail or Aspen, an all-day lift ticket was $4 higher than the ticket offered at nearby Bridger Bowl. In an attempt to alleviate this situation, management at Big Sky instituted a $9 "chair pass" for the 1977–78 season, entitling the holder to unlimited use of the three chairs, plus two rides per day on the gondola, to be taken between specified time periods. Because the gondola served primarily intermediate terrain, it was reasoned that the chair pass would appeal to the local, more expert skier. A triple chair serving the bowl area was located at the top of the gondola, and two rides on the gondola would allow those skiers to take ample advantage of the advanced terrain up there. Otherwise, all advanced terrain was served by another chair.

However, if Big Sky was to establish itself as a successful, nationally prominent destination area, Karen felt the attitudes and opinions of all skiers must be carefully weighed. Throughout the season she had made a special effort to grasp the general feeling toward rates. A $12 ticket, she discovered, was thought to be very reasonable by destination skiers, primarily because Big Sky was predominantly an intermediate area and the average destination skier was of intermediate ability; also because Big Sky was noted for its relative lack of lift lines, giving the skier more actual skiing time for the money. "Perhaps we should keep the price the same," she thought, "we do need more business. Other destination areas are likely to raise their prices and we should look good in comparison."

Also discussed was the possible abolition of the $9 chair pass. The question in Karen's mind was if its elimination would severely hurt local business or would it sell an all-lift $12 ticket to the skier who had previously bought only a chair pass. The issue was compounded by an unknown number of destination skiers who opted for the cheaper chair pass too.

Season-pass pricing was also an issue. Prices for the 1977–78 all-lift season pass had remained the same as last year, but a season chair pass had been introduced which was the counterpart of the daily chair lift pass. Karen did not like the number of season chair passes purchased in relation to the number of all-lift passes and considered recommending its abolition as well as an increase in the price of the all-lift pass. "I'm going to have to think this one out carefully," she thought, "because skiing accounted for about 40 percent of our total revenue this past season. I'll have to be able to justify my decision not only to Michigan but also to the Forest Service."

Price changes were not solely at the discretion of Big Sky management. As is the case with most larger western ski areas, the U.S. government owned part of the land on which Big Sky operated. Control of this land was the responsibility of the U.S. Forest Service, which annually approved all lift pricing policies. For the 1976–77 ski season, Forest Service action kept most lift rate increases to the national inflation rate. For the 1977–78 season, larger price increases were allowed for ski areas which had competing areas near by; Big Sky was considered to be such an area. No one knew what the Forest Service position would be for the upcoming 1978–79 season.

To help her in her decision, an assistant had prepared a summary of lift rates and usage for the past two seasons (Exhibit 3).

Room Rates

This area of pricing was particularly important because lodging accounted for about one-third of the past season's total revenue. It was also difficult because of the variety of accommodations (Exhibit 4) and the difficulty in accurately forecasting next season's demand. For example, the season of 1976–77 had been unique in that a good portion of the Rockies was without snow for the initial months of the winter, including Christmas. Big Sky was fortunate in receiving as much snow as it had, and consequently many groups and individuals who were originally headed for Vail or Aspen booked in with Big Sky.

Pricing for the 1977–78 season had been made on the premise that there would be a good amount of repeat business. This came true in part, but not as

Exhibit 3

(a) 1977–78 lift rates and usage summary (136 days operation)

Ticket	Consumer cost	Skier days*	Number season passes sold
Adult all-day all-lift	$ 12	53,400	
Adult all-day chair	9	20,200	
Adult half day	8	9,400	
Child all-day all-lift	8	8,500	
Child all-day chair	5	3,700	
Child half day	6	1,200	
Hotel passes[†]	12/day	23,400	
Complimentary	0	1,100	
Adult all-lift season pass	220	4,300	140
Adult chair season pass	135	4,200	165
Child all-lift season pass	130	590	30
Child chair season pass	75	340	15
Employee all-lift season pass	100	3,000	91
Employee chair season pass	35	1,100	37

(b) 1976–77 lift rates and usage summary (122 days operation)

Ticket	Consumer cost	Skier days	Number season passes sold
Adult all-day	$ 10	52,500	
Adult half day	6.50	9,000	
Child all-day	6	10,400	
Child half day	4	1,400	
Hotel passes[†]	10/day	30,500	
Complimentary	0	480	
Adult season pass	220	4,200	84
Child season pass	130	300	15
Employee season pass	100	2,300	70

*A skier day is defined as one skier using the facility for one day of operation.
[†]Hotel passes refers to those included in the lodging/lift packages.

Exhibit 4

(a) Nightly room rates,* 1977–1978

	Low season range	High season range	Maximum occupancy
Huntley Lodge			
Standard	$ 42–62	$ 50–70	4
Loft	52–92	60–100	6
Stillwater Condo			
Studio	40–60	45–65	4
One-bedroom	55–75	60–80	4
Bedroom w/loft	80–100	90–100	6
Deer Lodge Condo			
One-bedroom	74–84	80–90	4
Two-bedroom	93–103	100–110	6
Three-bedroom	112–122	120–130	8
Hill Condo			
Studio	30–40	35–45	4
Studio w/loft	50–70	55–75	6

(continued)

Exhibit 4 *(concluded)*

(b) Nightly room rates, 1976–1977

	Low season range	High season range	Maximum occupancy
Huntley Lodge			
Standard	$ 32–47	$35–50	4
Loft	47–67	50–70	6
Stillwater Condo			
Studio	39–54	37–52	4
One-bedroom	52–62	50–60	4
Bedroom w/loft	60–80	65–85	6
Deer Lodge Condo			
One-bedroom	51–66	55–70	4
Two-bedroom	74–94	80–100	6
Three-bedroom	93–123	100–130	8
Hill Condo			
Studio	28–43	30–45	4
Studio w/loft	42–62	45–65	6

*Rates determined by number of persons in room or condominium unit and do not include lift tickets. Maximums for each rate range apply at maximum occupancy.

Exhibit 5

(a) 1977–1978 Lodge-condominium occupancy (in room-nights*)

	December (26 days operation)	January	February	March	April (8 days operation)
Huntley Lodge	1,830	2,250	3,650	4,650	438
Condominiums[†]	775	930	1,350	100	90

(b) 1976–1977 Lodge-condominium occupancy (in room-nights)

	December (16 days operation)	January	February	March	April (16 days operation)
Huntley Lodge	1,700	3,080	4,525	4,300	1,525
Condominiums[‡]	600	1,000	1,600	1,650	480

(c) Lodge-condominium occupancy (in person-nights[§])

December 1977 (1976)	January 1978 (1977)	February 1978 (1977)	March 1978 (1977)	April 1978 (1977)
7,850 (6,775)	9,200 (13,000)	13,150 (17,225)	17,900 (17,500)	1,450 (4,725)

*A room-night is defined as one room (or condominium) rented for one night. Lodging experience is based on 124 days of operation for 1977–78, while Exhibit 3 shows the skiing facilities operating 136 days. Both numbers are correct.
[†]Big Sky had 92 condominiums available during the 1977–78 season.
[‡]Big Sky had 85 condominiums available during the 1976–77 season.
[§]A person-night refers to one person using the facility for one night.

much as had been hoped. Occupancy experience had also been summarized for the past two seasons to help Karen make her final decision (Exhibit 5).

As was customary in the hospitality industry, January was a slow period and it was necessary to price accordingly. Low season pricing was extremely important because many groups took advantage of these rates. On top of that, groups were often offered discounts in the neighborhood of 10 percent. Considering this, Karen could not price too high, with the risk of losing individual destination skiers, nor too low, such that an unacceptable profit would be made from group business in this period.

Food Service

Under some discussion was the feasibility of converting all destination skiers to the American Plan, under which policy each guest in the Huntley Lodge would be placed on a package to include three meals daily in a Big Sky-controlled facility. There was a feeling both for and against this idea. The parent company had been successfully utilizing this plan for years at its destination areas in northern Michigan. Extending the policy to Big Sky should find similar success.

Karen was not so sure. For one thing, the Michigan resorts were primarily self-contained and alternative eateries were few. For another, the whole idea of extending standardized policies from Michigan to Montana was suspect. As an example, Karen painfully recalled a day in January when Big Sky "tried on" another successful Michigan policy of accepting only cash or check payments for lift tickets. Reactions of credit-card-carrying skiers could be described as ranging from annoyed to irate.

If an American Plan were proposed for next year, it would likely include both the Huntley Lodge Dining Room and Lookout Cafeteria. Less clear, however, were prices to be charged. There certainly would have to be consideration for both adults and children and for the two independently operated eating places in the Mountain Mall (see Exhibit 6 for an identification of eating places in the Big Sky area). Beyond these considerations, there was little else other than an expectation of a profit to guide Karen in analysis.

The Telephone Call

"Profits in the food area might be hard to come by," Karen thought. "Last year it appears we lost money on everything we sold." (See Exhibit 7.) Just then the telephone rang. It was Rick Thompson, her counterpart at Boyne Mountain Lodge in Michigan. "How are your pricing recommendations coming?" he asked. "I'm about done with mine and thought we should compare notes."

"Good idea, Rick—only I'm just getting started out here. Do you have any hot ideas?"

"Only one," he responded. "I just got off the phone with a guy in Denver. He told me all of the major Colorado areas are upping their lift prices one or two dollars next year."

"Is that right, Rick? Are you sure?"

"Well, you know nobody knows for sure what's going to happen, but I think it's pretty good information. He heard it from his sister-in-law who works in Vail. I think he said she read it in the local paper or something."

"That doesn't seem like very solid information," said Karen. "Let me know if you hear anything more, will you?"

"Certainly. You know, we really should compare our recommendations before we stick our necks out too far on this pricing thing. Can you call me later in the week?" he asked.

"Sure, I'll talk to you the day after tomorrow; I should be about done by then. Anything else?"

"Nope—gotta run. Talk to you then. Bye," and he was gone.

"At least I've got some information," Karen thought, "and a new deadline!"

Exhibit 6   Eating places in the Big Sky area

Establishment	Type of service	Meals served	Current prices	Seating	Location
Lodge Dining Room*	A la carte	Breakfast Lunch Dinner	$2–5 2–5 7–15	250	Huntley Lodge
Steak House*	Steak/lobster	Dinner only	6–12	150	Huntley Lodge
Fondue Stube*	Fondue	Dinner only	6–10	25	Huntley Lodge
Ore House†	A la carte	Lunch Dinner	.80–4.00 5–12	150	Mountain Mall
Ernie's Deli†	Deli/restaurant	Breakfast Lunch	1–3 2–5	25	Mountain Mall
Lookout Cafeteria*	Cafeteria	Breakfast Lunch Dinner	1.50–3.00 2–4 3–6	175	Mountain Mall
Yellow Mule†	A la carte	Breakfast Lunch Dinner	2–4 2–5 4–8	75	Meadow Village
Buck's T–4†	Road house restaurant/bar	Dinner only	2–9	60	Gallatin Canyon (2 miles south of Big Sky entrance)
Karst Ranch†	Road house restaurant/bar	Breakfast Lunch Dinner	2–4 2–5 3–8	50	Gallatin Canyon (7 miles north of Big Sky entrance)
Corral†	Road house restaurant/bar	Breakfast Lunch Dinner	2–4 2–4 3–5	30	Gallatin Canyon (5 miles south of Big Sky entrance)

*Owned and operated by Big Sky of Montana, Inc.
†Independently operated.

Exhibit 7   Ski season income data (percent)

	Skiing	Lodging	Food and beverage
Revenue	100.0%	100.0%	100.0%
Cost of sales:			
Merchandise	0.0	0.0	30.0
Labor	15.0	15.9	19.7
Maintenance	3.1	5.2	2.4
Supplies	1.5	4.8	5.9
Miscellaneous	2.3	0.6	0.6
Operating expenses	66.2	66.4	66.7
Net profit (loss) before taxes	11.9	7.0	(25.2)

Case 27

Procter & Gamble Inc.: Downy Enviro-Pak*

In February 1989, Grad Schnurr, the brand manager for Downy fabric softener at Procter & Gamble (P&G) Inc., needed to work fast to develop plans to launch a refill pouch called an Enviro-Pak for the Downy product line. The introduction of such packaging would result in a reduction in the solid waste created by the Downy fabric softener. Several key decisions had to be made regarding pricing and promotion. Senior management had a keen interest in this project, especially after seeing the success of Loblaws's Green Product line. The environment was now a significant concern to consumers, and P&G Inc. wanted to be the first major consumer goods company in the market with their response.

Company History

Procter & Gamble was founded in Cincinnati, Ohio, in 1837 when William Procter, a candlemaker, and James Gamble, a soap maker, formed a partnership that grew to become a leading international company. By 1988, P&G was selling more than 160 brands in 140 countries and was a global leader in household cleaning, health care, personal care, and food product markets. Total sales exceeded $20 billion in 1988. P&G's leading brands include Tide laundry detergent, Pampers diapers, Ivory soap, Downy fabric softener, Crest toothpaste, Crisco oil, Duncan Hines baking mixes, and Vicks cold care products.

Procter & Gamble Inc. opened its first Canadian plant in 1915 in Hamilton, Ontario. It subsequently added three manufacturing sites in Belleville and Brockville, Ontario, and Pointe Claire, Quebec. P&G Inc. experienced substantial growth during the 1980s, with net sales doubling between 1978 and 1988; 1988 sales exceeded $1.2 billion, with net income of $78.9 million.

---

*This case was prepared by Janet Lahey, MBA student, and Chris Lane under the supervision of Professor Adrian B. Ryans for the sole purpose of providing material for class discussion at the Western Business School. Certain names and other identifying information may be disguised to protect confidentiality. It is not intended to illustrate either effective or ineffective handling of a managerial situation. Any reproduction, in any form, of the material in this case is prohibited except with the written consent of the School. Copyright 1990 © The University of Western Ontario. Used with permission.

P&G Inc. was organized into four divisions: Laundry and Cleaning Products, Health and Beauty Care, Food, and Paper Products. In an effort to push down decision making and increase responsiveness to the market, the company was organized on a category basis within each division (e.g., fabric softeners within the Laundry and Cleaning Products division). Each category had managers from Marketing, Finance, Sales, Product Supply, and Marketing Research assigned to it.

Marketing was organized on a brand management basis, with a brand manager and one or two assistant managers concentrating on the business of one product/brand, such as Tide detergent or Downy fabric softener. Promotions and projects within a brand were executed by business teams, which involved the other functional managers responsible for the category. During significant new product launches or promotions, these teams would meet every three or four weeks to review the critical path and discuss their progress.

Downy

Downy was a popular liquid fabric softener used in the washing machine to soften clothes, remove static from clothes, and leave them with a fresh scent. In early 1989, regular Downy was being sold in 1-liter, 1.5-liter, and 3-liter plastic jugs, and concentrated Downy was being sold in 500-milliliter, 1-liter, and 2-liter sizes. Overall, Downy was the number two brand in Canada in the liquid fabric softener category with a 12 percent share of the market. Its major competition consisted of a similar product called Fleecy, manufactured by Colgate-Palmolive, as well as fabric softener dryer sheets, which Procter & Gamble produced. There was little growth in this market segment, and competition usually took place on a price or incremental improvement (scent, efficacy) basis.

Pricing

The 3-liter bottle of Downy generated a contribution margin of 23 percent and was sold directly to the retail trade at $5.99. The average retail shelf price of $7.30 reflected typical retail trade margin levels of 18 percent (calculated on retail price). When Downy was on deal, the retail shelf price would fall to about $5.99 (retailers would still receive an 18 percent margin on the deal price). Downy appeared to be priced at a premium versus its competition, but on a price-per-use basis was on par with the major competitor.

Promotion

The 1989 Downy marketing plan included several promotions and incentives at both the consumer and trade levels. Events were scheduled to take place approximately every two months and would generally last four weeks. Approximately 70 percent of Downy was sold to the trade on deal.

Environmental Concern

In 1989, the environment had become a significant issue to Canadian consumers. David Nichols of Loblaws gained celebrity status when he launched an innovative line of "Green Products," which claimed to be "environmentally friendly." In Ontario alone, Loblaws sold more than $5 million of Green Products. It was clear that these products had a wide appeal. Business magazines were running articles concerning environmental management on a regular basis. One environmental concern, which was the primary focus of several lobby groups and which could be most readily addressed by consumers, was solid waste.

Landfill sites in urban communities like Toronto were projected to be full by the mid-90s. This posed a serious problem for government officials in determining locations for new sites, since "NIMBY" (not in my back yard) protests by the residents close to proposed landfill locations were increasingly effective. People were becoming aware of how much solid waste was being buried in the ground. As a result, some communities had started up "Blue Box" curbside recycling programs, which were run by the government and partially funded by industry. Household residents stored particular types of waste, such as newspapers, soft drink bottles, and tin cans in a blue plastic box, which were collected and sorted by municipal operators. The overwhelming success of these programs, with participation rates over 80 percent, indicated that citizens were highly concerned about protecting their environment and were willing to make an effort to reduce the amount of solid waste being sent to landfill sites.

Government Action

The Ontario Government had legislated new regulations for the soft drink industry under the Environmental Protection Act, requiring specific percentages of recyclable bottles. It had also stated a goal of a 25 percent reduction in the use of landfill sites by 1992. Other industries were speculating that the provincial government would soon require funding from them for recycling programs and were aware that legislation similar to the soft drink industry might also follow. Ontario was seen to be the leading province in dealing with environmental issues. Other provinces were expected to introduce similar programs after they had been proven in Ontario.

Procter & Gamble's Environmental Policy

P&G Inc. considered itself to be a community leader in terms of being a responsible business organization that contributed to the well-being of the environment. By 1989, it had already undertaken a number of environmental initiatives, including:

1. Using recycled materials for P&G product cartons and shipping containers. Laundry detergent cartons were made of 100 percent recycled paper.
2. Introducing a paper recycling program in the corporate head office.
3. Eliminating heavy metals from printing inks to facilitate safer incineration.

P&G Inc.'s efforts in the solid waste area were a major responsibility of a division general manager and the director of product development. The corporate policy followed the generally accepted ranking of waste management priorities: source reduction, reuse, and recycling.

European Enviro-Paks

In early 1989, Procter & Gamble Inc. was receiving consumer complaints regarding solid waste at an increasing rate. Disposable diapers were a particular area of concern. Calls about the environment had doubled in frequency over the past few months. P&G subsidiaries in Germany, Switzerland, and France had recently introduced "stand-up" pouches as refills for previously purchased bottles of Downy. These pouches (a type of Enviro-Pak) significantly reduced the solid waste generated by the Downy product. Grad Schnurr decided to review the results of the European launches to help him develop a strategy for a Canadian introduction (see Exhibit 1).

Exhibit 1   Procter & Gamble Inc.: Downy Enviro-Pak

	European Enviro-Pak results	
	Downy Enviro-Pak market share	*Enviro-Pak share of Downy business*
Germany	11.2%	26%
France	2.3	14
Switzerland	4.1	19
Austria	3.1	31
Spain	0.7	12
Italy	0.7	8

Source: Company records.

Product

A number of market research studies conducted in Europe indicated that the success of the pouch could be attributed primarily to its convenience and cost relative to the bottled Downy. Packages that reduced the amount of solid waste could generate further savings to German consumers, who were faced with financial penalties for excess garbage disposal.

Promotion

In Germany, the Downy pouch had been launched with substantial consumer and trade promotions, including in-store refill demonstrations and give-aways, trade samples followed by telephone calls for orders, shopping bag advertising, trade incentives for display, and direct delivery of display pallets.

Exhibit 2   Procter & Gamble Inc.: Downy Enviro-Pak

Downy Sales to the trade in Canada

	Shipments (000 cases)*	Market share (in percentage of dollar sales)
1988		
July	79	
August	72	13.8%
September	91	
October	78	12.6
November	95	
December	69	12.5
1989		
January	139	
February	96	12.6
March[†]	89	
April[†]	70	14.2
May[†]	73	
June[†]	100	11.8

*3-litre Downy was packed 6 bottles to a case.
[†]Forecast.
Source: Company records.

Pricing

The most popular package size for Downy in Europe was a 4-litre bottle. The European pouch had been originally priced at a 5 percent discount to this bottled version with very disappointing repurchase results. The problem stemmed from the promotional price of the 4-liter bottle, which often made the consumer price of the pouch more expensive. The trade was not reducing the pouch prices because they wished to retain the good margins they provided. P&G conducted a test market in one city with the pouch priced at a 15 percent discount to the bottle on a per-usage basis. This resulted in a significant volume improvement, with the pouch reaching a market share of 17 percent versus its previous share of 10 percent.

Share Results and Cannibalization

The pouch had been introduced in Germany and had achieved an 11 percent market share (see Exhibit 1). Although this was accompanied by a drop in the partner 4-litre size, the overall market share for Downy grew, taking Downy's share from 20 percent to 25 percent after the pouch was launched. Grad Schnurr wondered whether the same effect would occur in Canada, and what implications this had for the pricing of the pouch.

The Downy Enviro-Pak

The Downy pouch or Enviro-Pak provided a significant reduction in solid waste after use, containing 85 percent less plastic than the 3-litre bottle it would refill. The pouch was similar to a plastic milk bag, but had a gusseted bottom so it could

Exhibit 3   Procter & Gamble Inc.: Downy Enviro-Pak, proposed package

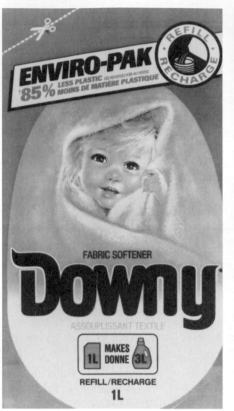
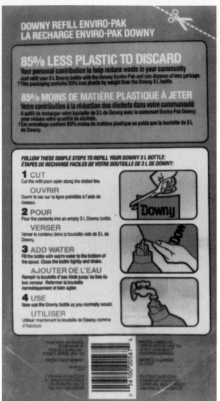

stand upright on the shelf. A consumer would cut the corner of the pouch off and then pour the product through a funnel into an empty 3-litre bottle. He or she would then add two litres of water, shake the bottle, and have three litres of fabric softener ready for use.

Grad Schnurr thought the Downy Enviro-Pak offered benefits for both consumers and the trade. Consumers would be attracted to the product for two reasons. First, by using the Enviro-Pak, they would be reducing the amount of household solid waste they generated. Second, the price could be lower than that of the regular bottle. Grad Schnurr recognized that the pouch represented a small inconvenience to consumers, as they had to do some preparation before they could use the product. Some consumers would also be concerned about spillage when they were refilling the bottle. These factors would need to be addressed through the Enviro-Pak's price and promotion plan.

The trade would also benefit in two ways. The pouches would attract environmentally conscious shoppers to their stores, away from competitors who did not carry such products. Also, the unique design of the Enviro-Pak provided more efficient use of space versus the bottled Downy. This second feature would provide decreased retailer handling and inventory costs.

Competitive Activity

Downy's three major competitors had also launched refill versions in Europe. No such activity had taken place in North America, but Canada would be a logical target for the next expansion, given the growing concern about the environment. However, Mr. Schnurr was unsure as to how applicable the German market results would be in predicting the response to the new package in Canada.

The logistics of the product launch also remained to be worked out. Given the likelihood of competitive activity in developing a more environmentally friendly package for Downy fabric softener, Grad Schnurr wasn't sure whether he should conduct a test market first or launch the Enviro-Pak in parts of Canada immediately. This decision was further complicated with trade rumours that Colgate-Palmolive was about to launch an environmental package. It would be much tougher trying to get retailers to list the Enviro-Paks if they already carried competitive versions. The brand that was able to introduce its environmental package first would gain an enviable reputation as a leading force in fighting the war on solid waste.

Manufacturing Issues

The manufacturing business team members estimated that their production schedule could support an August launch in Ontario and Quebec. These provinces were chosen for a number of reasons, including rising environmental awareness, potential volume, distribution time from plant, and competitive activity. The Hamilton plant estimated that it would take them an additional four months to get enough volume to fill the distribution pipeline and support ongoing shipments for the rest of the country. The cost of a packing line capable of producing 300,000 cases[1] annually of Enviro-Paks was estimated at $600,000.

Given the unique nature of this product, there was a high degree of uncertainty about the shipment forecasts. The last thing Grad Schnurr wanted was to have an overwhelming response to the Enviro-Pak with orders that P&G could not fill due to lack of supply.

Pricing

Grad Schnurr knew it would be vital to maintain the pouch price point below the comparable price of the 1.5-litre and 3-litre bottles. The pouch design provided a significant savings in the cost of goods sold. Its total delivered cost was 10 percent

---

[1]Each case would contain 12 Enviro-Paks.

less than the 3-litre bottle. Grad Schnurr had to consider the total contribution of the brand and how much of this saving should be passed on to the trade and consumer. He was considering two options:

1. *An everyday low retail price ($6.29).* This option would give the Enviro-Pak a discount versus the regular price of the 3-litre size ($7.30) using a cost-per-use comparison. The price to retailers would be either $5.16 or $4.74, depending on whether they were offered an 18 percent or 25 percent margin. The higher margin would help ensure fast acceptance, as retailers traditionally received 18 percent margins on the Downy bottle. To gain additional retailer support during the introductory period, retailers would be given a purchase allowance of $1.00 off each case. This amounted to an eleven-cent saving per bottle.

   In this scenario, there would be no special promotion or discount periods when the regular Downy product was on deal. One concern Grad Schnurr had with this option was that the Enviro-Pak would be priced above the 3-litre bottles when the bottles were featured on promotion at $5.99.

2. *A moderately lower retail price ($7.00), with featuring.* Under this scenario, the trade would be offered discount pricing for the Enviro-Pak coinciding with the regular Downy promotion schedule. The regular trade price would be $5.74, while the promotional offers would provide for a 20 percent discount, or a price of $4.59 for the trade and $5.60 for consumers.

Promotion

Grad Schnurr had put together a preliminary promotion plan, including trade discounts and television, radio, and print advertising. He was also considering using displayable shipping containers. These containers enabled retailers to build a display out of the Downy shipping containers by cutting off the top portion of each container and stacking them at aisle ends. The incremental cost of this style of container would be $0.95 per case.

   Given the unique environmental properties of the Downy Enviro-Pak, the launch would need some extra consideration to ensure the product was accepted by environmental groups, as well as the trade and consumers. This was evident in the problems Loblaws had faced when some of its Green Products were disputed by environmental groups such as Pollution Probe and Friends of the Earth. Grad Schnurr wanted to make sure that consumers accepted the Enviro-Pak as a valid environmental package without giving the impression that P&G was exploiting this concern for the sake of profits. He wondered how to go about this tactical issue. Should some of the environmental lobby groups be consulted before the launch? What if they did not support the idea? Would early consultation risk the security of the launch plans? Grad Schnurr needed to consult with Barry Smith, P&G Inc.'s public relations manager, to start planning their approach.

Part 8

Public Policy and Ethical Aspects of Marketing

The current environment of the marketing manager is undergoing rapid change and transition. Probably the most noteworthy of these developments, whether for better or for worse, is the increasing pervasiveness of public influences on marketing institutions and decision making. In this context, public influences are generally defined to include different levels of government (acting through legislation, regulation, or moral suasion), organized public groups (the consumerism movement, for example), individual advocates of change, and the force of changing public attitudes and opinion.

The cases in this section seek to develop an improved understanding of some of these trends and developments, and to provide practice for students in rendering decisions in the contemporary environment. The specific objectives of the cases are as follows:

1. To improve capacity for marketing decision making in situations where public influences and ethical considerations are involved.
2. To explore the nature and extent of public and ethical influences on marketing institutions and decision making.
3. To develop conceptual foundations leading to an improved understanding of contemporary developments in marketing.

Approaches to decision making in the area of marketing and public policy are not well established. One possible approach makes the following three assumptions:

1. Marketing and public policy decisions are made in a bargaining arena containing many interest groups.
2. Either explicit or implicit bargaining takes place among the interest groups in this arena whenever a marketing decision involves public influences.
3. Better decisions will be made if the objectives, motivations, and behaviors of each interest group are understood.

With these assumptions in mind, we present an approach to decision making in this area:

1. List and/or diagram the interest groups involved in a particular decision context. Note the interrelationships among them.
2. Identify the behavior of each group.
3. Attempt to explain this behavior by examining the objectives, motivations, and values of the people comprising the groups.
4. Identify what each group stands to lose or gain in the bargaining.
5. Identify what each group might be most willing to give up. What would they most want in return?
6. Based upon this analysis, predict the likely strategies of each group.
7. Make a decision based upon the anticipated reaction of each group to the alternatives you are considering. Be sure to have a contingency in case their reactions are not as you anticipated.

The ethical aspects of marketing are varied and complex. They fall in the so-called gray area of marketing decision making and behavior. The decision or behavior is itself legal, but may not be the right thing to do. The development of an approach to marketing ethics falls beyond the scope of this book. However, in this section we do present cases that explicitly raise ethics questions for marketers. Ethical issues are also present in some of the cases in other parts of the book.

Case 28

Nestlé and the Infant Food Controversy (A)*

In October 1978, Dr. Fürer, managing director of Nestlé S.A., headquartered in Vevey, Switzerland, was pondering the continuing problems his company faced. Public interest groups, media, health organizations, and other groups had been pressuring Nestlé to change its marketing practices for infant formula products, particularly in developing countries. Those groups had used a variety of pressure tactics, including consumer boycott in the United States over the past eight years. Critics of Nestlé charged that the company's promotional practices not only were abusive but also harmful, resulting in malnutrition and death in some circumstances. They demanded Nestlé put a stop to all promotion of its infant formula products both to consumers and health personnel.

Nestlé management had always prided itself on its high quality standards, its efforts to serve the best interests of Nestlé customers, and its contribution to the health and prosperity of people in developing countries. Nestlé management was convinced their infant formula products were useful and wanted; they had not taken the first signs of adverse publicity in the early 1970s very seriously. By 1978, massive adverse publicity appeared to be endangering the reputation of the company, particularly in Europe and North America. Despite support from some health officials and organizations throughout the world, Nestlé management in Vevey and White Plains, New York (U.S.A. headquarters), were seriously concerned. Dr. Fürer had been consulting with Mr. Guerrant, President of Nestlé U.S.A., in an effort to formulate a strategy. Of immediate concern to Nestlé management was the scheduled meeting of the National Council of Churches (USA) in November 1978. On the agenda was a resolution to support the critics of Nestlé

*This case was written by Aylin Kunt, research assistant under the supervision of Professors Christopher Gale and George Taucher in 1979. The earlier work of Professor James Kuhn of Columbia University is gratefully acknowledged. This version is a substantial revision of the earlier case and was prepared by Professor Michael R. Pearce. Copyright © 1981 by l'Institut pour l'Etude des Methodes de Direction de l'Entreprise (IMEDE), Lausanne, Switzerland, and The School of Business Administration, University of Western Ontario, London, Ontario, Canada. It is intended for classroom discussion and is not intended as an illustration of good or bad management practices.

who were leading the consumer boycott against Nestlé products in the United States. The National Council of Churches was an important, prestigious organization, which caused Nestlé management to fear that NCC support of the boycott might further endanger Nestlé.

Also of concern was the meeting of the World Health Organization (WHO) scheduled in the fall of 1979 to bring together the infant food manufacturers, public interest groups, and the world health community in an attempt to formulate a code of marketing conduct for the industry. Nestlé management, instrumental in establishing this conference, hoped that a clear set of standards would emerge, thus moderating or eliminating the attacks of the public pressure groups.

Dr. Fürer was anxious to clear up what he thought were misunderstandings about the industry. As he reviewed the history of the formula problem, he wondered in general what a company could do when subjected to pressure tactics by activist groups, and in particular, what Nestlé management should do next.

Nestlé Alimentana S.A.

The Swiss-based Nestlé Alimentana S.A. was one of the largest food products companies in the world. Nestlé had 80,000 shareholders in Switzerland. Nestlé's importance to Switzerland was comparable to the combined importance of General Motors and Exxon to the United States. In 1977, Nestlé's worldwide sales approximated 20 billion Swiss francs. Of this total, 7.3 percent were infant and dietetic products; more specifically, 2.5 percent of sales were accounted for by infant formula sales in developing countries.

Traditionally a transnational seller of food products, Nestlé's basic goal had always been to be a fully integrated food processor in every country in which it operated. It aimed at maintaining an important market presence in almost every nation of the world. In each country, Nestlé typically established local plants, supported private farms and dairy herds, and sold a wide range of products to cover all age groups. By the end of 1977, Nestlé had 87 factories in the developing countries and provided 35,610 direct jobs. Nestlé management was proud of this business approach and published a 228-page book in 1975 entitled *Nestlé in Developing Countries*. The cover of this book carried the following statement:

> While Nestlé is not a philanthropic society, facts and figures clearly prove that the nature of its activities in developing countries is self-evident as a factor that contributes to economic development. The company's constant need for local raw materials, processing, and staff, and the particular contribution it brings to local industry, support the fact that Nestlé's presence in the Third World is based on common interests in which the progress of one is always to the benefit of the other.

Although it neither produced nor marketed infant formula in the United States, the Nestlé Company, Inc. (White Plains) sold a variety of products such as Nescafé, Nestea, Crunch, Quik, Taster's Choice, and Libby and McNeil & Libby products throughout the United States.

With over 95 percent of Nestlé's sales outside of Switzerland, the company had developed an operating policy characterized by strong central financial control along with substantial freedom in marketing strategy by local managers. Each country manager was held responsible for profitability. Through periodic planning meetings, Nestlé management in Vevey ("the Centre") reviewed the broad strategy proposals of local companies. One area of responsibility clearly reserved by Vevey was the maintenance of the overall company image, although no formal public relations department existed. Marketing plans were reviewed in part by Vevey to see if they preserved the company's reputation for quality and service throughout the world.

Nestlé and the Infant Formula Industry

The international infant formula industry was composed of two types of firms, pharmaceutically oriented ones and food processing ones. The major companies competing in the developing countries were as follows:

Company	Brands
A. Pharmaceutical	
(U.S.) Wyeth Lab (American Home Products)	SMA, S26, Nursoy
(U.S.) Ross Lab (Abbott Laboratories)	Similac, Isomil
(U.S.) Mead Johnson (Bristol-Myers)	Enfamil, Olac, Prosobee
B. Food processing	
(U.S.) Borden	New Biolac
(Swit.) Nestlé	Nestogen, Eledon, Pelargon Nan, Lactogen
(U.K.) Unigate	

In addition to these six firms, there were about another dozen formula producers chartered in 1978 throughout the world.

The basic distinction between pharmaceutically oriented formula producers and food processing oriented producers lay in their entry point into the formula business. In the early 1900s, medical research laboratories of major pharmaceutical firms developed "humanized formulas," leading their parents into marketing such products. Essentially, a humanized formula was a modification of normal cow's milk to approximate more closely human milk. Generally speaking, the food processing companies had begun offering infant food as an extension of their full milk powdered products and canned milk.

As early as the 1800s, Nestlé had been engaged in research in the field of child nutrition. In 1867, Henri Nestlé, the founder of the company and the great-grandfather of infant formula, introduced the first specifically designed, commercially marketed infant weaning formula. An infant weaning formula is basically a cereal and milk mixture designed to introduce solids to a child of five–six months of age.

As of the 1860s, both Nestlé and Borden had been producing sweetened and evaporated milk. Nestlé very quickly recognized the need for better artificial infant food and steadily developed a full line of formula products in the early 1900s (for example, Lactogen in 1921, Eledon in 1927, Nestogen in 1930). Although it was a food processing company, Nestlé's product development and marketing were supervised by physicians.

In the United States in the early 1900s, the infant formula products developed by the medical laboratories were being used primarily in hospitals. Over time, the industry developed the distinction of formula products for "well babies" versus for "sick babies." In the latter category would be included special nutritional and dietary problems, such as allergies to milk requiring babies to have totally artificial formulas made from soybeans. Approximately 2 percent of industry volume was formula designed for "sick babies."

In the late 19th century and early years of the 20th century, Nestlé had developed a commanding position in the sweetened and evaporated milk market in the developing countries (also referred to as "the Third World"). Demand for these products was initially established among European colonials and gradually spread throughout the world and into the rising middle classes in many nations. Nestlé's early marketing efforts focused on switching infant feeding from the previously common use of sweetened and condensed milk to a more appropriate product, humanized infant formula.

By promoting a full product line through doctors (medical detailing), Nestlé achieved an overwhelmingly dominant market position in the European colonies, countries which later became independent "Third World" countries. Meanwhile, most of the competition developed quickly in the industrialized countries, so much so that Nestlé stayed out of the U.S. formula market entirely. Only late in the 1950s did significant intense competition, mainly from American multinationals, develop in Nestlé's markets in developing countries. These markets, with their high birth rates and rising affluence, became increasingly attractive to all formula producers. After the entry of American competitors, Nestlé's share of markets began to erode.

As of 1978, Nestlé accounted for about one-third to one-half of infant formula sales in the developing countries, while American companies held about one-fifth. The size of the total world market for infant formula was not exactly known because data on shipments of infant formula were not separated from other milk products, especially powders. Some sources guesstimated world sales to be close to $1.5 billion (U.S.), half of that to developing countries.

Traditional Methods of Promotion

Several methods had been used over the years to promote infant products in developing countries. Five major methods predominated:

1. *Media advertising*—All media types were employed including posters in clinics and hospitals, outdoor billboards, newspapers, magazines, radio, television, and loudspeakers on vans. Native languages and English were used.

2. *Samples*—Free sample distribution, either direct to new mothers or via doctors, was relatively limited until competition increased in the 1960s. Mothers were given either formula or feeding bottles or both, often in a

"new mother's kit." Doctors in clinics and hospitals received large packages of product for use while mother and baby were present. The formula
producers believed this practice helped educate new mothers on the use of
formula products, and hopefully, initiated brand preference. In some instances, doctors actually resold samples to provide an extra source of income for themselves or their institutions.

3. *Booklets*—Most formula marketers provided new mothers with booklets on
   baby care which were given free to them when they left the hospitals and
   clinics with their newborn infants. These booklets, such as Nestlé's *A Life
   Begins,* offered a variety of advice and advertised the formula products and
   other infant foods, both Nestlé and homemade.

4. *Milk nurses*—Milk nurses (also known as mothercraft nurses) were formula producer employees who talked with new mothers in the hospitals and
   clinics or at home. Originally, they were all fully trained nurses, instructed
   in product knowledge, then sent out to educate new mothers on the correct
   use of the new formula products. This instruction included the importance
   of proper personal hygiene, boiling the water, and mixing formula and water in correct quantities. These became a major part of many firms' efforts;
   for example, at one time Nestlé had about 200 mothercraft employees
   worldwide. The majority of milk nurses were paid a straight salary plus a
   travel allowance, but over time, some were hired on a sales-related bonus
   basis. Some companies, other than Nestlé, began to relax standards in the
   1960s and hired nonnursing personnel who dressed in nurses' uniforms and
   acted more in a selling capacity and less in an educational capacity.

5. *Milk banks*—Milk bank was the term used to describe a special distribution
   outlet affiliated with and administered by those hospitals and clinics which
   served very-low-income people. Formula products were provided to low-
   income families at much reduced prices for mothers who could not afford
   the commercial product. The producers sold products to those outlets at
   lower prices to enable this service to occur.

PAG 23

Nestlé management believed the controversy surrounding the sale of infant formula in developing countries began in the early 1970s. Many international organizations were concerned about the problem of malnourishment of infants in
the developing countries of South Asia, Africa, and Latin America. In Bogota
(1970) and Paris (1972), representatives of the Food and Agricultural
Organization (FAO), the World Health Organization (WHO), UNICEF, the
International Pediatric Association, and the infant formula industry including
Nestlé all met to discuss nutrition problems and guidelines. The result was a request that the United Nations Protein-Calorie Advisory Group (PAG), an organization formed in 1955, set guidelines for nutrition for infants. On July 18,
1972, the PAG issued Statement 23 on the "Promotion of special foods for vulnerable groups." This statement emphasized the importance of breast-feeding,

the danger of over-promotion, the need to take local conditions into account, the problem of misuse of formula products, and the desirability of reducing promotion but increasing education.

Statement 23 included the following statements:

> Breast milk is an optimal food for infants and, if available in sufficient quantities, it is adequate as the sole source of food during the first four to six months of age.

> Poor health and adverse social circumstances may decrease the output of milk by the mother . . . in such circumstances supplementation of breast milk with nutritionally adequate foods must start earlier than four to six months if growth failure is to be avoided.

> It is clearly important to avoid any action which would accelerate the trend away from breast-feeding.

> It is essential to make available to the mother, the foods, formulas, and instructions which will meet the need for good nutrition of those infants who are breast-fed.

Nestlé management regarded PAG 23 as an "advisory statement," so management's stance was to see what happened. None of the developing countries took any action on the statement. Nestlé officials consulted with ministers of health in many developing countries to ask what role their governments wished Nestlé to play in bringing nutrition education to local mothers. No major changes were requested.

At the same time, Nestlé Vevey ordered an audit of marketing practices employed by its companies in the developing nations. Based on reports from the field, Nestlé management in Vevey concluded that only a few changes in marketing were required, which they ordered be done. In Nigeria, the Nigerian Society of Health and Nutrition asked Nestlé to change its ads for formula to stress breast-feeding. Nestlé complied with this request, and its ads in all developing countries prominently carried the phrase "when breast milk fails, use . . ."

The British Contribution

In its August 1973 issue, the *New Internationalist,* an English journal devoted to problems in developing countries, published an article entitled "The Baby Food Tragedy." This was an interview with two doctors: Dr. R. G. Hendrikse, Director of the Tropical Child Health Course, Liverpool University, and medical researcher in Rhodesia, Nigeria, and South Africa, and Dr. David Morley, Reader in Tropical Child Health, University of London. Both doctors expressed concern with the widespread use of formula among impoverished, less-literate families. They claimed that in such cases, low family incomes prevented mothers from buying the necessary amount of formula for their children. Instead, they used smaller quantities of formula powder, diluting it with more water than recommended. Further, the water used was frequently contaminated. The infant thus received less than adequate nutrition, indeed often was exposed to contaminated formula. The malnourished child became increasingly susceptible to infections, leading to diarrheal diseases. Diarrhea meant the child could assimilate even less of the nutrients given to him because neither his stomach nor intestines were working properly. This vicious cycle could lead to death. The two doctors believed that local conditions made the use of commercial infant formula not only unnecessary, but likely difficult and dangerous. Breast-feeding was safer, healthier, and certainly less expensive.

The article, in the opinion of many, was relatively restrained and balanced. However, it was accompanied by dramatic photographs of malnourished black babies and of a baby's grave with a tin of milk powder placed on it. The article had a strong emotional impact on readers and reached many people who were not regular readers of the journal. It was widely reprinted and quoted by other groups. The journal sent copies of the article to more than 3,000 hospitals in the developing nations.

The two doctors interviewed for the article had mentioned Nestlé and its promotional practices. Accordingly, the editors of the *New Internationalist* contacted Nestlé S.A. for its position. The company response was published in the October issue of the *New Internationalist* along with an editorial entitled "Milk and Murder."

Nestlé S.A. responded in part as follows:

> We have carefully studied both the editorial and the interviews with Dr. Hendrickse and Dr. Morley published in the August edition of the *New Internationalist*. Although fleeting references are made to factors other than manufacturers' activities which are said to be responsible for the misuse of infant foods in developing countries, their readers would certainly not be in a position to judge from the report the immense socioeconomic complexities of the situation. . . .
>
> It would be impossible to demonstrate in the space of a letter the enormous efforts made by the Nestlé organization to ensure the correct usage of their infant food products, and the way in which the PAG guidelines have been applied by the Nestlé subsidiaries. However, if the editor of the *New Internationalist* (or the author of the article in question) wishes to establish the complete facts as far as we are concerned, then we should be happy to receive him in Vevey on a mutually agreeable date in the near future. We should certainly welcome the opportunity to reply to some of the sweeping allegations made against Nestlé either by implication or by specific references.

The editor of the *New Internationalist* refused the invitation to visit Nestlé's Vevey headquarters. Further, they maintained that PAG 23 guidelines were not being observed and did not have any provisions for enforcement.

In March 1974, War on Want published a pamphlet entitled *The Baby Killer.* War on Want was a private British group established to give aid to Third World nations. In particular, they were devoted "to make world poverty an urgent social and political issue." War on Want issued a set of recommendations to industry, governments, the medical profession, and others to deal with the baby formula problem as they saw it. See Exhibit 1.

EXHIBIT 1   War on want's recommendations

Industry

1. The serious problems caused by early weaning onto breast milk substitutes demand a serious response. Companies should follow the Swedish example and refrain from all consumer promotion of breast milk substitutes in high risk communities.
2. The companies should cooperate constructively with the international organizations working on the problems of infant and child nutrition in the developing countries.
3. Companies should abandon promotions to the medical profession which may perform the miseducational function of suggesting that particular brands of milk can overcome the problems of misuse.

Governments of developing countries

1. Governments should take note of the recommendations of the Protein Advisory Group for national nutrition strategies.
2. Where social and economic conditions are such that proprietary infant foods can make little useful contribution, serious consideration should be given to the curtailment of their importation, distribution, and/or promotion.
3. Governments should ensure that supplies are made available first to those in need—babies whose mothers cannot breast feed, twins, orphans, etc.—rather than to an economic elite, a danger noted by the PAG.

British Government

1. The British Government should exercise a constructive influence in the current debate.
2. The Government should insist that British companies such as Unigate and Glaxo set a high standard of behaviour and it should be prepared to enforce a similar standard on multinationals like Wyeth who export to developing country markets from Britain.
3. The British representative on the Codex Alimentarius Commission should urge the commission to consider all aspects of the promotion of infant foods. If necessary, structural alterations should be proposed to set up a subcommittee to consider broader aspects of promotion to enable the commission to fulfill its stated aims of protecting the consumer interests.

Medical profession

There is a need in the medical profession for a greater awareness of the problems caused by artificial feeding of infants and of the role of the medical profession in encouraging the trend away from breast-feeding.

Other channels

Practicing health workers in the Third World have achieved startling, if limited, response by writing to local medical journals and the press about any promotional malpractices they see and sending copies of their complaints to the companies involved. This could be done by volunteers and others not in the medical profession but in contact with the problem in the field.

In Britain, student unions at a number of universities and polytechnics decided to ban the use of all Nestlés products where they had control of catering following the initial exposé by the *New Internationalist* magazine. Without any clear objective, or coordination, this kind of action is unlikely to have much effect.

However, if the companies involved continue to be intransigent in the face of the dangerous situation developing in the Third World, a more broadly based campaign involving many national organizations may be the result. At the very least, trade unions, women's organizations, consumer groups, and other interested parties need to be made aware of the present dangers.

There is also a clear need to examine, on a community scale, how infant feeding practices are determined in Britain today. There is a long history of commercial persuasion, and artificial feeding is now well entrenched.

As has been shown, there are still risks inherent in bottle feeding even in Britain. The available evidence suggests that both mother and child may do better physically and emotionally by breast-feeding. An examination of our own irrational social practices can help the Third World to throw a light on theirs.

The Baby Killer was written by Mike Muller as an attempt to publicize the infant formula issue. Mr. Muller expanded on the *New Internationalist* articles, and in the view of many observers, gave reasonable treatment to the complexity of the circumstances surrounding the use of formula products in the developing countries. On the whole, it was an attack against bottle-feeding rather than an attack against any particular company.

Part of *The Baby Killer* was based on interviews the author had with three Nestlé employees: Dr. H. R. Müller, G. A. Fookes, and J. Momoud, all of Nestlé S.A. Infant and Dietctics Division. These Nestlé officials argued that Nestlé was acting as responsibly as it could. Further, they said that abuses, if they existed, could not be controlled by single companies. Only a drastic change in the competitive system could check abuses effectively. Mr. Muller apparently was not impressed by this argument, nor did he mention Nestlé management's stated willingness to establish enforceable international guidelines for marketing conduct. In *The Baby Killer,* Mr. Muller revealed he was convinced that Nestlé was exploiting the high birth rates in developing countries by encouraging mothers to replace, not supplement, breast-feeding by formula products. Mr. Muller offered as support for his stance a quotation from Nestlé's 1973 Annual Report:

> . . . the continual decline in birth rates, particularly in countries with a high standard of living, retarded growth of the market. . . . In the developing countries our own products continue to sell well thanks to the growth of population and improved living standards.

Dr. Fürer's reaction to *The Baby Killer* was that Mr. Muller had given too much weight to the negative aspects of the situation. Mr. Muller failed to mention, for example, that infant mortality rates had shown very dramatic declines in the developing countries. Some part of these declines were the result of improved nutrition, Dr. Fürer believed, and improved nutrition was partly the result of the use of formula products. Despite his strong belief that Nestlé's product was highly beneficial rather than harmful, Dr. Fürer ordered a second audit of Nestlé's advertising and promotional methods in developing countries. Again, changes were made. These changes included revision of advertising copy to emphasize further the superiority of breast-feeding, elimination of radio advertising in the developing world, and cessation of the use of white uniforms on the mothercraft nurses.

At the same time, on May 23, 1974, WHO adopted a resolution that misleading promotion had contributed to the decline in breast-feeding in the developing countries and urged individual countries to take legal action to curb such abuses.

The Third World Action Group

In June 1974, the infant formula issue moved into Switzerland. A small, poorly financed group called the Third World Action Group located in Bern, the capital of Switzerland, published in German a booklet entitled *Nestlé Kills Babies (Nestlé Totet Kinder)*. This was a partial translation of the War on Want publication *The Baby Killer.* Some of the qualifying facts found in Mr. Muller's booklet were omitted in *Nestlé Kills Babies,* while the focus was changed from a general attack on bottle-feeding to a direct attack on Nestlé and its promotional practices.

Nestlé top management was extremely upset by this publication. Dr. Fürer immediately ordered a follow-up audit of Nestlé's marketing practices to ensure stated corporate ethical standards were being observed. Nestlé management also believed that the infant formula issue was being used as a vehicle by leftist, Marxist groups intent on attacking the free-market system, multinational companies in general, and Nestlé in particular. Internal Nestlé memoranda of the time reveal the material available to management that supported their belief that the issue went beyond infant formula promotion. For example:

> Having a closer look at the allies of the AG3W in their actions, we realize that they happen to have the same aim. There are common actions with the Leninist progressive organizations (POCH), who are also considered to be pro-Soviet, with the Swiss communist party (PdA), and the communist youth organization (KJV), as well as with the revolutionary marxist alliance (RML). Since the AG3W has tried to coordinate the support of (only pro-communist) liberation movements with representatives of the communist bloc, it is not surprising that they also participate at the youth festival in Eastern Berlin.[1]

Believing the issue to be clearly legal, Nestlé management brought suit in July 1974 against 13 members of the Third World Action Group and against two newspapers who carried articles about *Nestlé Kills Babies.* Nestlé charged criminal libel, claiming that the company had been defamed because "the whole report charges Nestlé S.A. with using incorrect sales promotion in the third world and with pulling mothers away from breast-feeding their babies and turning them to its products." More specifically, Nestlé management claimed the following were defamatory:

The title "Nestlé Kills Babies."

The charge that the practices of Nestlé and other companies are unethical and immoral (written in the introduction and in the report itself).

The accusation of being responsible for the death or the permanent physical and mental damage of babies by its sales promotion policy (in the introduction).

The accusation that in less developed countries, the sales representatives for baby foods are dressed like nurses to give the sales promotion a scientific appearance.

The trial in Bern provided the Third World Action Group with a great deal of publicity, giving them a forum to present their views. Swiss television in particular devoted much time to coverage of the trial and the issues involved. The trial ended in the fall, 1976. Nestlé management won a judgment on the first of the libel charges (because of lack of specific evidence for the Third World Action

---

[1]Third World Action Group (AG3W), *Der Zürichbieter,* August 15, 1973.

Group), and the activists were fined 300 Swiss Francs each. Nestlé management dropped the remaining charges. In his judgment, the presiding judge added an opinion that became well-publicized:

> The need ensues for the Nestlé company to fundamentally rethink its advertising practices in developing countries as concerns bottle-feeding, for its advertising practice up to now can transform a life-saving product into one that is dangerous and life-destroying. If Nestlé S.A. in the future wants to be spared the accusations of immoral and unethical conduct, it will have to change its advertising practices.

The Controversy Spreads

While the trial was in process, various interest groups from all over the world became interested and involved in the infant formula controversy. In London, England, Mike Muller founded the Baby Foods Action Group. Late in 1974, the World Food Conference adopted a resolution recommending that developing-nation governments actively support breast-feeding. The PAG had been organizing a number of international regional seminars to discuss all aspects of the controversy. For example, in November 1974, during the PAG regional seminar in Singapore, the PAG recommended that the infant formula industry increase its efforts to implement Statement 23 and cooperate to regulate their promotion and advertising practices through a code of ethics.

The world health organizations kept up the pressure. In March 1975, the PAG again met:

> to discuss together the problem of deteriorating infant feeding practices in developing countries and to make recommendations for remedying the situation. The early discontinuance of breast-feeding by mothers in low-income groups in urban areas, leading to malnutrition, illness, and death among infants, has been a serious concern to all.

In May 1975, WHO, at its 14th plenary meeting, again called for a critical review of promotion of infant formula products.

In response, representatives of the major formula producers met in Zürich, Switzerland, in May 1975 to discuss the possibility and desirability of establishing an international code of ethics for the industry. Nine of the manufacturers, with the notable exceptions of Borden, Bristol-Myers, and Abbott, created an organization, called the International Council of Infant Food Industries (ICIFI), and a code of marketing conduct. This code went into effect November 1, 1975. Some firms also adopted individual codes, including Nestlé, with standards higher than the ICIFI code.

The ICIFI code required that ICIFI members assume responsibility to encourage breast-feeding, that milk nurses be paid on a strict salary basis and wear company uniforms, and that product labels indicate breast milk as the best infant food. At this time, Nestlé began to phase out use of mass media for infant formula in developing countries, but continued to distribute educational materials and product information in the hospitals and clinics. Nestlé management believed such advertising and promotion was of educational value to ensure proper use of formula and to decrease usage of sweetened and condensed milk for infant feeding.

ICIFI submitted its code of ethics to the PAG who submitted it to a number of third parties. On the basis of their opinions, the PAG refused to endorse the code, saying it did not go far enough, that substantial amendments were required. ICIFI rejected these suggestions because of difficult antitrust considerations, so the PAG withheld its approval of the code.

An important exception to ICIFI membership was Abbott Laboratories. While Abbott representatives had attended the meeting that led to the establishment of ICIFI, they decided not to join. Abbott, having recently had difficulties with the U.S. Food and Drug Administration regarding the marketing of cyclamates and artificial sweeteners, felt ICIFI was not an adequate response to the public pressure:

> The most important area is to reduce the impact of advertising on the low-income, poorly educated populations where the risk is the greatest. The ICIFI code does not address this very important issue.
>
> Our company decided not to join ICIFI because the organization is not prepared to go far enough in answering this legitimate criticism of our industry. We feel that for Abbott/Ross to identify with this organization and its code would limit our ability to speak on the important issues.

Abbott acted largely independently of the other producers. Later in 1977, Abbott management announced its intention to commit about $100,000 to a breast-feeding campaign in developing nations and about $175,000 to a task force on breast-feeding, infant formula, and Third World countries.

Developments in the United States

Although Nestlé U.S. neither manufactured nor marketed formula, management found itself increasingly embroiled in the controversy during the mid-1970s. The first major group to bring this matter to the public was the Interfaith Center on Corporate Responsibility (ICCR). The ICCR, a union of 14 Protestant denominations and approximately 150 Catholic orders and dioceses, was a group concerned about the social responsibility behaviour of corporations. The ICCR advised its members on this topic to guide decisions for the members' combined investment portfolio of several billion dollars. Formerly known as the Center of Corporate Responsibility, the ICCR was established under the tax-exempt umbrella of the American National Council of Churches when the U.S. Internal Revenue Service revoked the CCR tax exemption.

The ICCR urged its members to investigate the marketing practices of the leading American formula producers, American Home Products, Abbott Laboratories, and Bristol-Myers. Stockholder groups demanded from these companies, as they were entitled to do by American law, detailed information regarding market shares, promotion and advertising practices, and general company policies concerning the infant formula business.

Nestlé management believed that the ICCR was interested in ideology more than in baby formula. As support, they pointed to a statement made in a January edition of ICCR's *The Corporate Examiner:*

> The motivations, ethos, and operations of transnational corporations are inimical to the establishment of a new economic order. Both justice and stability are undermined in the fulfillment of their global vision.

Perhaps the major vehicle used by ICCR to get attention was a half-hour film entitled *Bottle Babies.* Well-known German filmmaker Peter Krieg began this film shortly after the Bern trial began. Nestlé Vevey management believed that the film was partially sponsored by the World Council of Churches to provide a public defense for the Third World Action Group position. Most of the filming was done in Kenya, Africa, in 1975 in a "documentary" style, although Nestlé management pointed out that the film was scripted and in their opinion, highly emotional and misleading. A letter (Exhibit 2) that Nestlé management later received written by Professor Bwibo of the University of Nairobi supported management's views about the *Bottle Babies* film.

ICCR distributed copies of the *Bottle Babies* film to church groups throughout the United States. Typically, the film was shown to a gathering of church members followed by an impassioned plea to write letters of protest and a request for funds to further the campaign. Since the film singled out Nestlé for attack in its last 10 minutes, Nestlé became symbolic of all that was wrong in the infant formula controversy in the minds of these religious groups. Nestlé management, however, was seldom asked for, or given an opportunity to present, its position on the issues.

While Nestlé felt the growing pressure of *Bottle Babies,* the major American formula producers faced a variety of ICCR-shareholder initiatives. ICCR requested detailed information from American Home Products, Abbott Laboratories, and Bristol-Myers. Each company responded differently.

American Home Products. After refusing to release all the information ICCR requested, AHP faced a resolution to be included in its proxy statement. ICCR dropped the resolution the day before printing, when AHP management agreed:

> To provide the requested information.

> To send a report to its shareholders saying that many authorities believe misuse of infant formula in developing countries could be dangerous, that the company promotes breast-feeding while making available formula for mothers who cannot or do not choose to breast-feed, that the company would promote to medical professionals only and that AHP was a member of ICIFI which was developing a voluntary code of promotional practices.

Abbott Laboratories. After a year and a half of meetings with ICCR, Abbott released most of the information ICCR wanted. Still, to obtain the rest of the data, ICCR shareholders filed a shareholder resolution. This proposal received less

EXHIBIT 2

14th April, 1978

Miss June Noranka
644 Summit Avenue
St. Paul
Minnesota 55105

Dear Miss Noranka:

Following your visit to Kenya and my office I write to inform you, your group, your colleagues, and any other person interested that the film Peter Krieg filmed in this department and the associated teaching areas, did not represent the right aspects of what we participated in during the filming.

The film which was intended to be a scientific and educational film turned out to be an emotional, biased, and exaggerated film—and failed to be a teaching film. It arouses emotions in people who have little chance to check these facts. No wonder it has heated the emotions of the Activists groups in America and I understand now spreading to Europe. I wish I was in an opportunity to be with your groups and we view the film together and I comment.

As a pediatrician, I would like to put on record that I have not seen the Commercial baby food companies pressure anybody to use their brands of milk. As for Nestlé, we have discussed with their Managing Directors, starting much earlier than the time of the film in 1971, as to the best way of approaching baby feeding and discussed extensively advertisement especially the material to be included. The directors have followed our advice and we are happy with their working conditions.

We are interested in the well-being of our children and we are Medical Scientists. So anything of scientific value we will promote but we will avoid imagined exaggerated and distorted views.

I am taking the liberty to copy this letter to Mr. Jones, managing director of Food Specialty in Nairobi who produce and make Nestlé's products here, for his information.

Yours sincerely,

NIMROD O. BWIBO
Professor & Chairman

---

than the three percent of the vote required by the Securities and Exchange Commission (SEC) in order to resubmit the proposal at a later time. Thus, it was not resubmitted.

Bristol-Myers. Bristol-Myers would not cooperate with ICCR, so one church shareholder with 500 shares, Sisters of the Precious Blood, filed a shareholder resolution in 1975 asking that the information be released. After receiving 5.4 percent of the vote and having aroused the concern of the Ford Foundation and the Rockefeller Foundation, it appeared the resolution would be launched again the next year. In August 1975, Bristol-Myers management published a report, "The Infant Formula Marketing Practices of Bristol-Myers Co. in Countries Outside the United States." The 1976 proxy included the Sisters' resolution and a statement entitled "Management's Position." The Sisters maintained the statement was false and misleading and filed suit against management; statements appearing in a proxy statement are required by law to be accurate.

In May 1977, a U.S. district court judge dismissed the case, saying the Sisters had failed to show irreparable harm to themselves as the law requires. The judge would not comment on the accuracy of the company's proxy report. The nuns appealed with the support of the SEC. In early 1978, the management of Bristol-Myers agreed to send a report outlining the dispute to all shareholders and to restrictions on company marketing practices, including a ban on all consumer-directed promotion in clinics, hospitals, and other public places and a stop to using milk nurses in Jamaica.

In 1977, Abbott management agreed to revise their code of marketing conduct and to eliminate the use of nurses' uniforms by company salespeople despite the fact some were registered nurses.

ICCR and its supporters also persuaded Representative Michael Harrington, Democrat–Massachusetts, to cosponsor a federal resolution requiring an investigation of U.S. infant formula producers.

The campaign against the formula producers took on a new dimension in mid-1977. A group called the Third World Institute, led by Doug Johnson at the University of Minnesota, formed the Infant Formula Action Coalition "INFACT" in June 1977. INFACT members were encouraged by ICCR and the Sisters, but felt that significant progress would not be made until Nestlé was pressured to change. INFACT realized that legal and shareholder action against a foreign-based company would be futile, so on July 4, 1977, INFACT announced a consumer boycott against those infant formula companies whose marketing practices INFACT found abusive. Despite the boycott's original target of several companies, Nestlé was the main focal point, especially after the other major companies made concessions to ICCR. INFACT began the boycott in front of Nestlé's Minneapolis offices with a demonstration of about 100 people. INFACT urged consumers to boycott over 40 Nestlé products.

Nestlé management in White Plains was not sure what response to take. Nestlé U.S. was not at all involved with infant formula, but was genuinely concerned about the publicity INFACT was getting. Nestlé S.A. management, on the other hand, originally did not think the boycott campaign would amount to anything, that it was a project of some college kids in the United States based on misinformation about events in other parts of the world.

In September and October 1977, Nestlé senior managers from Vevey and White Plains met with members of INFACT, ICCR, the Ford Foundation, and other interested groups. Nestlé management had hoped to resolve what they thought was a problem of poor communication by explaining the facts. Nestlé management argued the company could not meet competition if it stopped all promotion, which would mean less sales and less jobs in the developing nations. Further, management claimed: "We have an instructional and educational responsibility as marketers of these products and, if we failed in that responsibility, we could be justly criticized." INFACT members stated they found the talks useful in clarifying positions, but concluded Nestlé was unwilling to abandon all promotion of its formula products.

In November 1977, INFACT decided not only to continue the boycott, but also to increase it to a national scale. INFACT held a conference in Minneapolis on November 2–4, for more than 45 organizers from 24 cities. These organizers represented women's groups, college hunger-action coalitions, health professionals, church agencies, and social justice groups. A clearinghouse was established to coordinate boycott efforts and information collection. The group also agreed to assist ICCR in its shareholder pressure campaign and to press for congressional action. Later, INFACT petitioned all U.S. government officials, state and federal, for support of the boycott. On November 21, the Interfaith Hunger Coalition, a group affiliated with INFACT, demonstrated in front of Nestlé's Los Angeles sales office with about 150 people chanting "Nestlé kills babies." This demonstration received prominent media coverage as did other boycott activities. The combination of INFACT's boycott, ICCR's shareholder efforts, the exhibition of *Bottle Babies,* and the strong support of other U.S. activists (including Ralph Nader, Cesar Chavez, Gloria Steinem, and Dr. Benjamin Spock), resulted in an increasingly high profile for the infant formula controversy, even though Nestlé management believed there had been as yet no adverse effect on sales.

In early 1978, an unofficial WHO working group published the following statement:

> The advertising of food for nursing infants or older babies and young children is of particular importance and should be prohibited on radio and television. Advertising for mother's milk substitutes should never be aimed directly at the public or families, and advertising for ready-made infant food preparations should show clearly that they are not meant for less than three-month-old infants. Publicity for public consumption, which should in any case never be distributed without previous recommendation by the competent medical authority, should indicate that breast milk should always constitute the sole or chief constituent of food for those under three months. Finally, the distribution of free samples and other sales promotion practices for baby foods should be generally prohibited.

Nestlé management met again with INFACT representatives in February 1978. No progress was made in reconciling the two sides. Nestlé management could not accept statements from INFACT such as:

> The corporations provide the product and motivate the people to buy it, and set into motion a process that may cause the death of the baby. The corporations are responsible for that death. When the outcome is death, the charge against the corporation is murder.

Nonetheless, management learned what INFACT wanted:

> Stop all direct consumer promotion and publicity for infant formula.
> Stop employing "milk nurses" as sales staff.

Stop distributing free samples to clinics, hospitals, and maternity hospitals.

Stop promoting infant formula among the medical profession and public health profession.

To further publicize their campaign, INFACT representatives and their allies persuaded Senator Edward Kennedy, Democrat–Massachusetts, to hold Senate hearings on the infant formula issue in May 1978. CBS decided to make a TV report of the entire affair. To prepare for the hearings, INFACT organized a number of demonstrations across the United States. At one meeting on April 15, 1978, Doug Johnson said:

> The goal of the Nestlé's Boycott Campaign and of the entire infant formula coalition is to get the multinationals to stop promotion of infant formula. We're not asking them to stop marketing; we're not asking them to pull out of—out of the countries; we're simply asking them to stop the promotion, and in that I think we're—we're in agreement with a number of prestigious organizations. The World Health Organization recently asked the corporations to stop consumer advertising and to stop the use of free samples, and the International Pediatric Association did that several years ago. So, I think we're asking a very reasonable thing: to stop promoting something which is inappropriate and dangerous.

CBS filmed these demonstrations, but did not air them until after the Kennedy hearings.

The Kennedy Hearings and CBS Report

Senator Kennedy was chairman of the Subcommittee on Health and Scientific Research on Infant Nutrition. Both critics and members of the infant formula industry appeared before the Kennedy Committee in May 1978. Nestlé S.A. management decided not to send headquarters management or management from Nestlé U.S. Instead, they asked R. Oswaldo Ballarin, president and chairman of Nestlé, Brazil, to represent Nestlé at the hearings. Dr. Ballarin began with a statement prepared by Nestlé U.S., but Senator Kennedy soon interrupted him as the following excerpt from the testimony indicates:

Dr. Ballarin: United States Nestlé's Company has advised me that their research indicates this is actually an indirect attack on the free world's economic system: a worldwide church organization with its stated purpose of undermining the free enterprise system is at the forefront of this activity.

Senator Kennedy: Now you can't seriously expect . . . [Noise in background: gavel banging] We'll be in order . . . we'll be in order now please. We'll be in order. Uh, you don't seriously expect us to accept that on face value, after we've heard as . . . as you must've, Doctor . . . if I could just finish my question . . . the . . . the testimony of probably 9 different witnesses. It seemed to me that they were expressing a very deep compassion and concern about the well-being of infants, the most vulnerable in this . . . face of the world. Would you agree with me that your product should not be used where there is impure water? Yes or no?

Dr. Ballarin: Uh, we give all the instructions . . .

Senator Kennedy: Just . . . just answers. What would you . . . what is your position?

Dr. Ballarin: Of course not. But we cannot cope with that.

Senator Kennedy: Well, as I understand what you say, is where there's impure water, it should not be used.

Dr. Ballarin: Yes.

Senator Kennedy: Where the people are so poor that they're not gonna realistically be able to continue to purchase it, and which is gonna . . . that they're going to dilute it to a point, which is going to endanger the health, that it should not be used.

Dr. Ballarin: Yes, I believe . . .

Senator Kennedy: Alright, now . . . then my final question is . . . is what do you . . . or what do you feel is your corporate responsibility to find out the extent of the use of your product in those circumstances in the developing part of the world? Do you feel that you have any responsibility?

Dr. Ballarin: We can't have that responsibility, sir. May I make a reference to . . .

Senator Kennedy: You can't have that responsibility?

Dr. Ballarin: No.

Dr. Ballarin's testimony continued (for example of excerpts, see Exhibit 3), but Nestlé management believed little attention was paid to it. Mr. Guerrant, president of Nestlé U.S., was very angry and wrote a letter to Senator Kennedy on May 26, 1978, protesting against the way he had treated Dr. Ballarin (Exhibit 4).

EXHIBIT 3   Further excerpts from Dr. Ballarin's testimony

Nestlé recognized that even the best products will not give the desired results if used incorrectly. We, therefore, placed great weight on educational efforts aimed at explaining the correct use of our product. Our work in this field has received the public recognition and approval of the official Pediatric Associations in many countries. Such educational efforts never attempt to infer that our product is superior to breast milk. Indeed, we have devoted much attention to the promotion of breast-feeding, and educational material has always insisted that breast-feeding is best for the baby.

Nevertheless, many factors militate against exclusive breast-feeding in the rapidly growing cities of Brazil as well as other developing countries, and our products are seen today as filling a valid need, just as they did when they were first introduced over 50 years ago. In recognition of this, all such products are subject to strict price control, while in many countries which do not have a local dairy industry, they are classified as essential goods and imported free of duty. In many cases, official agencies establish what they consider to be a fair margin for the manufacturers.

It must be stressed that many problems remain to be solved. Our production is far from reaching the total needs of the population. Hence, many mothers in the poorer population groups continue to supplement breast-feeding with foods of doubtful quality. Owing to the lack of adequate medical services, especially in the rural areas, misuse of any supplement can occur and we are very conscious of the need to improve our efforts. These efforts depend on continued cooperation between the infant food industry and health professionals. We have to be more and more conscious of our responsibility to encourage breast-feeding while researching new foods and safer methods for feeding babies who cannot be exclusively breast-fed. The dilemma facing industry and the health service alike, is how to teach these methods without discouraging breast-feeding.

EXHIBIT 4   Excerpts from Mr. Guerrant's letter to Senator Kennedy

I am angry but more important deeply concerned about the example of our governmental processes exhibited this week by the Human Resources Subcommittee on Health and Scientific Research.

(continued)

It was the general consensus of several people in the audience that your position toward the manufacturers was "you are guilty until you prove your innocence." Objectivity would have been more becoming, Senator.

Secondly, it seemed equally probable that prior to the hearing the prepared statements were reviewed and you were quite prepared to rebuff Dr. Ballarin on his statement "undermining the free enterprise system." Unaccustomed to television and this type of inquisition, Dr. Ballarin, who appeared voluntarily, was flustered and embarrassed.

Probably, for this gathering, the statement was too strong (though nothing to compare with their theme "Nestlé kills babies") and should have been more subtle. But the point is well made, and your apparent denial of this possibility concerns me.

As you may know, this whole issue gained its greatest momentum a few years ago in Europe fostered by clearly identified radical leftist groups. Their stated purpose is opposition to capitalism and the free enterprise system. I submit that they are not really concerned with infants in the Third World but are intelligent enough to know that babies, especially sick and dying, create maximum emotional response. Further, they are clever enough to know that the people most easy to "use" for their campaign, to front for them, are in churches and universities. These are good people, ready to rise against oppression and wrong-doing without, regrettably, truthful facts for objective research. I know, as my father is a retired Presbyterian minister, and I have a very warm feeling toward members of the church, Protestant and Catholic.

People with far left philosophies are not confined to Europe and are certainly represented in many accepted organizations here and abroad. (Please take the time to read the enclosed report of the 1977 Geneva Consultation of the World Council of Churches.) Associated with the World Council is the National Council of Churches, and one of their units is the Interfaith Centre for Corporate Responsibility. One of their major spokespersons appears to be Leah Margulies, who was present in your hearing.

Now, just briefly to the very complex infant food issue. As the U.S. Nestlé Company does not manufacture or sell any infant food products, we are unhappy with the attempted boycott of our products—at least 95 percent of these manufactured in the United States. The jobs and security of about 12,000 good U.S. employees are being threatened.

From our associates in Switzerland, and Nestlé companies in the Third World, we have gathered hundreds of factual documents. Neither Nestlé nor the U.S. companies in this business claim perfection. Companies are comprised of human beings. However, virtually every charge against Nestlé has proved to be erroneous. Distorted "facts" and just pure propaganda have been answered by people with undeniable integrity and technical credentials. Quite some time ago, because of the accusations, Nestlé world headquarters in Switzerland studied every facet of their total infant food business, made immediate changes where warranted and established new and very clear policies and procedures regarding the conduct of this business.

I might add that Nestlé infant foods have undoubtedly saved hundreds of thousands of lives. There is not even one instance where proof exists that Nestlé infant food was responsible for a single death. The products are as essential in the Third World as in the industrialized world. Though the accusers use some statements by apparently qualified people, there is an overwhelming amount of data and number of statements from qualified medical, technical, and government representatives in the Third World confirming Nestlé's position.

At your hearing this week were the same identical charges made against Nestlé and the others years ago. These people will not recognize the changes made in marketing practices nor the irrefutable facts of the real infant health problems in the Third World. They continue to push the U.S. Nestlé boycott and continue to distribute the fraudulent film "Bottle Babies." (Please read Dr. Bwibo's letter enclosed.) Sincere, well-meaning church people continue to be used, as they have not had all the real facts available for analysis.

The above situation made me believe that the organizers must have some motivation for this campaign other than what appears on the surface. If it could possibly be what I think, then our representatives in government should proceed with caution, thorough study, and great objectivity, as your ultimate position can be of critical consequence. I am not a crusader, but I do feel the free enterprise system is best.

CBS aired its program on July 5, 1978. Again, Nestlé management was upset. In their view CBS had selected portions of the testimonies to make Nestlé management look inept and confused. Mr. Guerrant wrote a letter of protest to CBS president Richard Salant (Exhibit 5).

EXHIBIT 5   Excerpts from Mr. Guerrant's letter to CBS President Salant

---

In the first minute of the program the infant formula industry has been tried and convicted of causing infant malnutrition. The remainder of the program is devoted to reinforcing Mr. Myer's conclusion. Tools of persuasion include the emotionality of a needle sticking in a child's head and the uneasy answers of cross-examined industry witnesses who are asked not for the facts but to admit and apologize for their "guilt."

But CBS Reports chose to concentrate on the "rhetoric of concern" and the claims which permeate the rhetoric. Industry's response to the rhetoric is not glamorous but hits into the root causes of infant malnutrition—the poverty, disease, and ignorance existing in the areas of developing and developed countries. Those conditions are not easy for anthropologists, economists, scientists, or medical people to trace or explain. And certainly the reasons for them are not as identifiable as a major corporation. But in 30 minutes Mr. Myers and Ms. Roche identified four companies as a major reason for infant malnutrition.

One way Nestlé has attempted to meet the responsibility is by making capital investments in and transferring technology to the developing countries. Nestlé began this effort in 1921 in Brazil and now has almost 40,000 local employees working in 81 manufacturing facilities in 25 developing countries. Not only does Nestlé have a beneficial impact on those directly employed, the company also encourages and assists the development of other local supporting industries, such as the dairy industry and packaging plants.

Another way Nestlé meets its responsibility is to work with local governments and health authorities in educating consumers. Clinics, pamphlets, posters, books, and product labels emphasize the superiority of breast-feeding, demonstrate proper sanitation and diet for breast-feeding, and show in words and pictures how to correctly use formula products.

Neither of these positive approaches was covered in CBS Reports nor was there mention of the fact that infant mortality has declined worldwide over the past 30 years, nor that lack of sufficient breast milk is a major cause of infant malnutrition, nor that tropical diseases cause millions of deaths per year in developing countries. Any one of these facts would have provided some balance to the Myers-Roche report.

Following the Kennedy hearings, representatives of Nestlé S.A., Abbott, Bristol-Myers, and American Home Products met privately with Senator Kennedy to explore a suggestion for a further hearing. Meanwhile, the president of ICIFI wrote Kennedy, pointing out that this was an international and not a U.S. domestic issue—and should therefore be discussed at a forum sponsored by WHO. Kennedy accepted ICIFI's suggestion and requested the Director General of WHO to sponsor a conference at which the question of an international code could be discussed.

A consensus emerged that a uniform code for the industry was required and that Kennedy and ICIFI would suggest that WHO sponsor a conference with that aim in mind. The conference would be comprised of WHO officials, ICIFI members and other companies, health and government officials from the developing countries, and all appropriate concerned public groups. WHO accepted the idea and announced the conference date in the fall of 1979. Shortly after Nestlé management met with Kennedy, the National Council of Churches, comprised of about 30 major religious groups in the United States, announced that the question of supporting INFACT and ICCR would be discussed and decided at the NCC national conference in November 1978.

The Situation in October 1978

Dr. Fürer knew all senior Nestlé management felt personally attacked by critics of the industry. Not only was this the first major public pressure campaign ever encountered by Nestlé, but also Nestlé management felt its critics were using unfair tactics. For example, again and again they saw in boycott letters and articles a grotesque picture of a wizened child with a formula bottle nearby. Eventually this picture was traced to Dr. Derrick Jeliffe, an outspoken critic of the industry. He admitted to *Newsweek* he had taken the picture in a Caribbean hospital in 1964. Even though it seemed the media and many respected companies were against Nestlé, Dr. Fürer stated publicly:

> No one has the right to accuse us of killing babies. No one has the right to assert that we are guilty of pursuing unethical or immoral sales practices.

Nonetheless, under U.S. law a company is regarded as a public person which meant that the First Amendment applied; that is, Nestlé could not get legal relief against charges made by the critics unless the company could prove those charges were both wrong and malicious.

Further, Dr. Fürer was struck by the fact that all the demands for change were coming from developed countries. In fact, Nestlé had received many letters of support from people in the developing countries (Exhibit 6). Mr. Ernest Saunders, Nestlé vice president for infant nutrition products, summarized his view as follows:

> Government and medical personnel tell us that if we stopped selling infant foods we would be killing a lot of babies.

Dr. Fürer also believed that the scientific facts underlying the breast versus bottle controversy were not being given adequate attention (for example, see Exhibit 7) nor were the changes Nestlé and the other companies had made. Nestlé's policies regarding infant formula products were apparently not well known. Exhibit 8 includes excerpts from the latest edition, dated September 1, 1977.

EXHIBIT 6   Examples of support for Nestlé

---

1. I have been associated with the medical representatives of Nestlé in Kenya for the last five years. We have discussed on various occasions the problems of artificial feeding, in particular the use of proprietary milk preparations. We have all been agreed that breast-feeding should always come first. As far as I am aware, your representatives have not used any unethical methods when promoting Nestlé products in this country.

> M. L. Oduori, Senior Consultant
> Pediatrician
> Ministry of Health
> Kenyatta National Hospital, Nairobi,
> Kenya, Dec. 23, 1974

(continued)

EXHIBIT 6   *(concluded)*

2. You are not "killing babies," on the contrary your efforts joined with ours contribute to the improvement of the Health Status of our infant population.

   We consider your marketing policies as ethical and as not being opposite to our recommendations. We note with pleasure that you employ a fully qualified nurse and that during discussions with mothers she always encourages breast-feeding, recommending your products when only natural feeding is insufficient or fails.

   > Dr. Jerry Lukowski
   > Chief Gynecologist, Menelik Hospital
   > Ethiopia, Dec. 3, 1974

3. Over several decades I have had direct and indirect dealings with your organisation in South Africa in relation to many aspects of nutrition among the nonwhite population who fall under our care, as well as the supply of nutriments to the hospital and peripheral clinics.

   I am fairly well aware of the extent of your Company's contributions to medical science and research and that this generosity goes hand in hand with the highest ethical standards of advertising, distribution of products, and the nutrition educational services which you provide.

   At no time in the past have my colleagues or I entertained any idea or suspicion that Nestlé have behaved in any way that could be regarded as unethical in their promotions, their products or their educational programmes. On all occasions when discussion of problems or amendments to arrangements have been asked for, full cooperation has been given to this department.

   Your field workers have given and are giving correct priorities in regard to breast feeding, and, where necessary, the bottle feeding of infants.

   The staff employed to do this work have shown a strong sense of responsibility and duty towards the public whom they serve, no doubt due to the educational instruction they have themselves received in order to fit them for their work.

   > S. Wayburne, Chief Pediatrician
   > Baragwanath Hospital
   > Associate Professor of Pediatrics,
   > Acting Head of Department of
   > Pediatrics, University of
   > Witwatersrand/South Africa
   > Dec. 18, 1974

4. I have read about the accusation that "Nestlé Kills Babies" and I strongly refute it, I think it is quite unjustifiable.

   On my experience I have never seen any mother being advised to use artificial milk when it was not necessary. Every mother is advised to give breast foods to her baby. It is only when there is failure of this, then artificial foods are advised.

   I, being a working mother have brought up my five children on Nestlé Products and I do not see anything wrong with them. I knew I would have found it difficult to carry on with my profession if I had nothing to rely on like your products.

   Your marketing policies are quite in order as I knew them and they are quite ethical. As they stress on breast milk foods first and if this is unobtainable then one can use Nestlé's Products.

   > Mrs. M. Lema, Nursing Officer
   > Ocean Hospital
   > Dar-es-Salaam/TANZANIA
   > Dec. 16, 1974

5. On behalf of the Sisters of Nazareth Hospital, I thank you heartily for your generous contribution in giving us the Nestlé products in a way that we can assist and feed many undernourished children freely cured and treated in our hospital.

   Trusting in your continuous assistance allow me to express again my sincerest thanks, and may God bless you.

   > Nazareth Hospital
   > Nairobi, Kenya
   > September 9, 1978

6. I am very grateful for this help for our babies in need in the maternity ward.

   Another mission has asked me about this milk gift parcels, if there would be any chance for them. It is Butula Mission and they have a health centre with beds and maternity and maternal child health clinics. There is a lot of malnutrition also in that area, so that mothers often do not produce enough milk for their babies. It would be wonderful if you could help them also.

   > Nangina Hospital
   > Medical Mission Sisters
   > Funyula, Kenya
   > June 15, 1976

7. As a doctor who has practiced for 18 years in a developing country, I was angered by the collection of half-truths, judiciously mixed with falsehoods put out by the Infant Formula Action Coalition as reported in the *Newsweek* article on breast-feeding. Whether we like it or not, many mothers cannot or will not resort to breast-feeding. I do not believe that advertising has played any significant part in their decision. It is an inescapable necessity that specific, nutritionally balanced formulas are available. Otherwise, we would witness wholesale feeding with products that are unsuitable.

   I carry no brief for companies like Nestlé, but have always found it to be a company with the highest regard to ethical standards. Infant formulas have saved many thousands of lives. What alternative are their critics proposing?

   > D. C. Williams, M.D.
   > Kuala Lumpur
   > Malaysia

8. Surely, Nestlé is not to blame. There have been similar problems here but through the efforts of the Save the Children Fund and government assistance, feeding bottles can only be purchased through chemists or hospitals by prescription. In this way, the decision of whether to breast-feed or not is decided by qualified personnel.

   I would think that Americans would have better things to do than walk around disrupting commerce with placards.

   > Gail L. Hubbard
   > Goroka, Papua New Guinea

EXHIBIT 7 Examples of supplementary information on breast-feeding versus bottle-feeding

---

1. Findings of the Human Lactation Center (HLC).

   The HLC is a scientific research institute, a nonprofit organization dedicated to worldwide education and research on lactation. The HLC entered the breast/bottle controversy between the infant formula industry and the anti-multinational groups in an attempt to clarify certain issues. Eleven anthropologists, all women, studied infant feeding practices in 11 different cultures, ranging from a relatively urbanized Sardinian village to a very impoverished Egyptian agricultural village. Their findings:

   Poverty is correlated with infant morbidity (disease). Child health is associated with affluence.

   Infant mortality had decreased in the three decades prior to 1973 when food prices began to escalate.

   Breast milk is the best infant food but breast-feeding exclusively for most *undernourished* women in the less developed countries is inadequate beyond the baby's third month. Lack of sufficient food after this time is a major cause of morbidity and mortality whether or not the infant is breast-fed.

   Mixed feeding is an almost universal pattern in traditional cultures; that is, breast-feeding and supplementary feeding from early on and often into the second year.

   The preferred additional food for the very young child is milk. Most milk is fresh milk, unprocessed.

   (continued)

EXHIBIT 7 *(continued)*

Most women still breast-feed though many do not. The popular assumption that breast-feeding is being reduced has not been verified.

Third World women with the least amount of resources, time, or access to health care and weaning foods, have no choice but to breast-feed.

More than half the infants they bear do not survive due to lack of food for themselves and their children.

Women who are separated from close kin, especially the urban poor, lack mothering from a supportive figure. They find themselves unable to lactate adequately or lose their milk entirely. Without suitable substitutes, their infants die.

Middle class women in the less-developed countries, market women, the elite, and professional women are moving towards bottle feeding with infant formula in much the same way women turned from breast to bottle feeding in the western countries.

The current literature on breast-feeding in the developing countries is meager. Information on mortality, the incidence of breast-feeding, the content of infant food, and the amount of breast milk, tend to be impressionistic reports by well-meaning western or western trained persons often unaware of the complexities of feeding practices and insensitive to the real-life situation of the mothers. Judgments for action based on these inconclusive data could be dangerous.

Mothers have a sensitive and remarkable grasp of how best to keep their infants alive. Neither literacy nor what has been called "ignorance" determine which infants live and which die except as they are related directly to social class.

In seeking solutions to the problems of infant well-being in the developing world, we must listen to the mothers and involve them in the decisions which will affect their lives.

2. *The Feeding of the Very Young: An Approach to Determination of Policies,* report of the International Advisory Group on Infant and Child Feeding to the Nutrition Foundation, October 1978:

"Two basic requirements of successful feeding are: (1) adequate milk during the first four to six months of life, and (2) adequate complementary foods during the transition to adult diets. It is imperative that all societies recognize these requirements as a major component of nutrition policy. The extent to which mothers are able to meet both of these requirements will vary under different cultural and sociological circumstances. In all societies there will be some proportion of mothers who will not be able to meet them without assistance, and policy must be developed to protect those children who are at risk of malnutrition resulting from inadequacy in either one or both of these basic requirements."

Source: Nestlé memoranda.

(continued)

EXHIBIT 7 *(concluded)*

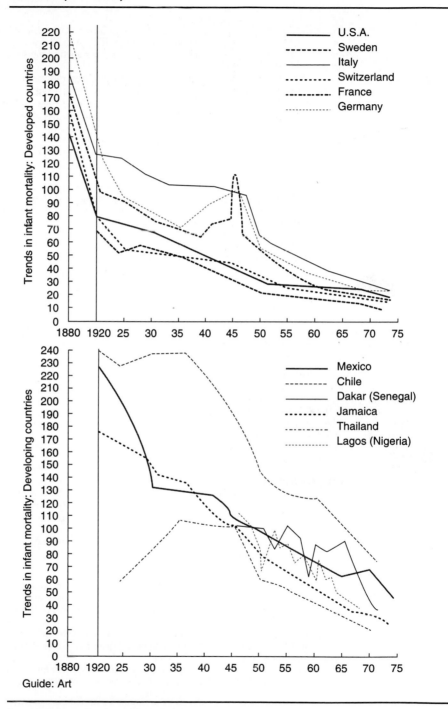

Guide: Art

Source: Demographic Yearbook, United Nations.

EXHIBIT 8   Excerpts from Nestlé directives on infant and dietetic products policy

Infant milks

It is recognized that breast milk is the best food for a baby. Our baby milks are therefore not intended to compete with breast milk, but to supplement breast feeding when the mother's own milk can no longer cover the baby's needs or to replace it when mothers cannot, or elect not to breast feed.

Three to four months after birth, the quantities of breast milk produced by the average mother become insufficient to satisfy the growing needs of the baby. The baby needs a supplement of water and food. From this moment on, in the poor communities of developing countries this baby is in danger because water is sometimes polluted and local foods, like plantain or manioc, are nutritionally inadequate. They are starchy foods with little food value and a young baby cannot digest them. Thus the highest infant mortality occurs precisely in areas where babies receive only mother's milk plus a supplement of unboiled local water and/or starchy decoctions.

This is not a Nestlé theory. This is a fact known by every Third World doctor and recently scientifically demonstrated by British researchers working in Africa.

The alternative to traditional local supplement is a properly formulated breast milk substitute, preferably a humanized formula. It is true that there is a risk of misuse, but these risks exist with a local supplement too, although the baby has a better chance of survival when the starting point is of high quality.

It is precisely to reduce the risks of misuse and thereby increase the chances of survival that we had developed over the years a comprehensive programme of information and education: contact with doctors, educative advertising, booklets, nurses; all this had the purpose of making the alternative to local supplements known and ensuring a proper and safe use of our products when needed. Nestlé policies are designed to avoid the unnecessary replacement of breast milk.

The real issue is not breast milk versus formula, as so often pictured, but breast milk plus formula plus education versus traditional foods like manioc.

Products must be in line with internationally recognized nutritional criteria and offer definite consumer benefits.

Distribution policy

It is a rule that PID products are never sold to mothers directly by us; distribution aims at making products available to prescribers and users under optimum safety and price conditions.

Within the limits set by the law and by the distribution structure, we practice mixed distribution (pharmacies and general food stores) and use the normal market channels. On the other hand, dietetic specialties and products designed for delicate or sick babies, which are basically sold on medical prescription, are sold only through pharmacies, unless special local conditions warrant mixed distribution.

Communication policy—direct contact with mothers

Medical representatives must not enter into direct contact with mothers, unless they are authorized to do so in writing by a medical or health authority and provided that they are properly qualified. Films may be shown with the agreement of the medical or public health authorities concerned.

Visits to mothers in their homes are not allowed unless the responsible medical authority has made a written request for a visit to take place.

Personnel policy

The main task of the medical promotion personnel consists in contacting the medical and paramedical professions and hospitals. They are not concerned with direct sales to mothers and cannot sell dietetic products other than, exceptionally and exclusively, to the trade or institutions.

Specialized training must be given to such staff, to enable them to render a genuine service to the medical and paramedical professions and give them scientific and unbiased information on product characteristics and utilization.

No sales-related bonus will be paid to any staff engaged in medical promotion or having direct contact with mothers. If a bonus is to be paid, it must depend on elements other than sales, such as personal qualities and qualifications.

Many members of management believed the attack against Nestlé was ideologically based. They gathered information about and quotations from many of the activist groups to support their position (for example, see Exhibit 9). Whatever their foundation, the critics seemed to Dr. Fürer to be gaining publicity and momentum. INFACT claimed at least 500 separate action committees in the United States, support in about 75 communities in Canada, as well as support in about 10 other countries. "The movement is snowballing," reported Gwen Willens of INFACT. "We're getting over 300 letters of support every day."

As Dr. Fürer consulted with senior management in Nestlé, he wondered what further steps Nestlé might take to deal with the controversy surrounding the marketing of infant formula products in the developing countries.

EXHIBIT 9   Examples of comments concerning the ideology of the activist group

Sue Tafler and Betsy Walker, "Why Boycott Nestlé?" in *Science for the People,* January/February 1978.

> Unfortunately, the power in many developing countries is not held by the people themselves, and local ruling elites often want to encourage corporate investment. . . . What the boycott will not do is overthrow capitalism. . . . The boycott can unite well-meaning groups that see themselves as apolitical with more openly political groups. . . . We can have the effect of politicizing others working in the coalition. If Nestlé does make some concessions to the demands of the boycott, the sense of victory can give encouragement to the organizers of the boycott to continue on to larger struggles.

T. Balasusiya, Centre for Society and Religion, Colombo, Sri Lanka, participant at the World Council of Churches meeting, January 1977.

> The capitalist system is the main cause of the increasing gap and within that system multinationals are a main form. Ideology of wealth is the practical religion of capitalist society. Churches are legitimizers of the system, so their first job is self-purification. There can be no neutrality between money and God.
>
> Our function is not to judge persons, but we have to judge systems. . . . What alternative solutions do countries propose that have rejected the capitalist system, e.g., USSR, China, Cuba, Tanzania? Capitalism is inherently contradictory to the Gospel.

M. Ritchie, at a conference, "Clergy and Laity Concerned," August 1978.

> It's not just on babies, it's not just multinational corporations, it's class conflict and class struggle. Broadening the constituency both of people interested in the infant formula issue . . . how the infant formula campaign and the people there link up completely in terms of support and action with other types of campaigns. . .
>
> I think ultimately what we're trying to do is take an issue-specific focus campaign and move it in conjunction with other issue-specific campaigns into a larger very class-wide very class-conscious campaign and reasserting our power in this country, our power in this world.

Douglas Johnson of INFACT, at an address in Washington, September 1978.

> Our hope is that we can use this [boycott] campaign as the forerunner of legislation for control of multinational corporations.

Source: Nestlé internal memoranda.

Case 29

InterMark: Designing UNICEF's Oral Rehydration Program in Zambia*

The setting sun gave a pink tone to the Washington skyline across the Potomac river and the jets glided over the river to National Airport in early August 1991. Allison Boyd enjoyed the view, but her thoughts were far away. For weeks she was occupied with the children of Zambia. As a project manager for InterMark, an international consulting firm, she had been working on UNICEF's oral rehydration program for reduction of diarrheal disease in Zambia for the past six months; her final recommendations were due in a week.

United Nations International Children's Emergency Fund (UNICEF) contracted with InterMark to recommend how UNICEF should spend their funds in the next three years to reduce the incidence of diarrheal disease, primarily through increased use of ORS. UNICEF spent $87,000 in 1991 to import ORS donated to the Ministry of Health for free distribution to hospitals and clinics. They were willing to spend as much as 30 percent more on purchase of ORS or alternative programs if it could be shown that their program objectives were likely to be met:

> Substantially reduce infant and child deaths and illnesses associated with diarrheal disease.
>
> Have a high likelihood of sustainability after three years when the aid is no longer available.

The assignment had been interesting and challenging. Two month-long visits to Zambia provided a large amount of information for her recommended program to increase the appropriate use of oral rehydration salts (ORS) in Zambia.

---

*This case was written by Professor Ron Stiff, University of Baltimore, and it was previously published by the *Case Research Journal.* © 1996. Used with permission.

Allison was expected to provide written recommendations and make a presentation to the UNICEF staff.

Zambia

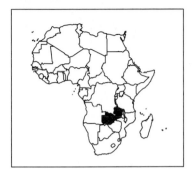

The Republic of Zambia (formerly Northern Rhodesia) attained independence from Britain in 1964. Zambia is situated on an elevated plateau in south-central Africa with a population of eight million in 1990 and an area of 752,614 sq. km., slightly larger than the state of Texas. As a land-locked country, it is dependent on either its neighbors or air transport for links with the outside world.

For many years, the mining of copper dominated the Zambian economy, although its contribution has declined significantly in recent years. The agricultural sector received the active support of the government and international donors, but has not achieved its potential and agricultural exports have declined. The per capita GNP, which stood at $290 U.S. in 1988, placed it in the low income economies as defined by the World Bank (18th poorest worldwide). Per capita GNP was expected to be as low as $150 U.S. per capita in 1991. Many households earned less than $40 U.S. per month.

Health Expenditures and Status

In 1986, the government spent $3.60 per capita for health care. Estimation of morbidity (illnesses) and mortality (deaths) levels and trends are uncertain in many developing countries, including Zambia, because of problems with the quality of measurements. The national infant mortality rate fell from around 130 deaths per 1,000 in the mid-1950s to about 120 in the mid-1960s, and thence to about 115 in the early 1970s. This was considerably higher than the infant mortality rate in the 25 highest-income countries, which was 9 deaths per 1,000 in 1988. Correspondingly, the proportion of children dying between birth and their fifth birthday (childhood mortality) fell from 22 percent to 20 percent, and thence to 19 percent, respectively, where it remained through 1991. One of every five children died before reaching age five.

The national figures were within the general range in Central and Southern Africa. These statistics concealed regional differentials in mortality that have clear implications for the delivery of health programs. Childhood mortality estimates for the 1960s showed a general pattern of highest mortality in the rural provinces, lowest mortality in the two most urbanized provinces, and an intermediate level in Southern province. The infant mortality rate for that period ranged from 82 (Copperbelt) to 175 (Eastern), giving a national average of 121.

Allison analyzed three Zambian statistical reports. She grouped provinces into three regions to evaluate geographical differences (Exhibit 1). She noted that the central provinces, along the main rail line, were far more urbanized than the provinces she grouped as northeastern and northwestern. The lower

Exhibit 1   Population statistics for Zambia

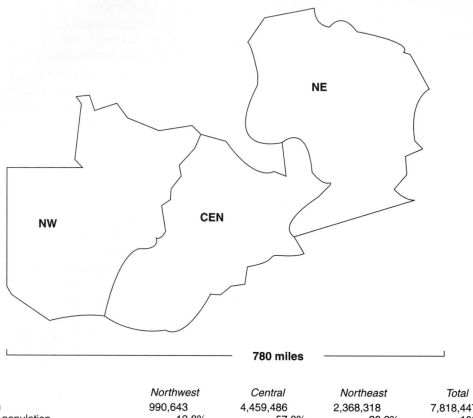

780 miles

	Northwest	Central	Northeast	Total
Population	990,643	4,459,486	2,368,318	7,818,447
Percent of population	12.8%	57.0%	30.2%	100%
Population under 5 years	200,704	903,492	479,821	1,584,017
Area, sq. km.	252,000	232,000	268,000	752,000
Pop. density/sq. km.	4	19	9	10
Percent urban	20.8%	68.4%	17.7%	48%
Population per physician—1988	12,926	17,380	23,449	15,544
Expected births	49,037	220,744	117,232	387,013
Percent births in medical units—1988	27.7%	37.2%	21.7%	31.3%

Sources: (1) *Country Profile, Republic of Zambia: 1989–1990,* Central Statistical Office, Lusaka. (2) *Bulletin of Health Statistics: 1978–1988,* Ministry of Health, Health Information Unit, Lusaka. (3) *Monthly Digest of Statistics: January 1991,* Central Statistical Office, Lusaka.
Notes: (1) Analysis combines Zambian provinces as: NW: Northwestern and Western; CEN: Central, Copperbelt, Lusaka, and Southern; NE: Eastern, Luapula, and Northern. (2) All 1990 except as noted.

population densities and less developed road systems in these areas made de-livery of health care services challenging.

This pattern fit well with what was known of background factors such as income levels, general economic development, nutrition, education, and fertility levels. The leading causes of mortality at Zambia's health centers in 1981 were: measles (26 percent), pneumonia (14 percent), malnutrition-anemia (14 percent),

TABLE 1   Diarrhea cases in health centers for children under 15 years of age

1986	805,880
1987	758,151
1988	842,142

Source: *Bulletin of Health Statistics: 1987–1988,* Ministry of Health, Health Information Unit, Republic of Zambia.

TABLE 2   Medical facilities

Hospitals	
Government	42
Mission	29
Mines	11
Clinics: Rural	
Government	643
Mission	64
Clinics: Urban	
Government	142
Mines	75
Total	1,006

Source: *Bulletin of Health Statistics: 1987–1988,* Ministry of Health, Health Information Unit, Republic of Zambia

TABLE 3   Health care providers

Physicians	500
Clinical officers	1,100
Nurses	5,250
Midwives	1,135
Health assistants	531
Community health workers	983

malaria (10 percent), and diarrheas (10 percent). The leading causes of outpatient morbidity in children under 15 years were respiratory illnesses, malaria, diarrhea, and injuries, most of which were preventable. Diarrhea cases for children under 15 years of age at health centers are shown in Table 1.

Public Sector Health Services

Most patients received free medical care through Ministry of Health, missionary, military, or mining company facilities. The medical facilities existing in 1988 are given in Table 2; the estimated number of health care providers in Table 3.

Private Sector Health Services

There were several private medical practitioners, primarily seeing patients in Zambia's capital, Lusaka. In addition, approximately 10,000 traditional healers provided services throughout the country. It was estimated that as many as 9 out of 10 patients sought help from "traditional" healers before coming for "scientific" treatment; some continued traditional medicine while hospitalized. The cost of the traditional healer's consultation fees could be greater than that paid to private medical doctors for the same symptoms.

Diarrhea Causes and Treatment

Diarrhea results from consuming contaminated food or water. The percentage of Zambian households supplied with piped water and sewage systems declined in the latter half of the 1980s. In 1991, about 50 percent of the total population had access to water defined as "reasonably" safe by World Health Organization standards.

Diarrhea was one of the most critical health problems in Zambia. For children under five years of age, who constituted over 18 percent of the total population, diarrhea was a leading cause of morbidity and mortality. In 1982, diarrhea accounted for up to 13.5 percent of total admissions, 19.2 percent of total outpatient visits, and 13.2 percent of total deaths in rural health centers. It was also responsible for 7.8 percent of total admissions, 17.3 percent of total outpatient visits, and 8.6 percent of total deaths in the hospitals.

Management of diarrhea cases involves restoring and maintaining fluids by oral rehydration and, in a few cases, intravenous therapy. Often, improving or maintaining nutritional status by appropriate feeding (including breast-feeding) during and after diarrhea, as well as treating fevers and other complications with drugs, is necessary. The most effective treatment is drinking oral rehydration salts (ORS), as recommended by the World Health Organization (WHO) and UNICEF. ORS contains three essential salts (the formulation of ORS has some similarities to sports drinks such as Gatorade). At the onset of diarrhea, weak tea and juice are often given to children, but a correctly prepared salt-sugar solution is better. ORS is, however, by far the most effective means of establishing rehydration. Health care educators consider it essential that parents understand that a dehydrated infant could die in less than 24 hours and know how to provide the child with the best available rehydration solution. Parents should be educated to recognize serious cases requiring that the child be taken to a trained health care provider.

Diarrhea produces severe dehydration especially damaging to the health of infants. ORS does not stop diarrhea but reduces dehydration by replacing fluids and electrolytes. Use of antidiarrheal drugs, such as kaolin, codeine, or activated charcoal, can cause severe life-threatening reactions in young children since these drugs do not reduce dehydration. Some pharmacists encouraged use of these drugs either because they were not educated in the use of ORS or they wanted to sell products that are higher priced than ORS.

Health care educators believe that ideal communications directed to parents include these informational items:

Diarrhea, any diarrhea, is a potentially serious illness for children.

A child who has diarrhea should receive appropriate and sufficient fluids and food while diarrhea persists and should receive extra fluids and food after an episode of diarrhea for a period equal to the duration of the illness.

The caretakers of a child with diarrhea should observe and monitor the child for danger signs, persistence of diarrhea, and the presence of blood in the stool.

Children with these danger signs must be taken for appropriate medical treatment as soon as possible.

Need and Demand for ORS

Without high-quality health statistics, determining the need and demand for ORS was difficult. In 1988, 842,142 new cases of diarrhea in children under 15 years of age were treated at hospitals or health centers. Many cases did not receive preadmission care. Additionally, the population under age five was increasing at a rapid rate. In 1991, 400,000 births were expected, with as many as 100,000 to new mothers who were unlikely to understand the proper care of sick infants since virtually no prenatal education was provided. It was estimated that there were about five episodes of diarrhea in each of the 1.6 million children under five years of age each year; at least one-third of these required ORS. There were at least one million more cases in older children and adults each year. Effective treatment required about two liters of ORS. Treating these cases with ORS would require six million one-liter packets (in Zambia, ORS was supplied as concentrated salts requiring the user to mix these with the correct quantity of water) or the equivalent in packets of other sizes. Only about two-thirds of this supply were available either through free distribution at health clinics or hospitals or for sale in the marketplace.

The actual demand for ORS was somewhat less than this estimate due to the difficulties in obtaining ORS and limited consumer awareness of its benefits. ORS supplied at no cost through hospitals and health centers by the Ministry of Health had limitations due to shortages, the distance and time involved in obtaining the ORS from these sources, and frequent long waiting lines for health care services. It was estimated that 25 percent of the population lay outside a 12-kilometer radius of a health clinic or hospital. Marketplace distribution was often ineffective since some segments of consumers were unable to pay for the ORS and/or unaware of its benefits. As with most products, demand varied with the price charged.

The need for education of parents was extensive. Many parents with children under 15 years of age were not knowledgeable about oral rehydration therapy. Adult literacy in 1985 was reported to be 67 percent; however, the average years of schooling was only 2.6 years, raising some questions regarding the published literacy statistics.

Analysis of Constraints

General Environment

Some constraints present in the general economic and social environment applied specifically to a control of diarrheal disease program—constraints to the supply of ORS, or constraints to the use of ORS by mothers. Other constraints applied more broadly to delivery of all primary health care service, but have a direct bearing on the success of the program.

Dispersed and remote rural population. Although Zambia has the most-highly urbanized population in sub-Saharan Africa, about 60 percent of the population live in rural areas where there were few points of population concentration. Household contact between mothers and the health system were common for the 75 percent of parents who lived within 12 kilometers of clinics (average of five contacts per year for children under one year of age); however, contact was far less likely for those who lived further away. Distribution of ORS packets was expensive and delays were frequent in many rural areas where the transportation infrastructure was weak.

Declining real incomes, especially for rural households. Cash available in households for purchases of ORS, radio batteries, public transport, and even "mealy meal" (the local term for corn meal, the major food staple) was increasingly scarce as the economic situation worsened. The long-standing decline in the terms of trade for agricultural products increased economic stress for rural households. The typical high-end expenditures for traditional medical treatment was generally between $1 and $5 (70 to 350 Zambian kwachas) for a routine course of treatment. Many households had monthly incomes of K2,800[1] or less. This highlighted the need for education about the most cost-effective medical treatments, such as ORS, for diarrhea.

Large proportion of female-headed households in rural areas. Female-headed households were a result of male labor migration to urban communities in search of higher wages. The approximately 25 percent of rural households headed by females were those most likely to be at the bottom of the income scale. Because these mothers needed to produce income, they were less likely to have time to seek health services, get health education, or give health care at the onset of diarrhea. These households were less likely to participate in, or benefit from, a program because of financial and time constraints.

Severely constrained national budget. The Zambia Ministry of Health could not afford to maintain the current level of health services throughout the national system. A disproportionately large share was being expended for curative services in the three major hospitals. To sustain and expand new programs like diarrheal disease control programs, additional funds or reallocations of existing health resources were needed. Allocations for the primary health care system, especially costs of training and supervision, would be crucial to the national diarrheal disease control program.

Health System Constraints

The general health system constraints in Zambia consisted of: shortages of staff, shortages of supplies, inadequate support measures, and lack of appropriate supervision at all levels. Field supervision suffered from shortages of staff and inadequate provision of transportation. The large percentage of attrition found among trained community health workers and other peripheral workers was felt by Allison to be the result of infrequent or nonexistent supervisory visits. It was likely that workers at remote rural health clinics felt isolated in any case, but to never have any contact with the supervisor encouraged high employee turnover. Ideally, the supervisor's role included in-service training, checking on procedures, reinforcement, and encouragement, all vital for good performance. This support was needed for the distant workers, and transportation was very important. Shortages of supplies lead to a decline in clinic attendance and an increase in the dependence on traditional healers that already represented a significant and important aspect of general health care activity.

Drastic cuts in the Ministry of Health budget made it likely that they could not afford to buy enough drugs, limiting expenditures to essential hospital supplies. It was likely that the Ministry of Health would encourage donor assistance for ORS rather than supporting their oral rehydration therapy program directly or by instituting a patient fee for drugs or services.

---

[1]Equivalent to $40 U.S.

Constraints Specific to Control of Diarrheal Disease

Inappropriate treatment methods for diarrhea. Allison visited hospitals and clinics with UNICEF physicians and observed inadequacies in diagnosis and treatment of diarrhea by all categories of health workers. There was a lack of awareness of the vital importance of oral rehydration therapy in clinical management and in home use for early prevention of dehydration. Health workers said that diarrheal disease was not strongly emphasized in their education, suggesting a need for refresher courses.

Another problem in the treatment of diarrhea was the clinical habit among all levels of health providers of not taking a careful and appropriate history and not fully examining the child when the chief complaint is "diarrhea." Clinical judgment ideally includes history and physical examination to arrive at the correct diagnosis and to begin appropriate case management. The pressure of long lines of patients may explain why health workers diagnosed only from chief complaints; nevertheless, inappropriate treatment caused the poorly treated patient to return the following day or to seek help elsewhere, perhaps at the local traditional healer.

The doctor or clinical officer often delegated to the nurse the dispensing of ORS and instruction to the parent. This put the therapy in the hands of the nurse who may not have the same degree of therapeutic credibility as the doctor or clinical officer (physician's assistant). Similarly, pharmacists may be the ones to instruct mothers and may recommend less effective treatment methods than oral rehydration therapy, either through lack of education or a desire to make profits on more expensive drugs which are often less effective or even harmful.

Expense of premixed ORS solutions. ORS can be manufactured either as a premixed solution or as a powdered concentrate in packets to be mixed with water by the consumer. Although premixed ORS has the advantages of being mixed in the correct proportions and sterile, it is significantly more expensive than using packets—as much as eight times more expensive per treatment. This can discourage use; therefore, packets have received considerably wider use than premixed solutions in developing countries.

Incorrect mixing of ORS in packets. ORS in packets requires careful mixing. Ideally, the solution is prepared with the correct amount of boiled water. Use of unboiled water, however, is unlikely to cause serious problems since it is likely that the patient has been using the unboiled water previously and has developed a resistance to most impurities. Mixtures that are too dilute are less effective than correctly prepared solutions. The most serious mixing problem is excessive concentrations of salts which can lead to severe illness and even death in infants.

Lack of universally available household liquid measure and lack of decision on packet size. Mixing instructions for ORS were complicated because there was no standardized single measuring container. For example, no standard one-liter bowl was commonly available. Once a standard packet size was selected, mothers could still be confused by having to use combinations of measuring containers. Until a standard size was decided, the national program would be delayed. One-liter, 750-ml, and 250-ml packets were being considered.

If production of either 250- or 750-ml packets was to proceed, the fact that one-liter packets had been in use for some time was likely to cause confusion and misuse at the household level, if not at hospitals and health clinics. Consequently, there was considerable concern over which size would be best.

Limitations and potential for home preparation of solutions. When ORS was not readily available throughout the health system, mothers needed to know how to prepare home-mixed solutions. The occasional unavailability of either salt or sugar made home preparation problematic; this was compounded by the frequent unavailability of mixing containers and/or teaspoons and the lack of consumer knowledge of oral rehydration therapy. Incorrect formulations can be harmful to children, especially infants.

Information provided to the mother when oral rehydration therapy is promoted did not state that ORS is not designed to stop the diarrhea. ORS maintains hydration through the disease course. Diarrhea often runs its course if the child is kept hydrated and there is not a serious underlying cause. This must be described carefully to the mother or father so that rapid cessation of the diarrhea is not expected. Unfortunately, if such information is not provided, parents who believed oral rehydration therapy should stop the diarrhea might not only end the therapy when diarrhea does not cease immediately, but also might be unlikely to employ oral rehydration therapy in future diarrheal episodes.

Program Alternatives

Several interrelated alternatives were under consideration for increasing the use of oral rehydration therapy using ORS. These alternatives are listed and discussed in succeeding paragraphs.

Supply alternatives:
   Zambian production: Produce ORS in-country
      By a government organization.
      By a private company.
   Importing: Import ORS.
Distribution alternatives:
   Ministry of Health: Increased distribution by Ministry of Health facilities.
   Private market distribution: Encourage distribution and sale in the private marketplace.
Packaging alternatives:
   Premixed ORS in bottles.
   One-liter packet.
   750 ml. packet.

250 ml. packet.

Combinations of packets.

Training of health care professionals.

Promotion of oral rehydration therapy.

Home preparation alternative.

Supply Alternatives

The major supply of ORS was from the Swedish International Development Agency (SIDA) who supplied one-liter packets of ORS in essential drug kits, monthly, to the 707 rural health clinics. Each sealed kit included 150 one-liter packets. As a result, the supply of ORS was greater in some rural health clinics than in urban areas. There was no inventory control in place to balance out supply and demand between the rural health clinics. Consequently, there could be several months' supply at some clinics while others stocked out. SIDA was considering increasing the ORS in kits to 200 each next year. They also considered supplying some stocks at the district level for reallocation to clinics on an as-needed basis, developing methods to reallocate inventories, and distribution to urban clinics. SIDA's policies of free distribution were likely to have an effect on the private marketplace for ORS.

UNICEF remained the most likely donor for additional ORS supplies; an option was to help the Ministry of Health by continuing to donate imported one-liter packets. In the past year, 1.2 million one-liter packets were donated at a total imported cost of $87,000—about K5 (kwacha is Zambian currency; K70 equaled $1 U.S.) per packet. UNICEF also had the option of supporting production by subsidizing the production of ORS packets by local manufacturers. UNICEF has done this in two countries (Haiti and Indonesia), paying the local producers the equivalent of the imported cost of packets.

The major constraint to this type of arrangement in Zambia was the high cost of the locally produced ORS packets. The approximate cost breakdown for local manufacturing of one-liter packets of ORS is given in Table 4.

Packets are produced for free distribution at health clinics and hospitals through the Ministry of Health by the parastatal company,[2] General Pharmaceutical Ltd. (GPL), and at various times for sale in the private sector by Cadbury Schweppes' Zambian operations and the Zambian firms Gamma Pharmaceuticals and Interchem. A UNICEF grant of $100,000 (estimated at half the total

TABLE 4   Local manufacturing costs for 1-liter package of ORS

Materials	K3.58	
Labor	80	
Direct costs		4.38
Factory OH	1.10	
Production cost		5.48
Company OH	1.33	
Exfac cost		6.81
Profit margin	1.19	
Mfg. price		K8.00

Notes: Costs are based on an annual production volume of two million packets. Retail price is higher due to markups. Costs for smaller packets are identical except that materials cost is less per packet. The current exchange rate is K70 per U.S. dollar.
Source: Company interviews.

---

[2]Parastatals are organizations that are partly or totally owned by the national government which generally controls the board of directors.

cost of setting up ORS manufacturing for two million annual packet production) in 1985 helped supply the equipment necessary for General Pharmaceutical to manufacture up to two million packets per year. GPL produced 1.4 million one-liter packets under the brand name "Madzi-a-moyi" (Water for Life) in the past year, but GPL ceased producing due to the high cost of imported raw materials and packaging.

A small amount of the GPL production was sold through about 100 parastatal pharmacies for K6 to K10. Although this price appears to be less than the manufacturer's cost, it results from these packets being produced in 1990 when the kwacha had not devalued to its current level. The retail price was expected to be higher if they resume production.

Gamma Pharmaceuticals and Interchem each had the capacity to manufacture two million packets of either one-liter, 250-ml, or 750-ml per year. Neither was producing ORS. Gamma used their machine to produce other products and Interchem had not been able to use their Korean-made machine for two years due to failure of a part. Distribution of drug products was either through deliveries to sales agents in the Copperbelt and Livingstone, or to general merchandise wholesalers who came to Lusaka to purchase ORS. There was also some direct distribution to pharmacies and other outlets in Lusaka.

The manufacturer's costs and prices were expected to be approximately the same for either manufacturer. Additional production capacity was expected to cost about $200,000 for each two million units produced per year for either one-liter, 250-ml, or 750-ml packet sizes. However, long delays were experienced in supplying equipment to GPL due to shipping delays, building construction problems, and the need to install a 3-phase electrical supply. Interchem's parent company was evaluating replacing the current machine.

Cadbury Schweppes had recently received Ministry of Health approval to market orange-flavored ORS in 250-ml packets using the brand name Oresa (Oral REhydration SAlts). They had manufactured 500,000 packets; 40,000 had been distributed directly to chemists (drug stores) to test market acceptance and the remainder was in inventory. The manufacturer's price was K12 with a suggested retail price of K15. Some chemists, however, charged K18. Flavored ORS was neither encouraged nor discouraged by WHO, although at one time they opposed flavored ORS due to its potential for unnecessary use and its increased cost relative to unflavored ORS. On the other hand, 300-ml soft drink bottles (Coke, Fanta, Torino, etc.) were widely available in Zambia (many were distributed by Cadbury) for mixing 250-ml ORS. Research at the University Teaching Hospital showed that children, even at very young ages, were more willing to drink flavored ORS and, as a result, consumed more total fluids than when given unflavored ORS. Cadbury Schweppes had the capacity to produce 18 million packets a year in one shift which is also used to produce powdered Kia-Ora, a children's drink (similar to Kool-Aid®). These could be either 250-ml flavored or 750- or 1,000-ml unflavored. The cost of unflavored ORS was expected to be about the same as for other local manufacturers. The per packet cost of 250-ml flavored ORS was slightly more than that of one liter of unflavored. Cadbury could also supply either flavored or unflavored ORS in bulk packages for hospitals and health clinics.

Flavored ORS had been imported in limited quantities. Small quantities of Rehidrat, from Searle, were available in lemon-lime 250-ml packets for K30. ORS imported for resale, however, was subject to a 100 percent import duty under import substitution laws. An additional 200,000 to 400,000 packets were supplied annually by the Red Cross, churches, and other nongovernment organizations.

Cadbury was the only firm that had the potential to produce ORS in bottles. It was expected that the cost for 250-ml bottles would be about the same as for soft drinks—K40 per bottle including a K20 bottle refund. Thus a two-liter treatment would cost the consumer K320 without refund and K160 if bottles are returned—considerably more than the cost of buying packets.

Considering the low incomes of many target consumers, a need may exist to price ORS cheaply to keep it affordable. This approach may be impossible without some type of subsidy. An ORS price subsidy to manufacturers or importers could create a financial burden that is unlikely to be sustainable over time. In the short term, UNICEF might use the value of the raw materials as a subsidy or provide promotional or educational services for branded products. Another option is for industry to offer a modest price to low-income consumers and still create revenues to help pay program costs by charging a much higher price for a different, more "modern" product aimed at higher-income consumers.

Distribution

Even if there was substantial donor support for free ORS distribution through clinics and hospitals, there was a need for other modes of access to ORS as well as a need to promote home-mix solutions. The commercial sector in Zambia offered several possibilities.

As a normal business practice in Zambia, a manufacturer established the recommended consumer price for his product. Trade discounts based on the recommended consumer price were 20 percent to retailers and 20 percent to trade channel members.

Allison conducted interviews with the general manager or the marketing manager of the major organizations that expressed an interest in distributing ORS. Each reached a large number of retail outlets, as shown in Table 5.

Table 5   Potential distribution outlets for ORS

	Outlets
Gamma Pharm.	1,000
Interchem	1,000
Cadbury Schweppes	5,000
Lyons Brooke Bond	2,200
Colgate & Palmolive	8,000

Gamma Pharmaceutical. Gamma Pharmaceutical, which started activities in 1984, manufactured pharmaceutical products for the Zambia market and for export. It sold its products to private pharmacies, government and industry health facilities, and retail outlets including supermarkets. Gamma had a fleet of six delivery trucks and one van, and two sales agents. Gamma was a sound, fast-growing company with a strong production and marketing team.

Interchem. Interchem manufactured a variety of pharmaceutical products. In addition to distributing ORS, their marketing manager was interested in resuming production. However, the decision rested with the board. They needed to either repair their existing packaging machine or purchase a new one; either would be expensive.

Cadbury Schweppes. Cadbury Schweppes is a major producer of soft drinks, drink syrups, and other consumer packaged goods. Cadbury distributed its products direct to their retail outlets. Cadbury was evaluating flavored ORS and deciding if they should introduce Oresa throughout Zambia. They had about 460,000 packets in inventory and could begin production of additional packets within a month.

Lyons Brooke Bond. Lyons Brooke Bond, Zambia, formerly a Lever Brothers company, is incorporated in Zambia. Lyons Brooke Bond manufactures and distributes processed food products. The managing director of the company has shown an interest in distributing ORS, although they did not handle any pharmaceutical products.

Colgate & Palmolive. Colgate, one of the largest distributors in Zambia, had five sales agents, four delivery vans, five freight trucks, and more than 10 large wholesalers. Colgate & Palmolive manufactured and distributed personal care and hygiene products.

Evaluation of Distribution Alternatives

A review of distribution capabilities in Zambia offered several options in terms of cost-effectiveness, marketing opportunities, and possible future self-sufficiency. Although historically the bulk of ORS had been distributed at no cost, there were vibrant commercial firms in Zambia that could be enlisted in the implementation of an ORS program. These firms had strong experience in marketing, sound management capabilities and financial stability, well-developed infrastructures that allowed them access to thousands of retail outlets, and were interested in participating in a marketing program as both good corporate citizens and as a potentially profitable business. Allison believed that the advantages to be derived from using private firms would be:

A good understanding of the marketing environment in Zambia, therefore, enhanced adaptability and flexibility.

Program management and administration at no cost or minimal cost to UNICEF and the Zambian government.

Reduced distribution costs and expanded distribution.

Willingness to make long-term financial commitment for sourcing commodities.

The possibility of achieving substantial cost recovery and, ultimately, self-sufficiency.

However, she felt that there were several unanswered questions:

> How much would private firms have to charge wholesalers?
>
> What would be the likely market price to the consumers?
>
> Would the market size be large enough to interest manufacturers?
>
> How much would free distribution by the Ministry of Health and the Swedish International Development Agency reduce manufacturers' interest?
>
> Would excess capacity be created, leading to an erosion of market share and profits leading to withdrawals from the market?
>
> Would quality control become a problem if the number of suppliers increased?

Packaging

ORS could be packaged as a premixed solution in bottles or cardboard containers, or as powdered salts in foil packets.

Premixed packages.

PROS:

ORS is sterile.

Correct concentration of ORS.

Less intense consumer education required for preparation.

Cadbury can produce in bottles.

CONS:

Only one firm has the capacity to produce bottles.

As much as eight times more expensive per treatment to the consumer than packets.

Require more space in delivery vehicles and on store shelves.

Use of bottles requires deposit and return system due to limited supply of bottles in Zambia.

No Zambian firm could produce cardboard container suitable for ORS.

Use of imported cardboard containers increases expense, waste, and litter.

Packets. It was felt that simple, consistent messages were needed in promotion of ORS packets and the associated training and education efforts. A single packet size is likely to be most effective; risk of confusion among mothers was possible if more than one packet size is available. Three packet sizes were possible for wide-spread production and distribution: 250 ml, 750 ml, and one liter. The following are the pros and cons:

250- and 750-ml-size packets.

PROS:

Bottle size was readily available. Concentrated drink syrup was widely used and distributed in 750-ml bottles. Schweppes, the largest manufacturer of syrups, expected no change in size and had placed a new order for 750-ml bottles. Soft drink bottles of 300-ml were widely available and could be used for 250-ml packets. Soft drinks were sold for K40 per bottle, including a K20 bottle refund.

Tea cups of 250 ml were widely available.

CONS:

Half a million one-liter packets were available in the distribution system.

Imported ORS was generally available in one-liter packets.

Changes in syrup bottle sizes could occur.

If parents mixed one-liter packets in 300- or 750-ml bottles, vomiting and serious heart and nervous problems could result, especially in younger children and if the 300-ml bottles were used.

One-liter-size packets.

PROS:

At least 500,000 existed in the supply system.

UNICEF's imported cost was less than local manufacturers' price.

UNICEF one-liter packets could be purchased in emergency shortages.

CONS:

If parents mixed 250- or 750-ml packets in one-liter containers, ORS was less effective (especially the 250-ml packets).

The variety of cup sizes available at retail outlets was increasing, with many cups of non-standard size available.

A key question was when local production could begin and whether local production would provide a substantial, reliable supply of acceptable quality. If production was delayed or unreliable, UNICEF or another supplier would have to fill the gap with one-liter packets.

Training of Health Care Professionals

Physicians, nurses, clinical officers, pharmacists, and traditional healers in their regular treatment and advice set the standards for medical care. If these professionals did not understand and have confidence in oral rehydration therapy, it was unlikely that they would establish oral rehydration as the standard treatment for diarrhea in Zambia.

Physicians needed training in appropriate clinical management of infants and children with diarrhea. Physicians needed to go beyond statements of symptoms as a basis for prescribing treatment for diarrhea. This included a patient history, an examination, and therapeutic management. Because physicians were opinion leaders, special efforts were desirable at the beginning of a program to inform them about oral rehydration therapy through seminars and refresher training courses.

Diarrhea Training Units

Diarrheal training units (DTU) had been effective in training health care workers in other developing countries. However, only one existed in Zambia. The purpose of a DTU was to develop the skills and confidence of physicians and nurses so they could give proper therapy to children with diarrhea. When participants attended clinical training, they developed skills in assessing and managing diarrhea. They learned to treat simple and complicated cases and how to communicate these skills to mothers and colleagues.

Experience suggested that a three- to five-day training course is needed to be effective. This approach made training expensive. Also, some professionals found it difficult to leave their responsibilities for the required period. Because DTUs emphasized individual and practical teaching, only relatively small numbers of professionals could be trained at any time. In effective DTUs, the number of participants ranged from five to 15. In addition, the need to have enough diarrhea cases of various types for each trainee to handle means that some DTUs could be run only during the rainy season.

Currently, the only DTU is a 1989 WHO-funded unit at the University Teaching Hospital in Lusaka that trains doctors and nurses. Allison felt that additional DTUs could be effective, but their costs needed to be evaluated. Costs involved in training are included in Exhibit 2.

Exhibit 2   Local costs for diarrheal training units (cost per unit per year)

Land cruiser truck (4WD)	K1,200,000
Annual fuel and maintenance	300,000
Driver	30,000
Trainers (if full time with program)	
Physician	72,000
Public health nurse	36,000
Public health trainer	36,000
Training materials	
For health care persons	120
For parents	10
Jugs (one liter or 750 ml)	100
Measuring spoons	30
Mugs (250 ml)	15
Banana cups (500 ml)	35
Posters (each)	500

Notes: (1) All costs are given in Zambian currency, the kwacha. In 1991, K70 equaled $1 U.S. (2) Room and board for all participants in training sessions was paid by the Ministry of Health, per diem paid to trainers when out of Lusaka.
Source: Interviews with health education professionals.

Promotion

There were an estimated three million radios in Zambia and two broadcasting stations. Both were state owned: *Radio Mulungushi,* a very popular station which is primarily urban, and *Radio Zambia,* primarily rural. There were as many as 250,000 television sets and one state-operated television station (operating from 5 P.M. to midnight weekdays, with longer hours on the weekend). There were seven major languages; therefore it was considered critical to advertise in English plus several other languages to reach the population effectively. A media rate card is provided in Exhibit 3.

Exhibit 3   Basic media rates for Zambia (1 December 1990)*

Television		Radio	
Time slot	*Rate for 1 ad*	*Time slot*	*Rate for 1 ad*
Prime time		"A" time	
60 sec.	K12,000	60 sec.	K1,800
45 sec.	9,600	45 sec.	1,500
30 sec.	6,000	30 sec.	1,200
15 sec.	3,600	15 sec.	900
7 sec.	3,000		
"A" time		"B" time	
60 sec.	K9,600	60 sec.	K1,440
45 sec.	6,600	45 sec.	1,200
30 sec.	4,200	30 sec.	900
15 sec.	3,000	15 sec.	720
7 sec.	2,160		
"B" time		"C" time	
60 sec.	K6,000	60 sec.	K1,080
45 sec.	6,600	45 sec.	780
30 sec.	3,600	30 sec.	720
15 sec.	1,800	15 sec.	540
7 sec.	1,200		

TV time distributions		Radio time distributions	
		"A" time	05:00 to 08:00
Prime time	18:55 to 20:00		12:00 to 14:00
			16:30 to 22:00
"A" time	07:00 to 11:00	Weekend	05:00 to 22:00
	20:00 to 23:00		
		"B" time	08:00 to 12:00
"B" time	06:00 to 07:00		14:00 to 16:30
	15:00 to 18:55		22:00 to 23:00
	23:00 to close	Weekend	22:00 to 23:00
		"C" time	23:00 to close
		Weekend	23:00 to 24:00

Press (one centimeter down by one column wide)	
Times of Zambia	K100.80
Zambia Daily Mail	70.87

*Gross rates include 20 percent sales tax.
Source: Zambia National Broadcasting Company Rate Card, 1991.

Message Content

A major challenge for ORS advertising is to persuade consumers that restoring the child's activity and preventing dehydration was a sufficient reason for using the product. Most communications/promotions efforts have chosen not to deliver negative messages such as "oral rehydration therapy does not stop diarrhea" or "antidiarrheals do not stop diarrhea," although both are factual. Programs have chosen to address these issues in other ways such as in scientific seminars for physicians or working to change national drug policies.

A second major challenge was not only to stimulate sales of the product, the traditional goal of advertising, but also to emphasize the correct mixture and utilization of ORS. ORS product advertising should include brand-specific advertising from the beginning for maximum effectiveness, but generic advertising may also be appropriate within the same campaign.

The Sustainability Issue

Any donor program is considered sustainable when the flow of benefits from the program can be maintained or enhanced when donor funding ceases. Thus, sustainability does not refer to each activity undertaken as part of a control of diarrheal disease (CDD) program, but refers to the lasting impact of the program. Seen in this perspective, the global smallpox eradication program achieved the ultimate in sustainability: the target population continues to receive the health benefits resulting from the eradication of the disease. Ultimately, the goal of any CDD effort is that there be a sustained reduction in morbidity and mortality from diarrhea because of the program.

There are various levels at which CDD activities take place, including strategies that have shorter- or longer-term impacts on diarrhea. For example, the installation of a water and sewer system might have a larger impact on diarrhea morbidity and mortality than an advertising campaign promoting oral rehydration therapy use; however, this is a longer-term, considerably more-expensive solution. Multiple actions are possible, but it is not possible to do everything and solve all of the problems. A more direct solution could be seeking ways to ensure that mothers and health workers maintain appropriate case management practices (oral rehydration therapy use being one of them) after the initial program investment has been made. More directly yet, one might concentrate on ways to sustain the resource base for program activities such as training, information systems, ORS production and distribution, or any other activities designed to reduce the incidence of diarrheal disease.

Donors want to invest in development efforts and then have the benefits resulting from their investment carry on without the need for continued outside support. The developing countries themselves would prefer to avoid recipient-country dependency on donor funding over the long term. This translates into donors trying to avoid paying recurrent costs, such as salaries, routine supervision, and transportation. When these costs are regularly paid by donors, the program is felt to be in jeopardy of being dropped, or critically under-funded when the donor project runs out and the program reverts from donor support to the routine government budget. If the government does not have sufficient funds to match the level of donor funding, the program's organization and activities may break down to the point where they are no longer effective. This situation describes what happens to an unsustainable program, one in which insufficient thought has been given to how the host country can support the program.

Developing UNICEF's ORS Program

Allison had to develop a program for UNICEF within a week. Among the alternatives she considered were:

How to increase the supply of ORS.
Increase imports.
Provide subsidies for local manufacturing.
How to make the distribution of ORS more effective.
How to educate effectively both health care providers and parents about when ORS is necessary and the correct use of ORS.
Should packet size be standardized at 250 ml, 750 ml, or one liter, or should a variety of sizes be available? Is there any role for premixed ORS?
To what extent should home preparation of alternative hydration solutions be encouraged?

She realized that she could recommend a variety of activities, but not everything could be accomplished in the UNICEF budget. She suspected that there were some actions that would greatly improve the functioning of the system and had begun to think about the flow of ORS from supply by the manufacturer to demand and use by the consumer. She was also concerned about the flow of ORS information. Where were the leverage points? How could appropriate use be achieved on a sustainable basis?

Case 30

Country Lass Fashions*

As New England regional manager for Country Lass Fashions, Jonathan Frank recognized that he was low man on the totem pole. Having recently earned his masters in retailing from Columbia University, he knew that his opinion was not regarded very highly yet in the organization, but he also knew that his company was in trouble.

Country Lass had been in business for over 30 years. With a reputation for good-quality products, the company's sales had slowly grown to over $9 million. But while its founders understood production and sales, Country Lass exhibited very little understanding of the market. Through ignorance or neglect, it appeared to violate all the standard practices of the industry. Country Lass made no funds available for cooperative advertising, permitted no returns of unsold merchandise, and had a policy of no markdown allowances. Its promotion was limited to advertising in high-circulation national magazines and major metropolitan newspapers. In short, in an industry known for good relations between manufacturers and retailers, Country Lass was conceding nothing.

This negative internal attitude was complicated by external pressures. Foreign producers, with much lower material and labor costs, were flooding the market with high-quality, inexpensive goods. Tariffs designed to keep foreign competitors away from the United States market also drove up the cost of imported fabric and textile machinery. In any event, these tariffs were replete with loopholes and were being scaled down and repealed by the federal government ostensibly to achieve a free-market economy. Finally, popular-priced competitors were offering stylish products which were currently very successful.

In this environment, Frank had to try to sell women's fashion goods. Inventory was piling up, especially blouses. Frank decided to take a chance with an idea he had been considering for some time. He had a good working relationship with Mary Blake, fashion editor for the *Boston Times*. If Blake could write

---

*This case was prepared by Mort Ettinger and Daniel Lindley of Salem State College, Salem, Massachusetts. Used with permission.

a fashion page featuring Country Lass blouses, Frank was sure he could sell two pages of advertising to retailers who carried Country Lass blouses. Retailers who purchased space would be eager to order blouses in advance of the publicity and tie-in advertising. Fliers could be prepared by the *Times* based on the story and the ads and sent to the retailers for display and distribution in their stores.

After talking with Blake and *Times* advertising manager Art Lester, Frank was sure he was on to something. The *Times* had once been a major newspaper in the Boston area, but it had suffered at the hands of its two major competitors, the *Globe* and the *Herald*. In fact, its single biggest advertiser was Lambert and Vaccaro, a large Boston department store, and one of Country Lass' largest accounts. Frank, Blake, and Lester were convinced that this idea would benefit all parties.

The next task facing Frank was to sell the advertising. The cost of display advertising was $74.65 per column inch; each page contained five 14-inch columns. The cost of two full pages came to $10,451. Frank figured that the top of each page could carry two 2 1/2 by 3 1/2 display ads at $653 each. The rest of each page could be divided into 35 boxes (1 by 1 1/2) and sold for $112 each.

Frank decided to sell the four display ads himself. Convinced that Lambert and Vaccaro would buy, Frank decided to save that store until last. The three remaining major department stores in Boston were easy to sell. Emmanuel's and Truman's did not want to be excluded. Flutey's was eager to be represented if Lambert and Vaccaro would be in the ad. But when Frank called on Muriel Lincoln, the head buyer for Lambert and Vaccaro, he ran into a problem he had not anticipated. Lincoln said she wanted nothing to do with the ad if Flutey's would appear in it.

By now nearly all the small ads had been sold. Many participating advertisers had already received tear sheets of the ad to display on the shopping floor and in dressing rooms of their stores and to send to preferred customers. Frank was in a tough spot. An idea came to him. He walked over to Flutey's and went straight to the buyer's office. "I'm in trouble," he said and explained the problem. Flutey's buyer reacted as he had hoped; she offered to buy the space that had been reserved for Lambert and Vaccaro in addition to the space already purchased.

Frank wasted no time in getting over to the *Boston Times* composing room. Within 30 minutes he had a final mock-up of the ad. Taking a short-cut to his office through Lambert and Vaccaro, Frank ran into Muriel Lincoln. He could not resist showing her the story and the accompanying ad. "Look how impressive this is. And to think, you could have been in it," he told her. She gave him an icy stare as they parted company.

When Jonathan Frank returned to his office there was an urgent phone message to call Art Lester. He could tell there was trouble when Lester's secretary forwarded the call. "I've got bad news," Lester started. "We have to pull the ad. Don't ask me why; I can't tell you. You have to trust me that there are important reasons. Don't take this personally."

Frank could not believe what he was hearing. After arguing, pleading, and, finally, reminding Lester of their close professional relationship over the years,

Frank learned that Lincoln had threatened to discontinue advertising with the *Times* if the ad and story ran. By now, inventory had been shipped. Retailers were planning in-store promotions and tie-ins to correspond to the advertising. If no large consumer response materialized, loyal retailers risked getting stuck with a large volume of perishable fashion merchandise, and salespeople risked antagonizing good customers.

Frank made two more phone calls. His attorney advised, "Never sue a newspaper." His insurance broker was only too happy to sell him a $1 million liability policy.

Part 9

Marketing Programs and Strategy

This section contains six cases which are comprehensive in nature, requiring the student to make a number of decisions in several different marketing decision areas. Thus, a great deal of integration is necessary. A decision in one of the marketing areas may have a significant impact on the other decisions which must be made to complete the marketing program.

In developing a complete marketing program for a product, one must start with the firm's overall goals and objectives. Then all the environmental factors such as demand, competition, marketing laws, distribution alternatives, and cost structure must be analyzed. At this point, a number of opportunities as well as potential problems will have been identified, and specific marketing objectives can be established.

The marketer must make a clear definition of the target market(s) to be served. This can be determined only after a thorough evaluation of all the alternative segments of the market, their needs, wants, attitudes and behavior, the strengths and weaknesses of the firm's products and those of competitors, and the potential profitability of various alternatives.

The next step in developing the marketing program is to search for the optimal marketing mix; that is, what is the best combination of product strategy, pricing strategy, promotion strategy, and distribution strategy? Typically, there will be a number of possible alternatives for each of these, so the marketer must determine the interrelationships among them and choose the optimal combination based upon a complete situation analysis.

The last step in the development of a marketing program is to create a plan for implementing the program. Without adequate implementation, even the best-designed plans will fail.

Case 31

Virgin Atlantic Airways*

June 1994. Virgin Atlantic Airways celebrated the 10th anniversary of its inaugural flight to New York. Richard Branson, the airline's chairman and founder, reminisced about its tremendous growth. In 10 short years, he had established Virgin Atlantic as Britain's second-largest long-haul airline, with a reputation for quality and innovative product development. Richard Branson turned his thoughts to the challenges that lay ahead.

The Origins of the Virgin Group

"Branson, I predict you will either go to prison, or become a millionaire." These were the last words that the 17-year-old Richard Branson heard from his headmaster as he left school. Twenty-five years later, Richard Branson ruled over a business empire whose 1993 sales exceeded £1.5 billion.[1] He had started his first entrepreneurial business at the age of 12, selling Christmas trees. Soon after leaving school, he set up *Student,* a national magazine, as "a platform for all shades of opinion, all beliefs and ideas . . . a vehicle for intelligent comment and protest." The magazine, whose editorial staff had an average age of 16, featured interviews by Richard Branson with celebrities and articles on controversial issues.

In 1970, Richard Branson founded a mail-order record business—called Virgin to emphasize his own commercial innocence. The first Virgin record shop was opened in London's Oxford Street in 1971, soon followed by a recording studio and a label which produced records for performers such as Phil Collins, Genesis, and Boy George. The Venue nightclub opened in 1978. In 1980, Virgin Records began expanding overseas, initially on a licensing basis; it later set up its own subsidiaries. Virgin Vision was created in 1983, followed by Virgin Atlantic Airways and Virgin Cargo in 1984, and Virgin Holidays in 1985.

---

*This case was prepared by Pantéa Denoyelle, Research Associate, under the supervision of Jean-Claude Larréché, Alfred H. Heineken Professor of Marketing, at INSEAD. It is intended to be used as a basis for class discussion rather than to illustrate either effective or ineffective handling of an administrative situation. Copyright © 1995 INSEAD, Fontainebleau, France. Used with permission.
[1]In June 1994, one pound sterling (£) = 1.51 U.S. dollars ($).

In November 1986, the Virgin Group, which included the Music, Communication, and Retail divisions, was floated on the London stock exchange. The airline, clubs, and holidays activities remained part of the privately-owned Voyager Group Ltd. In its first public year, Virgin Group Plc had profit of £13 million on £250 million turnover—far beyond expectations. Its public status, however, was short lived: Richard Branson believed he could not be an entrepreneur while chairing a public company. In October 1988, he regained full control by buying back all outstanding shares. The constraints that he had struggled with during the company's public life were replaced by an overwhelming sense of relief and freedom. A partnership with Seibu Saison International, one of Japan's largest retail and travel groups, was equally brief. In 1990, Richard Branson sold 10 percent of the equity of Voyager Travel Holdings, the holding company for Virgin Atlantic, to the Japanese group in return for an injection of £36 million of equity and convertible loan capital—only to buy out his Japanese partner for £45 million in 1991.

In 1992, Richard Branson sold Virgin Music (by then the world's sixth-largest record company) to Thorn EMI for £560 million. By 1994, the Virgin Group consisted of three holding companies: Virgin Retail Group, Virgin Communication, and Virgin Investments which controlled over 100 entities in 12 countries. Exhibit 1 summarizes the group's activities.

The Creation of Virgin Atlantic Airways

In 1984, Richard Branson was approached by Randolph Fields, a 31-year-old lawyer who wanted to start a transatlantic airline. Fields' plan was to operate a business-class-only B747 service to New York. Richard Branson quickly made up his mind. He announced that the new airline, to be named Virgin Atlantic Airways, would be operational within three months. Needless to say, his decision struck Virgin's senior management as completely insane.

Richard Branson, who knew nothing about the airline business, set out to learn from the downfall of Laker Air, an airline launched in 1970 by Freddie Laker with six planes and 120 employees. Laker Air was originally designed as a low-risk business, flying under contract for package-holiday firms; in 1971, however, it introduced a low-budget, no-frills service between London and New York. Laker's overconfidence led to several mistakes, including purchasing three DC–10s before the U.S. government had approved his London-New York line, and generally ordering more aircraft than he could afford. He accumulated a £350 million debt while the big transatlantic carriers slashed prices. This eventually led to Laker Airways' demise in 1981.

Richard Branson hired two former Laker executives, Roy Gardner (who later became Virgin Atlantic's co-managing director) and David Tait. Branson decided that his new airline should not be all business class, but combine an economy section with a first-class section at business-class prices. His goal was clear: "To provide all classes of travellers with the highest-quality travel at the lowest cost." Richard Branson also leased a second-hand 747. The contract he

EXHIBIT 1 The Virgin Group of Companies

Virgin consists of three wholly owned separate holding companies involved in distinct business areas from media and publishing to retail, travel and leisure. There are over 100 operating companies across the three holding companies in 12 countries worldwide.

Virgin Retail Group	*Virgin Communication*	*Voyager Investments*		
		Virgin Group	*Voyager Group*	*Virgin Travel Group*
Operates a chain of megastores in the U.K., Continental Europe, Australia, and Pacific selling music, video, and other entertainment products. Operates game stores in the U.K. Wholesale record exports and imports. *Note:* Marui of Japan owns 50 percent of Virgin Megastores Japan; W.H. Smith owns 50 percent of Virgin Retail U.K.	Publishing of computer entertainment software. Management of investments in broadcasting, including Music Box. Investments in related publishing and entertainment activities, television post-production services. Book publishing Virgin Radio, Britain's first national commercial contemporary music station.	Investments: joint ventures. Property developments Magnetic media distribution Management and corporate finance services to the Virgin organization.	Clubs & hotels. Airship and balloon operations. Storm model agency.	U.K.'s second-largest long-haul international airline: Virgin Atlantic Airways. Freight handling and packaging. Inclusive tour operations: Virgin Holidays.

Source: Virgin Atlantic.

negotiated with Boeing had a sell-back option at the end of the first, second, or third year; a clause protected Virgin against currency fluctuations. Another priority was to recruit air crew. Fortunately, British Airways had recently lowered the optional retirement age for its crew, creating a pool of experienced pilots from which Virgin could draw; this gave it the most experienced crew of any British airline.

Obtaining permission to fly to New York from American regulatory bodies was not easy; authorization to land at Newark was granted only three days before Virgin's first flight was scheduled. Forbidden to advertise in the U.S. until the approval, Virgin decided to launch a teaser campaign. Skywriters festooned the Manhattan sky with the words "WAIT FOR THE ENGLISH VIRGI. . . ."

Virgin Atlantic's inaugural flight took off from London on June 22, 1984, packed with friends, celebrities, reporters, and Richard Branson wearing a World War I leather flight helmet. Once the plane had taken off, passengers were surprised to see on the video screen the cockpit, where the crew—Richard Branson and two famous cricket players—greeted them. Although this was obviously a recording, it was a memorable moment for passengers.

Early Years (1984–89)

Virgin Atlantic's early years were slightly chaotic. "I love the challenge," Richard Branson said. "I suspect that before I went into the airline business, a lot of people thought I would never be able to make a go of it. It made it even more challenging to prove them wrong." Richard Branson's determination and enthusiasm, as well as the experienced management team that he assembled, made up for the initial amateurism.

Virgin Atlantic extended its operations progressively. Its early routes, all from London, were to New York (Newark since 1984 and John F. Kennedy airport since 1988), Miami (1986), Boston (1987), and Orlando (1988). Flights to Tokyo and Los Angeles were added in 1989 and 1990. In 1987, Virgin celebrated its one millionth transatlantic passenger. Until 1991, all Virgin flights left from London's Gatwick airport, which was much smaller than Heathrow. Virgin countered this commercial disadvantage with a free limousine service for upper class passengers and a Gatwick upper class lounge, inaugurated in 1990.

While Richard Branson had always befriended rock stars, he had otherwise kept a low profile. This changed when he launched the airline: "I knew that the only way of competing with British Airways and the others was to get out there and use myself to promote it," he explained. Richard made a point of being accessible to reporters and never missed an opportunity to cause a sensation, wearing a stewardess's uniform or a bikini on board, or letting himself be photographed in his bath. What really caught the public's attention were his Atlantic crossings. In 1986, his "Virgin Atlantic Challenger II" speedboat recorded the fastest time ever across the Atlantic with Richard Branson on board. Even more spectacular was the 1987 crossing of the "Virgin Atlantic Flyer"—the largest hot-air balloon ever flown and the first to cross the Atlantic. Three years later,

Richard Branson crossed the Pacific in another balloon from Japan to Arctic Canada, a distance of 6,700 miles, breaking all existing records with speeds of up to 245 miles per hour.

The Years of Professionalization (1989–94)

The professionalization of Virgin Atlantic's management began in 1989. Until then, Virgin Atlantic had had a flat structure, with 27 people reporting to Richard Branson directly. As the airline expanded, it had outgrown its entrepreneurial ways, and needed to become customer-driven.

Richard Branson asked Syd Pennington, a veteran Marks & Spencer retailer, to look into the airline's duty-free business in addition to his other responsibilities at Virgin Megastores. Some time later, Pennington, coming back from a trip, learned that he had been promoted to co-managing director of the airline. When Pennington expressed his surprise, Richard explained: "It's easier to find good retail people than good airline people." Syd Pennington saw that Virgin Atlantic lacked controls and procedures, and he devoted himself to professionalizing its management. His objective was to infuse the business with Richard Branson's charisma and energy while also making it effective enough to succeed. Exhibit 2 has a five-year summary of Virgin Atlantic's financial performance and labor force. Exhibit 3 shows the three-year evolution of passengers carried and market shares.

EXHIBIT 2   Financial results and labor force of Virgin Atlantic Airways

Financial year	Turnover (£m)	Profit (loss) before tax (£m)
1988–89	£106.7	£8.4
1989–90	208.8	8.5
1990–91	382.9	6.1
1991–92	356.9	(14.5)
1992–93	404.7	0.4

Note: The reporting year ends on 31 July until 1990, and on 31 October as of 1991. The 1990–91 period covers 15 months.

Year	Number of employees*
1988	440
1989	678
1990	1,104
1991	1,591
1992	1,638
1993	1,627
1994	2,602

*As of 31 December (31 May for 1994).
Source: Virgin Atlantic.

EXHIBIT 3   Market shares of Virgin Atlantic Airways (revenue passengers)

Route	1993	1992	1991
New York (JFK & Newark)	19.6%	17.2%	18%
Florida (Miami & Orlando)	33.2	30.6	25.2
Los Angeles	23.6	21.8	25.8
Tokyo	18.4	15.5	16
Boston	22.2	20	15.3
Total passengers carried	1,459,044	1,244,990	1,063,677

Note: Flights from Gatwick and LHR.
Source: Virgin Atlantic.

After years of campaigning, Virgin Atlantic was granted the right to fly out of Heathrow in 1991. Heathrow, Britain's busiest airport, handled 100,000 passengers a day—a total of 40 million in 1990, compared with 1.7 million at Gatwick. Virgin Atlantic was assigned to Heathrow's Terminal 3, where it competed with 30 other airlines serving over 75 destinations on five continents. In Richard Branson's eyes, gaining access to Heathrow was a "historic moment and the culmination of years of struggle." His dream to compete with other long-haul carriers on an equal footing had come true. A new era began for Virgin. Flying from Heathrow enabled it to have high load factors all year and to attract more business and full-fare economy passengers. It could also carry more interline flyers and more cargo, since Heathrow was the U.K.'s main air freight center. On the morning of the airline's first flight from Heathrow, a Virgin "hit squad" encircled the model British Airways Concorde at the airport's entrance and pasted it over with Virgin's logo. Richard Branson, dressed up as a pirate, was photographed in front of the Concorde before security forces could reach the site. A huge party marked the end of the day.

In April 1993, Virgin ordered four A340s from Airbus Industries, the European consortium in which British Aerospace had a 20 percent share. The order, worth over £300m, reflected the airline's commitment to new destinations. "We are proud to buy an aircraft which is in large part British-built, and on which so many jobs in the U.K. depend," said Richard Branson. The A340, the longest-range aircraft in the world, accommodated 292 passengers in three cabins, and had key advantages such as low fuel consumption and maintenance costs. When the first A340 was delivered in December, Virgin became the first U.K. carrier to fly A340s. Virgin also ordered two Boeing 747–400s and took options on two others. It also placed a $19 million order for the most-advanced in-flight entertainment system available, featuring 16 channels of video, which it planned to install in all three sections. In keeping with the airline's customization efforts, the new aircraft's cabin was redesigned. Upper class passengers would find electronically-operated 54-inch seats with a 55-degree recline and an on-board bar. There was a rest area for flight and cabin crew.

In June 1993, Virgin scheduled a second daily flight from Heathrow to JFK. "We've given travellers a wider choice on their time of travel," said Richard Branson. "The early evening departure is timed to minimize disruption to the working day, a welcome bonus to both busy executives and leisure travellers." In March 1994, Virgin put an end to British Airways' and Cathay Pacific's long-standing duopoly on the London-Hong Kong route, launching its own A340 service.

Virgin's first Boeing 747–400 was delivered in May 1994. Only days later, Virgin opened its San Francisco line (until then a British Airways-United duopoly). In a press release shown in Exhibit 4, Virgin emphasized the continuation of its expansion plans, the renewal of its fleet, and the "better alternative" that it offered customers on both sides of the Atlantic. During the inaugural flight, 150 guests—and some fare-paying flyers who had been warned that it would not be a quiet flight—were entertained with a fashion show and a jazz band. In San Francisco, the aircraft stopped near a giant taximeter. The door opened, Richard Branson appeared, and inserted a huge coin in the taximeter, out of which popped the Virgin flag. Airport authorities offered Richard Branson a giant cake decorated with a miniature Golden Gate Bridge. Guests were entertained for a whirlwind five days which included a tour of the Napa Valley and a visit to Alcatraz prison where Richard Branson was jailed in a stunt prepared by his team. Virgin also took advantage of the launch to unveil a recycling and environmental program. A stewardess dressed in green—rather than the usual red Virgin uniform—gave passengers information on the program, which had delivered savings of £500,000 since it was launched in late 1993.

At the time of Virgin's 10th anniversary, its fleet comprised eight B747–200s, a B747–400, and three A340s. The airline awaited delivery of its second B747–400 and fourth A340, and also planned to retire two older B747–200s by the end of 1994. By then, half of its fleet would be brand new. By comparison, the average age of British Airways' fleet was eight years.[2] Richard Branson planned to expand his fleet to 18 planes, which would serve 12 or 15 destinations by 1995. Proposed new routes included Washington, D.C., Chicago, Auckland, Singapore, Sydney, and Johannesburg. The London-Johannesburg license, granted in 1992, had been a major victory for Virgin; when exploited, it will end a 50-year duopoly enjoyed by British Airways and South African Airways.

All Virgin Atlantic planes were decorated with a Vargas painting of a red-headed, scantily dressed woman holding a scarf. The names of most Virgin aircraft

---

[2]British Airways' fleet had 240 aircraft, including some 180 Boeings, 7 Concordes, 10 A320s, 15 BAe ATPs, and 7 DC10s.

EXHIBIT 4   Press release for the opening of the San Francisco route

17th May 1994

New San Francisco Route Marks Continued Expansion
for Virgin Atlantic

A new service to San Francisco, its sixth gateway to the U.S., was launched today (17th May 1994) by Virgin Atlantic Airways, marking another stage in the airline's development as it approaches its tenth anniversary.

The daily Boeing 747 service from London's Heathrow airport follows further route expansion in February 1994, when the airline introduced a daily service to Hong Kong, using two of four recently acquired Airbus A340 aircraft.

Virgin Atlantic Chairman Richard Branson said: "San Francisco was always on our list of the 15 or so great cities of the world that we wanted to fly to, so it's a very proud moment for us finally to be launching this new service today.

"We regularly receive awards for our transatlantic flights so I hope that this new service will be able to provide consumers on both sides of the Atlantic with a better alternative to the current duopoly which exists on the San Francisco/London route.

"Today's launch is also the culmination of a number of significant developments at Virgin Atlantic, not least of which is our recent acquisition of two new Boeing 747–400s and four Airbus A340s. This comes on the back of our $19 million investment in new 14-channel in-flight entertainment, which, unlike other airlines, we have made available to all of our passengers."

Mr. Branson added that it was the airline's intention to have one of the most modern and passenger-friendly fleets in the world. Virgin's current fleet comprises: eight B747s, three A340s, and an A320, and two BAe 146 Whisper Jets which are jointly operated with franchise partners in Dublin and Athens.

A daily service will depart Heathrow at 11:15, arriving in San Francisco at 14:05 local time. Flights leave San Francisco at 16:45, arriving in the U.K. the following day at 10:45. For reservations call 0293 747747.

For further information:

James Murray
Virgin Atlantic Airways
Tel: 0293 747373

---

evoked the "Vargas Lady" theme, starting with its first aircraft, "Maiden Voyager". (Exhibit 5 lists the aircrafts' names.) The first A340, inaugurated by the Princess of Wales, was christened "The Lady in Red."

Virgin Classes

Richard Branson originally proposed to call Virgin's business and economy classes Upper Class and Riff Raff respectively; in the latter case, however, he bowed to the judgment of his managers, who urged him to desist. Virgin Atlantic strove to offer the highest-quality travel to all classes of passengers at the lowest cost, and to be flexible enough to respond rapidly to their changing needs. For instance, Virgin catered to the needs of children and infants with special meals, a children's channel, pioneering safety seats, changing facilities, and baby food.

"Offering a First Class service at less than First Class fares" had become a slogan for Virgin Atlantic. Marketed as a first class service at business class prices, Upper Class competed both with other carriers' first class and business class. Since its 1984 launch, this product had won every major travel industry award.

EXHIBIT 5 Virgin Atlantic fleet

Aircraft	Type	Name	Into Service
G-VIRG	B747-287B	Maiden Voyager	1984
G-VGIN	B747-243B	Scarlet Lady	1986
G-TKYO	B747-212B	Maiden Japan	1989
G-VRGN	B747-212B	Maid of Honour	28/08/89
G-VMIA	B747-123	Spirit of Sir Freddy	09/05/90
G-VOYG	B747-283B	Shady Lady	10/03/90
G-VJFK	B747-238B	Boston Belle	06/03/91
G-VLAX	B747-238B	California Girl	28/05/91
G-VBUS	A340-311	Lady in Red	16/12/93
G-VAEL	A340-311	Maiden Toulouse	01/01/94
G-VSKY	A340-311	China Girl	21/03/94
G-VFAB	B747-4Q8	Lady Penelope	19/05/94
G-VHOT	B747-4Q8		delivery 10/94
G-VFLY	A340-311		delivery 10/94

The Economy Class promised the best value for money, targeting price-sensitive leisure travellers who nevertheless sought comfort. It included three meal options, free drinks, seat-back video screens, and ice cream during movies on flights from London.

After years of operating only two classes, business and economy, Virgin had introduced its Mid Class in 1992 after realizing that 23 percent of Economy passengers travelled for business. Mid Class was aimed at cost-conscious business travellers who required enough space to work and relax. This full-fare economy class offered flyers a level of service usually found only in business class, with separate check-in and cabin, priority meal service, armrest or seat-back TVs, and the latest in audio and video entertainment. Exhibit 6 shows Virgin's three sections: Upper Class, Mid Class, and Economy.

EXHIBIT 6   Virgin Atlantic's three classes

Upper Class

- Reclining sleeper seat with 15″ more legroom than other airlines.
- Latest seat-arm video/audio entertainment.
- Unique Clubhouse lounge at Heathrow featuring health spa (includes hair salon, library, music room, games room, study, and brasserie).
- Virgin Arrival Clubhouse with shower, sauna, swimming pool, and gym.
- Inflight beauty therapist on most flights.
- Onboard lounges and stand-up bars.
- "Snoozzone" dedicated sleeping section with sleeper seat, duvet, and sleep suit.
- Complimentary airport transfers including chauffeur-driven limousine or motorcycle to and from airport.
- Free confirmable Economy ticket for round trip to U.S./Tokyo.

(continued)

EXHIBIT 6 *(Concluded)*

Mid Class

- Separate check-in and cabin.
- Most comfortable economy seat in the world with 38″ seat pitch (equivalent to many airlines' business class seat).
- Complimentary pre-takeoff drinks and amenity kits.
- Frequent Flyer programme.
- Priority meal service.
- Priority baggage reclaim.
- Armrest/seatback TVs and latest audio/video entertainment.

Economy Class

- Contoured, space-saving seats, maximizing legroom, seat pitch up to 34″.
- Three meal option service (including vegetarian) and wide selection of free alcoholic and soft drinks.
- Seatback TVs and 16 channels of the latest inflight entertainment.
- Pillow and blankets.
- Advance seat selection.
- Complimentary amenity kit and ice cream (during movies on flights from London).

Source: Virgin Atlantic.

Virgin's B747 configuration on the Heathrow/JFK route consisted of 50 seats in Upper Class, 38 in Mid Class, and 271 in Economy. The typical British Airways B747 configuration on the same route was 18 First Class seats, 70 seats in Club World, and 282 in World Traveller Class.[3]

Service the Virgin Way

Virgin Atlantic wanted to provide the best possible service while remaining original, spontaneous, and informal. Its goal was to turn flying into a unique experience, not to move passengers from one point to another. It saw itself not only in the airline business but also in entertainment and leisure. According to a staff brochure:

> "We must be memorable, we are not a bus service. The journeys made by our customers are romantic and exciting, and we should do everything we can to make them feel just that. That way they will talk about the most memorable moments long after they leave the airport."

Virgin Atlantic saw that, as it became increasingly successful, it risked also becoming complacent. The challenge was to keep up customers' interest by keeping service at the forefront of activities. Virgin was often distinguished for the quality and consistency of its service (as shown in Exhibit 7); it won the Executive Travel Airline of the Year award for an unprecedented three consecutive years. Service delivery, in other words "getting it right the first time," was of key importance. The airline was also perceived to excel in the art of service recovery, where it aimed to be proactive, not defensive. It handled complaints from Upper Class passengers within 24 hours, those from Economy Class flyers within a week. If a flight was delayed, passengers received a personalized fax of apology from Richard Branson or a bottle of champagne. Passengers who had complained were occasionally upgraded to Upper Class.

Innovation

Virgin's management, who wanted passengers never to feel bored, introduced video entertainment in 1989. They chose the quickest solution: handing out Sony Watchmans on board. Virgin later pioneered individual video screens for every seat, an idea that competitors quickly imitated. In 1994, Virgin's on-board entertainment offered up to 20 audio channels and 16 video channels, including a shopping channel and a game channel. A gambling channel would be introduced at year end. In the summer, a "Stop Smoking Program" video was shown on all flights—Virgin's contribution to a controversy over whether smoking should be permitted on aircraft.

---

[3]As of April 1994, the Club World and World Traveller (Euro Traveller for flights within Europe) were the names given to British Airways' former Business and Economy Classes, respectively.

EXHIBIT 7   Awards won by Virgin Atlantic

1994

Executive Travel:
Best Transatlantic Airline
Best Business Class
Best Inflight Magazine

Travel Weekly:
Best Transatlantic Airline

1993

Executive Travel:
Airline of the Year
Best Transatlantic Carrier
Best Business Class
Best Cabin Staff
Best Food and Wine
Best Inflight Entertainment
Best Airport Lounges
Best Inflight Magazine
Best Ground/Check-In Staff

Travel Weekly:
Best Transatlantic Airline

Travel Trade Gazette:
Best Transatlantic Airline

TTG **Travel Advertising Awards:**
Best Direct Mail Piece

1992

Executive Travel **(awards given for 91/92):**
Airline of the Year
Best Transatlantic Carrier
Best Long Haul Carrier
Best Business Class
Best Inflight Food
Best Inflight Entertainment
Best Ground/Check-In Staff

Business Traveller:
Best Airline for Business Class-Long Haul

Travel Weekly:
Best Transatlantic Airline

Travel Trade Gazette:
Best Transatlantic Airline

Courvoisier Book of the Best:
Best Business Airline

ITV Marketing Awards:
Brand of the Year—Service

Frontier Magazine:
Best Airline/Marine Duty Free

BPS Teleperformance:
UK Winner
Overall European Winner

Meetings and Incentive Travel:
Best U.K.-Base Airline

Ab-Road Magazine:
Airline "Would most like to fly"
Best Inflight Catering

1991

Executive Travel:
(Awards Given in 1992)

Business Traveller:
Best Business Class—Long Haul

Travel Weekly:
Best Transatlantic Airline

Travel Trade Gazette:
Best Transatlantic Airline
Most Attentive Airline Staff

Avion World Airline Entertainment Awards
Best Inflight Videos—Magazine Style
Best Inflight Audio—Programming
Best Inflight Audio of an Original Nature

Which Airline?:
Voted by the Reader as one of the Top Four Airlines in the World (the only British airline amongst these four)

The Travel Organization:
Best Long Haul Airline

Conde Nast Traveller:
In the Top Ten World Airlines

Air Cargo News:
Cargo Airline of the Year

1990

Executive Travel:
Airline of the Year
Best Transatlantic Carrier
Best Inflight Entertainment

Business Traveller:
Best Business Class—Long Haul

Travel News **(now** *Travel Weekly***):**
Best Transatlantic Airline
Special Merit Award to Richard Branson

Travel Trade Gazette:
Best Transatlantic Airline
Travel Personality—Richard Branson

Avion World Airline Entertainment Awards:
Best Overall Inflight Entertainment
Best Video Programme
Best Inflight Entertainment Guide

Onboard Services **magazine:**
Outstanding Inflight Entertainment Programme
Outstanding Entertainment (for Sony Video Walkmans)

The Travel Organization:
Best Long Haul Airline

1989

Executive Travel:
Best Transatlantic Airline
Best Business Class in the World
Best Inflight Entertainment

Business Traveller:
Best Business Class—Long Haul

World Airline Entertainment Awards:
Best Overall Inflight Entertainment
Best Inflight Audio Entertainment
Best Inflight Entertainment Guide (Outside Magazine)

Onboard Services **magazine:**
Overall Onboard Service Award (Upper Class)

Which Holiday?:
Best Transatlantic Airline

Nihon Keizai Shimbun **(Japan):**
Best Product in Japan—for Upper Class

1988

Executive Travel:
Best Business Class—North Atlantic

Business Traveller:
Best Business Class—Long Haul

Travel Trade Gazette:
Best Transatlantic Airline

1986

The Marketing Society:
Consumer Services Awards

What to Buy for Business:
Business Airline of the Year

Source: Virgin Atlantic.

The presence of a beauty therapist or a tailor was an occasional treat to passengers. The beautician offered massages and manicures. On some flights to Hong Kong, the tailor faxed passengers' measurements so that suits could be ready on arrival. In 1990, Virgin became the only airline to offer automatic defibrillators on board and to train staff to assist cardiac arrest victims. A three-person Special Facilities unit was set up in 1991 to deal with medical requests. Its brief was extended to handle arrangements for unaccompanied minors or unusual requests such as birthday cakes, champagne for newlyweds, public announcements, or midflight marriage proposals. The unit also informed passengers of flight delays or cancellations, and telephoned clients whose options on tickets had expired without their having confirmed their intention to travel. Another service innovation was motorcycle rides to Heathrow for Upper Class passengers. The chauffeur service used Honda PC800s with heated leather seats. Passengers wore waterproof coveralls and a helmet with a built-in headset for a cellular phone.

In February 1993, Britain's Secretary of State for Transport inaugurated a new Upper Class lounge at Heathrow: the Virgin Clubhouse. The £1 million Clubhouse, shown in Exhibit 8, had an unusual range of facilities: Victorian-style wood-panelled washrooms with showers and a grooming salon offering massages, aromatherapy, and haircuts; a 5,000-volume library with antique leather armchairs; a game room with the latest computer technology; a music room with a CD library; a study with the most recent office equipment. Many of the furnishings came from Richard Branson's own home: a giant model railway, the Challenger II trophy, a three-meter galleon model. A two-ton, five-meter table, made in Vienna from an old vessel, had to be installed with a crane. Upon the opening of the Hong Kong route, a blackjack table was added at which visitors received "Virgin bills" that the dealer exchanged for tokens. There was also a shoe-shine service. Passengers seemed to enjoy the lounge. One remarked in the visitors' book: "If you have to be delayed more than two hours, it could not happen in a more pleasant environment."

Customer Orientation, Virgin Style

Virgin tried to understand passengers' needs and go beyond their expectations. While it described itself as a "niche airline for those seeking value-for-money travel," its standards and reputation could appeal to a broad spectrum of customers. It managed to serve both sophisticated, demanding executives and easygoing, price-sensitive leisure travellers in the same aircraft. According to Marketing Director Steve Ridgeway, Virgin attracted a broader range of customers than its competitors because it managed this coexistence between passenger groups better. This had enabled the airline to reach high load factors soon after opening new lines, as shown in Exhibit 9.

Virgin Atlantic initially had marketed itself as an economical airline for young people who bought Virgin records and shopped at Virgin stores, but gradually its target shifted. The danger, which Richard Branson saw clearly, was that people would perceive it as a "cheap and cheerful" airline, a copy of the defunct Laker Airways. Richard Branson knew that his airline's survival depended on

EXHIBIT 8   Virgin Atlantic Clubhouse

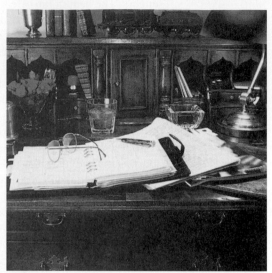

EXHIBIT 9   Load factors of Virgin Atlantic airways

Year	Newark	Miami	Tokyo	JFK	Los Angeles	Boston
1990–1991	82.0%	89.5%	65.9%	76.9%	84.5%	83.3%
1989–1990	83.3	92.1	68.3	74.2	79.8	
1988–1989	82.8	86.7	52.4			
1987–1988	77.1	85.0				
1986–1987	74.4	76.4				
1985–1986	72.9					
1984–1985	72.0					

Source: Virgin Atlantic promotional materials. This information is no longer made public since 1991.

high-yield business travellers. After establishing a strong base in leisure traffic, Virgin turned to the corporate segment and strove to establish itself as a sophisticated, business-class airline that concentrated on long-haul routes. The idea of fun and entertainment, however, was not abandoned. Upper Class was upgraded and incentives were added to attract the business traveller. By 1991, 10 percent of the airline's passengers and 35 to 40 percent of its income came from the business segment. Virgin's competitive advantage was reinforced through the combination of corporate travel buyers' price consciousness and the rising service expectations of travellers. Richard Branson actively wooed business customers by regularly inviting corporate buyers to have lunch at his house and seeking their comments.

As part of Virgin's drive to meet customers' standards, on each flight 30 passengers were asked to fill out a questionnaire. Their answers formed the basis of widely distributed quarterly reports. Virgin's senior managers flew regularly, interviewing passengers informally, making critical comments on the delivery of service, and circulating their reports among top management. Richard Branson himself, who welcomed every opportunity to obtain feedback from customers, took time to shake hands and chat with passengers. The preoccupation with service was so strong that staff were often more exacting in their evaluation of each other than the customers were.

Business executives, unlike younger leisure travellers, did not readily relate to other aspects of the Virgin world: the records, the Megastores, the daredevil chairman. Their good feelings about Virgin stemmed mainly from their positive experiences with the airline. These tough and demanding customers appreciated Virgin's style, service, innovations, and prices. Some were enthusiastic enough to rearrange their schedules in order to fly Virgin despite punctuality problems. Aside from complaints about flight delays, their only serious criticism was that Virgin did not serve enough destinations.

Virgin's People

Virgin Atlantic attracted quality staff despite the relatively low salaries it paid. In management's eyes, the ideal employee was "informal but caring": young, vibrant, interested, courteous, and willing to go out of his or her way to help customers. Richard Branson explained:

"We aren't interested in having just happy employees. We want employees who feel involved and prepared to express dissatisfaction when necessary. In fact, we think that the constructively dissatisfied employee is an asset we should encourage and we need an organization that allows us to do this—and that encourages employees to take responsibility, since I don't believe it is enough for us simply to give it."

Richard Branson believed that involving management and staff was the key to superior results: "I want employees in the airline to feel that it is *they* who can make the difference, and influence what passengers get," he said. He wrote to employees regularly to seek their ideas and to ensure that relevant news was communicated to them. His home phone number was given to all staff, who could call him at any time with suggestions or complaints.

Virgin Atlantic's philosophy was to stimulate the individual. Its dynamic business culture encouraged staff to take initiatives and gave them the means to implement them. Staff often provided insights into what customers wanted or needed—sometimes anticipating their expectations better than the customers themselves. Virgin Atlantic had a formal staff suggestion scheme and encouraged innovation from employees, both in project teams and in their daily work. Employees' suggestions were given serious consideration; many were implemented, such as the idea of serving ice cream as a snack, although formal marketing research had never shown the need for such a service.

Richard Branson himself was open to suggestions and innovations. He talked to everyone and was a good listener, inquisitive, and curious about all aspects of the business. He spent time with passengers, and visited the lounge without any advance notice. While he personified a "hands-on" approach to management, he never appeared controlling or threatening. His constant presence was a sign of involvement and a source of motivation for staff, who felt a lot of affection for him. It was not unusual to hear crew discuss his recent decisions or activities, mentioning "Mr. Branson" or "Richard" with admiration and respect.

In the difficult environment of the late 1980s and early 1990s, most airline employees were anxious to keep their jobs. With most operating costs—fuel prices, aircraft prices, insurance, landing and air traffic control fees—beyond management's control, labor costs were the main target of cutbacks. In 1993, the world's top 20 airlines cut 31,600 jobs, or 3.6 percent of their workforce, while the next 80 airlines added nearly 14,000, or 2.4 percent. That same year, Virgin Atlantic maintained its labor force, and was in the process of recruiting at the end of the year. In June 1994, Virgin Atlantic had 2,602 employees and recruited 880 cabin crew members. Opening a single long-haul line required hiring about 400 people.

The Airline Industry

Deregulation of the U.S. air transport industry in 1978 had reduced the government's role and removed protective rules, thereby increasing competition among American airlines. A decade later, deregulation hit Europe. The liberalization movement began in an effort to end monopolies and bring down prices. In fact, European carriers had been engaged in moderate competition in transatlantic travel while the domestic scheduled market remained heavily protected through bilateral agreements. European airlines were mostly state-owned in a regulated market where access was denied to new entrants. In April 1986, the European Court of Justice ruled that the Treaty of Rome's competition rules also applied to air transportation. Deregulation took place in three phases between 1987, when price controls were relaxed and market access was opened, and 1992, when airlines were allowed to set their own prices, subject to some controls.

In this atmosphere of deregulation and falling prices, traffic revenue grew briskly until 1990, when a global recession and the Gulf War plunged airlines into their worst crisis since World War II. The 22-member association of European airlines saw the number of passengers plummet by 7 million in 1991. Traffic recovered in 1992, when the world's 100 largest airlines saw their total revenue, measured in terms of tonnage or passengers, increase by just over 10 percent. However, the airlines recorded a net loss of $8 billion in 1992, after losses of $1.84 billion in 1991 and $2.66 billion in 1990. Some experts believed that the industry would ultimately be dominated by a handful of players, with a larger number of midsize carriers struggling to close the gap. Exhibits 10 and 11 show financial and passenger load data for some international airlines, while Exhibit 12 ranks Europe's top 20 airlines.

Virgin's Competitors

Virgin's direct competitor was British Airways (BA). Both carriers were fighting each other intensely on the most attractive routes out of London. BA, the number one British airline, was 15 times the size of second-placed Virgin. Exhibits 13 and 14 compare Virgin's and British Airways' flights and fares.

British Airways became the state-owned British airline in 1972 as the result of a merger between British European Airways and British Overseas Airways Corporation. In the early 80s, it was the clear leader in the highly lucrative and regulated transatlantic route, where operating margins were approximately 15 percent of sales. However, its overall profitability was shaky when Lord King became chairman in 1981. He transformed BA into a healthy organization and prepared it for its successful privatization in 1987. Since this time, BA has remarkably out-performed its European rivals.

British Airways traditionally benefited from a strong position at Heathrow, but competition toughened in 1991 when TWA and Pan Am sold their slots to American and United Airlines for $290 million and $445 million, respectively. In the same year, Virgin also received slots at Heathrow. These slot attributions so infuriated Lord King that he scrapped its annual £40,000 donation to Britain's ruling Conservative Party. At the time of the Heathrow transfer, BA scheduled 278 flights a week across the Atlantic from London, with 83,000 seats, while American had 168 flights with 35,000 seats and United 122 with 30,000. Virgin had 84 flights with 30,000 seats.

EXHIBIT 10   Financial results of selected international airlines

Airline company	Ranking 1992	Ranking 1991	Sales (U.S. $ million) 1992	% Change	Operating results (U.S. $ million)	Net results (U.S. $ million) 1992	Net results (U.S. $ million) 1991	Net margin (percent) 1992	Jet and turbo fleet	Total employees	Productivity (sales/employee) ($000)
American	1	1	$14,396	11.7%	$(25.0)	$(935.0)	$(239.9)	−6.5%	672	102,400	$140
United	2	2	12,889	10.5	(537.8)	(956.8)	(331.9)	−7.4	536	84,000	153
Delta	3	4	11,639	15.7	(825.5)	(564.8)	(239.6)	−4.9	554	79,157	147
Lufthansa	4	5	11,036	7.1	(198.5)	(250.4)	(257.7)	−2.3	302	63,645	173
Air France	5	3	10,769	−1.1	(285.0)	(617.0)	(12.1)	−5.7	220	63,933	168
British Airways	6	6	9,307	6.5	518.4	297.7	687.3	3.2	241	48,960	190
Swissair	16	16	4,438	7.0	152.8	80.7	57.9	1.8	60	19,025	233
TWA Inc	18	18	3,634	−0.7	(404.6)	(317.7)	34.6	−8.7	178	29,958	121
Singapore	19	19	3,443	5.4	548.0	518.5	558.4	15.1	57	22,857	150
Qantas	20	20	3,099	2.9	79.1	105.7	34.6	3.4	46	14,936	207
Cathay Pacific	21	21	2,988	11.3	464.0	385.0	378.0	12.9	49	13,240	225
Southwest	34	41	1,685	28.3	182.6	103.5	26.9	6.1	141	11,397	148
Virgin Atlantic	62	62	626	7.3	(22.0)	Not reported	3.8	Not reported	8	2,394	261

Source: "Much Pain, No Gain," *Airline Business* (September 1993). Productivity computed for this exhibit.

EXHIBIT 11   Passenger load factors of selected international airlines

Airline Company	1992 revenue Tonne km (million) Passenger	Freight	Total	Percent change	1992 revenue passenger km Million	Percent change	1992 passengers Million	Percent change	Passenger load factor 1992 percent	1991 percent	Year end	1992 rank
American	$14,223	$2,176	$16,399	19.7%	$156,786	18.3%	86.01	13.3%	63.7%	61.7%	Dec. 92	1
United	13,489	2,522	16,010	12.0	149,166	12.6	67.00	8.1	67.4	66.3	Dec. 92	2
Delta	11,761	1,765	13,525	20.2	129,632	19.6	82.97	11.8	61.3	60.3	Dec. 92	3
Lufthansa	5,882	4,676	10,725	14.4	61,274	17.1	33.70	14.2	65.0	64.0	Dec. 92	4
Air France	5,238	3,970	9,208	5.3	55,504	4.0	32.71	3.4	67.4	66.8	Dec. 92	5
British Airways	7,622	2,691	10,313	13.2	80,473	15.6	28.10	10.5	70.8	70.2	Mar. 93	6
Swissair	1,573	1,063	2,684	9.1	16,221	7.0	8.01	0.4	60.3	61.6	Dec. 92	16
TWA Inc	4,258	734	4,992	1.4	46,935	1.8	22.54	8.5	64.7	64.7	Dec. 92	18
Singapore Air.	3,675	2,412	6,086	14.2	37,861	8.5	8.64	6.3	71.3	73.5	Mar. 93	19
Qantas	2,684	1,220	3,904	4.9	28,836	7.2	4.53	9.4	66.2	66.0	Jun. 92	20
Cathay Pacific	2,695	1,671	4,366	13.3	27,527	12.7	8.36	13.1	73.5	73.6	Dec. 92	21
Southwest Air	2,032	49	2,082	23.4	22,187	22.0	27.84	22.6	64.5	61.1	Dec. 92	34
Virgin Atlantic	984	285	1,269	27.4	9,001	8.7	1.23	5.6	76.1	81.6	Oct. 92	62

Source: "Much Pain, No Gain," *Airline Business* (September 1993).

EXHIBIT 12   Europe's top 20 airlines (1993)

Rank	Airline company	Sales (U.S. $ million)	Global rank
1	Lufthansa	$11,036.5	4
2	Air France Group	10,769.4	5
3	British Airways	9,307.7	6
4	SAS Group	5,908.2	12
5	Alitalia	5,510.7	14
6	KLM Royal Dutch	4,666.3	15
7	Swissair	4,438.5	16
8	Iberia	4,136.7	17
9	LTU/LTU Sud	1,836.1	31
10	Sabena	1,708.3	33
11	Aer Lingus	1,381.0	38
12	Aeroflot	1,172.1	43
13	Finnair	1,132.2	45
14	TAP Air Portugal	1,110.1	47
15	Austrian Airlines	1,003.8	49
16	Britannia Airways	924.0	53
17	Olympic Airways	922.5	54
18	Turkish Airlines	736.5	59
19	Airlines of Britain Hldgs	687.7	61
20	Virgin Atlantic	626.5	62

Source: "Much Pain, No Gain," *Airline Business* (September 1993).

Despite these competitive pressures and the recent airline recession, British Airways remained one of the world's most profitable airlines. The largest carrier of international passengers, serving 150 destinations in 69 countries, it was making continuous progress in terms of cost efficiency, service quality, and marketing. BA recruited marketing experts from consumer goods companies who implemented a brand approach to the airline's classes. Some of the actions undertaken by BA in the early 90s included the relaunching of its European business class, Club Europe, with £17.5 million, and spending £10 million on new lounges (with a traditional British feel), check-in facilities, and ground staff at Heathrow. It was also rumored that BA was preparing to spend nearly £70 million on an advanced in-flight entertainment and information system for its long-haul fleet before the end of 1994.

British Airways and Virgin had fiercely competed against one another from the onset. One major incident that marked their rivalry was what became known as the "Dirty Tricks Campaign." In 1992, Virgin Atlantic filed a lawsuit against BA, accusing it of entering Virgin's computer system and spreading false rumors. In January 1993, Virgin won its libel suit against BA in London. The wide press coverage caused much embarrassment to British Airways. Later that year, Virgin filed a $325 million lawsuit in the Federal Court of New York, accusing BA of using its monopoly power to distort competition on North American routes.

In addition to British Airways, Virgin competed with at least one major carrier on each of its destinations. For instance, it was up against United Airlines to Los Angeles, American Airlines to New York, and Cathay Pacific to Hong Kong. Most of its competitors surpassed Virgin many times in terms of turnover, staff, and number of aircraft. Yet, Virgin was not intimidated by the size of its competitors; it saw its modest size as an advantage that enabled it to react quickly and remain innovative.

EXHIBIT 13   Virgin Atlantic and British Airways: Comparison of routes

Destination— from London to:	Airline	Frequency	Departure-arrival (local times)	Aircraft
New York (JFK)	Virgin Atlantic	Daily (LHR)	14:00–16:40 18:35–20:55	747
	British Airways	Daily (LHR)	10:30–09:20	Concorde
			11:00–13:40	747
			14:00–16:40	747
			18:30–21:10	747
			19:00–17:50	Concorde
		Daily (Gat)	10:40–13:20	D10
New York (Newark)	Virgin Atlantic	Daily (LHR)	16:00–18:40	747
	British Airways	Daily (LHR)	14:45–17:40	747
Boston	Virgin Atlantic	Daily (Gat.)	15:00–17:10	A340
	British Airways	Daily (LHR)	15:45–18:00	747
		Daily (LHR)	09:55–12:30	767
Los Angeles	Virgin Atlantic	Daily (LHR)	12:00–15:10	747
	British Airways	Daily (LHR)	12:15–15:15	747–400
		Daily (LHR)	15:30–18:30	747–400
Miami	Virgin Atlantic	W,F,S,Su (Gat.)	11:15–15:45	747
		Th (Gat.)	11:15–15:45	
	British Airways	Daily (LHR)	11:15–15:40	747
		Daily (LHR)	14:30–18:55	747
Orlando	Virgin Atlantic	Daily (Gat.)	12:30–16:40	747
	British Airways	Tu,W,Su (LHR)	11:15–19:15	747
		M,Th,F,S (Gat.)	11:00–15:10	747
San Francisco	Virgin Atlantic	Daily (LHR)	11:15–14:05	747
	British Airways	Daily (LHR)	13:15–16:05	747–400
		Daily (LHR)	10:50–13:40	747
Tokyo	Virgin Atlantic	M,T,Th,F,S,Su (LHR)	13:00–08:55 (next day)	747/A340
	British Airways	Daily (LHR)	12:55–08:45 (next day)	747–400
		M,T,Th,F,S,Su (LHR)	16:30–12:15 (next day)	747–400
Hong Kong	Virgin Atlantic	Daily	20:30–16:35 (next day)	A340
	British Airways	F	13:55–09:55 (next day)	747–400
		M,T,W,Th,S,Su	14:30–10:30 (next day)	747–400
		Daily	21:30–17:30 (next day)	747–400

Sources: "The Guide to Virgin Atlantic Airways," May/June 1994; "British Airways Worldwide Timetable," 27 March–29 October 1994.

EXHIBIT 14   Virgin Atlantic and British Airways fares (£)

Route	Virgin Atlantic			British Airways			
	Upper Class*	Mid Class*	Economy 21 day apex[†]	First Class*	Club*	Economy	21 day apex[‡]
New York	£1,195	£473	£489	£1,935	£1,061	£620	£538
San Francisco	1,627	595	538[§]	2,179	1,627	920	638
Los Angeles	1,627	604	538	2,179	1,627	920	638
Tokyo	1,806	783	993	2,751	1,806	1,580	993
Hong Kong	979	600	741	3,280	2,075	1,808	741
Boston	1,082	473	439	1,935	1,061	620	538
Miami	1,144	529	498	2,085	1,144	780	598
Orlando	1,144	529	498	2,085	1,144	780	598

* One-way weekend peak-time fares in pounds sterling (£).
[†] Economy fare for Virgin is "Economy 21 day apex" (reservation no later than 21 days prior to departure).
[‡] 21 day apex round-trip ticket.
[§] Between May 17 and June 30, 1994, a special launch fare round-trip ticket was sold at £299.

Virgin Atlantic's Management Structure

Virgin Atlantic's headquarters were in Crawley, a suburb near Gatwick. The airline had a loose organization combined with a high level of dialogue and involvement, as well as strong controls. A senior manager explained: "Our business is about independence, entrepreneurial flair, and people having autonomy to make decisions; yet we pay a great deal of attention to overhead and cost levels." Members of the management team, whose structure is shown in Exhibit 15, came from other airlines, other industries, or other divisions of the Virgin Group. The three top executives—comanaging directors Roy Gardner and Syd Pennington and finance director Nigel Primrose—reported directly to Richard Branson.

Gardner had joined Virgin Airways as technical director in 1984 after working at Laker Airways and British Caledonian Airways. He was responsible for the technical aspects of operations: quality, supplies, maintenance, emergency procedures. Pennington oversaw commercial operations, marketing, sales, and flight operations. Primrose, a chartered accountant with 20 years of international experience, had been part of the senior team that set up Air Europe in 1978 and Air UK in 1983 before joining Virgin Atlantic in 1986. He was Virgin Atlantic's company secretary with responsibility for route feasibility, financial planning, financial accounts, treasury, and legal affairs.

Steve Ridgeway headed the marketing department. After assisting Richard Branson in several projects, including the Transatlantic Boat Challenge, he had joined the airline in 1989 to develop its frequent traveller program, becoming head of marketing in 1992. Paul Griffiths, who had 14 years of commercial aviation experience, became Virgin Atlantic's director of commercial operations after spending two years designing and implementing its information management system. Personnel Director Nick Potts, a business studies graduate, had been recruited in 1991 from Warner Music U.K. where he was the head of the personnel department.

EXHIBIT 15   Virgin Atlantic Airways Ltd. organizational structure, May 1994

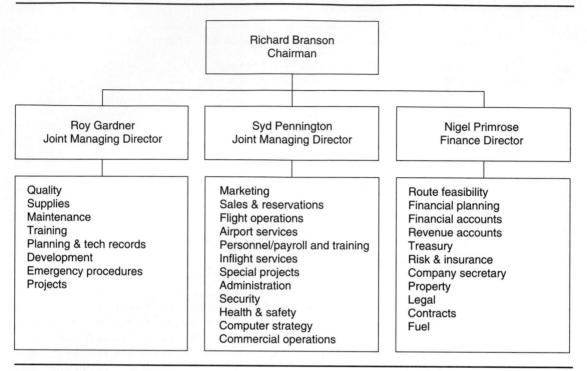

Source: Virgin Atlantic

Marketing Activities

Steve Ridgeway's marketing department covered a variety of activities, as shown in Exhibit 16. Some traditional marketing disciplines, such as advertising, promotions, planning, and the Freeway frequent flyer program, reported to Ruth Blakemore, head of marketing. Catering, retail operations (for example, duty-free sales), product development, and public relations reported directly to Steve Ridgeway.

Virgin Atlantic spent 2 percent of turnover on advertising, well below the 5 to 7 percent industry norm. Virgin's advertising had featured a series of short campaigns handled by various agencies. The winning of a quality award was often a campaign opportunity, as in Exhibit 17, as was the opening of a new line. On one April Fool's Day, Virgin announced that it had developed a new bubble-free champagne. It also launched ad hoc campaigns in response to competitors' activities, as in Exhibit 18. The survey in Exhibit 19 shows that Virgin Atlantic enjoyed a strong brand equity, as well as a high level of spontaneous awareness and a good image in the United Kingdom. In order to increase the trial rate, its advertising had evolved from a conceptual approach to more emphasis on specific product features.

EXHIBIT 16   Virgin Atlantic marketing department

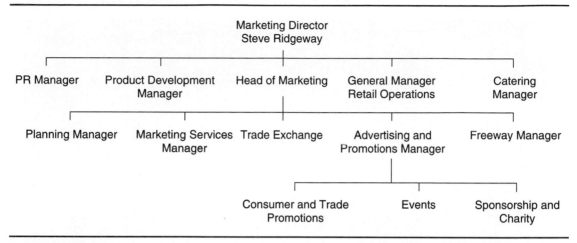

Source: Virgin Atlantic.

In 1990, the airline launched its Virgin Freeway frequent travellers program in Britain (it started in the U.S. in 1992). While Virgin Freeway was an independent division of the Virgin Travel Group, it operated within the airline's marketing department. Freeway miles were offered to members who flew Mid Class or Upper Class or who used the services of international companies such as American Express, Inter-Continental Hotels, British Midland, SAS, and others. Miles could be exchanged for free flights to Europe, North America, and Japan, as well as a wide range of activities: hot air ballooning, polo lessons, rally driving, luxury country getaways for two, five days skiing in the U.S. As part of the Freeway Program, Virgin offered a free standby ticket for every Upper Class ticket purchased.

The Virgin Freeway was run in partnership with SAS and other international groups which, according to Ruth Blakemore, enabled it to compete with British Airways. Virgin also had ties with SAS through another Freeway partner, British Midland, wholly owned by Airlines of Britain in which SAS had a 35 percent stake. Virgin delivered significant interline traffic to British Midland, and Blakemore believed that there was a useful common ground for all three to join forces against British Airways.

In May 1993, Virgin Atlantic unveiled a promotional campaign targeted at BA passengers who had never tried Virgin. Members of BA's Executive Club U.S.A. program who had accumulated 50,000 miles or more qualified for a free Upper Class Companion ticket on Virgin; those with 10,000 to 49,999 miles qualified for a free Mid Class ticket. The campaign was launched with a radio commercial in which Richard Branson said: "In recent years, Virgin has done about everything we can think of to get those remaining British Airways' passengers to try Virgin Atlantic."

The marketing department handled the franchising of the Virgin Atlantic brand, which included two routes. London-Athens, launched from Gatwick in

EXHIBIT 17   Virgin Atlantic advertising (1990)

They must be on a different planet.

It's a brave airline that claims to be the world's favourite.

Now it seems the world has a different idea.

For at the 1989 Executive Travel Airline of the Year Awards, Virgin Atlantic have emerged victorious.

Those most demanding and, dare one say, discerning of people, the readers of Executive Travel Magazine voted Virgin Atlantic, Best Transatlantic Carrier.

It's not just over the Atlantic that they hold sway.

For Virgin were also named Best Business Class in the World, above airlines they admire such as Singapore and Thai.

A choice that was quickly seconded by Business Traveller Magazine.

It's not hard to see why Virgin's Upper Class commands such respect.

AIRLINE OF THE YEAR AWARDS 1989

VIRGIN ATLANTIC AIRWAYS
EXECUTIVE TRAVEL MAGAZINE

Best Transatlantic Carrier
Best Business Class in the World
World's Best Inflight Entertainment

BUSINESS TRAVELLER MAGAZINE

World's Best Business Class

Passengers enjoy a free chauffeur driven car* to and from the airport plus a free economy standby ticket.†

On the plane there are first class sleeper seats that, miraculously, you can actually sleep in and on-board bars and lounges.

And your own personal Sony Video Walkman with a choice of 100 films.

As you might expect from Virgin, this entertainment is truly award winning. It helped scoop a third major award. Best In-Flight Entertainment.

So the next time you want to travel across the world in style, you know who to favour.

For details call *0800 800 400* or for reservations *0293 551616*, or see your travel agent.

*First 40 miles with our compliments. †Not available on Tokyo route.

LONDON · NEW YORK JFK AND NEWARK · MIAMI · MOSCOW · TOKYO

EXHIBIT 18 Virgin Atlantic advertising (Spring 1994) response to a British Airways campaign

The world's favourite airline?
Not in our book.

BEATS THE PANTS OFF BA!
VERY GOOD SERVICE.

JAMES ARMSTRONG
B. S. LIMITED

Excellent.
Keep BA on the run!

JEREMY HATTON
NORWICH CRUISE CENTRE

The best service from the best airline in the World!
Absolutely Fabulous - !!

VINCE CRAWLEY
COUNTRY CASUALS LTD

With a deal like this,
who the hell wants to
fly BA anyway!!

BOB BROWN
FILMCO EUROFORM

A previously dedicated and loyal
British Airways customer, now
a dedicated and loyal Virgin
customer!

ROBERT CASSON
PFIZER INC

Best Business Class price
service in the air.

GEOFF TOVEY
SMITHKLINE BEECHAM

Such a refreshing change from BA! Great
entertainment & service! - Looking forward
to another flight!

ANDREW TURNER
REED TRAVEL GROUP

I am your biggest fan -
I promise never to fly
another airline if I can
help it. It is always
a pleasure on Virgin!

KATHY BRADY
BANKERS TRUST

As ever, Virgin
leads the field.

PAUL JACKSON
CARLTON TV

My first time too on Virgin Atlantic and it's
unquestionably better than the equivalent BA.
The service, for example, was first class.

SHERBAN CANTACUZINO
ROYAL FINE ART COMMISSION

Virgin Atlantic's Upper Class costs the same as BA Club Class. And it's not just
the comments in our visitors' book that are better. Hope to see you soon.

Upper Class

Virgin atlantic

March 1992 in partnership with South East European Airlines of Greece, was transferred to Heathrow seven months later. London City Airport-Dublin, with City Jet, was launched in January 1994. In both cases, the aircraft and crew bore Virgin's name and colors, but Virgin's partner was the operator and paid royalties to Virgin for the use of its brand, marketing, and sales support, and for assistance in the recruitment and training of flight staff.

In April 1994, Virgin announced a partnership with Delta Air Lines—its first alliance with a major international airline. Delta would purchase a set percentage of seats on Virgin flights between London and Los Angeles, New York (Newark and JFK), Miami, San Francisco, Orlando, and Boston, which it would price and sell independently. The alliance, which increased Virgin's annual revenue by $150 million and gave Delta access to Heathrow, had received the blessing of the British government and was awaiting U.S. approval.

Virgin Atlantic's public relations department, known as "the press office" and led by James Murray, played an important role. "We are not here just to react to press inquiries," explained Murray. "We also try to gain publicity for the airline's products and services and to show how much better we are than the competition." Virgin Atlantic enjoyed excellent relations with the media—not the rule in the airline industry—because of a combination of factors: Richard Branson's persona, the airline's openness in dealing with the press, its "David vs. Goliath" quality, the news value of its innovations, and a good management of media relationships.

For instance, Virgin had readily accepted an invitation to participate in BBC television's prime time *Secret Service* series, in which investigators posing as customers test service at well-known firms. Failures in service delivery were exposed and discussed. British Airways, which the BBC had approached first, had declined. While the program did identify some shortcomings in Virgin's operations, including delays in meal service (due to oven problems) and in answering passenger calls, it gave a lively demonstration of the quality of service in Upper Class and of Virgin's willingness to take corrective action.

The public relations department comprised three people in Crawley and two in the group press office, where James Murray spent two days a week. Originally set up in Richard Branson's own house, the group press office had to move next door as the amount of work increased. Staff were on call round the clock, sometimes taking calls from journalists in the middle of the night. During a one-hour car ride with James Murray, the casewriters watched him handle a constant flow of requests ranging from invitations to the inaugural San Francisco flight to questions on Virgin's position on privatizing the Civil Aviation Agency or the possible banning of peanuts on flights after reports of allergy risks—all on the car phone.

A five-member Product Development department evaluated and developed innovations. It handled a broad range of new product activities—a new identity program for the aircraft, selection of seat design and internal decoration, the catering system, or new lounges—and coordinated the input from other departments. Typically, the marketing, engineering, commercial, and sales departments also participated in developing new products. For example, Airport Services played a crucial role in setting up the Clubhouse lounge.

By June 1994, Virgin had taken steps to correct its main weaknesses: the age of its fleet and its punctuality problems. More than half the fleet would be renewed by the end of the year, and Virgin was undertaking an "On-Time Initiative" in which cabin crew were to shut doors exactly 10 minutes before departure time, even if late passengers had not boarded—even Richard Branson, who was notorious for being late. Virgin was also implementing a new corporate identity program. In addition to the Virgin logo and the "Vargas Lady," all aircraft would bear the words *virgin atlantic* in large grey letters, as shown in Exhibit 20.

Challenges for the Future

During its first decade, Virgin Atlantic had confronted great challenges and survived the worst recession in the history of air transportation. Amidst rumors over the airline's financial health, Richard Branson had always stressed his personal commitment. "I would put everything I had into making sure that Virgin Atlantic was here in 20 years' time," he said.

Virgin Atlantic had demonstrated its capacity to innovate, to satisfy customers, and to be financially viable in difficult times. As the world economy began to recover, the airline was poised for a quantum leap in the scale of its operations. When Richard Branson had founded it in 1984, his ambition had been to build an airline unlike any other. Ten years later, what set Virgin apart was its reputation for giving customers what they wanted at prices they could afford, pioneering new concepts in service and entertainment, and restoring a sense of pleasure and excitement to long-distance travel.

The main challenge the airline faced as it celebrated its 10th anniversary was to foster this difference throughout the 1990s. What sort of airline should it be? How could it achieve that goal? How could it remain profitable? How could it retain its competitive edge in innovations? Was it possible to grow while retaining the organizational advantages of a small entrepreneurial company? How could it keep employees motivated and enthusiastic? How would it keep the momentum of its success? These were some of the questions that went through Richard Branson's mind as his 400 guests and himself watched a Virgin 747 Jumbo fly over the Thames and Westminster to mark Virgin's first decade.

EXHIBIT 19   Brand equity survey

	British Airways	Virgin Atlantic	American	United
Perceived strongest brand name in transatlantic travel (percent of respondents)	70%	24%	2%	1%
Spontaneous awareness (percent)	96%	74%	49%	22%
Usage (percent)	93%	48%	44%	23%
Rating of brand names (0–100 scale)	85	80	61	58

Source: Business Marketing Services Limited (BMSL). Based on 141 interviews of executives from the U.K.'s top 500 organisations.

EXHIBIT 20   Virgin Atlantic aircraft after new corporate identity program (1994)

Case 32

Dutch Food Industries Company*

In early September, Jan de Vries, product manager for Dutch Food Industries' new salad dressing product, was wondering what strategy to follow with respect to this new product. His assistant had prepared information concerning alternative promotional methods to use to introduce the new product, and he was concerned with exactly which of these he should recommend for the product's introduction. He also wondered what price the new product should retail for and when the company should introduce the new product. Mr. de Vries had to decide these issues in the next couple of days, as his report containing his recommendations on the introduction of the new salad dressing was due on the desk of the director of marketing the following Monday.

Company Background

The Netherlands Oil Factory of Delft, The Netherlands, was founded in 1884. This firm, which supplied edible oils to the growing margarine industry, merged in 1900 with a French milling company. The new firm then operated under the name Dutch Food Industries Company (DFI).

From this origin, the brand name DFI became increasingly strong and was eventually given to all of the company's branded products. More recently, the name was registered for use internationally.

In the course of the 1920s, DFI became an important factor in the margarine market. The company was a troublesome competitor for the Margarine Union, the company formed by the merger in 1927 of the two margarine giants, Van den Bergh and Jurgens. In 1928, an agreement was reached by which DFI joined the Margarine Union.

In 1930, the interests of the Margarine Union were merged with those of International Industries Corporation—a large, diversified, and international

*This case was written by Kenneth L. Bernhardt and James Scott, assisted by Jos Viehoff, graduate student, Netherlands School of Economics. Copyright © 1996 by Kenneth L. Bernhardt.

organization. It was in this way that DFI became a part of the International Industries complex of companies.

International Industries Corporation (IIC) is a worldwide organization with major interests in the production of margarine, other edible fats and oils, soups, ice cream, frozen foods, meats, cheeses, soaps, and detergents.

The total sales of IIC were more than $1 billion.[1] Profits before taxes were $56 million.

Within IIC, DFI proceeded with its original activities after its margarine factory was closed, namely developing its exports of oils and fats, its trade in bakery products, as well as a number of branded food products. The following list indicates the range of consumer products which the company marketed: table oil, household fats, mayonnaise, salad dressing (several varieties), tomato ketchup, peanut butter, and peanuts.

DFI's total annual sales were between $40 million and $60 million. Profits before taxes were between $5 million and $6 million.

Background on the Dressing Market

A large and growing percentage of Holland's population eats lettuce, usually with salad dressing, with their meals. Estimates indicated that 82 percent of the people ate lettuce with salad dressing regularly. The salad dressing market has extreme seasonal demand, as shown in Exhibit 1. This seasonal pattern coincides with the periods of greatest production of lettuce in Holland. Thus, 50 percent of the total year's volume for the salad dressing market occurs in the four months beginning in April. During this period, lettuce is plentiful and sells for approximately $.96 per head.

The total salad dressing market was growing at approximately 7 percent per year. DFI's share of the market had declined from 20.7 percent to 16.6 percent over the last five years. The total market for salad dressings at manufacturer's level was currently estimated at $15 million. The company was looking for ways to halt the decline in market share and, in fact, increase DFI's share of the growing market.

Historically, the salad dressing market was composed of two segments. The first was a 25 percent oil-based salad dressing, which comprised 90 percent of the total market. The other 10 percent of the market consisted of 50 percent oil-based salad dressing, a slightly creamier product. Previously, DFI, in an effort to increase its market share, had introduced a new product which was 50 percent oil based. Up to that time, DFI sold only 25 percent oil-based salad dressing. The product, called Delfine, was not successful in obtaining the desired volume and profit. While DFI still marketed Delfine, almost all of DFI's volume came from its 25 percent oil-based product, Slasaus.

---

[1] All financial data in this case are presented in U.S. dollars.

EXHIBIT 1 Seasonal analysis of salad dressing market (percentage of annual total market sales—bimonthly periods)

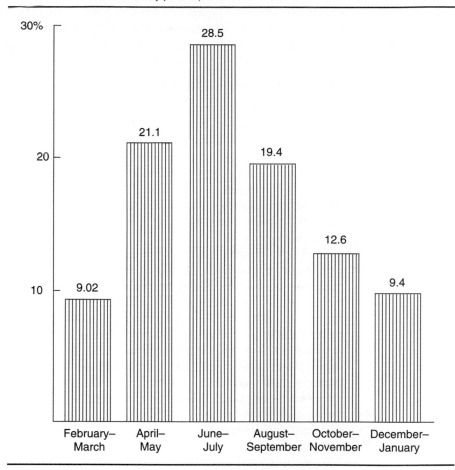

A research study was conducted to help the DFI marketing executives determine why Delfine was not successful. Several reasons emerged:

1. The potential of the 50 percent oil-based market was much smaller than originally anticipated, and only a small percentage of the total population was even interested in this product.
2. The consumers could detect only a small difference between the 25 percent oil-based and the 50 percent oil-based varieties when blind-tested. The difference was not noticeable enough for the consumers to prefer the 50 percent oil-based product.
3. The 50 percent oil-based salad dressing was more expensive, and the consumer was not willing to pay the difference for an apparently almost imperceptible difference.

Because the Delfine sales were well below expectations, DFI removed the heavy promotion support which it had been giving the product. The executives decided to wait for a significant breakthrough of a product with unique advantages. The Delfine experience indicated to them that it would take a totally new type of product for DFI to increase its market share significantly.

Background and Development of Slamix

Every two years, the company conducted a housewives' habits study in which a panel of 700 consumers was asked about their household and their food preparation habits. In August two years before, the company received the most recent study, called PMC–11. The housewives were asked how they prepared their lettuce and what ingredients they used. The results showed that an extremely large percentage of the housewives added not only salad dressing to lettuce, but also added other ingredients such as salt, pepper, eggs, onion, gherkins, and so on. Thus DFI executives got the idea that putting some of these ingredients in the salad dressing would result in a real convenience for the housewife, and DFI would have the significant new product for which they had been searching. The laboratory, in August of the same year, began developing a "dressed" salad dressing which included some of the ingredients which many housewives were accustomed to adding.

Early in the next year, a committee, called the Slamix Committee,[2] was formed to make sure that every part of the company was involved in the development of this new product. The committee, which was headed up by the product manager, had representatives from various parts of the company, including development, production, and marketing. The committee studied production problems, laboratory findings, and, in general, was charged with the responsibility of seeing that the development progressed as scheduled. The committee did not have decision-making powers, but either invited decision makers to important meetings or wrote reports to the people who were in a position to make the required decisions.

After several product tests concerned with taste and keeping properties were conducted at the factory, the company, one year after laboratory work began, undertook its first consumer test of the new "dressed" salad dressing. A panel of housewives was shown a bottle of the new product, which was a salad dressing containing pieces of gherkins, onions, and paprika. Several conclusions emerged from this study:

1. The "dressed" salad dressing was seen by the housewives as more than a salad dressing with ingredients. It was seen as a completely new product.
2. There were two sides to this newness:
   a. By looking at the product, they thought that it had a new taste.
   b. The convenience aspect was strongly stressed by the housewives.

---

[2]Literally translated, Slasaus means "lettuce sauce," and Slamix is literally "lettuce mix."

3. The housewives thought that the new product would be good for decorating the lettuce. With its new color (light red with colorful ingredients), they thought that they could decorate the lettuce much better than with present salad dressings which were creme-colored and very similar to mayonnaise.
4. When asked about the ingredients, one half of the housewives were favorable toward paprika, and half were against it. This apparently was a troublesome ingredient. However, because of the convenience aspect, gherkins and onions were favored by the housewives.

Later, a second consumer study was conducted by the Institute of Household Research in Rotterdam. A sample of 140 housewives who actually used salad dressing on lettuce was given a bottle of the new product to take home. Then, they were visited in their homes. Much useful information emerged from this study. After looking at the product, but before trying it, the housewives said that it looked like a fun product, it made them happy, and they thought that it would taste good. When asked what they thought the product contained, they said tomatoes, red paprika, celery, gherkins, and green paprika.

However, the company was disappointed with the housewives' overall evaluation of the product. Only 20 percent of the housewives said that they thought the product was very good, 11 percent did not like the product, and 69 percent of the housewives said that there were some favorable and some unfavorable aspects of the product. The main reason for the 80 percent unfavorable reaction was the consistency of the new salad dressing. It was too thin. The housewives could pour it too easily and it rapidly went to the bottom of the bowl. Because it fell to the bottom, the housewives said that it was much harder to decorate their salad. It was also uneconomical because they felt that they would put too much on if the product was that thin. There were also problems with taste. Many of the housewives thought it was too sour or too sharp. The paprika was the main reason for the dissatisfaction.

In spite of the above problems, there were several aspects of the study which encouraged the company to proceed with the development of this new product. When asked how they would change the ingredients in the "dressed" salad dressing, only 47 percent of the housewives suggested changes. Most recommended that more onions be added. The housewives were asked for their preference between DFI's Slasaus and the new "dressed" salad dressing. As shown in Exhibit 2, the housewives preferred the new product, except for its consistency. Sixty percent of the housewives said that they would buy the product if it were possible to buy it in the store. Since this was a very high positive response, the company was very encouraged.

The marketing, production, and development groups, coordinated by the Slamix Committee, began work on incorporating the required changes made evident by this consumer study. DFI's development group experimented with changes in the consistency, taste, and ingredients. The production group experimented with a new production process. DFI had intended to introduce the new "dressed" salad dressing in a few months. However, the top corporate executives

EXHIBIT 2   Preference test: Slasaus versus "dressed" salad dressing

Prefer	Taste	Appearance	Decoration aspects	Consistency	Convenience
"Dressed" salad dressing	59%	73%	46%	18%	50%
Slasaus	38	20	44	65	20
No preference/no difference	3	7	10	17	30
	100%	100%	100%	100%	100%

decided that, before the new product could be introduced, an extensive test of its keeping properties (vulnerability to deterioration) would have to be conducted.

The keeping-properties test showed that after several months the light red-colored product changed to a pink color. The difference in color was only slight, but DFI executives thought that the consumer reaction to this change should be tested. They decided that at the same time they would conduct a consumer test to find a name for this new product. A sample of 180 housewives from the Institute of Household Research was used to get at these questions. Only 2 out of the 180 housewives saw that there was a difference in color between the two bottles of the new product. When they were told that there was a slight difference and were shown the two bottles together, most of the housewives could not see the color change, and those that could were not unhappy about it.

The housewives were then asked what the name for this product should be. The phrase "mixed salad dressing" kept coming up. The housewives were then asked what they thought of two names which the company had screened, "Slamix" (lettuce mix) and "Spikkeltjessaus" (sauce with little spots). Eighty-one percent thought that Slamix was a very good name. Only 26 percent thought that Spikkeltjessaus was a good name. The name Slamix was chosen for the new product. Interestingly, that was the name that the company had used internally for the new product when it was first being developed.

A short time later, DFI had solved the color-change problem. The company now thought that it had a product ready to be marketed, so a final consumer test was undertaken to test the effect of all of the changes that had been made during the previous year.

Two versions of Slamix, a white one and a pink one, were tested at the Institute for Household Research. One hundred eighty housewives were asked what they thought of the product and whether they would buy it or not. The negative reactions to the product were minimal. Almost no negative comments were voiced. The problems of consistency, color, taste, and ingredients had apparently been solved. When asked if they would buy the product, 76 percent of those shown the pink product, and 70 percent of those shown the white product, responded in a positive manner. After tasting the two versions of Slamix, the housewives revealed a strong preference for the pink Slamix. The DFI executives felt that the product was now ready to be marketed.

DFI executives next reviewed the financial projections prepared by Mr. de Vries, the product manager. Almost no capital investment would be required as the Slamix would be produced by using present production facilities. Only a few machines, at a total cost of $25,000, would be required.

At an early stage in the development of the product, Slamix sales had been forecasted at 3.7 percent of the total market at the end of the first year. Encouraged by the results of the consumer tests, DFI executives revised their estimate of sales. The new forecast was for approximately 6.7 percent of the market. (See Exhibit 3.)

EXHIBIT 3   Forecast sales of Slamix

Year	Share of market (percent)
Original estimates:	
Year 1	3.7%
Year 2	3.9
Year 3	4.4
Revised estimates:	
Year 1	6.7
Year 2	11.7

The directors of the company thought that they finally had the product for which they had been waiting. The consumer tests were complete, and the product had found very high favor with the consumers. There was significant technological development involved in the product, and DFI executives thought that it would take considerable time for the competition to duplicate the product. The product manager's projected sales seemed reasonable. Mr. de Vries was asked to prepare a comprehensive report concerning the introductory marketing strategy to be used to introduce the new product.

Pricing Strategy

The first problem that the product manager had to resolve concerned the suggested retail price that the company should charge for Slamix. To help Mr. de Vries make his recommendation, the assistant product manager had made a list of the following considerations:

1. The company's total cost for a 0.30-liter-size bottle of Slamix was $0.40. This was 20 percent higher than DFI's regular salad dressing, Slasaus.
2. The gross margin for Slasaus was 22 percent. Because of the unique qualities of Slamix, large development costs, and possible substitution with Slasaus, a higher gross margin for Slamix might be considered.
3. DFI gave the wholesalers a 12.5 percent margin and retailers a 14.3 percent margin for Slasaus. Possibly these should be increased for Slamix to encourage greater acceptance and promotion by the trade channels of distribution.
4. The two leading salad dressings, Salata by Duyvis and Slasaus, both had a retail price of $.56 for the 0.30-liter bottle. The retail price for the 0.60-liter

bottle was $.96. Private-label salad dressings were $.44 for a 0.30-liter bottle. The average price for all salad dressings was approximately $.52.

5. DFI had conducted some research on the optimal price of Slamix. After using a sample of the product, 140 housewives were asked what price they would be willing to pay for Slamix. Their responses, by percent, were:

	Percent
$0.62 or less	45%
Between $0.62 and $0.80	41
$0.80 or more	14
Total	100%

The average price mentioned was $0.68.

The assistant product manager also prepared the table shown in Exhibit 4. The first column shows the retail price, and gives data that allows one to calculate trade margins and gross margin for Slasaus. The remaining six columns show alternative retail prices for Slamix, resulting from different trade margins and gross margins. Mr. de Vries wondered which of these prices he should recommend to the board of directors.

EXHIBIT 4   Alternative prices for Slamix*

	Slasaus	Slamix					
		1	2	3	4	5	6
Retail price	$0.56	$0.64	$0.68	$0.68	$0.72	$0.74	$0.76
Price to retailer	0.48	0.56	0.56	0.58	0.59	0.62	0.63
Price to wholesaler	0.42	0.50	0.50	0.52	0.52	0.56	0.56
Cost	0.33	0.40	0.40	0.40	0.40	0.40	0.40

* Selected figures in this table have been disguised.

Promotion Alternatives

The board of directors told the product manager that he had $600,000 for his promotion budget. Of this, $20,000 was to be allocated as Slamix's share of the general corporate advertising which aided all DFI products. The $600,000 was determined by using a percentage of the "expected gross profit of the first year" for Slamix.[3] DFI's policy was to break even in the third year of the new product, and make enough profits in years four and five to attain a total payback within five years.

The company had already given considerable thought to the sales message and the brand image desired for Slamix. The information below was sent to the advertising agency to help in planning the promotional program of the company:

---

[3]It was possible that the percentage could be greater than 100 percent. This would mean that the company was willing to spend more than the first year's gross profit for initial promotion.

Sales message. It is now possible, in a completely new way, to make delicious salad. Sla + Slamix = Sla Klaar. (Lettuce + Slamix = Lettuce Ready).

Supporting message. Slamix is a salad dressing with pieces of onion, gherkins, and paprika.

Desired brand image. With Slamix you can make, very easily and very quickly, a delicious salad that also looks nice. Slamix is a complete, good, handy product. DFI is a modern firm with up-to-date ideas.

Thus, the company wanted to get across three principal points. They are (1) that Slamix is a completely new product, (2) that it is convenient, and (3) that it is a salad dressing with ingredients making it a complete salad dressing.

The product manager was undecided as to how to divide the $580,000 among the following alternatives:

1. Television.
2. Radio.
3. Newspaper advertising.
4. Magazines.
5. Sampling.
6. Coupons.
7. Price-off promotion.
8. Key chain premiums.
9. Trade allowances.

Television

The product manager thought that television would be advantageous because of the ability to show the product in actual use—a housewife pouring Slamix onto the lettuce. The cost of using the television medium is shown in Exhibit 5. The company did not have a choice among the seven blocks of time, but had to take whatever was available. For planning, however, they figured an average cost of a 30-second ad would be $5,000. Mr. de Vries felt that at least 25 advertisements were necessary before the TV advertising would have maximum impact.

Radio

The chief attraction of radio was its extremely low price. Each 30-second radio ad cost $375 on Radio Veronica, a popular station during the daytime. Production costs for a radio ad were approximately $2,500. Only 60 percent of the households could receive Radio Veronica, mainly in the western part of the country. Mr. de Vries felt that if radio were used, a minimum of 100 spots should be purchased.

EXHIBIT 5 Data on Dutch television media

Station	Block number	Time	Cost of 30-second ad
Nederland 1	1	Before early news	$ 6,900
Nederland 1	2	After early news	6,900
Nederland 1	3	Before late news	8,800
Nederland 1	4	After late news	8,800
Nederland 2	5	After early news	1,500
Nederland 2	6	Before late news	2,500
Nederland 2	7	After late news	2,500
Average cost per 30-second TV ad			$ 5,000
Production cost for a TV ad			$21,000

TV coverage per 1,000 households = 850 or 85 percent. Only about one-half of the homes can receive Nederland 2.

Newspapers

De Vries thought the main advantages of newspapers would be the announcement effect and its influence with the local trade. Nationally, the cost of each half-page insertion would be $42,000.

Magazines

Magazines would be a desirable addition to the promotional program for several reasons. Due to the ability to use color, the company could show the product as it actually looked on the shelf. By using several women's magazines, the company could reach a select audience of people reading the magazine at its leisure. Data on selected Dutch magazines are shown in Exhibit 6. Mr. de Vries thought that if they were to use a magazine campaign, at least 10 insertions would be necessary before the advertising would be very effective. Of the possibilities in Exhibit 6, the agency thought that the combination of *Eva, Margriet,* and *AVRO-Televizier* would be most effective for DFI, since the combination would reach a large number of people at a relatively low cost.

Sampling

Although he realized that it was very expensive, Mr. de Vries considered the use of direct-mail sampling. A small 12 cm by 18 cm (approximately 5 × 7 inches) folder could be mailed to Holland's 3.7 million households for $100,000. The cost, however, would increase substantially if a small bottle of the product were to be included in the direct mailing. This cost would be 40 cents for handling, plus 45 cents for the actual sample. Thus, it would cost over $3 million to sample the whole country.

Coupon

Mr. de Vries was considering whether or not to include a coupon good for $.10 off the purchase of Slamix with one of the other DFI products—mayonnaise, for example. He estimated that 900,000 coupons would be distributed.

EXHIBIT 6   Data on selected Dutch magazines

Magazines	Type	Circulation	Frequency	Price for full-page ad		Cost per 1,000 circulation*
				Black and white	Color	
Eva	Women's	375,000	Weekly	$2,300	$4,200	$11.20
Margriet	Women's	825,000	Weekly	6,300	10,000	12.12
Libelle	Women's	570,000	Weekly	4,200	7,000	12.28
Prinses	Women's	213,000	Weekly	2,000	3,500	16.43
Panorama	General	403,000	Weekly	4,000	6,500	16.13
Nieuwe Revu	General	261,000	Weekly	2,750	4,600	17.62
Spiegel	General	175,000	Weekly	2,100	4,000	22.85
Het Beste	Digest	325,000	Monthly	2,900	4,900	15.08
Studio	TV Guide	575,000	Weekly	4,500	7,300	12.70
NCRV-gids	TV Guide	482,000	Weekly	4,300	7,100	14.73
Vara-gids	TV Guide	504,000	Weekly	4,500	7,100	14.09
AVRO-Televizier	TV Guide	950,000	Weekly	7,800	11,600	12.21
Combination of Eva, Margriet, and AVRO-Televizier				14,700	23,400	10.88

*Cost of one-page color ad, divided by circulation in thousands. With Eva as an example, cost per 1,000 circulation = $4,200/375 = $11.20.

At a redemption rate of 5 percent, the cost would, thus, be approximately $4,500, plus $2,000 for handling costs.

Price-Off Promotion

DFI made use of a reduced retail price for most of its new product introductions. Thus, the product manager thought it quite normal to consider the use of reducing the retail price by U.S. $.20 per bottle and identifying this price reduction on the label of the product. It was felt that this reduced price would encourage the housewives to try Slamix. It was also quite normal to follow up this sales promotion with a similar price reduction approximately five months after the product was introduced. This would encourage those who had still not tried the product to purchase a bottle and would encourage those who had already bought one bottle to continue purchasing the new product. The cost of this price-off promotion is shown in Exhibit 7.

EXHIBIT 7

Introduction:	
720,000 bottles at 20 cents off each	$144,000
Handling and display materials	7,500
Total	$151,500
Follow-up five months later:	
600,000 bottles at 20 cents off each	$120,000
Handling and display materials	7,500
Total	$127,500

Key Chain Premium

It was very unusual to use a free premium to introduce a new product, but Mr. de Vries was considering this alternative for several reasons. Many products in Holland at this time were using key chains as a premium. As shown in Exhibit 8, an extremely large percentage of the people in Holland were collecting key chains. The details of the research showed that mothers and daughters were more likely to collect key chains, especially if the children were between 8 and 11 years of age. Mr. de Vries felt that, if he used key chains as premiums for the introduction of Slamix, he could have a follow-up promotion five months later using either key chains or price-off deals. Selected cost information on the key chain promotion is shown in Exhibit 9.

Exhibit 8 Percentage of households collecting key chains

	June	July	September
Households with children	45	n.a.	n.a.
Households without children	5	n.a.	n.a.
Total (weighted average)	34	37	41

n.a. = not available.

Exhibit 9

Introduction:	
720,000 bottles = about 220 metric tons	
750,000 key chains at $.12	$ 90,000
Handling costs and display materials	25,000
Total	$115,000
Follow-up five months later:	
600,000 bottles = about 180 tons	
625,000 key chains at $.12	$ 75,000
Handling costs and display materials	20,000
Total	$ 95,000

Trade Allowances

The product manager also considered the use of trade allowances to encourage the retailers to accept and promote the new product. The company traditionally offered $.50 per case of 12 bottles. Thus, if it was decided that trade allowances were desirable, the cost would be $30,000 for the initial introduction and an additional $25,000 used during the follow-up promotion five months later. Trade allowances could be used together with either the price-off promotion or the key chain promotion. The product manager felt that trade allowances would not be very effective without one of the two consumer sales promotions.

Distribution

Outside of the question of what trade margins to use and whether or not to use trade allowances during the consumer sales promotions discussed above, Mr. de Vries did not see any problems with distribution. DFI had a sales force of approximately 50 persons who regularly called on 10,000 outlets in Holland. It was felt that the sales force could handle the introduction of the new product with no problem.

The last problem the product manager faced concerned the timing of the introduction of Slamix. The product would be ready for introduction in October. Mr. de Vries wondered whether the seasonal nature of the demand for the product would make it more desirable to hold off the introduction until March of the next year.

Case 33

Quaker State*

OIL CITY, PA   In the ultracompetitive motor-oil market, cutthroat discounting has become a way of life. So when Quaker State decided a year ago to stop slashing prices and emphasize quality, it was a big gamble.

The early results are in, and they aren't pretty. The company's nine-month revenue fell 9 percent, and fourth-quarter earnings are expected to show a big decline from a year earlier. The stock isn't far from its 52-week low. Wall Street is disenchanted.

The Wall Street Journal, Heard on the Street column, January 8, 1990

It has been three years since the devastating loss of 1987, and the Quaker State marketing strategy has been reworked again and again. With greater competition and new entrants, it appears Quaker State's future for the 1990s is in jeopardy. The relatively small independent oil company in Oil City has been repeatedly rumored as a takeover candidate. Management at Quaker State realize they need to regain past levels of profitability and market share to maintain their independence. There is no more room to gamble with the company's future and lose. The marketing strategy for the next year, 1991, and subsequent years, needs to identify and meet consumer needs.

The Passenger-Car Motor-Oil Market

The passenger-car motor-oil (PCMO) market can be characterized as a very competitive mature market with very little growth. Subsequently, the market is very price sensitive, and new product developments are closely watched by all competitors. The market is made up of the motor-oil specialist companies who produce and market strictly motor oil, and the gasoline companies who primarily market gasoline. Traditionally, the motor-oil specialists have been the market share leaders based on their distribution networks and their product innovation. However, during recent years the gasoline companies have increased their efforts

---

*This case was written by Craig F. Ehrnst under the supervision of Thomas C. Kinnear. The authors wish to thank the people at Quaker State without whose assistance this case would not have been possible. Copyright © 1990 by Thomas C. Kinnear.

to capture market share through mass merchandisers and other distribution channels formerly dominated by the motor-oil specialists.

Influenced by the automotive manufacturers, motor-oil quality has been increased to meet the performance needs of engines built in recent years. The higher quality standards have required increased research among motor-oil industry producers. These standards have been met with new additive packages to further prevent rust, corrosion, and sludge buildup. Most motor oil producers reformulated their products to meet the new industry standards during the mid-1980s. However, due to the nature of the competitive market, the full costs associated with the new additive packages have not been passed on to consumers. The reformulated products offered to consumers provide a higher-quality product to consumers and a lower margin for producers.

After reformulating their products, motor-oil producers took very aggressive positions to reintroduce their products. Advertising expenditures have essentially doubled, from estimates of $50 million in 1984 to well over $100 million in 1988 (see Exhibit 1). Promotional expenditures have also increased at a similar rate. The heavy advertising and promotional expenditures have been led by the motor-oil specialists. Their dependence on brand awareness is essential to pull their products through the distribution chain of mass merchandisers and auto parts stores.

EXHIBIT 1   Advertising and promotion expenditures

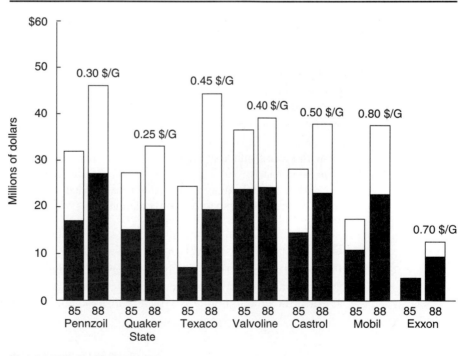

Motor Oil Classifications

The consumer is quality conscious but is probably unaware of measures to distinguish real quality from perceived quality motor oil. Fortunately, classification systems have been developed to measure motor-oil viscosity and engine service requirements (see Appendix A). First, the motor-oil viscosity standards, developed by the Society of Automotive Engineers (SAE), provide a guide for users to select motor oil according to the climate conditions of their automobiles. For example, a multigrade motor oil 5W–30 would perform better in subzero temperatures than a multigrade motor oil grade of 10W–30. Next, the engine service classification system, developed by motor-oil industry specialists, defines characteristics of a motor oil to help the consumer with the selection of appropriate products. Motor oil manufacturers label their product with a letter classification system according to recommended engine service requirements. For example, the motor oil with the letter designation "SG" is the recommended motor oil with the highest standards acceptable for 1989 gasoline engine warranty maintenance service. There are several other lower grades of motor oil, but the "SG" grade would be preferred because of its superior quality and because it can be substituted for other grades of motor oil.[1]

Both systems can provide the consumer with useful information, but typical consumers are probably not aware of the systems and they are most likely confused by the mix of numbers and letters used in the classification systems. Consumers will often rely on friends, their mechanics, or a salesperson when deciding which brand of motor oil to purchase. Appendix A provides a detailed overview of the two classification systems.

The Consumer Markets

The PCMO market is segmented by consumer usage into two principal areas—the do-it-yourselfer (DIYer) or the installed segments. Exhibit 2 illustrates the breakdown between the two primary market segments and their respective subsegments. The DIYers prefer to purchase their motor oil and install it themselves (or with the assistance of friends). There has been a decline in the DIYer market, from 70 percent in 1985 to 66 percent in 1988. In contrast, the installed segment has shown continued signs of growth, as service and convenience have influenced the buying perspectives of consumers.

The Do-It-Yourself Market

The DIYer has been the single largest market for two primary reasons: First, the DIYer wants to ensure that the oil change is done correctly. An individual's investment in an automobile is typically a substantial part of his or her income.

---

[1]Quaker State, "Oil and Lubricants Vital to Your Vehicle's Survival," May 1, 1989, pp. 6–9.

EXHIBIT 2   Distribution channel structure

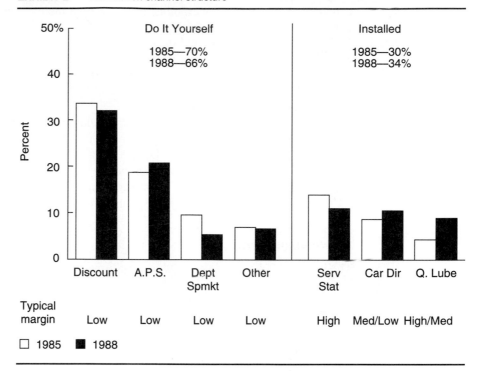

Therefore, it is worthwhile to protect their investments with the necessary motor oil changes. In addition, the DIYers are generally very proud of their cars and they don't mind changing their motor oil, but they don't particularly like it either. Rather, they change their own oil so they can be sure that it's done right. Second, the DIYers prefer changing their motor oil because they are price sensitive. Promotional discounts have been a common tradition in recent years, and thus the DIYers have become accustomed to discounted product prices.

Past industry surveys indicate that half of the DIYers are brand loyal for a variety of reasons. Perceived product quality and reliability are two reasons for maintaining this loyalty, but there is also a mixing problem that forces brand loyalty. The brand-loyal DIYer will purchase motor oil by the case, particularly if the brand is on sale. As the case empties, all of the single quart bottles may not be used up prior to the next oil change. The brand-loyal DIYer will consider the potential negative impacts of mixing two different brands of motor oil, and thus remain brand loyal to the last remaining quart of motor oil, rather than discarding it.

Approximately half of the DIYers are switchers who either switch and stick or switch less on the basis of quality and more based on price. The switch and stick DIYers switch brands of motor oil because of concerns with product quality or because they purchased a new car. Most automobile manufacturers have extended the life of engine warranties and are now more inclined to recommend specific brands of motor oil. With the combination of a new car purchase and the extended engine service warranties, it has become increasingly more important to maintain a single brand of motor oil throughout the ownership of the auto. The switch and stick DIYers are willing to try other motor oils perceived to better preserve and protect their automotive investment. The price-driven switchers see no problem in switching brands because they perceive no difference in the various brands of motor oil. The lowest-price motor oil will virtually guarantee their next purchase decision.

DIYers can be characterized as either brand loyal or switchers. They install their own motor oil not because they enjoy the task, but rather because they want to make sure that it is done right. DIYers are generally very price sensitive and more likely to become switchers when their preferred brand is not on sale. This market segment continues to be the larger of the two consumer markets, but the DIYer market has been declining and future growth is considered unlikely.

The "Installed" Market

The installed market consists of those consumers who have their cars' motor oil changed at service stations, car dealerships, or at quick-lube centers. Exhibit 2 shows the 4 percent growth in recent years of the installed market, as well as the rapid growth of the quick-lube centers, primarily at the expense of service stations. Price has not been as great a factor as convenience to these buyers. Based on consumer research, the installed market prefers a high-quality brand of motor oil that is expeditiously installed. Convenience to the consumer has become increasingly more important, as demographic trends indicate that more and more dual-income families have less free time available to do such things as changing their own motor oil.

The quick-lube centers have been one of the newest developments in the motor-oil industry. The rapid growth of quick-lube centers, which specialize in fast motor-oil changes (10 minutes or less), could be attributed to their convenience and expertise based on volume. The traditional quick-lube service center performs only motor oil changes in a three- to four-bay building. These buildings are frequently located near high-traffic centers, and some are converted service stations. The quick-lube service's bay doors are located in the front and back of the building in order for customers to drive in and out easily. The quick-lube centers also have a pit below the automobile service bay area for technicians to perform service without raising the car on a service platform, typical of most service stations. The pit reduces service time and provides added customer convenience since customers do not have to leave their cars.

Roughly half of the quick-lube centers are independently owned and they have been one of the fastest-growing businesses of the automotive service sector. Motor-oil specialist companies have been very aggressive in acquiring and building quick-lube centers. However, several major gasoline companies have been experimenting with building their own quick-lube centers, as well as modifying existing service stations.

Service stations have historically had the largest market share of the installed market, but they have lost market share to the quick-lube centers. Most service stations have not been regarded as very convenient to customers, nor have they been particularly price competitive. It is difficult for service stations to justify having a highly paid mechanic perform motor oil changes. Other service and preventive maintenance performed at service stations are preferred because of their higher profit margins. In addition, traditional service stations have been designed without pits because service platforms used to raise and lower cars are more desirable for other forms of maintenance. The service platforms are particularly advantageous because mechanics can obtain easier access to perform tire, brake, transmission, and other undercarriage repairs. The choice of a pit or a service platform is mutually exclusive. The pit requires a basement below the garage floor, while the service platform base is typically embedded in the garage floor.

Some industry analysts feel that the car dealerships offer another area of potential market growth. Extended engine service warranties are valid only with performed preventive maintenance, including frequent motor oil changes. The car dealerships have access to a large customer base, and they perform the majority of the manufacturers' service guarantees.

Growth in the installed market has also been fueled by environmental concerns about used motor oil and proposed legislation. Legislators have become increasingly concerned with the means of disposal of used motor oil, particularly by the typical DIYer. Currently, there is little incentive for a DIYer to return used motor oil to a community collection point, nor is there an incentive to create a collection point. While it is advantageous to recycle used motor oil, it is difficult to distinguish used motor oils from other more hazardous oils. There are significant health risks associated with unknowingly handling contaminated motor oil that may be a more harmful hazardous waste. Greater environmental awareness could lead to direct legislation affecting the DIYer and the future handling of used motor oil.

The installed market consumer prefers a high-quality motor oil conveniently installed. The recent growth in market share of quick-lube centers, and the frequency of discussed environmental legislation, make the installed market an attractive market for future growth.

Distribution

Motor-oil products are distributed from the blending plants to both mass merchandisers and motor-oil distributors. The mass merchandisers include discount and department stores such as Kmart, Montgomery Wards, Wal-Mart, Zayres, and others. The distributors handle distribution to smaller accounts such as individual quick-lube centers, service stations, grocery stores, drug stores, and hardware stores. Depending on the purchase volume, the accounts of auto parts stores could be handled as either mass merchandisers or distributors.

Generally, mass merchandisers purchase directly from the manufacturer and sell the motor oil by offering discounted prices to consumers. It is not uncommon for mass merchandisers to have their own private-label brands priced slightly less than the name-brand motor oils. The private-label brand is usually produced and packaged by a major oil company. The mass merchandiser's consumers are DIYers who are very price sensitive. Therefore, the mass merchandisers negotiate larger discounted volume purchases to resell name-brand motor oils at discounted prices across the country.

The distributors resell either a single company's products (as exclusive distributors) or they handle several different brands of motor-oil products for resale. This depends on the distributors' relationship with their suppliers. Some distributors are independently owned, while others are managed by motor oil companies. The relationship with the motor oil supplier may provide preference on whether the distributor handles more than one brand of motor oil. The distributors' consumer markets include both the DIYer and installed consumer. Pricing is extremely important to the independent distributors, as they are often in direct competition with the mass merchandisers for business.

Pricing

As a result of the cutthroat competition in the motor-oil industry, pricing has left most firms remaining in the industry with very small margins. The product pricing decisions are driven by competition for additional motor-oil market share. Although raw material cost may vary significantly from month to month, these price fluctuations are not passed on to consumers. There are a variety of reasons for current industry pricing practices, including factors affecting distribution channels, market share, and product image.

Mass merchandisers and large discounters have been particularly skillful in obtaining large volume discounts from most motor-oil producers. However, discounted volume sales to mass merchandisers can alienate the independent distributors. The independent distributors supply motor oil to both the installed and the DIYer consumer markets, while the mass merchandisers supply motor oil primarily to the DIYers. The pricing dilemma for motor-oil producers is extremely difficult. Independent distributors are very astute about product prices, and they sell motor oil to hundreds of service operations daily. Discounted motor oil offered at the mass merchandisers directly undercuts the distributors' price and is considered a threat to future business. As a result, motor-oil producers often deal with negotiated product pricing issues on a daily basis.

Market share is also an important factor in product pricing. The firms with large market shares—typically the motor oil specialists—have followed a more consistent pricing strategy ranging well within 50 cents per gallon of each other (see Exhibits 3 and 4). The gasoline companies, generally with lower market shares, have a larger variance in price range, as noted in Exhibit 4. Gasoline companies have virtually perfected instant price changes at the fuel pump, and they have not been afraid to frequently change the prices of their motor oil. Some firms with low market share have discounted their product price to tempt DIYers to switch brands. Havoline, owned by Texaco, has been particularly successful in

EXHIBIT 3   PCMO market share

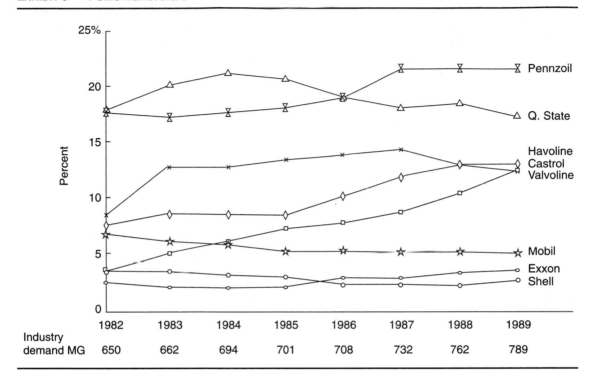

Industry demand MG	1982	1983	1984	1985	1986	1987	1988	1989
	650	662	694	701	708	732	762	789

gaining market share with this strategy, but it has been very costly. Depending on the firm's market share, pricing can influence the frequency of price changes and the price level.

Product image and positioning also significantly influence motor-oil pricing decisions. The motor-oil specialists have been the most successful in developing premium-brand images. The premium image commands a higher price and typically a higher demand. However, some gasoline companies have followed premium price strategies even though their product was not perceived to be a premium product.

Product pricing has been further complicated by product discounts offered to consumers and distributors. In the mid-1980s, the motor-oil industry quickly caught on to the concept of offering product coupon discounts to consumers. Rebates were readily available to most consumers by virtually all motor-oil producers in an effort to protect or capture market share. This rebating reduced margins and increased the intensity of competition among the key players. Overall, product pricing decisions must carefully weigh the trade-offs within distribution channels and brand-quality perceptions.

EXHIBIT 4   Retail pricing trends—Do it yourself

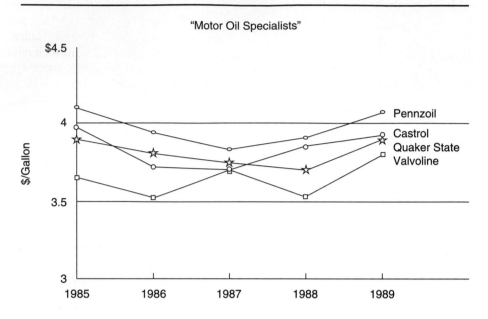

"Motor Oil Specialists"

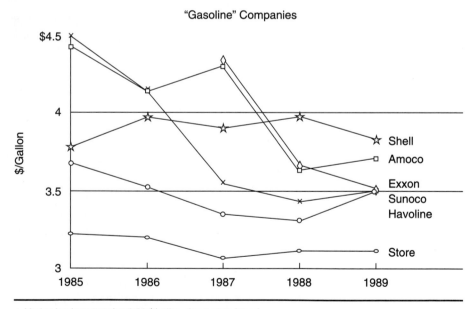

"Gasoline" Companies

+ Market leader averaging 0.80 $/gallon above store brand.

The PCMO Competitors

The competitors in the PCMO industry have each carefully positioned their products to meet specific market niches or to address future growth potential. Pennzoil and Quaker State have been successful in maintaining market leadership, but others such as Castrol and Havoline have successfully increased their respective market shares. A brief summary of all the key PCMO players follows.

Pennzoil

Pennzoil displaced Quaker State in 1986 as the market-share leader by capturing 21 percent of the PCMO market (see Exhibit 3). Their marketing strategy has been to remain as market leader by pushing their product hard into the quick-lube services. Pennzoil has approached the quick-lube market by franchising their name and flooding the quick-lube markets with their products. In 1988, Pennzoil claimed to have supplied about two-thirds of the motor oil sold in the booming U.S. quick-lube business. Pennzoil also has a long-term commitment with Jiffy Lube, the largest U.S. quick-lube franchise. The Pennzoil-Jiffy Lube relationship developed partly out of necessity, since Pennzoil was one of their largest creditors and Jiffy Lube had overbuilt their operations too quickly. Pennzoil stepped in with much needed cash, and over the following years Pennzoil has gained a greater controlling interest in Jiffy Lube.

Pennzoil has emphasized quality and brand loyalty to maintain their premium price level. As a result, Pennzoil users are brand loyal and less likely to become switchers. The 1988 annual report summarized part of their market approach:

> While motor oil sales were healthy in 1988, they failed to match the record levels of 1987. One major reason was deep discounting on the part of competitors, a tactic that tends to make motor oil a commodity. Pennzoil avoided this trap, unlike some of its competitors, and managed to hold market share, thanks to strong brand loyalty on the part of Pennzoil consumers. It finished the year comfortably ahead of its nearest competitor by a margin of several points.[2]

The motor oil and automotive products segment of Pennzoil had revenues of $1,312.2 million and an operating income of $110.8 million (excluding a $122 million write-down of assets) in 1988. Pennzoil earned a profit of $115.9 million and $168.7 million in 1987 and 1986.

Pennzoil's advertising and promotion has been directed at building their installed market position, while maintaining their DIYer position. Their advertising theme has stressed the multidimensional aspect of their motor oil to handle thermal breakdown, lubrication, and reduced friction; that is, "world-class protection." Given Pennzoil's strong cash position and their market leadership, Pennzoil will adamantly defend their market share against competitor's threats.

---

[2]Pennzoil, 1988 Annual Report, p. 14·

Castrol

Castrol has been one of the most successful marketers of PCMO in recent years. This is evidenced by their rise in market share from 5 percent in 1983 to almost 10 percent in 1988. Castrol has focused their product on the small car users, emphasizing their product as a high-performance motor oil developed for small-car engine needs. Their users are considered younger and more upscale and tend to drive cars with four-cylinder engines. Castrol users are in a class by themselves, with high brand loyalty and a specific market.

Castrol developed their market by focusing on the small-car DIYer and aggressively marketing the car dealers. Castrol has not directed any investment at the quick-lube business. Castrol has established their market niche as "an oil for small engine protection" tied to the advertising theme "engineered for smaller cars."

Havoline

Havoline has progressively increased its market share on a consistent basis. First, Havoline successfully dropped its name association with Texaco in the mid-1980s. Gasoline company motor oils in general are perceived negatively compared to their rivals, the motor-oil specialists. Second, Havoline has maintained a clear low-price strategy to obtain market share. While this strategy has been costly—a $25 million estimated loss in 1988 alone—market share has increased almost 2 percent for each of the last three years.

The Havoline users tend to be switchers who perceive their motor oil as a second choice, not as good as Pennzoil or Castrol, but effective. Havoline seems to be used because of price and product availability. Their advertising message has emphasized the formulation's ability to reduce sludge with the theme "more protection than you'll ever need."

Valvoline

Valvoline has had significant trouble in recent years, resulting in estimated break-even performance. Valvoline, owned by Ashland Oil, has been the price leader, but they have lost market share primarily due to the aggression of Texaco. Valvoline consumers are not as brand loyal as Pennzoil or Castrol consumers. When prices began to decline in the mid-1980s, Valvoline consumers departed.

Valvoline obtained brand awareness in the 1970s with their advertising theme using "Val the chimp" to make Valvoline a household name.[3] Television commercials and print advertising showing Val performing an oil change with Valvoline made it look easy. Clearly targeted at the DIYer, it was a creative advertisement that caught the public's attention. Today, Valvoline has switched its emphasis to the motor oil's product quality and brand image. The current

---

[3]"Val the Chimp Made Valvoline a Household Name," *The Oil Daily,* April 20, 1988, p. B–9.

advertising utilizes aggressive comparison advertising aimed specifically at the market leaders, such as Quaker State. Valvoline advertises that their motor oil is the highest-quality oil recommended by car manufacturers, with the theme "People who know, use Valvoline."

Others

The gasoline companies, Mobil, Exxon, Shell, and others, round out the rest of the PCMO business with break-even profits at best. Only Mobil has successfully utilized the gasoline company name with its name brand motor oil, particularly Mobil 1. Exxon has made some efforts recently to revitalize their brand, SUPERFLO, with heavy advertising and the building of experimental quick-lubes. Shell has introduced a reformulated motor oil specifically aimed at the rapidly expanding small truck market. The product, called Truckguard, offers the protection needed for small trucks, but there are no preliminary results to indicate success or failure of this product.

The PCMO industry remains a very competitive industry, and throughout the next few years margins are expected to remain low. The threat of new entrants is highly unlikely; however, there are clear opportunities for consolidations or external acquisitions in order to capture market share. Niche market segments have been successfully developed at the DIYer level to foster and maintain brand loyalty.

Finally, another factor to consider is the potential for a revolutionary development in the PCMO market. Environmental concerns about the illegal disposal of used motor oil have been increasingly brought to the attention of legislators. Legislation may be created to address this concern, possibly leading to the development of an engine sealed for life, with no oil added after the purchase of the car. Another possibility to consider is the usage of alternative fuels, such as methanol, requiring different lubrication needs. Any significant investment in this competitive industry should consider external factors which may affect the product life cycle of PCMO.

Quaker State—Background

Established in 1931, Quaker State has always been known as a leader in product innovation and in establishing motor oil standards. The founders of Quaker State pioneered one of the first brands of motor oil which was the oil of choice in the early days of the automobile. However, the PCMO environment has changed, and today Quaker State has lost both market share and past profit performance. In 1987, the company reported its first loss ever, $1.82 a share, and surrendered its number one market position to Pennzoil (See Exhibit 5). Overall, operating margins collapsed from 12.9 percent to 6.0 percent, reflecting deep product discounting. Quaker State's net income has fallen from profits of $50.3 million in 1986 to $14.9 million in 1988. The 1989 profits have fallen even further to $11.8 million on declining sales of $734.7 million. Within

EXHIBIT 5   Quaker State stock price

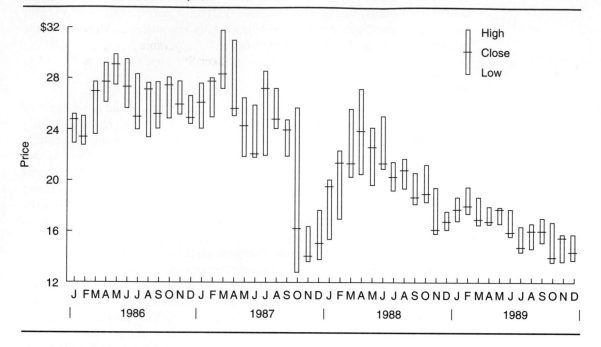

a 15-month period, the company switched chief executives three times.[4] These results have been disturbing for Quaker State and the marketing issues have not been resolved to restore past market share and operating profit performance.

Similar to other oil companies, Quaker State used the benefits of their abundant cash flow over the years to diversify their business away from the volatile motor oil business. Through various acquisitions, the firm is divided into five separate business units:

The petroleum operations still provide the majority of sales, profits, and proportionate assets. In order for Quaker State to have a successful recovery, the core motor oil business needs to be turned around.

		Percent	
1989 Data	*Sales*	*Profit*	*Assets*
1. Motor oil/auto	59%	41%	31%
2. Coal operations	13	22*	11
3. Insurance group	11	17	32
4. Truck-lite	7	20	6
5. Minit-lube, Inc.	10	0	20

*Includes +29 percent unusual item less −7 percent from operations.

---

[4]Kerry Hannon, "Run over by the Competition," *Forbes,* September 5, 1988, p. 80.

Quaker State's roots go back to the oil fields of Pennsylvania, first discovered at the turn of the century. The superior Pennsylvania crude oil enabled Quaker State to offer a premium-quality product, with refineries located near the producing fields in Pennsylvania. Today, the Pennsylvania fields are not nearly as productive as in prior years, and now Quaker State must obtain most of their raw materials from other sources.

Manufacturing

Motor oil is produced from a refined barrel of crude oil into a specialty product called a lube basestock. Typically, refinery production of lube basestock is less than 30 percent of all refinery output. The remaining 70 percent of the output is made up of gasoline, kerosene, and fuel oil, which can be sold to other consumer markets. The lube basestock is then blended with Quaker State's unique additive package and filled in the appropriate containers for consumer usage.

Quaker State's manufacturing facilities were designed to maximize motor-oil production, but overall this method of production is considered extremely inefficient. Essentially, 70 percent of their output is resold as undesirable products, with a break-even margin, at best. The major gasoline companies, on the other hand, maximize output streams by separating these streams and further refining the outputs into more valuable products.

Quaker State's cost structure on motor oil production has increased. The production inefficiencies have become more apparent as the availability of Pennsylvania-based crude oil has decreased and their outside purchases have increased. Recently it has been more efficient for Quaker State to purchase their lube basestock needs from the major gasoline companies and blend the motor oil at Quaker State packaging facilities. As a result, the future need of Quaker State's three refineries is extremely questionable. The 1987 loss included a $30 million write-down of assets related to the closure of the Ohio Valley Refinery. Their other refineries and some related plants have also been rumored to be on the auction block. Currently, it appears Quaker State's future will primarily be directed at blending and packaging their motor oil and marketing the product to consumers. Without raw material advantages, it is expected that this will increase their cost basis. However, it is probably the most attractive opportunity given the alternative—inefficiently producing motor oil with higher raw material costs and transportation costs.

Quaker State Marketing Strategies

In 1987, Quaker State realized the early results of a disastrous marketing strategy when it lost its number one market share to Pennzoil. With the assistance of the outside consulting firm, McKinsey & Co., management tried to force their distribution subsidiaries to carry Quaker State products exclusively, and to increase sales to mass merchandisers.[5] The company's profits plunged as its distributors

---

[5]Michael Schroeder, "Quaker State Switches into a Quick-Change Artist," *Business Week,* October 16, 1989, p. 126.

lost business to competitors with a larger variety of brands. In addition, distributors became increasingly upset with the company as the firm offered deep discounts to the mass merchandisers. The relationship between the motor oil distributors and Quaker State was significantly weakened in 1986.

Distribution

Jack W. Corn, a former distributor of the company's products, was brought in to turn the company around as the new president of Quaker State. He increased the company's investment in the firm's Minit-Lube shops, and he has attempted to patch up relations with the distributors. As noted in the 1988 annual report, Jack Corn stated:

> The first move we made was to change our program direction so that selling Quaker State would be attractive and profitable to independent distributors. In my opinion, that is the part of our business that has built consumer brand image and demand over the years. The independent distributors create the demand for the big mass merchandisers. And future demand depends on having a strong independent marketing force in as many markets as we can possibly have.[6]

In 1986, the company had 223 independent distributors handling their product. By 1988, the number of distributors dropped to 202. The firm appealed to their distributors by reversing past discount pricing strategies offered to the mass merchandisers. However, it is difficult to assess the extent of the damage done to the company's distribution network.

Pricing

In an effort to smooth the problems with the independent distributors, pricing policy became a critical issue. While pricing problems have always been a thorn in Quaker State's side, they became a larger problem. After discounting the company's products in 1986–87 and having several different price schedules for different consumers, Quaker State moved toward a uniform pricing policy. This meant that all customers, mass merchandisers, and distributors would pay comparable prices for the Quaker State products. However, in order to appease each of the distribution channels, Quaker State has priced their product in the low end of the motor oil price range (see Exhibit 4).

Products

The Quaker State product mix is illustrated in Appendix D. The product strategy for Quaker State has been to be a leader in product quality across all of their products. In 1988, the firm completed upgrading all of their motor oils to the highest

---

[6]Jack W. Corn, Quaker State, 1988 Annual Report, p. 15.

standards.[7] In 1989, Quaker State's 5W–30 and 10W–30 grades completed tests confirming that they qualify as "Energy Conserving II." This certified that these grades allowed motorists to achieve at least 2.7 percent greater mileage than a standard motor oil.[8]

Quaker State continues to improve product quality on a regular basis, and they anticipate matching any new product innovations that appear in the motor-oil market.

Packaging

Quaker State was one of the first major motor oils to change their product package from the can to the plastic bottle. In 1985, Quaker State also came up with an astute marketing innovation—a new easy-pour container. But its plastic can was round and hard to stack on store shelves. Pennzoil, 18 months later, produced a square container that fit more product on a tight shelf space. Quaker State was pushed aside, as it was less convenient to stack and reshelf.[9]

Minit-Lube Operations

Quaker State chose to expand its efforts in the quick-lube market with the additional acquisitions of quick-lube service centers. As of year-end 1989, the firm had over 450 Minit-Lube outlets either franchised or company owned. Mr. Corn has indicated that they would like to maintain a 60/40 percent owner/franchisee relationship.

The Minit-Lube outlets have focused their efforts on increasing the quality of service provided to customers. Quaker State is planning on a premium service worth a premium price. Quaker State has increased the prices at Minit-Lube operations to meet the high costs of the physical facilities.

Promotion

The promotion strategy for Quaker State has a focus for both the DIYer market and the installed market. First, the company continues to sponsor a racing program to demonstrate the high-quality attributes of the motor oil at major race events. Quaker State feels that the DIY user of motor oil is a "car-caring person who is intensely interested in auto racing."[10] The racing program has sponsored a number of racing events in NASCAR competition and international road races. The racing program emphasizes to DIYers the quality of Quaker State motor oil which can work for professionals, and, therefore, "it can work for you, too."

---

[7]Quaker State, 1988 Annual Report, p. 6.
[8]Quaker State, 1989 Annual Report, p. 6.
[9]Hannon, "Run over by the Competition," p. 80.
[10]Quaker State, 1988 Annual Report, p. 12.

Second, the company moved to enhance its position in the installed market by offering a lubrication limited warranty, available for new cars and good for 250,000 miles or 10 years (whichever comes first to the original owner)—see Appendix B. The warranty provides for repair or replacement of lubricated engine parts, provided certain rules are followed. The primary rule requires the owners to have their motor oil changed over 4,000 miles or four months by a professional installer who uses Quaker State.

Advertising

The emphasis on quality has been reduced in the 1990 print and commercial advertisements to stress Quaker State is "One Tough Motor Oil." This is supported with several different television advertisements emphasizing the 250,000-mile guarantee, NASCAR racing, and company testing of the product—sample advertisements are in Appendix B.

Appendix A   SAE Classifications

Over the years, the Society of Automotive Engineers (SAE) developed a classification system (Crankcase Oil Viscosity Classification—SAE J300–JUN 86) based on viscosity measurements. Thick, slow-flowing oils are assigned high numbers; thinner oils that flow more freely receive low numbers. Modified several times, the system establishes distinct motor oil viscosity grades: SAE OW, SAE 5W, SAE 10W, SAE 15W, SAE 20W, SAE 25W, SAE 20, SAE 30, SAE 40, and SAE 50.

EXHIBIT A–1   Viscosity: A measure of how much a fluid resists flowing. Motor oil is more viscous than water.

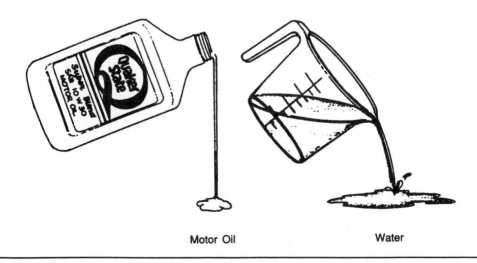

Motor Oil   Water

SAE: Society of Automotive Engineers

The "W" in the SAE grades stands for winter. Viscosity grades with the W classification are based on their maximum viscosity and borderline pumping temperatures at specific low temperatures. The W grades also are based on the minimum viscosity at $+100°C$. These oils are tested to ensure that they have proper flow characteristics and are suitable for use in cold seasons and climates. Oils without the W classification, on the other hand, are tested to ensure the proper viscosity at $+100°C$ only. Although SAE 20 and SAE 20W oils are separate classifications, each will generally meet the viscosity requirements of the other. Those that do meet the requirements are classified SAE 20W–20. This simple form of multigrading is one of the few possible without adding a viscosity index improver.

The viscosity index is an arbitrary scale in which oil from Pennsylvania crude is typically 100 and oils from naphthenic crudes are placed in the 0 to 70 range. These numbers are not related to the actual viscosity of the oil or its SAE number. Viscosity index numbers measure the change in viscosity as the operating temperatures change; the higher the number, the smaller the change. Motor oils used in a wide range of operating temperatures may have viscous polymers or polymeric compounds added to decrease this rate. Called "viscosity index improvers" because they raise the index number, these additives make possible the multigrade or "all-season" oils that have been marketed by U.S. oil companies for more than four decades.

Because the multigrades, such as SAE 5W–30, 10W–30, and 10W–40, are light enough to crank easily at low temperatures and heavy enough to perform well at high temperatures, they are among the most widely used motor oils. Table A–1 shows single and multigrade oils and the lowest temperatures at which they can be expected to perform satisfactorily.

TABLE A–1   SAE grades of motor oil*

Lowest temperature	Singlegrade oils	Multigrade oils
32°F/0°C	20, 20W, 30	10W–30, 10W–40, 10W–50, 15W–40, 20W–40, 30W–50
0°F/−18°C	10W	10W–30, 10W–40
Below 0°F/−18°C	5W	5W–20, 5W–30, 5W–40

*"Motor Oil Guide," American Petroleum Institute, Washington, D.C., 1982.

These grades refer to viscosity only and provide no information about the type or quality of an oil or its intended purpose. For this reason, another system was needed to take other factors into account. An early classification system developed by the American Petroleum Institute (API) classified engine oils as regular, premium, and heavy duty. A later API effort, in conjunction with the Society of Automotive Engineers (SAE) and the American Society for Testing and Materials (ASTM), described and classified the various service/engine-operating conditions as a basis for selecting the proper crankcase oil.

Engine Service Classifications

The changing requirements of the automobile industry, along with the need for more effective communication among engine manufacturers, the oil industry, and the consumer, led to a new API Engine Service Classification System. This system, developed by API, ASTM, and SAE, allows engine oils to be defined on the basis of performance characteristics and their intended types of service (see Table A–2). Together, the API and SAE systems define the characteristics of a motor oil to help consumer selection of appropriate products. Table A–3 shows the API classifications and SAE grades of Quaker State motor oils.

TABLE A–2   Service classification

Letter designation	API engine service description
SG	1989 gasoline engine warranty maintenance service. For passenger cars, vans, and light trucks beginning with the 1989 model year operating under manufacturer's recommended maintenance procedures. These oils provide improved control of engine deposits, oil oxidation, and engine wear relative to oils developed for previous categories. These oils also provide protection against rust and corrosion; they can be used where SF, SE, SF/CC, or SE/CC are recommended.
SF	1980 gasoline engine warranty maintenance service. For passenger cars and some trucks, beginning with 1980 models operating under engine manufacturers' warranties. These oils provide increased oxidation stability and better antiwear performance than the oils that meet the minimum requirements for the SE classification.
SE	1972 gasoline engine warranty maintenance service. For passenger cars and some trucks, beginning with 1972 (and some 1971 models) operating under engine manufacturers' warranties. These oils provide better protection than SC- and SD-classified oils.
SD	1968 gasoline engine warranty maintenance service. For passenger cars and some truck models operating under engine manufacturers' warranties in effect for model years 1968 through 1970, plus some 1971 or later models. These oils provide better protection than SC-classified oils.
SC	1964 gasoline engine warranty service. For passenger cars and some truck models operating under engine manufacturers' warranties in effect for model years 1964 through 1967.
SB	Minimum duty gasoline engine service. For engines operating under conditions mild enough to require only minimum protection through compounding.
SA	Formerly for utility gasoline and diesel engine service. For engines operated under conditions so mild that they do not need the protection of compounded oils; there are no performance requirements.
CE	Service typical of turbocharged or supercharged heavy-duty diesel engines manufactured since 1983 and operated under both low-speed, high-load and high-speed, high-load conditions. Oils designed for this service may also be used when previous API engine service categories for diesel engines are recommended.
CD-II	Service typical of two-stroke cycle diesel engines requiring highly effective control over wear and deposits. Oils designed for this service also meet all performance requirements of API Service Category CD.
CD-Diesel	Severe-duty diesel engine service. For certain naturally aspirated, turbocharged, or supercharged diesel engines in which effective control of wear and deposits is essential or when fuels ranging widely in quality (including high-sulfur content) are used. These oils provide protection from bearing corrosion and high-temperature deposits.
CC-Diesel	Moderate-duty diesel and gasoline engine service. For certain naturally aspirated, turbocharged, or supercharged diesel engines in moderate- to severe-duty service; also used for some heavy-duty gasoline engines.
CB-Diesel	Moderate-duty diesel engine service. For light- to moderate-duty diesel engines operating with lower-quality fuels that require greater protection against wear and deposits; occasionally used for light-duty gasoline engines.
CA-Diesel	Light-duty diesel engine service. For light- to moderate-duty diesel engines using high-quality fuels; sometimes used for gasoline engines in mild service.

TABLE A–3   Quaker State motor oils: SAE grades and API classifications

Product	SAE Grade	API Classification
Sterling	10W–30	SG–SF/CC–CD
Deluxe	10W–40	
Deluxe Performance	5W–30, 20W–50	
Super Blend	10W–30, 20W–40	SG–SF/CC–CD
HD	10W, 20W–20, 30, 40	
Turbo	10W–30	SG–SF/CC–CD
Regular	30	
Motorcycle Motor Oil (4-cycle)	20W–50	
HDX Universal Fleet	10W, 20W–20, 30, 40, 50 15W–40	CE, CD II, CD/SG–SF

Oil manufacturers are responsible for ensuring that a given motor oil has the performance characteristics essential for the recommended service classification(s). Engine manufacturers, on the other hand, are responsible for evaluating the class of service applicable to the engine's design and intended use and recommending the appropriate classification of oil for the engine. The consumer's responsibility lies in being aware of the engine manufacturer's recommendation and purchasing the proper oil.

Appendix B   Quaker State Advertising

EXHIBIT B–1

ONE TOUGH MOTOR OIL ANNOUNCES ONE TOUGH GUARANTEE...

250,000

TWO HUNDRED FIFTY THOUSAND MILES OR TEN YEARS.

Use Quaker State exclusively in your new car, and our limited guarantee will cover lubricated engine parts for 250,000 miles or ten years, whichever comes first.

How tough is today's Quaker State?

Tough enough to make this promise: Use only Quaker State in your new car's engine, and if any lubricated engine part not covered by the manufacturer's warranty or extended-service contract suffers an oil-related break-down during its first 250,000 miles or ten years, Quaker State will pay for the repair.

We'll guarantee lubricated parts in engines of all sizes—domestic or imported.

Quaker State's limited guarantee covers lubricated parts in engines of every single imported and domestic car or light truck sold in the United States. It even covers the deductible on any extended warranty you might have purchased from your new-car dealer. Enrollment is absolutely free.

See a copy of lubrication limited warranty and enrollment details at participating service centers.

Complete details and enrollment forms for the Quaker State 250,000-mile or ten-year guarantee are available at

participating Quaker State service centers. These include many new-car dealers, automotive service centers and fast lubes nationwide.

To participate in the guarantee program, enroll your new car at a participating service center within six months or 6,000 miles of purchase. Use only Quaker State Motor Oil, and have your oil and filter changed at a service center according to manufacturer's instructions for severe driving conditions but not to exceed 4,000 miles or four months between changes. Save your receipts.

How can Quaker State make a guarantee this tough?

Today's Quaker State has proven its toughness over and over again in the most rigorous tests that the world's auto makers have thrown at it. The result: Quaker State actually <u>exceeds</u> lubrication speci-fications for every single car sold in the United States. It takes a tough oil to offer a guarantee this tough. But Quaker State is One Tough Motor Oil.

 The Big Q is One Tough Motor Oil.

©1990 Quaker State Corporation. **DON'T POLLUTE. PLEASE DISPOSE OF USED MOTOR OIL PROPERLY.**

EXHIBIT B–2

QUAKER STATE --- ONE TOUGH MOTOR OIL BRINGS YOU A TOUGH NEW ADVERTISING CAMPAIGN!

EXHIBIT B–3

QUAKER STATE
ONE TOUGH MOTOR OIL
PRESENTS
A TOUGH ADVERTISING CAMPAIGN.

LEADERSHIP LEVELS OF QUAKER STATE
IMAGE ADVERTISING BEHIND OUR
"ONE TOUGH MOTOR OIL" THEME

- We will <u>dominate</u> television auto racing with our
  year round motor oil exclusivity on ESPN <u>and</u>
  major network races.

- We will <u>dominate</u> consumer magazines –
  automotive enthusiast, do-it-yourselfer,
  and outdoor publications.

- We will <u>dominate</u> broadcast advertising in
  major ADI's covering the U.S.

QUAKER STATE'S MEDIA SPENDING WILL BE UP +63% VERSUS 1989!

EXHIBIT B-4

"GUARANTEE"

LENGTH: 30 SECONDS

COMM'L NO.: QOAZ 0133

ANNCR: One tough motor oil announces one tough guarantee.

The Quaker State

250,000 mile or 10 year guarantee.

Register your new car at a participating service center.

Then use only Quaker State.

Have oil and filter changed as directed at a service center

and if any lubricated engine part suffers an oil related break down

within 250,000 miles

or 10 years

you're covered. Quaker State guarantees it in writing.

The Big Q

is one tough motor oil.

EXHIBIT B–5

"TESTED TOUGH"

LENGTH: 30 SECONDS

COMM'L NO.: QOAZ 0063

ANNCR: It's one of the most technologically advanced, most rigorously tested fluids on earth.

Relentlessly measured for maximum protection against the friction...(SFX)

the wear

and tear...(SFX)

the heat and stress of today's engines.

It is today's Quaker State.

In Europe, in Japan, in America

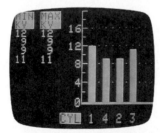

Quaker State quality has passed the most demanding tests

auto makers can throw at it.

At Quaker State we don't just say we're tough, we're tested tough.

The Big Q

is one tough motor oil.

EXHIBIT B–6

"TOUGH ENGINES"

LENGTH: 30 SECONDS

COMM'L NO.: QOAZ 0043

ANNCR: What makes a Quaker State engine so tough? One tough motor oil.

And being tough takes more than just talking tough.

There's a brand that says it's been engineered for smaller engines.

Well, Quaker State

has been tested tough for small engines

in Japan, in Europe and in America.

In fact, Quaker State has toughed out the most demanding specs

for every size engine in every size car sold in the U.S.

What makes any size Quaker State engine so tough?

Quality engineered Quaker State.

The Big Q

is one tough motor oil.

EXHIBIT B–7

"NASCAR"

LENGTH: 30 SECONDS

COMM'L NO.: QOAZ 0083

ANNCR: They got the green flag at Daytona.

Roared through Talladaga.

Left Darlington in the dust.

And which car piled up the most tough NASCAR miles in '89?

The Quaker State King Racing Buick.

Its engine getting maximum protection

from one tough motor oil. The same Quaker State you buy right off the shelf.

Only one car was tough enough to stack up NASCAR's highest mileage total.

Only one oil was tough enough to tough it out every single one of those miles.

Quaker State.

The Big Q

is one tough motor oil.

EXHIBIT B–8

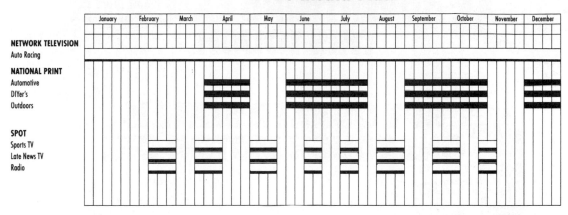

QUAKER STATE MOTOR OIL
1990 Media Plan

Ordering of Co-op Advertising Materials

To order materials call Customer Service at 1-800-759-2525 and give them the appropriate advertising material code number.

The following co-op advertising materials are available at no charge for use by case goods or bulk retailers:

	Order Code Number
Lube Warranty	
20 Second Television	3000559
45 Second Radio	3000560
30 Second Radio	3000561
16 1/2" x 11 1/4" Black & White Newspaper Ad	3000562
8 1/4" x 11 1/4" Black & White Newspaper Ad (Available 4/15)	3000563
Tested Tough (Beaker)	
20 Second Television	3000564
45 Second Radio	3000565
30 Second Radio	3000566
Tough Engines (Tested for all size engines)	
15 Second Television	3000568
45 Second Radio	3000569
30 Second Radio	3000570
Reprints of this Storyboard Handout	3000571
Copy of 1990 Ad Campaign Videotape	3000572

Retailers will have to produce their remaining portion of the co-op ad; plus buy and place the media. **All tags for these ads still must receive copy approval by Quaker State Marketing.** Please refer to the 1990 Retailer Merchandising Program for more information and details.

EXHIBIT B–9

IT TAKES A TOUGH OIL TO OFFER AN ADVERTISING CAMPAIGN THIS TOUGH.

BUT QUAKER STATE IS ONE TOUGH MOTOR OIL.

Appendix C

Annual income statement ($ millions)

	Dec. 1988	Dec. 1987	Dec. 1986	Dec. 1985	Dec. 1984
Sales	$869,104	$847,952	$899,065	$974,251	$924,630
Cost of goods sold	626,390	611,501	642,930	731,336	721,022
Gross profit	242,714	236,451	256,135	242,915	203,608
Selling, general, and administrative expense	190,977	183,958	139,716	132,037	114,780
Operating income before depreciation	51,737	52,493	116,419	110,878	88,828
Depreciation, depletion, and amortization	39,201	39,467	35,675	36,416	34,777
Operating profit	12,536	13,026	80,744	74,462	54,051
Interest expense	9,048	6,977	8,926	13,509	12,922
Nonoperating income/expense	8,341	11,744	18,070	18,752	10,322
Special items	5,804	−122,000	000	1,887	−24,695
Pretax income	17,633	−104,207	89,888	81,592	26,756
Total income taxes	2,700	−56,150	39,600	35,700	9,000
Minority interest	000	000	000	000	000
Income before extraordinary items and					
discontinued operations	14,933	−48,057	50,288	45,892	17,756
Extraordinary items	000	000	000	000	000
Discontinued operations	000	000	000	000	000
Net income	14,933	−48,057	50,288	45,892	17,756
Preferred dividends	000	000	000	000	000
Available for common	14,933	−48,057	50,288	45,892	17,756
Savings due to common stock equivalents	000	000	000	000	000
Adjusted available for common	$ 14,933	$−48,057	$ 50,288	$ 45,892	$ 17,756

Appendix D Quaker State's product mix

EXHIBIT D–1

Case 34

L.A. Gear*

September 13, 1989—The Los Angeles Palladium is packed with reporters waiting for L.A. Gear CEO Robert Y. Greenberg to formally introduce their new spokesperson, singer/entertainer Michael Jackson.

Taunted by rumors, the press wants to confirm the two-year, $20-million-plus stock option contract Jackson is reputed to have signed in exchange for starring in new commercials, wearing L.A. Gear footwear in his music videos, and designing a new line of apparel and shoes under their new 1990 campaign, UNSTOPPABLE.

Once the star appeared, however, he merely read a prepared statement about the alliance, blew a kiss to the crowd and left the stage, allowing no questions. Industry analyst Steven Levitt of Market Evaluations immediately cast doubts on the arrangement, predicting that Jackson would be valuable to L.A. Gear only if he sang in the commercials and if the target were narrowed to 6- to 11-year-old girls.

Thus, without direct confirmation on L.A. Gear's dealings, the press and the public were left to speculate on L.A. Gear's future marketing focus and strategy for the 90s for the $9 billion retail athletic footwear market, and its ability to achieve Greenberg's goal of "building the biggest brand name in the world."

Although Greenberg predicts that L.A. Gear will surpass both Reebok and Nike for sales within the next five years, there is still doubt within the industry that the upstart company will be able to successfully disseminate its trendy styles and its California moniker throughout the world.

Athletic Footwear Industry

The athletic footwear industry, expected to reach $5.4 billion in 1990, has seen rapid growth over the past 15 years, particularly during the past 5 years. Averaging 21 percent growth wholesale and 23 percent growth retail

---

*This case was written from public sources and from interviews with people knowledgeable about this industry by Joanne E. Novak, under the supervision of Thomas C. Kinnear. Copyright © 1990 by Thomas C. Kinnear.

between 1985 and 1990, the forces that have been driving the growth can be identified as:

- *Late 1970s*—The popularity of running.
- *Early 1980s*—The aerobics craze.
- *Early 1980s*—The emphasis on overall health and fitness.
  —The introduction of specialty shoes for each sport (basketball to boardsailing) or all sports (cross-training).
  —The emergence of technological innovations in material and design.
- *Late 1980s, early 1990s*—
  —The use of multimillion-dollar media campaigns and star-studded spokespeople.

From these trends, two distinct market segments have emerged—performance and fashion. There used to be classic, all-purpose, $15 sneakers—such as Converse "Chuck Taylor" All Stars, P.F. Flyers, and Keds—that could easily be replaced once they had worn out and that *never* would label their wearers as slaves to fashion. In the 90s, however, with numerous styles and new players vying for a piece of the market, athletic footwear can cost as much as $170 per pair and new styles appear every 8 to 10 months as manufacturers have decreased their new product introduction cycle. Today, athletic footwear is worn to make a statement.

Emergence of Fashion Segment

The development of the fashion segment began with "the runner's look." Running had become a popular sport, dominated by men, during the early 1970s. After American Frank Shorter won the gold medal for the marathon during the 1976 Olympics, however, many more Americans were inspired to run or jog for exercise. This boom created a demand for runners' apparel and running shoes—supplying growth to the athletic shoe industry from 1977 to 1983. The popularity of the sport eventually reached nonrunners who liked the image of the runner. This image spurred the purchase of running shoes for casual use and reflected the beginning of a nationwide trend toward a more casual lifestyle.[1]

The advent of aerobics in 1983 created a new fashion/fitness trend as women who aerobicized wanted apparel and footwear specific to the sport. They preferred stylish gear that was more comfortable, more colorful, and had more variety than traditional exercise outfits.

Thus, fashion was brought to the forefront and, for the first time, women were driving the market. By 1987, women bought sneakers more often than men and they bought more of them (Exhibits 1 and 2). The average woman in 1989 owned 2.6 pairs of sneakers compared with 2.5 pairs owned by the average man.

---

[1]Angela Hinton, et al., "Reebok and Nike: The Athletic Shoe Industry," University of Michigan Research Report for Prof. S. Hariharan, April 18, 1989.

EXHIBIT 1   Males/females purchases of athletic footwear (000s)

	Bought in last 12 months	Bought 1 pair	Bought 2 pairs	Bought >3 pairs
Males				
Total male population = 84,066				
Percent of total				
male population	20.80%	10.80%	6.00%	4.00%
Total buyers	17,467	9,105	5,027	3,336
Age 18–24	3,915	2,147	1,040	728
25–34	5,910	2,810	2,000	1,099
35–44	3,441	1,668	1,049	724
45–54	2,121	1,259	424	437
55–64	1,155	635	293	227
65+	925	584	220	122
Total shoes	>29,197	9,105	10,054	>10,008
Age 18–24	6,411	2,147	2,080	2,184
25–34	10,107	2,810	4,000	3,297
35–44	5,938	1,668	2,098	2,172
45–54	3,418	1,259	848	1,311
55–64	1,902	635	586	681
65+	1,390	584	440	366
Regions of Buying				
Northeast	4,346	2,258	1,279	809
Midwest	4,757	2,367	1,388	1,002
South	5,276	3,070	1,239	968
West	3,088	1,410	1,121	557
Females				
Total female population = 92,184				
Percent of total				
female population	28.20%	10.50%	6.30%	11.50%
Total buyers	26,033	9,636	5,827	10,571
Age 18–24	4,263	1,753	677	1,833
25–34	7,874	3,030	1,972	2,872
35–44	6,625	2,325	1,348	2,952
45–54	3,300	1,008	778	1,514
55–64	2,129	775	553	801
65+	1,841	745	498	559
Total shoes	>52,730	9,636	11,654	31,713
Age 18–24	8,606	1,753	1,354	5,499
25–34	15,590	3,030	3,944	8,616
35–44	13,877	2,325	2,696	8,856
45–54	7,106	1,008	1,556	4,542
55–64	4,284	775	1,106	2,403
65+	3,418	745	996	1,677
Regions of buying				
Northeast	6,809	2,449	947	3,413
Midwest	6,986	2,882	1,469	2,634
South	7,718	2,773	1,970	2,975
West	4,520	1,531	1,441	1,548

Source: Simmons, 1988.

EXHIBIT 2   Male/female spending patterns (000s)

Total male population = 84,066

Spending	Buyers	Percent who bought in last 12 months	Percent of total buyers
If men buy athletic footwear			
Spend < $15	4,032	23%	4.80%
Spend $15–$29	6,426	37	7.60
Spend ≥ $30	7,010	40	8.30

Total female population = 92,184
If women buy athletic footwear

Spend < $15	9,636	37%	10.50%
Spend $15–$29	5,827	22	6.30
Spend ≥ $30	10,571	41	11.50

77% of men who buy spend over $15.
63.5% of women who buy spend over $15.
Source: Simmons, 1988.

By the end of the decade, athletic footwear manufacturers were facing yet a different market. Inner-city kids began to define territories by brands of sneakers (i.e., on Boston's Intervale Street they would be seen only in Adidas sneakers, whereas Nike streets were Hamilton and Crawford); teenage girls developed sneaker etiquette, shunning boys donning sneakers incompatible with their own; and young urban professionals and teenagers bought several pairs of sneakers to match their wardrobes and their moods. They needed all-night dancing shoes, "impressing the ladies" shoes, and Saturday-at-the-park shoes to let their peers know they had style. As one teen simply said, "If I wear black, I wear black sneakers. If I wear red, I wear red sneakers. If I wear purple, I wear white sneakers."[2]

> Ten years ago, people had an average of 1.2 pairs of athletic shoes in their closets. In 1987, Reebok customers owned an average of 4.5 pairs. By the mid-90s, those same customers will own six to six and a half different pairs of sneakers apiece. Footwear will no longer be an accessory, it will be the main course.[3]
>
> Paul Fireman, *CEO,* Reebok

These wearers were shifting 40 percent of the athletic shoe demand (30 percent direct demand, 10 percent influential demand) to the 15- to 22-year-old age group and defining athletic footwear as *the* fashion statement.[4]

Acquisitions

Growth in the industry has been the result of not only these trends but also savvy marketing and new product design. Strength abroad and acquisitions of other footwear manufacturers has helped to grow market share (Exhibit 3). Reebok has

---

[2]"Much Ado About Rubber," CBS's *Sunday Today,* March 25, 1990.
[3]E. M. Swift, "Farewell My Lovely," *Sports Illustrated,* February 19, 1990, p. 80.
[4]Joseph Pereira, "The Well-Heeled," *The Wall Street Journal,* December 1, 1988, p. 1.

EXHIBIT 3   U.S. share of footwear market

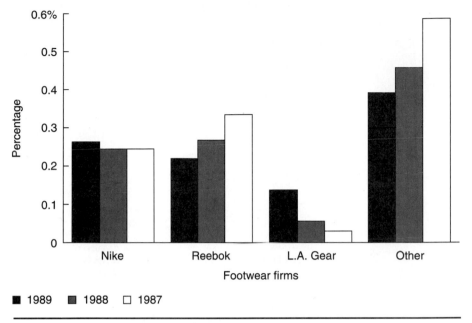

1989   1988   1987

Assumes total market = $9 billion.

brought several footwear manufacturers into its corporation: Rockport, 1985; Avia, 1987 (who previously bought Donnor, a hiking/walking shoe company, in 1986); Ellesse, 1987; Frye (boots), 1987; and Metaphors (women's casual shoes), 1987.

Interco, owner of the Florsheim brand, purchased Converse in 1986, and Yarsel Investment Corp. bought Pony (Exhibit 4).

Buyers

The athletic shoe manufacturers are forced to address the fashion issue. With their current penetration into the market at only 20 to 30 percent, footwear firms have a great potential to attract new buyers and penetrate the market further.

Buyers are not only serious athletes but also working women, casual or weekend athletes, and casual fashion wearers in search of comfortable, attractive shoes. Within each buyer segment, there are different priorities—performance, fashion, comfort, and price sensitivity—and for each buyer the priorities differ. Currently, 80 percent of all athletic shoe purchases are for casual use.[5]

---

[5]Ellen Paris, "Rhinestone Hightops, Anyone?" *Forbes,* March 7, 1988, p. 78.

EXHIBIT 4   Ownership of athletic footwear brands

Brand	Ownership
Adidas	Private
Autry	Private
Etonic	Private
Fila	Private
K–Swiss	Private
Kaepa	Private
Kangaroos	Private
Lotto	Private
New Balance	Private
Pony	Private
Spalding	Private
Tretorn	Private
Turntec	Private
Hyde	Public
L.A. Gear	Public
Nike	Public
Reebok	Public
Foot-Joy	Public, a division of American Brands
Converse	Public, a division of Interco
Avia	Public, a division of Reebok
Ellesse	Public, a division of Reebok
Keds	Public, a division of Stride-Rite
Brooks	Public, a division of Wolverine
Puma	Public, Germany
Asics Tigers	Public, Japan

Source: Drexel Burnham Lambert Industry Report, December 1987.

Additionally, more segments or subsegments have emerged within each segment: male/female; single sport user/multisport user; infant/toddler; young/old. Each of these subsegments has specific needs that they want addressed.

The market also can be segmented according to psychographic profiles. A recent Harvard Business School case study identified segments by athletic lifestyles: serious athletes, weekend warriors, and casual athletes. The case identified the serious athletes as the opinion leaders, prompting the manufacturers to cater to them. By satisfying this segment, it is assumed that other types of buyers would follow their lead.

Capabilities

The competition for these buyers has intensified. Nike and Reebok, the number one and number two U.S. market share holders, respectively, are fighting for more share in the media and the stores. They have invested millions of dollars on

EXHIBIT 5   Advertising and promotional expenditures (in $ millions)

	1986	1987	1988	1989	1990*
L.A. Gear	$2.6	$5.4	$12.6	$25	$50
Reebok		12	35	60	70
Nike	62.5	65.9	85.3	50	100

*Estimated for 1990.

For L.A. Gear, dollars include trade shows, trade and consumer publications (.12), merchandise, TV (.50), and specialty billboards. International advertising of $3 million is not included.

For Reebok, the $70 million is divided between $40 million domestic and $30 million in promotions. International advertising of $20 million is not included. Ten percent of expenditures in 1989 were for children's footwear.

For Nike, $25–$30 million will be spent on promotions in 1990.

Sources: Linda Williams, "On the Right Foot," *Los Angeles Times,* September 31, 1989, s. 4, p. 1.

"Reebok," *Adweek,* February 5, 1990, p. 12.

E. W. Swift, "Farewell My Lovely," *Sports Illustrated,* February 19, 1990, p. 80.

Nike 10–K 1988.

Reebok 10–K 1988.

David Jefferson, "Fashion Victim? L.A. Gear, Highflier in Sneakers, Discovers Perils of Shifting Fads," *The Wall Street Journal,* December 8, 1989, p. A16.

highly produced, star-studded media campaigns (Exhibit 5) and new product introductions that include air, color, and new materials (Exhibit 6). Reebok and Nike have been focused on performance, with technological attributes in the lead, for product differentiation.

This competition has forced a change to the product development and product life cycle for athletic footwear. The average product development cycle has been trimmed to 6 to 10 months, while the product life cycle has been shortened to 8 to 10 months. Nike is using CAD/CAM technologies to shorten their development time for the introduction of new products.

New styles appear with new technologies, materials, colors, or endorsers capitalizing on or creating the latest trends. For the buyer, there is more choice and more confusion about a brand and an athletic shoe's attributes. Also, with the possible eight-month turnaround for new styles—prices can conceivably rise every eight months. The largest retail hike in 1989 has been with basketball pump models retailing between $170 and $180. (Nike's Air Pressure, $175; Reebok's Pump, $170.)

Considering that the top three manufacturers use low-cost production facilities in South Korea and Taiwan and that it costs only $15 to $20 to manufacture a pair of sneakers that will retail at $60 to $100, in addition to manufacturing, the revenues from these athletic shoes support R&D, advertising and promotion, and company profits.

EXHIBIT 6   Reebok energy return system

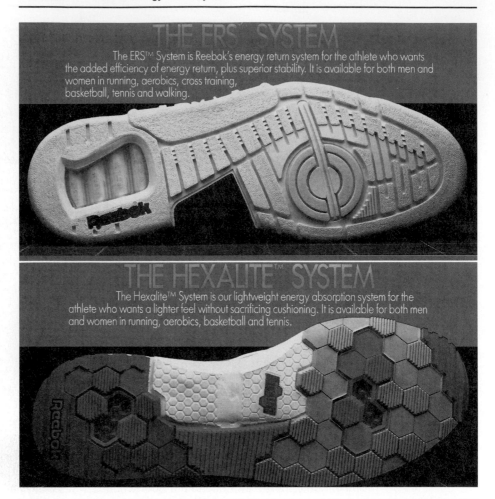

(continued)

EXHIBIT 6   *(concluded)*

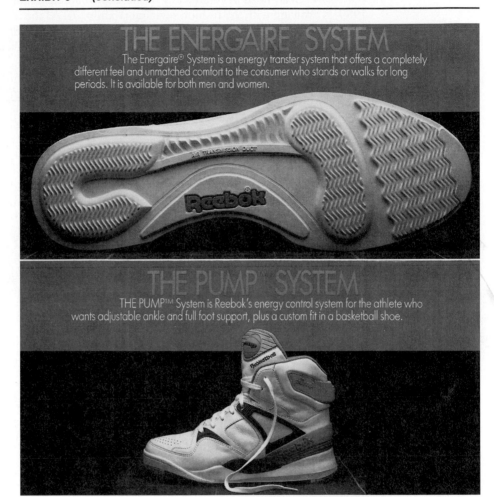

THE ENERGAIRE® SYSTEM

The Energaire® System is an energy transfer system that offers a completely different feel and unmatched comfort to the consumer who stands or walks for long periods. It is available for both men and women.

THE PUMP™ SYSTEM

THE PUMP™ System is Reebok's energy control system for the athlete who wants adjustable ankle and full foot support, plus a custom fit in a basketball shoe.

L.A. Gear, third in retail sales in the U.S. market, replacing Converse in 1989, is growing with the fashion segment (Exhibit 7). As the market expands to new users, however, old competitors (Keds, Converse, Adidas, and designers) are trying to capitalize on the industry's growth to recapture market share.

EXHIBIT 7   U.S. sales of athletic footwear

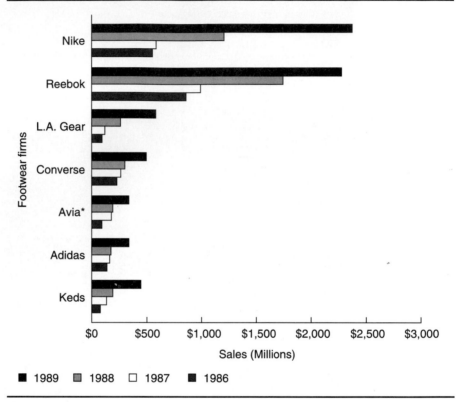

*Avia was purchased by Reebok in 1988.

With buyers willing to purchase several pairs of shoes for different uses, the market for performance shoes overlaps with the fashion shoe market. Thus, the two dimensions—fashion and performance—will not stay separated in the 90s. Manufacturers are faced with positioning themselves effectively in these markets to maintain, grow, or recapture market share.

Driving the 90s

Shoe design—with a technological or fashion emphasis—and advertising become two driving forces in the industry to support manufacturers' positioning. While technological innovations lead to a better-made shoe that has state-of-the-art fit and performance, heavy advertising and promotional activity serves to decrease brand blur and support manufacturers' unique images. The strength of a firm's R&D and image advertising is heavily correlated with leading market share and/or high sales growth.

L.A. Gear's performance over the past four years demonstrates how positioning and strategy can change the perceptions and performance of a company (Exhibit 8).

EXHIBIT 8   L.A. Gear financial statements

Statement of operations (in thousands)

	Year ended November 30				
	1988	*1987*	*1986*	*1985*	*1984*
Net sales	$223,713	$70,575	$36,299	$10,687	$9,007
Cost of sales	129,103	41,569	20,880	7,294	6,116
Gross profit	94,610	29,006	15,419	3,393	2,891
General and administrative expenses	54,024	20,559	10,263	2,722	2,685
Interest/factoring expenses	4,102	1,110	686	526	368
Provision for loss from litigation	0	0	2,295	0	0
Royalty income	−856	−604	−1,210	−285	−65
Earnings (loss) before income taxes, discontinued operations, and extraordinary item	37,340	7,941	3,385	430	−97
Income tax benefit (expense)	−15,310	−3,570	−1,634	−199	45
Earnings (loss) before discontinued operations and extraordinary item	22,030	4,371	1,751	231	−52
(Loss) from discontinued operations, net of income carryforward	0	0	−6	−31	−392
Earnings (loss) before extraordinary item	$ 22,030	$ 4,371	$ 1,745	$ 200	($444)
Extraordinary item—use of net operating loss carryforward	0	0	0	133	0
Net earnings (loss)	$ 22,030	$ 4,371	$ 1,745	$ 333	($444)

Consolidated balance sheet data L.A. Gear, Inc., and subsidiaries (in thousands)

	November 30	
	1988	*1987*
Assets		
Cash	$ 4,205	$ 3,245
Accounts receivable	49,526	15,148
Inventory	66,556	15,813
Prepaid expenses and other current assets	3,383	951
Total current assets	$123,670	$35,157
Property, equipment, net	3,110	
accumulated depreciation		1,010
Deferred tax charges	1,034	14
Other assets	1,019	613
Total assets	$128,833	$36,794

(continued)

EXHIBIT 8 *(concluded)*

Consolidated balance sheet data L.A. Gear, Inc., and subsidiaries *(in thousands)*

	November 30	
Liabilities and Shareholders' Equity		
Current liabilities:		
Line of credit	$ 57,230	$ 7,126
Accounts payable	7,748	3,886
Accrued expenses and other liabilities	10,029	585
Accrued loss from litigation	2,373	2,341
Accrued compensation	5,927	414
Income tax payable	4,217	323
Total current liabilities	$ 87,524	$ 14,675
Shareholders' equity		
Common stock	n/a	n/a
Preferred stock	n/a	n/a
Additional paid-in capital	13,008	15,848
Retained earnings	28,301	6,271
Total shareholders' equity	$ 41,309	$ 22,119
Total liabilities and shareholders' equity	$128,833	$ 36,794

L.A. Gear, Inc., and subsidiaries' consolidated statement of income and retained earnings *(thousands)*

	Three months ended February 28	
	1990	*1989*
Net sales	$187,281	$66,070
Cost of sales	113,605	37,486
Gross profit	73,676	28,584
Selling, general, and administrative expenses	46,498	17,419
Operating income	27,178	11,165
Interest expense, net	4,013	2,118
Income before income taxes	23,165	9,047
Income tax expense	9,266	3,689
Net income	$13,899	$5,358
Weighted average shares	20,022	17,311
Earnings per share	$0.69	$0.31

Source: L.A. Gear press release, February 1990.

Net sales increased 217 percent from 1987 to 1988 due to not only higher wholesale prices but also the number of shoes that were purchased—4.4 million units to 10.1 million units (Exhibit 9). Internationally, sales increased from $2.3 million to $20.5 million—a 791 percent gain.

By 1990, sales forecasts for L.A. Gear are projected to exceed $1 billion (Exhibit 10). First quarter 1990 results for revenue already show L.A. Gear exceeding industry analysts' forecasts of $160 million to $165 million. Their revenue grew 257 percent—from $66.1 million to $170 million.[6]

---

[6]"Nike, L.A. Gear, Reebok Are Expected to Post Increased 1st Quarter Earnings," *The Wall Street Journal,* March 29, 1990, p. A4.

EXHIBIT 9 U.S. sales of footwear market

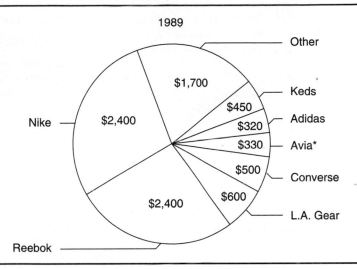

1989

Other — $1,700

Nike — $2,400

Keds — $450

Adidas — $320

Avia* — $330

Converse — $500

L.A. Gear — $600

Reebok — $2,400

*Avia was purchased by Reebok in 1988.

EXHIBIT 10 L.A. Gear sales

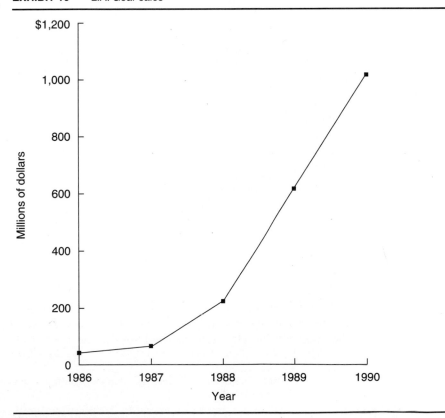

Note: Figure for 1990 was an estimate.

Greenberg notes, however,

> To achieve increased market penetration and to ensure that we meet the large customer demand for our products, we sold certain styles in the first quarter [1990] at gross profit margins lower than the Company's historic norms.
>
> This decision had its intended effect, increasing market share and retail shelf space for new styles . . . sales during the quarter were substantially in excess of analysts' expectations and the Company's gross and net profit margin percentages decreased somewhat during the period.[7]

By increasing their advertising and trade show presence during the late 1980s and increasing their marketing efforts in large department stores, L.A. Gear developed a stronger push strategy to help increase primary demand for their athletic and athletic-styled leisure footwear.

L.A. Gear's success has been reflected in its stock price (Exhibit 11). Previously considered only a trendy valley girl shoe company, L.A. Gear had the best performing stock in 1989, showing an increase of 185 percent total return to investors.

EXHIBIT 11   L.A. Gear common stock sale prices

	Sales prices	
	Low	High
1987		
First quarter	$ 1.63	$ 3.07
Second quarter	2.32	3.28
Third quarter	2.16	3.16
Fourth quarter	1.72	3.47
1988		
First quarter	$ 1.85	$ 4.47
Second quarter	3.91	6.97
Third quarter	5.82	9.88
Fourth quarter	8.38	11.38
1989		
First quarter	$10.00	$17.56
Second quarter	15.07	26.32
Third quarter	25.75	33.75
Fourth quarter	29.94	45.75

Note: Prices adjusted for an August 1988 and September stock split.
Source: L.A. Gear 10–K Report, February 28, 1990.

L.A. Gear

L.A. Gear found a niche in the fashion segment of the 1986 $5 billion athletic footwear industry and exploited it. Known as Good Times Industries until 1985, the company initially designed and sold roller skate shoes and owned roller

---

[7]L.A. Gear Press Release: L.A. Gear, Inc., Reports Significant Increases in Revenue and Net Income for First Quarter, 1990.

palaces. In 1983, the company introduced a canvas tie-on shoe with a flat rubber bottom from South Korea and called it The Street Walker. By 1985, the company—now L.A. Gear—had $10.7 million in sales of women's aerobic shoes and leather athletic-styled leisure shoes.

Greenberg says, "I was watching the popularity of athletic shoes as casual shoes."[8] As athletic shoes ceased to be worn for running and jumping, L.A. Gear provided shoes for wearers who chose athletic shoes as their casual shoe of choice. L.A. Gear now has an extensive product line (Exhibit 12).

An entrepreneur by nature, Greenberg began his retailing career in the 1960s selling wigs to beauty shops in Boston. He moved on to selling Wild Oats jeans to department stores in the 1970s, and in 1979 licensed Steven Spielberg's *E.T.* for use on kids' shoelaces. That venture reaped $3 million in 90 days.

Greenberg prides himself on being able to spot trends in his market and continues to introduce products that will appeal to his current customers. He readily acknowledges that designing for trends that take hold of young women can be risky, but he believes that if L.A. Gear stays in close touch with its shoe buyers, the company will only grow. Greenberg himself meets with his customers regularly—when he occasionally poses as a shoe salesman in a nearby mall.

Greenberg hopes to make L.A. Gear "America's No. 1 family brand" and has helped to generate enthusiasm for his goal—beginning with his executive officers (Exhibit 13). He has preprinted tee shirts and caps that say "L.A. Gear 1 in '91" for his executives.

Jonathan Ziegler, industry analyst with Sutro and Company, attributes L.A. Gear's success to good advertising and merchandising in Southern California. By placing their advertisements on MTV and cable stations, he says, L.A. Gear played to their target—the young female who would wear skirts and athletic shoes.[9]

> They identified a niche—the valley girl niche. . . . It's sort of like women in Reeboks and business suits. L.A. Gear hit the juniors with casual clothes and sneakers. It's not a technical shoe that would impress Michael Jordan [Chicago Bulls basketball star], but a fashion shoe that's got more look than technology.[10]
>
> John Horan—Publisher,
> *Sports Goods Management News*

As of 1988, L.A. Gear had 4.7 percent market share and currently has a 13 percent share. "There's no doubt that it was the name that caught on," says Gilbert Schwartzberg, executive vice president, L.A. Gear. "It has a magic to it . . . we are trying to capture that magic."[11]

---

[8]Linda Williams, "L.A. Gear Posts Huge Increases in Second Quarter Earnings," *Los Angeles Times,* June 29, 1988, s. 4, p. 1.

[9]Ibid.

[10]Ibid.

[11]Carl Lazzareschi, "A Great Leap Forward for L. A. Gear," *Los Angeles Times,* April 30, 1989, s. 4, p. B26.

EXHIBIT 12 L.A. Gear, Inc., product mix

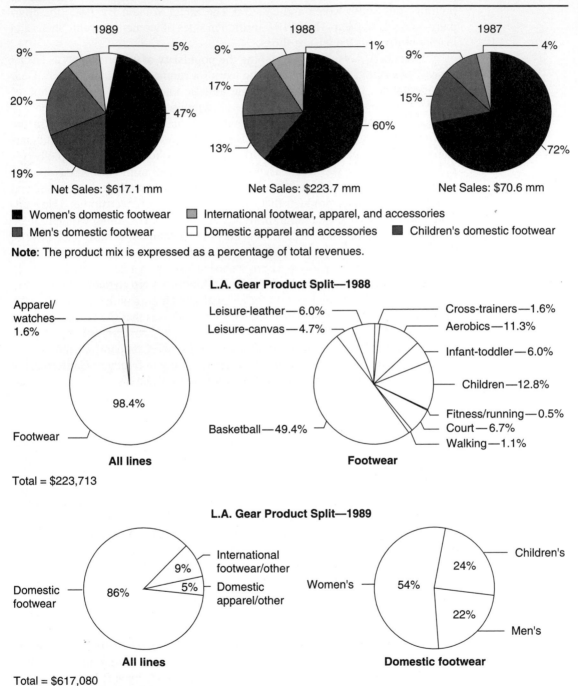

1989
Net Sales: $617.1 mm

9% — 5% — 47% — 19% — 20%

1988
Net Sales: $223.7 mm

9% — 1% — 17% — 60% — 13%

1987
Net Sales: $70.6 mm

9% — 4% — 15% — 72%

- ■ Women's domestic footwear
- ■ International footwear, apparel, and accessories
- ■ Men's domestic footwear
- □ Domestic apparel and accessories
- ■ Children's domestic footwear

Note: The product mix is expressed as a percentage of total revenues.

L.A. Gear Product Split—1988

Apparel/watches—1.6%

98.4%

Footwear

All lines

Total = $223,713

Leisure-leather—6.0%
Leisure-canvas—4.7%
Cross-trainers—1.6%
Aerobics—11.3%
Infant-toddler—6.0%
Children—12.8%
Fitness/running—0.5%
Court—6.7%
Walking—1.1%
Basketball—49.4%

Footwear

L.A. Gear Product Split—1989

Domestic footwear

86%
9% International footwear/other
5% Domestic apparel/other

All lines

Total = $617,080

Women's — 54%
Children's — 24%
Men's — 22%

Domestic footwear

Source: L.A. Gear press release, February 1990.

EXHIBIT 13   Corporate personnel (as of February 1989)

Full-time employees	431
Corporate management	42
Administration	38
Advertising and promotion	13
R & D	16
Sales, customer service	39
Jeanswear	3
Watches	1
International operations	13
Overseas offices	36
Technical reps	4
Warehousing	226
Directors and executive officers	*Age*
Allan E. Dalshaug, director	56
Robert Y. Greenberg, chairman of the board, president and director	48
Elliot J. Horowitz, executive vice president, chief financial officer and director	42
Sandy Saeman, executive vice president, secretary and director	41
Richard W. Schubert, director	37
Gil N. Schwartzberg, executive vice president and chief administrative officer	46
Stephen Williams, executive vice president	52
Donald B. Wasley, vice president—promotions	41
Larry Clark, vice president—product sourcing	31
Sudeepto Killick Datta, vice president—international operations and licensing	29
Ralph Hulit, vice president—marketing	45
Angelo Maccano, vice president—research and development	41
Ralph W. Polce, vice president—sales	50

Their tactic was to target their products to women, mainly teenagers, and stress the style of California. In its design studio, dozens of artists between ages 20 and 30 churn out prototypes with potential fads for the future. Their shoes are splashed with color, multiple laces, inlaid rhinestones, fringes, colored cutouts, neon trim, marbleized leather, vibrant lace colors, silver buckles, and leather lattices.

They exuded the Southern California lifestyle of "fun, colorful, fresh, and young," according to former L.A. Gear CFO Elliot Horowitz. By making themselves popular with trend-seeking women from coast to coast, L.A. Gear has developed a stronghold in the fashion segment.

L.A. Gear attributes their success to their ability to identify and respond promptly to changes in consumer preferences. Sales have skyrocketed from $9 million in 1984 to $223 million in 1988 to $600 million in 1989.

L.A. Gear believes their initial toehold into the market was due to Reebok's initial success in developing the demand for athletic shoes for women. With their soft-leather Freestyle aerobic shoes, they developed a strong niche. In 1986, however, when a fire devastated their Korean contract manufacturing plant, they had a shortage of inventory, and L.A. Gear stepped in with its soft-leather fashion shoe. Thus, L.A. Gear entered the industry in the fashion segment and positioned themselves to challenge Reebok on the fashion front.

Manufacturing

L.A. Gear manufactures their shoes using independent producers in Pusan, South Korea, and Taichung, Taiwan. The producers contract the manufacturing on a purchase order basis from L.A. Gear's Korean and Taiwan offices. Specifications for the shoes are predetermined in Los Angeles by management and a production design staff. The 32-member Korean staff and 4-member Taiwan staff only inspect the finished goods prior to shipment and arrange for the shipments.

L.A. Gear does not have a master manufacturing agreement with its producers, and they compete with other shoe companies, such as Reebok and Nike, for production capability. (Adidas, however, is unique and directly manufactures more than 6 percent of its products.) In fiscal 1988, L.A. Gear used 21 producers in Korea and 4 in Taiwan, 6 of which accounted for 57 percent of their total production.[12]

Distribution

L.A. Gear distributes its products in department stores, shoe stores, specialty stores, and sporting goods stores. Unlike its key competitors, Nike and Reebok, who rely on sporting goods outlets for 80 percent of their sales, L.A. Gear does not rely on any customer for more than 10 percent of total sales.[13]

L.A. Gear uses heavy promotions to create brand image and pull the buyers into the stores. Greenberg hopes to export that image and license it, predicting a Japanese opportunity of 500,000 pairs of sneakers sold to young women and teens. Greenberg says, "I want the distributor to set the course for the brand name to grow. If it's in lots of shoe store windows, then people will knock on our door asking to make L.A. Gear products—the name can go on anything."[14] In 1987, seven U.S. licensees put L.A. Gear's name on everything from doll clothes to sunglasses.

Sales

Domestic. L.A. Gear divides their sales into four divisions: (1) department stores and women's shoe stores, (2) sporting goods stores and athletic footwear stores, (3) men's stores, and (4) children's shoe stores. They use 102 independent, regional individual sales representatives divided among those divisions and employ their own national sales manager plus three to six regional sales managers per division. L.A. Gear employees sell L.A. Gear merchandise exclusively. This sales force calls on the trade and offers to assist in training their salespeople.

Additionally, L.A. Gear employs five national account managers and 14 technical representatives who assist in marketing. They are responsible for improved product displays and point-of-purchase advertisements.

---

[12]L. A. Gear 10–K Report, p. 8.
[13]L. A. Gear 10–K Report, p. 7.
[14]Ellen Paris, "Rhinestone Hightops, Anyone?" p. 78.

Since Reebok and Nike are offering the same services, the trade can be overwhelmed with the manufacturers' persistent sales and marketing forces. As the number of styles and shoes increase, their relationship with the trade becomes crucial since they control the limited shelf space. Many small retail outlets cannot stock all of the different footwear categories and hundreds of styles (Exhibit 14).

EXHIBIT 14   L.A. Gear product categories (as of first quarter 1989)

Type	Introduction date	Retail price range for selected styles	
Basketball	Apr. 1986	Shooter	$39.90
		B–424	77.90
Children's	Jun. 1985	Workout	19.90
		B–527	55.90
Aerobic	Feb. 1985	L.A. Impact	43.90
		CMR Trainer	55.90
Leisure	Feb. 1985	Canvas—Workout	21.90
		Surf Cat	37.90
		Leather—Westwood	29.90
		High Beach	53.90
Court (tennis, squash, racketball)	Sep. 1985		39.90
		T Slammer	61.90
		L.A. PRO	
Infant/toddler	Jun. 1986	Gidget	17.00
		Kids Rawhide	47.90
Walking	Dec. 1986	Streetwalker	23.90
		Imperial	59.90
Fitness/running	Aug. 1985 (men)	Skateboard	23.90
	Nov. 1986 (women)	Bandett 2	49.90
Apparel (312 combinations)	Oct. 1987 (men, jr. women)		
	Feb. 1989	Tees	
		Tank Tops	
		Sweatshirts	
		Sweatpants	
		Sweatshorts	
Jeanswear	Aug. 1988 (jr. women)	Pants	
		Jackets	
	Feb. 1989	Shorts	
		Skirts	
Watches (7 styles) (25 combinations of styles and colors)	Nov. 1988 (teen, jrs.)	Quartz/analog	$36–$38

Source: L.A. Gear 10–K, February 28, 1989.

L.A. Gear has only recently been able to penetrate the specialty store. They believe this penetration has been facilitated by their "open stock" system. This system lets retailers order as few as four pairs of shoes in any size, style, or color. According to Schwartzberg, they fill the order from their own inventory instead of reordering from the factory and are able to meet their customers' needs quickly.[15]

---

[15]L.A. Gear Press Release: Strategies for Continued Growth, 1990.

L.A. Gear has begun to diversify by entering the men's and children's market in 1986; the apparel market with sweatshirts, T-shirts, and shorts in 1987; and the watch and jean market in 1988.

Their watches are sold through six independent, regional sales representatives and some footwear sales representatives. Apparel is sold through 20 individual, regional sales representatives and some footwear sales representatives. Eight of these independent, regional representatives also sell Jeanswear. L.A. Gear employees sell watches, apparel, and Jeanswear, exclusively.

International. L.A. Gear only began selling overseas to Japan, Switzerland, and Germany in 1987. They now have agreements with 43 distributors in 77 countries for distribution of footwear and apparel. By 1991, they intend to be selling in 100 countries including the Soviet Union. They sell domestic designs in most foreign markets but have occasionally modified their product design in consideration of cultural norms.

After they had put a significant emphasis on international operations in early 1989, net sales from international operations increased from $2.3 million (3.3 percent of net sales) in fiscal 1987 to $20.5 million (9.2 percent of net sales) in fiscal 1988 to $52 million (8.67 percent of sales) in 1989. Killick Datta, vice president in charge of international operations and licensing, expects 1990 sales to reach $110 million. In five years, he predicts sales of $500 million. For 1988, approximately 61 percent of sales were in Canada, Japan, Italy, and England.

In early 1990, L.A. Gear signed a letter of intent with the Asics corporation of Japan for the marketing of L.A. Gear products in Japan. Greenberg indicated that Asic's strong distribution channel, their resources, and their selling experience in Japan would complement L.A. Gear's marketing skills and would help to get L.A. Gear products into the market quickly.

Distributors are given exclusive rights to distribute L.A. Gear to retailers in their specific geographic areas, but to maintain consistency in advertising and promotions, all materials they use must be approved in Los Angeles. Distributors, under the L.A. Gear contract, agree to spend 5 percent of their sales on advertising; they actually spend closer to 10 percent.

Datta believes L.A. Gear's utilization of distributors rather than an international sales force is not a deficiency in their strategy. He believes their distributors know the market "as well as you do or better."[16]

Although L.A. Gear considers their relationships abroad to be strong, they realize Reebok, Nike, and Adidas [industry leader worldwide] are more established in international markets and have greater financial resources at their disposal.

---

[16]Rose Horowitz, "Sports Shoe Makers in U.S. Lace Up for Global Race," *Journal of Commerce,* November 27, 1989, p. 5A.

Marketing

L.A. Gear conducts extensive marketing research—product testing, focus groups, store and consumer interviews, and surveys—to help determine designs and technological attributes consumers want and to evaluate the feasibility of expanding existing product lines. Besides point-of-purchase promotions, L.A. Gear channels their research findings into new product designs and image-oriented advertising.

They have developed the 12- to 25-year-old-market with their rhinestone-studded, pink and white basketball shoes, and they continue to make styles incorporating different gadgets. "Technical is another word for gadgetry," says Greenberg, "and we have gadgets in our products."[17] Further, he says, "whether they're technically fashionable or fashionably fashionable, it's all the same thing. . . . Everyone is playing the same game. I just say it."

In 1990, L.A. Gear will spend $50 million on footwear advertising with a heavy concentration on television. The remainder of their dollars will go to trade shows, consumer publications, merchandising, and specialty billboards (Exhibit 5).

L.A. Gear has built a 28,000-square-foot trade show booth with over 50 areas where they can show customers their products and write orders. The booth includes replicas of famous Los Angeles landmarks—the Beverly Hills and Bonaventure hotels, the Forum, the Coliseum, Santa Monica Pier, and City Hall—and illustrates L.A. Gear's commitment to the trade and various shows to spotlight their products.

Reebok and Nike have the resources to outspend L.A. Gear, but in the past, L.A. Gear has been able to effectively target a segment with their fashion message and build product image and brand awareness. As Elliot Horowitz, former CFO of L.A. Gear, says, "You get to a point where you can spend enough money on advertising and promotion that retailers will have to carry the brand. L.A. Gear has passed the critical mark where they are here to stay."[18]

For smaller players, the advertising war means more lost dollars in sales. Gary Jacobson, analyst for Kidder Peabody, estimates that the big three—Nike, Reebok, and L.A. Gear—will take another $250 million from the smaller makers. He adds, "If I were a small company, I'd be shaking in my shoes. No small company has the marketing dollars to compete nor the research and development dollars to thrive in a business built on the next big gimmick."[19]

As a solid player in the fashion segment, getting 75 percent of their sales from 15- to 25-year-old women, however, industry analysts caution that if L.A. Gear intends to go beyond $600 million in sales, they will need to be a major player in the men's market. In 1988, 10 percent of their market was sold to men and 15 percent to children. Industry analysts ask: "How long will women want to wear basketball shoes?"

"I may still have some reservations that they can just go in and penetrate that men's market," says James Hines, vice president and corporate director of marketing

---

[17]Ellen Benoit, "Lost Use," *Financial World,* September 20, 1988, pp. 28–31.
[18]Linda Williams, "On the Right Foot," *Los Angeles Times,* September 31, 1989, s. 4, p. 1.
[19]"Nike, L.A. Gear, Reebok Are Expected to Post Increased 1st Quarter Earnings," p. A4.

for footwear at Oshman's sporting goods chains. "It's pretty hard to go in from a dead start and compete." Greenberg sees it another way: "We are predators. Predators look at someone who has a nice big market share, go after it, and take it."[20]

For 1989, 23 percent of their sales were made to men, up from 10 percent in 1988. That is a small percentage attributable to men compared to their competitors with a 70 percent share. For 1990, analysts predict 40 percent of L.A. Gear's sales will be made up of men's footwear. Fifteen percent of L.A. Gear's sales are for children's shoes, and most of their buyers (men and women) have been leisure, nonathletic wearers. Competitors' product splits are shown in Exhibits 15 and 16.

EXHIBIT 15   Reebok product split—1988

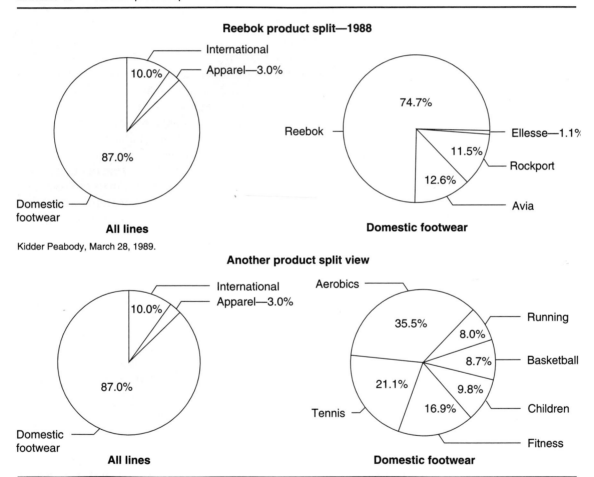

Reebok product split—1988

All lines

Kidder Peabody, March 28, 1989.

Another product split view

All lines

Domestic footwear

Reebok, 1989 Annual Report.

[20]Jobeth Daniel, "L. A. Gear Tries Full Court Press," *New York Times,* September 16, 1989, s. 3, p. F4.

EXHIBIT 16   Nike product split—1988

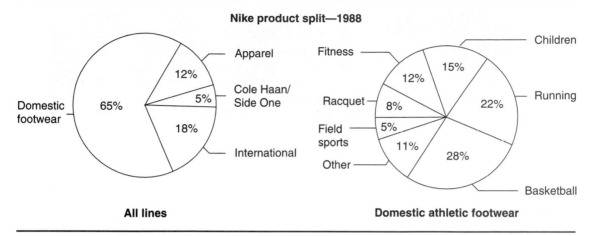

Nike product split—1988

All lines

Domestic footwear 65%

Apparel 12%

Cole Haan/ Side One 5%

International 18%

Domestic athletic footwear

Fitness 12%

Children 15%

Running 22%

Racquet 8%

Field sports 5%

Other 11%

Basketball 28%

Kidder Peabody, March 28, 1989; Nike, 1989 Annual Report.

Advertising

Greenberg had begun to follow the leaders with high-performance athletes as endorsers in late 1988 when he signed L.A. Laker's Kareem Abdul-Jabbar as spokesman. "We could have gone out and got some hotshot, but we wanted the Ambassador of Basketball," says Sandy Saeman, executive vice president, L.A. Gear. "Until someone else comes along who has played for 21 years, Kareem will be the ambassador."[21]

Featured in advertisements for Court Fire, Abdul-Jabbar continues to appear as their performance ambassador in the 1990 UNSTOPPABLE campaign (Exhibit 17). Industry analysts believe, however, "Jabbar will not be able to persuade serious athletes to wear L.A. Gear. Their male market is the boyfriends of the women buying hotshot—the men more concerned about making a fashion statement."

Additionally, L.A. Gear has enlisted L.A. Laker Mychal Thompson, Houston Rocket Akeen Olajuwon, Utah Jazz Karl Malone, and San Francisco 49er/Super Bowl MVP Joe Montana for their performance image. Montana, signed in 1990, will be marketing their Muscle High cross-training shoes.

Other members of their all star team include: Gary Grant, L.A. Clippers; Winston Garland, Golden State Warriors; Craig Hodges, Chicago Bulls; Scott Hastings, Detroit Pistons; Kenny "Sky" Walker, New York Knicks; Paul Pressey, Milwaukee Bucks; Purvis Short, New York Nets; Jedric Toney, Atlanta Hawks; Byron Nix, Indiana Pacers; and ESPN's "Body in Motion" star, Gil Janklowicz. L.A. Gear also utilizes noncelebrity advertising for 1990 (Exhibit 17).

---

[21]"Even without Layups Kareem Is a Shoo In," *Los Angeles Times,* January 17, 1989, s. 4, p. 20.

EXHIBIT 17   L.A. Gear advertising

EXHIBIT 17   *(concluded)*

Even though some industry analysts doubt Abdul-Jabbar's credibility as a performance spokesperson and see L.A. Gear's investment in celebrities as promoting a fashion image, with the signing of athletes L.A. Gear signals a clear indication of its step into the performance arena.

Fashion, however, will continue to be the main thrust of the company, and more ads will appear featuring children (Exhibit 18). Celebrities used to promote the fashion image are Heather Locklear, Priscilla Presley, and Michael Jackson. Greenberg does not see an identity blur for its customers. "This company is not a sporting goods company like Nike and Reebok. It's a fashion company. It's about looking pretty for women and looking good for men." He disagrees with industry analysts who claim the signing of Michael Jackson draws a clear line to teenagers and will clash with the image they are trying to create with Abdul-Jabbar.

For the spring of 1990, L.A. Gear has produced a black and white hightop similar to the space boot worn by Michael Jackson in his movie *Captain Eo,* with L.A. Gear embossed on the shoe in five places. More Jackson apparel and footwear under the MJ line will be incorporated throughout the next two years. Jackson's first commercial is scheduled for August 1990.

L.A. Gear produces their advertising in-house under the direction of Saeman, except for Hispanic and international business. Saeman indicated that Michael Jackson made the agreement with L.A. Gear since their creative process is tightly controlled.

Dissatisfaction in early March 1990 prompted Saeman to dismiss their agency with their Hispanic business and to contemplate hiring another agency or also bringing that business in-house.

Competitors

Others with strong positions in the performance arena are Nike, Adidas, and Converse. Nike's million dollar advertising campaigns in the past, Revolution in Motion (1988) and Just Do It (1989, 1990) have become the epitome of strong performance positioning.

Nike. Nike contracted with Chicago Bull Michael Jordan for another seven-year contract ($19 million) to market their Air line, enlisted baseball/football athlete Bo Jackson to promote their cross-training shoes, and signed Joan Benoit Samuelson to advertise their running shoes. Their past campaigns have stressed their state-of-the-art technology in a superior performance shoe.

Nike CEO Philip Knight, age 52, a University of Oregon graduate, started Blue Ribbon Sports in 1964 with Bill Bowerman, 78, his former track coach, to give the public these state-of-the art performance shoes. They imported and distributed Japanese-made Tiger brand track shoes, and in 1972 designed and introduced their own line. His goal was to finely tune shoes to human motion and physiology, and he began with a waffle iron sole.

EXHIBIT 18   L.A. Gear advertising

(continued)

EXHIBIT 18 *(continued)*

EXHIBIT 18   *(continued)*

EXHIBIT 18   *(concluded)*

Their sales have grown from $270 million in 1980 to $2,400 million in 1989. Knight saw his market share sink [...] and 1988, prompting him to decentralize decision making [...] Realizing that marketing and sales were taking precedenc[...] a group of his innovators, advance product engineers (A[...] mission to create more aggressive designs.

Working in a design shop apart from the main one, they created Nike STA[...] Pressure by reviving an old idea of incorporating several features of ski boots, basketball shoes, and hockey skates. Also, they created cross-trainers. "What Nike produces depends on whether the consumers will accept innovation in the marketplace," says Dr. Martyn Shorter, Nike sports research lab biomechanic.

Product strategy. Nike changed its outlook in the 80s from risk averse to adventuresome, prompted by the entrance of Reebok into their market. They became more innovative with new products and big technological changes instead of incremental improvements. "It was healthy for the company to get hit between the eyes," says C. Joseph LaBonte, now former president of Reebok, about Nike. "Nike got hot. God bless 'em."

Nike also changed their strategy. In 1987, Knight said, "For Nike to be a solid company in the long run, we have to concentrate on making the best-quality, best-performing shoe we can. The fashion business is just too hard to manage year in and year out."

In 1988, however, Nike purchased Cole Haan, a dress shoe marketer, and in early 1989 they introduced a new brand of shoes, Side One. These shoes were aimed at junior girls who wore fashion athletic shoes. Nike entered the fashion market—through the side door.

"Now more than ever, we know what the Nike name stands for and how far it can be stretched—and it can't be stretched that far," says Elizabeth Dolan, spokeswoman for Nike. She indicates that Nike has not compromised its name for the fashion segment, but they have entered the market. Side One competes directly with L.A. Gear and Reebok.

In late 1989, Nike had introduced its first non-Nike named brand—i.e., a line of women's casual footwear. For 1990, they plan to add a similar men's casual footwear line in a joint development project with Cole Haan. Keri Christenfeld, an analyst with Needham and Co., indicates both the performance and fashion dimensions are needed for athletic footwear manufacturers to gain market share.

She says that the strategy is a good one and the timing is good, especially as the boundaries blur between athletic and regular street shoes. The manufacturer that is able to capture the sales growth in the blurred area will most effectively be positioned for the growing industry.

Advertising strategy. For 1990, Nike has continued to use Just Do It in their television and print executions with Jordan and Jackson depicting hardcore performance and promoting their new technologies. They have expanded that slogan to address the market with a more personal health and personal winning strategy.

In their running and walking print advertisements, they tout exercise as physical therapy and stress management (Exhibit 19). Their Air line of print ads show how the hardcore athlete's driven to perform, but they have developed the runner's drive within a serene context: the busy city runner, the late-night loner, and the rural adventurer. The scene is vivid with one serious runner; his or her shoes are not visible (Exhibit 20).

EXHIBIT 19   Nike advertising

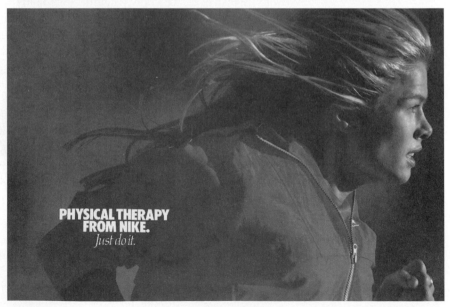

EXHIBIT 20   Nike advertising

(continued)

EXHIBIT 20 *(concluded)*

Consumers learn about new technologies from other players, too. Adidas and Converse introduced Torsion and Energy Wave, respectively, which give the consumer new attributes and materials to consider.

The new addition to Nike's 1990 campaigns is a series of Spike and Mike commercials—directed by and starring Spike Lee as a character named Mars Blackmon. Blackmon is a character from Lee's 1986 movie *She's Gotta Have It.* Lee's costar in the commercials is Michael Jordan.

"We want to show something that conveys the excitement of sports, but still brings our athletes across as human beings," says Dolan. She believes the Spike and Mike advertisements are particularly successful at conveying this with the awestruck fan and the athletic great. "That's kind of how we imagine people are responding to all our ads."[22]

Reebok. Unlike the successful performance campaigns, Reebok has not been successful with delivering a clear performance message to consumers: Life is not a spectator sport (performance), Let U.B.U. (fashion), Physics behind the Physiques (performance), and Legends (performance) have occurred since the 1983 Freestyle aerobic campaign. In 1988, their lack of success is reflected in Reebok's first-ever decline in earnings. Their campaigns have tried to produce both a performance image and a fashion image but have served to clutter the market rather than draw brand distinction.

In particular, their surrealistic, $10.6 million U.B.U. campaign—with such slogans as, "If U. ain't U., U. ain't nobody"—lasted only six months and was the object of competitors' mockery more than consumer's remembrances. "U. Gotta B. Kidding. Why pay for high-performance shoes if U. just want to bang around in sneakers?" (Keds).

With the numerous athletic footwear ads in the media, brand blur occurs where consumers may remember the ads but not the make of the shoe being promoted.

Paul Fireman, CEO of Reebok, acknowledges the problem with UBU. He says, "We had put together a campaign that would bring us awareness, bring us controversy. And that's what 'UBU' came from."[23] He believes Reebok's problem with the campaign was not knowing when to stop it. During its initial phase, in tests compared to Nike's Just Do It, Fireman indicates that consumers had a higher recall of UBU. "The unfortunate thing is that we didn't make a transition. . . . We probably should have shifted to a more normal approach. . . . We did not follow it through into the performance business."

Fireman has built Reebok through knowing when to make changes. His management style includes frequent personnel changes, internal reorganizations, and acquisitions to strengthen their market share. Reebok has had a cash surplus for the past 15 months, and Fireman confirms that if the right acquisition candidate came along, he would continue to build Reebok. "In a perfect world, we'd

---

[22]Gene Seymour, "Spike and Nike: The Making of a Sneaky Sneaker Commercial," *Entertainment,* March 30, 1990, p. 29.

[23]Pat Sloan, "Reebok Chief Looks Beyond Nike," *Advertising Age,* January 29, 1990, p. 16.

be in the $300 million-to-$400 million range (for an acquisition) . . . the company could deal with a $1 billion acquisition if we found the right one."[24]

He adds, for 1990, Reebok's most important focus is the international marketplace. He believes the international market has "the opportunity to be as big if not bigger than Reebok USA." He says that they are targeting their wholesale level to be $1 billion by the mid-1990s.[25]

Product strategy. Until 1989, Reebok had been known and had thought of itself as a "maker of stylish sneakers that give the wearer an edge in social competition."[26] But, in early 1989, while not forsaking the "image drive shoe," Reebok announced its intentions to get a larger piece of the performance-driven market. The growth in the market, they believed, was coming from the performance segment.

According to management consultant Heidi Steinberg, "They're defining their strategic outlook . . . And they're now defining themselves as a leisure/lifestyle company. They're not defining themselves as an athletic footwear company any longer."[27]

Advertising strategy. For early 1990, Reebok is showing product-specific advertisements (Exhibit 21):

- "If it's not one thing it's another" (cross-training).
- "Pump it up" (basketball).
- "Because its never the same game twice" (Energy System—all shoes).
- "Millions of girls want to be in her shoes, but she wants to be in ours" (dance).
- "Wear emblems, not labels" (fashion).
- "It's hard to improve a classic" (aerobics).
- "Go ahead, stick out your tongue" (fashion).
- "Training wheels for the feet" (children).
- "The Pump from Reebok. It Fits a Little Better Than Your Ordinary Athletic Shoe" (performance).

They continue to use Michael Chang, youngest champion of the French Open, as spokesman, and they have added singer/choreographer Paula Abdul to appeal to the younger consumers of their fast-growing competitor, L.A. Gear.

1990 Issues/Competitors' Actions—Reactions

Reebok

January 22, 1990—Reebok announced a split in its U.S. operations. To help keep pace with competitors in both fashion and performance markets, they are splitting into two units so they can focus their actions on performance and fashion, separately.

---

[24]Ibid.

[25]Ibid.

[26]Douglas McGill, "Reebok's New Models, Fully Loaded," *New York Times,* February 14, 1989, p. D1.

[27]Pat Sloan, "Reebok May Slip Back into Fashion," *Advertising Age,* September 4, 1989, p. 27.

EXHIBIT 21   Reebok advertising

(continued)

EXHIBIT 21   *(continued)*

While it may appear that we are stretching the truth, surprisingly it's a fact.

Every time your foot strikes the ground, the impact of three times your bodyweight is sent shuddering up your legs.

Armed with this and years of research, Reebok has developed the Sole Trainer™ 5000.

With the impact of three times your bodyweight in every stride, your lightweight shoe better be cushioned.

At only 10 ounces it's a lightweight shoe, but more importantly, it's exceptionally well-cushioned.

The secret lies in the midsole. It's comprised of Hexalite,™ a unique honeycomb of highly resilient yet light thermo plastic.

(Basically, the honeycomb, one of nature's lightest yet strongest designs, absorbs and spreads shock waves over a much larger area than EVA or polyurethane.)

The bottom line is that the Reebok Sole Trainer 5000 lets you run in a durable, lightweight shoe without sacrificing cushioning or comfort.

Now that should take a load off your mind.

EXHIBIT 21   *(continued)*

The revolutionary Agility™ shoes by Weebok® are designed to help beginning walkers the way training wheels help beginning riders – by giving them the extra balance and support they need.

The heart of the Agility system is a series of 10 strategically located pods on the sole. These pods follow the natural weight shift of the child's foot, while a snug-fitting heel cup helps

The Agility™ system's strategically located pods are designed to improve balance, traction and absorb shock.

to prevent unnecessary movement inside the shoe. At the same time, Agility shoes provide greater flexibility and breathability for your child's growing feet. Visit your local children's shoe store. Compare Agility™ with other shoes. We think you'll agree that all this comfort and technology is a terrific value.

Agility. It's one of the most important advances in children's footwear in 50 years.

Agility™ by Weebok®

Weebok® shoes are carefully fitted at select children's specialty and department stores. For more information, call **1-800-843-4444.**

(continued)

EXHIBIT 21 *(concluded)*

Citing that the structure will "enable us to move even more quickly to respond to consumer needs," Reebok claims it will shorten its product development cycle to three to six months for its lifestyle footwear. "Fashion is a very quick-moving phenomenon. To be competitive, we have to be able to do this."[28]

Some industry analysts believe the division of function will be a good move since marketing performance shoes is very different from marketing lifestyle shoes. Others, however, disagree, saying that with a split personality, Reebok has potential to further confuse the customer, disseminate uncoordinated messages, and develop a false belief that they can be all things to all people.

To complement the new structural change, the domestic and international advertising accounts are out to bid. There is speculation that two agencies may be assigned to the account, one for fashion and one for performance. Frank O'Connell, Reebok's U.S. division president, says, "We will choose the best creative in terms of advertising. We want spectacular advertising."[29] The company is looking for an umbrella campaign and hopes to have a new domestic agency by May 1, 1990.

February 19, 1990—There is speculation that Reebok's old agency now will be invited to bid for the business from which they were just dismissed. The speculation arose with the appointment of John Duerden as president of Reebok's new global marketing unit.

Duerden, the former international president, replaces Frank O'Connell. O'Connell's departure was due to Reebok's recent consolidation of U.S. and international business into one worldwide unit. This departure follows last December's resignation of C. Joseph LaBonte, Reebok international's president, and Mark Goldston, marketing chief.

March 26, 1990—Reebok's recent Pump advertisement touting the shoe's superior fit has been pulled after airing in only four spots. Reebok pulled the ad in response to customer concerns that people might imitate the bungee jumping sport shown in the commercial.

Once again, Reebok's advertising has been deemed controversial. While Reebok's premise for the ad is fit, for the first time, the company shows a competitor's shoe in the ad. In the ad, two jumpers, one wearing Reeboks, the other Nikes, leap from a Seattle bridge with bungee cords wrapped around their ankles. The elastic cord, which is supposed to prevent them from hitting bottom after their thrilling free-fall, ultimately works only for the wearer of the Reeboks. The audience sees the Reebok jumper hanging safely upside down while the Nike shoes float—empty—dangling in the wind.

---

[28]Joseph Pereira, "Reebok Sets Up Separate Units for Shoe Business," *The Wall Street Journal,* January 22, 1990.

[29]Pat Sloan and Jon Lafayette, "A Race for Reebok," *Advertising Age,* January 29, 1990, p. 3.

Nike

February 16, 1990—Nike filed a lawsuit accusing L.A. Gear of misappropriating their (Nike's) intellectual property by mimicking Air Jordan's (basketball shoes). The suit cites:

- Trade dress infringement.
- (L.A. Gear style MVP–1:) Mimicking of eight to nine attributes that give Air Jordan's their distinctive recognition.
- Creation of confusion in the minds of consumers.

Nike representatives state, "While imitation is a form of flattery, we think they (L.A. Gear) cross the line. . . . It's not one or two, but a bundle of them."[30]

L.A. Gear's MVP–1 style was introduced in 1989 and has produced $5 million in sales. Nike is asking for a restraining order, and as of March 1990 no decision has been reached.

Analysts

Industry analysts believe the high-tech emphasis coming from shoe manufacturers is not significant in creating consumer demand. "What matters," says Samuel Krause of Durham's Athleisure of Drayton Plains, Michigan, "is that the customer tries it and makes his own decision. It gives the customer a reason to buy the product."[31]

Analysts continue to speculate how successful footwear firms will be in the 1990s. With more players, the need for more resources and effective advertising and promotions and distribution expertise, they are uncertain as to which firm will take the number one position. Already retailers from a random survey have had their thoughts published in *Sporting Goods Business*'s March 1990 issue:

- 88.3 percent—Nike.
- 29.1 percent—L.A. Gear.
- 28.1 percent—Reebok.

With the results showing retailer's perceptions making L.A. Gear number 1 over Reebok, analysts point to L.A. Gear, in particular, trying to access their performance in the 80s and to project their success in the 90s.

They speculate whether L.A. Gear will have the products that will effectively meet their customers' constantly changing preferences, and if they will be able to keep a strong image in the consumers' minds as advertising wars escalate between the top athletic footwear players and the new entrants that may find a niche with a fad.

Clearly, the effectiveness of their product, marketing, and advertising strategies for the 1990s in developing consumer perceptions and preferences will be their major challenge.

---

[30]Ken Wells, "Is the Air Jordan Intellectual Property or Just Athletic?," *The Wall Street Journal,* February 16, 1990, p. B4.

[31]Douglas McGill, "Reebok's New Models, Fully Loaded," p. D6.

Case 35

Longevity Healthcare Systems, Inc.*

Kathryn Hamilton, president of Longevity Healthcare Systems, Inc., located in Grand Rapids, Michigan, was reviewing the 1993 annual statements. "We concluded another terrific year," she commented. "Our sales and earnings exceeded expectations, but I'm concerned about the next few years." Although Longevity was successful, it was beginning to experience competition and the uncertainty of health care reform. In February 1994, a large hospital in Grand Rapids, Michigan, had converted an entire wing to a long-term care facility. The hospital also initiated an aggressive sales and advertising campaign and was competing with Longevity for new nursing home residents.

Longevity's recent acquisition of seven nursing homes in Toledo, Ohio, was also proving to be an unprofitable venture. Many of the residents were on Medicare and Medicaid, and these health insurance programs generally did not reimburse the full costs of care. Additionally, the families of the Toledo residents were becoming value conscious and they frequently commented about the quality and cost of nursing care. Kathryn realized that, to improve the profitability, attention would have to be given to customer satisfaction and attracting more profitable private-pay residents. Health care reform was also a source of concern. It was her belief that reform of the health care industry would be comprehensive, with increased emphasis on cost control, competitive pricing, and quality of care. She wondered what effect reform would have on Longevity and what the timetable for legislative action would be.

While increased competition and health care reform seemed certain, the most profitable path for future growth was not clear because several marketing opportunities existed. An aging population had created a strong demand for long-term care

*This case was written by Professor Lawrence M. Lamont and Elizabeth W. Storey, Washington and Lee University. Case material is prepared as a basis for class discussion, and not designed to present illustrations of either effective or ineffective handling of administrative problems. The names of the firms, individuals, locations, and/or financial information have been disguised to preserve anonymity. Copyright © 1994, Lawrence M. Lamont. Used with permission.

in nursing homes. Alzheimer's disease was also becoming more common, and Longevity had recently lost some nursing home residents to Alzheimer's treatment centers because the company did not offer a specialized facility. Kathryn had to decide whether offering Alzheimer's treatment would be desirable.

Opportunities to expand existing businesses were also an option. The Grand Rapids pharmacy acquired in 1992 had been successfully phased into Longevity, and Kathryn was wondering if a similar acquisition would work in Toledo. However, she was concerned about the impact of reform on the pricing of prescription drugs and medical supplies. To date, the pharmacy had been very profitable, but what would the future hold?

Geographic expansion of the firm's nursing and subacute care facilities might also be a profitable avenue for growth. Industry consolidation was making it possible to acquire nursing homes and unprofitable hospitals that could be converted to health care facilities. However, Kathryn envisioned that a future industry trend might be toward vertical integration of health care services. If so, it might make sense to further integrate Longevity's business in the Grand Rapids and Toledo markets before committing to additional geographic expansion.

Beyond decisions on the future direction of Longevity, Kathryn wondered if it was time to begin thinking about a more formal approach to marketing. "I really need to get some ideas about marketing in our different businesses down on paper so I can see how they fit with my views on an overall corporate marketing strategy," she remarked.

History of Longevity Healthcare Systems, Inc.

In 1972, Kathryn Hamilton, R.N., was searching for a nursing home for her mother in Grand Rapids, Michigan. Discouraged by a six-month wait for admission, she decided to move her into the home she occupied with her husband, Richard. Dr. Hamilton, M.D., enjoyed a medical practice in Grand Rapids specializing in care for older adults.

A Nursing Home Business

In 1974, Richard's mother and father joined the household and Kathryn and Richard continued to learn how to care for older adults. In 1976, the Hamiltons leased a small, outdated, 40-bed hospital in a nearby suburb and converted it into a long-term care facility. Following certification, the facility was opened in 1977 as the Longevity Nursing Home. In addition to their parents, 10 other adults over 65 entered the home during the year. All were "private pay," meaning they paid directly for services with personal assets, but without government assistance. By 1979, the nursing facility was fully occupied with private pay residents. Longevity was incorporated, and Kathryn Hamilton became the president and its director of nursing, while her husband, Richard, provided medical services and continued his practice. The leased facility was purchased in 1979.

New Nursing Services

By 1980, Longevity found it necessary to add additional nursing services for aging residents. Two levels of care were added, and professional nurses were hired to provide the services. The new services were favorably received, and the referrals from residents and physicians kept the facility filled.

Expansion by Acquisition, 1980–85

The demand for nursing care was strong in the early 1980s, and Longevity expanded. Eight unprofitable nursing homes with a total of 480 beds were acquired in Grand Rapids and nearby communities. All of the homes were licensed, certified by Medicare and Medicaid, and occupied by residents requiring a variety of nursing services. Shortly after the acquisition, Dr. Hamilton left his medical practice to join Longevity full-time as its medical director. He added skilled nursing care for residents requiring 24-hour-a-day care, and rehabilitation services for those needing physical, speech, and occupational therapy.

Nursing Home Construction

From 1986 to 1988, Longevity expanded by constructing three 70-bed nursing homes in nearby communities. Each provided the full range of nursing and rehabilitation services and was licensed for Medicare and Medicaid patients.[1] The homes were quickly filled, and by the end of 1988 Longevity operated 12 nursing homes with a total of 730 beds. Employment had grown to 1,200 full-time and part-time employees.

New Business Opportunities

During a medical convention in 1990, Kathryn Hamilton noted a growing concern over the escalating costs of hospital care and the desire of insurance providers to shorten the hospitalization of patients requiring medical supervision, but not the other services traditionally provided by hospitals. Sensing an opportunity, the Hamiltons converted a 30-bed wing of one of the Grand Rapids nursing homes to a subacute care facility for patients that did not need the full services of a licensed acute care hospital.[2] For patients moved from a hospital to the Longevity facility, the needed care was provided for about half the cost.

---

[1]By 1988, all Longevity nursing homes were certified to receive Medicare and Medicaid patients. Medicare is a federally funded and administered health insurance program that reimburses health care facilities for nursing and medical services. Medicaid is a state-administered reimbursement program that covers skilled and intermediate long-term care for the medically indigent. The benefits paid by Medicaid programs vary from state to state.

[2]Medical services fall along a continuum from intensive care, acute care, subacute care, nursing care, and home health care. Hospitals offer intensive and acute care for patients with complex medical conditions. They have fully equipped operating and recovery rooms, radiology services, intensive and coronary care units, pharmacies, clinical laboratories, therapy services, and emergency services. Subacute care facilities owned by nursing homes serve the needs of patients who require nursing and medical care, but not many of the specialized services and equipment provided by an acute care hospital.

The subacute care facility was licensed in 1991 and it quickly filled with referrals from hospitals, physicians, and health care insurers.

The growing recognition that treating patients requiring subacute care in low-overhead nursing facilities was a cost-effective alternative, substantially increased the demand for Longevity's subacute care. In 1992, following marketing research, Longevity constructed a 50-bed subacute care facility near one of its nursing homes. It was completed in 1993 and, within a few months, operated at capacity with patients referred from insurance companies, physicians, and Longevity nursing homes.

As the demand for specialized nursing and medical care expanded, it became apparent that profitability could be improved by operating a pharmacy. In 1992, Longevity acquired a retail pharmacy in Grand Rapids from a retiring pharmacist. It was converted into an institutional pharmacy to provide prescriptions, medical equipment and supplies, and consulting services to Longevity facilities.

Geographic Expansion

Late in 1992, what appeared to be an exceptional business opportunity came to the attention of Kathryn and Richard Hamilton. A few hundred miles away, in Toledo, Ohio, a large health care company was selling seven unprofitable nursing homes with a total of 280 beds for $12,000,000. The homes were occupied primarily by Medicare and Medicaid patients and operated at 70 percent of capacity. The Hamiltons decided to take a one-year option on the facilities while they raised the money to complete the purchase. Eventually, 40 percent of Longevity's common stock was sold to a large insurance company, and some of the proceeds were used to exercise the purchase option. Kathryn Hamilton hired an experienced administrator and assigned him the task of returning the nursing homes to profitability. To reflect its broadening scope in the health care industry, the Hamiltons decided to change the company name to Longevity Healthcare Systems, Inc. As shown in Figures 1 and 2, Longevity ended 1993 with 12 nursing homes, two subacute care facilities, and a pharmacy located in Michigan, and 7 nursing homes located in Ohio. Tables 1 and 2 contain the financial statements for the year ending December 31, 1993. Table 3 presents a five-year sales and earnings history, while Table 4 provides some financial information for the pharmacy.

FIGURE 1 Longevity Healthcare Systems, Inc., historical development, 1972–1993

Date	Activity
1972–75	Nursing care for parents.
1976–77	Leased a 40-bed hospital and converted it to a nursing home.
1979	Business incorporated as Longevity Nursing Home.
1979	Corporation purchased leased nursing home.
1980–85	Acquired eight nursing homes in Grand Rapids area, 480 beds.
1986–88	Constructed three nursing homes in Grand Rapids area, 210 beds.
1990–91	Converted a 30-bed wing of Grand Rapids nursing home into subacute care.
1992–93	Constructed a 50-bed subacute care facility in Grand Rapids area.
1992	Acquired a retail pharmacy in Grand Rapids.
1992–93	Acquired seven nursing homes in Toledo area, 280 beds.
1993	Corporation name changed to Longevity Healthcare Systems, Inc.

FIGURE 2   Longevity Healthcare Systems, Inc., geographic location of facilities

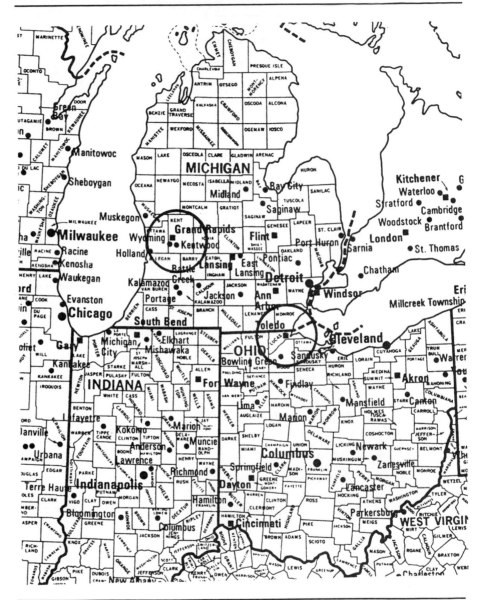

TABLE 1 Longevity Healthcare Systems, Inc., income statement (year ending 12-31-93)

Net revenues	
Basic LTC services	$45,500,000
Subacute medical services	9,000,000
Pharmacy services	3,000,000
Total revenues	$57,500,000
Operating expenses	
Salaries, wages, and benefits	$20,125,000
Patient services	21,275,000
Administrative and general	3,450,000
Depreciation and amortization	575,000
Total costs and expenses	$45,425,000
Income from operations	$12,075,000
Interest expense	1,726,111
Earnings before taxes	$10,348,889
Income taxes	4,139,555
Net income	$6,209,334
Net income per share	$0.78

TABLE 2 Longevity Healthcare Systems, Inc., balance sheet (years ending 12-31-93 and 12-31-92)

Assets	*1993*	*1992*
Current assets		
Cash and equivalents	$ 841,770	$ 501,120
Accounts receivable	3,265,584	2,702,552
Inventory	2,262,816	1,624,399
Property, plant, and equipment		
Land	9,959,051	7,690,249
Buildings and improvements	27,002,416	13,622,079
Equipment	2,917,136	2,179,842
Accumulated depreciation	(4,028,149)	(2,464,535)
Other assets		
Goodwill	791,794	655,278
Other long-term assets	5,163,275	4,063,190
Total assets	$48,175,693	$30,574,174
Liabilities and shareholders' equity		
Current liabilities		
Accounts payable	$ 1,250,201	$ 1,043,648
Accrued expenses	708,447	586,301
Accrued compensation	416,734	344,883
Current portion of long-term debt	2,041,995	2,700,120
Accrued interest	196,694	203,954
Long-term debt (net)	10,506,622	12,871,452
Shareholders' equity		
Common stock, $.01 par value	50,000	50,000
Additional paid-in capital	17,870,666	3,848,816
Retained earnings	15,134,334	8,925,000
Total liabilities and shareholders' equity	$48,175,693	$30,574,174

TABLE 3   Longevity Healthcare Systems, Inc., historical revenues and net income

Year	Revenues	Net Income
1993	$57,500,000	$6,209,334
1992	46,575,000	5,029,560
1991	37,260,000	3,017,736
1990	26,715,420	2,987,692
1989	21,799,783	1,334,147

TABLE 4   Longevity Healthcare Systems, Inc., selected pharmacy information (year ending 12-31-93)

Income statement	
Net revenue	$3,000,000
Operating expenses	2,430,000
Operating income	570,000
Net income	390,000
Financial ratios	
Current ratio	1.94
Inventory turnover	4.20
Profit margin (percent)	13.00%
Return on assets (percent)	9.29%

Longevity Marketing

Marketing was used to promote high occupancy in Longevity facilities, expand the percentage of private pay residents, and increase the profits of its institutional pharmacy. Operating information for the health care facilities is shown in Table 5, and the products and services marketed by Longevity are summarized in Figure 3.

TABLE 5   Longevity Healthcare Systems, Inc., operating information for facilities (year ending 12-31-93)

Payor mix	Grand Rapids	Toledo	Total
Private and other	69.7%	18.7%	44.2%
Medicare	8.4	17.8	13.1
Medicaid	21.9	63.5	42.7
Occupancy	96.4%	81.2%	88.8%
No. of beds	780	280	1,060

Nursing care was marketed locally. The administrator and admissions director of each facility designed a marketing strategy to increase awareness of the nursing home and its services in the market it served. Personal selling using telemarketing and direct contact was targeted to referral sources such as physicians, hospital administrators, home health agencies, community organizations and churches, senior citizens groups, retirement communities, and the families of

FIGURE 3   Longevity Healthcare Systems, Inc., products and services

Business	Products/services
Nursing care	Custodial care
	Assisted living
	Intermediate nursing care
	Skilled nursing care
Subacute care for	Lung and heart disease
	Coma, pain, and wound care
	Spinal cord injuries
	Head injuries
	Intravenous therapy
	Joint replacements
Rehabilitation services	Occupational therapy
	Physical therapy
	Speech therapy
Institutional pharmacy	Prescription drugs
	Nonprescription drugs
	Medical supplies
	Medical equipment
	Consulting services

prospective residents. Longevity also distributed promotional literature discussing its philosophy of care, services, and quality standards. Frequently the literature was provided to prospective residents and their families when they inquired about nursing or toured the facilities.

Marketing for subacute care was directed by Kathryn Hamilton who contacted insurance companies, managed care organizations such as HMOs, hospital administrators, and other third-party payors to promote Longevity's services.[3] Kathryn also attended professional meetings where she maintained contact with the various referral sources.

The products and services of the institutional pharmacy were marketed by the pharmacy manager and his assistant by direct contact with Longevity facilities, other nursing homes, hospitals, clinics, and home health agencies. In addition to drugs and medical supplies, management also provided consulting services to help ensure quality patient care. These services were especially valuable because they enabled the nursing homes to admit patients that required more complex and profitable medical services.

---

[3]Managed care organizations provide health care products which integrate financing and management with the delivery of health care services through a network of providers (such as nursing homes and hospitals) who share financial risk or who have incentives to deliver cost-effective services. An HMO (Health Maintenance Organization) provides prepaid health care services to its members through physicians employed by the HMO at facilities owned by the HMO or through a network of independent physicians and facilities. They actively manage patient care to maximize quality and cost effectiveness.

Nursing Home Services

Longevity nursing homes provided room and board, dietary services, recreation and social activities, housekeeping and laundry services, four levels of nursing care, and numerous specialized services. Custodial care was provided to residents needing minimal care. Assisted living was used by persons needing some assistance with personal care such as bathing and eating. Intermediate care was provided to residents needing more nursing and attention, but not continual access to nurses. Finally, skilled nursing care was available to residents requiring the professional services of a nurse on a 24-hour-a-day basis. Rehabilitation therapy was also available for residents that had disabilities or were returning from hospitalization for surgery or illness. Rehabilitation was an important part of Longevity's care because it helped residents improve their quality of life.

Most of the residents in Longevity nursing homes were female and over 65. Although rates depended on accommodations and the services used, a typical nursing home bed generated monthly revenues of $4,415. It was common for a resident to initially enter the nursing home needing only custodial care or assisted living and to progress to higher levels of nursing care as they aged. Table 6 provides a typical schedule of monthly charges for a resident in a semi-private room with seven hours of therapy.

TABLE 6   Longevity Healthcare Systems, Inc., example resident statement for nursing care (per month)*

Semi-private room, $105.00 per day	$3,150.00
Basic telephone service	15.00
Rehabilitation therapy, 7.0 hours per month	840.00
Pharmacy and other specialized services	360.00
Miscellaneous personal expenses	50.00
Total	$4,415.00
Per day	147.17

*Based on private pay. Includes room and board, 24-hour professional nursing care, meals, housekeeping and linen services. Social and recreational activity programs are also included.

All of the Longevity nursing homes were licensed in their respective states. Generally, the licenses had to be renewed annually. For renewal, state health care agencies considered the physical condition of the facility, the qualifications of the administrative and medical staff, the quality of care, and the facilities compliance with the applicable laws and regulations.

Subacute Care

Longevity marketed subacute care for patients with more complex medical needs that required constant medical supervision, but not the expensive equipment and services of an acute care hospital. Subacute care generated higher profit margins than nursing care, although patient stays in the facility were usually shorter.[4] Daily patient rates varied from $250.00 to $750.00, depending on the services and equipment required. Longevity's services included care for patients with lung and heart disease, spinal cord and head injuries, joint replacements, coma, pain and wound care, and intravenous therapy. Services at the subacute care facilities were not limited to the elderly. Younger patients discharged from hospitals were attractive because of their longer life expectancy and eventual need for nursing and rehabilitation. Based on an average rate of $1,000 per day charged by acute care hospitals, Longevity knew that its prices were substantially lower for comparable services. Like the nursing homes, the subacute care facilities were subject to licensing by the state health care agencies and certification by Medicare. All Longevity subacute care facilities were licensed and certified.

Pharmacy Products and Services

Longevity provided pharmacy products and services to nursing homes, retirement communities, and other health care organizations. The pharmacy's products were frequently customized with special packaging and dispensing systems and delivered daily. The pharmacy also consulted on medications and long-term care regulations, and provided computerized tracking of medications, medical records processing, and 24-hour emergency services.

The Market for Long-Term Health Care

Long-term health care includes basic health care (such as that provided in nursing homes), rehabilitation therapy and Alzheimer's care, institutional pharmacy services, subacute care, and home health care. In recent years, spending for these and other health care services has increased significantly. For example, in 1993, one out of every seven dollars that Americans spent went to purchase health care. Total expenditures are projected to increase from $585.3 billion in 1990 to $3,457.7 billion in 2010, an annual growth rate of over 9 percent.

Nursing homes are important providers of long-term health care. Expenditures for nursing home care are expected to increase at a comparable rate, from $53.1 billion in 1990 to $310.1 billion in 2010. This industry consists of about 16,000 licensed facilities with a total of 1,700,000 beds. It includes a large number of small, locally owned nursing homes and a growing number of regional and national companies. The industry is undergoing restructuring in response to stricter regulation, increasing complexity of medical services, and competitive pressures. Smaller, local operators who lack sophisticated management and financial resources are being acquired by larger, more established companies. At present, the 20 largest firms operate about

---

[4]Longevity profit margins for subacute care facilities were about 25 percent higher than for nursing care facilities. The length of stay was usually 20 to 45 days versus eight months for private pay nursing care and two years for Medicaid patients.

18 percent of the nursing facilities. Consolidation is expected to continue, but the long-term outlook is extremely positive for the businesses that survive. Nursing home revenues increased by about 12 percent in 1993 and they are expected to experience similar gains in 1994. Several factors account for the optimistic outlook:

Favorable Demographic Trends

Demographic trends, namely growth in the elderly segment of the population, are increasing the demand for health care and the services of nursing homes. Most of the market for nursing care consists of men and women 65 years of age and older. Their number was approximately 25 million in 1980 and is projected to increase to 35 million by 2000 and to 40 million by the year 2010. The 65-and-over segment suffers from a greater incidence of chronic illnesses and disabilities and currently accounts for about two-thirds of the health care expenditures in the United States.

Pressures to Control Costs

Government and private payers have adopted cost control measures to encourage reduced hospital stays. In addition, private insurers have begun to limit reimbursement to "reasonable" charges, while managed care organizations are limiting hospitalization costs by monitoring utilization and negotiating discounted rates. As a result, hospital stays have been shortened and many patients are discharged with a continuing need for care. Because nursing homes are able to provide services at lower prices, the cost pressures have increased the demand for nursing home services and subacute care following hospital discharge.

Advances in Medical Technology

Advances in technology leading to improved medications and surgical procedures have increased life expectancies. Adults over age 85 are now the fastest-growing segment of the population, and their numbers are expected to double over the next 20 years. Many require skilled care and the medical equipment traditionally available only in hospitals. Nursing homes are acquiring some of the specialty medical equipment and providing skilled nursing care to older adults through subacute care facilities.

Limited Supply of Nursing Beds

The supply of nursing home beds has been limited by the availability of financing and high construction and start-up expenses. Additionally, the supply has been constrained by legislation limiting licenses for new nursing beds in states that require a demonstration of need. The effect has been to create a barrier to market entry and conditions where demand for nursing home services exceeds the available supply in many states.

National Health Care Reform

The next decade will be a period of reform for the health care system. Although it is not clear how comprehensive the reform will be and how it will be financed, the focus will be to control costs and provide universal access to quality health care. The most likely plan will probably reform the health insurance industry, build on the current employer-financed approach, and call for market incentives to control costs. To ensure universal access, insurance and managed care companies will be prohibited from dropping, rejecting, or pricing out of the market anyone with an expensive medical condition.

Reform will affect long-term care providers, such as nursing homes, in several ways. It will regulate the insurance companies to make health insurance more price competitive and affordable. This change will favorably impact long-term health care providers by increasing the number of residents paying with insurance benefits. Reform may also extend Medicare coverage for home health care. A change such as this would encourage more older adults to receive health care at home instead of at a nursing facility, resulting in an unfavorable impact.

Employers will also have incentives to control costs and deliver quality care. Increasingly they will rely on managed care organizations, such as HMOs, who are likely to contract lower-cost providers, such as nursing homes, for subacute care and other cost-effective services. Companies capable of providing a variety of health care services at attractive prices should see opportunities to expand demand.

Institutional pharmacies will also be impacted by health care reform. President Clinton's Health Security Act called for the addition of prescription drug coverage to the Medicare program. If adopted, this provision would probably decrease prices of prescription drugs by regulation of pharmaceutical manufacturers. Price decreases, either legislated or achieved through managed care and the market system, may allow institutional pharmacies to enjoy higher profit margins while still providing medications at affordable prices to patients.

Regulation and Competition

Health care providers are regulated at the state and federal levels. Regulation impacts financial management and the quality and safety of care. Ensuring that health care facilities are in compliance with regulatory standards is an important aspect of managing a health care business. In addition, management is increasingly confronted with competition. Nursing homes and subacute care facilities compete for patients who are able to select from a variety of alternatives to meet their needs. Managed care and insurance organizations also negotiate aggressively with health care providers to ensure quality care at attractive prices.

Financial Regulation

The Health Care Financing Administration (HCFA) is the federal regulatory agency for Medicare and Medicaid. Both programs are cost-based and use a per-diem payment schedule that reimburses the provider for a portion of the costs of care. Each facility must apply to participate in the Medicare and Medicaid programs and then have its beds certified to provide skilled nursing, intermediate, or other levels of care. A nursing home may have a mix of beds at any time, but it must match patient services to each bed. A facility cannot place a Medicare patient requiring skilled nursing care in a bed certified for intermediate care without recertifying the bed for skilled care. Recertification often required a month or more.

Quality and Safety of Care

Much of the current regulation facing nursing homes was developed in the Omnibus Budget Reconciliation Act of 1987 (OBRA 87). Facilities that participate in Medicare and Medicaid must be regularly inspected by state survey teams under contract with HCFA to ensure safety and quality of care. OBRA 87 also established a resident "bill of rights" that essentially converted nursing homes from merely custodial facilities into centers for rehabilitation. Nursing homes are now required to establish a care plan for patients and conduct assessments to ensure that the facility achieves the highest practical well-being for each resident.

Competition

Longevity competes with acute care and rehabilitation hospitals, other nursing and subacute care facilities, home health care agencies, and institutional pharmacies. Some offer services and prices which are comparable to those offered by Longevity.

Nursing homes compete on the basis of their reputation in the community, the ability to meet particular needs, the location and appearance of the facility, and the price of services. When a nursing facility is being selected, members of a prospective resident's family usually participate by visiting and evaluating nursing homes over a period of several weeks.

Some of the competing nursing homes in Grand Rapids and Toledo are operated by nonprofit organizations (churches and fraternal organizations) that can finance capital expenditures on a tax-exempt basis or receive charitable contributions to subsidize their operations. They compete with Longevity on the basis of price for private pay residents.

Longevity competes for subacute care patients with acute care and rehabilitation hospitals, nursing homes, and home health agencies. The competition is generally local or regional and the competitive factors are similar to those for nursing care, although more emphasis is placed on support services such as third-party reimbursement, information management, and patient record keeping. Insurance and managed care organizations exert considerable influence on the decision and increase the competition by negotiating with several health care providers.

The institutional pharmacy market has no dominant competitor in the markets served by Longevity. Twenty percent of the market is accounted for by the institutional pharmacies owned by nursing homes. Independent institutional pharmacies control about 35 percent of the market, and retail pharmacies supply the remainder. Retail pharmacies are steadily being acquired by nursing homes and independents to gain market share and achieve economies of scale in purchasing prescriptions and medical supplies. Institutional pharmacies compete on the basis of fast, customer-oriented service, price, and the ability to provide consulting and information management services to customers.

Marketing Issues and Opportunities

Kathryn Hamilton believed that Longevity could improve its marketing. She was concerned about the efforts of individual nursing homes and the need to improve the marketing of subacute care to managed care providers. Finally, she believed that customer satisfaction would become an important competitive factor and Longevity would need to assess the reactions of nursing home residents and their families to the quality of its services.

Continued growth was also on Kathryn's mind. Population demographics and health care reform would create outstanding opportunities for businesses that could design and implement successful marketing strategies. For some time, she had been thinking about expanding into Alzheimer's treatment because of the demographics and the growing need for facilities in the Grand Rapids area. Additionally, she saw an opportunity to further integrate Longevity by establishing a pharmacy in Toledo or by acquiring nursing homes in a new market such as South Bend, Indiana. Each marketing opportunity seemed to make sense, so the final choices would be difficult.

Local Marketing of Health Care Services

Although local marketing had worked well, duplication of effort and overlapping market areas were becoming problems as the number of nursing homes in a market increased. Kathryn wondered what the marketing strategy for nursing home services should be and whether the marketing efforts of the Grand Rapids and Toledo nursing homes could be coordinated in each area to eliminate duplication and preserve local identity. One approach she was considering was to hire a marketing specialist to work with the nursing homes to attract more private pay customers. Advertising was a related issue because it had not been used and Kathryn questioned whether it should be part of the marketing strategy. Should an advertising campaign be created for all of the nursing homes in a market, or should it be left to nursing home administrators to decide if advertising was appropriate in their strategy? If advertising were to be used, then a decision would have to be made on the type of advertising, the creative strategy, and the appropriate media.

Marketing Subacute Care

Subacute care was viewed as an attractive marketing opportunity because of the profit margins. However, to further penetrate the market, a marketing strategy would have to be developed. Kathryn noted that managed care organizations and other referral sources were like organizational buyers as they made decisions on subacute care for the cases they managed. Instead of marketing the service to physicians and patient families, Longevity would negotiate directly with HMOs and insurance companies to determine services and a rate structure based on the patient's medical needs. Personal selling would be used to build a relationship with the case managers for both the insurance company and the hospital. The marketing objective was to convince the insurance companies that the subacute unit could achieve the same patient outcomes at a lower cost than a hospital. If a marketing strategy could be developed along with appropriate staffing, it might be desirable to expand this part of Longevity's business. Economics favored conversion of a wing of an existing nursing home into a subacute care facility at a cost of $25,000 per bed. One possibility existed in Toledo where an unprofitable 80-bed facility was operating at 60 percent of capacity. If part of the facility were upgraded to subacute care, she expected that, within a short time, it would operate at capacity.

Customer Satisfaction

Occasional complaints from nursing home residents about the price and quality of care were of concern to management. Since Longevity depended on referrals, customer satisfaction was an important element of a successful marketing strategy. In thinking about the issue, Kathryn noted that the license renewal process generally assured the maintenance of high standards in each facility, but it focused heavily on the inputs necessary to provide quality nursing care and not on customer satisfaction. Kathryn needed to decide what should be done to monitor individual nursing homes to assure customer satisfaction with Longevity's services.

Acquisition of a Toledo Pharmacy

One marketing opportunity being considered was the acquisition of a Toledo pharmacy. From management's perspective, an acquisition was interesting because it further integrated the existing health care operations and provided an incremental source of earnings from the Toledo market.

Management had identified an institutional pharmacy serving 15 nursing homes with 700 beds. It was offered at a cash price of $1,050,000 and generated annual revenues of approximately $1,450 per bed served. The pharmacy was quite profitable, with an average profit margin of 12.5 percent over the past 5 years. To consider the profitability of the acquisition, Kathryn believed it was reasonable to assume that the pharmacy would be able to serve the Longevity facilities in Toledo and retain 60 percent of the nursing home beds it presently served if it was staffed with appropriate marketing support.

One concern was the impact of health care reform. Most of the nursing homes served by the pharmacy had a high percentage of Medicare and Medicaid patients. If the reimbursement rates for prescription drugs and medical supplies were to decline, then what seemed to be an attractive opportunity could quickly change.

Alzheimer's Treatment

Alzheimer's treatment was being considered because the demand for care was not being met and the development of a cure or drug therapy for the disease was progressing slowly. Kathryn believed that the demand for Alzheimer's treatment would grow at least as fast as the over-65 population. Projections from the U.S. Department of Health and Human Services indicated that, by the year 2000, the Alzheimer's care market would increase by 50 percent from the present base of 4,000,000 presently suffering from the disease.

Longevity was considering establishing an Alzheimer's wing in two of the Grand Rapids nursing homes that served areas near older community residents. Each unit would serve 30 patients and it would be self-contained and secured to protect residents against their wandering habits. The furniture and fixtures would also be renovated to meet the needs of the Alzheimer's patient, including softer colors, more subdued lighting, a separate nurses station, and a secured entrance. If an existing facility was converted, about six nursing rooms would have to be taken out of service to provide a separate activity and dining space. However, management reasoned that the revenue loss would be offset by average monthly revenues of $3,400 per patient and 15 percent lower costs than those for the average nursing home resident. Alzheimer's patients frequently required less costly care because of their younger age, better health, and a tendency to use fewer services. Longevity management had secured cost estimates that indicated the conversion costs would be $2,000 to $3,000 per bed.

In thinking about the opportunity, Kathryn also recalled that Alzheimer's units typically had occupancy levels above 95 percent. Patients averaged a three-year length of stay and were almost always private pay. The marketing for Alzheimer's units focused on Alzheimer's associations, Alzheimer support groups, and church groups. Kathryn would have to decide how to position and market the Alzheimer's units so they would not appear to conflict with or be confused with the nursing home services. This would be a difficult but important marketing challenge because nursing homes that were known to operate Alzheimer's units tended to have better relationships with referral sources. Apparently they were perceived as providing an important community service.

Toward a Comprehensive Marketing Strategy

As Kathryn Hamilton completed her review of the financial statements, she was reminded of the need to make improvements in Longevity's marketing strategies. "I wish I could just write a one-paragraph statement of the corporate marketing strategy for this company. Then I could address each of the marketing issues and opportunities using my corporate strategy as a guide," she remarked.

Certainly one issue was improving existing marketing efforts. Marketing of nursing care, subacute care, and the institutional pharmacy had been reasonably successful, but Kathryn felt uneasy about going another year without making needed changes. Since most of Kathryn's time was now needed to manage the business, additional marketing personnel would be necessary to develop and implement the marketing strategies for the various services. How many people would be needed and how the marketing effort would be organized also had to be decided.

Because Longevity was still evolving as a company with an uncertain marketing strategy, the most profitable direction for future growth was also important. Selecting attractive marketing opportunities was complicated because the choice depended on financial resources. Should Longevity expand the institutional pharmacy business, the subacute care business, or would resources be better utilized by offering Alzheimer's care? Each would bring Longevity closer to becoming an integrated health care provider.

Just as Kathryn moved to turn her personal computer off for the day, she noticed an electronic mail message from the administrator of the Toledo nursing homes. It said that, for the first quarter of 1994, the seven nursing homes were breaking even at 81 percent occupancy and 25 percent private pay residents. When she arrived home that evening, she was greeted by her husband, Richard, who mentioned that she had received a telephone call from a commercial real estate broker in South Bend, Indiana. The broker had located five nursing homes with a total of 450 beds that were being sold in a bankruptcy proceeding for $5,000,000. During dinner that evening, Richard mentioned that they needed to discuss the South Bend opportunity because the homes were attractively priced in a desirable market. It was his belief that, in the future, the most profitable health care businesses would be vertically integrated and geographically diversified. Kathryn nodded in agreement as he handed her the summary information provided in Table 7, and mentioned that a decision would have to be made in five days. She thought to herself, "I wonder if it's financially possible?"

TABLE 7   Longevity Healthcare Systems, Inc., selected demographic information

	Grand Rapids*		Toledo		South Bend†	
Retired	235,513	18.9%	161,630	19.9%	119,401	20.0%
Age, household head						
55–64	77,383	12.4	54,421	13.2	40,661	13.4
65–74	71,142	11.4	52,772	12.8	39,448	13.0
75 and older	56,165	9.0	40,816	9.9	30,951	10.2
Median age	44.5		46.1		46.7	
Lifecycle stage						
Married, 45–64	87,992	14.1	58,544	14.2	44,910	14.8
Married, 65+	61,157	9.8	42,053	10.2	34,289	11.3
Single, 45–64	44,932	7.2	31,746	7.7	23,365	7.7
Single, 65+	56,789	9.1	43,702	10.6	30,951	10.2
Median income	$32,928		$32,194		$31,264	
Adult population	1,246,101		812,212		597,003	
Nursing Facilities‡	439		988		590	
Total Nursing Beds	49,927		92,518		64,263	

* Includes Kalamazoo and Battle Creek, Michigan.
† Includes Elkhart, Indiana.
‡ Statewide statistics for certified Medicare and Medicaid facilities and beds.
Source: *The Lifestyle Market Analyst, 1993. Health Care Financing Administration, 1991.*

Case 36

Cima Mountaineering, Inc.*

Introduction

"What a great hike," exclaimed Anthony Simon as he tossed his Summit HX 350 hiking boots into his car. He had just finished hiking the challenging Cascade Canyon Trail in the Tetons north of Jackson, Wyoming. Anthony hiked often because it was a great way to test the hiking boots made by Cima Mountaineering, Inc., the business he inherited from his parents and owned with his sister, Margaret. As he drove back to Jackson, he began thinking about next week's meeting with Margaret, the president of Cima. During the past month they had been discussing marketing strategies for increasing the sales and profits of the company. No decisions had been made, but the preferences of each owner were becoming clear.

As illustrated in Table 1, sales and profits had grown steadily for Cima and by most measures the company was successful. However, growth was beginning to slow as a result of foreign competition and a changing market. Margaret observed that the market had shifted to a more casual, stylish hiking boot that appealed to hikers interested in a boot for a variety of uses. She favored a strategy of diversifying the company by marketing a new line of boots for the less experienced, weekend hiker. Anthony also recognized that the market had changed, but he supported expanding the existing lines of boots for mountaineers and hikers. The company had been successful with these boots and Anthony had some ideas about how to extend the lines and expand distribution. "This is a better way to grow," he thought. "I'm concerned about the risk in Margaret's recommenda-

*Lawrence M. Lamont is Professor of Management at Washington and Lee University. Eva Cid and Wade Drew Hammond are seniors in the class of 1995 at Washington and Lee, majoring in Management and Accounting respectively.

Case material is prepared as a basis for class discussion, and not designed to present illustrations of either effective or ineffective handling of administrative problems. Some names, locations, and financial information have been disguised. Copyright © 1995, Washington and Lee University.

TABLE 1   Cima Mountaineering, Inc., revenues and net income, 1990–1995

Year	Revenues	Net income	Profit margin (percent)
1995	$20,091,450	$857,134	4.27%
1994	18,738,529	809,505	4.32
1993	17,281,683	838,162	4.85
1992	15,614,803	776,056	4.97
1991	14,221,132	602,976	4.24
1990	13,034,562	522,606	4.01

tion. If we move to a more casual boot, then we have to resolve a new set of marketing and competitive issues and finance a new line. I'm not sure we can do it."

When he returned to Jackson that evening, Anthony stopped by his office to check his messages. The financial statements shown in Table 2 and Table 3 were on his desk, along with a marketing study from a Denver consulting firm. Harris Fleming, vice president of marketing, had commissioned a study of the hiking boot market several months earlier to help the company plan for the future. As Anthony paged through the report, two figures caught his eye. One was a segmentation of the hiking boot market (see Figure 1) and the other was a summary of market competition (see Figure 2). "This is interesting," he mused. "I hope Margaret reads it before our meeting."

TABLE 2   Cima Mountaineering, Inc., income statement (years ended 12-31-95 and 12-31-94)

	1995	1994
Net sales	$20,091,450	$18,738,529
Cost of goods sold	14,381,460	13,426,156
Gross margin	5,709,990	5,312,373
Selling and admin. expenses	4,285,730	3,973,419
Operating income	1,424,260	1,338,954
Other income (expenses)		
Interest expense	(160,733)	(131,170)
Interest income	35,161	18,739
Total other income (net)	(125,572)	(112,431)
Earnings before income taxes	1,298,688	1,226,523
Income taxes	441,554	417,018
Net income	$857,134	$809,505

TABLE 3   Cima Mountaineering, Inc., balance sheet (years ending 12-31-95 and 12-31-94)

	1995	1994
Assets		
Current assets		
Cash and equivalents	$ 1,571,441	$ 1,228,296
Accounts receivable	4,696,260	3,976,608
Inventory	6,195,450	5,327,733
Other	270,938	276,367
Total	12,734,089	10,809,004
Fixed assets		
Property, plant, and equipment	3,899,568	2,961,667
Less: Accumulated depreciation	(1,117,937)	(858,210)
Total fixed assets (net)	2,781,631	2,103,457
Other assets		
Intangibles	379,313	568,087
Other long-term assets	2,167,504	1,873,151
Total Assets	$18,062,537	$15,353,699
Liabilities and shareholder equity		
Current liabilities:		
Accounts payable	$ 4,280,821	$ 4,097,595
Notes payable	1,083,752	951,929
Current maturities of LT debt	496,720	303,236
Accrued liabilities:		
Expenses	2,754,537	2,360,631
Salaries and wages	1,408,878	1,259,003
Other	1,137,940	991,235
Total current liabilities	11,162,648	9,963,629
Long-term liabilities		
Long-term debt	3,070,631	2,303,055
Lease obligations	90,313	31,629
Total long-term liabilities	3,702,820	2,334,684
Other liabilities		
Deferred taxes	36,125	92,122
Other noncurrent liabilities	312,326	429,904
Total liabilities	14,672,043	12,820,339
Owner's equity		
Retained earnings	3,390,494	2,533,360
Total liabilities and owner's equity	$18,062,537	$15,353,699

FIGURE 1   Cima Mountaineering, Inc., segmentation of the hiking boot market

	Mountaineers	Serious hikers	Weekenders	Practical users	Children	Fashion seekers
Benefits	Durability/ruggedness Stability/support Dryness/warmth Grip/traction	Stability Durability Traction Comfort/protection	Lightweight Comfort Durability Versatility	Lightweight Durability Good value Versatility	Durability Protection Lightweight Traction	Fashion/style Appearance Lightweight Inexpensive
Demographics	Young Primarily male Shops in specialty stores and specialized catalogs	Young, middle aged Male and female Shops in specialty stores & outdoor catalogs	Young, middle aged Male and female Shops in shoe retailers, sporting goods stores, and mail order catalogs	Young, middle aged Primarily male Shops in shoe retailers and department stores	Young marrieds Male and female Shops in department stores and outdoor catalogs	Young Male and female Shops in shoe retailers, department stores and catalogs
Lifestyle	Independent Risk taker Enjoys challenge	Nature lover Outdoorsman Sportsman Backpacker	Recreational hiker Social, spends time with family & friends Enjoys the outdoors	Practical Sociable Outdoors for work and recreation	Enjoys family activities Enjoys outdoors & hiking Children are active and play outdoors Parents are value conscious	Materialistic Trendy Socially conscious Nonhikers Brand name shoppers Price conscious
Examples of brands	Asolo Cliff Raichle Mt. Blanc Salomon Adventure 9	Raichle Explorer Vasque Clarion Tecnica Pegasus Dry Hi-Tec Piramide	Reebok R-Evolution Timberland Topozoic Merrell Acadia Nike Air Mada, Zion Vasque Alpha	Merrell Eagle Nike Air Khyber Tecnica Volcano	Vasque Kids Klimber Nike Merrell Caribou	Nike Espirit Reebok Telos Hi-Tec Magnum
Estimated market share	5% Slow growth	17% Moderate growth	25% High growth	20% Stable growth	5% Slow growth	28% At peak of rapid growth cycle
Price range	$210–$450	$120–$215	$70–$125	$40–$80	Will pay up to $40	$65–$100

Adventuresome

FIGURE 2   Cima Mountaineering, Inc., summary of competitors

Company	Location	Mountaineering (styles)	Hiking (styles)	Men's	Women's	Children's	Price range
Raichle	Switzerland	Yes (7)	Yes (16)	Yes	Yes	Yes	High
Salomon	France	Yes (1)	Yes (9)	Yes	Yes	No	Mid
Asolo	Italy	Yes (4)	Yes (26)	Yes	Yes	No	High
Tecnica	Italy	Yes (3)	Yes (9)	Yes	Yes	No	Mid/high
Hi-Tec	U.K.	Yes (2)	Yes (29)	Yes	Yes	Yes	Mid/low
Vasque	Minnesota	Yes (4)	Yes (18)	Yes	Yes	Yes	Mid/high
Merrell	Vermont	Yes (5)	Yes (31)	Yes	Yes	Yes	Mid
Timberland	New Hampshire	No	Yes (4)	Yes	No	No	Mid
Nike	Oregon	No	Yes (5)	Yes	Yes	Yes	Low
Reebok	Massachusetts	No	Yes (3)	Yes	Yes	Yes	Low
Cima	Wyoming	Yes (3)	Yes (5)	Yes	Yes	No	High

Source: Published literature and company product brochures, 1995.

History of Cima Mountaineering

As children, Anthony and Margaret Simon watched their parents make western boots at the Hoback Boot Company, a small business they owned in Jackson, Wyoming. They learned the craft as they grew up and joined the company after college.

In the late 1960s, the demand for western boots began to decline and the Hoback Boot Company struggled to survive. By 1975, the parents were close to retirement and they seemed content to close the business, but Margaret and Anthony decided to try to salvage the company. Margaret, the oldest, became president and Anthony became the executive vice president. By the end of 1976, sales had declined to $1.5 million and the company earned profits of only $45,000. It became clear that, to survive, the business would have to be refocused on products with a more promising future.

Refocusing the Business

As a college student, Anthony attended a mountaineering school north of Jackson in Teton National Park. As he learned to climb and hike, he became aware of the growing popularity of the sport and the boots being used. Because of his experience with western boots, he also noticed their limitations. Although the boots had good traction, they were heavy, uncomfortable, and had little resistance to the snow and water always present in the mountains. He convinced Margaret that Hoback should explore the possibility of developing boots for mountaineering and hiking.

In 1977, Anthony and Margaret began 12 months of marketing research. They investigated the market, the competition, and the extent to which Hoback's existing equipment could be used to produce the new boots. By the summer of 1978, Hoback had developed a mountaineering and a hiking boot that were ready for testing. Several instructors from the mountaineering school tested the boots and gave them excellent reviews.

The Transition

By 1981, Hoback was ready to enter the market with two styles of boots, one for the mountaineer who wanted a boot for all-weather climbing and the other for men and women who were advanced hikers. Both styles were made of water-repellent leather uppers and cleated soles for superior traction. Distribution was secured through mountaineering shops in Wyoming and Colorado.

Hoback continued to manufacture western boots for its loyal customers, but Margaret planned to phase them out as the hiking boot business developed. However, because they did not completely understand the needs of the market, they hired Harris Fleming, a mountaineering instructor, to help them with product design and marketing.

A New Company

During the 1980s, Hoback prospered as the market expanded along with the popularity of outdoor recreation. The company slowly increased its product line and achieved success by focusing on classic boots that were relatively insensitive to fashion trends. By 1986, sales of Hoback Boots had reached $3.5 million.

Over the next several years, distribution was steadily expanded. In 1987, Hoback employed independent sales representatives to handle the sales and service. Before long, Hoback boots were sold throughout Wyoming, Colorado, and Montana by retailers specializing in mountaineering and hiking equipment. Margaret decided to discontinue western boots to make room for the growing hiking boot business. To reflect the new direction of the company, the name was changed to Cima Mountaineering, Inc.

Cima Boots "Take Off"

The late 1980s were a period of exceptional growth. Demand for Cima boots grew quickly as consumers caught the trend toward healthy, active lifestyles. The company expanded its line for advanced hikers and improved the performance of its boots. By 1990, sales had reached $13 million and the company earned profits of $522,606. Margaret was satisfied with the growth, but she was concerned about low profitability as a result of foreign competition. She challenged the company to find new ways to design and manufacture boots at lower cost.

Growth and Innovation

The next five years were marked by growth, innovation, and increasing foreign and domestic competition. Market growth continued as hiking boots became popular for casual wear in addition to hiking in mountains and on trails. Cima and its competitors began to make boots with molded footbeds and to utilize materials that reduced weight.[1] Fashion also became a factor, and companies like Nike and Reebok marketed lightweight boots in a variety of materials and colors to meet the demand for styling in addition to performance. Cima implemented a computer-aided design (CAD) system in 1993 to shorten product development and devote more attention to design. Late in 1994, Cima restructured its facilities and implemented a modular approach to manufacturing. The company switched from a production line to a system in which a work team applied multiple processes to each pair of boots. Significant cost savings were achieved as the new approach improved the profit and quality of the company's boots.

The Situation in 1995

As the company ended 1995, sales had grown to $20.0 million, up 7.2 percent from the previous year. Employment was at 425 and the facility was operating at 85 percent of capacity producing several styles of mountaineering and hiking boots. Time-saving innovations and cost reduction had also worked, and profits reached an all-time high. Margaret, now 57, was still president and Anthony remained executive vice president.

Cima Marketing Strategy

According to estimates, 1994 was a record year for sales of hiking and mountaineering boots in the United States. Retail sales exceeded $600 million and about 15 million pairs of boots were sold. Consumers wore the boots for activities ranging from mountaineering to casual social events. In recent years, changes were beginning to occur in the market. Inexpensive, lightweight hiking boots were becoming increasingly popular for day hikes and trail walking, and a new category of comfortable, light "trekking" shoes were being marketed by the manufacturers of athletic shoes.

Only a part of the market was targeted by Cima. Most of its customers were serious outdoor enthusiasts. They included mountaineers who climbed in rugged terrain and advanced hikers who used the boots on challenging trails and extended backpacking trips. The demand for Cima boots was seasonal and most of the purchases were made during the summer months when the mountains and trails were most accessible.

---

[1]Two processes are used to attach the uppers to the soles of boots. In classic welt construction, the uppers and soles are stitched. In the more contemporary method, a molded polyurethane footbed (including a one-piece heel and sole) is cemented to the upper with a waterproof adhesive. Many mountaineering boots use classic welt construction because it provides outstanding stability, while the contemporary method is often used with hiking boots to achieve lightweight construction. Cima used the classic method of construction for mountaineering boots and the contemporary method for hiking boots.

Positioning

Cima boots were positioned as the best available for their intended purpose. Consumers saw them as durable and comfortable with exceptional performance. Retailers viewed the company as quick to adopt innovative construction techniques, but conservative in styling. Cima intentionally used traditional styling to avoid fashion obsolescence and the need for frequent design changes. Some of the most popular styles had been in the market for several years without any significant modifications. The Glacier MX 350 shown in Figure 3 and the Summit HX 350 boot shown in Figure 4 are good examples. The MX 350, priced at $219, was positioned as a classic boot for men with a

FIGURE 3   Cima Mountaineering, Inc., the Glacier MX 350 mountaineering boot

FIGURE 4   Cima Mountaineering, Inc., the Summit HX 350 hiking boot

unique tread design for beginning mountaineers. The Summit HX 350 was priced at $159 and was a boot for men and women hiking rough trails. Figure 5 describes the items in the mountaineering and hiking boot lines, and Table 4 provides a sales history for Cima boots.

Product Lines

Corporate branding was used, and "Cima" was embossed into the leather on the side of the boot to enhance consumer recognition. Product lines were also

FIGURE 5   Cima Mountaineering, Inc., mountaineering and hiking boot lines

Product line	Description
Glacier	
MX 550	For expert mountaineers climbing challenging mountains. Made for use on rocks, ice, and snow. Features welt construction, superior stability and support, reinforced heel and toe, padded ankle and tongue, step-in crampon insert, thermal insulation, and waterproof inner liner. Retails for $299.
MX 450	For proficient mountaineers engaging in rigorous, high-altitude hiking. Offers long-term comfort and stability on rough terrain. Features welt construction, deep cleated soles and heels, reinforced heel and toe, padded ankle and tongue, step-in crampon insert, and waterproof inner liner. Retails for $249.
MX 350	For beginning mountaineers climbing in moderate terrain and temperate climates. Features welt construction, unique tread design for traction, padded ankle and tongue, good stability and support, and a quick-dry lining. Retails for $219.
Summit	
HX 550	For experienced hikers who require uncompromising performance. Features nylon shank for stability and rigidity, waterproof inner liner, cushioned midsole, high-traction outsole, and padded ankle and tongue. Retails for $197.
HX 450	For backpackers who carry heavy loads on extended trips. Features thermal insulation, cushioned midsole, waterproof inner liner, excellent foot protection, and high-traction outsole. Retails for $179.
HX 350	For hikers who travel rough trails and a variety of backcountry terrain. Features extra cushioning, good stability and support, waterproof inner liner, and high-traction outsole for good grip in muddy and sloping surfaces. Retails for $159.
HX 250	For hikers who hike developed trails. Made with only the necessary technical features, including cushioning, foot and ankle support, waterproof inner liner, and high-traction outsole. Retails for $139.
HX 150	For individuals taking more than day and weekend hikes. Versatile boot for all kinds of excursions. Features cushioning, good support, waterproof inner liner, and high-traction outsoles for use on a variety of surfaces. Retails for $129.

TABLE 4   Cima Mountaineering, Inc., product line sales

Year	Unit sales (percent)		Sales revenue (percent)	
	Mountaineering	Hiking	Mountaineering	Hiking
1995	15.00%	85.00%	21.74%	78.26%
1994	15.90	84.10	22.93	77.07
1993	17.20	82.80	24.64	75.36
1992	18.00	82.00	25.68	74.32
1991	18.80	81.20	26.71	73.29
1990	19.70	80.30	27.86	72.14

branded, and alphabetic letters and numbers were used to differentiate items in the line. Each line had different styles and features to cover many of the important uses in the market. However, all boots had features that the company believed were essential to positioning. Standard features included water-repellent leather uppers and high-traction soles and heels. The hardware for the boots was plated steel and the laces were tough, durable nylon. Quality was emphasized throughout the product lines.

Glacier Boots for Mountaineering

The Glacier line featured three boots for men. The MX 550 was designed for expert all-weather climbers looking for the ultimate in traction, protection, and warmth. The MX 450 was for experienced climbers taking extended excursions, while the MX 350 met the needs of less-skilled individuals beginning climbing in moderate terrain and climates.

Summit Boots for Hiking

The Summit line featured five styles for men and women. The HX 550 was preferred by experienced hikers who demanded the best possible performance. The boot featured water-repellent leather uppers, a waterproof inner liner, a cushioned midsole, a nylon shank for rigidity, and a sole designed for high traction. It was available in grey and brown with different types of leather.[2] The Summit HX 150 was the least-expensive boot in the line, designed for individuals who were beginning to hike more than the occasional "weekend hike." It was a versatile boot for all kinds of excursions and featured a water-repellent leather upper, a cushioned midsole, and excellent traction. The HX 150 was popular as an entry-level boot for outdoor enthusiasts.

Distribution

Cima boots were distributed in Arizona, California, Colorado, Idaho, Montana, Nevada, New Mexico, Oregon, Washington, Wyoming, and western Canada through specialty retailers selling mountaineering, backpacking, and hiking equipment. Occasionally, Cima was approached by mail order catalog companies and chain sporting goods stores offering to sell their boots. The company considered the proposals, but had not used these channels.

Promotion

The Cima sales and marketing office was located in Jackson. It was managed by Harris Fleming and staffed with several marketing personnel. Promotion was an important aspect of the marketing strategy, and advertising, personal selling, and

---

[2]Different types of leather are used to make hiking boots. *Full Grain:* High-quality, durable, upper layer of the hide. It has a natural finish, and is strong and breathable. *Split Grain:* Underside of the hide after the full grain leather has been removed from the top. Light weight and comfort are the primary characteristics. *Suede:* A very fine split-grain leather. *Nubuck:* Brushed full-grain leather. *Waxed:* A process in which leather is coated with wax to help shed water. Most Cima boots were available in two or more types of leather.

Mountaineering and hiking boots are made water repellent by treating the uppers with wax or chemical coatings. To make the boots waterproof, a fabric inner liner is built into the boot to provide waterproof protection and breathability. All Cima boots were water repellent, but only those styles with an inner liner were waterproof.

sales promotion were used to gain exposure for Cima branded boots. Promotion was directed to consumers and to the retailers that stocked Cima mountaineering and hiking boots.

Personal Selling

Cima used 10 independent sales representatives to sell its boots in the western states and Canada. Representatives did not sell competing boots, but they sold complementary products such as outdoor apparel and equipment for mountaineering, hiking, and backpacking. They were paid a commission and handled customer service in addition to sales. Management was also involved in personal selling. Harris Fleming trained the independent sales representatives and often accompanied them on sales calls.

Advertising and Sales Promotion

Advertising and sales promotion were also important promotional methods. Print advertising was used to increase brand awareness and assist retailers with promotion. Advertising was placed in leading magazines such as *Summit, Outside,* and *Backpacker* to reach mountaineers and hikers with the message that Cima boots were functional and durable with classic styling. In addition, cooperative advertising was offered to encourage retailers to advertise Cima boots and identify their locations.

Sales promotion was an important part of the promotion program. Along with the focus on brand name recognition, Cima provided product literature and point-of-sale display materials to assist retailers in promoting the boots. In addition, the company regularly exhibited at industry trade shows. The exhibits, staffed by marketing personnel and the company's independent sales representatives, were effective for maintaining relationships with retailers and presenting the company's products.

Pricing

Cima selling prices to retailers ranged from $64.50 to $149.50 a pair depending on the style. Mountaineering boots were more expensive because of their construction and features, while hiking boots were priced lower. Retailers were encouraged to take a 50 percent markup on the retail selling price, so retail prices shown in Figure 5 should be divided by two to get the Cima selling price. Cima priced its boots higher than competitors, supporting the positioning of the boots as the top-quality product at each price point. Payment terms were net 30 days (similar to competitors) and boots were shipped to retailers from a warehouse located in Jackson, Wyoming.

Segmentation of the Hiking Boot Market

As Anthony reviewed the marketing study commissioned by Harris Fleming, his attention focused on the market segmentation shown in Figure 1. It was interesting, because management had never seriously thought about the segmentation in the market. Of course, Anthony was aware that not everyone was a potential customer for Cima boots, but he was surprised to see how well the product lines met the needs of mountaineers and serious hikers. As he reviewed the market segmentation, he read the descriptions for mountaineers, serious hikers, and weekenders carefully because Cima was trying to decide which of these segments to target for expansion.

Mountaineers

Mountain climbers and high-altitude hikers are in this segment. They are serious about climbing and enjoy risk and adventure. Because mountaineers' safety may often depend on their boots, they need maximum stability and support, traction for a variety of climbing conditions, and protection from wet and cold weather.

Serious Hikers

Outdoorsmen, who love nature and have a strong interest in health and fitness, comprise the serious hikers. They hike rough trails and take extended backpacking or hiking excursions. Serious hikers are brand conscious and look for durable, high-performance boots with good support, comfortable fit, and good traction.

Weekenders

Consumers in this segment are recreational hikers who enjoy casual, weekend, and day hikes with family and friends. They are interested in light, comfortable boots that provide good fit, protection, and traction on a variety of surfaces. Weekenders prefer versatile boots that can be worn for a variety of activities.

Foreign and Domestic Competition

The second part of the marketing study that caught Anthony's attention was the analysis of competition. Although Anthony and Margaret were aware that competition had increased, they had overlooked the extent to which foreign boot makers had entered the market. Apparently, foreign competitors had noticed the market growth and they were aggressively exporting their boots into the United States. They had established sales offices and independent sales agents to compete for the customers served by Cima. The leading foreign brands such as Asolo, Hi-Tec, Salomon, and Raichle were marketed on performance and reputation, usually to the mountaineering, serious hiker, and weekender segments of the market.

The study also summarized the most important domestic competitors. Vasque and Merrell marketed boots that competed with Cima, but others were offering products for segments of the market where the prospects for growth were better. As Anthony examined Figure 2, he realized that the entry of Reebok and Nike into the hiking boot market was quite logical. They had entered the market as consumer preference shifted from wearing athletic shoes for casual outdoor activities to a more rugged shoe. Each was marketing footwear that combined the appearance and durability of hiking boots with the lightness and fit of athletic shoes. The result was a line of fashionable hiking boots that appealed to brand- and style-conscious teens and young adults. Both firms were expanding their product lines and moving into segments of the market that demanded lower levels of performance.

Margaret and Anthony Discuss Marketing Strategy

A few days after hiking in Cascade Canyon, Anthony met with Margaret and Harris Fleming to discuss marketing strategy. Each had read the consultant's report and studied the market segmentation and competitive summary. As the meeting opened, the conversation developed as follows:

Margaret: "It looks like we will have another record year. The economy is growing and consumers seem confident and eager to buy. Yet, I'm concerned about the future. The foreign bootmakers are providing some stiff competition. Their boots have outstanding performance and attractive prices. The improvements we made in manufacturing helped to control costs and maintain margins, but it looks like the competition and slow growth in our markets will make it difficult to improve profits. We need to be thinking about new opportunities."

Harris: "I agree, Margaret. Just this past week we lost Rocky Mountain Sports in Boulder, Colorado. John Kline, the sales manager, decided to drop us and pick up Asolo. We were doing $70,000 a year with them and they carried our entire line. We also lost Great Western Outfitters in Colorado Springs. They replaced us with Merrell. The sales manager said that the college students there had been asking for the lower-priced Merrell boots. They bought $60,000 last year."

Anthony: "Rocky Mountain and Great Western were good customers. I guess I'm not surprised though. Our Glacier line needs another boot and the Summit line is just not deep enough to cover the price points. We need to have some styles at lower prices to compete with Merrell and Asolo. I'm in favor of extending our existing lines to broaden their market appeal. It seems to me that the best way to compete is to stick with what we do best, making boots for mountaineers and serious hikers."

Margaret: "Not so fast, Anthony. The problem is that our markets are small and not growing fast enough to support the foreign competitors who have entered with excellent products. We can probably hold our own, but I doubt if we can do much better. I think the future of this company is to move with the market. Consumers are demanding more style, lower prices, and a lightweight hiking boot that can be worn for a variety of uses. Look at the segmentation again. The "Weekender" segment is large and it's growing. That's where we need to go with some stylish new boots that depart from our classic leather lines."

Anthony: "Maybe so, but we don't have much experience working with the leather and nylon combinations that are being used in these lighter boots. Besides, I'm not sure we can finance the product development and marketing for a new market that already has plenty of competition. And, I'm concerned about the brand image that we have worked so hard to establish over the past 20 years. A line of inexpensive, casual boots just doesn't seem to fit with the perception consumers have of our products."

Harris: "I can see advantages to each strategy. I do know that we don't have the time and resources to do both, so we had better make a thoughtful choice. Also, I think we should reconsider selling to the mail order catalog companies that specialize in mountaineering and hiking equipment. Last week, I received another call from REI requesting us to sell them some of the boots in our Summit line for the 1997 season. This might be a good source of revenue and a way of expanding our geographic market."

Margaret: "You're right, Harris. We need to rethink our position on the mail order companies. Most of them have good market penetration in the East where we don't have distribution. I noticed that Gander Mountain is carrying some of the Timberland line and that L.L. Bean is carrying some Vasque styles along with their own line of branded boots."

Anthony: "I agree. Why don't we each put together a proposal that summarizes our recommendations and then we can get back together to continue the discussion."

Harris: "Good idea. Eventually we will need a sales forecast and some cost data. Send me your proposals and I'll call the consulting firm and have them prepare some forecasts. I think we already have some cost information. Give me a few days and then we can get together again."

The Meeting to Review the Proposals

The following week, the discussion continued. Margaret presented her proposal, which is summarized in Exhibit 1. She proposed moving Cima into the "Weekender" segment by marketing two new hiking boots. Anthony countered with the proposal summarized in Exhibit 2. He favored extending the existing lines by adding a new mountaineering boot and two new Summit hiking boots at lower price points. Harris presented sales forecasts for each proposal and, after some discussion and modification, they were finalized as shown in Table 5. Cost information was gathered by Harris from the vice president of manufacturing and it is presented in Table 6. Following a lengthy discussion in which Margaret and Anthony were unable to agree on a course of action, Harris Fleming suggested that each proposal be explored further by conducting marketing research. He proposed the formation of teams from the Cima marketing staff to research each proposal and present it to Margaret and

EXHIBIT 1   Cima Mountaineering, Inc.: Margaret's marketing proposal

Memorandum

To: Anthony Simon, Executive Vice President
            Harris Fleming, Vice President of Marketing

From: Margaret Simon, President

Re: Marketing Proposal

I believe we have an excellent opportunity to expand the sales and profits of Cima by entering the "Weekender" segment of the hiking boot market. The segment's estimated share of the market is 25 percent, and, according to the consultant's report, it is growing quite rapidly. I propose that we begin immediately to develop two new products and prepare a marketing strategy as discussed below:

Target Market and Positioning

Male and female recreational hikers looking for a comfortable, lightweight boot that is attractively priced and acceptable for short hikes and casual wear. Weekenders enjoy the outdoors and a day or weekend hike with family and friends.

    The new boots would be positioned with magazine advertising as hiking boots that deliver performance and style for the demands of light hiking and casual outdoor wear.

Product

Two boots in men's and women's sizes. The boots would be constructed of leather and nylon uppers with a molded rubber outsole. A new branded line would be created to meet the needs of the market segment. The boots (designated WX 550 and WX 450) would have the following features:

	WX 550	WX 450
Leather and nylon uppers	X	X
Molded rubber outsole	X	X
Cushioned midsole	X	X
Padded collar and tongue	X	X
Durable hardware and laces	X	X
Waterproof inner liner	X	

    Uppers: To be designed. Options include brown full grain, split grain, or suede leather combined with durable nylon in two of the following colors: beige, black, blue, gray, green, and slate.

    Boot design and brand name: To be decided.

Retail Outlets

Specialty shoe retailers carrying hiking boots and casual shoes, and sporting goods stores. Eventually, mail order catalogs carrying outdoor apparel and hiking, backpacking, and camping equipment.

Promotion

Independent sales representatives.
Magazine advertising.
Co-op advertising.
Point-of-sale display materials.
Product brochures.
Trade shows.

Suggested Retail Pricing

WX 550: $89.00
WX 450: $69.00

Competitors

Timberland, Hi-Tec, Vasque, Merrell, Asolo, Nike, and Reebok.

Product Development and Required Investment

We should allow about one year for the necessary product development and testing. I estimate these costs to be $350,000. Additionally, we will need to make a capital expenditure of $150,000 for new equipment.

EXHIBIT 2   Cima Mountaineering, Inc.: Anthony's marketing proposal

---

Memorandum

To: Margaret Simon, President
Harris Fleming, Vice President of Marketing

From: Anthony Simon, Executive Vice President

Re: Marketing Proposal

We have been successful with boots for mountaineers and serious hikers for years, and this is where our strengths seem to be. I recommend extending our Glacier and Summit lines instead of venturing into a new, unfamiliar market. My recommendations are summarized below:

Product Development
Introduce two new boots in the Summit line (designated HX 100 and HX 50) and market the Glacier MX 350 in a style for women with the same features as the boot for men. The new women's Glacier boot would have a suggested retail price of $219.99, while the suggested retail prices for the HX 100 and the HX 50 would be $119.00 and $89.00, respectively, to provide price points at the low end of the line. The new Summit boots for men and women would be the first in the line to have leather and nylon uppers as well as the following features:

	HX 100	*HX 50*
Leather and nylon uppers	X	X
Molded rubber outsole	X	X
Cushioned midsole	X	X
Padded collar and tongue	X	X
Quick dry lining	X	X
Waterproof inner liner	X	

The leather used in the uppers will have to be determined. We should consider full-grain, suede, and nubuck since they are all popular with users in this segment. We need to select one for the initial introduction. The nylon fabric for the uppers should be available in two colors, selected from among the following: beige, brown, green, slate, maroon, and navy blue. Additional colors can be offered as sales develop and we gain a better understanding of consumer preferences.

Product Development and Required Investment
Product design and development costs of $400,000 for the MX 350, HX 100, and HX 50 styles and a capital investment of $150,000 to acquire equipment to cut and stitch the nylon/leather uppers. One year will be needed for product development and testing.

Positioning
The additions to the Summit line will be positioned as boots for serious hikers who want a quality hiking boot at a reasonable price. The boots will also be attractive to casual hikers who are looking to move up to a better boot as they gain experience in hiking and outdoor activity.

Retail Outlets
We can use our existing retail outlets. Additionally, the lower price points on the new styles will make these boots attractive to catalog shoppers. I recommend that we consider making the Summit boots available to consumers through mail order catalog companies.

Promotion
We will need to revise our product brochures and develop new advertising for the additions to the Summit line. The balance of the promotion program should remain as it exists since it is working quite well. I believe the sales representatives and retailers selling our lines will welcome the new boots since they broaden the consumer appeal of our lines.

Suggested Retail Pricing

MX 350 for women:	$219.00
HX 100:	$119.00
HX 50:	$ 89.00

Competitors
Asolo, Hi-Tec, Merrell, Raichle, Salomon, Tecnica, and Vasque.

TABLE 5   Cima Mountaineering, Inc., sales forecasts for proposed new products (pairs of boots)

	Project 1		Project 2		
Year	WX 550	WX 450	MX 350	HX 100	HX 50
2001–02	16,420	24,590	2,249	15,420	12,897
2000–01	14,104	21,115	1,778	13,285	11,733
1999–00	8,420	12,605	897	10,078	9,169
1998–99	5,590	8,430	538	5,470	5,049
1997–98	4,050	6,160	414	4,049	3,813

Note: Sales forecasts are expected values derived from minimum and maximum estimates.

Some cannibalization of existing boots will occur when the new styles are introduced. The sales forecasts provided above have taken in account the impact of sales losses on existing boots. No additional adjustments need to be made.

Forecasts for WX 550, WX 450, HX 100, and HX 50 include sales of both men's and women's boots.

TABLE 6   Cima Mountaineering, Inc., cost information for mountaineering and hiking boots

	Inner liner	No inner liner
Retail markup	50%	50%
Marketing and manufacturing costs		
Sales commissions	10	10
Advertising and sales promotion	5	5
Materials	42	35
Labor, OHD, and transportation	28	35

Cost information for 1997–98 only. Sales commissions, advertising and sales promotion, materials, labor, OHD, and transportation costs are based on Cima selling prices.

After 1997–98, annual increases of 3.0 percent apply to marketing and manufacturing costs, and 4.0 percent apply to Cima selling prices.

EXHIBIT 3   Cima Mountaineering, Inc.: Harris Fleming's memorandum to the marketing staff

Memorandum

To: Marketing Staff

Cc: Margaret Simon, President
Anthony Simon, Executive Vice President

From: Harris Fleming, Vice President of Marketing

Subject: Marketing Research Projects

Attached to this memorandum are two marketing proposals (see Exhibits 1 and 2) under consideration by our company. Each proposal is a guide for additional marketing research. You have been selected to serve on a project team to investigate **one** of the proposals and report your conclusions and recommendations to management. At your earliest convenience, please complete the following.

Project Team 1: Proposal to enter the "Weekender" segment of the hiking boot market.

Review the market segmentation and summary of competition in Figures 1 and 2. Identify consumers that would match the profile described in the market segment and conduct field research using a focus group, a survey, or both. You may

(continued)

EXHIBIT 3   *(concluded)*

also visit retailers carrying hiking boots to examine displays and product brochures. Using the information in the proposal, supplemented with your research, prepare the following:

1. A design for the hiking boots (WX 550 and WX 450). Please prepare a sketch that shows the styling for the uppers. We propose to use the same design for each boot, the only difference being the waterproof inner liner on the WX 550 boot. On your design, list the features that your proposed boot would have, considering additions or deletions to those listed in the proposal.
2. Recommend a type of leather (from among those proposed) and two colors for the nylon to be used in the panels of the uppers. We plan to make two styles, one in each color for each boot.
3. Recommend a brand name for the product line. Include a rationale for your choice.
4. Verify the acceptability of the suggested retail pricing.
5. Prepare a magazine advertisement for the hiking boot. Provide a rationale for the advertisement in the report.
6. Convert the suggested retail prices *in the proposal* to the Cima selling price and use the sales forecasts and costs (shown in Tables 5 and 6) to prepare an estimate of before-tax profits for the new product line covering a five-year period starting in 1997–98. Assume annual cost increases of 3.0 percent and price increases of 4.0 percent beginning in 1998–99. Discount the future profits to present value using a cost of capital of 15.0 percent. Use 1996–97 as the base year for all discounting.
7. Determine the payback period for the proposal. Assume product development and investment occurs in 1996–97.
8. Provide your conclusions on the attractiveness of these styles to mail order catalog companies and their customers. You may wish to review current mail order catalogs to observe the hiking boots featured. Assuming Cima is successful selling to mail order catalog companies, estimate the percentage of our sales that could be expected from these customers.
9. Prepare a report that summarizes the recommendations of your project team including the advantages and disadvantages of the proposal. Be prepared to present your product design, branding, pro-forma projections, payback period, and recommendations to management shortly after completion of this assignment.
10. Summarize your research and list the sources of information used to prepare the report.

Project Team 2: Proposal to extend the existing lines of boots for mountaineers and hikers.

Review the market segmentation and summary of competition in Figures 1 and 2. Identify consumers that match the profile described in the market segment and conduct field research using a focus group, a survey, or both. You may also visit retailers carrying hiking boots to examine displays and product brochures. Using the information in the proposal, supplemented with your research, prepare the following.

1. Designs for the hiking boots (HX 100 and HX 50). Please prepare sketches showing the styling for the uppers. We propose to use a different design for each boot, so you should provide a sketch for each. On each sketch, list the features that your proposed boots would have, considering additions or deletions to those listed in the proposal.
    No sketch is necessary for the mountaineering boot, MX 350, since we will use the same design as the men's boot and build it on a women's last.
2. Recommend one type of leather (from among those proposed) and two colors for the nylon to be used in the panels of the uppers. We plan to make two styles, one in each color for each boot.
3. Verify the market acceptability of the suggested retail pricing.
4. Prepare a magazine advertisement for your hiking boots. Include a rationale for the advertisement in the report.
5. Using the suggested retail prices *in the proposal,* convert them to the Cima selling prices and use the sales forecasts and costs (shown in Tables 5 and 6) to prepare an estimate of before-tax profits for the new products covering a five-year period starting in 1997–98. Assume annual cost increases of 3.0 percent and price increases of 4.0 percent beginning in 1998–99. Discount the profits to present value using a cost of capital of 15.0 percent. Use 1996–97 as the base year for all discounting.
6. Determine the payback period for the proposal. Assume product development and investment occurs in 1996–97.
7. Provide your conclusions on the attractiveness of these styles to mail order catalog companies and their customers. You may wish to review current mail order catalogs to observe the hiking boots featured. Assuming Cima is successful selling to mail order catalog companies, estimate the percentage of our sales that could be expected from these customers.
8. Prepare a report that summarizes the recommendations of your project team including the advantages and disadvantages of the proposal. Be prepared to present your product design, pro-forma projections, payback period, and recommendations to management shortly after completion of this assignment.
9. Summarize your research and list the sources of information used to prepare the report.

Anthony at a later date. Harris presented his directions to the teams in the memorandum shown in Exhibit 3. The discussion between Margaret and Anthony continued as follows:

Margaret: "Once the marketing research is completed and we can read the reports and listen to the presentations, we should have a better idea of which strategy makes the best sense. Hopefully, a clear direction will emerge and we can move ahead with one of the proposals. In either case, I'm still intrigued with the possibility of moving into the mail order catalogs, since we really haven't developed these companies as customers. I just wish we knew how much business we could expect from them."

Anthony: "We should seriously consider them, Margaret. Companies like L.L. Bean, Gander Mountain, and REI have been carrying a selection of hiking boots for several years. However, there may be a problem for us. Eventually, the catalog companies expect their boot suppliers to make them a private brand. I'm not sure this is something we want to do since we built the company on a strategy of marketing our own brands that are made in the U.S.A. Also, I'm concerned about the reaction of our retailers when they discover we are selling to the catalog companies. It could create some problems."

Harris: "That is a strategy issue we will have to address. However, I'm not even sure what percentage of sales the typical footwear company makes through the mail order catalogs. If we were to solicit the catalog business, we would need an answer to this question to avoid exceeding our capacity. In the proposals, I asked each of the teams to provide an estimate for us. I have to catch an early flight to Denver in the morning. It's 6:30, why don't we call it a day."

The meeting was adjourned at 6:35 P.M. Soon thereafter, the marketing teams were formed, with a leader assigned to each team.